ARCO

POLICE OFFICER

14th Edition

Hugh O'Neill
Hy Hammer
Eve P. Steinberg

MACMILLAN • USA

Fourteenth Edition

Macmillan General Reference
A Simon & Schuster Macmillan Company
1633 Broadway
New York, NY 10019-6785

Library of Congress Number: 98-88336

ISBN: 0-02-862808-X

Manufactured in the United States of America

10 9 8 7 6 5 4 3 2 1

CONTENTS

What This Book Will Do for You

You want to become a Police Officer. That's great. Every city, every town, every county, every state needs qualified and enthusiastic new recruits to maintain staffing at full level and to cover all posts. You have made a good start toward joining the police force by buying this book.

This book has been carefully researched and has been written to help you through the application and screening process. The information in this book will prepare you for the written exam, forewarn you as to the physical skills on which you must concentrate, and give you valuable tips for your interview and psychological screening.

It is important that you allow the book to help you. Read it carefully. Do not skip over any information. Information about police work itself and the organization of police forces should help psych you for the job. You should get more and more excited about the work as you read about all the possible assignments. The information about the screening process itself should calm you and help to allay your fears. Taken step-by-step the process is not so frightening. Each step has a purpose. There is a way to handle each one. Once you know what to expect, half the battle is won. Thorough preparation for the written exam should win the other half of the battle. If you are prepared, you can feel self-confident. If you feel confident, you can answer questions quickly and decisively, finish the exam, and earn a high score.

So make a study schedule. Assign yourself a period of time each day to devote to preparation for the police screening process. A regular time is best, but the important thing is daily study. Choose a quiet, well-lighted spot with as few distractions as possible. Try to arrange not to be interrupted.

Begin at the beginning of the book. Read. Underline points that you consider significant. Make marginal notes. Flag the pages that you think are especially important with little "post it"™ notes. We have highlighted some pages with colored paper. Read these pages more than once.

The bulk of this book consists of police examinations, real examinations given to candidates by the City of New York within the past several years and practice exams that we have created using questions that have appeared on police exams over the years. Before you attempt these exams, study the three chapters about Police Judgment Questions, Reading-Based Questions, and Observation and Memory. These chapters give you help with the three most common kinds of police exam questions. Many police forces test only in these three areas. Each chapter begins with instructions about the topic and the kind of question. Each gives practical suggestions about how to answer the questions. Read the instructions in each chapter. Try the practice questions in each chapter. Then study the answer explanations. You can learn a great deal from answer explanations. Even when you have answered correctly, the explanation may bring out points that had not occurred to you. This same suggestion—read *all* the explanations—applies throughout this book, to the exams as well as to the instructional chapters.

When you feel that you are well prepared, move on to the exams. If possible, answer an entire exam in one sitting. If you must divide your time, divide into no more than two sessions per exam. You need not do the first exam first. The practice exams are somewhat shorter than the actual New York City exams. It might be wise to save the longest exams for a weekend.

When you do take the exams, treat them with respect. Time yourself accurately and do not peek at the correct answers. Remember, you are taking these for practice; they will not be scored; they do not count. So learn from them. Learn to think; learn to reason like a police officer; learn to pace yourself so that you can answer all the questions. Then learn from the explanations.

IMPORTANT: Do not memorize questions and answers. Any question that has been released will not be used again. You may run into questions that are very similar, but you will not be tested with any of these exact questions. These questions will give you good practice, but they will not give you the answers to any of the questions on your exam.

With all of this emphasis on time, you may be wondering if it is wise to guess. The best policy is, of course, to pace yourself so that you can read and consider each question. Sometimes this does not work. Most civil service exam scores are based only on the number of questions answered correctly. This means that a wild guess is better than a blank space. There is no penalty for a wrong answer, and you just might guess right. If you see that time is about to run out, mark all the remaining spaces with the same answer. By the law of averages, some will be right.

Far better than a wild guess is an educated guess. You make this kind of guess not when you are pressed for time but when you are not sure of the correct answer. Usually, one or two of the choices are obviously wrong. Eliminate the obviously wrong answers and try to reason among those remaining. Then, if necessary, guess from the smaller field. The odds of a right answer increase if you guess from a field of two instead of from a field of four. When you make an educated guess or a wild guess in the course of the exam, you might want to make a note next to the question number in the test booklet. Then, if there is time, you can go back for a second look.

Unless you have applied to a very small police force, your exam will be machine scored. You will mark your answers on a separate answer sheet. Each exam in this book has its own answer sheet so that you can practice marking all your answers in the right way. Tear out the answer sheet before you begin each exam. Do not try to flip pages back and forth. Since your answer sheet will be machine scored, you must fill it out clearly and correctly. You cannot give any explanations to the machine. This means:

1. Blacken your answer space firmly and completely. ● This is the only correct way to mark the answer sheet. ◐, ⊗, ⊘, and ∅ are all unacceptable. The machine might not read them at all.

2. Mark only one answer for each question. If you mark more than one answer you will be considered wrong even if one of the answers is correct.

3. If you change your mind, you must erase your mark. Attempting to cross out an incorrect answer like this ▨ will not work. You must erase any incorrect answer completely. An incomplete erasure might be read as a second answer.

4. All of your answering should be in the form of blackened spaces. The machine cannot read English. Do not write any notes in the margins. If you have done any figuring in the margins of the test booklet itself, be sure to mark the letter of your answer on the answer sheet. Correct answers in the test booklet do not count. Only the answer sheet is scored.

5. MOST IMPORTANT: Answer each question in the right place. Question 1 must be answered in space 1; question 52 in space 52. If you should skip an answer space and mark a series of answers in the wrong places, you must erase all those answers and do the questions over, marking your answers in the proper places. You cannot afford to use the limited time in this way. Therefore, as you answer *each* question, look at its number and check that you are marking your answer in the space with the same number.

6. In general, because of the risk of getting out of line on the answer sheet, we recommend that you answer every question in order, even if you have to guess. Make it an educated guess if you can. If not, make it a wild guess. Just mark the question number in the test booklet so that you can try again if there is time.

Caution: Answer sheets are not all alike. The most common arrangement of answer sheets is in columns, that is, with one number below the other. However, some exams, including most New York City Civil Service exams, present the answer sheet in rows, that is, across the page. Take a good look at your answer sheet before you begin to answer questions.

On the examination day assigned to you, allow the test itself to be the main event of the day. Do not squeeze it in between other activities. Arrive rested, relaxed, and on time. In fact, plan to arrive early. Leave plenty of time for traffic tie-ups or other complications that might upset you and interfere with your test performance.

In the test room, the examiner will hand out forms for you to fill out. He or she will give you the instructions that you must follow in taking the examination. The examiner will tell you how to fill in the grids on the forms. Time limits and timing signals will be explained. If you do not understand any of the examiner's instructions, ASK QUESTIONS. Make sure that you know exactly what to do.

At the examination, you must follow instructions exactly. Fill in the grids on the forms carefully and accurately. Filling in the wrong grid may lead to loss of veterans' credits to which you may be entitled or to an incorrect address for your test results. Do not begin until you are told to begin. Stop as soon as the examiner tells you to stop. Do not turn pages until you are told to. Do not go back to parts you have already completed. Any infraction of the rules is considered cheating. If you cheat, your test paper will not be scored, and you will not be eligible for appointment.

Once the signal has been given and you begin the exam, read every word of every question. Be alert for exclusionary words that might affect your answer: words like "not," "most," "least," "all," "every," and "except."

Read all the choices before you mark your answer. It is statistically true that most errors are made when the last choice is the correct answer. Too many people mark the first answer that seems correct without reading through all the choices to find out which answer is *best*.

If you happen to finish before time is up, return to difficult questions that you marked in the booklet and try them again. There is no bonus for finishing early, so use all your time to perfect your exam paper.

ORGANIZATION OF A MUNICIPAL POLICE FORCE

The entire criminal justice system in the United States starts with the police, and it is the municipal police officer who is most familiar to the average person. Municipal police departments, in both personnel and management practices, are generally organized along semimilitary lines. Police officers wear uniforms, usually blue or brown; they are ranked according to a military system, such as sergeant, lieutenant, captain, colonel; and they are governed by specific, written rules and regulations. Highly trained police officers are found in both large and small cities. Of the more than 17,000 cities in the United States, 55 have populations exceeding a quarter of a million, and these employ about one-third of all police personnel. It is in the cities that American police problems are concentrated, and these problems present the greatest challenges to law enforcement.

All police agencies, large or small, have similar problems and responsibilities. Each engages in common activities that prevent crime and disorder, preserve the peace, and protect individual life and property. Police work is often thought of as a matter of confrontations between police officers and hardened criminals; this frequently is so. In many instances, however, police officers deal with quite different and surprisingly varied situations.

Police activities can be divided into two functions: line and staff. Line functions involve activities that result directly in meeting police service goals; staff activities help administrators organize and manage the police agency. The line functions common to most municipal police departments include patrol, investigation, vice, traffic, juvenile, and crime prevention.

Line Functions

At the center of police law enforcement is patrol. It involves movement of uniformed police personnel, on foot or in vehicles, through designated areas. In most departments, at least half of all police personnel are assigned to patrol. Officers on patrol have a variety of duties that include: interviewing and interrogating suspects and arresting lawbreakers; controlling crowds at public gatherings; enforcing laws regulating public conduct; intervening in personal, family, and public disputes; issuing warnings and citations; and providing miscellaneous services to members of the public. Although patrol officers spend more time carrying out routine police services than in catching criminals, their importance cannot be underestimated. Because their primary duties are performed on the street, patrol officers are the most visible representatives of local government.

Investigation activities come into play when patrol officers are unable to prevent a crime or to arrest a suspect in the act of committing a crime. Investigative specialists, better known as detectives, help to solve crimes by: skillful questioning of victims, witnesses, and suspects; by gathering evidence at crime sites; and by tracing stolen property or vehicles connected with crime. Detectives investigate many types of crimes including murder, manslaughter, robbery, rape, aggravated assault, burglary, auto theft, forgery, embezzlement, and weapons violations. They spend considerable time reviewing physical evidence, clues, interviews, and methods used by the criminal that may provide a break in solving a case. In addition, investigations are coordinated by use of information provided by patrol officers, laboratory personnel, records clerks, and concerned citizens. All of these may lead to the identification of the guilty individual.

Vice operations in the local police agency are aimed at illegal activities that corrupt and destroy the physical, mental, and moral health of the public. Enforcement activities in vice operations are directed principally against illegal gambling, narcotics violations, traffic in liquor, prostitution, pandering, pornography, and obscene conduct. Organized crime is involved in many vice crimes, and vice crimes are directly linked to other types of street crime. For example, gambling is associated with loansharking, and prostitution and drug abuse are linked with robbery. Patrol units have the primary responsibility of enforcing vice laws and can significantly prevent such illegal activities, particularly in high crime areas. In order to be effective, however, there must be a continual exchange of information and coordinated effort between vice units and all other elements of the police department, as well as cooperation with federal law enforcement agencies such as the Drug Enforcement Agency and the Bureau of Alcohol, Tobacco, and Firearms.

Traffic law enforcement seeks the voluntary compliance of citizens with traffic regulations to provide maximum movement of traffic with a minimum of interruption. As no shame is associated with most traffic violations, and the public often breaks traffic regulations without realizing it, breaking these laws is made an unpleasant experience by enforcing penalties such as fines, loss of license, or imprisonment. In addition to vehicular traffic enforcement, uniformed police officers also engage in pedestrian control, traffic direction, investigation of accidents, and traffic education. There is an important relationship between traffic law enforcement and other police services. Stopping a motorist for a routine vehicle check or for a traffic violation often results in an arrest for a nontraffic-related reason, such as weapons or drug possession, stolen vehicle, or flight to avoid prosecution in another jurisdiction. As in the case of other police assignments, traffic officers give court testimony and are often involved in civil cases because of traffic accident investigations.

Most municipal police agencies have specific policy guidelines for dealing with juveniles. However, there may be differences in approach or philosophy among various departments depending on the needs of individual communities. In some cases, police officers are given special training and are assigned to juvenile activities on a full-time basis. In other police departments, the training in this area is minimal, and officers rely on the traditional police methods in dealing with juveniles. A juvenile becomes a delinquent by commiting an act which, if he or she were an adult, would be a crime. The police, however, have greater responsibilities in juvenile matters than merely enforcing laws by taking youthful offenders into custody. Police juvenile efforts are aimed at identifying neglected and dependent children, detecting and preventing predelinquent behavior, finding and investigating delinquency breeding-grounds within the community, and proper disposition of juvenile cases.

The last of the basic line functions of the municipal police agency involves crime prevention. When citizens are hostile to the police agency in their community, it is as real a threat to peace and order as would be police indifference to the needs of the citizens. Police serve all segments of the community, but they cannot preserve law and order and control crime unless the public cooperates and participates in the law enforcement process. Hostility between citizens and police not only creates explosive situations, but, more importantly, can promote crime in the community. Crime is both a police and social problem that will continue to grow unless the public becomes more involved. Community relations programs, for example, help to close the gap between citizens and police by making each aware of the other's problems and providing the impetus to settle their differences. In some municipalities, police agencies have introduced crime prevention techniques such as neighborhood security and watch programs. These encourage citizens to take security measures in their homes and businesses and to report any suspicious persons or activities in the neighborhood.

Staff Functions

Staff functions are activities performed by police officers to help administrators organize and manage the police agency. Personnel recruitment (which includes selection and training), planning, finance, employee services, public relations, and use of civilian personnel are examples of staff work.

Staff is the costliest and most important of all the resources committed to the law enforcement process, and a police agency is only as able and effective as its personnel. To varying degrees, every police department engages in recruitment, selection, and training of personnel. It sets qualifications, recruits candidates, tests and screens applicants, and places them in training facilities. The police department also reviews performance during probation and develops salary schedules and lines of promotion for police officers. In addition, staff units are responsible for providing ongoing training to police officers at all levels in the department as a means of keeping them up-to-date on the latest developments in law enforcement. All of these factors are important because the quality of the personnel and their training determine the character of police performance, and, in the final analysis, the quality of police leadership.

To be effective, police departments must plan and organize numerous activities that characterize around-the-clock operations. The unpredictable nature of police work, however, and the problems that arise from emergency situations sometimes make planning difficult. Work schedules, paydays, patrol assignments, uniforms, and equipment all require planning; this, in turn, involves administrative staff and line operations, extradepartmental plans, and research and development. Good planning by the police agency produces effective police service in the community.

Budgeting is an important part of the staff functions of police personnel. These responsibilities include, but are not limited to, fiscal planning and preparation of cost estimates for personnel, equipment, facilities, and programs necessary to meet the established goals of the police department.

The staff must also provide employee services to members of the police agency. They must explain benefits and help employees and their families to obtain all the services to which they are entitled. For example, in cases of illness, injury, or death, specialists in employee benefits take care of matters with a minimum of inconvenience to the officers and their families.

Police personnel also engage in public relations activities. This entails the development of programs that acquaint the community with police goals and help to gain public support for police activities. Duties include providing information to the press and public, maintaining liaison with community representatives, and working with educational organizations to improve relations with youth in the community.

A number of staff positions and auxiliary staff positions can be filled by handicapped personnel.

A widespread practice is the use of civilian personnel in certain jobs within police agencies. Civilian personnel are assigned to duties that do not require the exercise of police authority or the application of the skills and knowledge of the professional police officer. Work typically performed by civilians includes clerical or secretarial work, maintenance or sanitation work, prisoner booking, and motor vehicle maintenance. Many civilian employees develop an interest in regular police work, and, if they meet the requirements for sworn status, become potential candidates for the police officer position. Some police departments will help pay for the schooling required for their civilian employees to meet the educational standards of the department. Some offer part-time training to their employees.

Besides these primary staff functions, important auxiliary staff services help line and administrative personnel to meet police objectives. These services include crime laboratory, property and detention, transportation, communications, and information systems. In addition, many police departments have intelligence operations and systems of internal discipline. Brief descriptions of these auxiliary services follow.

Auxiliary Staff Services

CRIME LABORATORY

Because solutions to many crimes are found through the application of the physical and biological sciences, the crime laboratory is of great value to law enforcement officers. In an initial critical phase, police officers or specially trained evidence technicians identify, collect, and preserve physical evidence at scenes of crime. Overlooking, contaminating, or accidentally destroying evidence can hinder the progress of an investigation. After the evidence reaches the crime laboratory, qualitative, quantitative, and interpretive analyses are performed by forensic personnel. Crime laboratory personnel are responsible for fingerprint operations, ballistics, polygraph tests, blood and alcohol tests, and examination of questioned documents. Owing to the considerable expense involved with operating crime laboratory facilities, not all police agencies have them. Local and regional laboratories have therefore been established in most states to provide services to law enforcement agencies from different jurisdictions.

PROPERTY AND DETENTION

Regardless of their size, locale, or functions, police agencies are responsible for evidence, personal property, and articles of value confiscated when carrying out police business. In addition, they must take inventory, inspect, replace, and maintain departmental property and facilities. Each police department must ensure the safekeeping of all property and evidence and make provisions for its storage, retrieval, and disposition to authorized police personnel.

Detention activities in a police agency involve temporary confinement of persons arrested and awaiting investigation or trial and permanent imprisonment in city or county facilities for those sentenced by the court. Typical activities include booking, searching, fingerprinting, photographing, and feeding prisoners.

TRANSPORTATION

Police mobility is crucial to crime prevention. Police officers must have the capability of moving safely and swiftly to meet their responsibilities. Police transportation activities center around the acquisition, use, maintenance, cost, and safety of a variety of vehicles. These include automobiles (patrol and unmarked), motorcycles, trucks, buses, motor scooters, aircraft (helicopters and planes), watercraft, and horses. By developing and maintaining an efficient transportation program, the police agency increases its effectiveness and ability to enforce the law.

COMMUNICATIONS

Communications in a police agency are the lifeline of the organization. Most police department communications systems have three parts: the telephone communications system, command and control operations, and radio communications. Though communications systems differ among departments throughout the country because of variation in staffing and funding, they generally operate as follows:

Telephone communications systems aim to reduce crime through rapid and accurate communication with the public. The telephone is the primary link between the police and the community, and, in an emergency, the public must be able to contact the police immediately. This is vitally important because rapid police response to an emergency call can mean the difference between life and death or between the capture and escape of suspects.

Command and control means coordinating operations of radio-equipped field units through exchange of information between field units and communications centers. In its simplest form, it is the receipt, processing, and dispatching of information received in telephone complaints to field units for action. This process becomes more complex as calls increase. In large departments, the use of automated command control equipment is widespread. Regardless of department size, rapid and accurate command and control operations are needed to ensure the safety of the community.

Radio communications, an integral part of police operations, involve use of radio frequencies by command control and police officers both to receive and transmit information. The efficiency of radio communications, however, is often impaired because frequency ranges are limited. In recent years, frequency congestion has been the result of increasing use of communication devices by the public and business. Efforts to solve this problem are receiving constant attention by law enforcement agencies at all levels. Where possible, in addition to radio-equipped vehicles, police departments provide police officers with specialized equipment such as miniature transceivers, mobile and portable radio units, and walkie-talkies. The object is to provide continuous communication among commanders, supervisors, and field personnel.

POLICE INFORMATION SYSTEMS

Another staff service, the information system, can also significantly affect efforts to reduce crime. Such a system consists of three components: reporting, collection and recording of crime data, and information storage and retrieval.

Reporting means thorough and precise reporting of all crimes that come to the department's attention. Included are telephone and field investigation reports and warrant information received from judicial agencies. Such information can assist criminal investigation and is useful in other parts of the criminal justice system.

Collection and recording of crime data helps evaluate crime conditions and the effectiveness of police operations. The data is obtained from the department's reportable incident files, such as precinct and field unit activity logs, accident reports, and criminal investigation reports, as well as summary dossier files consisting of fingerprints, name index to fingerprints, and criminal histories.

Information storage and retrieval, the third part of police information systems, supports police in the field by providing quick and accurate criminal information on request. Field personnel have access, for example, to arrest records, outstanding warrants, stolen vehicles, and serially identified stolen weapons and property. Development of good information systems for police officers contributes significantly to the effectiveness of the police agency.

INTELLIGENCE

Intelligence operations, still another staff service, also contribute to efficient police work. Information is gathered to keep police officials attuned to happenings in their areas of jurisdiction by providing insight into community conditions, potential problem areas, and criminal activities—all essential to law enforcement. This work deals with activities that present a threat to the community. The most common targets of intelligence investigations are organized crime and individuals or groups who cause public disorder. To be effective, intelligence activities must be continuous; the data gathered must be used to plan and carry out crime-fighting programs.

INTERNAL DISCIPLINE

Another auxiliary staff service is internal discipline. Discipline and accountability are vital to any police agency in maintaining its integrity. Internal discipline, also known as internal affairs, involves investigation of complaints related to police department services and personnel. Complaints are lodged by citizens or police personnel themselves. Depending on whether the charges are substantiated, complaints can lead to departmental discipline, dismissal, arrest, prosecution, and imprisonment of those found guilty. By protecting the public from police misconduct and corruption and by taking positive action against employees found guilty of misconduct, the department strengthens morale and gains the support of the community it serves.

When all of the line and staff functions performed in police agencies of any size are considered, it is obvious that effective administration is not easily attained. Large agencies tend to use police officers as specialists in specific types of operations, while smaller departments use officers as generalists performing a wide variety of functions. There are merits to both systems, and their use is generally dictated by the needs and composition of the communities in which they are located.

In addition to the local police agencies in municipalities, other special-purpose public police forces are found in many cities throughout the United States. Their jurisdictions include parks, harbors, airports, sanitation departments, transit systems, housing facilities, and ports. Some of these agencies have full police officer powers within their jurisdictions, while others have more limited authority.

WHAT POLICE OFFICERS DO

The fundamental purpose of the police throughout America is crime prevention through law enforcement, and, to most citizens, the most visible representative of this effort is the uniformed Police Officer. There is no more important police function than day-to-day patrol activities, for the effectiveness of police agencies depends on it. After their basic training, most Police Officers are assigned to patrol duty, and their specific duties and responsibilities are numerous and varied. Unlike the specialist, **Patrol Officers** must perform well in a variety of tasks. Regardless of police department size, these officers have two basic responsibilities: to prevent criminal activities and to furnish day-to-day police service to the community. Patrol Officers protect the public, interpret and enforce the law, control traffic, and perform preliminary investigations. They frequently face situations that require swift yet sound decisions. For example, they must decide whether to take no action in an incident or to offer advice, whether to warn or to arrest persons, perhaps using firearms or substantial force. In some situations they must determine the difference between crime and bizarre behavior or between disturbing the peace and legitimate dissent by citizens. Regardless of the circumstances, their first duty is protection of constitutional guarantees, and their second duty is enforcement of the law.

Police Officers patrol assigned sectors in motor vehicles or on foot, working alone or with a partner, paying close attention to area conditions and inhabitants. During patrol, Police Officers observe suspicious behavior, conditions, or illegal activities in their sector and report incidents by radio to a superior officer prior to taking action. They investigate incidents and question the individuals involved to determine violations of the law. They respond to radio calls sent by police dispatchers or superior officers ordering them to the scene of incidents such as burglaries, bank robberies, homicides, rapes, suicides, assaults, and crimes in progress. They make preliminary investigations, question victims and witnesses, recover stolen property, and take evidence into possession. Where indicated, they arrest suspects at crime scenes or after pursuit and use physical force and firearms to subdue them. When making arrests, they advise suspects of their constitutional rights, as required by law, and transport them in police vehicles to police booking and detention facilities prior to court arraignment. At the time of trial, Police Officers testify in court to provide evidence for prosecuting attorneys.

Traffic control is an essential part of police patrol activities. Police Officers direct and control pedestrian and vehicular traffic in high density areas to ensure safe and rapid movement, observe parked and moving vehicles for evidence of traffic violations, and issue citations for violations of traffic regulations. Other responsibilities include maintaining order and traffic flow during public gatherings, demonstrations, and emergencies such as riots, fires, explosions, auto accidents, and natural disasters, using crowd control and traffic-direction techniques to carry out such assignments. They administer first aid to victims of accidents or crimes and arrange for the dispatch of medical units to the scene. In cases of traffic accidents, they investigate circumstances and causes and record findings for subsequent use by the parties involved and their attorneys.

Assignment to patrol duty requires performance of a number of miscellaneous tasks. Police Officers check entrances and exits of commercial facilities for security during hours of darkness. In some police departments, officers inspect residential buildings for safety and suggest methods of improving security, such as installing special locks, alarms, or improved lighting in entry areas. They inspect premises of public, licensed business establishments to enforce laws, local ordinances, and regulations concerning their operation. Police Officers also provide information and assistance to inquiring citizens, help to settle domestic disputes when called to the scene, and may lend assistance in cases of emergency childbirth. They note conditions that are hazardous to the public such as obstructions, potholes, inoperable street lamps, and defective traffic signals, and report them for appropriate action. At the conclusion of each daily work tour, a Police Officer prepares a written activity report that describes arrests, incidents, and all relevant information gathered and submits it to a superior officer, usually a Police Sergeant.

As noted previously, Police Officers on patrol duty are generalists who perform a number of police functions well. However, many aspects of modern police service are complex and require use of specialized personnel. The degree of specialization within a police agency varies with the size and resources of the department and needs of the community. Small communities usually require less specialization while highly populated areas make specialists a necessity. In small police agencies, specialists are generally used on a part-time basis, while the larger departments usually employ full-time specialists. The following are some examples of the various specialized assignments carried out by Police Officers.

SPECIALIZED ASSIGNMENTS

Bomb Squad Officers are highly trained police personnel who respond to incidents of bomb threats and report to locations where bombs have been detonated. Sophisticated equipment and specially trained dogs may be used to locate and disarm explosive and incendiary devices, many of them real and others cleverly constructed hoaxes.

Community Relations Officers help to develop and maintain contact between the police department and community groups, organizations, and schools in the area. Their objective is to promote understanding of the police role in the community, develop closer working relationships, and keep open the lines of communication between citizens and the police department. These officers meet with members of the community and assist in developing police-sponsored programs to help reduce crime. Other duties include conducting tours of police facilities and addressing student and civic groups on relevant topics such as drug abuse, crime prevention, and traffic safety.

Canine Officers team with specially trained dogs to provide assistance to other police units within the department. For example, they are called to different scenes where their special skills are used to conduct building searches, track suspects in wooded or mountainous terrain, locate lost persons, or help in crowd-control operations. Canine Officers personally train their dogs with the help of professional instructors and are responsible for the animals' general care as well.

Crime Prevention Officers conduct security surveys of multiple dwelling and commercial establishments and suggest methods of improving security, such as the use of burglar alarms, window gates, and better locking devices. Speaking before civic groups to inform citizens of crime prevention and safety methods and presenting slides and movies that demonstrate various crime prevention programs may be other job duties. In some departments, Crime Prevention Officers analyze information contained in police reports for indications of crime patterns or trends. They then alert police units to potential problem areas and methods of operation used by perpetrators. This often effects a reduction in criminal activities.

Emergency Service Officers are highly trained police personnel who are brought into situations that other Police Officers are not equipped to handle. Examples of problems dealt with range from people threatening to jump from bridges or high buildings to persons trapped in automobile wreckage or threatened by a dangerous animal. Such cases require a special expertise, and these officers have the equipment and training needed to do the job.

In some police agencies, Police Officers are assigned to **Fugitive Search Units** where they are responsible for conducting investigations to locate and return fugitives for prosecution by criminal justice agencies. Data received from national, regional, and state crime information centers is examined and employers and other law enforcement agencies are contacted to develop leads. Once a fugitive is located, these officers obtain the legal documents necessary for custody and may be required to travel to other criminal justice agencies throughout the country to return prisoners wanted for unlawful flight.

Harbor Patrol is a specialized unit in which Police Officers are responsible for patrolling municipal harbors to detect and apprehend criminals and to aid persons in distress. Patrol is usually in power launches and may involve rescuing drowning victims, recovering bodies, or assisting ships in distress. These officers also cooperate with other law enforcement agencies in an effort to apprehend criminals and prevent smuggling or entry of illegal aliens.

Hostage Negotiation Teams are another area in which some Police Officers may specialize. Members of these units are specially trained officers who have the difficult task of rescuing hostages from their captors without bloodshed or violence. This is hardly easy because persons holding hostages are often nervous and desperate. Such situations require cool, calm, and logical actions on the part of each officer.

Police Officers in certain police departments are members of **Intelligence Units**. These units gather and compile information about community conditions, potential problems, organized crime, and lawlessness in the form of civil disorder. To obtain this data, officers often work undercover to infiltrate organized crime and terrorist groups or seemingly legitimate businesses used as fronts for criminal activities. They coordinate their activities with other law enforcement agencies, and furnish current information about the location and activities of members of organized crime and subversive groups to local, state, and federal agents.

Police Officers assigned to **Juvenile Units** have the responsibility of conducting juvenile investigations, providing assistance to field officers in matters involving juvenile problems, and of coordinating efforts with other agencies such as courts, schools, and social service and counseling agencies. Juvenile Officers investigate not only juvenile offenses but also cases of lost or runaway children to discover their whereabouts and to locate their parents. They take into custody delinquent or neglected children and refer cases involving serious offenses to the juvenile court system. They also patrol neighborhoods where youths gather, investigate reports of large gatherings that might indicate trouble, and enlist the help of the community in preventing potential juvenile problems.

Mounted Police Officers are specially trained officers who patrol their assigned areas on horseback or motorcycle. Officers on horseback perform the basic duties of the Patrol Officer but their skills are particularly effective in crowd-control activities. Through skillful handling of their mounts, these officers preserve order where large crowds congregate, such as at parades and sporting events, and, in cases of riot or civil unrest, disperse unruly crowds. Officers patrolling on motorcycles perform important traffic-control duties in congested areas by helping to facilitate the flow of traffic. In many cases, patrol cars are unable to reach the scene of disturbances or accidents, and motorcycle officers, first on the scene, provide assistance to sick or injured persons, direct traffic around fires or explosions, and perform general police work by keeping order and apprehending criminals.

Another specialized assignment that may be available to Police Officers is the **Property Unit**. Property Officers are responsible for property confiscated as evidence, removed from suspects, lost or stolen, or purchased by police department officials. Work also involves keeping detailed records of all properties under their control and, when authorized, releasing property to arresting officers for use as evidence in legal proceedings. They return personal property to suspects being released from custody and contact owners of lost or stolen property to claim articles upon proof of ownership. Property Officers keep extensive records of articles confiscated during arrests, such as narcotics and firearms, and arrange for their transfer to official disposal sites when required by law. Responsibility may also include receiving and examining property purchased by the department to verify the completeness and satisfactory condition of these purchases against invoices or other records.

Aviation programs in which Police Officers are trained as **Police Pilots** provide another area of police specialization. Because aircraft are not restricted by roads or traffic congestion, larger areas can be patrolled, and aircraft can be used for aerial surveillance missions, high-speed transportation, and police rescue missions. Police pilots may fly helicopters, conventional fixed-wing aircraft, or Short Takeoff and Landing (STOL) aircraft in carrying out their assignments. Helicopters are very effective in urban patrol as part of helicopter-automobile patrol teams. They can shorten response time to crime scenes, hover, or patrol at slow speeds to observe ground activities or illuminate an area at night. Conventional fixed-wing aircraft are very effective in highway speed enforcement as part of air-ground teams and in search and surveillance operations. Unlike the helicopter, however, they cannot hover or cruise at reduced speeds needed in urban areas. STOL aircraft combine some of the characteristics of the helicopter with those of conventional, fixed-wing aircraft. These aircraft can take off and land in shorter distances than those required for other fixed-wing aircraft. Faster than most helicopters, they can cruise at slower speeds than other fixed-wing craft and can stay airborne without refueling twice as long as rotary-wing aircraft. Regardless of the type of aircraft they fly, Police Pilots play a crucial role in law enforcement activities.

In some departments, cases of rape and sexual assault are the responsibility of Police Officers assigned to **Sex Crimes Units**. These crimes create special problems for both victims and the criminal justice system. Fear of harassment or humiliation during police investigations and medical examinations makes victims reluctant to report such crimes and to go through the ordeal of a trial. Sex Crimes Units are staffed with both male and female officers who are specially trained and sensitive to the plight of victims and can provide needed support during medical examinations, interviews with police and public prosecutors, and subsequent investigations. In some departments, rape victims, if they so desire, can deal exclusively with other women who act both as interviewers and as criminal investigators. These officers can also provide referral to community agencies that give special help to victims of sex crimes.

Anti-Crime or Street-Crime Units are a successful innovation being used by many departments throughout the country. Police Officers assigned to these units work in high-crime areas, out of uniform, and pose as unsuspecting citizens from various walks of life. Their objective is to present themselves as targets for assaults and robberies and to apprehend suspects who attempt to commit such crimes. These decoys team with backup units in the area so that a response is made when suspects attempt to carry out crimes against the decoy officers. Members of these units also conduct surveillance activities on stakeouts.

Many police agencies have developed **Tactical Forces**—highly mobile units that can be deployed rapidly against special crime problems. Normally made up of Police Officers from within the police agency, and varying in size from a few officers on small forces to several hundred on larger forces, these units are motorized and assigned to areas where patterns of serious crimes are occurring. The work can be varied and officers may find themselves working in plainclothes on a robbery detail and then be abruptly assigned to work in uniform on a different type of assignment. When no specific crime problems occur in a particular area, these officers are deployed over a wider area and then, if needed, can be called back quickly to work as a unit on a particular case. In some police agencies, these officers are members of specially trained units, such as sniper-suppression teams and special weapons attack teams (SWAT), which are used during specified emergency situations. The overall purpose of Tactical Forces is to strengthen the regular patrol force and help the line units to meet their goals.

Police Instructors are another example of the varied specializations into which Police Officers may move. These training officers instruct police recruits in basic phases of police work and in the duties and responsibilities of the Police Officer. They conduct lectures, discussions, and demonstrations and use audio-visual materials to teach basic core skills to new personnel. Subject matter of the training sessions includes criminal law, traffic regulations, human relations, criminal investigation, patrol techniques, report writing, firearms, and physical training. In addition to training police recruits, Police Instructors train veteran officers through inservice courses and refresher sessions. Some instructors specialize in one area of training. The educational and background qualifications for this position vary among departments.

Traffic Officers are members of specialized police units whose aim is to produce voluntary obedience to traffic regulations and provide maximum mobility of traffic with a minimum of interruption. These enforcement units operate in preselected locations in which high rates of vehicular and pedestrian accidents, auto thefts, and traffic-law violations occur. Traffic enforcement is closely related to other police activities because, in many instances, persons stopped for traffic violations are found to be involved in criminal activities or are fugitives wanted in another jurisdiction.

In addition to the Police Officers who work in local and county police agencies, there are others who are employed by special purpose public police forces in many cities throughout the United States. Some typical examples include park, harbor, airport, sanitation, transit, housing, and port police forces. Some of these agencies have full peace-officer powers within their limited jurisdictions while others have limited authority.

Housing Authority Officers patrol grounds, cellars, roofs, stairwells, and elevators of public housing projects. Officers are assigned to housing projects around the clock based on the incidence of crime in various locations. They conduct investigations of all crimes and disturbances on properties within their jurisdiction and apprehend and arrest suspects, using physical force or firearms if necessary.

Transit Authority Officers enforce the law and provide security services for municipal transit systems. These officers patrol subway stations, trains, and bus terminals, particularly during the high-crime late night hours. They apprehend and arrest suspects and use physical force and firearms if necessary to carry out their duties. The jurisdiction of Transit Officers is not limited to Transit Authority property. They have full police powers to enforce all local, state, and federal laws anywhere in the city.

Port Authority Police may be employed by an authority created to administer a port that spans more than one city or state. The Port Authority of New York and New Jersey is one example of such a port authority. Port Authority Police are responsible for policing and providing security in bus, rail, and air terminals; tunnels and bridges; and any properties or facilities operated by the Port Authority. Port Authority Officers enforce the law and apprehend and arrest suspects using physical force or firearms if necessary. Other responsibilities include controlling traffic and crowds and handling emergency situations occurring within their jurisdiction.

WORKING CONDITIONS

Police Officers work in many locations, which range from boroughs, townships, and counties to urban areas of varying sizes. Working conditions vary considerably according to location, size, organization, and jurisdiction of the police agency. Those who work in small towns and rural communities most certainly face problems different from those met by their counterparts in the inner cities of larger urban areas. There are definite differences in pace, types of criminal activities encountered, and availability of manpower and services needed to provide adequate police protection to the public. But all Police Officers, regardless of where they work, share certain problems. They constantly deal with human suffering, yet must always maintain self-control and act in a calm, efficient manner. They face danger, difficulty, and frustration, perhaps daily, but can do little to prevent it from happening. They also share the problems of long, irregular hours and, in some communities, a lack of public support for police officers.

As a rule, most Police Officers, while conducting patrols or carrying out other assignments, work outdoors in all types of weather. Some officers on special duty may perform their duties indoors at police facilities. Depending on the size of the department, Police Officers work alone or may have a partner. Because police agencies operate 24 hours a day, officers are usually required to work five-day rotating shifts, including holidays and weekends. Police Officers are on call at all times and, during periods of emergency or manpower shortages, are required to work additional tours of duty. All Police Officers, regardless of where they work or the size of the employing police agency, *must live with the very real threat of physical injury or death*. The apprehension of suspects who may be armed and dangerous, situations involving high-speed chases, or the rescue of individuals attempting suicide are some of the possibilities that make this work *hazardous*. Such hazards should be fully considered by individuals thinking about a police career. In most police agencies, Police Officers have fringe benefits that include some or all of the following: paid vacation, sick leave, and holidays; overtime pay; life, medical, and disability insurance; uniform allowances; tuition assistance or refund programs for college studies; and retirement pension. In some departments, officers may retire after 20 years of service if they are from 50 to 55 years of age. In departments with different standards, Police Officers may retire after 20 years of service regardless of age.

TRAINING AND PROMOTION OPPORTUNITIES

Following the completion of training, new officers are assigned to work under the supervision of a veteran officer. The experienced officer evaluates their work performance from time to time during the probationary period, which may last one year to 18 months. New officers may also team with experienced officers who provide them with practical instruction and field experience. After successfully completing the probationary period, these officers become permanent licensed or certified law enforcement officers; then they are sworn in and awarded a badge.

Once entry into this work is made, promotional prospects are generally good and are usually governed by merit or civil service system regulations. Police Officers as a rule become eligible for promotion after a specified number of years (three to five in most police agencies). Promotions are made according to the officer's position on a promotion list, determined by scores on a written, competitive examination as well as ratings of on-the-job performance. The first promotional level for uniformed Police Officers is the position of Sergeant. Thereafter they are eligible to compete for other positions such as Lieutenant Captain, or higher command positions the titles of which vary among police agencies throughout the country. A Police Officer might instead opt for lateral promotion into the Detective division. The officer would then begin as a Police Detective, moving up the ranks to Detective Sergeant, Detective Lieutenant, Detective Captain, and even beyond as merited by education, performance, and scores on competitive examinations.

Police Detective

DUTIES OF THE JOB

Police Detectives, key members of the police law enforcement team, conduct investigations to prevent crime, protect life and property, and solve criminal cases, which can range from misdemeanors to homicide. As a rule, crimes are initially investigated by uniformed Police Officers who are dispatched to crime scenes to apprehend suspects, question witnesses, and preserve evidence. If arrests are not made or the crime remains unsolved, Detectives take over the criminal investigation. Working in plainclothes, Detectives assigned to a case report to the scene, where possible, and determine the nature of the incident, exact location and time of the occurrence, and probable reason for the crime. They obtain reports from uniformed Police Officers; question witnesses, victims and suspects if they have been apprehended; and arrange for official statements to be given at a police station or headquarters. In addition, they search the area carefully to detect clues and gather evidence for use in the investigation. Detectives then direct Evidence Technicians to examine the scene to locate and lift latent fingerprints and to photograph the scene and any evidence obtained for eventual use in preparing the case for court. In some police departments, Detectives trained in fingerprinting and photography perform these duties themselves.

In seeking solutions to crimes, Detectives use all the resources of the police agency, such as ballistics experts, police chemists, laboratory technicians, computers, and speedy communication systems. Once all of the available information has been compiled, they analyze the results to determine the direction the investigation will take. Detectives study the files and records of suspects, if any, evaluate police laboratory findings, and prepare detailed reports including descriptions of evidence, names and statements of witnesses and victims, circumstances of the crime, and statements made by suspects. In attempts to develop leads, copies of fingerprints found at the crime scene may be transmitted to the State Crime Information Center (S.C.I.C.) and National Crime Information Center (N.C.I.C.) for comparison with those found at scenes in other localities. Information may also be given to police artists in their own departments or state and local law enforcement agencies for use in preparing composite sketches of suspects. Members of police patrol units are advised about crimes occurring in various areas and about the methods of operation used by perpetrators. In many instances, Police Detectives question informants on their knowledge of a crime or on their information about the personal habits, associates, characteristics, and aliases of crime suspects.

As evidence begins to develop, court-approved wire tapping or electronic surveillance methods may be used to gather data pertinent to the investigation. Detectives conduct surveillance of suspects on foot or in vehicles to uncover illegal activities; they participate in stakeouts at specific locations to gather evidence or prevent commission of crimes. When all investigative efforts have been made, each Detective prepares a written progress report of the case assigned and submits it to the Detective Sergeant or other superior officer for criticism and suggestions. At this point, the Detective usually plans what action is to be taken to resolve the case based on the evidence gathered and the recommendations of Supervisory Officers. Police Detectives arrest, or participate in the arrest of, suspects based on this evidence and as authorized by appropriate legal warrants.

During the process of arrest, they are authorized to use firearms and/or physical force where necessary to subdue suspects. At the time of arrest, they advise suspects of their constitutional rights and escort them to the police station or headquarters for booking, interrogation, and detention. Suspects are turned over to designated police personnel for fingerprinting, photographing, recording of personal effects, and checking of their records by the records section of the department against outstanding warrants in other jurisdictions.

An important responsibility of Police Detectives involves the preparation of criminal cases scheduled for trial. This entails preparing a written summary of facts gathered during the investigation, including evidence obtained and official statements made by witnesses, victims, Police Officers, and defendants. Prior to trial, Detectives usually review the case summary with the prosecutor to detect legal flaws; they may have to supply supplemental data to strengthen the case for the prosecution. Detectives spend many hours in court testifying as arresting officers and appearing as witnesses for the prosecution. In instances of unsolved cases, Detectives usually forward copies of the fingerprints gathered during the investigation to the Federal Bureau of Investigation (FBI) for comparison with prints which will be recorded during future arrests made nationwide by other law enforcement agencies.

The duties just described are common to Police Detectives in most local, county, and state investigative units. The increasing complexities of police work, however, have caused many agencies to use Detectives as specialists in various types of investigations. The size and resources of the department plus the needs of the community determine the extent of such specialization. Detectives in small police agencies tend to specialize less and are usually generalists who investigate a wide range of crimes. Detectives in large departments in heavily populated urban or suburban areas are more likely to specialize. The following are examples of some of the specialized assignments carried out by Police Detectives.

SPECIALIZED ASSIGNMENTS

Bombing/arson cases are those in which Detectives investigate incidents of suspected arson or the use or presence of explosive devices. Arson is the intentional or attempted destruction, by fire or explosion, of the property of another, or of one's own property, with the intent to defraud. Bombing incidents involve detonation or attempted detonation of an explosive or incendiary device for a criminal purpose or with disregard for the safety and property of others. In some departments, Detectives supervise or actually remove suspected explosive devices to the safe areas, using special skills and equipment to reduce the risk to police personnel and public safety.

Detectives assigned to **Burglary/Robbery Units** specialize in the investigation of such incidents to solve current criminal cases and to prevent future crimes of this sort. Burglary is the actual or attempted entry of a structure, with or without force, with the intent to steal or commit a felony (serious crime). Robbery is the unlawful taking or attempted taking of property in the immediate possession of another person by force or threat of force, with or without a deadly weapon.

Detectives, Fraud and Embezzlement, specialize in crimes involving embezzlement, fraud, forgery, and counterfeiting. Embezzlement is the illegal appropriation of entrusted property with the intention of defrauding the legal owner or beneficiary. Fraud involves deceit or intentional misrepresentation with the aim of illegally depriving a person of his/her property or legal rights. Forgery is the creation or alteration of a written or printed document with the intention to defraud by claiming it is the act of an unknown second party. In a check forgery, for example, the forged signature is accepted as being legitimate and the transaction is completed. Counterfeiting involves manufacture of a copy or imitation of a negotiable instrument with value set by law. Examples include currency, coins, postage, food stamps, and bearer bonds. The investigations into these "white-collar crimes" bring Detectives into close association with representatives of banks, brokerage firms, hotels, and retail establishments, as well as law enforcement agencies.

Homicide Detectives investigate criminal homicide cases in which one person is killed by another or other cases where death appears imminent as the result of aggravated assault. Criminal homicides are those that involve the death of another person without justification or excuse and include acts such as murder and voluntary, involuntary, and vehicular manslaughter.

Detectives assigned to a **Juvenile Section or Division** specialize in investigating cases involving juveniles (youths under 18 years of age who are subject to the jurisdiction of a juvenile court). These Detectives investigate all cases of juvenile crimes. They maintain surveillance in areas where youths gather to keep abreast of happenings and to develop case leads and arrest juveniles suspected of violating the law. Cases involving serious offenses are referred to the Juvenile Court, and parents or guardians are notified to advise them of circumstances in the case. Meetings may also be held with parents or guardians of juveniles in detainment, but not arrested or charged, to stress the need for increased supervision to prevent development of delinquent behavior.

Narcotics Detectives conduct specialized investigations to identify and apprehend persons suspected of illegal use or sale of narcotics and dangerous drugs. Narcotics Detectives examine physicians' and pharmacists' records to determine the legality of sales and to monitor the distribution of narcotics and the quantity of drugs in stock. They must often perform undercover work to investigate known or suspected drug suppliers and handlers who have been identified through surveillance or informants. Detectives purchase narcotics from suspects for use as evidence and arrest individuals identified as distributors, suppliers, and pushers. Narcotics Detectives also work on a cooperative basis with other police agencies involved in narcotics investigations and with federal agencies such as the Drug Enforcement Administration (DEA).

Detectives in some police agencies are part of **Organized Crime Activities Units** and specialize in investigating such activities. They gather data about members of organized criminal groups through the use of informers, surveillance, and infiltration by undercover officers. Not only are cases involving members of organized crime solved by such efforts, but numerous criminal acts are prevented from occurring at all. Often, participation in the Federal Organized Strike Force Programs and work with members of law enforcement agencies from all levels of government is part of these Detectives' assignments.

Motor Vehicle Theft and Truck Hijacking is another type of investigative specialization. Detectives question salvage and junkyard operators, motor vehicle and motor parts dealers, owners of retail stores, and pawnbrokers to uncover possible leads. They check inventories and records to make certain that stocks are legitimate. They maintain surveillance of known thieves and fences who illegally dispose of stolen property, use informers, and take suspects into custody when sufficient evidence has been gathered. Other duties include identification of stolen property and making arrangements for its return to owners.

Investigation of establishments and persons suspected of violating morality and antivice laws pertaining to liquor, gambling, and prostitution is the concern of **Vice Squad Detectives**. They monitor places where liquor is sold to check on hours of operation, underage patrons, and general adherence to the law. Establishing surveillance of suspects and locations to gather evidence of gambling and/or prostitution activities and working undercover to gain access are also part of the job. When sufficient evidence is gathered, necessary legal warrants are obtained, raids on suspects' establishments are conducted, and accused persons are taken into custody. In addition to those just mentioned, Detectives may, in some police agencies, specialize in the investigation of sex offenses, kidnappings, bank robberies, and missing person cases.

Working Conditions

Local, county, and state police agencies employ Detectives. Working conditions differ widely according to the size, location, organization, and jurisdiction of the police agency. During investigations, considerable time is spent in office work, reviewing files, gathering data, evaluating and preparing reports, meeting with other Police Officers, and making telephone inquiries. A good deal of time is also spent away from police officers working in a variety of locations, in all kinds of weather, reporting to crime scenes, questioning suspects and witnesses, conducting surveillance and stakeouts, and making arrests. Detectives drive unmarked police vehicles. They may work alone or with partners. Their basic work schedule is rotating shifts of five days a week, eight hours a day, including weekends and holidays. At times they work long, irregular hours; a considerable amount of overtime may be necessary during the investigation of certain cases. As with other Police Officers, Detectives are on call at all times and may be recalled to duty during periods of emergency. *Although detective work is a challenging career, there are times when it is tedious, routine, and frustrating.* Furthermore, *Detectives are often exposed to the risks of bodily injury and death* during the course of criminal investigations.

In most police agencies, Detectives receive fringe benefits including some or all of the following: paid vacation, sick leave, and holidays; overtime pay; life, medical, and disability insurance; tuition assistance or refund programs for college studies; and retirement pension. In some departments, Detectives can retire after 20 years of service if they are in the 50- to 55-year age bracket. Other departments have different standards, and Detectives may retire after 20 years of service regardless of age.

Training and Promotion Opportunities

After successfully completing their training, new Detectives remain on probation. They are assigned to work with experienced investigative personnel who provide practical guidance and assistance under actual field conditions. After demonstrating the ability to perform this job on an independent basis, newly hired Detectives are permanently assigned.

Advancement prospects for Detectives are governed by work performance, as well as the personnel practices and size of the agency. Promotional opportunities are usually good and are made according to merit system or civil service regulations. Detectives are, as a rule, eligible for promotion after satisfactory service for a specified period of time, say two to four years. When skills are developed through training, experience, and further education, it is possible to compete for the position of Sergeant, the first step in the promotion ladder. Subsequently, qualified candidates can compete for such positions as Lieutenant, Captain, and other high-level jobs known in different parts of the country by various titles such as Inspector, Major, Lieutenant Colonel, and Colonel.

POLICE RECRUIT QUALIFICATIONS

Entry requirements for Police Officers vary to a certain degree among police agencies throughout the country. As a rule, however, applicants must be U.S. citizens between the ages of 20 and 35 at the time of appointment to service. Time served in the military is usually deducted from a candidate's chronological age in meeting the upper age requirement. Most police agencies require completion of high school or its equivalent as the educational minimum, although some insist on completion of a specified number of college credits and, in some instances, a college degree. Secondary and postsecondary courses helpful in preparing for police work include government, English, psychology, sociology, American history, physics, and foreign languages. In addition, over 1000 junior colleges, colleges, and universities offer programs in police science or criminal justice. The vast majority of police agencies in the United States operate under civil service systems and select candidates accordingly. Candidates must pass a competitive examination and obtain a qualifying rating on an interview conducted by senior police officers. Each applicant must pass a comprehensive medical examination, which in some agencies includes psychological and psychiatric evaluations to determine emotional stability and acceptability for police work. Performance tests designed to gauge strength, agility, and stamina must be passed, and departmental standards with regard to height, weight, and eyesight must also be met. Because good judgment and a sense of responsibility are essential in police work, a thorough background investigation is conducted to assess general character, past history, honesty, and general suitability for this work. As a rule, possession of a valid driver's license is also required prior to employment by the police agency. Meeting the preceding requirements is the typical way of beginning a police career. In some localities, however, young high school graduates or law enforcement students in college can enter this field as police cadets or interns. These individuals, hired as paid civilian employees of the police agency, perform nonenforcement duties and attend classes to learn basic police skills. Those who successfully complete this type of program and meet the basic entry requirements for Police Officer may be appointed to the regular force at age 21.

Newly hired Police Officers enter training on a probationary basis prior to being assigned to duty. Programs vary widely with regard to length and content. In small departments, there is less formal instruction and a greater degree of on-the-job training as a means of developing skills. In large police agencies, formalized programs of instruction are the rule and may last from several weeks to six months, depending on department policy and availability of training facilities. Newly hired officers receive instruction in a variety of subjects including criminal law; motor vehicle codes; arrest, search, and seizure procedures; constitutional law; civil rights; methods of patrol, surveillance, and communications; traffic control; accident investigation; laws of evidence; crime prevention and criminal investigation procedures; pursuit driving; armed and unarmed defense tactics; use of various types of firearms; physical conditioning; crowd control; first aid; community relations; preparation of reports; court procedures; use of legal warrants; police ethics; and departmental regulations. Some departments combine this formal training with field experience to reinforce concepts learned in the classroom.

Following the completion of training, new officers are assigned to work under the supervision of an experienced officer. The experienced officers with whom probationary officers are teamed provide them with practical instruction and field experience and evaluate their work performance from time to time during the probationary period. Probation may last from a year to 18 months, after which the new officer becomes a permanent member of the force.

Police officers usually become eligible for promotion after a specified length of service. In a large department, promotion may allow an officer to specialize in one type of police work such as laboratory work, traffic control, communications, or work with juveniles. Promotions to the rank of sergeant, lieutenant, and captain are usually made according to a candidate's position on a promotion list, as determined by scores on a written examination and on-the-job performance.

Many types of training help police officers improve their performance on the job and prepare for advancement. Through training given at police department academies and colleges, officers keep abreast of crowd-control techniques, civil defense, legal developments that affect their work, and advances in law enforcement equipment. Many police departments encourage officers to work toward college degrees, and some pay all or part of the tuition.

IMPORTANT NOTE: If you are a veteran of the United States Armed Forces, be sure to make this fact known. Veterans receive some form of employment preference when they apply for any government position—local, state, or federal. The veteran's preference sometimes takes the form of points added to the examination score. For some positions, the maximum age of entry is raised by the number of years served. Service-connected disability, if it is not disqualifying for the job, can add still more weight to the application. Even if your experience in the Armed Forces was such that it cannot be counted towards the experience requirements of the position, be sure that you get credit for the very fact of that service.

A TYPICAL NOTICE OF EXAMINATION

POLICE OFFICER, EXAM. NO. . . . . . .

Job Description

To perform general police duties and related work in the New York City Police Department.

EXAMPLES OF TYPICAL TASKS: Patrols an assigned area on foot or in a vehicle; apprehends crime suspects; intervenes in various situations involving crimes in progress, aided cases, complaints, emotionally disturbed persons, etc.; responds to and investigates vehicular accidents; investigates specific offenses; interacts with prisoners; operates and maintains patrol vehicle; issues summonses; obtains information regarding incidents by interviewing witnesses, victims, and/or complainants; safeguards and vouchers found, seized, or recovered property; provides information to the public; handles situations involving maltreated, abused, or missing children; interacts with juveniles; prepares forms and reports; testifies in court.

OTHER JOB FACTORS: Listed below are examples of physical activities that Police Officers perform and environmental conditions in which their activities are conducted. This is not a comprehensive listing, only an indication of some of the job factors.

Works outdoors in all kinds of weather; walks and/or stands in an assigned area during a tour; drives or sits in a patrol car during a tour while remaining alert; runs after a fleeing suspect; climbs up stairs; carries an injured adult with assistance; grips persons to prevent escape; restrains a suspect by use of handcuffs; detects odors such as those caused by smoke or gas leaks; engages in hand to hand struggles to subdue a suspect resisting arrest; may be physically active for prolonged periods of time; understands verbal communication over the radio with background noise; reads and writes under low light conditions; carries or wears heavy equipment; wears bulletproof vest.

Police Officers are required to work Saturdays, Sundays, holidays, nights and change tours or work overtime when ordered as permitted by the Collective Bargaining Agreement.

Requirements

Candidates must have successfully completed either 60 semester credits from an accredited college or university or two years of full-time U.S. military service.

CHARACTER AND BACKGROUND: Proof of good character and satisfactory background will be absolute prerequisites to appointment. The following are among the factors which would ordinarily be cause for disqualification: (a) conviction of an offense, the nature of which indicates lack of good moral character or disposition towards violence or disorder, or which is punishable by one or more years of imprisonment; (b) repeated convictions of an offense, where such convictions indicate a disrespect for the law; (c) discharge from employment, where such discharge indicates poor behavior or inability to adjust to discipline; (d) dishonorable discharge from the Armed Forces; and (e) persons who have been convicted of petit larceny.

In accordance with provisions of law, persons convicted of a felony are not eligible for appointment to the title of Police Officer.

LICENSE REQUIREMENT: On the date of appointment, possession of a valid unrestricted New York State Driver License is required. Employees must maintain such license during their employment.

MEDICAL, PSYCHOLOGICAL, AND PHYSICAL STANDARDS: Eligibles must pass medical and psychological tests. Eligibles will be rejected for any medical condition which impairs their ability to perform the duties of the position in a reasonable manner, or which may reasonably be expected to render them unfit to continue to perform those duties in a reasonable manner. All employees must be medically, psychologically and physically fit to perform the full duties of the position and must continue to meet prescribed standards throughout their careers. Periodic testing may be required. Medical Standards are available at the Application Section of the Department of Personnel, 18 Washington Street, New York, NY 10004.

Candidates may be required to pass a qualifying physical test.

DRUG TESTING: A drug screening test will be conducted as part of a pre-employment screening process. Drug tests will also be administered to all Probationary Police Officers during Academy Training and again as part of the medical examination at the end of probation. All employees may again be drug tested on a random basis after their probationary periods are completed. Any member of the NYC Police Department found in possession of or using illegal drugs will be terminated.

Employees may be drug tested on a random basis as a prerequisite for assignment or promotion.

MINIMUM AGE REQUIREMENT: Eligibles must have attained age 22 to be appointed. Candidates who are too young for appointment on the date the lists are terminated will have no further opportunity for appointment from these lists.

Applicants must be at least 18 1/2 years of age by the last date of the application period to take this examination.

CITIZENSHIP REQUIREMENT: United States citizenship is required at the time of appointment.

All qualification requirements mentioned above must be met by the date of appointment.

Applicants may be summoned for the test prior to a review of their qualifications.

TEST INFORMATION

TEST DESCRIPTION: Written, multiple-choice test, weight 100.

The written test may include questions requiring any of the following abilities: written comprehension, written expression, memorization, problem sensitivity, number facility, deductive reasoning, inductive reasoning, information ordering, spatial orientation and visualization

The passing score will be determined after an analysis of the results.

Five points will be added to the written test score of those candidates who qualify for the New York City Residency Credit. To be eligible for the residency credit, a candidate must have achieved a passing score on the written examination and be a resident of New York City: (1) on the date of the written examination; and (2) on the date the eligible list is established. Candidates seeking residency credit must apply by completing the required forms on the date of the written test.

Eligibility for the residency credit will be investigated. As in the case of any intentional misrepresentation of a material fact on an employment application, candidates who claim residency credit and who are determined to have intentionally misrepresented facts concerning City residency shall be disqualified and their names shall be removed from the eligible list.

SELECTIVE CERTIFICATION: The eligible list resulting from this examination may be selectively certified to fill positions which require a working knowledge of both English and another language. Those who pass the written test and are placed on the eligible list may be permitted to take a qualifying oral test to determine ability to speak and understand other languages as needed. Candidates wishing to take such a qualifying test must indicate at the time of the written test the language for which they wish to be tested. Eligibles may be called to the qualifying oral test as needed. Only those eligibles who pass this qualifying oral test will be eligible for such selective certification.

APPOINTMENT INFORMATION

INVESTIGATION: Candidates are subject to investigation before appointment. At the time of investigation, candidates will be required to pay a fee for fingerprint screening.

At the time of investigation and at the time of appointment, candidates must present originals or certified copies of all required documents and proof, including but not limited to proof of date and place of birth by transcript of record of the Bureau of Vital Statistics or other satisfactory evidence, naturalization papers if necessary, proof of any military service, and proof of meeting educational requirements.

Any willful misstatement or failure to present any documents required for investigation will be cause for disqualification.

PROBATIONARY PERIOD: The probationary period is 24 months. Among other requirements, each appointee will be required to pass the Police Academy firearms, academic, physical performance, and driving tests.

FIREARMS QUALIFICATION: Candidates must qualify and remain qualified for firearms' usage as a condition of employment for the duration of their tenure. A firearms qualification test will be administered annually to determine qualification.

RESIDENCY REQUIREMENT: The New York State Public Officers Law requires that any person employed as a Police Officer in the New York City Police Department must be a resident of the City of New York or of Nassau, Westchester, Suffolk, Orange, Rockland or Putnam counties.

ENGLISH REQUIREMENT: Candidates must be able to understand and be understood in English. (See General Examination Regulation E.9)

PROOF OF IDENTITY: Under the Immigration Reform and Control Act of 1986, you must be able to prove your identity and your right to obtain employment in the United States prior to employment with the City of New York.

PROMOTION OPPORTUNITIES: Employees in the title of Police Officer are accorded the opportunity to be promoted to the title of Sergeant and are also accorded an opportunity to be designated Detective.

Currently, educational requirements for appointment to successive ranks are: (1) Sergeant—satisfactory completion of two years (64 credits) of coursework at an accredited college or university; (2) Lieutenant—satisfactory completion of three years (96 credits) of coursework at an accredited college or university; (3) Captain—attainment of a Baccalaureate degree from an accredited college or university. College credits which are earned as a result of satisfactorily completing the Police Academy curriculum can be used towards meeting the educational requirements.

APPLICATION INFORMATION

APPLICATION PERIOD: From February 7 through March 26. Application forms may be obtained in person or by mail from the Application Section, New York City Department of Personnel, 18 Washington Street, New York, NY 10004. Properly completed **ORIGINAL** application forms (**NO COPIES**) must be submitted only by mail to the **New York City Department of Personnel, Bowling Green Station, P O Box 996, New York, NY 10274-0996.** Applications must be postmarked no later than the last date of the application period.

In addition to the above, applications will also be available at all NYC Police Department precincts.

APPLICATION FEE: Payable by money order ONLY. Money orders should be made payable to the New York City Department of Personnel. The social security number of the candidate and the number(s) of the examination(s) for which he or she is applying must be written on the money order. Cash and checks will *not* be accepted. The application fee will be waived for a New York City resident receiving public assistance who submits a clear photocopy of a current Medicaid card along with the application. Applicants should retain their money order receipt as proof of filing until they receive notice of their test results.

TEST DATE: The multiple-choice test is expected to be held on Saturday, June 15.

ADMISSION CARD: Applicants who do not receive an admission card at least 4 days prior to the tentative test date must appear at the Examining Service Division of the Department of Personnel, 2 Washington Street, Manhattan, 17th floor, during normal business hours on one of the 4 days preceding the test date to obtain an admission card.

Accommodations are available for applicants who provide satisfactory proof of disability. Applications for accommodations must be submitted as early as possible and in no event later than 30 work days before the test or part of a test for which accommodation is requested. Consult General Examination Regulation E.10 for further requirements.

The Department of Personnel makes provisions for candidates claiming inability to participate in an examination when originally scheduled because of the candidate's religious beliefs. Such candidates should consult General Examination Regulation E.11.2 for applicable procedures in requesting a special examination. Such requests must be submitted no later than 15 days before the scheduled date of the regular examination.

LIST TERMINATION: The eligible list will be terminated one year from the date it is established, unless extended by the City Personnel Director.

THE POLICE OFFICER
SCREENING PROCESS

WHY DO PEOPLE BECOME POLICE OFFICERS?

The police officer on the beat or in the patrol car is a familiar figure on the American scene. Except among certain criminal elements, the officer is highly respected. Law abiding citizens are reassured by the presence of police officers whether those officers are directing traffic, discouraging crime by their visible presence, or helping citizens during actual or potential emergencies.

The respect commanded by the police officer makes him or her a role model to all young children. At some time in his or her childhood, nearly every youngster wants to grow up to be a police officer. Many retain this career goal into their teen years and take active steps to join a police force as they become young adults.

A combination of factors makes police work attractive. The idealistic young person—yes, despite the cynics, there are a great many idealistic young Americans—sees police work as a worthwhile activity. A police officer serves the community. His or her work is absolutely vital to the welfare of the public. Police work gives an opportunity to serve while gaining respect and earning a good living.

The material benefits of police work are very real. Police officers are well-paid public servants; their salary levels are above average, and they receive excellent benefits packages. Police officers can look forward to health and life insurance coverage, to generous time-off and vacation allotments, to opportunities for increased responsibility, advancement, and promotions, and to early, well-paid retirement.

A police department never shuts down. This twenty-four-hour, year-round coverage means that police officers sometimes must work nontraditional hours. While the odd working hours may at times interfere with sleep patterns, they offer benefits as well. Family men, in particular, find it a real asset to have some "prime time" hours at home with their children. Police officers with rotating shifts may have opportunities to share school events or afternoon leisure time with their growing families. Traditional 9-to-5 workers miss these opportunities. Flexible work schedules allow the police officer to attend to personal business without having to borrow precious vacation days. In addition, local police officers do not travel. They are not required to spend long periods on the road away from their homes and families. Police scheduling is one of the appealing features that draws people into this field and that adds to the competitiveness of entry.

One final aspect of police work that draws people into the field is the potential for excitement. A desire for excitement in one's everyday work is not a reason in itself for entering a police force, but it can be an added attraction. Much police work is routine and boring, but the possibility of variety and excitement does exist. Many desk or production jobs are routine and boring with no prospects for interesting relief. Police departments are careful to avoid hiring candidates who seek police work only for the excitement, but they look favorably upon candidates who welcome the challenge of the unexpected.

The popularity of police work makes the field a highly competitive one to enter. There are many more aspiring police officers than there are openings on the force. This situation allows police departments to be very selective in the hiring process. Since they have a large applicant pool, they can afford to hire only those applicants who they feel will succeed in their police training and who they expect to become superior police officers.

The police department is looking for a combination of positive traits in each prospective police officer. The screening process takes each applicant through a series of steps, each designed to measure another trait. The recruit must successfully pass through each of these stages. Failure at any stage eliminates the candidate. Let us discuss the desired traits and the reasons they are so important to the police force.

Traits of a Police Officer

1. **The police officer must be intelligent.** First of all, the recruit must be intelligent enough to make it through the police academy or whatever training program the particular department offers. The recruit must read well to comprehend written materials, must have good listening skills, and must remember what he or she has been taught. The recruit must be able to synthesize material, that is, be able to learn rules and then be able to apply them to hypothetical or actual situations. Remembering information is not enough. The candidate must convince the examiners that he or she can understand, interpret, and apply information in the field. The intelligent police officer can separate what is important from what is less important, can make quick judgments, and can express him- or herself well in speech and in writing. Most police departments begin the applicant screening process with a written test. Written tests require a minimum of administrative time. They can be administered to a large number of applicants at one sitting. Applicants who do not score well on the written test are dropped from consideration. There is no reason to spend time administering medical exams, physical performance tests, psychological exams, or interviews to candidates who do not demonstrate the intelligence to learn the job and to serve as effective police officers.

2. **The police officer must be healthy and physically strong and agile.** Police work is physically taxing. The officer must be able to spend many hours on his or her feet, to move quickly, to see and hear accurately, and to lift, move, or carry as the emergency requires. Obviously, a police officer who is often ill or who cannot perform all physical activities adequately is not acceptable. Police departments have strict medical standards so that they hire only recruits in excellent health. A great many medical conditions that are not so severe as to interfere with everyday life nor with most occupations are disqualifying for the police officer. Likewise, police departments have carefully devised physical performance tests of strength, speed, and agility. The applicant who cannot qualify on the tests does not show great promise for success as a police officer. Medical and physical screening are important hurdles in the selection process.

3. **The police officer must be emotionally stable.** A police officer carries a gun. Obviously, anyone who is armed must be even tempered, well adjusted, and impartial. When it comes to dealing with firearms, there is no room for error. It is vital that the police officer not become excited nor fire too soon. The police officer must be able to size up a situation without fear or prejudice, then act appropriately. The police officer cannot be ruled by anger; at the same time, the police officer cannot hesitate when prompt action is required. Police brutality, insult, and behavior on the basis of preconceived opinions have no place anywhere in the police force. Choosing the most stable recruits from among the applicants is one

of the more difficult tasks for those in charge of hiring. Applicants who have done well on the written exam and who have passed medical examination and physical fitness tests must often submit to psychological examinations. Psychological examinations are not always satisfactory, but police departments must rely on them to eliminate those candidates who appear to be less than perfectly well adjusted and stable. Because psychological testing tends to be inexact, the test results are often confirmed through interviews. Through a psychological test (often more than one) and interviews, each applicant who has reached this stage of the screening process must prove the stability required for responsible behavior in the police role.

4. **The police officer must be self-confident and tactful.** These personality aspects are the final refinements upon which hiring decisions are based. These judgments are based upon interviews. The police officer must have the self-confidence to make quick decisions and to stick with them. Unwavering decisions and firm actions are vital in maintaining control. Tactful, gentle, but firm: these are the hallmarks of the effective, successful police officer. The interviewer hopes to choose the applicants who best display these qualities in a fine, delicate balance. The judgment cannot be entirely objective, but the interviewer does his or her best. The police officer candidate, in turn, can make a conscious effort to impress the interviewer as a tactful, thoughtful person who can communicate and take over effectively under pressure.

The Written Examination

Step one in the screening process is nearly always the written examination. Police departments want to avoid any possible accusation of favoritism or prejudice in hiring, so they invariably use written examinations to screen out unqualified candidates. The written examination is in almost all cases a multiple-choice examination. Multiple choice assures objectivity. If the questions are well designed, each question has only one right answer. Such exams are easy to score and are generally considered to be fair. The unique feature of entry-level examinations is that they do not presuppose any knowledge. The applicant taking a police officer entry exam is not expected to know police rules, regulations, or procedures. On the other hand, the candidate is expected to reason and even to think like a police officer. Questions that evaluate the candidate's thinking and reasoning processes will include all the necessary information with which to reason. This means that police officer exams tend to include many lists of rules and procedures. They often include long excerpts from manuals and rulebooks. The test taker must read and understand the rules that are the basis for each judgment or reasoning question and then must think through the best answer.

READING-BASED QUESTIONS

By now you should have gathered that much of the measure of police intelligence is based upon how well you read and what you do with that which you read. Reading-based questions include questions of fact to be extracted directly from reading passages, questions of inference from reading passages, questions that require a choice of actions based upon rules and a fact situation, and questions of judgment of the behavior of others, again based upon both rules and a fact situation. They may also probe your ability to interpret and judge from what you read by presenting a series of definitions and descriptions of situations and then asking you to classify the situations based on the fact situations.

Since reading-based questions of one form or another constitute the bulk of all police exams, we have devoted a full chapter in this book to preparing you for these questions.

PRACTICAL JUDGMENT QUESTIONS

Closely related to reading-based questions are questions of practical police judgment. These are questions that present you with a fact situation and require you to make a spot decision for appropriate action in that situation. The judgment questions do not presuppose knowledge of the proper police action. Your answer should be based upon good judgment and common sense. However, some familiarity with "police thinking" should stand you in good stead with these questions. The good judgment that you demonstrate in police practical judgment questions should predict the same good judgment in actual police situations. The chapter Police Judgment Quizzer prepares you for police judgment questions and introduces you to "police thinking," which you can then combine with your own common sense in answering the questions. The Judgment Quizzer will give you lots of practice with this important question type, and the answer explanations will all contribute to training you to "think right."

OBSERVATION AND MEMORY QUESTIONS

The intelligent police officer not only reads well but is able to choose a course of action on the basis of knowledge from reading and can make good judgments in both emergency and nonemergency situations. He or she must also be a keen observer with a good memory. Observation with instant forgetting is totally useless. Observation and memory questions, which appear on many, though by no means all, police officer exams, serve to identify those recruits who are wide awake and know what to watch for. In a way, they also are a test of judgment, for the test-taker must be able to decide what to focus on. Obviously, no one can notice and remember every detail of a scene or event. The intelligent observer can choose what is most important and commit it to memory. The test situation is not, of course, the same as real life. If your exam does not include this type of question, it is because your police department considers observation and memory questions on a written test to be too artificial to be truly predictive. Since this type of question does appear frequently, we have included a chapter for instruction and practice. The information will prove useful whether or not you must answer observation and memory questions on your exam; you will certainly need to sharpen these skills in order to perform your police duties.

GRAMMAR AND EFFECTIVE EXPRESSION QUESTIONS

Another important line of questioning on police entrance exams has to do with grammar and effective expression. The reason for these questions is obvious. A police officer must communicate in both speech and in writing; his or her message must come across clearly and accurately. All important information must be included, and it must be stated in logical order. There must be no opportunity for misinterpretation or misunderstanding. Police recruits should present their best language skills along with their other qualifications. Grammar and effective expression are, of course, also related to reading. The person who has done extensive reading should be aware of ways to best express information in clear and orderly fashion. We will not attempt to teach grammar at this late stage. Your logical thinking and your eye for what "looks right" will have to see you through. However, we can forewarn you of various forms that grammar and effective expression questions may take and how to approach them.

Your exam may offer you four sentences and ask you to choose the sentence that is wrong with respect to grammar or English usage. This type of question can prove quite difficult. Often two or even three sentences appear to be wrong. Draw upon your school training. Try the sentences aloud (very softly). You may have to weed out the sentences that you are sure are correct, then guess from among the remaining ones.

Another approach is to offer you four sentences, often all attempting to give the same information, and to ask you which one is best. This is a little easier. Concentrate on literal reading of each sentence. Be sure that the one you choose says what you think it means.

Other exams may ask your advice in rephrasing an awkward sentence or in repositioning a sentence or paragraph for more reasonable presentation.

A common effective expression question gives a series of sentences in random order. You must choose the logical progression of steps—what happened first, next, and so on.

A final form of this question is one that presents a list of facts, then asks you to include all these facts in a statement of one or two sentences. You must take care to include all the facts and to express them in an unambiguous way. Read each choice literally to catch word orders that may make the meaning incorrect or even ridiculous. Check the list of facts often to ensure that all facts are presented clearly and appropriately in the statement.

Related to questions of effective expression are questions of what information is important to include in a statement or report. This type of question relies on judgment as well as on knowing the best way of expressing information. Put yourself in the position of the person receiving and having to act on the information. What would be most useful? What do you need to know? In what order would you find the information most helpful?

Reading Maps

Except in cases of extreme emergency, police officers are required to obey all traffic laws. The police officer who goes to the scene of an accident by entering a one-way street in the wrong direction is likely to create another accident. On the other hand, time may be of the essence. A victim may have injuries that require immediate attention. An officer may have to choose the most efficient legal way to get there. Map questions on police exams involve a combination of reading, logical thinking, and common sense. The police candidate can learn how to use maps effectively while undergoing training; however, the applicant who comes with a well-developed skill will be able to spend more time getting specialized police training. Concentrate on map questions on your exam. Read carefully. Put yourself in the driver's seat, and follow all instructions. Do not hesitate to turn the test booklet as needed to maintain your sense of direction.

FILLING OUT FORMS

Police officers must fill out forms and must read and follow them. A few police exams include questions based upon a form, instructions for filling out the form, and a fact situation. There is no trick to these questions. Read carefully. Be especially alert to instructions which read "fill in blank 3 only if such and such" or "leave number 7 blank unless this and that both apply." Exclusionary and inclusive words present the keys in answering many form questions.

MISCELLANEOUS QUESTIONS

There is a variety of miscellaneous questions that appear on isolated police qualification exams. Some or all or none of them may occur on yours. If they are included, they tend not to comprise a significant part of the exam. These questions include arithmetic, synonyms, verbal analogies, spelling, and various types of coding questions. Read directions carefully, then do your best with these.

The Medical Examination

The police officer's beat must be covered at all times. This means that the assigned officer must show up. Otherwise, the scheduling officer must find a substitute and must rearrange the work tours of many other officers. The candidate with a history of frequent illness or one with a chronic ailment that may periodically crop up and interfere with attendance is not an acceptable candidate. Likewise, the applicant with an underlying physical condition that presents no problems in everyday life but which might be aggravated under the stressful activity of a police officer must be rejected.

Every candidate under consideration must undergo a thorough medical examination performed by a department physician or by a physician designated by the department. This examination most often occurs after the applicant has passed the written exam and before the test of physical fitness or physical performance. Occasionally, the candidate is required to have a preliminary medical examination by his or her own physician and to present a note attesting to adequate health and fitness for taking the performance test. A medical examination comes before the physical test so that candidates whose health might be jeopardized by the strenuous activity of the physical test are screened out ahead of time. The police department does not want its applicants collapsing on the floor of the physical testing arena. Only the background check may occur either before or after the medical exam. Since both medical exam and background check require an investment of time by police personnel and yet neither depends upon the other, they may be done in either order. Disqualification on the basis of either background check or medical exam stops the screening process and eliminates the candidate from further consideration.

The medical exam will resemble an army physical more than a visit to your personal physician. You will start by filling out a lengthy questionnaire relating to your medical history. This questionnaire will be used by the physician to single out special health areas for consideration. It may also be used by the personal interviewer when you approach the final step of the screening process.

Do not lie on the medical questionnaire. Your medical history is a matter of record at school, in your service dossier, and in the hospital or clinic files. If you lie you will be found out. If the medical condition does not disqualify you, the fact of your untruthfulness will. On the other hand, there is no need to tell more than is asked. You do not need to expand upon your aches and pains. You needn't make an illness or injury more dramatic than it was. Stick to the facts and do not raise any questions. If you have any current concerns, the police department's examining officer is not the person to ask.

Your medical examination almost certainly will include height and weight measurement, chest x-ray, eye test, hearing test, blood tests, urinalysis, cardiogram, blood pressure, and actual visual and physical examination by the doctor. If you have any doubts as to how you will fare with any of these examinations, you might want to consult your personal physician ahead of time. You may be able to correct a borderline situation before you appear for the exam.

Most police departments provide candidates with height-weight standards and with lists of medical requirements before their scheduled medical examinations. If you receive these, look them over carefully. If they present any problems to you, see your doctor. Your worry may be misplaced, or it may be real. Possibly you will have to change your career goals. Or, likely, you can correct the situation, pass the medical exam, and go on to serve on the police force.

Not all police departments have the same standards for medical conditions. Some will accept conditions that are absolutely disqualifying in others. The height-weight charts and the list of medical requirements on the following pages are illustrative. They are typical of those of many police departments. They should serve you as a general guide at this time. If your own medical position is way out of line, you may need to reconsider or embark on a major health reform campaign right away. Once you get your own department's official set of guidelines, follow those standards rather than the ones printed here.

Height and Weight for Females
Acceptable Weight in Pounds According to Frame

Height	Small Frame	Medium Frame	Large Frame
	lb.	lb.	lb.
4'10"	92–98	96–107	104–119
4'11"	94–101	98–110	106–122
5'	96–104	101–113	109–125
5'1"	99–107	104–116	112–128
5'2"	102–110	107–119	115–131
5'3"	105–113	110–122	118–134
5'4"	108–116	113–126	121–138
5'5"	111–119	116–130	125–142
5'6"	114–123	120–135	129–146
5'7"	118–127	124–139	133–150
5'8"	122–131	128–143	137–154
5'9"	126–135	132–147	141–158
5'10"	130–140	136–151	145–163
5'11"	134–144	140–155	149–168
6'	138–148	144–159	153–173
6'1"	142–152	148–163	157–177

Body Fat Percentage (Maximum allowed)

Age Group	20–29	30–39
Females	26.1	27.1

Height and Weight for Males
Acceptable Weight in Pounds According to Frame

Height	Small Frame	Medium Frame	Large Frame
	lb.	lb.	lb.
5'3"	115–123	121–133	129–144
5'4"	118–126	124–136	132–148
5'5"	121–129	127–139	135–152
5'6"	124–133	130–143	138–156
5'7"	128–137	134–147	142–161
5'8"	132–141	138–152	147–166
5'9"	136–145	142–156	151–170
5'10"	140–150	146–160	155–174
5'11"	144–154	150–165	159–179
6'	148–158	154–170	164–184
6'1"	152–162	158–175	168–189
6'2"	156–167	162–180	175–194
6'3"	160–171	167–185	178–199
6'4"	164–175	172–190	182–204
6'5"	168–179	176–194	186–209
6'6"	172–183	180–198	190–214

Body Fat Percentage (Maximum allowed)

Age Group	20–29	30–39
Males	18.9	22.0

NOTE: Although the above tables commence at a specified height, no minimum height requirement has been prescribed. This table of height and weight will be adhered to in all instances except where the Civil Service examining physician certifies that weight in excess of that shown in the table (up to a maximum of twenty pounds) is lead body mass and not fat. Decision as to frame size of a candidate shall be made by the examining physician.

The following tests will be part of the physical examination:

- Vision
- Hearing
- Serology
- Urinalysis
- Chest X-Ray
- Blood Pressure
- Electrocardiogram

ONE LARGE CITY'S MEDICAL REQUIREMENTS

Candidates are required to meet the physical and medical requirements stated below and in the announcement at the time of the medical examination, at the time of appointment, and at appropriate intervals thereafter.

1. **Weight.** Candidates should have weight commensurate to frame. Weight should not interfere with candidate's ability to perform the duties of the position of Police Officer.

2. **Vision.** Candidates must have binocular visual acuity not less than 20/20 with or without correction; if correction is required, binocular visual acuity not less than 20/40 without correction. Binocular peripheral vision should not be less than 150 degrees.

3. **Color Vision.** Be able to distinguish individual basic colors against a favorable background.

4. **Hearing.** Candidates must be able to pass an audiometric test of hearing acuity in each ear. A binaural hearing loss of greater than 15% in the frequency ranges of 500, 1000, 2000 Hz would be considered disqualifying. Hearing appliances should correct the deficiency so the binaural hearing loss in the combined frequency level of 500, 1000, 2000 Hz is no greater than 15%.

5. **Heart.** Candidates must be free of functionally limiting heart disease. Must have a functional cardiac classification of no greater than Class I. This determination to be made clinically or by cardiac stress test.

6. **Lungs.** The respiratory system must be free of chronic disabling conditions that would interfere with the candidate's performance of required duties.

7. **Diabetes.** Candidates who are diabetic must not require insulin injections or oral hypoglycemic agents for control.

8. **Neurological Health.** Candidates must be free of neurological disorders that may affect job performance. Candidates with epilepsy or seizure disorders must provide evidence of one-year seizure free history without drug control.

9. **Musculoskeletal Health.** Candidates must be free of musculoskeletal defects, deformities, or disorders which may affect job performance. Functional use of the arms, hands, legs, feet and back must be demonstrable at the examination. Candidates will be asked to demonstrate physical fitness through tests of strength, agility, flexibility and endurance.

10. **Hernia.** Candidates must be free of abdominal and inguinal herniae which would interfere with job performance.

11. **Blood / Vascular Health.** Candidates must be free of blood or vascular disorders that interfere with the performance of duties. Candidates with uncontrolled high blood pressure will be disqualified remediable.

12. **Mental Health.** Candidates must be free of mental illness, serious emotional disturbances or nervous disorders and from alcoholism or drug dependence or abuse.

13. **General Medical Statement.** Candidates must be free of any medical and/or nervous condition that would jeopardize safety and health of others. Candidates with communicable diseases will be disqualified remediable.

3

MEDICAL REQUIREMENTS FROM OTHER POLICE DEPARTMENTS

Medical standards do indeed vary from department to department, so if you appear to be borderline or even not qualified for one department, it is worthwhile to look into the specifics in another department or jurisdiction. The variations are most notable in standards for vision and hearing. Some police officers are permitted to wear glasses or contact lenses; most are not. Some may have limited color blindness. Furthermore, some jurisdictions will happily employ officers who have had their vision surgically corrected by orthokeratology, radial keratotomy, or epikeratoplasty while in other jurisdictions these procedures are automatically disqualifying. It is worthwhile to do some research before you begin the application process.

38.

While there is indeed variation in the standards of the various police departments, there is more similarity than difference. The greater variation comes in the way the departments state their requirements. Here are formulations from two more police jurisdictions.

Sample Medical Requirements from a Second Police Department

3

The duties of these positions involve physical exertion under rigorous environmental conditions; irregular and protracted hours of work; patrol duties on foot, motor vehicle, and aircraft; and participation in physical training. Applicants must be in sound physical condition and of good muscular development.

Vision

- Binocular vision is required and must test 20/40 (Snellen) without corrective lenses,
- Uncorrected vision must test at least 20/70 in each eye,
- Vision in each eye must be corrected to 20/20,
- Near vision, corrected or uncorrected, must be sufficient to read Jaeger Type 2 at 14 inches, and
- Ability to distinguish basic colors by pseudoisochromatic plate test (missing no more than four plates) is required, as is normal peripheral vision.

Hearing

- Without using a hearing aid, the applicant must be able to hear the whispered voice at 15 feet with each ear; or
- Using an audiometer for measurement, there should be no loss of 30 or more decibels in each ear at the 500, 1,000, and 2,000 levels.

Speech

- Diseases or conditions resulting in indistinct speech are disqualifying.

Respiratory System

- Any chronic disease or condition affecting the respiratory system of a nature that would impair the full performance of duties of the position is disqualifying; e.g., conditions that result in reduced pulmonary function, shortness of breath, or painful respiration.

Cardiovascular System

The following conditions are disqualifying:

- Organic heart disease (compensated or not),
- Hypertension with repeated readings which exceed 150 systolic and 90 diastolic without medication, and
- Symptomatic peripheral vascular disease and severe varicose veins.

Gastrointestinal System

- Chronic symptomatic diseases or conditions of the gastrointestinal tract are disqualifying.
- Conditions requiring special diets or medications are disqualifying.

Endocrine System

- Any history of a systemic metabolic disease, such as diabetes or gout, is disqualifying.

Genito-Urinary Disorders

- Chronic, symptomatic diseases or conditions of the genito-urinary tract are disqualifying.

Extremities and Spine

- Any deformity or disease that would interfere with range of motion, or dexterity, or that is severe enough to affect adversely the full performance of the duties of the position is disqualifying.

Hernias

- Inguinal and femoral hernias with or without the use of a truss are disqualifying. Other hernias are disqualifying if they interfere with performance of the duties of the position.

Nervous System

- Applicants must possess emotional and mental stability with no history of a basic personality disorder.
- Applicants with a history of epilepsy or convulsive disorder must have been seizure free for the past two years without medication.
- Any neurological disorder with resulting decreased neurological or muscular function is disqualifying.

Miscellaneous

Though not mentioned specifically above, any other disease or condition that interferes with the full performance of duties is also grounds for medical rejection.

Before entrance on duty, all applicants must undergo a pre-employment medical examination and be medically suitable to perform the full duties of the position efficiently and without hazard to themselves and others. Failure to meet any one of the required medical qualifications will be disqualifying for appointment. These standards are considered minimum standards and will not be waived in any case. Applicants found to have a correctable condition may be restored to any existing list of eligibles for further consideration for appointment when the disqualifying condition has been satisfactorily corrected or eliminated.

Statement of Medical Requirements from a Third Department

NOTE: Candidates are required to meet the physical and medical requirements stated below and in the announcement at the time of the medical examination, at the time of appointment, and at appropriate intervals thereafter.

1. **Height and Weight**—Will not interfere with the candidate's ability to perform the essential functions of the position. All candidates will be evaluated for stamina and vigor to demonstrate their physical fitness through tests of strength, agility, flexibility, and endurance.

2. **Speech**—Must be free of speech pathology which would interfere with the ability to communicate clearly.

3. **Vision**—Distant visual acuity should be correctable to better than, or equal to 20/30 (Snellen) in each eye; if correction is required, binocular visual acuity not less than 20/70 without correction. Binocular peripheral vision should not be less than 170 degrees.

4. **Color Vision**—Perception of color is deemed acceptable if the candidate correctly reads nine (9) or more of the first thirteen (13) plates of the 24-plate edition of the Ishihara Test. If the candidate's color perception is deemed unacceptable through the use of said test and he/she believes the results to be incorrect, such an individual may at his/her own expense take the Farnsworth-Munsell 100-Hue Test. (a) The test must be taken under the supervision of an ophthalmologist having the proper equipment and utilizing the standards established by the Municipal Police Training Council. (b) If the candidate takes and completes the Farnsworth-Munsell 100-Hue Test, the specialist shall certify in writing whether or not the candidate meets the required color perception standards. (c) Both eyes should be examined together and scored as such. (d) If a candidate fails the initial test, he/she must, upon request, be immediately retested and the lower total error score used for purposes of qualification. A total error score of not more than 124 is deemed acceptable. (e) The use of any lens by an officer candidate in order to meet the color perception standard is not acceptable.

5. **Hearing**—The average hearing level (HL) for the three (3) test frequencies of 500, 1000, and 2000 Hz will not exceed 25 dB in either ear, and no single hearing level will exceed 30 dB at any of these 3 test frequencies in either ear. Hearing loss at 3000 Hz will not exceed 40 dB HL in either ear. Use of hearing aids is permitted as long as they are self-contained and fit within (auricular) or behind or over (post-auricular) the ear. Candidates with hearing aids, at their own expense, must provide evidence from a licensed audiologist, using functional gain or real ear measurements, that their aid(s) meet the stipulated manufacturer's standards. *Recourse Testing:* If the candidate's pure tone screening test is deemed unacceptable, such candidate may at his/her own expense have an audiological evaluation administered by a NYS licensed audiologist, including: 1. hearing sensitivity,

2. speech discrimination in quiet, 3. speech discrimination in noise. Testing should be performed in a sound-treated environment meeting the 1969 ANSI or any subsequent standard. The CID W-22 word lists should be presented at 50 dB HL via a calibrated speed audiometer through a single speaker stationed at 0 degrees azimuth with the candidate seated at approximately 1 meter (39 inches) from the speaker. Speech (hearing) discrimination testing in a background of broad-band noise should be conducted in the same sound field environment. Again, using a different version of one of the CID W-22 word lists presented at 50 dB HL, a competing noise should be simultaneously presented at 40 dB HL (S/N=+10) through the same speaker (0 degrees azimuth) as the test words or through a separate speaker located at 180 degrees azimuth. The minimal acceptable standard of speech (hearing) discrimination shall be a score no poorer than 90% in quiet and 70% in noise on two of the pre-recorded versions of the CID W-22 word lists. An open-test response format should be utilized with the candidate responding in writing.

6. **Cardiovascular**—Candidate must have a functional and therapeutic cardiac classification no greater than NYS Class IA. This determination must be made clinically or by cardiac stress test. Candidates with uncontrolled high blood pressure will be restricted pending remediation.

7. **Respiratory System**—The respiratory system must be free of chronically disabling conditions that would interfere with the candidate's ability to perform the essential functions of the position.

8. **Diabetes**—Candidates who are diabetic must provide evidence of satisfactory medical control. Candidates will be evaluated on a case-by-case assessment as to the control of diabetes and presence and severity of symptoms and complications.

9. **Neurological Health**—Candidates must be free of neurological disorders that would interfere with the candidate's ability to perform the essential functions of the position. Candidates with any type of epilepsy or seizure disorders must provide evidence of one-year seizure free history with or without drug control.

10. **Musculoskeletal Health**—Candidates must have no defects, deformities, or disorders that will interfere with the candidate's ability to perform the essential functions of the position. The use of prostheses or braces is allowed as long as the candidate can perform the full range of duties of the position and no security risk is posed.

11. **General Medical Statement**

A. Candidates must be free of any medical condition, including alcohol abuse, and/or psychiatric disorder, that would jeopardize the safety and health of the public and/or other employees, or would clearly interfere with the ability to perform the essential functions of the position.

B. Candidates may not have a medical problem that prevents them from working mandatory unscheduled overtime.

C. Candidates found to be abusing legal drugs or using illegal drugs will be disqualified.

Physical Performance Tests

The physical performance requirements for all law enforcement officers—police officers, state troopers, corrections officers, special agents—are very similar. All law enforcement officers must be able to jump into action in an instant, must be able to move very quickly, must be strong, must have the stamina to maintain speed and strength for a long time, and must be able to continue physically stressful activity at a high level while withstanding discomfort and pain. The ideal law enforcement officer is "Superman." The actual officer does well to approach those qualities.

While all departments have similar physical performance requirements, each tends to measure fitness in its own way. Because physical ability is absolutely vital to the officer's effectiveness and survival on the job, departments place a great deal of emphasis on their physical performance tests. In some jurisdictions, the physical performance test is a competitive test. This means that the test is scored, and the numerical score contributes to the candidate's place on the eligibility list. In other jurisdictions, the physical performance test is qualifying. This means that the candidate must pass the test in order to be hired, but ranking on the list is based on other factors. Either way, you must be well prepared for the performance test. All tests are not alike. The following selection of tests of physical fitness and agility will introduce you to many different tasks. Read them through and note the variations. Try each out to the extent that you can without the actual testing course. See how you do. You may need to get yourself into a regular body-building routine some time before you are called for examination. Strength and fitness cannot be developed overnight. You will need to work yourself up to par over a long period. Set up a program and get started right away. You will not be called for a physical fitness test until after you have passed the written examination and the medical examination. The background check may also be conducted before your physical fitness test. Chances are that you will not be called for a physical fitness test until there is some possibility that your place on the list will soon be reached. The hiring process moves along slowly, but it does move. You have time, but not that much time. Start now. Buy a book, join a gym or a fitness class, design a program of your own, or turn to the appendix of this book. You can pick and choose from among the suggested activities or follow the entire fitness course.

1. TYPICAL QUALIFYING PHYSICAL FITNESS TEST FOR POLICE OFFICER

Instructions for Candidates

These subtests are electronically timed by your stepping on the Start Mat and the Finish Mat.

Stair Climb / Restrain: (One Trial)
(Maximum Time Allowed: Two Minutes)

In this subtest, you will be expected to run up 3 flights of stairs, down 1 flight, push and pull a box 5 times, and run 5 feet to the finish line.

- On the signal GO, step on the Start Mat, run up the stairs on your right, continue up to the landing on the third floor.

- Both feet must be placed on the landing.
- Run quickly down one flight of stairs and into the lobby.
- Grab the box and pull it towards you until the front of the box reaches the tape on the floor.
- Now push it back to its starting position.
- Repeat 4 more times as the examiner announces the count.
- After the last trip, turn RIGHT and step on the Finish Mat.

Dummy Drag: (Two Trials)
(Maximum Time Allowed: One Minute)

In this subtest, you will be expected to drag a dummy 30 feet.

- Step on the Start Mat.
- Grab the dummy under the shoulders.
- Holding the dummy in this position, move backwards around the traffic cone set 15 feet away and return.
- Place the dummy EXACTLY as you found it in the starting position.
- Step on the Finish Mat.

Wall Climb / Obstacle Run: (Two Trials)
(Maximum Time Allowed: One Minute)

In this subtest, you will be expected to go over the five-foot wall and continue through the obstacle run.

- Step on the Start Mat.
- Run to the wall and go over. You are NOT allowed to use the support bars.
- Follow the tape on the floor around the cones.
- If you miss a cone or go around it the wrong way, you must go back and go around the cone CORRECTLY.
- If you knock a cone over, you must STOP and set it up before you continue.
- Step on the Finish Mat.

2. ANOTHER PHYSICAL FITNESS TEST

Medical evidence to allow participation in the physical fitness test may be required, and the Department of Personnel reserves the right to exclude from the physical test any eligibles who, upon examination of such evidence, are apparently medically unfit. Eligibles will take the physical fitness test at their own risk of injury, although efforts will be made to safeguard them.

Candidates must complete the *entire* course consisting of seven events in not more than *65 seconds*.

Candidates who do not successfully complete events 3, 5, and 6 will fail the test.

Description of Events

1. Run up approximately 40 steps.

2. Run approximately 40 yards, following a designated path including at least four 90 degree turns, to a sandbag.

3. Push the sandbag, weighing approximately 100 pounds, forward a distance of approximately five yards and then back to its original position. (Failure to meet all of the conditions for this event will result in failure of the test as a whole.)

4. Run approximately 10 yards to a dummy, weighing approximately 110 pounds, which is hanging with its lowest point approximately 3 feet above the floor.

5. Raise the dummy so as to lift the attached ring off the metal pipe. Allow the dummy to slide onto the floor or place it on the floor. You must not drop it or throw it down. (Failure to meet all of the conditions for this event will result in failure of the test as a whole.)

6. Step up approximately 18 inches and walk across a 12-foot beam by placing one foot in front of the other until you reach the other end. (You must be in control at all times, and falling off the beam will result in failure of the test as a whole.)

7. Run approximately 10 yards to the finish line.

Candidates who fail the test on their first trial will be allowed a second trial on the same date after a rest period.

Candidates who do not successfully complete all the events in their proper sequence will fail the test.

3. PHYSICAL AGILITY TEST

The first part of the test will consist of the first seven (7) elements described below, all of which are essential for the satisfactory performance of the duties of the position.

All elements are scored on a pass/fail basis, and candidates must satisfactorily complete each element of the test in order to successfully complete the test. Candidates who fail the test will not be appointed to the position. Unsuccessful candidates will be considered for retesting at a future date.

Element I

Stair Climb: This task consists of safely going up and down one flight of stairs.

Element II

Ladder Ascent: The candidate safely climbs to a height of approximately 12 feet, the ladder encased by a standard industrial safety cage with an interior dimension of approximately 30 inches, until the designated rung is touched. The candidate then descends to the floor in a safe manner.

Element III

Suspended Dummy Raise: A rescue dummy simulating a body weighing 120 pounds is hanging by a rope. The dummy must be raised vertically (3 inches) until the noose pressure is off the neck and held there for a period of five (5) consecutive seconds. The dummy must be raised by facing it and using hands and arms (as in a "bear hug").

Element IV

Body Transport: A 160-pound dummy is placed on a blanket. The candidate must pull the weighted blanket a total distance of 30 feet.

Element V

Obstacle Vault: This task consists of getting over a three-foot-high obstacle in a safe manner. Hurdling or diving is not permitted.

Element VI

Door Lock and Unlock: This task consists of properly unlocking a standard use security cell door, using the assigned key, going through the door, and relocking the same door.

Element VII

Load and Unload: This task consists of properly loading and unloading a weapon, 4-inch revolver, observing all specified safety regulations. Live ammunition will not be used.

Element VIII

Three-Minute Step Test: In addition, the agility test includes an element to screen for cardiovascular disease: For 3 minutes, the candidate will lift one foot at a time while stepping on and off a 12-inch bench at a rate of 24 times per minute. The candidate must keep pace with a metronome set at 96 beats per minute. After the 3 minutes of stepping, the candidate will sit down and relax without talking. A 60-second heart count will be taken starting 5 seconds after the completion of stepping. There is no pass/fail on this test. Instead, EHS medical staff will consider the results of this test along with other aspects of the examination to determine if a candidate is capable of performing the essential duties of a police officer.

4. PHYSICAL PERFORMANCE TEST

There are six test parts designed to assess: strength to push, pull, drag and lift; cardio-respiratory endurance for strenuous work and running; abdominal strength and spine flexibility to avoid low back pain, problems of strains and loss of mobility and agility. The physical performance test consists of the following:

1. **Push-ups:** This is a standard push-up where the back and legs are kept straight. The event starts in the up position and the count occurs when the applicant returns to the up position after having touched an audible beeper on the mat with his/her chest. The applicant is to do as many push-ups as possible in 60 seconds.

2. **Grip:** Using a hand grip dynamometer, the applicant squeezes the meter while keeping the arm extended parallel to the leg. Both right and left grips are tested and recorded in kilograms of pressure.

3. **Obstacle Course:** The total distance for this obstacle course is 90 feet and it is run for time. The applicant runs 20 feet, crawls 6 feet through a 2 1/2-foot high simulated tunnel, runs 20 feet, and climbs a 6-foot 6-inch barrier with footholds and handholds. The applicant then runs 20 feet to and around a set of pylons, then back to the barrier, which has footholds and handholds on it. After climbing the barrier a second time, the applicant runs 4 feet to the stop position.

4. **165-Pound Drag:** The applicant drags a 165-pound life-form dummy 30 feet for time. The dummy is gripped in the armpits and dragged backwards.

5. **95-Pound Carry.** The applicant lifts a 95-pound bag, which has handholds, runs with it 30 feet, and places it on a 32-inch platform for time.

6. **1/2-Mile Shuttle Run:** The applicant runs between two pylons placed 88 feet apart for a total of 15 round trips for time.

Examinees are encouraged to practice ahead of time for the physical performance test. All physical tests, and especially the 1/2-mile run, are aided by conditioning ahead of time. Physical training for law enforcement positions requires that new hires be physically fit when they are hired.

5. QUALIFYING PHYSICAL AGILITY TEST

NOTE: The qualifying physical agility test is a series of 6 sub-tests in 4 events that take place consecutively. There are only two rest periods permitted, each rest period lasting only 2 minutes. **You must pass all 6 sub-tests;** a fail in any one sub-test will cause you to fail the entire test. A pass in one sub-test cannot be used to cover a fail in a different sub-test. **You must pass all 6 sub-tests.**

300 Yard Run—Explanation of sub-tests 1, 2, and 3: You will run 6 continuous laps along an oblong course where you will be timed at the 50-yard point (1 lap), then at the 100-yard point (2 laps), and finally at the 300-yard point (6 laps).

1. **50 yard run:** Run a distance of 50 yards as fast as possible. Maximum allowable time is 13 seconds. You will be timed at the 50-yard point.

2. **100 yard run:** Run a distance of 100 yards as fast as possible. Maximum allowable time is 28 seconds. You will be timed at the 100-yard point.

3. **300 yard run:** Run a distance of 300 yards as fast as possible. Maximum allowable time is 1 minute 20 seconds (80 seconds). You will be timed at the 300-yard point (conclusion of the run).

A 2-MINUTE REST PERIOD IS PERMITTED AT THIS POINT

4. **Fire extinguisher carry:** Carry a fully loaded fire extinguisher weighing about 25 pounds a distance of 50 feet as fast as possible. Maximum allowable time is 10 seconds.

5. **Stair climb:** Run down 3 flights of stairs and climb back up 3 flights of stairs as fast as possible. Maximum allowable time is 45 seconds.

A 2-MINUTE REST PERIOD IS PERMITTED AT THIS POINT

6. **Deadweight drag:** Drag a bag weighing 50 pounds a distance of 50 feet as fast as possible. Maximum allowable time is 8 seconds.

6. PHYSICAL ASSESSMENT

This phase is intended to give an overall measurement of a candidate's physical fitness and preparation for Police Academy training. Blood pressure and vision will be measured, and candidates must fall within required levels to continue in the process, which includes:

1. A 1.5-mile run measuring cardiovascular efficiency.

2. Push-ups measuring shoulder muscular endurance.

3. Sit-ups measuring abdominal and hip flex or muscle strength.

4. An agility run measuring quickness, speed, and balance.

5. A vertical jump measuring leg muscle strength and explosiveness.

6. A sit and reach test measuring thigh and back muscle extensiveness.

7. A grip test measuring wrist and finger muscle strength.

8. A measure of body fat composition.

7. PHYSICAL FITNESS TEST

The candidates who qualify on the medical examination will be required to pass the qualifying physical fitness test. A total score of twenty is required for passing this test; the scores attained on the five individual tests are added together to obtain your final score.

Test I: Trunk Flexion Test (Three Chances)

Candidates will assume a sitting position on the floor with the legs extended at right angles to a line drawn on the floor. The heels should touch the near edge of the line and be five inches apart. The candidate should slowly reach with both hands as far forward as possible on a yardstick that is placed between the legs with the fifteen-inch mark resting on the near edge of the heel line. The score is the most distant point (in inches) reached on the yardstick with fingertips.

Rating	Trunk Flexion (Inches)	Points
Excellent	22 and over	6
Good	20–21	5
Average	14–19	4
Fair	12–13	3
Poor	10–11	2
Very Poor	9 and under	1

Test II: Hand Grip Strength Test (Three Chances)

The candidate places the dynamometer (hand grip tester) at the side and, without touching the body with any part of the arm, hand, or the dynamometer, should grip the dynamometer as hard as possible in one quick movement. The best of the three tries will be recorded.

Rating	Hand Grip in Kg.	Points
Excellent	65 and above	6
Good	57–64	5
Average	45–56	4
Fair	37–44	3
Poor	30–36	2
Very Poor	29 and under	1

Test III: Standing Broad Jump (Three Chances)

Candidates will be permitted three chances in consecutive order, and the longest distance will be credited. Candidates will be required to jump from a standing position, both feet together. Distance of jump will be recorded from starting point to back of heels. It is each candidate's responsibility to have a non-skid surface on the soles of his or her sneakers.

Rating	Distance	Points
Excellent	7'10" or better	6
Good	7'0" to 7'9"	5
Average	6'1" to 6'11"	4
Fair	5'6" to 6'0"	3
Poor	5'0" to 5'5"	2
Very Poor	Less than 5'	1

Test IV: One Minute Sit-Up Test

The candidate will start by lying on the back with the knees bent so that the heels are about eighteen inches away from the buttocks. An examiner will hold the ankles to give support. The candidate will then perform as many correct sit-ups (elbows alternately touching the opposite knee) as possible within a one-minute period. The candidate should return to the starting position (back to floor) between sit-ups.

Rating	Sit-Ups in 1 Minute	Points
Excellent	35	6
Good	30–34	5
Average	20–29	4
Fair	15–19	3
Poor	10–14	2
Very Poor	9 and under	1

Test V: Three Minute Step Test

The candidate will step for three minutes on a one-inch bench at a rate of twenty-four steps per minute. The time will be maintained by a metronome. Immediately after the three minutes of stepping, the subject will sit down and relax without talking. A sixty-second heart rate count is taken starting five seconds after the completion of stepping.

Rating	Pulse	Points
Excellent	75–84	6
Good	85–94	5
Average	95–119	4
Fair	120–129	3
Poor	130–139	2
Very Poor	Over 140	1

SLIDING SCALE STANDARDS

The Americans with Disabilities Act requires that age not be a consideration in hiring except where youth, or maturity, is a bona fide qualification for performance of the job. The federal government has established 37 as the highest age at which persons can and may effectively enter certain federal law enforcement positions. In order to establish an age-based hiring limit, each jurisdiction must justify the age it has chosen. At this time, not all guidelines are clear. Each jurisdiction makes its own interpretation of the requirements of the Americans with Disabilities Act, and its interpretation remains in effect until challenged and overturned by a court of law. Some states have chosen to take the Act at face value and have done away with upper age limits altogether.

When states, or jurisdictions within those states, discard upper age limits, they open themselves to new complications. According to the US Justice Department, physical fitness standards that are the same for everyone violate the Americans with Disabilities Act. In response to this determination, many jurisdictions have relaxed the physical fitness requirements for their police officers. These last two are recently announced Physical Fitness Screening Tests that take into consideration both age and sex.

8. PHYSICAL FITNESS SCREENING TEST

Candidate will go from Stations I through IV in order. Each station is pass/fail. Candidate must pass each station in order to proceed to the next station. Candidate will be allowed up to three minutes rest between stations. Once a station is started, it must be completed according to protocol. See the chart below:

Station I: Sit-up—Candidate lies flat on the back, knees bent, heels flat on the floor, fingers interlaced behind the head. Monitor holds the feet down firmly. In the up position, candidate should touch elbows to knees and return with shoulder blades touching floor. To pass this component, candidate must complete the requisite number of correct sit-ups in one minute.

Station II: Flex—Candidate removes shoes and places feet squarely against box with feet no wider than eight inches apart. Toes are pointed directly toward ceiling, knees remain extended throughout test. With hands placed one on top of the other, candidate leans forward without lunging or bobbing and reaches as far down the yardstick as possible. The hands must stay together and the stretch must be held for one second. Three attempts are allowed with the best of three recorded to the nearest 1/4 inch to determine whether the candidate passed/failed.

Station III: Bench—Monitor loads weights to 1/2 of candidate required weight. Candidate is permitted to "press" this weight once. Monitor increases weight to 2/3 of candidate required weight. Candidate is permitted to "press" this weight once. The required test weight is then loaded. The candidate has up to four (4) attempts to "press" required (maximum) weight. In order to pass, buttocks must remain on the bench. Candidate will be allowed up to two minutes rest between each "press." (Universal Bench Press Equipment)

Station IV: 1.5 Mile Run—Candidate must be successful on Stations I, II & III in order to participate in Station IV. It will be administered on a track. Candidate will be informed of his/her lap time during the test.

Scoring Chart

Age/Sex		Test		
Male	**Sit-up**	**Flex**	**Bench**	**1.5 Mi Run**
20–29	38	16.5	99	12.51
30–39	35	15.5	88	13.36
40–49	29	14.3	80	14.29
50–59	24	13.3	71	15.26
60+	19	12.5	66	16.43
Female				
20–29	32	19.3	59	15.26
30–39	25	18.3	53	15.57
40–49	20	17.3	50	16.58
50–59	14	16.8	44	17.54
60+	6	15.5	43	18.44

9. Physical Ability Test

The Physical Ability Test is designed to assess the following fitness components:

- **Flexibility**—the ability of muscles and joints to operate through a normal range of motion without injury.
- **Dynamic Strength**—the ability of the muscles to generate force to perform repeated tasks over an extended period of time.
- **Cardiovascular Endurance**—the ability of the heart and vascular system to transport and utilize oxygen for sustained activity involving stamina.

The Physical Ability Test for candidates consists of four (4) subtests scored in a pass/fail manner. The minimum performance score on each and every subtest must be met in order to continue through the selection process. A schedule of minimum physical fitness standards is included on a chart following the description of the subtests.

Subtest I—Sit-Ups

The candidate shall start in the supine position with knees bent, heels flat on the floor, and fingers interlaced and placed behind the head. The candidate's feet will be held down at the ankle. The candidate shall raise the upper body touching the elbows to the knees, and then return down until the shoulder blades touch the floor. The candidate may rest in the up position only. <u>The candidate must perform at least the minimum required number of correct sit-ups in one minute. Only sit-ups that are performed correctly will be counted.</u>

Starting position (down)   Up position

Subtest II—Flexibility—Sit and Reach

The candidate shall sit on the floor, remove shoes and place feet squarely against a measuring box. The candidate's feet shall be no wider than eight inches apart. Knees shall remain extended throughout the test. The candidate's hands are placed exactly together, one on top of the other, fingers extended. A yardstick is placed on top of the box such that the 15-inch mark is flush with the edge of the box at the candidate's feet. The zero end of the yardstick is extended toward the candidate's upper body. The candidate will lean forward without lunging or bobbing and must reach as far down the yardstick as possible. The hands must stay together and even. Exhaling on the reach is recommended. Three reaches are allowed, if needed, and recorded to the nearest 1/4 inch. <u>The candidate must reach the minimum required distance in inches as listed.</u>

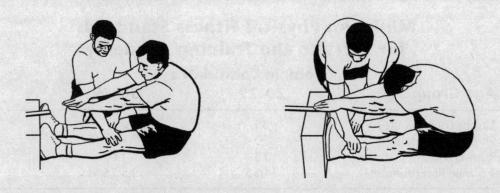

Subtest III—Push-ups

An administrator will hold a three (3) inch measuring device directly between and in line with the candidate's hands on the floor under the candidate performing the push-up. The candidate will start with his/her hands placed approximately shoulder-width apart on the floor and elbows fully extended. The back and remainder of the body should be kept straight at all times. From this full extension, known as the "up" position, the candidate will lower the body toward the floor until the sternum touches the device being held by the administrator. The candidate then returns to the fully extended "up" position. This completes one repetition. The candidate may rest in the up position only. <u>The candidate must perform at least the minimum required number of correct push-ups. Only push-ups that are performed correctly will be counted.</u>

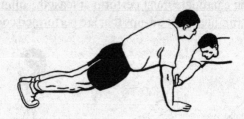

Starting position (up)

Down position (two views)

Subtest IV—1.5 Mile Run

Candidates should refrain from smoking or eating for two hours preceding the test. Adequate time will be allowed for stretching and warm-up prior to the test. The candidate will run 6 laps on a 440 yard (1/4 mile) track to complete the 1.5 mile run as fast as possible. <u>The candidate must perform the 1.5 mile run within the required time limit.</u> Time will be allowed for stretching and cool-down following the test.

Minimum Physical Fitness Standards for Entry to the Training Academy

Female Candidates

Age Group	20–29	30–39
Sit-ups (one minute)	35	27
Sit & Reach (inches)	20	19
Push-ups	18	14
1.5 Mile Run (minutes)	14:55	15:26

Male Candidates

Age Group	20–29	30–39
Sit-ups (one minute)	40	36
Sit & Reach (inches)	17.5	16.5
Push-ups	33	27
1.5 Mile Run (minutes)	12:18	12:51

Academy Physical Training—The Physical Training course design is based upon the Physical Ability Test Standards candidates were required to meet in order to enter the Academy. In order to graduate, recruits will be expected to perform the same exercises. However, minimum graduation standards reflect the improvement gained from training.

Physical Fitness Levels—(Graduation Standard)

Female Recruits

Age Group	20–29	30–39
Sit-ups (one minute)	41	32
Sit & Reach (inches)	21.5	20.5
Push-ups	23	18
1.5 Mile Run (minutes)	13:53	14:24

Male Recruits

Age Group	20–29	30–39
Sit-ups (one minute)	45	41
Sit & Reach (inches)	19.5	18.5
Push-ups	41	34
1.5 Mi. Run (minutes)	10:47	11:34

The Background Check

The police officer is in a position of public trust. He or she must be deserving of that trust. The police department must feel very certain that the police officer will not use his or her position for personal gain, will not use it to harass individuals or groups that he or she dislikes, will not be easily corrupted, and will not take advantage of privileged knowledge.

The standard predictor of future behavior is past behavior. The police department must find out how you have behaved in the past. It will do this by first having you fill out a questionnaire. As with the medical questionnaire, there is no point in lying or cheating. You will be found out and will be disqualified. State the facts clearly. Explain fully and factually.

If you have a totally clean record and face no problems in your personal or family life, then you need have no concern about the background check. Fill in the blanks. List references, and inform those people whose names you have given, so that they are not upset when they are contacted by the police.

Most people have something in their backgrounds that can spark more inquiry. The problem may be financial: If you are strapped for money, the police department may fear that you might be corruptible. The problem may be marital: The police department may worry that you will be distracted. The problem may be one of frequent job changes: The police department questions your stability and the value of investing in your training. The problem may be one of poor credit: Are you responsible and reliable? Or the problem may be one of a brush with the law, minor or major. Most minor infractions can be explained at an interview; reassure the interviewer that these were youthful indiscretions unlikely to recur. Arrests for felonies, and, worse still, convictions present greater obstacles. It may be wise to consult an attorney who specializes in expunging criminal records to see what can be done to clear your name. Some offenses are absolutely disqualifying. You may as well know ahead of time and take all possible steps to make yourself employable by the police department.

A felony record needs the services of an attorney. So might multiple misdemeanor convictions. You can help yourself in many other situations. If you have a poor credit rating, pay up and have your rating upgraded. If you are behind on alimony payments, catch up. If you have an unanswered summons, go to court and answer it. Pay your parking tickets. Even if these past problems turn up in the background check, your positive attitude in clearing them up will be in your favor.

Be sure that you are able to document any claims you make with reference to diplomas, degrees, and honors. You may have to produce these at an interview. Likewise, be certain that you understand the nature and gravity of the problems in your background. Be prepared to admit that you misbehaved and to reassure the examiners that you have matured into a responsible citizen.

The Psychological Evaluation

THE PURPOSE OF THE PSYCHOLOGICAL EVALUATION

Some jurisdictions subject all police officer candidates to a psychological evaluation before appointment; others, because of the expense involved, limit psychological evaluations to those cases where there are signs that one might be necessary. However, in all cases the sole purpose of a psychological evaluation is to determine the candidate's mental fitness for performing the specific duties of a police officer. The evaluation is not concerned with other aspects of mental well-being. In fact, because of this exclusive focus on police work, a candidate might be judged psychologically unfit to be a police officer even if he or she is perfectly suited for other types of employment.

What makes police work so different from other occupations? Soon after orientation and the usual training at the police academy, the police officer begins functioning more or less independently. Although the officer functions under supervision, that supervision is present only periodically; and although the officer should be guided by the department's rules of procedure, many times the officer will be thrust into situations where immediate action is required to save lives or protect property. For example, the officer who answers the call of a pregnant woman about to give birth must take decisive action at once. In such situations, there is no time to consult the rules of procedure. The officer must do whatever is necessary right away.

Another crucial difference is that the police officer carries a gun as part of the job. Prudent use of this weapon requires not only conformance to the rules of procedure but also a good sense of police judgment. The officer who must decide in an emergency whether to use that gun must have a very high degree of psychological stability.

Psychological evaluations of police officer candidates are usually conducted by a psychologist or psychiatrist who is trained to detect signs of deficiencies that could interfere with the proper performance of police work. The job is twofold: to look for signs of potential trouble and to evaluate the sincerity of the candidate. For example, consider the possible responses when the psychologist asks, "Why do you want to become a police officer?" A proper response would be "I want a career in the public service, and I feel that effective law enforcement will make for a better society for my children and eventually for my grandchildren." There is nothing wrong with this response. The only thing to be judged is the sincerity of the candidate. Now look at the following response to the same question: "I have always liked uniforms. They bring respect and admiration, and they permit you to perform your duties without interference." Something is wrong here. Or consider this response: "I hate criminals. They take advantage of the weak and elderly. They are cowards, and I want to do everything I can to eliminate them." This intense hatred may indicate the need for further investigation of this candidate's psychological stability.

TYPICAL EVALUATION QUESTIONS

The questions that you will be asked will, for the most part, be quite predictable. The majority of them will be based on your responses to application forms and other papers that you have been required to file. The psychologist will ask you to amplify or to explain the personal data that you listed on those papers. Sometimes you will be asked to describe your feelings about events that happened to you. Also, as a way of encouraging you to talk, you may be asked more open-ended questions about your personal likes, dislikes, or emotions.

You may also be asked your opinion about what you might do in a hypothetical police work situation, but such questions are unlikely to form the bulk of the evaluation. In this case, the psychologist is not testing your knowledge of police procedures, but only your ability to make reasoned judgments and to avoid rash behavior. Because most of the questions you will be asked are predictable, it is relatively easy to prepare answers for them. Begin your preparation by looking over the application forms that you filled out and any other papers that you were required to file. You should be able to pick out the points that a psychologist will want you to clarify or explain.

Typical questions you might encounter include the following:

- Why did you choose your area of concentration in school?
- What particularly interests you about that subject?
- Why did you transfer from school x to school y?
- How did you get the job with _____?
- Which of the duties described in your second job did you like best? Which least? Why?
- What did you do during the nine months between your second and third jobs?
- Explain the circumstances of your leaving a particular job.
- Please clarify: armed forces service, arrest record, hospitalization record, etc., as applicable.

Other questions are much like those asked at a routine job interview. They can be anticipated and prepared for as well.

- Why do you want to leave the kind of work you are doing now?
- Why do you want to be a police officer?
- How does your family feel about your becoming a police officer?
- What do you do in your leisure time?

- Do you have any hobbies? What are they? What do you particularly like about _____?
- What is your favorite sport? Would you rather play or watch?
- How do you react to criticism? If you think the criticism is reasonable? If you consider the criticism unwarranted?
- What is your pet peeve?
- What are your greatest strengths? Weaknesses?
- What could make you lose your temper?
- Of what accomplishment in your life are you most proud?
- What act do you most regret?
- If you could start over, what would you do differently?
- What traits do you value most in a co-worker? In a friend?
- What makes you think you would make a good police officer?

Still other questions may be more specific to police work. You should have prepared answers to:

- How much sleep do you need?
- Are you afraid of heights?
- What is your attitude toward irregular hours?
- Do you prefer working alone or on a team?
- Are you afraid of dying?
- What would you do with the rest of your life if your legs were crippled in an injury?
- How do you deal with panic? Your own? That of others?
- What is your attitude toward smoking? Drinking? Drugs? *Playboy* magazine? Gambling?
- What is your favorite TV program? How do you feel about watching news? Sports? Classical drama? Rock music? Opera? Game shows?

Now make a list of your own. The variety of evaluation questions is endless, but most can be answered with ease. Preparation makes the whole process much more pleasant and less frightening.

There is one question that strikes terror into the heart of nearly every candidate for police officer or any other job. This question is likely to be the first and, unless you are prepared for it, may well throw you off your guard. The question is, "Tell me about yourself." For this question you should have a prepared script (in your head, not in your hand). Think well ahead of time about what you want to tell. What could the psychologist be interested in? This question is not seeking information about your birthweight nor about your food preferences. The psychologist wants you to tell about yourself with relation to your interest in and qualifications for police work. Think of how to describe yourself with this goal in mind. What information puts you into a good light with reference to the work for which you are applying? Organize your presentation. Then analyze what you plan to say. What is a psychologist likely to pick up on? To what questions will your speech lead? You must prepare to answer these questions to which you have opened yourself.

Towards the end of the evaluation, the psychologist will most likely ask if you have any questions. You undoubtedly will have had some beforehand and should have come prepared to ask them. If all of your questions have been answered in the course of the evaluation, you may tell this to the psychologist. If not, or if the evaluation has raised new questions in your mind, by all means ask them. The evaluation should serve for your benefit; it is not just to serve the purposes of the Police Department.

The invitation of your questions tends to be the signal that the evaluation is nearly over. The psychologist is satisfied that he or she has gathered enough information. The time allotted to you is up. Be alert to the cues. Do not spoil the good impression you have made by trying to prolong the evaluation.

SHOULD YOU REVEAL PERSONAL OPINIONS AND FEELINGS?

The psychologist does not expect candidates to be devoid of personal feelings. After all, everyone has likes and dislikes. However, the mature, psychologically stable person is able to keep those feelings from interfering with the performance of job duties. The police officer will encounter a very wide variety of people on the job. Some the officer may find personally likeable; others may be unlikeable, even downright unpleasant. However, whatever the officer's true feelings about the persons encountered, he or she must service those individuals in an effective manner or serious repercussions—even loss of life—may result. This type of behavior takes mental maturity and stability, qualities every officer must possess. It is these qualities that the psychologist is looking for at the evaluation, not an absence of personal feelings. The successful candidate does not have to like everyone he or she meets. What is important is the ability to control personal feelings in order to function effectively.

Sometimes during an evaluation a candidate will express "extreme" views on certain subjects. Unlike more typical opinions or feelings, these may indeed be cause for disqualification. An obvious example is a display of unreasoning dislike for people from a particular ethnic or religious background. To the psychologist, this is a sure sign of trouble. The candidate who says, "People from ethnic group x are always the ones who commit the violent crimes" will never be appointed a police officer.

SHOULD YOU VOLUNTEER INFORMATION?

One very important point to remember at the evaluation is to limit your responses to what is asked. An evaluation session of this type is one of the very few opportunities most people have to reveal their true inner selves to others. The psychologist knows this and will often encourage the person being evaluated to talk freely and openly about personal matters and opinions. An unthinking candidate may use this opportunity to bring up matters that ordinarily he or she would never discuss. The talkative candidate might even know that he or she is getting in too deep but may be unable to refrain from continuing. The psychologist will encourage this type of individual to talk at length in order to reveal personal matters that will indicate the level of the candidate's psychological stability.

One device that psychologists use to make candidates keep talking is to assume a facial expression that indicates that further explanation is expected. It is very important not to respond to this suggestion! If you do, you are likely to say things that can only be harmful to you. Try to be satisfied with your original response, and have the maturity to stand by it no matter what expression you see on the psychologist's face. Display a sense of self-assurance that convinces the psychologist that you are satisfied with your answers.

How to Explain Problem Incidents in Your Past

One concern of many police officer candidates is how to handle questions about problem incidents in their past. More than a few candidates have at some time—usually in their youth—gotten into trouble in some incident involving property damage or even personal injury to others. Such incidents almost always come to light during the candidate's background check, often through school, court, or military records. If you have such an incident in your past and are questioned about it by the psychologist, the wisest course is to accept full responsibility for it and to attribute it to your youthful immaturity at the time. Claiming that the record is false or giving excuses for your bad behavior is not likely to be regarded favorably. The psychologist is much more apt to respond positively if you accept responsibility and—just as important—you attribute any such incident to an immature outlook that you have now outgrown. One mistake of this type will not necessarily disqualify you if you can convince the psychologist that you have become a fully responsible adult and will never do anything of the kind again.

"Pencil-and-Paper" Evaluations

As part of the psychological evaluation, some jurisdictions use standardized personality tests that you answer by marking a sheet of paper. These tests may contain a hundred or more questions. Your responses help the psychologist determine your specific personality traits. Your answer to any one question by itself usually means very little, but your answers to a group of questions, taken together, will have significance to the psychologist. Your wisest course when taking one of these written personality tests is to give honest, truthful answers. Any attempt to make yourself appear different from the way you really are is not likely to be successful.

Keep a Positive Attitude

One final word of advice: it is important to approach all psychological evaluations with a positive attitude. Think of the evaluation not as an ordeal that you must endure, but rather as an opportunity to prove that you are qualified to become a police officer. In truth, the psychologist will be looking for traits that qualify you, not ones that disqualify you. And if disqualifying evidence exists, it is the psychologist's responsibility to consider every factor before making a negative recommendation. So go into the evaluation with confidence and be prepared to "sell" yourself to the psychologist. You will be given every chance to prove your worth.

Evaluation Checklist

Here are some valuable points to remember as you prepare for the psychological evaluation.

1. Get a good night's sleep the night before the evaluation.

2. Do not take any medication beforehand to calm yourself. You may be tested for drugs before the evaluation.

3. Dress neatly and conservatively.

4. Be polite to the psychologist or psychiatrist.

5. Respond to all questions honestly and forthrightly.

POLICE JUDGMENT QUIZZER

About the Police Judgment Quizzer

Early Police Officer examinations were a strange mixture of questions covering municipal government, municipal geography, spelling, grammar, first aid, everything, in fact, that every person should know something about, but very little that was specific to measuring the ability of future police officers to do their job well. As testing methods matured and examiners gained experience in mass testing, they determined that the best measure of a good police officer is a measure of his or her judgment in actual police situations. So the emphasis shifted from factual to actual exams. "Let the questions supply the facts," the examiners reasoned, "and let the aspiring police officers display their judgment in choosing the correct answers."

What Would You Do If . . .

This is the essential form of the practical question on police officer exams. Assume you are a police officer. Here is a given situation. How would you respond to it? This is a very subtle and efficient method of testing. Questions are often based on actual patrol situations. What would you do if you saw a woman walking down the street dressed only in a sheet and leading a doe on a leash? Arrest her? On what charge? Take the doe to an animal shelter? Take the woman to a doctor? Ask her for her phone number? It actually happened. What would you do?

TEST-TAKING STRATEGY FOR PRACTICAL JUDGMENT QUESTIONS

Police applicants are placed in a peculiar position by practical judgment questions in that the correct answers for these questions are influenced by actual police department procedures. As an applicant taking the exam, you are not expected to know the police department's policies or procedures. Yet test-makers often assume that police departmental policies or procedures are just common sense. To do really well on practical judgment questions, you need something more than common sense. You need a good understanding of ordinary police department policies and procedures as they apply to routine patrol situations. This is the reason why close relatives of police officers tend to earn high scores on the police officer exam. Their familiarity with "police language" and "police thinking" stands them in good stead when they must choose the correct answers to police practical judgment questions.

This chapter will familiarize you with many of the "common sense" ideas that underlie police practical judgment questions. The chapter will serve as "your brother the police officer," teaching you to think like a patrol officer. By the time you have finished studying this material, you will be thinking like a patrol officer. You will then be prepared to score high on your police officer exam.

THE POLICE ROLE

To start with, you must understand the role of a police officer. This role varies according to size, location, and philosophy of the police department. State police find that their role encompasses major problems like traffic pileups and serious accidents, as well as the more routine problems of stranded motorists. Small-town police find that they have a broad role in maintaining public safety and assuring law and order. Big-city police tend to have a more narrow role because in big cities other agencies take on primary responsibility for certain tasks: medics handle health situations beyond emergency first-aid; traffic department personnel deal with many traffic situations; social workers handle many crises concerning the elderly, children, and the mentally ill. Part of your preparation for your own exam should be acquiring some familiarity with the ordinary role of police officers in the department to which you are applying.

With this information in mind, you must follow one basic rule when answering police practical judgment questions—fulfill the police role and only the police role. This means:

1. Be professional. Avoid emotional responses, show of bias, or incurring any kind of indebtedness to persons on your beat.

2. Avoid all roles other than the police role, e.g., parent, physician, tradesman, private security, etc. Sometimes you may find it hard to draw the line, such as that between emergency first-aid and the role of the medic. In an emergency where time is pressing, the police officer must provide assistance to people to the full extent of his or her competence. Where more time is available, leave doubtful roles to others.

3. Fulfill the police role of assisting endangered people twenty-four hours a day. Be prepared to assist in keeping the peace at any time and to take the initiative in urgent situations. Fulfilling the police role does not necessarily mean making arrests when there is no great need to do so. In practical judgment questions, think of the police role as one of keeping the peace rather than one of making arrests, especially in the off-duty situation.

4. Avoid even the slightest appearance of corruption. Maintain police integrity. Avoid all partiality. Do not accept any gifts or favors. Do not refer business to any particular businessman, company, or professional person.

POLICE PRIORITIES

A *hierarchy* is an arrangement of things according to their importance. Something near the top of a hierarchy is more important than something near the bottom of the hierarchy. Basically it is an arrangement of things or activities according to their priorities.

There are five basic functions in police work. These have a definite hierarchical order. If an officer finds him- or herself in a situation in which several of these functions must be done, the officer should consider the hierarchical order, or order of priorities, and act in accordance with the position of each function in that order.

1. *Assist endangered people*. Essentially this means assisting:
   a. seriously injured persons.
   b. physically endangered persons (e.g., victims of a crime in progress, drowning persons, etc.).

2. *Keep the peace*. Calm any major disorder. Prevent tumult, aggression, or destruction of property.

3. *Enforce the law*. Where no actual harm to persons or property is threatened, peace-keeping and maintaining order may be adequate. Where there is unlawful injury or loss, arrest may be necessary in addition to the restoring of order.

4. *Assist people who are not immediately endangered but who need help*. This means assisting:
   a. physically or mentally needy persons: children, the elderly, the handicapped, the homeless, and persons who appear to be sick, mentally ill, or intoxicated.
   b. crime victims, lost persons, and stranded persons.

5. *Maintain order on the beat*. This involves:
   a. Investigating suspicious persons or circumstances. Something is suspicious if it is *unusual* for the time or the place or the persons involved.
   b. Regulating the use of streets and sidewalks for safety and for the efficient flow of traffic.
   c. Knowing the beat. You must be familiar with the physical features of the beat, you must be aware of routine events, and you must develop positive contacts with the people on the beat.
   d. Making recommendations that will improve safety or flow of traffic in the area. Remember to stay "professional" by recommending only activities, not particular products or businesses.

THE PRINCIPLE OF USE OF MINIMUM NECESSARY FORCE

Many police practical judgment questions concern the possible use of force. Police officers are empowered to use force, even deadly force, under certain circumstances. In general, common sense should rule judgments about the use of force. There are some basic principles that are part of "common sense."

Police officers should always handle problems with the *minimum amount of force necessary* to resolve the problem. Never use more force than the problem deserves. Obviously, a police officer should not shoot somebody for failing to show identification, even if the person were being unreasonably stubborn. A police officer's action should not cause greater harm than the problem the officer is trying to resolve. In other words, a problem should not be handled in such a way as to create an even bigger problem.

When a police officer is evaluating the gravity of a situation to determine how much force is necessary (or when a candidate is making this choice in an examination), the officer must consider the physical setting, the actual actions and the apparent intentions of the people involved, and the intent of the law. Differences in physical settings require differences in policies and regulations. Big-city police departments, for example, practically never permit police officers to fire warning shots, to shoot at moving vehicles, or to shoot at people on public streets. It is assumed that such shooting would endanger innocent bystanders. On the other hand, state police departments often do allow warning shots, shooting at moving vehicles, and even shooting at people on the road because they assume a highway setting without any innocent bystanders in the line of fire.

THE VALUE HIERARCHY

Occasionally a police officer has to make a quick decision in a situation that involves value conflicts. For example, it may be necessary to choose between risking serious injury to a hostage or letting a dangerous criminal escape. Such a decision involves a value judgment. An officer makes the decision based on the order of priorities.

If a police department's hierarchy of values is spelled out clearly, officers are assisted in making rapid and proper judgments. Police exam candidates can rely on the same list of priorities. The list below is the value hierarchy that has been the basis for practical judgment questions on police officer exams for many years. In order of priority:

1. Protection of life and limb.
2. Obeying orders in an emergency situation.
3. Protection of property.
4. Obeying orders in a non-emergency situation.
5. Maintaining the assigned role.
6. Efficiency in getting the job done.
7. Avoiding blame or earning praise or respect.

Use the hierarchy of values in making decisions. If a situation presents a conflict of values, always choose the value that is highest on the list. Here are two examples:

Example 1. You are assigned to stay in a particular spot during an emergency situation, but by leaving that spot you will save a life. You are justified in choosing to save a life (1) rather than obeying orders (2). The understanding is, of course, that leaving your spot will not result in other lives being lost. "Protecting life and limb" is your number one priority, the highest value in the police hierarchy of values.

Example 2. You are assigned to watch a prisoner, and a fellow officer is assigned to write up the arrest report. Stay in your own role even if you are more skilled than the other officer at writing up arrest reports. The conflict is between carrying out an assigned duty (5) and getting a job done efficiently (6). Choose the higher priority.

One more: You are patrolling alone at night, and you come across a business that has been burglarized with the front door smashed in. At this hour you are expected to be making a routine check of illegal parking on a certain street. The police department might be criticized by residents if the illegal parking is not acted on, but the store is likely to be further burglarized if you leave this spot. Stay where you are and protect the property (3) rather than carrying out your assigned illegal parking patrol (5) or concerning yourself with criticism of the department (7). Always choose the highest value.

Please note that no value is given to the officer's personal gains or benefits or reputation. Personal consideration is *never* a good reason for doing anything so far as a civil service exam question is concerned.

As the hierarchy of values suggests, the best reason for any action is the protection of life and limb. If safety is a real issue in the fact pattern of the question, then safety is the number one priority in choosing the answer. Sometimes there is no real issue of safety. In such a case, the next value assumes the greatest importance. If there is an emergency situation and you have been given specific orders, your priority is to carry out those orders. If not, the next priority is the protection of property. Property includes public property and police department property as well as private property. If there are no threats to property, you are expected to carry out routine, non-emergency orders and to fulfill your assigned duties. Doing what you were told to do and carrying out your routine assignments as a police officer take priority over efficiency. A police force is a highly organized bureaucracy. The organization will function best as a whole if each person does just his or her own assigned job.

Read each question carefully. Is there really something in the question situation to indicate that there is an issue of life and limb at stake? Would a proposed answer based on efficiency really be possible and efficient? Be realistic. Unless told otherwise, assume that the officer is an ordinary police officer and not a sharpshooter or a trained firefighter.

When all other reasoning fails you, answer to the Chief. In other words, the Chief of Police is testing you for your job. If you are faced with a difficult choice in making a decision, imagine that the question is being asked you personally by the Chief of Police. Give the answer the Chief would want you to give.

ANSWERING THE QUESTIONS

This quizzer contains questions that have actually appeared on examinations for entry-level law enforcement positions conducted over a considerable number of years. The questions have been carefully screened for current relevancy.

Answering these questions will accomplish much in preparing you to do your best on the examination. Ideally, you can consider yourself well prepared if on the day of the examination you are thinking like a police officer. This quizzer will help you get in that frame of mind. Most of the questions found here concern incidents that a police officer may encounter on a daily basis.

The position of police officer is unique in that, although it is an entry-level position, it involves a great deal of responsibility and requires the ability to make reliable on-the-spot decisions. Therefore, accurate judgment is perhaps the most important qualification of the police officer. In order to make accurate police decisions, the officer must thoroughly understand the duties of the position and the police officer's role in society.

By the time you finish the Police Judgment Quizzer, you no doubt will be thinking like a police officer, and you thus will be well on your way towards earning that high examination score.

Choose from among the four suggested answers the *best* answer to each question. Write the letter of your answer choice beside the corresponding question number. The correct answers appear on page 50. Following the answer key is a full explanation of the police reasoning behind each correct answer choice.

1. An off-duty police officer was seated in a restaurant when two men entered, drew guns, and robbed the cashier. The officer made no attempt to prevent the robbery or apprehend the criminals. Later he justified his conduct by stating that an officer, when off duty, is a private citizen with the same duties and rights of all private citizens. The officer's conduct was

   (A) wrong; a police officer must act to prevent crimes and apprehend criminals at all times
   (B) right; the police officer was out of uniform at the time of the robbery
   (C) wrong; he should have obtained the necessary information and descriptions after the robbers left
   (D) right; it would have been foolhardy for him to intervene when outnumbered by armed robbers

2. While you are on traffic duty, a middle-aged man crossing the street cries out with pain, presses his hand to his chest, and stands perfectly still. You suspect that he may have suffered a heart attack. You should

   (A) help him to cross the street quickly in order to prevent his being hit by moving traffic

   (B) permit him to lie down flat in the street while you divert traffic
   (C) ask him for the name of his doctor so that you can summon him
   (D) request a cab to take him to the nearest hospital for immediate treatment

3. Assume that you have been assigned to a traffic post at a busy intersection. A car bearing out-of-state license plates is about to turn into a one-way street going in the opposite direction. You should blow your whistle and stop the car. You should then

   (A) hand out a summons to the driver in order to make an example of him, since out-of-town drivers notoriously disregard our traffic regulations
   (B) pay no attention to him and let him continue in the proper direction
   (C) ask him to pull over to the curb and advise him to get a copy of the latest New York City traffic regulations
   (D) call his attention to the fact that he was violating a traffic regulation and permit him to continue in the proper direction

4. Assume that you are a police officer. A woman has complained to you about a man's indecent exposure in front of her house. As you approach the house, the man begins to run. You should

   (A) shoot to kill as the man may be a dangerous maniac
   (B) fire a warning shot to try to halt the man
   (C) summon other police officers in order to apprehend him
   (D) pursue and try to seize the man

5. You have been assigned to a patrol post in the park during the winter months. You hear the cries of a boy who has fallen through the ice. The first thing you should do is to

   (A) rush to the nearest telephone and call an ambulance
   (B) call upon a passerby to summon additional police officers
   (C) rush to the spot from which the cries came and try to save the boy
   (D) rush to the spot from which the cries came and question the boy concerning his identity so that you can summon his parents

6. While you are patrolling your post, you find a flashlight and a screwdriver lying near a closed bar and grill. You also notice some jimmy marks on the door. You should

   (A) continue patrolling your post after noting in your memorandum book what you have seen
   (B) arrest any persons standing in the vicinity
   (C) determine whether the bar has been robbed
   (D) telephone the owner of the bar and grill to relate what you have seen outside the door

7. You are on your way to report for an assignment when you see two men fighting on the street. For you to attempt to stop the fight would be

   (A) unjustified; it is none of your business
   (B) justified; a fight between individuals may turn into a riot
   (C) unjustified; you may get hurt with the result that you will not be able to report for duty
   (D) justified; as a police officer, it is your duty to see that the public peace is kept

8. Suppose a police officer's tour of duty extends from 12:00 midnight to 8:00 A.M. While on the first round of her tour, she notices that the night light in the front of a small candy store is out. In the past, the proprietor has always left the light on. The door to the store is locked. Of the following, the most appropriate action for the officer to take *first* is to

   (A) use her flashlight to light the store interior so that she may inspect it for unusual conditions
   (B) continue on her beat, since the light probably burned out
   (C) break open the door lock to conduct a thorough search of the store
   (D) call the storekeeper to say that the night light is out

9. While on patrol at 2 A.M., you notice a man and a woman walking down the street and arguing in loud tones. They do not see you as you are standing in the shadows. The pair stops in front of a large apartment house. The man takes a bunch of keys from his pocket and finds the one that will open the door. While he is doing this, the woman taps her foot impatiently. At this point, as the two are entering the apartment house, you should

   (A) notify headquarters of the incident
   (B) permit them to enter but follow closely behind them to see what they do
   (C) ignore the incident and continue on your patrol
   (D) force them to show identification

10. While patrolling a post late Saturday night, a police officer notices a well-dressed man break a car window with a rock, open the front door, and enter the car. He is followed into the car by a female companion. Of the following, the most essential action for the officer to take is to

    (A) point a gun at the car, enter the car, and order the man to drive to the station house to explain his actions
    (B) approach the car and ask the man why it was necessary to break the car window
    (C) take down the license number of the car and note the description of both the man and the woman in the event that the car is later reported as stolen
    (D) request proof of ownership of the car from the man

11. Assume that a police officer is assigned to duty in a radio patrol car. The situation in which it would be *least* advisable for the officer to use the siren to help clear traffic when answering a call is when a report has come in that

    (A) a man is involved in an argument with a cleaning store proprietor
    (B) a man is holding up a liquor store
    (C) two cars have crashed, resulting in loss of life
    (D) two gangs of juveniles are engaged in a street fight

12. You notice that a man is limping hurriedly, leaving a trail of blood behind him. You question him and his explanation is that he was hurt accidentally while he was watching a man clean a gun. You should

    (A) let him go as you have no proof that his story is not true
    (B) have him sent to the nearest city hospital under police escort so that he may be questioned further after treatment
    (C) ask him whether the man has a license for his gun
    (D) ask him to lead you to the man who cleaned his gun so that you may question him further about the accident

13. At 10 A.M. on a regular school day, a police officer notices a boy about 11 years old wandering in the street. When asked why he is not in school, the boy replies that he attends school in the neighborhood, but that he felt sick that morning. The officer then takes the boy to the principal of the school. This method of handling the situation was

    (A) bad; the officer should have obtained verification of the boy's illness
    (B) good; the school authorities are best equipped to deal with the problem
    (C) bad; the officer should have obtained the boy's name and address and reported the incident to the attendance officer
    (D) good; seeing the truant boy escorted by a police officer will deter other children from truancy

14. "A police officer should know the occupations and habits of the people on his or her beat. In heavily populated districts, however, it is too much to ask that the officer know all the people on the beat." If this statement is correct, which of the following would be the most practical course for a police officer to follow?

    (A) Concentrate on becoming acquainted with the oldest residents on his or her beat.
    (B) Limit his or her attention to people who work as well as live in the district.
    (C) Limit his or her attention to people with criminal records.
    (D) Concentrate on becoming acquainted with key people such as janitors and local merchants.

15. Police officers are instructed to pay particular attention to anyone apparently making repairs to an auto parked in the street. The most important reason for this rule is that

    (A) the person making the repairs may be stealing the auto
    (B) the person making the repairs may be obstructing traffic
    (C) working on autos is prohibited on certain streets
    (D) many people injure themselves while working on autos

16. A police officer, walking his beat at 3 A.M., notices heavy smoke coming out of a top floor window of a large apartment house. Of the following, the action the officer should take *first* is to:

    (A) make certain that there really is a fire
    (B) enter the building and warn all the occupants of the apartment house
    (C) attempt to extinguish the fire before it gets out of control
    (D) call the fire department

17. Inspections of critical points on a post are purposely made at irregular intervals to

    (A) permit leaving the post when arrests are necessary
    (B) make it difficult for wrongdoers to anticipate the inspections
    (C) allow for delays due to unusual occurrences at other points
    (D) simplify the scheduling of lunch reliefs and rest periods

18. A police officer making her rounds notices that one storekeeper has not cleared the snow from the sidewalk in front of his store. After reminding the storekeeper that he is breaking the law if the sidewalk is not cleared, the officer also points out that a dangerous situation may arise if ice forms. This method of handling the situation is usually

(A) bad; the storekeeper broke the law and should be punished
(B) good; the storekeeper will clear the sidewalk and no one will be hurt
(C) bad; the police officer should have forced the storekeeper to clear the sidewalk of snow immediately
(D) good; threatening severe punishment is the most desirable method to achieve compliance with the law

19. "Because the woman had been acting suspiciously, the police officer halted her for questioning. Immediately a man joined the two. Though the police officer directed his questioning at the woman, it was the man who responded." On the basis of these data, it is *most* reasonable to infer that

(A) the woman is incapable of speech or is intellectually incompetent
(B) an effort is being made to conceal information
(C) the police officer's suspicions are badly grounded
(D) what appears to be suspicious is often proved to be law abiding

20. "The woman approached the police officer with the tearful request that he call her at home in order to put the fear of the law into her 11-year-old son. The boy, she said, was associating with a group of wild, older youths who were leading the boy astray." The officer should have

(A) complied with the the woman's request
(B) obtained further information before committing himself to any cooperative relations with the woman
(C) cooperated with the woman in whatever manner seemed appropriate, provided that the boy's history has been reported accurately by his mother
(D) denied the woman's request

21. Suppose that, at 11 A.M., while you are patrolling your post, a young girl runs up to you, saying that a man has just dropped dead on the street a block away. Of the following, your *first* action under the circumstances should be to

(A) request the young girl to describe the man who is said to be dead
(B) approach furtively the scene of the alleged death in order to investigate all the circumstances fully
(C) proceed immediately to the place where the man is alleged to have dropped dead
(D) request the young girl to identify herself

22. A group of boys about 17 years of age is standing on a street corner, talking loudly, shouting, and, in general, making a good deal of noise in a residential district in the early hours of the morning. A police officer who comes upon this scene should attempt to

(A) arrest the boy who appears to be the leader
(B) arrest the entire group
(C) disperse the group
(D) summon assistance

23. Suppose that, in the course of your duties, you are called to the scene of a disturbance in which some seven or eight people are involved. Of the following, the action most likely to end the disturbance quickly and effectively is for you to

(A) divide the disorderly group immediately into three approximately equal sections
(B) take the nearest person promptly into custody and remove that person from the scene
(C) announce your authority and call for order in a firm and decisive manner
(D) question a bystander in detail about the reasons for the disorder

24. A newly appointed officer of a uniformed force may *least* reasonably expect an immediate supervising officer to

(A) help him or her avoid errors
(B) give him or her specific instructions
(C) check on the progress he or she is making
(D) make all necessary decisions for him or her

25. In lecturing on the law of arrest, an instructor remarked: "To go beyond is as bad as to fall short." The one of the following that most nearly expresses the same thing is

(A) never undertake the impossible
(B) extremes are not desirable
(C) look before you leap
(D) too much success is dangerous

26. In addressing a class, an instructor remarked: "Carelessness and failure are twins." The one of the following that most nearly expresses the same thing is

(A) negligence seldom accompanies success
(B) incomplete work is careless work
(C) conscientious work is never attended by failure
(D) a conscientious person never makes mistakes

27. The primary function of a police department is

(A) the prevention of crime
(B) the efficiency and discipline of its members
(C) to preserve property values
(D) to minimize conflicts

28. Law enforcement officials receive badges with numbers on them so that

(A) their personalities may be submerged
(B) they may be more easily identified
(C) they may be spied upon
(D) their movements may be kept under constant control

29. The best attitude for an officer to take is to

(A) be constantly on the alert
(B) be hostile
(C) vary watchfulness with the apparent necessity for it
(D) regard tact as the most effective weapon for handling any degree of disorder

30. Ten percent of the inmates released from a certain prison are arrested as parole violators. It follows that

(A) 90 percent have reformed
(B) 10 percent have reformed
(C) none has reformed
(D) none of the foregoing is necessarily true

31. A certain committee found that over 90 percent of the murders in the United States are committed by use of pistols. It follows that

(A) almost all murders are caused by the possession of pistols
(B) 90 percent of all murders can be eliminated by eliminating the sale and use of pistols
(C) the pistol is a mechanical aid to crime
(D) no information is available with regard to the way murders happen

32. A criminal is typically one who

(A) has a peculiarly shaped head
(B) exhibits a most degenerate kind of behavior
(C) is an intelligent, well-educated person
(D) looks like other people

33. There would be no crime if there were no

(A) weapons
(B) criminals
(C) stupid laws
(D) private property

34. An officer receives instructions from his supervisor that he does not fully understand. For the officer to ask for a further explanation would be

(A) good; chiefly because his supervisor will be impressed with his interest in his work
(B) poor; chiefly because the supervisor's time will be needlessly wasted
(C) good; chiefly because proper performance depends on full understanding of the work to be done
(D) poor; chiefly because officers should be able to think for themselves

35. Which of the following statements concerning the behavior of law enforcement officers is most accurate?

(A) A show of confident assurance on the part of a law enforcement officer will make it possible to cover a shortage of knowledge in any given duty.
(B) In ordinary cases, when a newly appointed officer does not know what to do, it is always better to do too much than to do too little.
(C) It is not advisable that officers recommend the employment of certain attorneys for individuals taken into custody.
(D) A prisoner who is morose and refuses to talk will need less watching by an officer than one who is suicidal.

36. In dealing with children, a law enforcement officer should always

(A) treat them the same as adults
(B) instill in them a fear of the law
(C) secure their confidence
(D) impress them with the right of the law to punish them for their wrongdoings

37. The one of the following which is the most probable reason for the considerably increasing proportion of serious crimes committed by women is

(A) that the proportion of women in the population is increasing
(B) the increasing number of crime gangs in operation
(C) the success of women in achieving social equality with men
(D) the increasing number of crime stories in the movies and on television

38. Increased police vigilance would probably be *least* successful in preventing

(A) murder
(B) burglary
(C) prostitution
(D) auto theft

39. It frequently happens that a major crime of an unusual nature is followed almost immediately by an epidemic of several crimes, in widely scattered locations, with elements similar to the first crime. Of the following, the most likely explanation for this situation is that

(A) the same criminal is likely to commit the same type of crime
(B) a gang of criminals will operate in several areas simultaneously
(C) newspaper publicity on a major crime is apt to influence other would-be criminals
(D) the same causes which are responsible for the first crime are also responsible for the others

40. "A member of the department shall not indulge in intoxicants while in uniform. A member of the department, not required to wear a uniform, and a uniformed member, while out of uniform, shall not indulge in intoxicants to an extent unfitting him or her for duty." It follows that a

(A) member off duty, not in uniform, may drink intoxicants to any degree desired
(B) member on duty, not in uniform, may drink intoxicants

(C) member on duty, in uniform, may drink intoxicants
(D) uniformed member, in civilian clothes, may not drink intoxicants

41. The reason police officers have greater authority than private citizens in making arrests is

(A) to protect citizens against needless arrest
(B) to ensure a fair trial
(C) that they have greater knowledge of the law
(D) that they are in better physical shape

42. "The treatment given to the offender cannot alter the fact of the offense, but we can take measures to reduce the chances of similar acts occurring in the future. We should banish the criminal, not in order to exact revenge nor directly to encourage reform, but to deter him or her and others from further illegal attacks on society." According to this quotation, the principal reason for punishing criminals is to

(A) prevent the commission of future crimes
(B) remove them safely from society
(C) avenge society
(D) teach them that crime does not pay

43. When arrested, boys under 16 years of age are not brought to the same place of detention as older men. The reason for this separation is most likely to

(A) keep them with others of their own age
(B) protect them from rough police methods
(C) help them get sound legal aid
(D) keep them from contact with hardened criminals

44. Many criminals dress well and look intelligent but have no regard for a human life if it stands in their way. A reasonable conclusion from this statement is that

(A) it is almost certain death to combat a criminal
(B) criminals are frequently intelligent
(C) even some intelligent people have no regard for human life
(D) a well-dressed person may be a criminal

45. A police officer stationed along the route of a parade has been ordered not to allow cars to cross the route while the parade is in progress. An ambulance driver on an emergency run attempts to drive an ambulance across the route while the parade is passing. Under these circumstances, the officer should

(A) ask the driver to wait while the officer calls headquarters and obtains a decision

(B) stop the parade long enough to permit the ambulance to cross the street

(C) direct the ambulance driver to the shortest detour available, which will add at least ten minutes to the run

(D) hold up the ambulance in accordance with the order

46. An off-duty police officer in civilian clothes riding in the rear of a bus notices two teenage boys tampering with the rear emergency door. The most appropriate action for the officer to take is to

(A) tell the boys to discontinue their tampering, pointing out the dangers to life that their actions create

(B) report the boys' actions to the bus operator and let the bus operator take whatever action is deemed best

(C) signal the bus operator to stop, show the boys the police badge, and then order them off the bus

(D) show the boys the police badge, order them to stop their actions, and take down their names and addresses

47. Assume that you are on your way home late at night. You notice smoke pouring out of one of the windows of a house in which several families reside. Your first consideration under these circumstances should be to

(A) determine the cause of the smoke

(B) arouse all the residents in the house

(C) carry out to safety any persons overcome by smoke

(D) call the fire department to the scene

48. While present at a performance in a theater, you are notified that there is a fire under the stage. Under these circumstances, you would *least* expect to

(A) transmit the alarm from the nearest box

(B) remove fire appliances from their places

(C) ascertain whether there is a fire

(D) announce to the audience that there is a fire in the theater and everyone should leave quietly

49. You notice something unusual on your post. You should immediately

(A) report the matter in writing to your superior

(B) look up the rules on the matter

(C) investigate the matter

(D) wait for a time to see whether anything will happen

50. A police officer is summoned into a subway station where a man has collapsed and is lying unconscious on the floor. His breath smells strongly of alcohol. For the officer to summon medical aid immediately is

(A) undesirable; the man is merely intoxicated and can be handled by the police officer alone

(B) desirable; the man's unconsciousness may have a medical cause

(C) undesirable; the commotion caused by the incident will be aggravated by the appearance of an ambulance

(D) desirable; medical aid is necessary to help him regain consciousness in any event

51. A police officer notices a two-year-old child standing by himself in front of a supermarket and crying. Which of the following actions should the officer take *first*?

(A) Call the precinct to find out if the child has been reported missing.

(B) Look for possible identification on the child's clothing.

(C) Take the child to the police precinct until he is claimed.

(D) Inquire in the supermarket in an attempt to find his parent.

52. At a crowded bus stop, a police officer notices that a child about seven years old has been pushed out of the bus involuntarily. The crowd piling into the bus is so thick that the child is unable to get back into it. After the bus has gone, the officer learns from the child that her mother was on the bus but was probably unable to get out because of the crowd pushing in. The child knows her own address, a considerable distance away, and in an opposite direction from the one in which she was traveling. Of the following, the best action for the officer to take *first* is to

(A) take the child home
(B) explain to the child how to go home and let her go alone
(C) leave the child with instructions to wait until her mother returns
(D) wait at the stop with the child long enough to give the mother a chance to return from the next stop

53. Which of the following is the most accurate statement concerning the proper attitude of a police officer towards persons in his or her custody?

(A) Ignore any serious problems of those in custody, if they have no bearing on the charges preferred.
(B) Do not inform the person who has been arrested of the reason for the arrest.
(C) Do not permit a person in custody to give vent to feelings at any time.
(D) Watch a brooding or silent person more carefully than one who loudly threatens suicide.

54. Two rival youth gangs have been involved in several minor clashes. The officer working in the area believes that a serious clash will occur if steps are not taken to prevent it. Of the following, the *least* desirable action for the officer to take in the effort to head off trouble is to

(A) arrest the leaders of both gangs as a warning
(B) warn the parents of the dangerous situation
(C) obtain the cooperation of religious and civic leaders in the community
(D) report the situation to a superior

55. If, while you are on traffic duty at a busy intersection, a pedestrian asks you for directions to a particular place, the best course of conduct is for you to

(A) ignore the question and continue directing traffic

(B) tell the pedestrian to ask an officer on foot patrol
(C) answer the question in a brief, courteous manner
(D) leave your traffic post only long enough to give clear and adequate directions

56. Suppose that, while you are patrolling your post, a middle-aged woman informs you that three men are holding up a nearby bank. You rush immediately to the scene of the holdup. While you are still about 75 feet away, you see the three men, revolvers in their hands, emerge from the bank and run towards what is apparently their getaway car, which is pointed in the opposite direction. Of the following, your *first* consideration in this situation should be to

(A) enter the bank in order to find out what the men have taken
(B) maneuver quickly so as to get the getaway car between you and the bank
(C) make a mental note of the descriptions of the escaping men for immediate alarm
(D) draw your gun and shout for the men to surrender

57. A storekeeper has complained to you that every day at noon several peddlers congregate outside his store in order to sell their merchandise. You should

(A) inform him that such complaints must be made directly to the Police Commissioner
(B) inform him that peddlers have a right to earn their living too
(C) make it your business to patrol that part of your post around noon
(D) pay no attention to him as this storekeeper is probably a crank inasmuch as nobody else has complained

58. A police officer is approached by an obviously upset woman who reports that her husband is missing. The *first* thing the officer should do is to

(A) check with the hospitals and the police station
(B) tell the woman to wait a few hours and call the police station if her husband has not returned
(C) obtain a description of the missing man so that an alarm can be broadcast
(D) ask the woman why she thinks her husband is missing

59. When approaching a suspect to make an arrest, it is *least* important for the police officer to guard against the possibility that the suspect may

(A) be diseased
(B) have a gun
(C) use physical force
(D) run away

60. An acceptable proof of the present address of the person to whom a police officer is issuing a summons would logically be

(A) a recent photograph
(B) society membership cards
(C) recently postmarked letters addressed to that person
(D) the deed to a house

61. "In any uniformed service, strict discipline is essential." Of the following, the best justification for requiring that subordinates follow the orders of superior officers without delay is that

(A) not all orders can be carried out quickly
(B) it is more important that an order be obeyed accurately than promptly
(C) prompt obedience makes for efficient action in emergencies
(D) some superior officers are too strict

62. Suppose that you receive directions from your supervisor that you do not altogether understand. Of the following, the best action for you to take is to

(A) request a more experienced employee to assist you in your work
(B) go ahead and do the best you can
(C) follow only those directions that you understand perfectly
(D) ask your supervisor to repeat those instructions that are not clear

63. As a police officer, if you think of an idea for improving the police protection in certain areas, your best procedure would be to

(A) get the opinions of all the people working in those areas
(B) suggest it to your superiors immediately
(C) forget it because the department has experts thinking about such problems all the time
(D) consider the idea carefully before suggesting it.

64. A person is making a complaint to an officer which seems unreasonable and of little importance. Of the following, the best action for the officer to take is to

(A) criticize the person making the complaint for taking up valuable time
(B) laugh over the matter to show that the complaint is minor and silly
(C) tell the person that anyone responsible for the grievance will be arrested
(D) listen to the person making the complaint and tell him or her that the matter will be investigated

65. When reporting a robbery to headquarters over the police telephone system, a police officer should make the report as brief as possible so as to avoid

(A) long entries in the record book
(B) confusing the listener
(C) errors in fact
(D) tying up the line

66. Police officers are instructed to confer with the assistant district attorney before preparing a formal written complaint. The most probable reason is to

(A) keep it brief
(B) agree on the facts of the case
(C) avoid legal errors
(D) assure a conviction

67. In submitting a report of an unusual arrest or other unusual occurrence, the first paragraph of the report should contain

(A) a brief outline of what occurred
(B) your conclusions and recommendations
(C) the authority and reason for the investigation of the arrest or occurrence
(D) complete and accurate answers to the questions who?, what?, where?, when?, why?, and how?

68. "If an officer is not relieved at the expiration of a tour of duty, he or she shall not abandon the post, but shall communicate with the desk officer or control sergeant and comply with the instructions received." Of the following, the best reason for this rule is that

(A) it gives the officer definite control over all earned overtime

(B) the service given to an officer's relief may be repaid at another time when he or she is late

(C) it gives the officer a chance to make up time which he or she may owe due to previous lateness

(D) it is necessary for the safety of the public that a post be manned at all times

69. A factory manager asks a police officer to escort the payroll clerk to and from the local bank when payroll money is withdrawn. The police officer knows that it is against departmental policy to provide payroll escort service. The officer should

(A) refuse and explain why he or she cannot do what is requested

(B) refer the manager to the precinct commander

(C) tell the manager that police officers have more important tasks to perform

(D) advise the manager that he or she will provide this service if other duties do not interfere

70. A police officer in civilian clothes appearing as a witness in a court must wear his or her shield over the left breast. This procedure

(A) helps the officer in reporting for duty promptly if called

(B) impresses the judge

(C) identifies the witness as a police officer

(D preserves order

71. The printed departmental rules may logically be expected to include information on

(A) which posts are the most dangerous

(B) where to purchase uniforms and equipment cheaply

(C) how many days a week overtime work will be required

(D) what must be included in an accident report

72. Orders issued to police officers remain in effect until cancelled. An example of an order that will be be fulfilled at a definite time known in advance is one which

(A) warns police officers to be on the look-out for certain known hoodlums

(B) informs police officers of a new reporting procedure

(C) assigns additional police officers to the entertainment district area on New Year's Eve

(D) reminds police officers of a rule that is sometimes overlooked

73. Certain orders and instructions are transmitted by means of bulletins posted on the precinct bulletin boards. Such a bulletin order would most likely be rescinded if it

(A) conflicted with another order that was issued later

(B) was not readily understood by the entire force

(C) had been in force for a long time

(D) was frequently violated

74. A thorough knowledge of printed departmental regulations will help a police officer to know

(A) how to recognize a forgery

(B) when it is proper to make an arrest

(C) how to take care of the police uniform

(D) when to expecct vandalism

75. According to the police manual, when circumstances permit, not more than one prisoner shall be confined in a cell. Of the following, the most important reason for this regulation is to

(A) ensure reasonable privacy for the prisoners

(B) minimize the development of troublesome situations

(C) protect the civil rights of the prisoners

(D) separate the hardened from the less hardened criminals

76. "Parking is prohibited here," the police officer said. "You'll have to move further down." The driver then informed the police officer that he was a good friend of an important local political figure and indicated that the officer should attend to other more significant matters. Of the following courses of action, the one that the officer ought to select is to

(A) permit the driver to park there for a brief time

(B) request the name of the alleged important political figure

(C) insist that the car be parked elsewhere

(D) attract the attention of bystanders to the incident in order to demonstrate police impartiality

77. Suppose that while you are directing traffic at Columbus Circle, a young man approaches and asks "How can I get to Columbus Circle?" You should say

(A) "On your way, young man."

(B) "This seems paradoxical. You seek what you have."

(C) "Columbus Circle is at 59th Street and Broadway."

(D) "This is Columbus Circle. Where do you want to go?"

78. A motorist who has been stopped by an officer for speeding acts rudely. He hints about his personal connections with high officials in the city government and demands the officer's name and shield number. The officer should

(A) ask the motorist why he wants the information and give it only if the answer is satisfactory

(B) give both name and shield number without comment

(C) ignore the request since both name and shield number will appear on the summons the officer will issue

(D) give name and shield number but increase the charges against the motorist

79. At 3:00 A.M. while on his tour of duty, a police officer notices a traffic light at an intersection is not operating. There is little traffic at night at this intersection. Under these circumstances, the most appropriate action for the police officer to take is to

(A) report this matter to a superior at the end of his tour of duty

(B) station himself at the intersection to direct traffic until the appearance of daylight reduces the hazard of a collision

(C) report this matter immediately to the precinct

(D) post a sign at the intersection stating that the traffic light is not operating

80. "While Police Officer Y was patrolling his post, he noticed that a traffic light at an important intersection was not operating. Traffic was beginning to become snarled. He immediately stepped out into the intersection and directed traffic until the traffic load eased up, whereupon he resumed his patrol." Of the following, the chief criticism of Officer Y's action in this situation is that he should

(A) have remained at the intersection directing traffic until the end of his tour of duty

(B) not have attempted to direct traffic at all, since that is not his duty

(C) have called his superior so that his regular post could have been covered

(D) not have waited until traffic eased up before taking the responsibility of leaving his post

81. "Driver 1 claimed that the collision occurred because, as he approached the intersection, Driver 2 started to make a left turn suddenly and at a high speed, even though the light had been red for 15 to 20 seconds." Suppose that you have been assigned to make a report on this accident. The position of the vehicles after the accident is indicated in the diagram below. The point in each case indicates the front of the vehicle. On the basis of this diagram, the best reason for concluding that Driver 1's statement is false is that

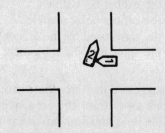

(A) Driver 2's car is beyond the center of the intersection

(B) Driver 2's car is making the turn on the proper side of the road

(C) Driver 1's car is beyond the sidewalk line

(D) Driver 1's car is on the right-hand side of the road

82. While patrolling a bridge approach road alone in a radio car, you are signaled to stop by a private car traveling in the opposite direction. The driver tells you that be was robbed by two men in a sedan ahead of him. Your car cannot cross the concrete safety-strip to get into the other lane. Of the following, the best course of action for you to take is to

(A) tell the driver you cannot cross to his lane and ask him to report the matter
(B) leave your car where it is, cross over to the private car, and use it to pursue the suspects
(C) notify headquarters over your radio
(D) make a U-turn in your car and chase the suspect vehicle on the wrong side of the parkway

83. "A courteous warning by an officer to a vehicle operator who has committed a minor traffic violation is usually more effective than a summons." Of the following statements, the one that best supports this point of view is:

(A) An officer should issue a summons whenever one is called for and never show favoritism.
(B) A warning should always be issued for a first offense.
(C) The inconvenience and expense of a summons will keep most motorists from repeating the offense.
(D) The operator who receives a warning for a minor violation will try to avoid repeating the offense.

84. A police officer using hand signals is directing traffic at a congested intersection. It is *least* important that

(A) the officer be visible
(B) the officer be accessible
(C) the signs used by the officer be uniform
(D) the signs used by the officer be simple

85. It is suggested that an officer should keep all persons away from the area of an accident until an investigation has been completed. This suggested procedure is

(A) good; witnesses will be more likely to agree on a single story
(B) bad; such action blocks traffic flow and causes congestion
(C) good; objects of possible use as evidence will be protected from damage or loss

(D) bad; the flow of normal pedestrian traffic provides an opportunity for an investigator to determine the cause of the accident

86. Before permitting automobiles involved in an accident to depart, a police officer should take certain measures. Of the following, it is *least* important that the officer make certain that

(A) both drivers are properly licensed
(B) the automobiles are in safe operating condition
(C) the drivers have exchanged names and license numbers
(D) he or she obtains the names and addresses of drivers and witnesses

87. A radio motor patrol team arrives on the scene a few minutes after a pedestrian has been killed by a hit-and-run driver. After obtaining a description of the car, the first action the officer should take is to

(A) radio a description of the fleeing car to precinct headquarters
(B) try to overtake the fleeing car
(C) obtain complete statements from everyone at the scene
(D) inspect the site of the accident for clues

88. The most effective method of crime prevention is, in general,

(A) severe punishment of malefactors
(B) probation
(C) parole
(D) eradication of causal factors

89. A businessman requests advice concerning good practice in the use of a safe in his office. Of the following points, which should be stressed in the use of safes?

(A) A safe should not be placed where it can be seen from the street.
(B) The combination should be written down and carefully hidden in the office.
(C) A safe located in a dark place is more tempting to a burglar than one that is located in a well-lighted place.
(D) Factors of size and weight alone determine the protection offered by a safe.

90. It has been claimed that a person who commits a crime sometimes has an unconscious wish to be punished, which is caused by strong unconscious feelings of guilt. Of the following actions by a criminal, the one which may be partly due to an unconscious desire for punishment is

(A) claiming that he or she doesn't know anything about the crime when questioned by the police

(B) running away from the state where the crime was committed

(C) revisiting the place where the crime was committed

(D) taking care not to leave any clues at the scene of the crime

91. Which of the following statements about fingerprints is *least* accurate?

(A) The value of fingerprints left at the scene of the crime does not vary with the distinctness of the fingerprint impressions.

(B) It is of value to fingerprint a person with an abnormal number of fingers.

(C) Fingerprints of different persons have never been found to be alike.

(D) The prime value of fingerprints lies in their effectiveness in identifying people.

92. According to a police manual, the delivery for laboratory examination of any article required as evidence must be made by the member of the force finding or coming into the possession of such evidence. Of the following, the most likely reason for this procedure is that it

(A) assists in the establishment of the authenticity of the evidence

(B) encourages a more careful search of the crime scene for all physical evidence that may be related to the crime

(C) ensures that the evidence will be properly marked or tagged for future identification

(D) prevents the undue delay that might result from a delivery through official channels

93. You are getting the description of a lost diamond bracelet. Of the following, the most important piece of information, in addition to knowing that the missing item is a diamond bracelet, is

(A) value—$10,000

(B) design—two intertwining snakes

(C) diamonds—many small and several large diamonds

(D) owner—Mrs. H. Jones

94. You are watching a great number of people leave a ball game. Of the persons who are described below, the one whom it would be easiest to spot would be

(A) female; age 15; height 5′6″; weight 130 lbs.; long straight black hair

(B) male; age 50; height 5′8″; weight 150 lbs.; missing toe on right foot

(C) male; age 60; height 5′7″; weight 170 lbs.; all false teeth

(D) male; age 25; height 6′3″; weight 220 lbs.; pockmarked

95. You are preparing a description of a woman to be broadcast. Of the following characteristics, the one which would be of most value to an officer driving a squad car is

(A) wanted for murder

(B) age 45 years

(C) height 6′1″

(D) smokes very heavily

96. Assume that on a hot summer day, you are stationed on the grass at the south bank of a busy parkway looking at southbound traffic for a light blue 1974 Ford two door sedan. If traffic is very heavy, which of the following additional pieces of information would be most helpful to you in identifying the car?

(A) All chrome is missing from the left side of the car.

(B) There is a bullet hole in the left front window.

(C) The paint on the right side of the car is somewhat faded.

(D) The front bumper is missing.

97. You are watching a great number of people leave a sports arena after a boxing match. Of the characteristics listed below, the one which would be of greatest value to you in spotting a man wanted by the department is
    (A) height: 5'3"; weight: 200 lbs.
    (B) eyes: brown; hair: black, wavy; complexion: sallow
    (C) that he frequents bars and grills and customarily associates with females
    (D) scars: thin ½" scar on left upper lip; tattoos: on right forearm—"Pinto"

98. "Social Security cards are not acceptable proof of identification for police purposes." Of the following, the most important reason for this rule is that the Social Security card
    (A) is easily obtained
    (B) states on its face "for Social Security purposes—not for identification"
    (C) is frequently lost
    (D) does not contain a photograph, description, or fingerprints of the person

99. "Photographs of suspected persons should not be shown to the witness if the suspect himself can be arrested and placed on view for identification." This recommendation is
    (A) inadvisable; this procedure might subject the witness to future retribution by the suspect
    (B) advisable; a photograph cannot be used for identification purposes with the same degree of certainty as the suspect in person
    (C) inadvisable; the appearance of the suspect may have changed since the commission of the crime
    (D) advisable; photography as an art has not achieved an acceptable degree of perfection

100. Stationed at a busy intersection, you are given the description of a vehicle that has been stolen. Of the following characteristics, the one which will permit you to eliminate most easily a large number of vehicles is
    (A) no spare tire
    (B) make—Buick, two-door sedan, 1976
    (C) color—black
    (D) tires—750 × 16, white-walled

101. If a sick or injured woman, to whom a male police officer is rendering aid, is unknown and the officer has reason to believe that her clothing contains means of identification, he should
    (A) immediately search the clothing for such identification and remove any identification found therein
    (B) send for a female officer to search the clothing before the woman is sent to a hospital
    (C) ask any female present to search the clothing for such identification
    (D) accompany her to the hospital and there seek the necessary information from the hospital authorities.

102. Which of the following means of avoiding identification would be most likely to meet with success?
    (A) growing a beard
    (B) shaving off the beard if there was one originally
    (C) burning the fingers so as to remove the fingerprints
    (D) changing the features by facial surgery

103. In asking a witness of a crime to identify a suspect, it is a common practice to place the suspect with a group of persons and ask the witness to pick out the person in question. Of the following, the best reason for this practice is that it will
    (A) make the identification more reliable than if the witness were shown the suspect alone
    (B) protect the witness against reprisals
    (C) make sure that the witness is telling the truth
    (D) help select other participants in the crime at the same time

104. Suppose that a police officer observes an individual acting suspiciously while in a department store. Of the following, the most desirable procedure for her to follow is to
    (A) arrest the person
    (B) warn the salespeople that this person may be a thief
    (C) continue to observe this person until sufficient data is present for the formulation of a final decision
    (D) telephone headquarters for assistance as there may soon be a disturbance

105. A police officer who is off duty observes a woman busily engaged in examining fabrics at a counter in a large store. The woman's handbag is open. A number of other persons are at this counter also engaged in examining fabrics. Of the following, the best procedure for the officer to follow *first* is to

   (A) tell the woman that her handbag is open
   (B) keep the woman under close observation
   (C) direct a clerk to inform the woman that her handbag is open
   (D) approach the woman and engage her in conversation, by asking a question like, "Do you have the time? My watch seems to have stopped."

106. "The four witnesses to the bank robbery, including the bank president and the cashier, were left together for one hour in the president's office at the bank before they were questioned." This kind of procedure is

   (A) desirable and considerate as there is no point in treating respectable citizens as criminals
   (B) unwise as it permits undue pressure to be brought upon some of the witnesses
   (C) unwise as it permits an exchange of actual and imagined details that may result in invalid testimony
   (D) wise as it keeps the witnesses all in one place

107. Assume that you are questioning a victim in order to obtain a description of a mugger. Of the following, the best example of the type of question to be avoided is:

   (A) Did you notice any scars or unusual features?
   (B) Did he wear a brown or black coat?
   (C) What color were his shoes?
   (D) Approximately how tall was he?

108. Suppose that you are questioning witnesses to a hit-and-run accident. Of the following, the information that will probably be *least* valuable for the purpose of sending out an alarm for the hit-and-run automobile is the

   (A) direction which the automobile took after the accident
   (B) number of occupants in the automobile at the time of the accident
   (C) speed at which the automobile was moving when it struck the victim
   (D) part of the automobile that struck the victim of the accident

109. The marks left on a bullet by a gun barrel are different from those left by any other gun barrel. This fact is most useful in directly identifying the

   (A) direction from which a shot was fired
   (B) person who fired a particular gun
   (C) gun from which a bullet was fired
   (D) bullet that caused a fatal wound

110. Uniformed officers are constantly urged to consider every revolver loaded until proven otherwise. Of the following, the best justification for this recommendation is that

   (A) no time is lost when use of the revolver is required
   (B) there are many accidents involving apparently empty revolvers
   (C) less danger is involved when facing armed criminals
   (D) ammunition deteriorates unless replaced periodically.

111. Of the following, the best method to use in shooting a revolver is to keep

   (A) both eyes closed
   (B) both eyes open
   (C) the right eye open
   (D) the left eye open

112. A police officer should fire a pistol

   (A) only as a last resort
   (B) at no time
   (C) primarily to inspire fear
   (D) to impress upon citizens the need for respect

113. The police officer must inform the person arrested of his or her authority and of the cause of arrest except when the

   (A) crime charged is a felony
   (B) person arrested is a habitual offender
   (C) officer is in uniform so that authority is apparent
   (D) person is arrested in the actual commission of the crime

114. "A woman about thirty years of age accosted a police officer with the complaint that her husband had just attacked her with a pair of scissors. 'My husband nearly gouged my eyes out,' the woman said. 'He poked me in the face not once but four or five times. He cut my face into ribbons. He's a dangerous man and I want him arrested. I have five or six witnesses to the attack.' The officer saw no marks on the woman's face." On the basis of these data, the officer may most reasonably take the position that

    (A) the husband ought to be taken into custody immediately
    (B) the woman's story is at least partially inaccurate
    (C) no scissors were involved in the accident
    (D) the incident occurred some time ago

115. Generally, before making an arrest for a serious crime, the police officer must have facts to provide a reasonable basis for believing the person to be guilty." The best reason for this rule is to

    (A) reduce the number of arrests
    (B) protect himself or herself against being charged with false arrest
    (C) safeguard the rights of citizens against improper arrest
    (D) place the burden of disproving the charges upon accused

116. Suppose that a police officer arrests a man accused of molesting a young girl. In an instance of this type, the officer should

    (A) behave toward the accused in the same manner as toward any other individual accused of a crime
    (B) be a little rough in handling the man
    (C) inform the man in no uncertain terms that the act of which he is accused is most contemptible
    (D) assume that the man is psychopathic and rightfully a case for institutionalization

117. Suppose that a police officer is summoned by a Mr. Smith who accuses a Mr. Jones of having aided a Mr. Brown to do an injury to Mr. Smith. The nature of the claimed injury is not such as to give the officer the right to make an arrest. The officer should *first*

    (A) prove to Mr. Smith that there is insufficient merit in his case

    (B) refer Mr. Smith to the captain of the precinct
    (C) explain to Mr. Smith the reason why an arrest cannot be made
    (D) refer Mr. Smith to the nearest court

118. When sent to make an arrest, a police officer should be sure he or she is arresting the correct person in order to avoid

    (A) publicity
    (B) detaining an innocent person
    (C) having to use force
    (D) having to appear in court

119. If a police officer is called upon to eject a disorderly person from a bus station, the most important consideration must necessarily be to

    (A) avoid damaging transit system property
    (B) earn good public opinion
    (C) avoid endangering other passengers
    (D) get the person off the property

120. "When making arrests, the police officer should treat all suspects in the same manner." This suggested rule is

    (A) undesirable; the specific problems presented should govern the officer's actions
    (B) desirable; this is the only democratic solution to the problem
    (C) undesirable; persons who are only suspected are not criminals and should not be treated as such
    (D) desirable; only by setting up fixed and rigid rules can officers know what is expected of them

121. A police officer observes a young man who is obviously very excited, walking unusually fast, and repeatedly halting to look behind him. Upon stopping the young man, the officer finds that he is carrying a gun and has just held up a liquor store a few blocks away. This incident illustrates that

    (A) circumstances that are not suspicious in themselves frequently provide clues for the solution of crimes
    (B) an experienced officer can pick the criminal type out of a crowd by alert observation
    (C) action is always to be preferred to thought
    (D) a police officer should investigate suspicious circumstances

122. A police officer positively recognizes a woman on a busy street as one wanted for passing bad checks. Of the following, the most appropriate action for the officer to take is to

(A) approach and then arrest the woman
(B) follow the women until a place is reached where there are few people, then take out a gun, and arrest the woman
(C) immediately take out a gun, stop the woman, and search her
(D) follow the woman as she may lead the way to associates.

123. A woman has her husband arrested for severely beating their five-year-old son. A crowd of angry neighbors has gathered around the husband. In making the arrest, the arresting officer should

(A) treat the husband like any other person accused of breaking the law
(B) deal with the husband sympathetically since the man may be mentally ill
(C) handle the husband harshly since his crime is a despicable one
(D) treat the husband roughly only if he shows no remorse for his actions

124. The purpose of a raid is to

(A) apprehend criminals
(B) disclose the members of a certain criminal group
(C) secure the probable cause required for the issuance of a search warrant
(D) know the fields of observation from a suspected place

125. There has been a series of burglaries in a residential area consisting of one-family houses. You have been assigned to select a house in this area in which detectives can wait secretly for an attempted burglary of that house so that the burglars can be apprehended in the act. Which of the following would be the best house to select for this purpose?

(A) The house that was recently burglarized and from which several thousand dollars worth of clothing and personal property were taken.

(B) The house whose owner reports that several times the telephone has rung, but the person making the call hung up as soon as the telephone was answered.
(C) The house that is smaller and looks much less pretentious than other houses in the same area.
(D) The house that is occupied by a widower who works long hours but who lives with an invalid mother requiring constant nursing service.

126. Suppose that a police officer observes a young girl picking up small articles of merchandise as she passes from one counter to another of a large department store. The girl does not stop to pay for any of the articles. For the officer to wait until the girl is about to leave the store before apprehending her is

(A) inadvisable; she may escape
(B) advisable; evidence is thereby more firmly established
(C) inadvisable if she has an accomplice waiting outside
(D) advisable if the police officer has a witness to confirm the observations

127. Jones is accused of having assaulted Smith at a particular time and place. Police investigation disclosed that Jones was present at the time and place where the alleged assault took place. This information makes admissible the conclusion that

(A) Jones assaulted Smith
(B) Smith assaulted Jones
(C) Jones may have assaulted Smith
(D) Smith may have assaulted Jones

128. Suppose that a lawyer is attacked in a washroom by a man who delivered several blows from behind with a carpenter's mallet. From this information only, it is safe to infer

(A) that the attacker is young and strong
(B) that the mallet was either recently purchased or stolen
(C) that the washroom is located in an office building
(D) none of the foregoing

129. Suppose that a police officer is seeking information designed to locate the perpetrator of a known assault. Of the following, the question that would be most useful in assisting the officer to ascertain the identity of the guilty person is

(A) Where did the assault occur?
(B) At what time did the assault occur?
(C) Who was the victim of the assault?
(D) Who was the assailant?

130. During a quarrel on a crowded city street, one man stabs another and flees. A police officer arriving at the scene a short time later finds the victim unconscious, calls for an ambulance, and orders the crowd to leave. The officer's action is

(A) bad; there may have been witnesses to the assault among the crowd
(B) good; it is proper first aid procedure to give an injured person room and air
(C) bad; the assailant is probably among the crowd
(D) good; a crowd may destroy needed evidence

131. Green is accused on apparently good evidence of having stolen a radio from Brown at 8:30 P.M., January 18. If Green is able to prove that at 10:00 P.M. of the same day he was not in possession of any radio, Green has

(A) proved his innocence
(B) yet to establish his innocence
(C) implied his guilt since evidence for the period 8:30 P.M. to 10:00 P.M. is absent
(D) proved that Brown is mistaken or lying

132. Clothes valued at $800 as well as $1000 in cash were stolen from the home of one of the residents of a police officer's post. The officer learns that Albert Jones, a man 27 years old and not known ever to possess more than a few dollars at one time, has, shortly after the occasion of the robbery, displayed what seemed to be a large roll of bills. The officer may most profitably take, as the basis for first action, the position that

(A) a large roll of bills is sometimes obtained as the result of a burglary
(B) despite the fact that the clothing is valued at $800, a considerably smaller sum is likely to be realized when the clothing is sold to a secondhand dealer
(C) Albert Jones may recently have gotten a job
(D) reputation must be distinguished from character

133. A resident on your post informs you that a valuable diamond ring has been stolen from her apartment. About two weeks later, a boy gives you what appears to be a diamond ring that he says be found on the street. Of the following, the question that would be *least* significant in this situation is:

(A) Did the boy actually find the ring on the street?
(B) Is this the same ring the resident mentioned?
(C) Was the ring really stolen?
(D) Did the resident wait for more or less than two hours before reporting the theft of the ring?

134. "Goods valued at $75,000 were reported burglarized from a loft. Investigation proved conclusively that it was impossible for burglars either to have entered or left the loft building without having been detected." On the basis of these data, the police officer may most reasonably deduce that

(A) more than $75,000 worth of goods were stolen
(B) the burglary was committed by a person unfamiliar with the habits of the people in the loft where the crime occurred
(C) what was reported to be a burglary is actually an assault
(D) the alleged crime did not occur

135. Suppose that a police officer observes that a certain company on his post pays out a large sum in cash weekly in payroll. If the officer were asked to suggest the best method for eliminating the possibility of a successful payroll robbery in this company, he would suggest

(A) the hiring of several armed guards
(B) that payday occur at irregular intervals
(C) that payment be made at a place other than at the offices of the company
(D) payment by check

136. "Many thieves conceal themselves in a building during business hours, and, when they have accomplished their purpose, escape through a rear door or window." The reason for such concealment in the building is most probably that after business hours

(A) without a key, locked doors are sometimes difficult to open

(B) poor lighting is conducive to undetected criminal activity

(C) to accomplish a purpose, one must have a goal

(D) rear doors ordinarily serve as exits

137. "When investigating a burglary, a police officer should obtain as complete descriptions as possible of articles of value that were stolen, but should list, without describing, stolen articles that are relatively valueless." This suggested procedure is

(A) poor; what is valueless to one person may be of great value to another

(B) good; it enables the police to concentrate on recovering the most valuable articles

(C) poor; articles of little value frequently provide the only evidence connecting the suspect to the crime

(D) good; the listing of the inexpensive items is probably incomplete

138. Looking through the window of a jewelry store, a police officer sees a man take a watch from the counter and drop it into his pocket while the jeweler is busy talking to someone else. The man looks around the store and then walks out. The officer should

(A) stop the man and bring him back into the store so that both he and the jeweler can be questioned

(B) ignore the incident; if the man were performing an illegal act, the jeweler would have called for help

(C) arrest the man, take him to the station house, and then return to obtain the jeweler's statement

(D) ignore the incident; if the man were a thief, the jeweler would not have left the watches unattended

139. A radio police officer who responded at 2 A.M. to a radio call that a burglary had been committed in an apartment heard the sound of clashing tools coming from the adjoining apartment. For the officer to investigate the noise would be

(A) undesirable; the officer may not search without a warrant

(B) desirable; the thief may be found

(C) undesirable; unusual noises in apartments are common

(D) desirable; the victim would tend to be impressed by the concern shown

140. Assume that you are driving a police car, equipped with a two-way radio, along an isolated section of the parkway at 3 A.M. You note that the headlights of a car pulled to the side of the road are blinking rapidly. When you stop to investigate, the driver of the car informs you that he was just forced to the side of the road by two men in a green station wagon, who robbed him of a large amount of cash and jewelry at gunpoint and then sped away. Your *first* consideration in this situation should be to

(A) drive rapidly along the parkway in the direction taken by the criminals in an effort to apprehend them before they escape

(B) question the driver carefully, looking for inconsistencies indicating that he made up the whole story

(C) obtain a complete listing and identification of all materials lost

(D) notify your superior to have the parkway exits watched for a car answering the description of the getaway car

141. A police officer finds a man dying in one of the city parks. There are several stab wounds in the man's chest and his skull is fractured. Just before dying, the man manages to say that he was the victim of an assault and robbery. Upon investigation by the officer, a bloodstained shoemaker's awl is found nearby. Of the following, the most useful assumption to make *first* in attempting to solve the crime is that

(A) for some reason the man lied, so tentatively, his statement ought to be disregarded

(B) there were no witnesses to the possible crime

(C) the awl was deliberately placed near the scene of the crime to mislead the police

(D) the murderer had access to shoemaker's tools

142. "At 2 A.M., while patrolling your post, you find the body of a man lying on the street. A knife is protruding from the man's back." On the basis of these data only, it is *least* likely that the man was lying

    (A) on his left side
    (B) face downward
    (C) on his back
    (D) on his right side

143. In a recent case of suicide, the body was found slumped in a chair and no revolver, knife, or razor was found in the room. Of the following, the most reasonable hypothesis from the data given is that

    (A) the person had taken some poison
    (B) the person had hanged himself
    (C) the person had died as a result of a heart attack
    (D) the murderer had taken the weapon

144. Suppose that while patrolling your post in an unfrequented area at 1:00 A.M., you find a man sprawled on the ground in an alley. The man's throat has been cut and he is dead. There is considerable blood on the ground, but the man does not appear to be bleeding. Of the following, the *first* step you should take is to

    (A) straighten the man out so he is resting comfortably
    (B) telephone your precinct
    (C) investigate to determine whether the blood on the ground is the blood of the dead man
    (D) carry the man out to the street

145. Suppose that A, the proprietor of a fur business, is found dead at his place of business at 8:00 A.M. His death appears to have occurred as a result of the fact that he is hanging from a rope tied to a water pipe. In the pockets of A's trousers are a number of pawn tickets for furs and a lapsed insurance policy for $10,000. On the basis of this information only, the best inference is that

    (A) A committed suicide because of business difficulties
    (B) A had been working late and was murdered by thieves
    (C) A's death is the consequence of an accident

    (D) it is safe only to declare that A probably did not commit suicide. The fact that so few articles were found in his pockets is a substantial basis for extended additional investigation

146. When the bodies of two women were found stabbed in an inner room of an apartment, it was first believed that it was a case of mutual homicide. Of the following clues found at the scene, the one that indicates that it was more likely a case of murder by a third party is the fact that

    (A) the door to the apartment was found locked
    (B) there were bloodstains on the outer door of the apartment
    (C) there was a switchblade knife in each body
    (D) no money could be found in the room where the bodies were

147. "The questioning of witnesses is often much less truth-revealing than are physical clues found at the scene of the crime." Of the following, the chief justification for this statement is that

    (A) most witnesses rarely tell the truth
    (B) physical clues are always present if examination is thorough
    (C) questioning of witnesses must be supported by other evidence
    (D) the memory of witnesses is often unreliable

148. Jones, who is suspected of having committed a crime of homicide at 8:30 P.M. in the building where he lives, claims that he could not have committed the act because he worked overtime until 8:00 P.M. In order to prove that Jones actually could not have committed the act in question, it is most important to know

    (A) how long it takes to get from Jones' building to Jones' place of work
    (B) if there are any witnesses to the fact that Jones worked overtime
    (C) Jones' reputation in the community
    (D) what kind of work Jones does

149. A police officer on a post hears a cry for help from a woman in a car with two men. He approaches the car and is told by the woman that the men are kidnapping her. The men claim to be the woman's husband and doctor, and they state that they are taking her to a private mental hospital in Westchester County. Of the following, the officer should

(A) take all of them to the station house for further questioning

(B) permit the car to depart on the basis of the explanation

(C) call for an ambulance to take the woman to the nearest city mental hospital

(D) accompany the car to the private mental hospital

150. Suppose that a seven-year-old boy has been kidnapped as he was returning home from a playground at dusk. The following day, his parents received an anonymous letter that told them the child was well and designated a close friend of the family, who was known to be very fond of the boy, as an intermediary to arrange payment of a ransom. On the basis of these data only, we may most reasonably assume that

(A) the friend kidnapped the boy

(B) the friend was probably an accessory in the kidnapping

(C) further investigation is necessary to determine the identity of the kidnapper

(D) the boy is dead

151. The most frequent cause among the following for making a person a criminal is

(A) mental retardation

(B) good education

(C) bad environmental conditions

(D) superior ability in a trade

152. A view widely held among criminologists is that the severity of laws dealing with criminals is not so effective a deterrent to crime as is

(A) the enactment of less severe laws, coupled with lenient administration

(B) a well-organized parole system for even the most hardened criminals

(C) psychiatric treatment, as most crimes are committed by persons with emotional and mental difficulties

(D) certainty that the criminal will be apprehended and sentenced properly

153. A representative group of young criminals in a certain state were found to be normal in intelligence, but 86 percent were behind from one to six grades in school. The best inference from these data is that

(A) lack of intelligence is highly correlated with delinquency

(B) criminals should be removed from the school system

(C) educational maladjustments are closely associated with delinquency

(D) the usual rate at which criminals progress educationally represents the limit of their learning powers

154. "One study shows that boys' clubs and similar programs aimed at the prevention of crime and the rehabilitation of the juvenile delinquent tend to attract the good boys, while the bad boys stay away." This quotation implies most directly that the number of instances in which juvenile delinquents are rehabilitated through such programs as boys' clubs is

(A) relatively large

(B) relatively small

(C) a quantity the size of which cannot be estimated even loosely and approximately

(D) greater for good boys than for bad boys

155. Two police officers patrolling the downtown business streets at 1 A.M. observe a young girl dressed in a manner to attract attention, walking slowly down the street. The girl approaches a young man, who disregards her. After a short time, she approaches another man, who also disregards her. The officers should

(A) follow the girl until they are in a position to make a double arrest

(B) ignore the situation, since the girl is obviously not a professional prostitute

(C) approach and question the men as well as the girl since they may give evidence to prove solicitation

(D) separate, one continuing to observe the girl, the other calling the Missing Persons Bureau to check up on descriptions of missing girls

156. "Where a satisfactory adjustment can be made without arresting the delinquent minor, it is done. Court action is only taken where it seems best for the minor or the community." Of the following, the best justification for this procedure is that

(A) court cases are costly to the community
(B) rehabilitation of the delinquent minor is of primary importance
(C) arresting minors may become a source of inconvenience if not discouraged
(D) juvenile delinquency can increase if juvenile delinquents are not arrested

157. Suppose that, while on patrol late at night, you find a woman lying in the street, apparently a victim of a hit-and-run accident. She seems to be injured seriously, but you wish to ask her one or two questions in order to help apprehend the driver of the hit-and-run car. Of the following, the first question to ask is:

(A) Which direction did the car go?
(B) What time did it happen?
(C) What kind of car was it?
(D) How many persons were in the car?

158. Of the following, the information that would be *least* helpful to the police officer assigned to the case of a 14-year-old girl who has been reported by her mother as a runaway is

(A) the possible cause for her running away
(B) a detailed description of her clothing
(C) a detailed description of her scholastic abilities
(D) a detailed description of her features

159. A plainclothes police officer in a market comes upon a woman who is complaining that a fruit dealer has fraudulent scales. Upon questioning, she offers as evidence a bag of grapes she has just purchased. Of the following, the most appropriate action for the officer to take would be to

(A) buy some fruit from the dealer and later check the weight on scales known to be true
(B) return with the woman to the dealer and ask him to weigh the grapes again
(C) take the woman's bag of grapes and weigh it on true scales to verify her claim
(D) weigh the bag of grapes on a nearby dealer's scale as a check

160. A violin is reported as missing from the home of Mrs. Brown. It would be *least* important to the police, before making a routine check of pawn shops, to know that this violin

(A) is of a certain unusual shade of red
(B) has one tuning key with a chip mark on it in the shape of a triangle
(C) has a well-known manufacturer's label stamped inside the violin
(D) has a hidden number given to the police by the owner

161. Merely looking at a criminal is enough to tell an intelligent officer

(A) how educated the person is
(B) whether the person will be a troublemaker
(C) whether the person is truly a criminal
(D) little or nothing

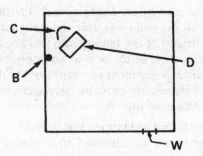

162. Assume that you are investigating a case of reported suicide. You find the deceased sitting in a chair, sprawled over his desk, a revolver still clutched in his right hand. In your examination of the room, you find that the window is partly open. Only one bullet has been fired from the revolver. The bullet has lodged in the wall. Assume that the diagram above is a scale drawing of the scene. D indicates the desk, C indicates the chair, W indicates the window, and B indicates the bullet. Of the following, which indicates most strongly the deceased did not commit suicide?

(A) the distance between the desk and the bullet hole
(B) the relative position of the bullet hole and the chair
(C) the fact that the window was partly open
(D) the relative position of the desk and the window.

163. As the police officer approaches a lighted delicatessen late at night, two men emerge and walk rapidly in the opposite direction. Suspicious of the behavior of these men, the officer looks through the window into the store. Of the following, the circumstances tending most strongly to confirm his suspicions are

(A) several persons are waiting to be served inside the store
(B) the clerk is standing at the counter with his back to the officer
(C) the clerk and a customer are engaged in a conversation
(D) no one at all is visible inside the store

164. About 9:00 P.M., a police officer observed two men loitering near a neighborhood movie theater. He had not seen either man in the neighborhood before. The agent for the theater usually deposited the night receipts in the local bank's night deposit vault between 9:00 and 9:15 P.M. The most appropriate action for the officer to take was to

(A) station himself so that he could observe their actions until the theater's money had been deposited
(B) demand that they tell him their place of residence and the reason for their presence near the theater
(C) pay no further attention since they were obviously waiting for someone in the theater
(D) enter the theater by the side entrance and warn the manager to be prepared for a possible robbery attempt

165. The proprietor of a tavern summons a police officer and turns over a loaded revolver that was found in one of the tavern's booths. The *least* appropriate action for the officer to take is to

(A) unload the gun and place it in an inside pocket
(B) determine exactly when the revolver was found
(C) obtain the names or descriptions of the persons who occupied the booth before the revolver was found
(D) question the proprietor very closely concerning the matter

166. Assume that you have stopped a 1978 Dodge four-door sedan, which you suspect is a car reported as stolen the day before. The items of information that would be most useful in determining whether or not this is the stolen car is that

(A) the stolen car's license number was QA2356; this car's license number is U21375
(B) the stolen car's engine number was AB6231; this car's engine number is CS2315
(C) the windshield of the stolen car was not cracked; this car's windshield is cracked
(D) the stolen car had whitewall tires; this car does not have whitewall tires

167. Crime statistics indicate that property crimes such as larceny, burglary, and robbery are more numerous during winter months than in summer. The explanation that most adequately accounts for this situation is that

(A) human needs, such as clothing, food, heat, and shelter, are greater in summer
(B) criminal tendencies are generally aggravated by climatic changes
(C) there are more hours of darkness in winter and such crimes are usually committed under cover of darkness
(D) urban areas are more densely populated during winter months, affording greater opportunity for such crimes

168. Blackmail is an especially troublesome problem for the police. The best justification for this statement is that the

(A) victim of a blackmail plot usually hesitates to cooperate with the police for fear of publicity
(B) blackmailer is usually a hardened criminal who will not hesitate to murder the victim
(C) facts constituting the subject matter of a blackmail are seldom known to the victim
(D) victim of a blackmail plot is usually anxious to expose all details to the police

169. In some states, statutes forbid the payment of ransom to kidnappers. Such statutes are

(A) actually in violation of the due process of law clause of the federal constitution
(B) necessary to encourage kidnappers to return the kidnapped person unharmed
(C) harmful because kidnapping is encouraged by such legislation
(D) examples of laws that protect society although sometimes working hardships on individuals

170. Any change in insurance coverage immediately prior to a fire should be investigated. Strange as it may seem, most such changes made by convicted arsonists are made to a smaller amount. The most probable reason for such changes is that the arsonist

(A) was trying to divert suspicion
(B) decided to set the fire after the change was made
(C) did not have enough money to pay for the full amount
(D) reduced the insurance to the amount he or she expected to be lost in the fire

ANSWER KEY

We are providing this key to the correct answers so that you can check your answers quickly and easily. Be sure to continue and study all the answer explanations that follow. The explanations point out the police reasoning and judgment involved in the correct answer choices.

1. A	18. B	35. C	52. D	69. A	86. C	103. A	120. A	137. C	154. B
2. A	19. B	36. C	53. D	70. C	87. A	104. C	121. D	138. A	155. C
3. D	20. D	37. C	54. A	71. D	88. D	105. A	122. A	139. B	156. B
4. D	21. C	38. A	55. C	72. C	89. C	106. C	123. A	140. D	157. C
5. C	22. C	39. C	56. C	73. A	90. C	107. B	124. A	141. D	158. C
6. C	23. C	40. B	57. C	74. B	91. A	108. C	125. B	142. C	159. A
7. D	24. D	41. C	58. D	75. B	92. A	109. C	126. B	143. A	160. C
8. A	25. B	42. A	59. A	76. C	93. B	110. B	127. C	144. B	161. D
9. C	26. A	43. D	60. C	77. D	94. D	111. B	128. D	145. A	162. B
10. D	27. A	44. D	61. C	78. B	95. C	112. A	129. D	146. B	163. D
11. A	28. B	45. B	62. D	79. C	96. D	113. D	130. A	147. D	164. A
12. B	29. A	46. A	63. D	80. C	97. A	114. B	131. B	148. A	165. A
13. B	30. D	47. D	64. D	81. A	98. D	115. C	132. A	149. A	166. B
14. D	31. C	48. D	65. D	82. C	99. B	116. A	133. D	150. C	167. C
15. A	32. D	49. C	66. C	83. D	100. C	117. C	134. D	151. C	168. A
16. D	33. B	50. B	67. A	84. B	101. D	118. B	135. D	152. D	169. D
17. B	34. C	51. D	68. D	85. C	102. D	119. C	136. A	153. C	170. A

ANSWER EXPLANATIONS

1. **(A)** A police officer is always a police officer, even when not officially on duty. Off-duty status does not relieve a police officer from fulfilling the police role.

2. **(A)** The first thing to do is to protect the man's life by escorting him out of danger. Securing medical assistance should follow.

3. **(D)** Obviously, going the wrong way on a one-way street creates a dangerous situation for many people. By stopping the driver, you have averted the danger. The out-of-towner has not actually committed a violation, he was just about to. It would be wise to point out to him exactly how one-way streets are marked in your town.

4. **(D)** If the man is that close, you may be able to catch him yourself. Summoning other officers might lose valuable time and allow the man to escape. The offense is not such as to warrant shooting the man nor endangering bystanders by discharging your gun.

5. **(C)** Drowning occurs very quickly. Try to rescue the boy.

6. **(C)** Anything unusual should be investigated as soon as possible. The first thing to do is to determine whether or not a burglary has occurred. Then the premises should be secured and the owner notified. If the premises were not entered, they should be kept under surveillance in case the burglar returns.

7. **(D)** Stopping fights is part of keeping the peace and of maintaining order on your beat.

8. **(A)** A burglar may be inside and have turned off the light to escape detection. If there is no evidence of intruders, the storekeeper should be called to turn on the light or to replace the burned-out bulb. This question illustrates the need for a police officer to be observant and to remember how things usually appear on the beat.

9. **(C)** No one has broken the law, and there is nothing suspicious in anyone's behavior. People are entitled to argue. There is no reason to suspect that the keys on the man's key ring were not his own.

10. **(D)** You can assume that these people are up to no good. The quickest way to find this out is to ask for registration papers, for proof of ownership. If the keys were simply locked inside the car, the owner should readily clear up your suspicion. If ownership cannot be proved, arrest is indicated.

11. **(A)** An argument in a cleaning store is not an emergency situation. There is no need to disrupt traffic nor to create alarm. On the other hand, the situation could lead to blows so the officer should stop in to try to calm the tempers.

12. **(B)** Your first consideration must be protection of life and limb. Get the man to the hospital for medical attention but have him escorted for futher questioning. Gunshot wounds always should be investigated.

13. **(B)** Absolutely. Schools are prepared to deal with unauthorized absences and with children's illness.

14. **(D)** Janitors and local merchants tend to be out on the street often and are very aware of what is happening in the neighborhood. These people also would prefer to avoid having any trouble in the area and, if on friendly terms with a trusted police officer, are likely to alert the officer to situations they feel the officer should know about.

15. **(A)** The owner may indeed be caring for his or her car, in which case the owner can prove ownership. An open hood can also be a sign of car theft by means of jump start or of battery theft in progress.

16. **(D)** A police officer is a police officer, not a firefighter. It is the job of firefighters to ascertain whether or not there really is a fire and to put it out. Fires spread rapidly. The practical move is to call the fire department rather than trying to run through the building alone trying to rouse all occupants.

17. **(B)** A pattern of regular inspections gives fair notice to prospective wrongdoers as to when no one will be looking.

18. **(B)** No storekeeper wants the liability of a pedestrian's being injured because of his fail-

ure to do what was required. Pointing out the danger to the storekeeper should be sufficient.

19. **(B)** It may well be that the man is simply a "take charge" type. However, you must answer by choosing one of the four statements. Of these, it is most likely that the man feels better equipped to answer so as to conceal some information.

20. **(D)** The police officer must maintain the role of police officer. He may not assume the role of parent. Rather than simply turning the woman down, he might suggest that she contact the proper social agency.

21. **(C)** Rush to the scene. The girl may have misjudged the situation and the man may be in need of emergency medical assistance. If the man is indeed dead, his body should not lie in the street unattended.

22. **(C)** Dispersing a noisy group of teenagers is generally sufficient to quiet things down.

23. **(C)** Seven or eight people do not constitute an unruly crowd. The appearance of a person of authority demanding order should end the disturbance.

24. **(D)** A newly appointed officer assumes some responsibility immediately. The supervising officer will give guidance but will not make all decisions.

25. **(B)** Common sense. Extremes are not desirable. You must respect the rights of the innocent even as you make sure to arrest the guilty.

26. **(A)** The careless person is not likely to succeed; the negligent person will probably fail.

27. **(A)** You have four choices. Of these, crime prevention is the primary function of a police department.

28. **(B)** Police badges serve as identification of the police officers.

29. **(A)** The police officer must be alert at all times.

30. **(D)** If 10 percent of the inmates released from a prison are arrested as parole violators, the one conclusion that may be drawn is that 10 percent have violated parole and have been caught. The statement gives no basis for any other conclusions.

31. **(C)** Murders are not caused by pistols; pistols are often used in the commission of murders. Clearly the pistol is a mechanical aid to crime, and some crimes might be avoided if pistols were unavailable, but there is no one-to-one correspondence between pistols and murders.

32. **(D)** A police officer cannot allow his or her professional judgment to be influenced in any way by misinformation or personal prejudice.

33. **(B)** This is a truism. Common sense should give you the answer.

34. **(C)** The officer must understand what he or she is to do in order to do it. Watch out for distracting answers like that offered by choice (A). Self-interest is never the reason for doing anything when taking a civil service exam.

35. **(C)** Remember not to step out of the police officer's role. The police officer must never recommend individuals, not even a choice of individuals. The most the police officer may do is recommend that the individual contact the local bar association or consult directories in a library.

36. **(C)** In police exams, older children are generally referred to as juveniles. "Children" means young children. In dealing with children, whether protecting them or arresting them, the police officer must secure their confidence to get maximum cooperation.

37. **(C)** Criminal behavior is not exempt from the struggle for equality.

38. **(A)** Since murder is often a crime of passion, the police may have little means to foresee or prevent it. Burglary, prostitution, and auto theft are premeditated and, to some extent, visible. Police vigilance can help prevent opportunities for such crimes to occur.

39. **(C)** This phenomenon is called "copycat crime." It is an unfortunate but unavoidable consequence of a free press.

40. **(B)** This question requires careful reading and interpreting rather than judgment. A member on duty but not in uniform may drink intoxicants but not to an extent to make him- or her unfit for duty. Judgment enters into the situation in that the officer must judge for him- or herself at what point to stop drinking.

41. **(C)** Police officers are trained in the law and in the law of arrest. They are better able to judge when arrest is called for.

42. **(A)** Imprisonment serves to prevent that offender's commission of future crimes, at least so long as the offender remains in prison. It is hoped that the imprisonment of offenders serves to deter others from crime and thus further prevents the commission of future crimes.

43. **(D)** Boys under sixteen are very impressionable and learn readily. Society's interests are best served by not allowing them contact with hardened criminals.

44. **(D)** According to the statement, it is certainly true that a well-dressed person may be a criminal. Statement (C) is on its face also true, but the statement speaks only of criminals who *look* intelligent, not of criminals who *are* intelligent.

45. **(B)** The police officer's first priority is to save lives. An ambulance on an emergency run is on a mission to save a life. Lifesaving supersedes all other orders.

46. **(A)** Even though in civilian clothes and off duty, the police officer has the duty to save lives. By educating the youngsters in the dangers of their actions, the police officer may be saving their lives and possibly the lives of other passengers on very crowded buses. One must hope that this instruction will also restrain them from tampering with emergency doors in future bus rides.

47. **(D)** Even when the fire is in a house rather than an apartment building, your first duty is to summon firefighters. They most likely can save more lives than you can alone by attempting to rouse residents.

48. **(D)** Common sense. No responsible person would start a stampede in a crowded theater by shouting "Fire!" In addition, as a police officer you must never contribute to disorder.

49. **(C)** Your job is to investigate anything unusual along your beat and to deal with threats to persons or property.

50. **(B)** Remain in the police role. A police officer is a police officer, not a paramedic.

Send for professional assistance and leave medical decisions to medical personnel.

51. **(D)** This is a true common-sense question. An inquiry over the supermarket's public address system is most likely to produce a parent who had not yet missed the child. If not, proceed with other actions.

52. **(D)** Again common sense. The mother is most likely to return to the spot at which she became separated from the youngster.

53. **(D)** If you do not really know the answer to this question, you can reach it by a process of elimination. (A) is incorrect because a medical problem cannot be ignored; (B) is incorrect because the person must be informed of the reason for arrest; (C) is incorrect because the person is certainly allowed to speak and to express feelings. (D) is your best choice. While all suicide threats must be taken seriously, the person newly taken into custody may well be blustering. Suicide in custody is a serious problem. The silent, brooding, distressed prisoner must be carefully watched.

54. **(A)** Note the word *least*. Arresting the leaders who have not been involved in criminal activity would be illegal and foolhardy. Gang members are very loyal to their own, and you could start a riot. All the other choices represent potentially positive steps.

55. **(C)** The police officer is the department's representative to the public. The officer should be as helpful as possible without neglecting assigned duties.

56. **(C)** Your first consideration is public safety. You are outnumbered by armed men who are desperate to escape. If you shout, they are likely to shoot, thereby endangering bystanders in the intervening 75 feet. Do your best to identify the men so that officers better positioned to apprehend them can be alerted by alarm.

57. **(C)** Police presence is often sufficient to discourage prohibited activity. The police officer should always attempt to accomplish his or her purpose with the least aggressive action.

58. **(D)** The woman is upset, but you must not act too hastily. Ascertain that the husband is really missing before you spend time getting a description and searching for the man.

59. **(A)** Even in this age of AIDS, the officer must be *least* concerned with diseases the suspect may carry. The officer must be more concerned with the possibility that the suspect will use a gun or physical force to resist arrest or that he or she will try to flee.

60. **(C)** Of course, a person may be having mail directed to an address from which he or she has recently moved or even where he or she has never lived; however, it is most likely that mail delivered to an address is meant for persons who reside there. Of the choices, this is clearly the best.

61. **(C)** Your superiors have the advantage of years of training and experience. Their judgment is quicker, and they must be obeyed without question at the site of an emergency.

62. **(D)** You are likely to see this type of question more than once. You *must* know what you are to do. If you do not understand, ask.

63. **(D)** Of course there are experts trying to improve the police system, so you should not rush to present every idea. On the other hand, as an active police officer you are in daily contact with the special demands of your work. If you have a good idea, consider it carefully, then present it to your superiors.

64. **(D)** Public relations is important, and a little tact can work wonders. You can be polite and noncommital and satisfy the complainant.

65. **(D)** Obviously, the police emergency telephone lines must be kept open to receive emergency calls. Further, the less time spent talking, the sooner there will be action.

66. **(C)** The police role is to perform police work. The police officer is not a lawyer and is not expected to understand the fine points of preparation of legal documents. An assistant district attorney is equipped to give proper legal advice.

67. **(A)** An introductory statement describing the occurrence establishes the framework on which to hang details and conclusions.

68. **(D)** Both common sense and proper police practice require that a police officer's post be covered at all times. In answering questions on a civil service exam, personal gain is *never* the correct answer.

69. **(A)** A police officer must adhere to rules and regulations and so cannot provide a prohibited service. On the other hand, it is easy to be polite and caring. Explain to the manager the reason for your refusal.

70. **(C)** The police badge is an identifying emblem. The police officer who serves as a witness must be identified as such.

71. **(D)** To answer this question, read through the choices and find which one constitutes a rule. Obviously that is the one which will appear in printed departmental rules.

72. **(C)** Obviously, an order which concerns police activity on New Year's Eve will be fulfilled on New Year's Eve.

73. **(A)** Two conflicting orders cannot remain in effect at the same time. If a new order is issued and conflicts with a previously issued order, the previous order is thereby rescinded.

74. **(B)** Read carefully. The question asks about printed department rules and regulations. You can eliminate choices (A) and (D). Regulations may include standards for condition of the uniform but not instructions for its care. Rules for arrest procedure belong in the printed regulations.

75. **(B)** Pure common sense. Overcrowding leads to friction. Furthermore, convicts in constant close proximity have more opportunity to plan trouble together.

76. **(C)** A police officer must never bow to political pressure nor give the appearance of doing so. The officer must politely but firmly insist upon obedience to the law.

77. **(D)** A police officer must be polite and helpful.

78. **(B)** It is true that the officer's name and shield number will appear on the summons,

but there is no harm in giving these to the motorist. Professional behavior requires that the summons be given without further discussion.

79. **(C)** Since there is not much danger of traffic accidents caused by the malfunctioning light at this hour, report the matter immediately to allow maximum opportunity for the light's repair before morning traffic. Then post a temporary sign to alert traffic until the light is repaired. If the light cannot be repaired in time, your prompt report to the precinct allows time for a special officer to be assigned to direct traffic in the morning.

80. **(C)** A police officer must make quick judgments on the job. The assigned post must be covered; yet emeregencies must be dealt with. Snarled traffic could have waited the brief time it would have taken for Officer Y to contact his precinct.

81. **(A)** You do not need to have had training in investigation of traffic accidents to recognize from the diagram that car 2 is too far beyond the center of the intersection to have been attempting a left turn. Driver 1 is trying to cover himself with a false statement about driver 2.

82. **(C)** You have a radio. Use it. The alleged robbers should be pursued promptly and safely.

83. **(D)** The vast majority of people wish to be law-abiding citizens. A summons must be issued for a major offense, even if it is a first offense, but a courteous warning may be sufficient for a minor offense that the operator may not even have recognized as an offense.

84. **(B)** The police officer directing traffic at a congested intersection must be visible, must use simply understood signals, and must consistently use the same signals. It is *least* important that the officer be physically accessible to motorists or to pedestrians.

85. **(C)** Access to the area of an accident should be limited to those who are attending to the injured. Beyond lifesaving, the first priority is to preserve evidence. Inconvenience to the public is a later consideration.

86. **(C)** The police role at the scene of a property-damage accident is to be certain that both drivers are licensed drivers and are authorized to drive the vehicles, that the automobiles are safe to operate on the public roadway, and that information has been obtained for police files as to those involved in the accident and witnesses. It is not the role of the police officer to be concerned with the parties' arrangements to collect damages from one another.

87. **(A)** A hit-and-run driver must be pursued and apprehended as quickly as possible. The efficient way to intercept the hit-and-run car is to radio a description of the car to precinct headquarters for instant broadcast to patrol cars in the vicinity.

88. **(D)** The accepted answer is that eradication of the cause of crime should be the most effective means of crime prevention.

89. **(C)** There is no question that fewer crimes are committed in locations with high visibility. A safe in a well-lighted place is more secure from tampering than one in a dark place. It is permissible and advisable to give this type of general safety advice to businesspeople. On the other hand, were a businessperson to ask for advice about the best kind of safe, the police officer would have to decline. A police officer cannot recommend products or merchants.

90. **(C)** The person with an unconscious wish to be punished, also known as a "death wish," will draw attention to him- or herself with respect to the crime. Revisiting the crime scene is a common means of doing this. The other choices represent efforts to avoid detection and punishment.

91. **(A)** Read carefully. *The least accurate* format of the question makes it tricky to answer. Choices (B), (C), and (D) make correct, positive statements. Choice (A) makes a wrong statement. The value of fingerprints left at the scene of the crime *does* vary with the distinctness of the fingerprint impressions. Clearer fingerprints are more valuable.

92. **(A)** In general, the fewer people who handle a piece of evidence, the fewer things can go wrong. Personal delivery of the evidence

makes for less hearsay. Choice (C) is incorrect because of the strong word "ensures." Evidence can still be mismarked even with personal delivery and initially correct information.

93. **(B)** The description that focuses on the unique character of a missing item is most useful for search and recovery.

94. **(D)** Descriptions (B) and (C) are of no use whatsoever. Watching people leave a ball game, you have no way of knowing who is missing a toe nor who has false teeth. Choice (A) describes a very typical young girl. Choice (D) is a big man who stands out in a crowd, and his pockmarked face is further visible identification.

95. **(C)** Common sense. How many 6'1" women do you see roaming the streets?

96. **(D)** As the car is coming towards you, the most useful information is that the front bumper is missing. A bullet hole would be too small to see in a moving car on a busy highway.

97. **(A)** A 5'3" man weighing 200 lbs. is obese and very short. He should be relatively easy to spot if you are alerted to watch for him. All these identification judgment questions are meant to test your judgment as to what you would report if other officers needed to search on the basis of your descriptions.

98. **(B)** A Social Security card is not acceptable proof of identification for any purpose because it does not identify. The Social Security card contains no picture and no descriptive text of any sort.

99. **(B)** One picture may be worth a thousand words, but a good look at the person in the flesh leads to greater ease and accuracy of identification than does studying photographs.

100. **(C)** On a busy highway, tire size and spare would be impossible to determine. Make of car is also difficult to screen quickly. Color is obvious, and many cars are not black.

101. **(D)** The key is that the woman is sick or injured and needs medical attention. The first step is to get her to the hospital. Identification is secondary.

102. **(D)** Surgery would be most successful. Few criminals resort to surgery to avoid identification because of the time and pain involved and the need to find a competent person to perform the operation confidentially.

103. **(A)** Identification from a lineup is more reliable. The witness cannot simply say "yes" or "no."

104. **(C)** Citizens have rights that may not be abridged unless they commit some infraction. Suspicious actions are no grounds for arrest, alarm, or embarrassment of the person. The police officer who considers behavior suspicious is, in effect, facing an unusual situation on the post. Continued observation is called for.

105. **(A)** An open handbag is a danger to the woman's property. By all means bring the open handbag to the woman's attention.

106. **(C)** You want the personal recollection of each individual witness, not the consensus of a committee.

107. **(B)** Questions should be of the open sort, such as, "Was the mugger wearing an outer garment?" Giving an either-or choice limits the answer and may miss important descriptive information.

108. **(C)** The speed at which an automobile was traveling when it hit a victim may affect the extent of damage to the vehicle, but it is the *least* valuable information from among the choices. The direction in which the automobile fled can direct the chase; the number of occupants helps with identification; the part of the automobile that struck the victim may be distinctively damaged.

109. **(C)** Markings on a bullet left by a gun barrel serve the same purpose as fingerprints. Since barrel markings are unique, they effectively identify the gun from which the bullet was fired.

110. **(B)** Common sense. Read the newspapers for confirmation.

111. **(B)** You need proper depth vision to shoot accurately. Depth vision is achieved with both eyes open.

112. **(A)** Of course; there are police regulations concerning the firing of guns. Common

sense dictates that the officer has a pistol to use if necessary, but that there must be a very good reason to use that gun.

113. **(D)** A person who is in the physical process of committing a crime is fully aware of that fact. When arresting such person, it is unnecessary to tell the person that he or she is being arrested because he or she is in the process of committing a crime.

114. **(B)** The woman's intact, scarless face must certainly lead the police officer to question her story. The correct answer choice is generous in giving the benefit of some credence to the woman. The situation bears investigation for the sake of the woman who might likely require psychiatric attention.

115. **(C)** Our Constitution protects the rights of the individual. A police officer must learn to recognize reasonable basis for arrest so as to protect the rights of the innocent while taking into custody those who, on the basis of evidence, appear to be guilty.

116. **(A)** Professionalism requires that a police officer not allow personal prejudices nor emotions to interfere with the manner in which he or she performs duties. In giving the reason for arrest, the officer must state the facts without commentary.

117. **(C)** Much of the work of a police officer falls into the realm of public relations. The officer must be patient and tactful in explaining action or inaction on the specific complaint.

118. **(B)** The civil rights of the innocent citizen must be protected. The possibility of personal embarrassment or embarrassment of the police force are not the paramount considerations.

119. **(C)** The number one priority is the safety of the general public.

120. **(A)** This is not an attitude question; it is an action question. Situations vary greatly. Procedures differ on the basis of circumstances such as: Is the suspect armed? Is the suspect injured and in need of immediate medical attention? Is the suspect in the midst of a crowd? Does the suspect hold hostages? Is the suspect at home in bed?

121. **(D)** Do not read extra meaning into a straightforward question. The young man was acting suspiciously, and the officer correctly investigated his suspicious behavior. The fact that the man had indeed committed a crime confirms that investigation of suspicious incidents is worthwhile and may produce results.

122. **(A)** Where a police officer is positive of his or her identification and where immediate arrest threatens no danger, he or she should inform the suspect of the reason for the arrest and should take the suspect into custody.

123. **(A)** Once again, professionalism is the key to the answer. The police officer must not let any personal feelings intrude upon performance of duties.

124. **(A)** The ultimate purpose of a raid upon a premises, with legal search warrant already in hand, is to secure evidence that leads to the apprehension of criminals or to apprehend the criminals themselves.

125. **(B)** Eliminate choice (A). The burglars know there is nothing more to steal in that house. Eliminate choice (C). Burglars tend to hit houses that look as if the takings would be more worthwhile. Eliminate choice (D). This house is never unoccupied so would be difficult to burglarize. Chances are that the party that calls the house in choice (B) and hangs up when the phone is answered is waiting for a time when the phone is not answered and the house is presumably unattended as an opportunity to burglarize.

126. **(B)** The police officer must continue to observe the young girl but cannot apprehend her until she signals intent to steal the merchandise by leaving the store without paying. Merely carrying merchandise around in the store is not a prohibited activity.

127. **(C)** You must not jump to conclusions. The fact that Jones was present at the time and place of the assault does not mean that he actually committed the assault. On the other hand, the possibility cannot be ruled out, since he was there. If it had been proven that Jones had been elsewhere at the time of the assault, then it could have been

positively stated that Jones did not assault Smith.

128. **(D)** From this fact statement, we know only that the lawyer was attacked from behind in a washroom by a male who had access to the washroom and to a carpenter's mallet. No conclusions can be drawn.

129. **(D)** The only way to ascertain identity is to know who the person is.

130. **(A)** The officer's immediate sending for an ambulance is correct. However, once the injured is medically cared for, the officer's next responsibility is to learn what happened. Among the bystanders, a witness or several witnesses may be able to describe the circumstances of the stabbing and possibly to identify or at least to describe the assailant.

131. **(B)** Green must prove that he did not steal the radio. One-and-one-half hours is ample time to fence a radio, so nonpossession is not automatic proof of innocence.

132. **(A)** Note that the question merely suggests the given facts as a basis for first action, not that Jones should be assumed guilty. Much police investigative work is based upon reasonable assumptions.

133. **(D)** The length of time that the resident waited before reporting the theft of the ring is totally irrelevant. All the other questions are valid ones.

134. **(D)** If burglary was physically impossible at this site and time, then, from among the choices, we must assume that the crime of burglary did not occur and that the report is a false one. Beyond the scope of the question, an investigator might reasonably suspect an internal theft with the claim of burglary as coverup.

135. **(D)** Since the question has to do with protection of property, the police officer is within the scope of the police role to make a suggestion. The suggestion, without reference to a specific bank or payroll service, is entirely proper.

136. **(A)** The thief who is already inside the premises to be burglarized avoids the risk of attracting attention by the act of forcing entrance.

137. **(C)** Thieves are likely to be careful with items of value but to pay less attention to articles they consider worthless. This carelessness combined with care taken by police officers can lead to apprehension of the thieves.

138. **(A)** Immediate confrontation will ascertain that the watch was indeed taken from the given jewelry store. If, by chance, the man was authorized to take the watch (if, for example it had been repaired for him), then the matter will be readily clarified. If the police officer has indeed observed the man in the process of stealing the watch, this prompt action will make for a neat case.

139. **(B)** A police officer must investigate unusual occurrences. The sound of clashing tools at 2 A.M. is certainly worth investigating, especially in an apartment next door to one in which there had just been a burglary.

140. **(D)** You can't catch the robbers yourself; they have already gone too far. On the other hand, you must not allow them to exit the parkway while you are questioning the victim. Radio to have the exits monitored. A limited access parkway offers possibilities for interception of thieves that are absent on city streets.

141. **(D)** The only immediate assumption is that the murderer had access to shoemaker's tools. This is a useful piece of knowledge. If no shoe repair shop has reported a theft, the field of suspects can be reasonably narrowed.

142. **(C)** Common sense. For the knife to be protruding from his back, the man is unlikely to be lying on his back.

143. **(A)** Read carefully. The question describes a suicide, thereby eliminating choices (C) and (D). A body slumped in a chair is not consistent with hanging.

144. **(B)** The man is dead; there is nothing you can do for him now. On the other hand, there is a body on the ground. Phone your precinct at once. Investigation of circumstances of death will follow.

145. **(A)** The pawn tickets serve as a very good clue. A man in the fur business should sell furs, not pawn them. Obviously, this man

was in deep financial trouble. The lapsed insurance policy is further indication of desperation. No businessman willingly allows insurance of property or self (the question does not specify which) to lapse.

146. **(B)** The blood on the door bears investigation. It was likely left by the murderer at exit.

147. **(D)** Unfortunately, observation is often incomplete and memory may fill in the gaps or even distort the facts.

148. **(A)** The first question to be raised is the amount of time taken to travel from Jones' place of work to his home. If it is determined that it does indeed take longer than one half hour, then Jones must supply proof that he really was working at 8 P.M. If the distance can be covered in less than a half hour, whether or not Jones was really working at 8 P.M. is irrelevant.

149. **(A)** This is an unusual situation that bears investigation. Admission to a private mental hospital is not an emergency situation, especially since the alleged patient will be under observation at the station house, so by all means bring the whole party in for questioning.

150. **(C)** With these facts, the only certainty is that further investigation is warranted on an urgent basis.

151. **(C)** Bad environmental conditions—poverty, poor housing, lack of opportunity, immoral companions—combine to create criminals.

152. **(D)** It is generally assumed that the best deterrent to crime is the expectation that one will be caught and swiftly punished.

153. **(C)** A person who is normal in intelligence but is below grade level in school is educationally maladjusted. The fact that 86 percent of delinquents appear to be normally intelligent but below grade level points to a close association of educational maladjustment with delinquency. With this information, we can describe a correlation but not a causal relationship. The data do not indicate that educational maladjustment causes delinquency nor that delinquency leads to educational maladjustment, only that they are related.

154. **(B)** Unfortunately, the boys who might be most helped by boys' clubs do not join.

155. **(C)** A man who has responded to a prostitute is unlikely to cooperate with the police, but a man who has spurned her advances will probably answer your questions. Both the girl and one or two men should be questioned, for the girl will undoubtedly deny that she is soliciting. Indeed, it may be that she is not, and, if police officers approach her, she may ask for needed instructions or assistance. You must not assume guilt without first investigating.

156. **(B)** The expectation and hope is that minors are not incorrigible; that is, their behavior can be corrected and improved. If this can be accomplished without arrest, so much the better.

157. **(C)** The most important information when seeking a hit-and-run vehicle is the appearance of the car. Of the choices, "What kind of car was it?" is by far the most useful.

158. **(C)** One of the last things a runaway is likely to do is to enroll in a school. Therefore, knowledge of her scholastic abilities would not be very helpful in the search for the girl. Detailed description of her features would be most helpful.

159. **(A)** The officer cannot be certain that the woman has not eaten some grapes; therefore, no determination can be made on the basis of the bag she presents. The officer must buy his own fruit to check the weights.

160. **(C)** The label of the well-known manufacturer is found in many violins. It does not distinguish this violin from many other violins. All the other choices would help in making a positive identification.

161. **(D)** This is a probe of your prejudices. Looks tell nothing about intelligence, personality, or character.

162. **(B)** For the deceased to have committed suicide with the bullet lodged as indicated, the shot would have had to come from a revolver in his left hand. The revolver is in his right hand.

163. **(D)** It is most unlikely that a lighted delicatessen is left unattended late at night. The officer should confirm suspicions further by

entering the delicatessen to search for foul play with reference to the proprietor or employees.

164. **(A)** Loitering just before theater deposits are about to be made could be either a coincidence or a plan for robbery. People do loiter around theaters waiting for others or just passing the time away. You must be prepared, but you can take no action unless some crime is committed. The best action is to keep the men under observation until the money has been safely deposited.

165. **(A)** This is unintelligent handling of evidence. Fingerprints and ballistics evidence may be destroyed. It would be wise to close off the booth to the public so as to safeguard possible clues such as match covers, bits of paper with notes on them, and fingerprints on drinking glasses.

166. **(B)** Comparison of engine numbers is usually the determining factor in establishing whether or not a car is indeed the stolen one in question. Engine numbers are changed only with great difficulty; it is most unlikely that this would be accomplished in one day. This 1978 Dodge is probably not the car that was reported stolen. License plates and tires are easily changed and cannot serve as positive identification of stolen cars. A stolen car can easily acquire a cracked windshield.

167. **(C)** Statistical studies show that crimes against property reach a maximum in winter months when human needs are greatest. During winter months, crimes such as larceny, burglary, and robbery show a decided increase for the further reason that longer periods of darkness reduce probability of detection. Crimes against persons and morals (assaults, rapes, homicides, etc.) show an increase during the warm months when the contacts between persons are more frequent.

168. **(A)** The very subject matter of the blackmail is precisely the reason the victim is unlikely to cooperate with the police. The victim of a blackmail plot usually has some secret that he or she does not wish to reveal to the public by way of the police. It may concern some event, scandalous or otherwise, which occurred in the past and which if revealed may hold him or her up to public ridicule. Because of this, victims are reluctant to cooperate with the police in the prosecution of blackmailers.

169. **(D)** This is a situation in which individual interests must be subverted for the common good. The individual family wants its kidnapped member back at any price. However, allowing kidnappers to profit from kidnapping encourages other kidnappers. The principle is the same as the principle of not negotiating with terrorists. Wrongdoers must not achieve their goals through their wrongdoing. Hopefully, prospective kidnappers who know that they will fail in their attempt to collect ransom will be discouraged from kidnapping.

170. **(A)** As strange as it may seem, intent to defraud the insurer may not always be manifested by increasing insurance just before have the commission of the crime. There have been many instances in which the insurance was deliberately reduced in order to divert suspicion.

READING-BASED QUESTIONS

A recent survey of police officer examinations given nationwide indicates that there is wide variation in the subject matter of these exams. The single topic that is common to all exams is reading. Some exams include classic reading comprehension questions that present a passage and then ask questions on the details of the passage and, perhaps, on its meaning. Other exams require candidates to indicate proper behavior based on their reading of printed procedures and regulations. Still another type of reading-based question requires candidates to reason and choose next steps on the basis of information presented in a reading passage. There are, of course, nearly as many variations of the reading-based question as there are testmakers. In fact, reading skill enters into form-completion questions, arithmetic problems based on fact situations, and police judgment questions as well.

Before you begin to devote attention to strategies for dealing with reading-based questions, give some thought to your reading habits and skills. Of course, you already know how to read. But how well do you read? Do you concentrate? Do you get the point on your first reading? Do you notice details?

Between now and the test day, you must work to improve your reading concentration and comprehension. Your daily newspaper provides excellent material to improve your reading. Make a point of reading all the way through any article that you begin. Do not be satisfied with the first paragraph or two. Read with a pencil in hand. Underscore details and ideas that seem to be crucial to the meaning of the article. Notice points of view, arguments, and supporting information. When you have finished the article, summarize it for yourself. Do you know the purpose of the article? The main idea presented? The attitude of the writer? The points over which there is controversy? Did you find certain information lacking? As you answer these questions, skim back over your underlinings. Did you focus on important words and ideas? Did you read with comprehension? As you repeat this process day after day, you will find that your reading will become more efficient. You will read with greater understanding, and will get more from your newspaper.

One aspect of your daily reading that deserves special attention is vocabulary building. The effective reader has a rich, extensive vocabulary. As you read, make a list of unfamiliar words. Include in your list words that you understand within the context of the article, but that you cannot really define. In addition, mark words that you do not understand at all. When you put aside your newspaper, go to the dictionary and look up *every* new and unfamiliar word. Write the word and its definition in a special notebook. Writing the words and their definitions helps seal them in your memory far better than just reading them, and the notebook serves as a handy reference for your own use. A sensitivity to the meanings of words and an understanding of more words will make reading easier and more enjoyable even if none of the words you learn in this way crops up on your exam. In fact, the habit of vocabulary building is a good lifetime habit to develop.

Success with reading questions depends on more than reading comprehension. You must also know how to draw the answers from the reading selection, and be able to distinguish the *best* answer from a number of answers that all seem to be good ones, or from a number of answers that all seem to be wrong.

Strange as it may seem, it's a good idea to approach reading comprehension questions by reading the questions—not the answer choices, just the questions themselves—before you read the selection. The questions will alert you to look for certain details, ideas, and points of view. Use your pencil. Underscore key words in the questions. These will help direct your attention as you read.

Next skim the selection very rapidly to get an idea of its subject matter and its organization. If key words or ideas pop out at you, underline them, but do not consciously search out details in the preliminary skimming.

Now read the selection carefully with comprehension as your main goal. Underscore the important words as you have been doing in your newspaper reading.

Finally, return to the questions. Read each question carefully. Be sure you know what it asks. Misreading of questions is a major cause of error on reading comprehension tests. Read *all* the answer choices. Eliminate the obviously incorrect answers. You may be left with only one possible answer. If you find yourself with more than one possible answer, reread the question. Then skim the passage once more, focusing on the underlined segments. By now you should be able to conclude which answer is *best*.

Reading-based questions may take a number of different forms. In general, some of the most common forms are as follows:

1. **Question of fact or detail**. You may have to mentally rephrase or rearrange, but you should find the answer stated in the body of the selection.
2. **Best title or main idea**. The answer may be obvious, but the incorrect choices to the "main idea" question are often half-truths that are easily confused with the main idea. They may misstate the idea, omit part of the idea, or even offer a supporting idea quoted directly from the text. The correct answer is the one that covers the largest part of the selection.
3. **Interpretation**. This type of question asks you what the selection means, not just what it says. On police exams, the questions based upon definitions of crimes, for example, fall into this category.
4. **Inference.** This is the most difficult type of reading comprehension question. It asks you to go beyond what the selection says, and to predict what might happen next. You might have to choose the best course of action to take, based upon given procedures and a fact situation, or you may have to judge the actions of others. Your answer must be based upon the information in the selection and your own common sense, but not upon any other information you may have about the subject. A variation of the interference question might be stated as, "The author would expect that...." To answer this question, you must understand the author's point of view, and then make an inference from that viewpoint based upon the information in the selection.
5. **Vocabulary**. Some police reading sections, directly or indirectly, ask the meanings of certain words as used in the selection.

Let's now work together on some typical reading comprehension selections and questions.

Selection for Questions 1 to 4

The recipient gains an impression of a typewritten letter before beginning to read the message. Factors that give a good first impression include margins and spacing that are visually pleasing, formal parts of the letter that are correctly placed according to the style of the letter, copy that is free of obvious erasures and overstrikes, and transcript that is even and clear. The problem for the typist is how to produce that first, positive impression of her work.

There are several general rules that a typist can follow when she wishes to prepare a properly spaced letter on a sheet of letterhead. The width of a letter should ordinarily not be less than four inches, nor more than six inches. The side margins should also have a proportionate relation to the bottom margin, as well as the space between the letterhead and the body of the letter. Usually the most appealing arrangement is when the side margins are even, and the bottom margin is slightly wider than the side margins. In some offices, however, a standard line length is used for all business letters, and the secretary then varies the

spacing between the date line and the inside address according to the length of
the letter.

1. The best title for the preceding paragraph is   1. Ⓐ Ⓑ Ⓒ Ⓓ
   (A) Writing Office Letters
   (B) Making Good First Impressions
   (C) Judging Well-Typed Letters
   (D) Good Placing and Spacing for Office Letters

2. According to the preceding paragraphs, which of the following might   2. Ⓐ Ⓑ Ⓒ Ⓓ
   be considered the way that people quickly judge the quality of work
   that has been typed?
   (A) by measuring the margins to see if they are correct
   (B) by looking at the spacing and cleanliness of the typescript
   (C) by scanning the body of the letter for meaning
   (D) by reading the date line and address for errors

3. According to the preceding paragraphs, what would be definitely   3. Ⓐ Ⓑ Ⓒ Ⓓ
   undesirable as the average line length of a typed letter?
   (A) 4″
   (B) 5″
   (C) 6″
   (D) 7″

4. According to the preceding paragraphs, when the line length is kept   4. Ⓐ Ⓑ Ⓒ Ⓓ
   standard, the secretary
   (A) does not have to vary the spacing at all because this also is
       standard
   (B) adjusts the spacing between the date line and inside address for
       different lengths of letters
   (C) uses the longest line as a guideline for spacing between the date
       line and inside address
   (D) varies the number of spaces between the lines

Begin by skimming the questions and underscoring key words. Your underscored questions should look more or less like this:

1. The best title for the preceding paragraphs is
2. According to the preceding paragraphs, which of the following might be considered the way that people quickly judge the quality of work that has been typed?
3. According to the preceding paragraphs, what would be definitely undesirable as the average line length of a typed letter?
4. According to the preceding paragraphs, when the line length is kept standard, the secretary does what?

Now skim the selection. This quick reading should give you an idea of the structure of the selection and of its overall meaning.

Next read the selection carefully and underscore words that seem important or that you think hold keys to the question answers. Your underscored selection should look something like this:

The recipient gains an impression of a typewritten letter before beginning to read the message. Factors that give a good first impression include margins and spacing that are visually pleasing, formal parts of the letter that are correctly placed according to the style of the letter, copy that is free of obvious erasures and overstrikes, and transcript that is even and clear. The problem for the typist is how to produce that first, positive impression of her work.

There are several general rules that a typist can follow when she wishes to prepare a properly spaced letter on a sheet of letterhead. The width of a letter should ordinarily not be less than four inches, nor more than six inches. The side margins should also have a proportionate relation to the bottom margin, as well as the space between the letterhead and the body of the letter. Usually the most appealing arrangement is when the side margins are even, and the bottom margin is slightly wider than the side margins. In some offices, however, a standard line length is used for all business letters, and the secretary then varies the spacing between the date line and the inside address according to the length of the letter.

Finally, read the questions and answer choices, and try to choose the correct answer for each question.

The correct answers are: 1. **(D)**, 2. **(B)**, 3. **(D)**, 4. **(B)**. Did you get them all right? Whether you made any errors or not, read these explanations.

1. **(D)** The best title for any selection is the one that takes in all of the ideas presented without being too broad or too narrow. Choice (D) provides the most inclusive title for this passage. A look at the other choices shows you why. Choice (A) can be eliminated because the passage discusses typing a letter, not writing one. Although the first paragraph states that a letter should make a good first impression, the passage is clearly devoted to the letter, not the first impression, so choice (B) can be eliminated. Choice (C) puts the emphasis on the wrong aspect of the typewritten letter. The passage concerns how to type a properly spaced letter not how to judge one.

2. **(B)** Both spacing and cleanliness are mentioned in paragraph 1 as ways to judge the quality of a typed letter. The first paragraph states that the margins should be "visually pleasing" in relation to the body of the letter, but that does not imply margins of a particular measure, so choice (A) is incorrect. Meaning is not discussed in the passage, only the look of the finished letter, so choice (C) is incorrect. The passage makes no mention of errors, only the avoidance of erasures and overstrikes, so choice (D) is incorrect.

3. **(D)** This answer comes from the information provided in paragraph 2, that the width of a letter "should not be less than four inches nor more than six inches." According to this rule, seven inches is an undesirable line length.

4. **(B)** The answer to this question is stated in the last sentence of the reading passage. When a standard line length is used, the secretary "varies the spacing between the date line and the inside address according to the length of the letter." The passage offers no support for any other choice.

Let us try another together.

Selection for Questions 5 to 9

Cotton fabrics treated with the XYZ Process have features that make them far superior to any previously known flame-retardant-treated cotton fabrics. XYZ

Process treated fabrics endure repeated laundering and dry cleaning; are glow resistant as well as flame resistant; when exposed to flames or intense heat form tough, pliable, and protective chars; are inert physiologically to persons handling or exposed to the fabric; are only slightly heavier than untreated fabrics; and are susceptible to further wet and dry finishing treatments. In addition, the treated fabrics exhibit little or no adverse change in feel, texture, and appearance, and are shrink-, rot-, and mildew-resistant. The treatment reduces strength only slightly. Finished fabrics have "easy care" properties in that they are wrinkle resistant and dry rapidly.

5. It is most accurate to state that the author in the preceding selection presents   5. Ⓐ Ⓑ Ⓒ Ⓓ
   - (A) facts but reaches no conclusion concerning the value of the process
   - (B) a conclusion concerning the value of the process and facts to support that conclusion
   - (C) a conclusion concerning the value of the process unsupported by facts
   - (D) neither facts nor conclusions, but merely describes the process

6. Of the following articles, for which is the XYZ process most suitable?   6. Ⓐ Ⓑ Ⓒ Ⓓ
   - (A) nylon stockings
   - (B) woolen shirt
   - (C) silk tie
   - (D) cotton bedsheet

7. Of the following aspects of the XYZ process, which is *not* discussed in the preceding selection?   7. Ⓐ Ⓑ Ⓒ Ⓓ
   - (A) costs
   - (B) washability
   - (C) wearability
   - (D) the human body

8. The main reason for treating a fabric with the XYZ Process is to   8. Ⓐ Ⓑ Ⓒ Ⓓ
   - (A) prepare the fabric for other wet and dry finishing treatment
   - (B) render it shrink-, rot-, and mildew-resistant
   - (C) increase its weight and strength
   - (D) reduce the chance that it will catch fire

9. Which of the following would be considered a minor drawback of the XYZ process?   9. Ⓐ Ⓑ Ⓒ Ⓓ
   - (A) it forms chars when exposed to flame
   - (B) it makes fabrics mildew-resistant
   - (C) it adds to the weight of fabrics
   - (D) it is compatible with other finishing treatments

Skim the questions and underscore the words which you consider to be key. The questions should look something like this:

5. It is most accurate to state that the author in the preceding selection presents
6. Of the following articles, for which is the XYZ process most suitable?
7. Of the following aspects of the XYZ process, which is *not* discussed in the preceding selection?
8. The main reason for treating a fabric with the XYZ process is to
9. Which of the following would be considered a minor drawback of the XYZ process?

Skim the reading selection. Get an idea of the subject matter of the selection and of how it is organized.

Now read the selection carefully and underscore the words which you think are especially important. This fact-filled selection might be underlined like this:

Cotton fabrics treated with the XYZ Process have features that make them far superior to any previously known flame-retardant-treated cotton fabrics. XYZ Process treated fabrics endure repeated laundering and dry cleaning; are glow resistant as well as flame resistant; when exposed to flames or intense heat form tough, pliable, and protective chars; are inert physiologically to persons handling or exposed to the fabric; are only slightly heavier than untreated fabrics; and are susceptible to further wet and dry finishing treatments. In addition, the treated fabrics exhibit little or no adverse change in feel, texture, and appearance, and are shrink-, rot-, and mildew-resistant. The treatment reduces strength only slightly. Finished fabrics have "easy care" properties in that they are wrinkle resistant and dry rapidly

Now read each question and all its answer choices, and try to choose the correct answer for each question.

The correct answers are: 5. (B), 6. (D), 7. (A), 8. (D), 9. (C). How did you do on these? Read the explanations.

5. **(B)** This is a combination main idea and interpretation question. If you cannot answer this question readily, reread the selection. The author clearly thinks that the XYZ process is terrific and says so in the first sentence. The rest of the selection presents a wealth of facts to support the initial claim.

6. **(D)** At first glance you might think that this is an inference question requiring you to make a judgement based upon the few drawbacks of the process. Closer reading, however, shows you that there is no contest for correct answer here. This is a simple question of fact. The XYZ Process is a treatment for cotton fabrics.

7. **(A)** Your underlinings should help you with this question of fact. Cost is not mentioned; all other aspects of the XYZ Process are. If you are having trouble finding mention of the effect of the XYZ Process on the human body, add to your vocabulary list "inert" and "physiologically."

8. **(D)** This is a main idea question. You must distinguish between the main idea and the supporting and incidental facts.

9. **(C)** Obviously a drawback is a negative feature. The selection mentions only two negative features. The treatment reduces strength slightly, and it makes fabrics slightly heavier than untreated fabrics. Only one of these negative features is offered among the answer choices.

You should be getting better at reading and at answering questions. Try this next selection on your own. Read and underline the questions. Skim the selection. Read and underline the selection. Read questions and answer choices and mark your answers. Then check your answers against the answers and explanations that follow the selection.

Selection for Questions 10 to 12

Language performs an essentially social function: It helps us get along together, communicate, and achieve a great measure of concerted action. Words are signs that have significance by convention, and those people who do not adopt the conventions simply fail to communicate. They do not "get along," and a social force arises that encourages them to achieve the correct associations. By "correct" we mean as used by other members of the social group. Some of the vital points about language are brought home to an English visitor to America, and vice versa, because our vocabularies are nearly the same—but not quite.

10. As defined in the preceding selection, usage of a word is "correct" when it is

    10. Ⓐ Ⓑ Ⓒ Ⓓ

  (A) defined in standard dictionaries
  (B) used by the majority of persons throughout the world who speak the same language
  (C) used by the majority of educated persons who speak the same language
  (D) used by other persons with whom we are associating

11. In the preceding selection, the author is concerned primarily with the

    11. Ⓐ Ⓑ Ⓒ Ⓓ

  (A) meaning of words
  (B) pronunciation of words
  (C) structure of sentences
  (D) origin and development of language

12. According to the preceding selection, the main language problem of an English visitor to America stems from the fact that an English person

    12. Ⓐ Ⓑ Ⓒ Ⓓ

  (A) uses some words that have different meanings for Americans
  (B) has different social values than the Americans
  (C) has had more exposure to non-English speaking persons than Americans have had
  (D) pronounces words differently than Americans do

The correct answers are: 10. **(D)**, 11. **(A)**, 12. **(A)**.

10. **(D)** The answer to this question is stated in the next-to-last sentence of the selection.

11. **(A)** This main idea question is an easy one to answer. You should have readily eliminated all of the wrong choices.

12. **(A)** This is a question of fact. The phrasing of the question is quite different from the phrasing of the last sentence, but the meaning is the same. You may have found this reading selection more difficult to absorb than some of the others, but you should have had no difficulty answering this question by eliminating the wrong answers.

Now try this reading selection and its questions. Once more, explanations follow the correct answers. Follow the procedure you have learned, and be sure to read the explanations even if you have a perfect score.

Selection for Questions 13 to 18

Since almost every office has some contact with data-processed records, a Senior Stenographer should have some understanding of the basic operations of data processing. Data processing systems now handle about one third of all office paper work. On punched cards, magnetic tape, or on other mediums, data are recorded before being fed into the computer for processing. A machine such as the key punch is used to convert the data written on the source document into the coded symbols on punched cards or tapes. After data has been converted, it must be verified to guarantee absolute accuracy of conversion. In this manner data becomes a permanent record that can be read by electronic computers that compare, store, compute, and otherwise process data at high speeds.

One key person in a computer installation is a programmer, the man or woman who puts business and scientific problems into special symbolic languages that can be read by the computer. Jobs done by the computer range all the way from payroll operations to chemical process control, but most computer applications are directed toward management data. About half of the programmers employed by business come to their positions with college degrees; the remaining half are promoted to their positions, without regard to education, from within the organization on the basis of demonstrated ability.

13. Of the following, the best title for the preceding selection is

    13. Ⓐ Ⓑ Ⓒ Ⓓ

(A) The Stenographer as Data Processer
(B) The Relation of Key Punching to Stenography
(C) Understanding Data Processing
(D) Permanent Office Records

14. According to the preceding selection, a Senior Stenographer should understand the basic operations of data processing because

    14. Ⓐ Ⓑ Ⓒ Ⓓ

(A) almost every office today has contact with data processed records by computer
(B) any office worker may be asked to verify the accuracy of data
(C) most offices are involved in the production of permanent records
(D) data may be converted into computer language by typing on a key punch

15. According to the preceding selection, the data that the computer understands is most often expressed

    15. Ⓐ Ⓑ Ⓒ Ⓓ

(A) as a scientific programming language
(B) as records or symbols punched on tape, cards, or other mediums
(C) as records on cards
(D) as records on tape

16. According to the preceding selection, computers are used most often to handle

    16. Ⓐ Ⓑ Ⓒ Ⓓ

(A) management data
(B) problems of higher education
(C) the control of chemical processes
(D) payroll operations

17. Computer programming is taught in many colleges and business schools. The preceding selection implies that programmers in industry

    17. Ⓐ Ⓑ Ⓒ Ⓓ

(A) must have professional training
(B) need professional training to advance
(C) must have at least a college education to do adequate programming tasks
(D) do not need college education to do programming work

18. According to the preceding selection, data to be processed by computer should be

    18. Ⓐ Ⓑ Ⓒ Ⓓ

(A) recent
(B) complete
(C) basic
(D) verified

The correct answers are: 13. **(C)**, 14. **(A)**, 15. **(B)**, 16. **(A)**, 17. **(D)**, 18. **(D)**.

13. **(C)** Choosing the best title for this selection is not easy. Although the Senior Stenographer is mentioned in the first sentence, the selection is really not concerned with stenographers or with their relationship to key punching. Eliminate choices (A) and (B). Permanent office records are mentioned in the selection, but only along with other equally important uses for data processing. Eliminate choice (D). When in doubt, the most general title is usually correct.

14. **(A)** This is a question of fact. Any one of the answer choices could be correct, but the answer is given almost verbatim in the first sentence. Take advantage of answers that are handed to you in this way.

15. **(B)** This is a question of fact, but it is a tricky one. The program language is a symbolic language, not a scientific one. Reread carefully and eliminate choice (A). (B) includes more of the information in the selection than either (C) or (D), and so is the best answer.

16. **(A)** This is a question of fact. The answer is stated in the next to the last sentence.

17. **(D)** Remember that you are answering the questions on the basis of the information given in the selection. In spite of any information you may have to the contrary, the last sentence of the selection states that half the programmers employed in business achieved their positions by moving up from the ranks without regard to education.

18. **(D)** Judicious underlining proves very helpful to you in finding the correct answer to this question buried in the middle of the selection. Since any one of the answers might be correct, the way to deal with this question is to skim the underlined words in the selection, eliminate those that are not mentioned, and choose the appropriate answer.

On police exams, many reading passages will relate to legal definitions, laws, and police procedures. When reading these passages, you must pay special attention to details relating to exceptions, special preconditions, combinations of activities, choices of actions, and prescribed time sequences. Sometimes the printed procedure specifies that certain actions are to be taken only when there is a combination of factors such as that a person actually breaks a window *and* has a gun. At other times, the procedures give choices of action under certain circumstances. You must read carefully to determine if the passage requires a combination of factors or gives a choice, then make the appropriate judgment. And when a time sequence is specified, be certain to follow that sequence in the prescribed order.

The remaining selections in this chapter are based on police-type questions. Beyond requiring reading comprehension skills, they require the special police exam emphasis we have just discussed.

Selection for Questions 19 to 23

If we are to study crime in its widest social setting, we will find a variety of conduct that, although criminal in the legal sense, is not offensive to the moral conscience of a considerable number of persons. Traffic violations, for example, do not brand the offender as guilty of moral offense. In fact, the recipient of a traffic ticket is usually simply the subject of some good-natured joking by friends. Although there may be indignation among certain groups of citizens against gambling and liquor law violations, these activities are often tolerated, if not openly supported, by the more numerous residents of the community. Indeed, certain social and service clubs regularly conduct gambling games and lotteries for the purpose of raising funds. Some communities regard violations involving the sale of liquor with little concern in order to profit from increased license fees and taxes paid by dealers. The thousand and one forms of political graft and corruption which infest our urban centers only occasionally arouse public condemnation and official action.

19. According to the passage, all types of illegal conduct are   19. Ⓐ Ⓑ Ⓒ Ⓓ

    (A) condemned by all elements of the community
    (B) considered a moral offense, although some are tolerated by a few citizens
    (C) violations of the law, but some are acceptable to certain elements of the community
    (D) found in a social setting and therefore not punishable by law

20. According to the passage, traffic violations are generally considered   20. Ⓐ Ⓑ Ⓒ Ⓓ
    by society to be

    (A) crimes requiring the maximum penalty set by the law
    (B) more serious than violations of the liquor laws
    (C) offenses against the morals of the community
    (D) relatively minor offenses requiring minimum punishment

21. According to the passage, a lottery conducted for the purpose of rais-   21. Ⓐ Ⓑ Ⓒ Ⓓ
    ing funds for a church

    (A) is considered a serious violation of the law
    (B) may be tolerated by a community that has laws against gambling
    (C) may be conducted under special laws demanded by the more numerous residents of a community
    (D) arouses indignation in most communities

22. On the basis of the passage, the most likely reaction in the commu-   22. Ⓐ Ⓑ Ⓒ Ⓓ
    nity to a police raid on a gambling casino would be

    (A) more an attitude of indifference than interest in the raid
    (B) general approval of the raid
    (C) condemnation of the raid by most people
    (D) demand for further action, since this raid is not sufficient to end gambling activities

23. Of the following, which best describes the central thought of this pas-   23. Ⓐ Ⓑ Ⓒ Ⓓ
    sage and would be most suitable as a title?

    (A) Crime and the Police
    (B) Public Condemnation of Graft and Corruption
    (C) Gambling Is Not Always a Vicious Business
    (D) Public Attitude Toward Law Violations

The correct answers are: 19. (C), 20. (D), 21. (B), 22. (A), 23. (D).

19. (C) The words "although" and "occasionally," which pop up in this passage, are the clues to the answer. Although illegal conduct is, by definition, violation of law, much illegal conduct is not repulsive to many elements of the community. Choice (A) is a direct contradiction of the meaning of the passage as is choice (B). (D) is unsupported by the passage.

20. (D) The third sentence supports this answer. The fourth sentence directly contradicts choice (B) in its statement that gambling and liquor law violations may raise some indignation.

21. **(B)** The clear implication is that law-abiding citizens readily engage in gambling and lotteries for fund-raising purposes. Nothing is said about special laws enabling this activity, so (C) is not a correct choice.

22. **(A)** Since gambling is not considered a serious criminal activity by the bulk of the populace, a raid on a gambling establishment would meet with indifference rather than with either approval or disapproval.

23. **(D)** Choice (A) is too broad; the passage deals specifically with certain kinds of crime. (B) is opposite in thought to the content of the passage. (C) is too narrow since other crimes are discussed in addition to gambling.

Selection for Questions 24 to 26

The law enforcement agency is one of the most important agencies in the field of juvenile delinquency prevention. This is so, however, not because of the social work connected with this problem, for this is not a police matter, but because the officers are usually the first to come in contact with the delinquent. The manner of arrest and detention makes a deep impression on the delinquent and affects his or her lifelong attitude toward society and toward the law. The juvenile court is perhaps the most important agency in this work. Contrary to general opinion, however, it is not primarily concerned with putting children into correctional schools. The main purpose of the juvenile court is to save the child and to develop his or her emotional makeup so that he or she can grow up to be a decent and well-balanced citizen. The system of probation is the means by which the court seeks to accomplish these goals.

24. According to the passage, police work is an important part of a program to prevent juvenile delinquency because   24. Ⓐ Ⓑ Ⓒ Ⓓ

   (A) social work is no longer considered important in juvenile delinquency prevention
   (B) police officers are the first to have contact with the delinquent
   (C) police officers jail the offender in order to be able to change his or her attitude toward society and the law
   (D) it is the first step in placing the delinquent in jail

25. According to the passage, the chief purpose of the juvenile court is to   25. Ⓐ Ⓑ Ⓒ Ⓓ

   (A) punish the child for the offense
   (B) select a suitable correctional school for the delinquent
   (C) use available means to help the delinquent become a better person
   (D) provide psychiatric care for the delinquent

26. According to the passage, the juvenile court directs the development of a delinquent under its care chiefly by: 26. Ⓐ Ⓑ Ⓒ Ⓓ

   (A) placing the child under probation
   (B) sending the child to a correctional school
   (C) keeping the delinquent in prison
   (D) returning the child to his or her home

The correct answers are: 24. **(B)**, 25. **(C)**, 26. **(A)**.

24. **(B)** The correct answer is stated in the second sentence: "...officers are usually the first to come in contact with the delinquent." The point with reference to social work

is not that social work is unimportant but that it is not a police matter. Choices (C) and (D) are in direct contradiction to the passage.

25. **(C)** The purpose of the juvenile court is to choose the best possible method to "save the child." The passage implies that punishment and reform school are not the methods of choice, that probation is preferred. While psychiatric care may be the correct method in some cases, it is not mentioned in the passage and is certainly not the best answer choice.

26. **(A)** Some questions are easier than others. Careful reading makes this answer obvious.

Selection for Question 27

When a person commits a traffic infraction, a Police Officer should:

1. Inform the violator of the offense committed.
2. Request the violator to show his or her driver's license, vehicle registration, and insurance identification card. Failure to produce this required material may result in additional tickets. (Taxis, buses, and other rented vehicles do not require insurance identification cards.)
3. Enter only one infraction on each ticket.
4. Use a separate ticket for each additional infraction.

27. Police Officer Herrmann has been assigned to curb traffic violations at the intersection of Main Street and Central Avenue. Officer Herrmann observes a taxi cab going through a red light at this intersection and signals the driver to pull over. The officer informs the cab driver of his violation and asks for the required material. The driver surrenders his license and registration to the officer. Police Officer Herrmann should

27. Ⓐ Ⓑ Ⓒ Ⓓ

(A) issue the cab driver a ticket for the red light violation and issue him a separate ticket for not surrendering his insurance card
(B) issue the cab driver one ticket including both the red light violation and the absence of the insurance card
(C) issue the cab driver a ticket only for the red light violation
(D) issue the cab driver a ticket only for not having an insurance card

The correct answer is **(C)**.

27. **(C)** The taxi driver violated the law by going through a red light. Officer Herrmann correctly informed the driver of this infraction and must issue a ticket. If the violator had been driving a private automobile, Officer Herrmann would have had to issue a separate ticket for his not producing an insurance card (see rules 3 and 4). However, in this case, the exception applies. The exception is that taxis, along with buses and rented vehicles, do not need to have insurance identification cards. You have to read carefully to determine exactly which rule applies in this case.

Selection for Questions 28 to 29

Police Officers while on patrol may observe a recently vacated building that can create a safety hazard. In such situations, Police Officers should follow these procedures, in the order given:

1. Walk through the vacated building to determine if a safety hazard exists.
2. If a safety hazard exists, notify the supervisor on patrol.
3. Write an entry in the Activity Log.
4. Report the facts concerning the safety hazard in the vacant building to the Telephone Switchboard Operator.
5. Place barriers in front of the vacated building if directed by the Patrol Supervisor.

28. Police Officer Wolff notes that a building on his patrol route has recently been vacated. What action should Officer Wolff take next?   28. Ⓐ Ⓑ Ⓒ Ⓓ

(A) Report the safety hazard in the vacant building to the Telephone Switchboard Operator.
(B) Radio the supervisor on patrol.
(C) Make an entry in his Activity Log.
(D) Determine if there is a safety hazard.

29. Police Officer Furumoto has noticed a safety hazard in a vacant building. He first notified the supervisor on patrol and then made an entry in the Activity Log. He is about to place barriers in front of the building to safeguard the public. Officer Furumoto is acting   29. Ⓐ Ⓑ Ⓒ Ⓓ

(A) correctly. Public safety is the police officer's first duty.
(B) incorrectly. The Patrol Supervisor has not directed him to place barriers.
(C) incorrectly. He must first report the safety hazard to the Telephone Switchboard Operator.
(D) incorrectly. He should radio for additional police officers to assist him in protecting the public from this hazard.

The correct answers are: 28. (D), 29. (C).

28. (D) The introductory sentence says that a recently vacated building can create a safety hazard, not that it necessarily does so. Officer Wolff must enter the building and look around to determine whether or not there is indeed a safety hazard. Only if he decides that there is a hazard, should he proceed with notification and other actions.

29. (C) The procedure lists steps to be taken in the order given. While Officer Furumoto is justly concerned with public safety, the hazard in the vacant building hardly constitutes a pressing emergency. Having made the entry in the Log, his next act must be to notify the Telephone Switchboard Operator. Then he must await instructions from the Patrol Supervisor. The Supervisor may feel that the hazard does not warrant barricades.

Selection for Questions 30 to 31

Police Officer DiSisto has observed that there is a pattern to criminal activity in her sector. She has noticed that burglaries tend to occur on High Street while auto thefts occur on York Street. Most rapes take place on Chapel Street and most assaults on Whitney. The rapes occur between 10 P.M. and 4 A.M., auto thefts between midnight and 6 A.M., burglaries between 10 A.M. and 4 P.M., and assaults between 6 P.M. and 10 P.M. Auto thefts seem most common on Monday, Tuesday, and Thursday. Assaults occur most often on Friday, Saturday, and Sunday. Most rapes happen over the weekend and most burglaries on Monday, Wednesday, and Saturday.

30. Police Officer DiSisto would most likely be able to reduce the incidence of rape by concentrating her patrol on

30. Ⓐ Ⓑ Ⓒ Ⓓ

(A) York Street between midnight and 8 A.M.
(B) Chapel Street between 7 P.M. and 3 A.M.
(C) High Street between 2 A.M. and 10 P.M.
(D) Chapel Street between 4 P.M. and midnight

31. Auto theft has been a special problem in the precinct, and Police Officer DiSisto's supervisor has requested that she make a special effort to eliminate auto theft on her patrol. Officer DiSisto should request assignment to patrol on

31. Ⓐ Ⓑ Ⓒ Ⓓ

(A) Sunday through Thursday from 10 P.M. to 6 A.M.
(B) Friday through Wednesday from 3 A.M. to 11 A.M.
(C) Monday through Friday from 8 A.M. to 4 P.M.
(D) Wednesday through Sunday from 2 P.M. to 10 P.M.

The correct answers are: 30. **(B)**, 31. **(A)**.

30. **(B)** You must read for details and then use these details to reason. This type of question highlights the value of reading the questions before you read the paragraph. Question 30 deals with rape; question 31 with auto theft. In your initial reading of the paragraph, you will underscore details concerning rape and auto theft, ignoring information relating to burglary and assault. With your information thus narrowed, note that the rape area is Chapel Street. Eliminate choices (A) and (C). The rapes occur in the six-hour span from 10 P.M. to 4 A.M. Choice (B) covers five hours of this six-hour span while (D) covers only the two hours from 10 P.M. to midnight.

31. **(A)** Approach this question in the same way. Auto theft appears to be a mid-week event. Only choices (A) and (C) include the three target days of Monday, Tuesday, and Thursday. Auto thefts occur under cover of darkness making (C) a poor choice.

Selection to Question 32

Harassment occurs when a person annoys or alarms another person, but does not intend or cause physical injury.

Menacing occurs when a person threatens to cause serious physical injury to another person, but does not cause a serious physical injury.

Assault occurs when a person causes physical injury to another person.

32. On a foggy Friday night after work, a group of men met at the Jolly-O Tavern for a few beers. The conversation centered on the merits of the two local hockey teams, and Warren Wu stoutly defended his favorite team against that of Tomas Ramos. Ramos could stand just so much taunting. As he became more angry, Ramos told Wu that he had better "shut up" before he, Tomas Ramos, knocked Wu's block off. Wu continued to praise his team, whereupon Ramos gave him such a punch to the jaw that Wu's lip was split and a tooth was knocked out. Based on the definitions above, Ramos should be charged with

32. Ⓐ Ⓑ Ⓒ Ⓓ

(A) harassment, menacing, and assault
(B) menacing and assault
(C) assault
(D) no crime

The correct answer is (C).

32. **(C)** The fact of assault seems clear. Ramos caused physical injury to Wu. According to the definitions, assault is the only charge. Harassment requires that no injury be intended, but Ramos stated intent to harm Wu. Menacing requires that no injury be caused. These definitions are mutually exclusive. Only one can apply. Definitions of other crimes may allow for one definition to be included within another. Careful reading is the number one requirement.

Use the skills and techniques you have just developed to practice with the traditional-style reading comprehension questions in the following chapter. Then apply your new expertise to the exams in this book and to your Police Officer exam.

Before you begin the exercises, review this list of hints for scoring high on reading comprehension questions.

1. Read the questions and underline key words.

2. Skim the selection to get a general idea of the subject matter, the point that is being made, and the organization of the material.

3. Reread the selection giving attention to details and point of view. Underscore key words and phrases.

4. If the author has quoted material from another source, be sure that you understand the purpose of the quote. Does the author agree or disagree?

5. Carefully read each question or incomplete statement. Determine exactly what is being asked. Watch for negatives or all-inclusive words such as *always, never, all, only, every, absolutely, completely, none, entirely, no.*

6. Read all the answer choices. Eliminate those choices that are obviously incorrect. Reread the remaining choices and refer to the selection, if necessary, to determine the *best* answer.

7. Avoid inserting your own judgments into your answers. Even if you disagree with the author or even if you spot a factual error in the selection, you must answer on the basis of what is stated or implied in the selection.

8. Do not allow yourself to spend too much time on any one question. If looking back at the selection does not help you to find or figure out the answer, choose from among the answers remaining after you eliminate the obviously wrong answers, mark the question in the test booklet, and go on. If you have time at the end of the exam or exam portion, reread the selection and the question. Often a fresh look provides new insights.

PRACTICE WITH READING COMPREHENSION QUESTIONS

1. "The force reconciling and coordinating all human conflicts and directing people in the harmonious accomplishment of their work is the supervisor. To deal with people successfully, the first one a supervisor must learn to work with is him- or herself." According to the quotation, the most accurate of the following conclusions is:

   (A) Human conflicts are the result of harmonious accomplishment.
   (B) A supervisor should attempt to reconcile all the different views subordinates may have.
   (C) A supervisor who understands him- or herself is in a good position to deal with others successfully.
   (D) The reconciling force in human conflicts is the ability to deal with people successfully.

2. "Law must be stable and yet it cannot stand still," means most nearly that

   (A) law is a fixed body of subject matter
   (B) law must adapt itself to changing conditions
   (C) law is a poor substitute for justice
   (D) the true administration of justice is the firmest pillar of good government.

3. "The treatment to be given the offender cannot alter the fact of the offense; but we can take measures to reduce the chance of similar acts occurring in the future. We should banish the criminal, not in order to exact revenge nor directly to encourage reform, but to deter that person and others from further illegal attacks on society." According to the quotation, prisoners should be punished in order to

   (A) alter the nature of their offenses
   (B) banish them from society
   (C) deter them and others from similar illegal attacks on society
   (D) directly encourage reform.

4. "On the other hand, the treatment of prisoners on a basis of direct reform is foredoomed to failure. Neither honest persons nor criminals will tolerate a bald proposition from anyone to alter their characters or habits, least of all if we attempt to gain such a change by a system of coercion." According to this quotation, criminals

   (A) are incorrigible
   (B) are incapable of being coerced
   (C) are not likely to turn into law-abiding citizens
   (D) possess very firm characters.

5. "While much thought has been devoted to the question of how to build walls high enough to keep persons temporarily in prison, we have devoted very little attention to the treatment necessary to enable them to come out permanently cured, inclined to be friends rather than enemies of their law-abiding fellow citizens." According to this quotation, much thought has been devoted to the problem of prisons as

   (A) vengeful agencies
   (B) efficient custodial agencies
   (C) efficient sanatoria
   (D) places from which society's friends might issue.

6. "Community organization most often includes persons whose behavior is unconventional in relation to generally accepted social definition, if such persons wield substantial influence with the residents." The inference one can most validly draw from this statement is that

   (A) influential persons are often likely to be unconventional
   (B) the success of a community organization depends largely on the democratic processes employed by it
   (C) a gang leader may sometimes be an acceptable recruit for a community organization
   (D) the unconventional behavior of a local barkeeper may often become acceptable to the community.

7. "The safeguard of democracy is education. The education of youth during a limited period of more or less compulsory attendance at school does not suffice. The educative process is a lifelong one." The statement most consistent with this quotation is:

(A) The school is not the only institution that can contribute to the education of the population.
(B) All democratic peoples are educated.
(C) The entire population should be required to go to school throughout life.
(D) If compulsory education were not required, the educative process would be more effective.

8. "The police officer's art consists in applying and enforcing a multitude of laws and ordinances in such degree or proportion and in such manner that the greatest degree of social protection will be secured. The degree of enforcement and the method of application will vary with each neighborhood and community." According to this statement,

(A) each neighborhood or community must judge for itself to what extent the law is to be enforced

(B) a police officer should only enforce those laws that are designed to give the greatest degree of social protection
(C) the manner and intensity of law enforcement is not necessarily the same in all communities
(D) all laws and ordinances must be enforced in a community with the same degree of intensity.

9. "As a rule, police officers, through service and experience, are familiar with the duties and the methods and means required to perform them. Yet, left to themselves, their aggregate effort would disintegrate and the vital work of preserving the peace would never be accomplished." According to this statement, the most accurate of the following conclusions is:

(A) Police officers are sufficiently familiar with their duties as to need no supervision.
(B) Working together for a common purpose is not efficient without supervision.
(C) Police officers are familiar with the methods of performing their duties because of rules.
(D) Preserving the peace is so vital that it can never be said to be completed.

Answer questions 10 through 12 on the basis of the information given in the following passage.

Criminal science is largely the science of identification. Progress in this field has been marked and sometimes very spectacular because new techniques, instruments, and facts flow continuously from the scientists. But the crime laboratories are understaffed; trade secrets still prevail; and inaccurate conclusions are often the result. However, modern gadgets cannot substitute for the skilled intelligent investigator; he or she must be their master.

10. According to this passage, criminal science

(A) excludes the field of investigation
(B) is primarily interested in establishing identity
(C) is based on the equipment used in crime laboratories
(D) uses techniques different from those used in other sciences.

11. Advances in criminal science have been, according to the passage,

(A) extremely limited
(B) slow but steady
(C) unusually reliable
(D) outstanding.

12. A problem that has not been overcome completely in crime work is, according to the passage,

(A) unskilled investigators
(B) the expense of new equipment and techniques
(C) an insufficient number of personnel in crime laboratories
(D) inaccurate equipment used in laboratories.

13. "While the safe burglar can ply his or her trade the year round, the loft burglar has more seasonal activities, since only at certain periods of the year is a substantial amount of valuable merchandise stored in lofts." The generalization, which this statement best illustrates, is that

   (A) nothing is ever completely safe from a thief
   (B) there are safe burglars and loft burglars
   (C) some types of burglarly are seasonal
   (D) the safe burglar considers safecracking a trade.

Answer questions 14 through 17 on the basis of the information given in the following passage.

When a vehicle has been disabled in a tunnel, the officer on patrol in this zone shall press the emergency truck light button. In the fast lane, red lights will go on throughout the tunnel; in the slow lane, amber lights will go on throughout the tunnel. The yellow zone light will go on at each signal control station throughout the tunnel and will flash the number of the zone in which the stoppage has occurred. A red flashing pilot light will appear only at the signal control station at which the emergency truck button was pressed. The emergency garage will receive an audible and visual signal indicating the signal control station at which the emergency truck button was pressed. The garage officer shall acknowledge receipt of the signal by pressing the acknowledgement button. This will cause the pilot light at the operated signal control station in the tunnel to cease flashing and to remain steady. It is an answer to the officer at the operated signal control station that the emergency truck is responding to the call.

14. According to this passage, when the emergency truck light button is pressed,

   (A) amber lights will go on in every lane throughout the tunnel
   (B) emergency signal lights will go on only in the lane in which the disabled vehicle is located
   (C) red lights will go on in the fast lane throughout the tunnel
   (D) pilot lights at all signal control stations will turn amber.

15. According to this passage, the number of the zone in which the stoppage has occurred is flashed

   (A) immediately after all the lights in the tunnel turn red
   (B) by the yellow zone light at each signal control station
   (C) by the emergency truck.at the point of stoppage
   (D) by the emergency garage

16. According to the passage, an officer near the disabled vehicle will know that the emergency tow truck is coming when

   (A) the pilot light at the operated signal control station appears and flashes red
   (B) an audible signal is heard in the tunnel
   (C) the zone light at the operated signal control station turns red
   (D) the pilot light at the operated signal control station becomes steady.

17. Under the system described in the passage, it would be correct to come to the conclusion that

   (A) officers at all signal control stations are expected to acknowledge that they have received the stoppage signal
   (B) officers at all signal control stations will know where the stoppage has occurred
   (C) all traffic in both lanes of that side of the tunnel in which the stoppage has occurred must stop until the emergency truck has arrived
   (D) there are two emergency garages, each able to respond to stoppages in traffic going in one particular direction.

Answer questions 18 through 20 on the basis of the information given in the following passage.

The use of a roadblock is simply an adaptation of the military practice of encirclement by the police. Successful operation of a roadblock plan depends almost entirely on the amount of advance study and planning given to such operations. A thorough and detailed examination of the roads and terrain under the jurisdiction of a given police agency should be made with the locations of the roadblocks pinpointed in advance. The first principle to be borne in mind in the location of each roadblock is the time element. Its location must be at a point beyond which the fugitive could not have possibly traveled in the time elapsed from the commission of the crime to the arrival of the officers at the roadblock.

18. According to the passage,

(A) military operations have made extensive use of roadblocks

(B) the military practice of encirclement is an adaptation of police use of roadblocks

(C) the technique of encirclement has been widely used by military forces

(D) a roadblock is generally more effective than encirclement.

19. According to the passage,

(A) advance study and planning are of minor importance in the success of roadblock operations

(B) a thorough and detailed examination of all roads within a radius of fifty miles should precede the determination of a roadblock location

(C) consideration of terrain features is important in planning the location of roadblocks

(D) a roadblock operation can seldom be successfully undertaken by a single police agency.

20. According to the passage,

(A) the factor of time is the sole consideration in the location of a roadblock

(B) the maximum speed possible in the method of escape is of major importance in roadblock location

(C) the time the officers arrive at the site of a proposed roadblock is of little importance

(D) a roadblock should be sited as close to the scene of the crime as the terrain will permit.

Answer questions 21 through 22 on the basis of the information given in the following passage.

A number of crimes, such as robbery, assault, rape, certain forms of theft, and burglary, are high visibility crimes in that it is apparent to all concerned that they are criminal acts prior to or at the time they are committed. In contrast to these, check forgeries, especially those committed by first offenders, have low visibility. There is little in the criminal act or in the interaction between the check passer and the person cashing the check to identify it as a crime. Closely related to this special quality of the forgery crime is the fact that, while it is formally defined and treated as a felonious or "infamous" crime, it is informally held by the legally untrained public to be a relatively harmless form of crime.

21. According to the passage, crimes of "high visibility"

(A) are immediately recognized as crime by the victims

(B) take place in public view

(C) always involve violence or the threat of violence

(D) are usually committed after dark.

22. According to the passage

(A) the public regards check forgery as a minor crime

(B) the law regards check forgery as a minor crime

(C) the law distinguishes between check forgery and other forgery

(D) it is easier to spot inexperienced check forgers than other criminals.

Answer questions 23 and 24 on the basis of the information given in the following passage.

The racketeer is primarily concerned with business affairs, legitimate or otherwise, and preferably those that are close to the margin of legitimacy. The racketeer gets the best opportunities from business organizations that meet the need of large sections of the public for goods or services that are defined as illegitimate by the same public, such as prostitution, gambling, illicit drugs, or liquor. In contrast to the thief, the racketeer and the establishments controlled deliver goods and services for money received.

23. It can be deduced from the passage that suppression of racketeers is difficult because

(A) victims of racketeers are not guilty of violating the law
(B) racketeers are generally engaged in fully legitimate enterprises
(C) many people want services that are not obtainable through legitimate sources
(D) laws prohibiting gambling and prostitution are unenforceable.

24. According to the passage, racketeering, unlike theft, involves

(A) objects of value
(B) payment for goods received
(C) organized gangs
(D) unlawful activities.

25. "In examining the scene of a homicide, one should not only look for the usual, standard traces—fingerprints, footprints, etc.—but should also have eyes open for details that at first glance may not seem to have any connection with the crime." The most logical inference to be drawn from this statement is that

(A) in general, standard traces are not important
(B) sometimes one should not look for footprints
(C) usually only the standard traces are important
(D) one cannot tell in advance what will be important.

Answer questions 26 and 27 on the basis of the information given in the following passage.

If a motor vehicle fails to pass inspection, the owner will be given a rejection notice by the inspection station. Repairs must be made within ten days after this notice is issued. It is not necessary to have the required adjustment or repairs made at the station where the inspection occurred. The vehicle may be taken to any other garage. Reinspection after repairs may be made at any official inspection station, not necessarily the same station that made the initial inspection. The registration of any motor vehicle for which an inspection sticker has not been obtained as required, or which is not repaired and inspected within ten days after inspection indicates defects, is subject to suspension. A vehicle cannot be used on public highways while its registration is under suspension.

26. According to the passage, the owner of a car that does not pass inspection must

(A) have repairs made at the same station that rejected the car
(B) take the car to another station and have it reinspected
(C) have repairs made anywhere and then have the car reinspected
(D) not use the car on a public highway until the necessary repairs have been made.

27. According to the passage, the one of the following which may be cause for suspension of the registration of a vehicle is that

(A) an inspection sticker was issued before the rejection notice had been in force for ten days
(B) it was not reinspected by the station that rejected it originally
(C) it was not reinspected either by the station that rejected it originally or by the garage that made the repairs
(D) it has not had defective parts repaired within ten days after inspection.

28. A statute states: "A person who steals an article worth less than $100 where no aggravating circumstances accompany the act is guilty of petit larceny. If the article is worth $100 or more, it may be larceny second degree." If all you know is that Edward Smith stole an article worth $100, it may reasonably be said that

(A) Smith is guilty of petit larceny
(B) Smith is guilty of larceny second degree
(C) Smith is guilty of neither petit larceny nor larceny second degree
(D) precisely what charge will be placed against Smith is uncertain.

Answer questions 29 through 30 on the basis of the information given in the following passage.

The City Police Department will accept for investigation no report of a person missing from his residence if such residence is located outside of the city. The person reporting same will be advised to report such fact to the police department of the locality where the missing person lives, which will, if necessary, communicate officially with the City Police Department. However, a report will be accepted of a person who is missing from a temporary residence in the city, but the person making the report will be instructed to make a report also to the police department of the locality where the missing person lives.

29. According to the passage, a report to the City Police Department of a missing person whose permanent residence is outside of the city will

(A) always be investigated provided that a report is also made to local police authorities
(B) never be investigated unless requested officially by local police authorities
(C) be investigated in cases of temporary residence in the city, but a report should always be made to local police authorities
(D) always be investigated and a report will be made to the local police authorities by the City Police Department.

30. Mr. Smith of Oldtown and Mr. Jones of Newtown have an appointment in the city, but Mr. Jones doesn't appear. Mr. Smith, after trying repeatedly to phone Mr. Jones the next day, believes that something has happened to him. According to the passage, Mr. Smith should apply to the police of

(A) Oldtown
(B) Newtown
(C) Newtown and the city
(D) Oldtown and the city.

31. A police department rule reads as follows: "A Deputy Commissioner acting as Police Commissioner shall carry out the orders of the Police Commissioner, previously given, and such orders shall not, except in cases of extreme emergency, be countermanded." This means most nearly that, except in cases of extreme emergency,

(A) the orders given by a Deputy Commissioner acting as Police Commissioner may not be revoked
(B) a Deputy Commissioner acting as Police Commissioner should not revoke orders previously given by the Police Commissioner
(C) a Deputy Commissioner acting as Police Commissioner is vested with the same authority to issue orders as the Police Commissioner
(D) only a Deputy Commissioner acting as Police Commissioner may issue orders in the absence of the Police Commissioner.

32. "A 'crime' is an act committed or omitted in violation of a public law either forbidding or commanding it." This statement implies most nearly that

(A) crimes can be omitted
(B) a forbidding act, if omitted, is a crime
(C) an act of omission may be criminal
(D) to commit an act not commanded is criminal.

33. "He who by command, counsel, or assistance procures another to commit a crime is, in morals and in law, as culpable as the visible actor himself, for the reason that the criminal act, whichever it may be, is imputable to the person who conceived it and set the forces in motion for its actual accomplishment." Of the following, the most accurate inference from this statement is that

(A) a criminal act does not have to be committed for a crime to be committed

(B) acting as counselor for a criminal is a crime
(C) the mere counseling of a criminal act can never be a crime if no criminal act is committed
(D) a person acting only as an adviser may be guilty of committing a criminal act.

34. "A 'felony' is a crime punishable by death or imprisonment in a state prison, and any other crime is a 'misdemeanor.'" According to this quotation, the decisive distinction between "felony" and "misdemeanor" is the

(A) degree of criminality
(B) type of crime
(C) place of incarceration
(D) judicial jurisdiction.

Question 35 is to be answered on the basis of the information given in the following passage.

If the second or third felony is such that, upon a first conviction, the offender would be punishable by imprisonment for any term less than his or her natural life, then such person must be sentenced to imprisonment for an indeterminate term, the minimum of which shall be not less than one-half of the longest term prescribed upon a first conviction, and the maximum of which shall be not longer than twice such longest term; provided, however, that the minimum sentence imposed hereunder upon such second or third felony offender shall in no case be less than five years; except that where the maximum punishment for a second or third felony offender hereunder is five years or less, the minimum sentence must be not less than two years.

35. According to this passage, a person who has a second felony conviction shall receive as a sentence for that second felony an indeterminate term

(A) not less than twice the minimum term prescribed upon a first conviction as a maximum
(B) not less than one-half the maximum term of the first conviction as a minimum
(C) not more than twice the minimum term prescribed upon a first conviction as a minimum
(D) with a maximum of not more than twice the longest term prescribed for a first conviction for this crime.

ANSWER KEY

1. C	8. C	15. B	22. A	29. C
2. B	9. B	16. D	23. C	30. B
3. C	10. B	17. B	24. B	31. B
4. C	11. D	18. C	25. D	32. C
5. B	12. C	19. C	26. C	33. D
6. C	13. C	20. B	27. D	34. C
7. A	14. C	21. A	28. D	35. D

ANSWER EXPLANATIONS

1. **(C)** Before understanding and working with others, one must first understand one's own motivation and working habits. The supervisor with good self-understanding is an effective supervisor.

2. **(B)** Adaptation is changing in response to changing conditions without a total change of substance.

3. **(C)** This quotation expresses the philosophy that the purpose of punishment is neither to make the offender "pay for his/her crime" nor to reform the offender, but rather to protect society from the specific criminal and to serve, by example, as a deterrent to others.

4. **(C)** The philosophy expressed here is "Once a criminal, always a criminal." Attempts at reform and rehabilitation are futile. (Remember: Answer questions based on reading passages on the information in the passages. You may disagree; you may even know that the information is incorrect. However, your answer must be based on the passage, not upon your opinions or your knowledge.)

5. **(B)** This question deals with a philosophy contrary to those expressed in the previous two questions. It states that we have devoted attention to means of making prisons secure places in which to keep offenders but have not given much thought to rehabilitation.

6. **(C)** You may find this principle difficult to accept, but it does represent accepted practice in many quarters. The concept is that if the person with leadership qualities—even if with antisocial behaviors—is drawn into the mainstream, that person can learn to accept certain norms of the majority and transmit these more acceptable attitudes and behaviors to the group that respects him or her. The term used to describe the drawing into the inner circle of the unconventional leader is "co-opting."

7. **(A)** Since education continues throughout life, yet schooling is of limited duration, obviously education occurs in places other than schools.

8. **(C)** The needs and desires of communities vary, therefore degree and manner of enforcement of different laws in different communities will also vary.

9. **(B)** The meaning of this quotation is that good intentions and thorough knowledge of duties are not sufficient. Organization and supervision are vital to efficient operation of the police function.

10. **(B)** The science of identification is primarily interested in establishing identity.

11. **(D)** Marked and spectacular progress is outstanding.

12. **(C)** Understaffed laboratories have insufficient personnel.

13. **(C)** The concept may be novel to you, but the question itself is an easy one. The answer is stated directly in the paragraph.

14. **(C)** See the second sentence. When a reading passage is crammed with details, most of the questions will be strictly factual.

15. **(B)** See the third sentence.

16. **(D)** See the last two sentences.

17. **(B)** The yellow zone light goes on at each signal control station and flashes the number of the zone in which the stoppage has occurred, so all officers receive this information.

18. **(C)** If the military practice of encirclement was adapted for use by the police, we may assume that it was widely and successfully used. Choice (B) reverses the order of the adaptation.

19. **(C)** This is the clear implication of the third sentence.

20. **(B)** The roadblock must be placed beyond the point that the fugitive could have possibly reached, so maximum speed of escape is vitally important in the establishment of a roadblock.

21. **(A)** See the first sentence.

22. **(A)** See the last sentence.

23. **(C)** The racketeer provides goods and services that are officially illegal but that are desired by otherwise respectable members of

the general public. Since the public wants these services, active effort to suppress the providers is unlikely.

24. **(B)** See the last sentence.

25. **(D)** The police officer must always be observant and alert to both abnormalities and routine details in the environment. This useful quality in a police officer is the reason many police officer exams include a section testing powers of observation and memory.

26. **(C)** The state is not concerned with who makes repairs nor with who does the inspection, only that these be accomplished.

27. **(D)** See the next-to-last sentence.

28. **(D)** Beware of qualifying words and definite statements. If the article is worth $100 or more, it *may* be larceny second degree, but not necessarily.

29. **(C)** See the last sentence.

30. **(B)** Mr. Jones is a resident of Newtown, so the missing person report must be filed with the Newtown police. The meeting of Smith and Jones was to have taken place in the city, but Jones was not a temporary resident of the city, so the city police are not involved in this case.

31. **(B)** The word "countermand" means "revoke." The Deputy Commissioner carries out the orders of the Police Commissioner and revokes them only in cases of extreme emergency.

32. **(C)** An act of omission, if it is in violation of a public law commanding said act, is a crime. The act of omission is not a crime if it is not in violation of a public law.

33. **(D)** The person who conceives and sets in motion the forces for the accomplishment of a crime—in other words, the advisor who convinced another to commit a criminal act, may well be deemed guilty of committing the criminal act.

34. **(C)** Imprisonment in a state prison is incarceration in the state prison. Imprisonment or incarceration in any other institution is the punishment for a misdemeanor. Crimes are defined by the place of incarceration or imprisonment.

35. **(D)** You may have to do some very careful reading and rereading to find the answer to this question. You will find it in the last clause before the first semicolon.

OBSERVATION AND MEMORY

To function effectively, a police officer must possess a keen memory for details. He or she must be on the constant alert for physical characteristics that will help to identify key people, places, or things, thereby leading to the apprehension of a criminal or the solution of a criminal investigation.

Most people have distinguishing features that are difficult to disguise: the contour of the face; the size, shape, and position of the ears; the shape of the mouth. Any of these may be sufficient for an officer to detect an individual wanted for criminal activities. On the other hand, the color or style of an individual's hair or the first impression of his or her face may change drastically with the addition of a wig, mustache, or beard. In addition, eye color can be altered with tinted contact lenses. Therefore, the police officer must focus attention on those physical features that cannot be changed easily and might serve as the basis of a positive identification of that person at some time in the future.

Observation is not limited to the act of seeing. In addition, the officer must learn to recognize and recall distinctive features of people, places, and things. An official record in the memorandum book may serve as a refresher for the facts stored in the officer's mental record. The officer should be aware of the people who frequent his or her post, and of the surrounding buildings and stores on that post, so that important details may be brought to bear in a case when necessary. An officer without a keen sense of recall cannot perform his or her duties effectively.

Because police departments all over the country recognize the importance of a good memory for details and a good sense of recall in the officer's job, examinations for the position frequently contain sections that evaluate these skills. To best sharpen your memory and sense of recall, you must practice using these skills. You need only walk around your neighborhood and observe. Keep your eyes open to everything you see. Later try to recall details of buildings or people that you saw. Remember, your environment is your study aid: Virtually any place you go, you can practice observing and recalling details.

Police Observation of Persons, Places, and Things

The police officer must be thoroughly observant at all times. The nonobservant officer is soon found out by the criminal element who will take advantage of this deficiency to commit crimes on the officer's post. Good observation is a matter of training and knowledge. A police officer may have perfect eyesight yet be blind when it comes to observing matters calling for police action.

Many dangerous criminals have been arrested by virtue of a police officer's keen observation. An officer should observe the customary activities on his or her post as well as the people who live in or frequent it, so that the officer can quickly spot a stranger or an unusual activity. Some places will call for more observation than others: banks, jewelry stores, taverns, service stations, and any place where crime is likely to occur or where the criminal element may gather.

An essential element in observation is the ability to remember details. Officers should practice observation by giving themselves such tests as describing a man or a woman encountered casually or trying to remember details on a billboard. The identification of persons, places, and things depends on accurate observation. Many witnesses testify inaccurately in court because they failed to observe properly at the time of the incident's occurrence. A failure of this kind is *inexcusable* on the part of an officer.

Memory is a very individualized skill. Some people remember details of what they see and hear, others remember only the most obvious facts. Some people memorize easily, others find memorizing very difficult. Some people remember forever, others forget in a short time. Some people can memorize in a systematic manner, others are haphazard in their methods or have no method at all. Systematic observation tends to lead to more efficient memorization. Some sort of meaningful grouping of people and activities helps to secure the descriptions, the activities, and the interactions in your mind. Whether the material is pictorial or narrative, try to organize it in some meaningful way.

We really cannot tell you how to memorize. We can, however, teach you how to look at pictures and point out the details on which you should concentrate.

Photograph for Exercise 1

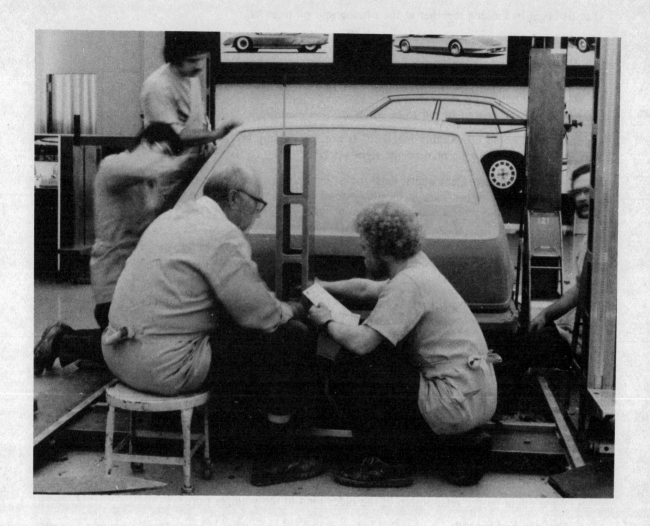

(Photograph courtesy of General Motors)

Exercise 1

Let us begin by looking together at the photograph on page 89.

Start with the people:

1. How many people are in the photograph?

2. How many men? How many women?

3. What do the people appear to be doing?

4. Are the people all working together? If not, how many are working alone? How many together? Is the man on the right working?

5. Note the clothing. Dark pants, dark socks, light shirts crossed across the chest and tied in back. The two men in the foreground have on the same type of shoes, but the other visible pair of shoes is a different type.

6. Note glasses. Which men wear them?

7. Note hair. Which men have dark hair? Which light? Can you describe the hairstyles of the light-haired men?

8. One man is sitting on a stool. Which man? How many legs does the stool have? Of what does the stool appear to be made? Does it move on casters?

9. Which of the men have beards? Mustaches?

10. Is anyone wearing a watch? Who?

Observe the action:

11. What does the man in the right foreground have in his hand? What is he probably doing?

12. What does the man who is standing appear to be doing? What about the man kneeling beside him?

13. What might be the relationship of the older man to the younger ones?

Note the background:

14. There are pictures of cars on the walls. Parts of how many cars are visible? How many tires are shown?

15. What else can be seen on the walls? Telephone? Calendar? Bookcase?

16. Is the car on which the men are working up on a lift?

17. How many levels of floor are visible? Is the floor clean?

18. There is a number on one piece of equipment. Did you notice the number? Remember it!

A good question writer could easily develop ten questions based upon these observations. Would you have noticed everything and made note as well about what was not there at all?

In looking at a photograph, focus first on the people. Notice their clothing, physical features, and activities. Count, but also make note of which person or persons are wearing what, doing what, interacting with whom, and so on. Then notice the prominent objects. Next, turn your attention to the background, floors, walls, etc. Finally, start at the left side of the photograph and move your eyes very slowly to the right, noticing special details such as numbers, calibrations, dirt spots, unidentified objects, etc. If you work very hard at noticing, you are likely to remember what you noticed, at least for the duration of the exam.

Photograph for Exercise 2

(Photograph courtesy of The Coleman Company, Inc.)

Exercise 2

Let us look at another photograph on page 91.

1. The people in the picture are...number, sex, age.

2. The people are wearing...notice the boy's belt, label on jeans (even if you cannot read it, you should notice that it is there), long-sleeved plaid shirts.

3. Notice hair color, type (curly or straight), and length.

4. Note that no shoes are visible; neither person wears glasses nor a watch nor hat.

5. What is the boy doing? What is the girl doing?

6. Who is standing? Who sitting? On What?

7. On what is the soda can resting? On what is the cooler resting?

8. What else is on the table? Notice lantern, covered pot, box, and coffeepot.

9. How many slats make up the table? The bench?

10. What is on the ground? Snow? Sand? Gravel? Lawn? Rocks? Flowers? Wild grasses?

11. The day is...cold? warm? rainy? cloudy? sunny? Where is the sun in the picture?

12. In the background are (is)...mountains? trees? water? boats? tents? more grass? other people? animals?

13. What can you see in the sky? What is on or in the water? What else is there on the land?

14. Does the cooler have a handle on top? Where? Is it all one color? How many colors? Describe the design of the cooler.

15. Where is the fill valve on the lantern?

16. Does the coffeepot have a handle?

17. Does the tent have a visible window?

18. Describe the end of the bench? Squared off? Rounded? Other?

How did you do with this photograph? Are you developing skill at noticing everything?

Photograph for Exercise 3

(Photograph courtesy of The Coleman Company, Inc.)

Exercise 3

Study the photograph on page 93. On a plain piece of paper make as comprehensive a list as you can. Try to notice every detail on which you could possibly be quizzed. When you have completed your list, compare it with ours, which follows. If you noticed everything that we did, you are becoming very observant. Perhaps you found details that we missed. If so, congratulate yourself and keep up the good work.

Here is our list:

1. There are four people in the photograph, two adults and two children.

2. Two people are in a canoe, a man and a child.

3. The man in the canoe is sitting in the stern (rear) and is paddling on his left side.

4. The child in the canoe is in the bow (front) and is paddling on his right side.

5. The child in the canoe is blond, the man is dark-haired. Both are wearing shirts with long sleeves.

6. A woman and a little girl are standing on the shore.

7. The little girl is blonde; the woman's hair is darker.

8. Both the woman and the girl are wearing jackets. The little girl's jacket is a winter jacket with a fleece-lined hood.

9. In the foreground is a cooler with white top, white handle and drainage valve.

10. On top of the cooler is a soda can.

11. Also in the foreground is a light colored tent of modified quonset shape.

12. A door flap of the tent is rolled back.

13. The opening of the tent is screened.

14. The water is calm.

15. The bank is grassy.

16. The body of water is lined with trees and shrubs.

17. Not visible: sky, end of body of water, background beyond the tree line, other people, and animals.

By now your powers of observation should be considerably keener.

Photograph for Exercise 4

Exercise 4

Make this exercise an observation and memory exercise rather than just an observation exercise. Study the photograph on page 95 for five minutes. Make mental notes of as many details as you possibly can, but do not do any writing while you look at the photo. Then close the book and write as many details as you can remember. When you have written all that you can remember, draw a line on your paper and reopen the book. Add to the list details that you forgot and details that you previously overlooked. Then compare your list with ours.

1. The scene is a classroom. The students are women; the instructor is a man.

2. The students are all seated; the teacher is standing.

3. The teacher has dark, curly hair. He wears white pants and a white knit, collared sport shirt with some dark strips.

4. The teacher wears a watch on his left wrist and a bracelet on his right. He has something in each hand.

5. The teacher has some slender object in each breast pocket.

6. The teacher is not wearing glasses. He is clean shaven. His mouth is closed.

7. Parts of thirteen students are visible.

8. The class is racially mixed.

9. The students are wearing a uniform that consists of a white short-sleeved blouse with cuffs on the sleeves and wide pointed collar, dark slacks, and dark overblouse vest.

10. Footwear is not part of the uniform though low white shoes seem to be favored.

11. One student is wearing a long-sleeved print shirt under her uniform blouse. That student is black and wears glasses.

12. Most students are seated on folding chairs with writing arms. One student is sitting in a chair without an arm. That student is closest to the camera. She has her notebook open on her lap, wears her hair in a bun, has side combs in her hair and loop earrings, is wearing white shoes, and has a watch on her left wrist and a ring on one finger of her left hand.

13. The students all appear to be very attentive.

14. While some students are holding pen or pencil, none appears to be writing, and some even have notebooks closed.

15. There is a cane leaning on the wall right next to the door.

16. The room lighting is not visible.

17. The floor is made of square tiles.

18. On the floor in the foreground can be seen parts of three suitcases or large briefcases and two large plastic bags with something dark inside each.

19. Beside the teacher is a low table. On that table is a model of a woman's head and a spray bottle.

20. Behind the low table is a white cabinet with two doors. On top of the cabinet is a book and two small unidentifiable objects.

21. Part of a second white cabinet is visible beside the first.

22. In the left background is a sink with a depression in its front rim.

23. On a shelf behind the sink is a stack of unidentifiable objects.

24. Pasted on the wall over and around the door are sixteen separate pictures. Some of these feature only one woman; some have a number of smaller snapshots on a standard size background.

25. The largest number of separate heads one can count in any one of these pictures is seven. (Top picture of far left group.)

26. The part of the room to the right is deeper than that on the left.

27. There is a dark colored, molded shape chair behind the instructor.

28. Two students are supporting their chins with one hand. One student is using her left hand, the other her right.

29. Of all the students, only one is obviously wearing glasses.

30. One student is wearing high-heeled open shoes.

Exercise 5
Observation and Recognition of Faces

This exercise measures your ability to recognize the basic differences and similarities in the faces of people. Many alleged criminals being sought by the police disguise their facial features to make it difficult for the police to apprehend them. Aside from surgery, there are many things that the wanted person can do to make recognition difficult. The addition and removal of beards and mustaches, or even change in hair color or hair style, are relatively easy to accomplish. As noted previously, tinted contact lenses, now very common, can alter the color of eyes. However, there are some features that an individual cannot change easily. These are the features a police officer should concentrate on when attempting to identify wanted persons: the size, shape, and position of the ears; the shape of the jaw. The shape of the nose and the jaw are difficult to change without surgery. The police officer should also recognize that the wanted male with a distinctive jaw would likely try to disguise that feature by growing a beard.

DIRECTIONS: Answer the following ten questions by selecting the face, labeled (A), (B), (C), or (D), which is most likely to be the same as that of the suspect on the left. You are to assume that no surgery has taken place since the sketch of the suspect was made. Only observation and recognition are factors in this exercise. Do not try to memorize features of these faces. Circle the letter of the face you choose. Explanations follow the last question.

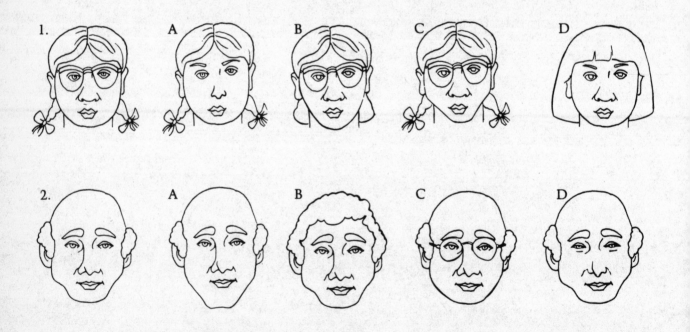

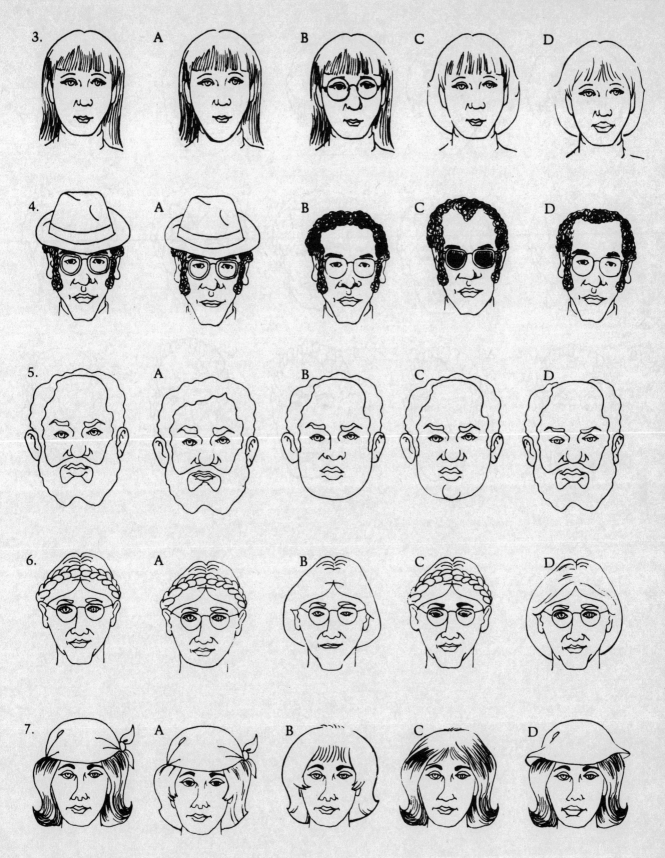

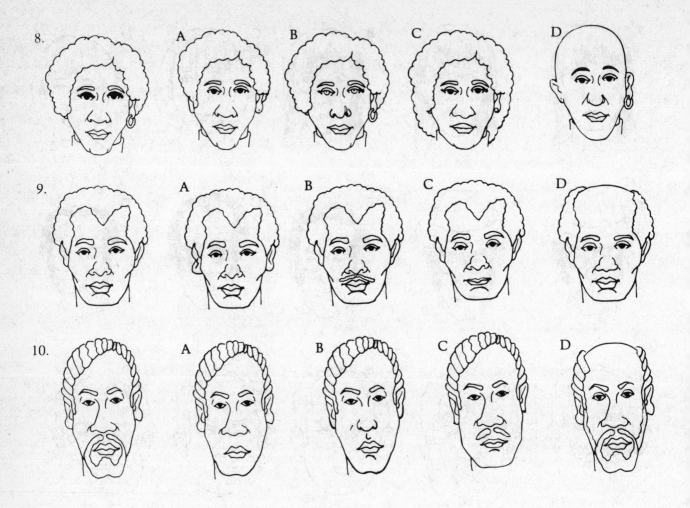

ANSWER KEY

1. D	3. C	5. C	7. B	9. B
2. B	4. D	6. D	8. A	10. A

ANSWER EXPLANATIONS

1. **(D)** Choice (A) has a different nose; (B) and (C) have different chins.

2. **(B)** Choice (A) has a longer face; (C) has a fuller face with different chin; (D) has a different nose.

3. **(C)** Choice (A) has a longer face; (B) has dark eyes; (D) has much fuller lips.

4. **(D)** Choice (A) has thinner lips; (B) has a different nose; (C) has different ears.

5. **(C)** Choice (A) has a different mouth; (B) has a different nose; (D) has different eyes.

6. **(D)** Choice (A) has a different chin; (B) has a different mouth; (C) has different eyes.

7. **(B)** Choice A has different eyes; (C) has a different nose; (D) has a different mouth.

8. **(A)** Choice (B) has different eyes and nose; (C) has a wider face at the jaw line; (D) has different nose and chin. It would appear that the original face has larger eyes than any of the choices. Be aware that makeup can create illusions in the original face as well as in the choices.

9. **(B)** Choice (A) has different ears; (C) has a different mouth; (D) has less prominent nostrils. The difference in hairline may also be significant. The original could be wearing a wig, but judging from his hairstyle that is unlikely.

10. **(A)** Choice (B) has a different nose; (C) has different ears; (D) has different eyes and, again, the original's hairline suggests that it is natural, not a wig.

ANSWER SHEET

NEW YORK CITY EXAM—OCTOBER 29, 1988

1. Ⓐ Ⓑ Ⓒ Ⓓ 2. Ⓐ Ⓑ Ⓒ Ⓓ 3. Ⓐ Ⓑ Ⓒ Ⓓ 4. Ⓐ Ⓑ Ⓒ Ⓓ 5. Ⓐ Ⓑ Ⓒ Ⓓ

6. Ⓐ Ⓑ Ⓒ Ⓓ 7. Ⓐ Ⓑ Ⓒ Ⓓ 8. Ⓐ Ⓑ Ⓒ Ⓓ 9. Ⓐ Ⓑ Ⓒ Ⓓ 10. Ⓐ Ⓑ Ⓒ Ⓓ

11. Ⓐ Ⓑ Ⓒ Ⓓ 12. Ⓐ Ⓑ Ⓒ Ⓓ 13. Ⓐ Ⓑ Ⓒ Ⓓ 14. Ⓐ Ⓑ Ⓒ Ⓓ 15. Ⓐ Ⓑ Ⓒ Ⓓ

16. Ⓐ Ⓑ Ⓒ Ⓓ 17. Ⓐ Ⓑ Ⓒ Ⓓ 18. Ⓐ Ⓑ Ⓒ Ⓓ 19. Ⓐ Ⓑ Ⓒ Ⓓ 20. Ⓐ Ⓑ Ⓒ Ⓓ

21. Ⓐ Ⓑ Ⓒ Ⓓ 22. Ⓐ Ⓑ Ⓒ Ⓓ 23. Ⓐ Ⓑ Ⓒ Ⓓ 24. Ⓐ Ⓑ Ⓒ Ⓓ 25. Ⓐ Ⓑ Ⓒ Ⓓ

26. Ⓐ Ⓑ Ⓒ Ⓓ 27. Ⓐ Ⓑ Ⓒ Ⓓ 28. Ⓐ Ⓑ Ⓒ Ⓓ 29. Ⓐ Ⓑ Ⓒ Ⓓ 30. Ⓐ Ⓑ Ⓒ Ⓓ

31. Ⓐ Ⓑ Ⓒ Ⓓ 32. Ⓐ Ⓑ Ⓒ Ⓓ 33. Ⓐ Ⓑ Ⓒ Ⓓ 34. Ⓐ Ⓑ Ⓒ Ⓓ 35. Ⓐ Ⓑ Ⓒ Ⓓ

36. Ⓐ Ⓑ Ⓒ Ⓓ 37. Ⓐ Ⓑ Ⓒ Ⓓ 38. Ⓐ Ⓑ Ⓒ Ⓓ 39. Ⓐ Ⓑ Ⓒ Ⓓ 40. Ⓐ Ⓑ Ⓒ Ⓓ

41. Ⓐ Ⓑ Ⓒ Ⓓ 42. Ⓐ Ⓑ Ⓒ Ⓓ 43. Ⓐ Ⓑ Ⓒ Ⓓ 44. Ⓐ Ⓑ Ⓒ Ⓓ 45. Ⓐ Ⓑ Ⓒ Ⓓ

46. Ⓐ Ⓑ Ⓒ Ⓓ 47. Ⓐ Ⓑ Ⓒ Ⓓ 48. Ⓐ Ⓑ Ⓒ Ⓓ 49. Ⓐ Ⓑ Ⓒ Ⓓ 50. Ⓐ Ⓑ Ⓒ Ⓓ

51. Ⓐ Ⓑ Ⓒ Ⓓ 52. Ⓐ Ⓑ Ⓒ Ⓓ 53. Ⓐ Ⓑ Ⓒ Ⓓ 54. Ⓐ Ⓑ Ⓒ Ⓓ 55. Ⓐ Ⓑ Ⓒ Ⓓ

56. Ⓐ Ⓑ Ⓒ Ⓓ 57. Ⓐ Ⓑ Ⓒ Ⓓ 58. Ⓐ Ⓑ Ⓒ Ⓓ 59. Ⓐ Ⓑ Ⓒ Ⓓ 60. Ⓐ Ⓑ Ⓒ Ⓓ

61. Ⓐ Ⓑ Ⓒ Ⓓ 62. Ⓐ Ⓑ Ⓒ Ⓓ 63. Ⓐ Ⓑ Ⓒ Ⓓ 64. Ⓐ Ⓑ Ⓒ Ⓓ 65. Ⓐ Ⓑ Ⓒ Ⓓ

66. Ⓐ Ⓑ Ⓒ Ⓓ 67. Ⓐ Ⓑ Ⓒ Ⓓ 68. Ⓐ Ⓑ Ⓒ Ⓓ 69. Ⓐ Ⓑ Ⓒ Ⓓ 70. Ⓐ Ⓑ Ⓒ Ⓓ

71. Ⓐ Ⓑ Ⓒ Ⓓ 72. Ⓐ Ⓑ Ⓒ Ⓓ 73. Ⓐ Ⓑ Ⓒ Ⓓ 74. Ⓐ Ⓑ Ⓒ Ⓓ 75. Ⓐ Ⓑ Ⓒ Ⓓ

76. Ⓐ Ⓑ Ⓒ Ⓓ 77. Ⓐ Ⓑ Ⓒ Ⓓ 78. Ⓐ Ⓑ Ⓒ Ⓓ 79. Ⓐ Ⓑ Ⓒ Ⓓ 80. Ⓐ Ⓑ Ⓒ Ⓓ

81. Ⓐ Ⓑ Ⓒ Ⓓ 82. Ⓐ Ⓑ Ⓒ Ⓓ 83. Ⓐ Ⓑ Ⓒ Ⓓ 84. Ⓐ Ⓑ Ⓒ Ⓓ 85. Ⓐ Ⓑ Ⓒ Ⓓ

86. Ⓐ Ⓑ Ⓒ Ⓓ 87. Ⓐ Ⓑ Ⓒ Ⓓ 88. Ⓐ Ⓑ Ⓒ Ⓓ 89. Ⓐ Ⓑ Ⓒ Ⓓ 90. Ⓐ Ⓑ Ⓒ Ⓓ

91. Ⓐ Ⓑ Ⓒ Ⓓ 92. Ⓐ Ⓑ Ⓒ Ⓓ 93. Ⓐ Ⓑ Ⓒ Ⓓ 94. Ⓐ Ⓑ Ⓒ Ⓓ 95. Ⓐ Ⓑ Ⓒ Ⓓ

96. Ⓐ Ⓑ Ⓒ Ⓓ 97. Ⓐ Ⓑ Ⓒ Ⓓ 98. Ⓐ Ⓑ Ⓒ Ⓓ 99. Ⓐ Ⓑ Ⓒ Ⓓ 100. Ⓐ Ⓑ Ⓒ Ⓓ

101. Ⓐ Ⓑ Ⓒ Ⓓ 102. Ⓐ Ⓑ Ⓒ Ⓓ 103. Ⓐ Ⓑ Ⓒ Ⓓ 104. Ⓐ Ⓑ Ⓒ Ⓓ 105. Ⓐ Ⓑ Ⓒ Ⓓ

106. Ⓐ Ⓑ Ⓒ Ⓓ 107. Ⓐ Ⓑ Ⓒ Ⓓ 108. Ⓐ Ⓑ Ⓒ Ⓓ 109. Ⓐ Ⓑ Ⓒ Ⓓ 110. Ⓐ Ⓑ Ⓒ Ⓓ

111. Ⓐ Ⓑ Ⓒ Ⓓ 112. Ⓐ Ⓑ Ⓒ Ⓓ 113. Ⓐ Ⓑ Ⓒ Ⓓ 114. Ⓐ Ⓑ Ⓒ Ⓓ 115. Ⓐ Ⓑ Ⓒ Ⓓ

116. Ⓐ Ⓑ Ⓒ Ⓓ 117. Ⓐ Ⓑ Ⓒ Ⓓ 118. Ⓐ Ⓑ Ⓒ Ⓓ 119. Ⓐ Ⓑ Ⓒ Ⓓ 120. Ⓐ Ⓑ Ⓒ Ⓓ

121. Ⓐ Ⓑ Ⓒ Ⓓ 122. Ⓐ Ⓑ Ⓒ Ⓓ 123. Ⓐ Ⓑ Ⓒ Ⓓ 124. Ⓐ Ⓑ Ⓒ Ⓓ 125. Ⓐ Ⓑ Ⓒ Ⓓ

126. Ⓐ Ⓑ Ⓒ Ⓓ 127. Ⓐ Ⓑ Ⓒ Ⓓ 128. Ⓐ Ⓑ Ⓒ Ⓓ 129. Ⓐ Ⓑ Ⓒ Ⓓ 130. Ⓐ Ⓑ Ⓒ Ⓓ

131. Ⓐ Ⓑ Ⓒ Ⓓ 132. Ⓐ Ⓑ Ⓒ Ⓓ 133. Ⓐ Ⓑ Ⓒ Ⓓ 134. Ⓐ Ⓑ Ⓒ Ⓓ 135. Ⓐ Ⓑ Ⓒ Ⓓ

136. Ⓐ Ⓑ Ⓒ Ⓓ 137. Ⓐ Ⓑ Ⓒ Ⓓ 138. Ⓐ Ⓑ Ⓒ Ⓓ 139. Ⓐ Ⓑ Ⓒ Ⓓ 140. Ⓐ Ⓑ Ⓒ Ⓓ

141. Ⓐ Ⓑ Ⓒ Ⓓ 142. Ⓐ Ⓑ Ⓒ Ⓓ 143. Ⓐ Ⓑ Ⓒ Ⓓ 144. Ⓐ Ⓑ Ⓒ Ⓓ 145. Ⓐ Ⓑ Ⓒ Ⓓ

146. Ⓐ Ⓑ Ⓒ Ⓓ 147. Ⓐ Ⓑ Ⓒ Ⓓ 148. Ⓐ Ⓑ Ⓒ Ⓓ 149. Ⓐ Ⓑ Ⓒ Ⓓ 150. Ⓐ Ⓑ Ⓒ Ⓓ

TEAR HERE

Practice Examination 1

Department of Personnel

Social Security No. _____
Room No. _____
Seat No. _____
School _____

Police Officer Series
Examination No. 7197

First Memory Booklet
October 29, 1988

DO NOT OPEN THIS BOOKLET UNTIL THE SECOND SIGNAL IS GIVEN!

Write your Social Security Number, Room Number, Seat Number, and School in the appropriate spaces at the top of this page.

You *must* follow the instructions found on the TEST INSTRUCTION SHEET.

ANYONE DISOBEYING ANY OF THE INSTRUCTIONS FOUND ON THE TEST INSTRUCTION SHEET MAY BE DISQUALIFIED— RECEIVE A ZERO ON THE ENTIRE TEST.

This booklet contains one scene. Try to remember as many details in the scene as you can. You should pay equal attention both to objects and to people shown in the scene.

DO *NOT* WRITE OR MAKE *ANY* NOTES WHILE STUDYING THE SCENE.

DO NOT OPEN THIS BOOKLET UNTIL THE
SECOND SIGNAL IS GIVEN!

[NOTE: You will have five (5) minutes to study the scene shown.]

The New York City Department of Personnel makes no commitment, and no inference is to be drawn, regarding the content, style, or format of any future examination for the position of Police Officer.

DEPARTMENT OF PERSONNEL

Social Security No. _____

Room No. _____

Seat No. _____

School _____

POLICE OFFICER SERIES
EXAMINATION NO. 7197

Second Memory Booklet
October 29, 1988

DO NOT OPEN THIS BOOKLET UNTIL THE FOURTH SIGNAL IS GIVEN!

Write your Social Security Number, Room Number, Seat Number, and School in the appropriate spaces at the top of this page.

You *must* follow the instructions found on the TEST INSTRUCTION SHEET.

ANYONE DISOBEYING ANY OF THE INSTRUCTIONS FOUND ON THE TEST INSTRUCTION SHEET MAY BE DISQUALIFIED— RECEIVE A ZERO ON THE ENTIRE TEST.

This booklet contains Questions 1 through 6, which are based on Scene 1 as shown in the First Memory Booklet. Answer Questions 1 through 6 after the fourth signal. At the *FIFTH SIGNAL*, you should turn to Scene 2. Try to remember as many details in the scene as you can. You should pay equal attention both to objects and to people shown in the scene.

DO NOT OPEN THIS BOOKLET UNTIL THE FOURTH SIGNAL IS GIVEN!

[Note: You will have five (5) minutes to study the scene shown.]

The New York City Department of Personnel makes no commitment, and no inference is to be drawn, regarding the content, style, or format of any future examination for the position of Police Officer.

Answer questions 1 through 6 solely on the basis of sketch number 1.

1. Which one of the following vehicles is parked on Elm Road?

   (A) A police car
   (B) An ambulance
   (C) A tow truck
   (D) A fire truck.

2. What are the words printed on the side of the bus?

   (A) Northside Bus   (C) Eastside Bus
   (B) Southside Bus   (D) Westside Bus.

3. The man with the gun is wearing a

   (A) white shirt with black stripes
   (B) tee shirt with the words SPOT NEWS
   (C) sweat shirt with the word ACE
   (D) white shirt with black dots.

4. The taxi which is being repaired is parked in a

   (A) No Standing Zone
   (B) No Parking Zone
   (C) Towaway Zone
   (D) Authorized Vehicles Only Zone.

5. The license plate number of the vehicle which is closest to the person lying on the street is

   (A) G498   (C) 302L
   (B) 8K46   (D) 31S4.

6. The person in the second floor window is directly above

   (A) Uncle Dan's Lunch
   (B) Mandley Discount Clothing Outlet
   (C) Cafeteria Europa
   (D) M & P Music World.

DEPARTMENT OF PERSONNEL

Social Security No. _____
Room No. _____
Seat No. _____
School _____

POLICE OFFICER SERIES
EXAMINATION NO. 7197

Question Booklet
October 29, 1988

Written Test: Weight 100
Time Allowed: 4½ Hours

DO NOT OPEN THIS BOOKLET UNTIL THE SEVENTH SIGNAL IS GIVEN!

Record your answers on the Official Answer Sheet before the last signal. If you wish, you may also record your answers in the Question Booklet before the last signal is given. This will be your only official record of answers.

This Question Booklet contains procedures and definitions which are to be used to answer certain questions. These procedures and definitions are not necessarily those of the New York City Police Department. However, you are to answer these questions solely on the basis of the material given.

After the seventh signal is given, open this Question Booklet and begin to work. You will have 4½ hours to complete this test. Answer questions 7 through 11 before answering any other questions.

You may make notes in this booklet and use the scrap paper on your desk. If you need additional scrap paper, ask the monitor.

Remember, only your Official Answer Sheet will be rated, so be sure to mark *all* your answers on the Official Answer Sheet before the eighth signal. *No additional time* will be given for marking your answers after the test has ended.

DO NOT OPEN THIS BOOKLET UNTIL THE SEVENTH SIGNAL IS GIVEN!

The New York City Department of Personnel makes no commitment, and no inference is to be drawn, regarding the content, style, or format of any future examination for the position of Police Officer.

Answer questions 7 through 11 solely on the basis of sketch 2.

7. The robbery at knifepoint is occurring on

   (A) The corner of Brady Avenue and E. 7th Street
   (B) Brady Avenue in front of Mario's Pizza Hole
   (C) The corner of Brady Avenue and W. 7th Street
   (D) Brady Avenue in front of Sparta Senior Center.

8. The street musician is standing closest to

   (A) Crane Hotel
   (B) The subway entrance
   (C) Mario's Pizza Hole
   (D) Blair Savings Bank.

9. The youth holding the knife is wearing a

   (A) black ski cap, plaid shirt, and white pants
   (B) white ski cap, plaid shirt, and black pants
   (C) black baseball cap, white shirt, and plaid pants
   (D) white baseball cap, white shirt, and black pants.

10. Which one of the following best describes the person holding the gun?

    (A) White male, white pants, and a plaid shirt.
    (B) Asian male, black pants, and a heart print shirt.
    (C) White male, plaid pants, and a black jacket.
    (D) Black male, black pants, and a white jacket.

11. What is the number on the shirt of the man running towards the subway?

    (A) 49
    (B) 54
    (C) 45
    (D) 94.

Please check your Answer Sheet to make sure that you have written in and blackened your Social Security number correctly. If you have not yet written in and blackened your Social Security number, please do so immediately. If you have incorrectly written in or blackened your Social Security number, please correct the mistake immediately. Failure to correctly blacken your Social Security number may result in your Answer Sheet NOT being rated.

Answer questions 12 through 14 solely on the basis of the following passage.

At 11:30 P.M., while parked in front of 945 Howard Street, Police Officers Abbott and Johnson received a radio call of a family dispute at 779 Seward Street, Apartment 1928. The radio dispatcher informed the Officers that the call came from Mrs. Debra Lacoste who lives in Apartment 1930. The officers arrived at the location and heard yelling and screaming. When the Officers knocked on the door a woman crying hysterically opened the door. The woman, Gloria Ross, informed the Officers that her husband, Sam Ross, was in her apartment. She said he was drunk, had yelled at her, and had made threats to hurt her if she did not let him see his children. Mrs. Ross then presented a letter to Officer Abbott, which he recognized as being an Order of Protection issued by Family Court. The Order of Protection stated that Mr. Ross was not to be seen anywhere near his wife, including her residence and place of employment. Furthermore, the Order stated that he had no right to see the children or to yell at his wife or use obscene language in his wife's presence. Mrs. Ross told the Officer that she wanted her husband arrested for violating the Order of Protection. Officer Johnson quickly read the Order of Protection and informed Officer Abbott that the Order was valid. Officer Abbott ordered Sam Ross to turn around with his hands behind his back and Officer Abbott handcuffed him and placed him under arrest.

12. Which of the following persons first made the authorities aware of the family dispute?

    (A) A neighbor
    (B) The victim
    (C) A Police Officer
    (D) The suspect.

13. The Police Officers responded to a report of a disturbance at

    (A) 945 Howard Street, Apartment 1928
    (B) 779 Seward Street, Apartment 1930
    (C) 779 Seward Street, Apartment 1928
    (D) 945 Howard Street, Apartment 1930.

14. Which of the following actions caused Mr. Ross to be arrested?

    (A) He called his children on the telephone.
    (B) He tried to visit his children.
    (C) He waited for his wife in front of her job.
    (D) He yelled at his children.

Answer question 15 solely on the basis of the following information.

Sexual Abuse 3rd Degree—occurs when a person intentionally subjects an individual to sexual contact without the individual's consent.

15. Which one of the following situations is the best example of Sexual Abuse in the Third Degree?

(A) Joe is riding a crowded train and bumps into JoAnn when the train comes to a sudden stop.

(B) When Jean carelessly steps on Bob's toe, Bob curses at her and uses sexually explicit language.

(C) John is standing on a crowded train and starts rubbing himself against a woman's buttocks.

(D) Bill accidentally brushes his newspaper against a woman's chest while he is reading on a crowded train.

Answer question 16 solely on the basis of the following information.

Police Officers are required to provide assistance to sick or injured persons. Upon arrival at the scene of a sick or injured person a Police Officer should do the following in the order given:

1. Give reasonable aid to the sick or injured person.
2. Request an ambulance or doctor, if necessary.
3. Wait outside to direct the ambulance, or have some responsible person do so.
4. Make a second call in 20 minutes if ambulance does not arrive.

16. Police Officer Jones, while on patrol, is approached by John Rutherford who informs the Officer that his business partner, Silvio Monteleone, tripped on the 5th floor stairs outside his apartment located at 1276 Stork Lane. When Officer Jones and Rutherford arrive at the scene, the Officer finds that Silvio may have broken his right arm. At 12:20 P.M. Officer Jones radios for an ambulance to take Silvio to the hospital. While waiting, Officer Jones attempts to locate a blanket to place over Silvio who is lying on a cold tile floor. After knocking at three apartments, Officer Jones receives a blanket from Mrs. Flores. It is now 12:35 P.M. and the ambulance has not arrived. The next step Officer Jones should take is to

(A) call his patrol supervisor

(B) send Silvio's friend John down to the street to direct the medical personnel

(C) call the ambulance a second time to request assistance

(D) radio for a patrol car to transport Silvio to the hospital

17. Sergeant Burroughs assigns Police Officer Holland to patrol the area between Webster and St. Paul Avenues. She informs Officer Holland that over the past month there has been a sharp increase in the number of burglaries. She instructs Officer Holland to pay close attention to any suspicious activities. To which one of the following situations should Officer Holland give the most attention?

(A) Two young children who knock on doors and run away.
(B) Two teenagers who live around the corner, sitting on the stairs of a building listening to the radio.
(C) A group of elderly men sitting on a bench in front of a row of buildings.
(D) Two men going from door to door asking if Mr. Jones is home.

18. While on patrol, Police Officer Fuentes is approached by a woman who states that she has just been robbed. Officer Fuentes obtains the following information relating to the robbery:

Place of Occurrence:	168 Delancey Street
Time of Occurrence:	5 minutes earlier
Description of Suspect:	Male, white, 6 feet tall, wearing a black jacket, grey pants, and white sneakers
Direction of Flight:	Northbound on Delancey Street

Officer Fuentes radios this information to the other Officers. Which one of the following expresses the above information *most clearly* and *accurately*?

(A) I have a robbery. The suspect is six feet tall wearing a black jacket, grey pants, and white sneakers. The robbery occurred five minutes ago at 168 Delancey Street. A white male fled northbound on Delancey Street.
(B) A robbery occurred five minutes ago at 168 Delancey Street. The suspect fled northbound on Delancey Street. He is a white male, approximately 6 feet tall, wearing a black jacket, grey pants, and white sneakers.
(C) I have a robbery. The suspect fled northbound on Delancey Street and is a male, approximately 6 feet tall five minutes ago. Suspect is white and is wearing a black jacket, grey pants, and white sneakers. The robbery occurred at 168 Delancey Street.
(D) A robbery has occurred at 168 Delancey Street. The suspect is wearing white sneakers. He fled northbound wearing a black jacket on Delancey Street and he is approximately 6 feet tall, wearing grey pants. The robbery took place five minutes ago with a white male.

19. Police Officer Waters was the first person at the scene of a fire which may have been the result of arson. He obtained the following information:

Place of Occurrence:	35 John Street, Apartment 27
Time of Occurrence:	4:00 P.M.
Witness:	Daisy Logan
Incident:	Fire (possible Arson)
Suspect:	Male, white, approximately 18 years old, wearing blue jeans and a plaid shirt, running away from incident.

Officer Waters is completing a report on the incident. Which one of the following expresses the above information *most clearly* and *accurately*?

(A) At 4:00 P.M., Daisy Logan saw a white male, approximately 18 years old who was wearing blue jeans and a plaid shirt, running from the scene of a fire at 35 John Street, Apartment 27.

(B) Seeing a fire at 35 John Street, a white male approximately 18 years old, wearing blue jeans and a plaid shirt was seen running from Apartment 27 at 4:00 P.M. reported Daisy Logan.

(C) Approximately 18 years old and wearing blue jeans and a plaid shirt, Daisy Logan saw a fire and a white male running from 35 John Street, Apartment 27 at 4:00 P.M.

(D) Running from 35 John Street, Apartment 27, the scene of the fire, reported Daisy Logan at 4:00 P.M., was a white male approximately 18 years old and wearing blue jeans and a plaid shirt.

20. Police Officer Sullivan obtained the following information at the scene of a two-car accident:

Place of Occurrence:	2971 William Street
Drivers and Vehicles Involved:	Mrs. Wilson, driver of blue 1984 Toyota Camry; Mr. Bailey, driver of white 1981 Dodge Omni
Injuries Sustained:	Mr. Bailey had a swollen right eye; Mrs. Wilson had a broken left hand

Which one of the following expresses the above information *most clearly* and *accurately*?

(A) Mr. Bailey, owner of a white, 1981 Dodge Omni, at 2971 William Street, had a swollen right eye. Mrs. Wilson, with a broken left hand, is the owner of the blue 1984 Toyota Camry. They were in a car accident.

(B) Mrs. Wilson got a broken left hand and Mr. Bailey a swollen right eye at 2971 William Street. The vehicles involved in the car accident were a 1981 Dodge Omni, white, owned by Mr. Bailey, and Mrs. Wilson's blue 1984 Toyota Camry.

(C) Mrs. Wilson, the driver of the blue 1984 Toyota Camry, and Mr. Bailey, the driver of the white 1981 Dodge Omni, were involved in a car accident at 2971 William Street. Mr. Bailey sustained a swollen right eye, and Mrs. Wilson broke her left hand.

(D) Mr. Bailey sustained a swollen right eye and Mrs. Wilson broke her left hand in a car accident at 2971 William Street. They owned a 1981 white Dodge Omni and a 1984 blue Toyota Camry.

Answer question 21 solely on the basis of the following information.

When a Police Officer observes a person who is in possession of a firearm, the Officer is required to:

1. Ask the person to produce identification and the pistol license.
2. Verify the pistol license, if it is questionable, by telephoning the New York City Police Department License Division during business hours between 9:00 A.M. and 5:00 P.M., Monday to Friday.
3. Make an Activity Log entry including the person's name, address, date of birth, and the pistol license number and expiration date.
4. Remove person to station house if license has expired.
5. If license is valid, return all identification and notify Desk Officer.

21. At 3:00 P.M. on September 10, 1988, Police Officer Rogers sees a man walking towards him with a gun in his waistband. The Officer stops the man and asks him for identification and his pistol license. The man gives the Officer his pistol license and driver's license. The information on the pistol license identifies the man as John Wilson, residing at 4 Auburn Street, Apt. #1B. Mr. Wilson is 34 years old, and was born on May 15, 1954. His pistol license number is 71554, and the expiration date is September 9, 1988. His driver's license indicates the same name, address, and date of birth. The Officer makes an Activity Log entry listing all of the required information obtained from Mr. Wilson, returns both licenses to him, and then notifies the Desk Officer. In this situation, the actions taken by Officer Rogers were

(A) proper, primarily because Mr. Wilson was not a New York City resident
(B) improper, primarily because the Officer did not verify the pistol license with the License Division
(C) proper, primarily because he returned the pistol license to Mr. Wilson and notified the Desk Officer that the license was valid
(D) improper, primarily because Mr. Wilson should have been brought to the station house.

Answer question 22 solely on the basis of the following information.

Police Officers must sometimes rely on eyewitness accounts of incidents, even though eyewitnesses may make mistakes with regard to some details.

22. Police Officer Colon responded to a report of a purse snatch on 110th Street. Upon arrival at the scene she interviewed the complainant, Mrs. Smith, and three other witnesses who had been standing at a bus stop. The witnesses saw two men fleeing from the scene in a black car. The following are license plate numbers provided by the complainant and witnesses. Which one of these numbers should Officer Colon consider most likely to be correct?

(A) P-51856
(B) T-58166
(C) P-51886
(D) T-41685

Answer question 23 solely on the basis of the following information.

When Police Officers receive a report of a missing person they should do the following in the order given:

1. Report to the location of the complainant who reported the missing person.
2. Interview the complainant.
3. Obtain a physical description of the missing person and a description of the clothes worn by the missing person.
4. Determine where the missing person was last seen.
5. Start a search at the location where the missing person was last seen.
6. Request a Patrol Supervisor to respond to the scene.

23. Police Officer Jane Anderson responds to a report of a missing 15-year-old at 187 Rockwell Avenue, Apt. 6F. The teenager's mother, the complainant, informs Officer Anderson that her son is 5'5", 140 lbs., and was wearing a red striped shirt and black shorts. Police Officer Anderson should next

   (A) search the apartment building for the teenager
   (B) begin searching the neighborhood
   (C) ask the mother where her son was last seen
   (D) request a Patrol Supervisor to respond to the scene.

Answer question 24 solely on the basis of the following information.

Grand Larceny 4th Degree—occurs when a person steals property and:

1. the value of the property is more than one thousand dollars; or
2. the property, regardless of its nature and value, is taken from the victim; or
3. the property consists of one or more firearms.

24. Which one of the following is the best example of Grand Larceny in the Fourth Degree?

   (A) Samuel, a security guard working at Beacon's Warehouse, enters an unauthorized area and steals a clock radio.
   (B) Jonathan enters Lacy's Department Store, loads $500 worth of merchandise into a large shopping bag, and leaves the store.
   (C) Harry is walking down the street at night when a shabbily dressed woman pulls out a gun and tells him to put his hands up.
   (D) Mildred discovers that the man, who just bumped into her, has stolen her wallet containing $20 in cash from her pants pocket.

25. Officer Johnson has issued a summons to a driver and has obtained the following information:

Place of Occurrence:	Corner of Foster Road and Woodrow Avenue
Time of Occurrence:	7:10 P.M.
Driver:	William Grant
Offense:	Driving through a red light
Age of Driver:	42
Address of Driver:	23 Richmond Avenue

Officer Johnson is making an entry in his memo book regarding the incident. Which one of the following expresses the above information *most clearly* and *accurately*?

(A) William Grant, lives at 23 Richmond Avenue at 7:10 P.M., went through a red light. He was issued a summons at the corner of Foster Road and Woodrow Avenue. The driver is 42 years old.

(B) William Grant, age 42, who lives at 23 Richmond Avenue, was issued a summons for going through a red light at 7:10 P.M. at the corner of Foster Road and Woodrow Avenue.

(C) William Grant, age 42, was issued a summons on the corner of Foster Road and Woodrow Avenue for going through a red light. He lives at 23 Richmond Avenue at 7:10 P.M.

(D) A 42-year-old man who lives at 23 Richmond Avenue was issued a summons at 7:10 P.M. William Grant went through a red light at the corner of Foster Road and Woodrow Avenue.

26. Police Officer Frome has completed investigating a report of a stolen auto and obtained the following information:

Date of Occurrence:	October 26, 1988
Place of Occurrence:	51st Street and 8th Avenue
Time of Occurrence:	3:30 P.M.
Crime:	Auto Theft
Suspect:	Michael Wadsworth
Action Taken:	Suspect arrested

Officer Frome is preparing a report on the incident. Which one of the following expresses the above information *most clearly* and *accurately*?

(A) Arrested on October 26, 1988 was a stolen auto at 51st Street and 8th Avenue at 3:30 P.M. driven by Michael Wadsworth.

(B) For driving a stolen auto at 3:30 P.M., Michael Wadsworth was arrested at 51st Street and 8th Avenue on October 26, 1988.

(C) On October 26, 1988 at 3:30 P.M. Michael Wadsworth was arrested at 51st Street and 8th Avenue for driving a stolen auto.

(D) Michael Wadsworth was arrested on October 26, 1988 at 3:30 P.M. for driving at 51st Street and 8th Avenue. The auto was stolen.

Answer questions 27 and 28 solely on the basis of the following information.

As a result of numerous interviews of complainants and witnesses of violent crimes, Officer Wells has noticed a serious rise in the number of certain crimes in his patrol area over the past three months. He has observed that most of the rapes take place on E. 98th Street between Lott Avenue and Herk Place; assaults happen on Lott Avenue between Chester Avenue and E. 98th Street; and the majority of the robberies occur on Lott Avenue between E. 98th Street and Hughes Place. The assaults take place between 1:00 A.M. and 3:00 A.M. All of the robberies happen between 1:00 A.M. and 6:00 A.M. and most of the rapes happen between 8:00 A.M. and 11:00 A.M. The rapes usually occur on Mondays and Wednesdays, the robberies on Fridays and Saturdays, and the assaults on Saturdays and Sundays.

27. Officer Wells would most effectively reduce the number of robberies by patrolling

(A) Lott Avenue between E. 98th Street and Hughes Place on Fridays and Saturdays between 1:00 A.M. and 8:00 A.M.
(B) Lott Avenue between E. 98th Street and Chester Avenue on Saturdays and Sundays between 1:00 A.M. and 6:00 A.M.
(C) E. 98th Street between Lott Avenue and Herk Place on Saturdays and Sundays between 1:00 A.M. and 3:00 A.M.
(D) E. 98th Street between Herk Place and Chester Avenue on Mondays and Wednesdays between 8:00 A.M. and 11:00 A.M.

28. Officer Wells has been informed by his supervisor that he will be assigned to a patrol each week that would allow him to concentrate on reducing the number of rapes. What would be the most appropriate patrol for Officer Wells to work?

(A) Tuesday through Saturday, 8:00 P.M. to 4:00 P.M.
(B) Monday through Friday, 7:30 A.M. to 3:30 P.M.
(C) Wednesday through Sunday, noon to 8:00 P.M.
(D) Monday through Friday, 3:00 P.M. to 11:00 P.M.

29. Police Officers are required to remove potentially dangerous property from a prisoner prior to placing him in a jail cell. Which of the following items should be removed from a prisoner?

(A) An empty wallet.
(B) A gold wedding ring.
(C) A box of cough drops.
(D) A pair of shoe laces.

Answer question 30 solely on the basis of the following information.

When a Police Officer makes an arrest, the Officer should do the following in the order given:

1. Inform the prisoner of the reason for the arrest.
2. Handcuff the prisoner's hands behind his back.
3. Search the prisoner and the nearby area for weapons and evidence.
4. Advise the prisoner of his legal rights before questioning.

30. Police Officer Golden arrests Roy Owen and informs Mr. Owen that he is being arrested for the robbery of a jewelry store. While properly handcuffing the prisoner, the Officer notices a small handgun in Mr. Owen's back pants pocket. The Officer finishes handcuffing the prisoner and then removes the handgun from his pants pocket. The Officer should next

(A) inform the prisoner of his rights
(B) question the prisoner
(C) return, with the prisoner, to the jewelry store
(D) search the prisoner and the immediate area for weapons and evidence.

31. Police Officer Wright has finished investigating a report of Grand Larceny and has obtained the following information:

Time of Occurrence:	Between 1:00 P.M. and 2:00 P.M.
Place of Occurrence:	In front of victim's home, 85 Montgomery Avenue
Victim:	Mr. Williams, owner of the vehicle
Crime:	Automobile broken into
Property Taken:	Stereo valued at $1,200

Officer Wright is preparing a report on the incident. Which one of the following expresses the above information *most clearly* and *accurately*?

(A) While parked in front of his home Mr. Williams states that between 1:00 P.M. and 2:00 P.M. an unknown person broke into his vehicle. Mr. Williams, who lives at 85 Montgomery Avenue, lost his $1,200 stereo.
(B) Mr. Williams, who lives at 85 Montgomery Avenue, states that between 1:00 P.M. and 2:00 P.M. his vehicle was parked in front of his home when an unknown person broke into his car and took his stereo worth $1,200.
(C) Mr. Williams was parked in front of 85 Montgomery Avenue, which is his home, when it was robbed of a $1,200 stereo. When he came out he observed between 1:00 P.M. and 2:00 P.M. that his car had been broken into by an unknown person.
(D) Mr. Williams states between 1:00 P.M. and 2:00 P.M. that an unknown person broke into his car in front of his home. Mr. Williams further states that he was robbed of a $1,200 stereo at 85 Montgomery Avenue.

Answer questions 32 through 35 solely on the basis of the following passage.

Police Officers Grice and Sexton were working a 4:00 P.M. to midnight tour of duty on Friday, December 5, when they were assigned to investigate a burglary. They were told to respond to 355 Grand Street, the 14th floor, Apartment 1402, and to speak to the complainant, Ms. Starr. Upon arrival, Officer Sexton interviewed Ms. Starr, who stated that when she returned home from work at approximately 6:10 P.M. she was unable to unlock her door because the keyhole had been stuffed with toothpicks. After the door was opened by building maintenance, she entered her apartment and saw that her jewelry box had been emptied and was laying on the floor.

Officer Grice, who is qualified in the recovery of fingerprints, dusted the jewelry box and the front door in an attempt to recover any fingerprints that the burglar may have left. The Officers also interviewed Mrs. Caputo, who lives in Apartment 1404 and Mr. Babbit who lives in Apartment 1407. Both individuals stated that they neither saw nor heard anything unusual.

The next night, Saturday, December 6, Officers Grice and Sexton responded to Apartment 1514 in the same building on a call of a burglary. The complainant, Ms. Chung, stated that when she returned home from shopping she discovered that her lock had been stuffed with chewing gum and that her apartment had been burglarized. Officer Grice dusted the front door and a dresser, which had been opened, for prints.

Ten days after the last burglary, Detective Carrano, who had been assigned to investigate the burglaries, was informed by Mr. Hunt of the fingerprint identification unit that the prints recovered from both apartments belonged to Peter Remo of 355 Gravel Street, Apartment 1705. Later that evening after obtaining an arrest warrant, Detective Carrano arrested Peter Remo for the burglaries.

32. Who lived on the same floor as Ms. Starr?

(A) Ms. Chung (C) Mr. Babbit
(B) Peter Remo (D) Mr. Hunt.

33. Who was responsible for recovering the fingerprints that were used to identify Peter Remo?

(A) Officer Grice (C) Detective Carrano
(B) Mr. Hunt (D) Officer Sexton.

34. When was Peter Remo arrested?

(A) December 5 (C) December 15
(B) December 6 (D) December 16.

35. Why was Ms. Starr unable to unlock her door?

(A) She lost her keys.
(B) Chewing gum had been stuffed into the lock.
(C) Her keys had been taken from her jewelry box.
(D) The lock was stuffed with toothpicks.

Answer question 36 solely on the basis of the following information.

Upon arriving at the scene of any offense committed between members of the same family or household, a Police Officer should do the following in the order given:

1. Ascertain all the facts.
2. Obtain medical assistance, if needed.
3. Determine whether:
   a. a family offense has been committed; or
   b. an Order of Protection has been obtained by the complainant in order to keep the offender from entering the complainant's home or workplace.
4. Begin a search of the immediate area for the offender, if the offender has fled the scene.
5. If the search produces no results advise the complainant/victim to call the police when the offender returns.
6. Prepare a Complaint Report.

36. Police Officer Laura Molina responds to 285 Oak Street, Apartment 3A, in regard to a possible violent family offense. Upon arrival, Police Officer Molina is met at the apartment door by Ms. Martin. Officer Molina notices that Ms. Martin had been bleeding from a cut over her right eye. Ms. Martin tells Police Officer Molina that she and her husband had been having serious marital problems for the past six months. She said that just last week she had gotten an Order of Protection against her husband. However, her husband had returned to their home drunk and hit her on the head with a glass bottle. Police Officer Molina noticed broken glass on the floor in the living room. Police Officer Molina asked Ms. Martin if she needed an ambulance, but Ms. Martin told the Officer that she did not. Ms. Martin further explained that after her husband hit her, he ran out of the apartment. Ms. Martin added that he was wearing white sneakers, green army fatigue pants, and a light blue shirt. The next step P.O. Molina should take is to

(A) call an ambulance
(B) search the area for Mr. Martin
(C) prepare a Complaint Report
(D) advise Ms. Martin to call the police when her husband returns.

Answer question 37 solely on the basis of the following information.

When handcuffing a prisoner, a Police Officer should:

1. Handcuff person with hands behind his back.
2. Search person for weapons, evidence, or contraband.
3. Escort person to station house and inform the supervisor of the charges.
4. Remove handcuffs and place the person in a cell.

37. While on patrol, Police Officer Lewis arrests Robert Hendricks for assaulting his wife, Mrs. Hendricks. Police Officer Davis, who is also on patrol, arrives to assist Officer Lewis and observes her handcuffing the prisoner with his hands in front of his body. When Officer Lewis begins to search the prisoner for weapons, the prisoner swings his arms around and hits Officer Lewis on the side of the head. Officer Davis then steps in to subdue the prisoner. A patrol car arrives to transport the prisoner to the station house. There, Officer Lewis informs the Supervisor of the charges against the prisoner, removes the handcuffs, and places him in a cell. In this situation, Officer Lewis' actions were

   (A) improper, primarily because she should not have removed the handcuffs from the prisoner until he was safely in his cell
   (B) proper, primarily because she did not place the handcuffs on the legs or ankles of the prisoner
   (C) improper, primarily because the prisoner's hands were not handcuffed behind his back
   (D) proper, primarily because she placed the handcuffs on the prisoner in the presence of another Police Officer.

Answer question 38 solely on the basis of the following information.

Police Officers must sometimes rely on eyewitness accounts of incidents, even though eyewitnesses may make mistakes with regard to some details.

38. While crossing the street, Robert Green was struck by a delivery truck. Police Officer Luther was called to the scene and spoke with four witnesses who saw the truck that struck Mr. Green. The following are descriptions of the truck given by the witnesses. Which one of the descriptions should Officer Luther consider most likely to be correct?

   (A) A brown GMC truck, Plate G-1843
   (B) A black Ford truck, Plate G-1854
   (C) A brown Ford truck, Plate G-1845
   (D) A brown Ford truck, Plate C-1845.

Answer question 39 solely on the basis of the following information.

Police Officers may be required to safeguard the property of a deceased person who lived alone. When safeguarding the property, a Police Officer should do the following in the order given:

1. Request a Patrol Supervisor to respond to the scene.
2. In the presence of the Patrol Supervisor, search the body for valuables and documents concerning identity.
3. Remove all property except clothing.
4. Enter in Memo Book a complete list of property removed from deceased.
5. Complete the Property Clerk's Invoice Work Sheet indicating what property was removed.
6. Deliver all property and the Property Clerk's Invoice Work Sheet to the Desk Officer at the precinct.

39. Police Officer Frey responds to 220 E. 5th Street, Apt. 8M. He finds Mr. Johnson lying dead on the living room floor. The building superintendant, who had let Officer Frey into the apartment, informs Officer Frey that Mr. Johnson lived alone. The Officer radios the dispatcher and requests the Patrol Supervisor to respond to the scene. When Sergeant O'Malley, the Patrol Supervisor arrives, he and Officer Frey search the body. They find a wallet with various personal papers and $3,200 in cash. Officer Frey removes the property. The next step Officer Frey should take is to

(A) continue searching the area around the body for any additional property
(B) deliver the property to the precinct and give it to the Desk Officer
(C) prepare the Property Clerk's Invoice Work Sheet
(D) make a Memo Book entry listing the wallet and its contents.

40. On August 31st at 2:30 P.M., Police Officer Jones is assigned to a post at the West Side Shopping Mall. Captain Franks tells Officer Jones that there has been a sharp increase in shoplifting at the mall over the past three weeks. He instructs the Officer to watch closely any persons whose behavior appears to be suspicious. Officer Jones observes the following four situations. Which person should Officer Jones watch more closely?

(A) A woman who is dressed in jeans and a winter overcoat is looking at a display counter in a dress shop.
(B) A woman with a large shopping bag who appears to be counting money while leaving a store.
(C) An old man who is pushing a stroller with a two-year-old child in the toy department of a large store.
(D) Two teenaged boys who are looking in the display window of an electronics store.

Answer questions 41 through 42 solely on the basis of the following map. The flow of traffic is indicated by the arrows. If there is only one arrow shown, then traffic flows only in the direction indicated by the arrow. If there are two arrows shown, then traffic flows in both directions. You must follow the flow of traffic.

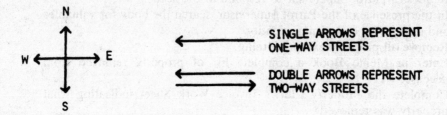

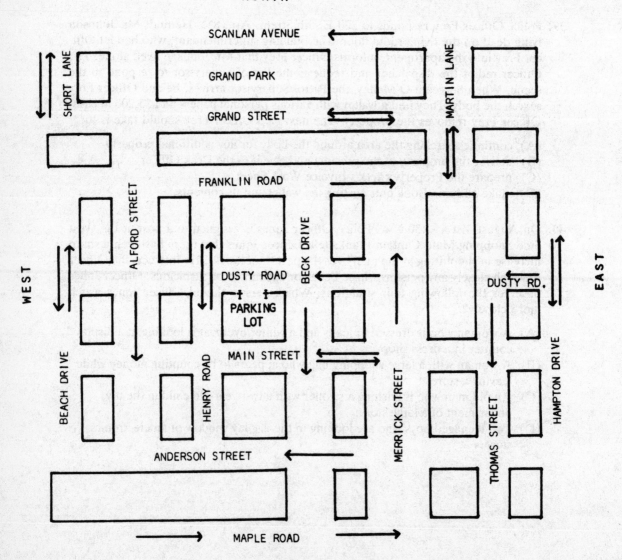

41. Police Officers Gold and Warren are at the intersection of Maple Road and Hampton Drive. The radio dispatcher has assigned them to investigate an attempted auto theft in the parking lot on Dusty Road. Which one of the following is the shortest route for the Officers to take in their patrol car to get to the entrance of the parking lot on Dusty Road, making sure to obey all traffic regulations?

(A) Travel north on Hampton Drive, then west on Dusty Road to the parking lot entrance.

(B) Travel west on Maple Road, then north on Beck Drive, then west on Dusty Road to the parking lot entrance.

(C) Travel north on Hampton Drive, then west on Anderson Street, then north on Merrick Street, then west on Dusty Road to the parking lot entrance.

(D) Travel west on Maple Road, then north on Merrick Street, then west on Dusty Road to the parking lot entrance.

42. Police Officer Gladden is in a patrol car at the intersection of Beach Drive and Anderson Street when he spots a suspicious car. P.O. Gladden calls the radio dispatcher to determine if the vehicle was stolen. P.O. Gladden then follows the vehicle north on Beach Drive for three blocks, then turns right and proceeds for one block and makes another right. He then follows the vehicle for two blocks and then they both make a left turn and continue driving. P.O. Gladden now receives a call from the dispatcher stating the car was reported stolen and signals for the vehicle to pull to the side of the road. In what direction was P.O. Gladden heading at the time he signaled for the other car to pull over?

(A) North   (C) South

(B) East   (D) West.

Answer question 43 solely on the basis of the following information.

Criminal Possession of Stolen Property 3rd Degree—occurs when a person knowingly possesses stolen property in order to benefit himself or another person who does not own the property.

43. Which one of the following situations is the best example of Criminal Possession of Stolen Property in the Third Degree?

(A) Police Officers enter Mr. Hanson's home and discover a stolen television. Hanson shows the Officers a receipt for the television from what he thought was an honest dealer.

(B) While walking to work, Anne finds a diamond ring in the street and keeps it.

(C) John purchases what he believes is an expensive stolen stereo, which is actually a low-priced stereo that the dealer obtained properly.

(D) Tim warns his customers that the stereos he has for sale are stolen and shouldn't be brought to authorized dealers for repairs.

44. Police Officer Fontaine obtained the following details relating to a suspicious package:

Place of Occurrence:	Case Bank, 2 Wall Street
Time of Occurrence:	10:30 A.M.
Date of Occurrence	October 10, 1988
Complaint:	Suspicious package in doorway
Found by:	Emergency Service Unit

Officer Fontaine is preparing a report for department records. Which one of the following expresses the above information *most clearly* and *accurately*?

(A) At 10:30 A.M. the Emergency Service Unit reported they found a package on October 10, 1988 which appeared suspicious. This occurred in a doorway at 2 Wall Street, Case Bank.

(B) A package which appeared suspicious was in the doorway of Case Bank. The Emergency Service Unit reported this at 2 Wall Street at 10:30 A.M. on October 10, 1988 when found.

(C) On October 10, 1988 at 10:30 A.M. a suspicious package was found by the Emergency Service Unit in the doorway of Case Bank at 2 Wall Street.

(D) The Emergency Service Unit found a package at the Case Bank. It appeared suspicious at 10:30 A.M. in the doorway of 2 Wall Street on October 10, 1988.

45. Police Officer Reardon receives the following information regarding a case of child abuse:

Victim:	Joseph Mays
Victim's Age:	10 years old
Victim's Address:	Resides with his family at 42 Columbia Street, Apartment 1B
Complainant:	Victim's uncle, Kevin Mays
Suspects:	Victim's parents

Police Officer Reardon is preparing a report to send to the Department of Social Services. Which one of the following expresses the above information *most clearly* and *accurately*?

(A) Kevin Mays reported a case of child abuse to his ten-year-old nephew, Joseph Mays, by his parents. He resides with his family at 42 Columbia Street, Apartment 1B.

(B) Kevin Mays reported that his ten-year-old nephew, Joseph Mays, has been abused by the child's parents. Joseph Mays resides with his family at 42 Columbia Street, Apartment 1B.

(C) Joseph Mays has been abused by his parents. Kevin Mays reported that his nephew resides with his family at 42 Columbia Street, Apartment 1B. He is ten years old.

(D) Kevin Mays reported that his nephew is ten years old. Joseph Mays has been abused by his parents. He resides with his family at 42 Columbia Street, Apartment 1B.

46. While on patrol Police Officer Hawkins was approached by Harry Roland, a store owner, who found a leather bag, valued at $200.00, outside his store. Officer Hawkins took the property into custody and removed the following

- 2 Solex watches, each valued at $500.00
- 4 14-kt. gold necklaces, each valued at $315.00
- Cash $519.00
- 1 diamond ring valued at $400.00

Officer Hawkins is preparing a report on the found property. Which one of the following is the total value of the property and cash found?

(A) $1,734.00   (C) $3,179.00
(B) $3,171.00   (D) $3,379.00.

Answer question 47 solely on the basis of the following information.

During the month of September, three rapes were committed near Pier 21 on Westerly Avenue. The description of each of the suspects given by the victims, is as follows:

Rape No. 1—Male, white, mid thirties, 5'8", 190 lbs., long wavy hair, wearing dark sunglasses, black jacket, green pants, black boots, moustache.

Rape No. 2—Male, white, late 20's, 5'8", slim build, moustache, closely cropped hair, brown eyes, black jacket, blue jeans, black boots.

Rape No. 3—Male, white, 35, 5'7", 180 lbs., long hair, moustache, dark glasses, blue denim jacket, blue jeans, black boots.

On October 3, 1988, a fourth rape was committed. The suspect was arrested by Police Officer Jackson. The description of the suspect is as follows:

Rape No. 4—Male, white, 30–35, 5'7", 185 lbs., long curly hair, moustache, grey jacket, blue jeans, baseball cap, white boots.

47. Based on the above descriptions of the suspects in the first three rapes, Officer Jackson should consider the suspect in the fourth rape as a suspect in

(A) Rape No.1, but not Rape No. 2 or Rape No.3
(B) Rape No.1 and Rape No. 3, but not Rape No. 2
(C) Rape No. 2 and Rape No. 3, but not Rape No. 1
(D) Rape No. 1, Rape No. 2, and Rape No. 3.

Answer question 48 solely on the basis of the following information.

When a warrant has been issued for the arrest of a parent who has physically abused or neglected a child, Police Officers should do the following in the order given:

1. Respond to the location and arrest the parent(s) named in the warrant if the parent is present.
2. Remove the child from the home, even if parent named in warrant is not present and an arrest is not made.
3. Deliver the child to Family Court between the hours of 9 A.M. and 5 P.M.
4. If Family Court is not in session, bring the child to the precinct station house and locate temporary housing.
5. If either the child or parent is not home, attempt to locate child or parent.

48. Officers Batts and Peters are informed by the Desk Officer that a warrant has been issued for the arrest of Mr. Hughes. It has been reported that Mr. Hughes has physically abused his five-year-old son, Michael. The Officers arrive at the Hughes home at 1:00 A.M. They find Michael at home alone. When asked where his parents are, he informs the Officers that his father went away yesterday and that his mother doesn't live with them. Michael tells the Officers that his uncle has been visiting but hasn't been home all day. The Officers return to the station house with Michael and locate temporary housing for him. What should the Officers do next?

(A) Attempt to locate Michael's uncle.
(B) Take Michael to Family Court.
(C) Try to locate Michael's parents.
(D) Hold Michael in the station house until his mother is located.

Answer question 49 solely on the basis of the following information.

Police Department policy requires that a vehicle pursuit should be ended whenever the pursuit causes a greater risk to Police Officers and the public than the danger to the community if the suspect is not caught. If the chase is ended, the Officers should attempt to obtain enough information to apprehend the suspect at a later time.

49. Officer Jordan is in her patrol car when she sees a blue Ford, license plate #7744-AEK, hit an unoccupied red Chevrolet, and speed away from the scene of the accident. Officer Jordan pursues the blue Ford at 80 M.P.H. on a busy street. While in pursuit, Officer Jordan weaves in and out of traffic, causing some cars to skid and swerve. After a few blocks the blue Ford skids and Officer Jordan's car crashes into it. Officer Jordan immediately arrests the driver of the Ford. In this situation Officer Jordan's actions were

(A) proper, primarily because it is her duty to arrest criminal suspects
(B) improper, primarily because Officer Jordan should not have pursued the blue Ford without knowing how badly the red Chevrolet was damaged
(C) proper, primarily because Officer Jordan arrested the driver without causing serious injury to another person
(D) improper, primarily because Officer Jordan should have discontinued the pursuit and tried to arrest the suspect at another time.

50. While on patrol, Police Officer Blake observes a man running from a burning abandoned building. Officer Blake radios the following information:

Place of Occurrence:	310 Hall Avenue
Time of Occurrence:	8:30 P.M.
Type of Building:	Abandoned
Suspect:	Male, white, about 35 years old
Crime:	Arson

Officer Blake is completing a report on the incident. Which one of the following expresses the above information *most clearly* and *accurately*?

(A) An abandoned building located at 310 Hall Avenue was set on fire at 8:30 P.M. A white male, approximately 35 years old, was observed fleeing the scene.
(B) A white male, approximately 35 years old, at 8:30 P.M. was observed fleeing 310 Hall Avenue. The fire was set at an abandoned building.
(C) An abandoned building was set on fire. A white male, approximately 35 years old, was observed fleeing the scene at 8:30 P.M. at 310 Hall Avenue.
(D) Observed fleeing a building at 8:30 P.M. was a white male, approximately 35 years old. An abandoned building, located at 310 Hall Avenue, was set on fire.

Answer question 51 solely on the basis of the following information.

Police Officers must sometimes rely on eyewitness accounts of incidents, even though eyewitnesses may make mistakes with regard to some details.

51. While on patrol, Police Officer Hanson was approached by a woman who was screaming that her pocketbook had just been stolen. Officer Hanson questions four witnesses who saw the robbery. The following are descriptions of the suspect given by the witnesses. Which one of the descriptions should Officer Hanson consider most likely to be correct?

(A) Male, white, 40 years old, wearing a black hat and red sneakers.
(B) Male, black, 25 years old, wearing a black hat and red sneakers.
(C) Male, white, 25 years old, wearing a black hat and red sneakers.
(D) Male, white, 20 years old, wearing a grey hat and maroon sneakers.

52. Police Officers may be required to transport to a hospital persons who are in need of immediate treatment when an ambulance is not immediately available. It would be most appropriate for a Police Officer to transport which one of the following individuals?

(A) An elderly woman who twists her ankle while walking to the grocery store.
(B) A 4-year-old boy who trips and breaks his arm while walking to school with his mother.
(C) A man who has a heart attack and is lying unconscious in the street.
(D) A man who bangs his forehead in a car accident and claims he might have a broken nose.

53. Police Officer Winters responds to a call regarding a report of a missing person. The following information was obtained by the Officer:

Time of Occurrence:	3:30 P.M.
Place of Occurrence:	Harrison Park
Reported by:	Louise Dee—daughter
Description of Missing Person:	Sharon Dee, 70 years old, 5'5", brown eyes, black hair—mother

Officer Winters is completing a report on the incident. Which one of the following expresses the above information *most clearly* and *accurately*?

(A) Mrs. Sharon Dee, reported missing by her daughter Louise, was seen in Harrison Park. The last time she saw her was at 3:30 P.M. She is 70 years old with black hair, brown eyes, and 5'5"

(B) Louise Dee reported that her mother, Sharon Dee, is missing. Sharon Dee is 70 years old, has black hair, brown eyes, and is 5'5". She was last seen at 3:30 P.M. in Harrison Park.

(C) Louise Dee reported Sharon, her 70-year-old mother at 3:30 P.M., to be missing after being seen last at Harrison Park. Described as being 5'5", she has black hair and brown eyes.

(D) At 3:30 P.M. Louise Dee's mother was last seen by her daughter in Harrison Park. She has black hair and brown eyes. Louise reported Sharon is 5'5" and 70 years old.

Answer questions 54 through 57 solely on the basis of the following passage.

While working an 8:00 A.M. to 4:00 P.M. shift on January 14, 1988, Police Officers Jones and Smith received a radio call at 1:45 P.M. to investigate a report of a man with a gun in front of 103 Lexington Avenue. Mary Holmes had called 911 from her home at 1:43 P.M. and explained that two days ago while on her way home from work, she had been threatened by a man with a gun in front of her home at 113 Lowell Street. She told the police operator that the same man was now standing in front of Harry's Lounge at 103 Lexington Avenue, drinking a beer. She described him as being between 30 and 40 years old, 5'6", 160 lbs., wearing a gray coat, gray brim hat, and gold wire rim glasses. The Officers responded to the location and observed a male fitting the description given by Miss Holmes. The Officers approached the suspect and, while searching his right front waist band, Officer Jones found a chromeplated .38 caliber revolver licensed and registered under the name of Joseph Fitz. Miss Holmes was brought to the scene and identified the suspect as the person who had threatened her earlier. Officer Smith then placed the man, identified as Joseph Fitz, under arrest.

54. On what day did the suspect threaten Miss Holmes?

(A) January 10   (C) January 14
(B) January 12   (D) January 16.

55. Officer Jones recovered the gun from the suspect's

(A) left front waist band   (C) left rear waist band
(B) right rear waist band   (D) right front waist band.

56. Miss Holmes stated that the suspect had threatened her in front of

(A) Harry's Lounge   (C) a bar
(B) her home   (D) her office.

57. Joseph Fitz was arrested because he

(A) illegally possessed a weapon
(B) was drinking in a public place
(C) committed a robbery two days earlier
(D) was identified as the suspect in a previous incident.

58. While on patrol, Police Officers Mertz and Gallo receive a call from the dispatcher regarding a crime in progress. When the Officers arrive they obtain the following information:

Time of Occurrence:	2:00 P.M.
Place of Occurrence:	In front of 2124 Bristol Avenue
Crime:	Purse Snatch
Victim:	Maria Nieves
Suspect:	Carlos Ortiz
Witness:	Jose Perez, who apprehended the suspect

The Officers are completing a report on the incident. Which one of the following expresses the above information *most clearly* and *accurately*?

(A) At 2:00 P.M., Jose Perez witnessed Maria Nieves. Her purse was snatched. The suspect, Carlos Ortiz was apprehended in front of 2124 Bristol Avenue.
(B) In front of 2124 Bristol Avenue, Carlos Ortiz snatched the purse belonging to Maria Nieves. Carlos Ortiz was apprehended by a witness to the crime after Jose Perez saw the purse snatch at 2:00 P.M.
(C) At 2:00 P.M., Carlos Ortiz snatched a purse from Maria Nieves in front of 2124 Bristol Avenue. Carlos Ortiz was apprehended by Jose Perez, a witness to the crime.
(D) At 2:00 P.M., Carlos Ortiz was seen snatching the purse of Maria Nieves as seen and apprehended by Jose Perez in front of 2124 Bristol Avenue.

59. Police Officers Willis and James respond to a crime in progress and obtain the following information:

Time of Occurence:	8:30 A.M.
Place of Occurrence:	Corner of Hopkin Avenue and Amboy Place
Crime:	Chain snatch
Victim:	Mrs. Paula Evans
Witness:	Mr. Robert Peters
Suspect:	white male

Officers Willis and James are completing a report on the incident. Which one of the following expresses the above information *most clearly* and *accurately*?

(A) Mrs. Paula Evans was standing on the corner of Hopkin Avenue and Amboy Place at 8:30 A.M. when a white male snatched her chain. Mr. Robert Peters witnessed the crime.
(B) At 8:30 A.M., Mr. Robert Peters witnessed Mrs. Paula Evans and a white male standing on the corner of Hopkin Avenue and Amboy Place. Her chain was snatched.
(C) At 8:30 A.M., a white male was standing on the corner of Hopkin Avenue and Amboy Place. Mrs. Paula Evans' chain was snatched and Mr. Robert Peters witnessed the crime.
(D) At 8:30 A.M., Mr. Robert Peters reported he witnessed a white male snatching Mrs. Paula Evans' chain while standing on the corner of Hopkin Avenue and Amboy Place.

Answer question 60 solely on the basis of the following information.

When a Police Officer reasonably suspects that a person has committed, is committing, or is about to commit a crime, the Officer, in order to protect himself from being injured, should do the following in the order given:

1. Stop the person and request identification and an explanation of the person's conduct.
2. Frisk the person by running hands over the person's clothing if the Officer thinks his life may be in danger.
3. Search the person by placing hands inside pockets and interior parts of the person's clothing if a frisk reveals an object that appears to be a weapon.
4. Prepare a Stop and Frisk Report for each person stopped if:
   a. person was stopped by use of force; or
   b. person was stopped and frisked or searched; or
   c. person was stopped and arrested.

60. Police Officers Darcey and Sanchez are investigating a report of a man with a gun on the corner of Boston Road and Montana Avenue. The Officers stop a man fitting the description they were given. Officer Darcey asks the man why he is in the area. Officer Darcey then asks the man for some proper identification. He then frisks the man and feels an object which seems to be an address book in the man's shirt pocket. Officer Darcey should next

(A) complete a Stop and Frisk Report
(B) search the man's clothing
(C) request the man's identification and an explanation of his conduct
(D) place the man under arrest for possession of a weapon.

Answer question 61 solely on the basis of the following information.

Robbery 3rd Degree—occurs when a person forcibly steals property.

61. Which one of the following situations is the best example of Robbery in the Third Degree?

(A) Stephanie was riding the train to Coney Island. When the train reached her stop, she realized her briefcase was missing.
(B) June was walking north on 119 Avenue to the bus stop when Sam approached her and snatched her bag. As she struggled with the attacker, he knocked her to the ground and fled south on 119 Avenue.
(C) Clifton was riding the train to Chambers Street during rush hour when Joe brushed past him, picked his pocket, and got off at the next stop.
(D) Denise's purse was hanging on the back of her chair while she ate at a local coffee shop, when Bill slit the purse strap with a razor and fled with the purse.

Answer question 62 solely on the basis of the following information.

Police Officer Gray has been instructed by his supervisor to help search for a suspected murderer who was seen running into an abandoned building after committing the crime. The description of the suspect is as follows:

Male, white, about 38 years old, 6'5", 225 lbs., short hair, gray pants, brown sweat shirt, brown construction boots, moustache, 2" scar above right eye.

Officer Gray has also been informed that there were three other murders committed on the same block since the beginning of the year and has been given the following descriptions of the suspects:

Murder No. 1—Male, white, 40 years old, 6'4", 220 lbs., short black hair, black pants, brown shirt, black jacket, construction boots, moustache, scar on face.

Murder No. 2—Male, white, 25 years old, 6'3", 170 lbs., short afro, gray pants, brown sweat shirt, brown boots, moustache, beard.

Murder No. 3—Male, white, 35 years old, 6'0", 225 lbs., black hair, gray pants, brown sweat shirt, brown shoes, moustache, long sideburns.

62. Based on the above descriptions of the suspects in the three previous murders, Officer Gray should tell his supervisor that the suspect in the last murder should also be considered a suspect in

(A) Murder No. 1, but not Murder No. 2 or Murder No. 3
(B) Murder No. 3, but not Murder No. 1 or Murder No. 2
(C) Murder No. 1 and Murder No. 2, but not Murder No. 3
(D) Murder No. 2 and Murder No. 3, but not Murder No. 1.

Answer question 63 solely on the basis of the following information.

When a Police Officer responds to the scene of an incident, the Officer may find it necessary to request the immediate assistance of another Department such as Fire, Sanitation, etc.

63. In which of the following incidents would an Officer most likely request the assistance of another Department?

(A) A man reports that he was robbed at gunpoint.
(B) Two teenage boys are caught spray-painting their names on a factory wall.
(C) A truck carrying a poisonous liquid overturns and spills the liquid onto a crowded street.
(D) A box of jewelry is found in the basement of an apartment house.

Answer question 64 solely on the basis of the following information.

When a juvenile, who is less than 16 years old, is arrested by a Police Officer and charged with a felony, the Officer must take the following steps in the order given:

1. Transport juvenile to Central Booking.
2. Place juvenile in a cell separate from adult prisoners.
3. Notify juvenile's parents of arrest.
4. Deliver arrest report to Central Booking Supervisor.
5. Have juvenile fingerprinted and photographed.
6. Deliver juvenile to Spofford Juvenile Center for detention.

64. Police Officer Wilson arrested 15-year-old Johnny Leon after Leon was seen threatening and eventually hitting Mr. Perez over the head with an ax handle. Leon was charged with Assault 1st Degree. Officer Wilson placed Leon in the patrol wagon. When they arrive at Central Booking, Officer Wilson should next

(A) ensure that Leon is not put in a cell with adult prisoners
(B) telephone Leon's parents
(C) have Leon fingerprinted and photographed
(D) submit arrest report to Supervisor at Central Booking.

Answer question 65 solely on the basis of the following information.

When evidence is required for presentation in court, a Police Officer must:

1. Request evidence from the Officer assigned to the Property Clerk facility where it is stored.
2. Give the Officer the Property Clerk's Index Number.
3. Present shield and identification card.
4. Sign a receipt for evidence.

65. Police Officer Dana is informed that she is scheduled to testify in court about a narcotics arrest she made four months ago. The case involves evidence stored at the Property Clerk's Office. Since Officer Dana was scheduled to work on patrol that day, she appears at the Property Clerk's Office in full police uniform. She requests the evidence from Officer Baskin, who is assigned to the Property Clerk's Office, and gives the clerk the correct Property Clerk's Index Number. Officer Dana presents her shield to Officer Baskin and signs a receipt for the evidence. She then proceeds to court. Officer Dana's actions in this situation were

(A) proper, primarily because she was scheduled to work patrol that day
(B) improper, primarily because a patrol supervisor should have been present to witness the transfer of property
(C) proper, primarily because the evidence was critical to the case
(D) improper, primarily because she did not show proper identification to Officer Baskin.

66. Police Officers Cleveland and Logan responded to an assault that had recently occurred. The following information was obtained at the scene:

Place of Occurrence:	Broadway and Roosevelt Avenue
Time of Occurrence:	1:00 A.M.
Crime:	Attempted robbery, assault
Victim:	Chuck Brown, suffered a broken tooth
Suspect:	Lewis Brown, victim's brother

Officer Logan is completing a report on the incident. Which one of the following expresses the above information *most clearly* and *accurately*?

(A) Lewis Brown assaulted his brother Chuck on the corner of Broadway and Roosevelt Avenue. Chuck Brown reported his broken tooth during the attempted robbery at 1:00 A.M.

(B) Chuck Brown had his tooth broken when he was assaulted at 1:00 A.M. on the corner of Broadway and Roosevelt Avenue by his brother, Lewis Brown, while Lewis was attempting to rob him.

(C) An attempt at 1:00 A.M. to rob Chuck Brown turned into an assault at the corner of Broadway and Roosevelt Avenue when his brother Lewis broke his tooth.

(D) At 1:00 A.M., Chuck Brown reported that he was assaulted during his brother's attempt to rob him. Lewis Brown broke his tooth. The incident occurred on the corner of Broadway and Roosevelt Avenue.

67. Police Officer Mannix has just completed an investigation regarding a hit-and-run accident which resulted in a pedestrian being injured. Officer Mannix has obtained the following information:

Make and Model of Car:	Pontiac, Trans Am
Year and Color of Car:	1986, white
Driver of Car:	Male, black
Place of Occurrence:	Corner of W. 15th Street and 8th Avenue
Time of Occurrence:	1:00 P.M.

Officer Mannix is completing a report on the accident. Which one of the following expresses the above information *most clearly* and *accurately*?

(A) At 1:00 P.M., at the corner of W. 15th Street and 8th Avenue, a black male driving a white 1986 Pontiac Trans Am was observed leaving the scene of the accident after injuring a pedestrian with the vehicle.

(B) On the corner of W. 15th Street and 8th Avenue, a white Pontiac, driven by a black male, a 1986 Trans Am injured a pedestrian and left the scene of the accident at 1:00 P.M.

(C) A black male driving a white 1986 Pontiac Trans Am, injured a pedestrian and left with the car while driving on the corner of W. 15th Street and 8th Avenue at 1:00 P.M.

(D) At the corner of W. 15th Street and 8th Avenue, a pedestrian was injured by a black male. He fled in his white 1986 Pontiac Trans Am at 1:00 P.M.

Answer questions 68 and 69 solely on the basis of the following information.

Police Officer Jones has been made aware by merchants on her post that an increase in crimes has been occurring in her area. All of the assaults seem to take place on Pitt Avenue between Van Syck Street and Stone Street. Most of the robberies take place on Pitt Avenue between Amboy Place and Herzl Street. All of the larcenies take place on Amboy Place between Pitt Avenue and East Avenue. The robberies usually occur on Fridays and Saturdays; the larcenies occur on Sundays and Mondays; and the assaults occur on Wednesdays and Thursdays. Most of the larcenies occur between 4:00 P.M. and 8:00 P.M, all of the robberies occur between 1:00 P.M. and 3:00 P.M., and the assaults occur between 1:00 A.M. and 4:00 A.M.

68. In order to reduce the number of larcenies, Officer Jones should inform the merchants that she will increase patrol on

   (A) Pitt Avenue between Amboy Place and Herzl Street on Sundays and Mondays between 4:00 P.M. and 8:00 P.M.
   (B) Amboy Place between Pitt Avenue and East Avenue on Mondays and Tuesdays between 3:00 A.M. and 8:00 A.M.
   (C) Amboy Place between East Avenue and Pitt Avenue on Sundays and Mondays between 3:00 P.M. and 10:00 P.M.
   (D) Herzl Street between Amboy Place and Pitt Avenue on Wednesdays and Thursdays between 1:00 A.M. and 9:00 A.M.

69. Officer Jones would be most effective in reducing the number of robberies if she patrolled from

   (A) 10:00 A.M. to 6:00 P.M., Monday through Friday
   (B) 1:00 P.M. to 9:00 P.M., Saturday through Wednesday
   (C) 1:00 A.M. to 9:00 A.M., Wednesday through Sunday
   (D) 8:00 A.M. to 4:00 P.M., Tuesday through Saturday.

70. Under certain circumstances, Police Officers are required to request the assistance and advice of a supervisor. Which one of the following situations would most likely require a supervisor?

   (A) Two men are verbally arguing over a parking space.
   (B) Several teenagers are listening and dancing to loud music in the schoolyard.
   (C) A woman threatens to jump from the twelfth floor of a building.
   (D) A man complains that his next door neighbor smokes marijuana in the building hallways.

Answer question 71 solely on the basis of the following information.

Reckless Endangerment 1st Degree—occurs when, under circumstances that clearly show a total disregard for human life, a person acts in a manner that creates a grave risk of death to another person.

71. Which one of the following is the best example of Reckless Endangerment in the First Degree?

   (A) James, while attending a football game where his favorite team is losing, fires a rifle into the stands to get the crowd to stop cheering for the opposing team.
   (B) A woman threatens to kill herself if her husband is not immediately released from prison.
   (C) A motorist whose gas pedal is stuck hits a woman who is pushing a baby carriage down the block, causing her death.
   (D) A person continues to throw garbage out of his second floor window into an empty lot, even after he is warned he could injure someone.

Answer question 72 solely on the basis of the following information.

When a Police Officer recovers a stolen vehicle, the following should be done in the order given:

   1. Make a Memo Book entry describing the vehicle and where the vehicle was found.
   2. Notify the Desk Officer.
   3. Prepare a Property Clerk's Invoice.
   4. Notify the owner, if known.

72. While on patrol, Police Officer Vasquez notices an unoccupied vehicle with lit headlights on the corner of 101st and Kane Avenue. She recalls seeing that same vehicle parked in the same place with its engine running one hour earlier. Officer Vasquez requests the radio dispatcher to run a check on the vehicle's Florida license plate ZBF293. She is informed that the vehicle is registered to Ms. Patti Tucci of Miami Beach. Officer Vasquez notices that the steering column of the vehicle has been broken. Officer Vasquez suspects that the vehicle has been stolen. Officer Vasquez should next

   (A) notify the owner of the vehicle
   (B) record all details related to the vehicle in her Memo Book
   (C) prepare a Property Clerk's Invoice
   (D) call the Desk Officer.

Answer question 73 through 76 solely on the basis of the following passage.

On April 6, at 5:25 A.M., while patrolling the #8 train southbound to Brooklyn, Transit Police Officer O'Rourke noticed a young woman at the end of the car who appeared to be ill. Officer O'Rourke approached the woman and asked her if she was feeling all right. The woman was crying and began speaking incoherently. Officer O'Rourke escorted the woman off the train at the next southbound #8 platform in order to obtain information from her. After speaking with her for fifteen minutes, Officer O'Rourke learned that her name was Carol Rivers and that she had been assaulted and sexually molested while waiting for the southbound #8 train about a half hour before meeting the Officer. Miss Rivers described the suspect as a white male, in his forties, with gray hair, glasses, a red shirt, black pants, and a brown hat. The suspect fled on a northbound #8 train with the victim's pocketbook. Officer O'Rourke then radioed for an ambulance to respond to the location to assist Miss Rivers.

The next day at approximately 5:30 A.M., while Officer O'Rourke was standing on the subway platform waiting to board the uptown #7 train to Queens, he noticed an individual coming down the steps from the southbound platform. The man was in his forties, with gray hair, dark glasses, and the same clothing described by Miss Rivers the day before, except for his shirt, which was white. Office O'Rourke, believing the man to be the same perpetrator, decided to follow him in order to observe the suspect's actions. The man was walking alongside a woman on the northbound platform and attempted to snatch her pocketbook. The woman held onto her purse and started to yell for the police. The man immediately released his hold on the pocketbook and ran down the platform onto an awaiting #7 train to Manhattan. Officer O'Rourke pursued the man onto the train and subsequently placed him under arrest two stations later.

73. Officer O'Rourke requested that the ambulance respond to the subway platform of the

(A) northbound #8 train
(B) uptown #7 train
(C) downtown #7 train
(D) southbound #8 train.

74. At approximately what time was Miss Rivers assaulted?

(A) 4:55 A.M.
(B) 5:10 A.M.
(C) 5:25 A.M.
(D) 5:40 A.M.

75. The suspect arrested by Officer O'Rourke was wearing a

(A) red shirt and blue pants
(B) white shirt and black pants
(C) red shirt and black pants
(D) white shirt and red pants.

76. On April 7, Officer O'Rourke boarded a train to

(A) Manhattan
(B) Queens
(C) the Bronx
(D) Brooklyn.

77. Police Officer Brown has responded to a domestic dispute and has obtained the following information:

Time of Complaint:	3:20 P.M.
Complainant:	Mrs. Jenny Shawn
Address of Complainant:	39 Waring Place
Complaint:	Husband and wife screaming, and threatening each other with knives
People involved:	Mr. and Mrs. George Roberts

Officer Brown is completing a report on the incident. Which one of the following expresses the above information *most clearly* and *accurately*?

(A) At 39 Waring Place Mrs. Jenny Shawn called the police because Mr. and Mrs. George Roberts were screaming and threatening each other with knives at 3:20 P.M.

(B) At 3:20 P.M., Mrs. Jenny Shawn reported Mr. and Mrs. George Roberts to the police. At 39 Waring Place they were screaming and threatening each other with knives.

(C) Mrs. Jenny Shawn reported to the police of 39 Waring Place at 3:20 P.M., that Mr. and Mrs. George Roberts were screaming and threatening each other with knives.

(D) At 3:20 P.M., Mrs. Jenny Shawn, of 39 Waring Place, called the police because Mr. and Mrs. George Roberts were screaming and threatening each other with knives.

78. While on patrol, Police Officer Beckman witnesses the following incident:

Incident:	Person hit by brick that was thrown from 12th floor of a building
Place of Incident:	In front of 227 20th Street
Time of Incident:	11:21 A.M.
Victim:	Mr. George Manson, Injured
Suspect:	Mr. Brian Mor

Officer Beckman is completing a report regarding this incident. Which one of the following expresses the above information *most clearly* and *accurately*?

(A) At 11:21 A.M., in front of 227 20th Street a brick was thrown. Mr. George Manson was walking and injured by Mr. Brian Mor on the 12th floor of a building.

(B) A brick was thrown from the 12th floor window of a building in front of 227 20th Street. Mr. George Manson was walking at 11:21 A.M. and was injured by Mr. Brian Mor.

(C) Mr. Brian Mor threw a brick in front of 227 20th Street. At 11:21 A.M. Mr. George Manson was injured when walking from the 12th floor of a building.

(D) At 11:21 A.M., Mr. George Manson was walking in front of 227 20th Street. He was injured by a brick that Mr. Brian Mor threw from the 12th floor of a building.

Answer question 79 solely on the basis of the following information.

When a Police Officer investigates a complaint of a rape or an attempted rape, the Officer should do the following in the order given:

1. Interview the complainant and witnesses and attempt to obtain the facts.
2. Search for and remove any evidence from the location of the complaint.
3. Notify the Sex Crime Squad if the victim was raped.
4. Prepare a Complaint Report Worksheet.
5. Notify supervisor upon completion of investigation.

79. Police Officers King and Ross respond to 110-30 11th Avenue. Upon arriving at the location they find Mary Jones and Sam Dean sitting on the front steps of the building. Mr. Dean informs the Officers that as he was walking home he heard screams, ran into an alley, and discovered a man threatening Mary Jones with a knife. Mr. Dean ran towards the man who dropped his knife and ran away. Mary Jones confirms what Mr. Dean told the Officers and added that when the man had threatened her with a knife he said he was going to rape her. She said that if Mr. Dean hadn't chased the man away she would have been raped. The next step that Officers King and Ross should take is to

(A) prepare a Complaint Report Worksheet
(B) interview Mr. Dean
(C) search for the knife
(D) call the Sex Crime Squad.

Answer question 80 solely on the basis of the following information.

Police Officer Selma is assigned to patrol Blum and Tan Streets in order to reduce the sale of drugs. Officer Selma is informed that drugs are being sold at 416 Blum Street in Apt. 1A and at 428 Tan Street in Apt. 1B. Most of the drug sales in Apt. 1A occur between 10:30 A.M. and 4:00 P.M. Most of the drug sales in Apt. 1B take place from 5:00 P.M. to 8:00 P.M. Officer Selma is also informed that most of the drug sales are taking place on Thursdays and Sundays on Tan Street and Wednesdays and Fridays on Blum Street.

80. Officer Selma would most likely reduce the number of drug sales taking place in Apt. 1A by patrolling in the area of

(A) 428 Tan Street from 9:00 A.M. to 5:00 P.M.
(B) 416 Blum Street from 9:00 A.M. to 5:00 P.M.
(C) 428 Tan Street from 3:00 P.M. to 11:00 P.M.
(D) 416 Blum Street from 3:00 P.M. to 11:00 P.M.

Answer question 81 solely on the basis of the following information.

When a Police Officer stops a vehicle and discovers that the operator is driving with a suspended license, the Officer should

1. Take away the driver's license.
2. Give the operator of the vehicle a receipt for the license.
3. If the operator has two or more unrelated suspensions, or if the driver's license has been revoked for any reason, arrest the motorist.
4. Do not mark or mutilate the license in any manner.
5. Have the violator's vehicle parked in a legal parking area until removed by a licensed operator.

81. Police Officers Wells and Cortese, while on patrol, observed the driver of a blue Firebird make an illegal U-turn at an intersection. Officer Wells directed the driver to pull over to the curb. The Officer approached the driver and requested his driver's license and car registration. While inspecting the license, Officer Wells noticed that the license had been revoked. Officer Wells took the license, issued a receipt, and placed the driver under arrest. Officer Cortese legally parked the car under a tree. In this situation the actions taken by Officers Wells and Cortese were

(A) proper, primarily because the driver had a revoked license
(B) improper, primarily because he should have taken the license and registration
(C) proper, primarily because the driver almost caused an accident
(D) improper, primarily because the vehicle should have been removed by a licensed driver.

Answer question 82 solely on the basis of the following information.

Under certain circumstances Police Officers may be required to use their hand guns.

82. In which one of the following situations would it be most appropriate for an Officer to remove his gun from his holster?

(A) A man enters a subway station without paying a fare and as he runs towards a train he knocks a woman to the ground.
(B) A person grabs a woman's handbag and runs down a crowded street.
(C) A woman hits a young boy with her car and begins to drive away without stopping.
(D) A person is swinging an axe in a crowded area and threatens to kill anyone who comes near him.

83. Police Officer Spencer received the following information from a Grand Larceny victim:

Time of Occurrence:	3:45 P.M.
Place of Occurrence:	Uptown #4 train, 14th Street station
Victim:	Louis Smith
Witness:	Cindy Lewis (Smith's girlfriend)
Description of Suspect:	Unknown
Crime:	Grand Larceny, chain snatch

Officer Spencer is completing a report on the Grand Larceny. Which one of the following expresses the above information *most clearly* and *accurately*?

(A) Cindy Lewis stated that at 3:45 P.M., while aboard the uptown #4 train, an unknown man reached into the train while it was stopped at the 14th Street station and snatched the chain of her boyfriend, Louis Smith.

(B) A male, unidentified by Louis Smith, reached in and stole his chain from an uptown #4 train at the 14th Street station. Cindy Lewis said she was his girlfriend and unable to identify the suspect, who did the snatch at 3:45 P.M.

(C) On the #4 train going uptown, Louis Smith had his chain snatched at the 14th Street station when a man reached in the train. He was traveling with his girlfriend, Cindy Lewis, and they were both unable to identify him when it occurred at 3:45 P.M.

(D) At 3:45 P.M., Cindy Lewis was unable to identify the man who snatched her boyfriend's chain at the 14th Street station. They were traveling uptown on the #4 train when someone reached in and took Smith's chain.

84. While on patrol, Officer Casio responds to a Grand Larceny. The following details were obtained at the scene:

Time of Crime:	Between 9:30 P.M. and midnight
Place of Crime:	In front of 119-30 Long Street
Crime:	Car theft
Vehicle stolen:	1983 Renault
Victim:	Sam Andrews
Suspect:	Unidentified

Officer Casio is completing a report on the incident. Which one of the following expresses the above information *most clearly* and *accurately*?

(A) Between 9:30 P.M. and midnight, Sam Andrews was in front of 119-30 Long Street. A 1983 Renault was stolen by an unidentified person.

(B) An unidentified person stole Sam Andrews' 1983 Renault from in front of 119-30 Long Street between 9:30 P.M., and midnight.

(C) An unidentified person in front of 119-30 Long Street stole a car between 9:30 P.M. and midnight. Sam Andrews has a 1983 Renault.

(D) A 1983 Renault was stolen in front of Sam Andrews at 119-30 Long Street between 9:30 P.M. and midnight by an unidentified person.

Answer questions 85 through 87 solely on the basis of the following map. The flow of traffic is indicated by arrows. If there is only one arrow shown, then traffic flows only in the direction indicated by the arrow. If there are two arrows shown, then traffic flows in both directions. You must follow the flow of traffic.

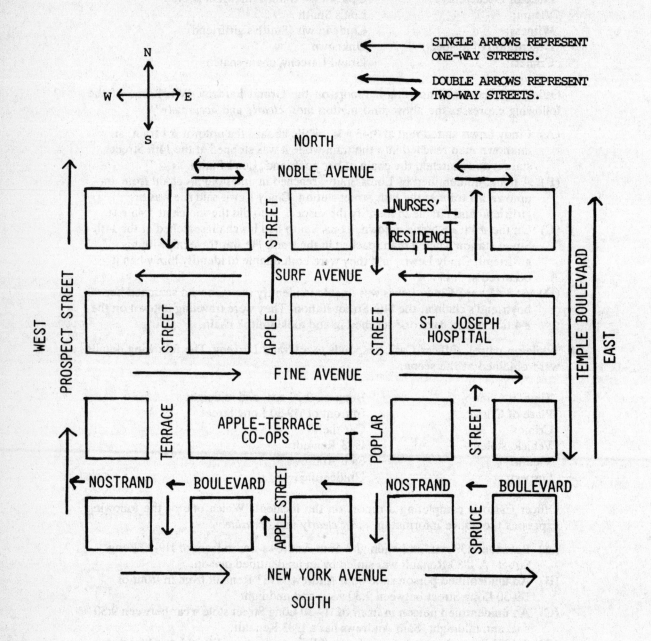

SINGLE ARROWS REPRESENT ONE-WAY STREETS.

DOUBLE ARROWS REPRESENT TWO-WAY STREETS.

85. Police Officers Gannon and Vine are located at the intersection of Terrace Street and Surf Avenue when they receive a call from the radio dispatcher stating that they need to respond to an attempted murder at Spruce Street and Fine Avenue. Which one of the following is the shortest route for them to take in their patrol car, making sure to obey all traffic regulations?

    (A) Travel west on Surf Avenue, then north on Prospect Street, then east on Noble Avenue, then south on Poplar Street, then east on Fine Avenue to Spruce Street.
    (B) Travel east on Surf Avenue, then south on Poplar Street, then east on Fine Avenue to Spruce Street.
    (C) Travel west on Surf Avenue, then south on Prospect Street, then east on Fine Avenue to Spruce Street.
    (D) Travel south on Terrace Street, then east on Fine Avenue to Spruce Street.

86. Police Officers Sears and Ronald are at Nostrand Boulevard and Prospect Street. They receive a call assigning them to investigate a disruptive group of youths at Temple Boulevard and Surf Avenue. Which one of the following is the shortest route for them to take in their patrol car, making sure to obey all traffic regulations?

    (A) Travel north on Prospect Street, then east on Surf Avenue to Temple Boulevard.
    (B) Travel north on Prospect Street, then east on Noble Avenue, then south on Temple Boulevard to Surf Avenue.
    (C) Travel north on Prospect Street, then east on Fine Avenue, then north on Temple Boulevard to Surf Avenue.
    (D) Travel south on Prospect Street, then east on New York Avenue, then north on Temple Boulevard to Surf Avenue.

87. While on patrol at Prospect Street and New York Avenue, Police Officers Ross and Rock are called to a burglary in progress near the entrance to the Apple-Terrace Co-ops on Poplar Street midway between Fine Avenue and Nostrand Boulevard. Which one of the following is the shortest route for them to take in their patrol car, making sure to obey all traffic regulations?

    (A) Travel east on New York Avenue, then north on Poplar Street.
    (B) Travel north on Prospect Street, then east on Fine Avenue, then south on Poplar Street.
    (C) Travel north on Prospect Street, then east on Surf Avenue, then south on Poplar Street.
    (D) Travel east on New York Avenue, then north on Temple Boulevard, then west on Surf Avenue, then south on Poplar Street.

88. While on patrol, Officer Smith responded to the scene of a robbery. Upon his arrival, Mrs. Mary Taylor told Officer Smith that the following items were taken from her at gun point:

- Cash $150.00
- 3 bracelets, each valued at 95.00
- 2 rings, each valued at 70.00
- 1 leather handbag, valued at 100.00

Later that day, Mary Taylor telephoned Officer Smith and informed him that she found a receipt for the leather bag that was taken, and it is actually valued at $159.00.

Officer Smith is preparing a Complaint Report on the robbery. Which one of the following is the total value of the property and cash taken from Mrs. Taylor

(A) $415.00   (C) $675.00
(B) $474.00   (D) $734.00

Answer question 89 solely on the basis of the following information.

Three rapes occurred in the 141st Precinct during the month of April. The reported description of each of the suspects is as follows:

Rape No. 1—Male, white, about 25 years old, short brown hair, gray pants, white tank top shirt, black shoes, scar above right eye and across right cheek, earring in left ear.

Rape No. 2—Male, white, early 40's black hair, gray pants, white shirt, black shoes, black suit jacket, wearing sun glasses.

Rape No. 3—Male, white, 21 years old, black hair, blue dungarees, white sneakers, black leather vest, white T-shirt, tattoo on left arm, earring in right ear.

On April 21, Police Officer Johnson arrested a suspect during an attempted rape. The description of the suspect is as follows:

Rape No. 4—Male, white, 20 years old, short black hair, blue jeans, white sneakers, white T-shirt, tattoo of a ghost on left arm, earring in left ear.

89. Based on the descriptions of the suspects in the first three rapes, Officer Johnson should consider the suspect in the fourth rape as a suspect in

(A) Rape No. 1, but not Rape No. 2 or Rape No. 3
(B) Rape No. 3, but not rape No. 1 or No. 2
(C) Rape No. 1 and Rape No.3, but not Rape No. 2
(D) Rape No. 1 and Rape No. 2, but not Rape No. 3

90. While on patrol, Police Officer Rucco witnesses a robbery and apprehends the suspect. The following information relates to this incident:

Place of Robbery:	In front of 311 Sutter Avenue
Victim:	Veronica Stables, not injured
Suspect:	Male, white, wearing blue jeans, white sneakers, leather jacket
Action Taken:	Suspect apprehended and arrested on the corner of Canal and Vestry Streets.

Officer Rucco is completing a report on the incident. Which one of the following expresses the above information *most clearly* and *accurately*?

(A) Wearing blue jeans, white sneakers, and a leather jacket in front of 311 Sutter Avenue, Veronica Stables was robbed by the suspect and not injured. The white male was apprehended and arrested on the corner of Canal and Vestry Streets.

(B) On the corner of Canal and Vestry Streets was apprehended and arrested a white male. Veronica Stables was robbed and not injured by the suspect wearing blue jeans, white sneakers, and a leather jacket in front of 311 Sutter Avenue.

(C) A white male wearing blue jeans, white sneakers, and a leather jacket in front of 311 Sutter Avenue was apprehended and arrested on the corner of Canal and Vestry streets. Veronica Stables was not injured and robbed by the suspect.

(D) A white male wearing blue jeans, white sneakers, and a leather jacket robbed Veronica Stables in front of 311 Sutter Avenue. The suspect was apprehended and arrested on the corner of Canal and Vestry Streets.

Answer question 91 solely on the basis of the following information.

Police Officers may arrest a person for driving while under the influence of alcohol and then test the person for alcohol use at a police facility. Upon making such an arrest, a Police Officer should do the following in the order given:

1. Remove the prisoner to the precinct station house.
2. Inform the Desk Officer of the arrest.
3. Request the Communications Division to dispatch Highway Police Officers to the testing location where the alcohol test will be conducted.
4. Remove the prisoner to the testing location in order to have the Highway Police Officers conduct a chemical test of the prisoner.
5. Record the results of the test on an Intoxicated Driver Examination Report.
6. Return the prisoner to the precinct station house.

91. While on patrol, Police Officers Riglioni and Cardaci observe the driver of a red Chevrolet driving erratically. The Officers stop the vehicle and ask the driver to get out. The driver gets out of the vehicle and is obviously drunk. The Officers arrest the driver for operating a vehicle while under the influence of alcohol. The Officers take the prisoner to the precinct station house and report the arrest to the Desk Officer. The next step the Officers should take is to

(A) request the Communications Division to send the Highway Police
(B) bring the prisoner to the testing location
(C) conduct a test to determine if the prisoner is drunk
(D) complete the Intoxicated Driver Examination Report.

Answer question 92 solely on the basis of the following information.

Police Officers must sometimes rely on eyewitness accounts of incidents, even though eyewitnesses may make mistakes with regard to some details.

92. Mrs. Levy was the victim of a hit-and-run accident. When Police Officer Murphy arrived at the scene, he interviewed four witnesses who saw a black car strike the victim and leave the scene. The following are license plate numbers provided by the four witnesses. Which one of these numbers should Officer Murphy consider most likely to be correct?

(A) P-82324   (C) F-83424
(B) P-82342   (D) F-62323.

Answer question 93 solely on the basis of the following information.

When Police Officers respond to investigate a complaint of unnecessary loud noise, they should do the following in the order given:

1. Respond to the location of the unnecessary noise.
2. Interview the complainant, if possible.
3. Interview the violator.
4. Correct the condition by advising and warning the violator.
5. Give the violator a summons if the warning is ignored.
6. Make a Memo Book entry concerning the incident.
7. Report all actions taken to the Desk Officer.

93. While on patrol, Police Officer Ryan receives a call at 3 A.M. to respond to 225 Kent Street, Apt. 4J, concerning a complaint of loud music. Upon his arrival, the Officer is met by Mr. Templer who states that his neighbor has been continuously playing his stereo very loudly. As the Officer is speaking to Mr. Templer, he hears a loud stereo playing from the next-door apartment. Officer Ryan goes to the apartment and informs the violator, Mr. Nelson, that Mr. Templer has complained about the noise. Mr. Nelson immediately apologizes for playing his stereo loudly and then lowers the stereo saying he will be more thoughtful in the future. Police Officer Ryan should next

(A) interview Mr. Templer
(B) give Mr. Nelson a summons
(C) make a Memo Book entry
(D) give Mr. Templer a summons.

94. When a motorist commits a traffic violation, a Police Officer may give the motorist either a warning or a traffic ticket. In which one of the following situations should a Police Officer issue a traffic ticket instead of a warning?

(A) A woman is adjusting her child's seat belt while driving.
(B) A man who is driving on a busy street turns his head away from the road to watch a young woman pass by.
(C) A woman who is applying lipstick while driving goes through a stop sign.
(D) A man who is talking to his friend comes to a sudden halt at a red traffic light.

Answer question 95 solely on the basis of the following information.

Grand Larceny 2nd Degree—occurs when a person steals property and when the value of the property is greater than $1500.

Unauthorized Use of a Vehicle—occurs when a person knowingly takes, operates, rides in or otherwise uses a vehicle without the consent of the owner.

95. Will Walker, a car mechanic at a gas station, repairs Mr. Smith's car. Knowing that Mr. Smith is away, Walker decides to borrow the car for the weekend. He drives the car home, parks it on the street, and accidentally leaves the keys in the ignition. Several hours later, Ben Barnes walks past the car and notices the keys in the ignition. Knowing that the car is worth at least $7,000, Barnes breaks into the car and drives it away. Barnes later sells the car to a used car salesman for $8,000. In this situation

   (A) both Barnes and Walker should be charged only with Grand Larceny 2nd Degree
   (B) Barnes should be charged with Grand Larceny 2nd Degree and Unauthorized Use of a Vehicle, and Walker should be charged with Unauthorized Use of a Vehicle
   (C) both Barnes and Walker should be charged only with Unauthorized Use of a Vehicle
   (D) Barnes should be charged with Unauthorized Use of a Vehicle and Walker should be charged with Grand Larceny 2nd Degree and Unauthorized Use of a Vehicle.

96. Police Officer Clay obtained the following information at the scene of burglary:

Time of Occurrence:	3:00 P.M.
Place of Occurrence:	350 Lenox Avenue
Suspect:	Male
Crime:	Burglary; TV and VCR stolen
Witness:	Ed Simms
Victim:	Mrs. Lester

   Police Officer Clay is preparing a report on the burglary. Which one of the following expresses the above information *most clearly* and *accurately*?

   (A) At 3:00 P.M., Mrs. Lester's house at 350 Lenox Avenue was burglarized. Ed Simms reported seeing a man leaving Mrs. Lester's house with a TV and VCR.
   (B) Mrs. Lester's house was burglarized at 3:00 P.M. A man took a TV and a VCR. Mr. Ed Simms saw a man. She lives at 350 Lenox Ave.
   (C) At 350 Lenox Ave., Mrs. Lester's house was burglarized. Mr. Ed Simms saw a man leaving her house at 3:00 P.M. He was carrying a TV and a VCR.
   (D) Ed Simms stated that he witnessed a burglary. It happened at 350 Lenox Ave., at 3:00 P.M. A man took a TV set and a VCR from Mrs. Lester's house.

Answer question 97 solely on the basis of the following information.

While on patrol in September 1988, Police Officer Harris received several reports from people who were robbed as they exited the Georgia Street subway station. The description of each suspect is as follows:

Robbery No. 1—Male, black, early 20's, 5'10", 180 lbs., dark hair, moustache, blue jeans, black jacket, running shoes.

Robbery No. 2—Male, black, 25 to 30 years old, 5'9", 165 lbs., dark hair, dark moustache, glasses, black jeans, green sweat shirt, running shoes.

Robbery No. 3—Male, black, 40 to 45 years old, 5'8", 150 lbs., dark hair, clean shaven, blue jeans, black jacket, running shoes.

On October 6, 1988, a woman was robbed by a male who was loitering near the Georgia Street subway station. Police Officer Harris witnessed the robbery and apprehended the suspect four blocks away. The description of the suspect is as follows:

Robbery No. 4—Male, black, 20-25 years old, 5'10", 175 lbs., dark hair, moustache, blue jeans, black jacket, black cap, sneakers.

97. Based on the above description of the suspects in the first three robberies, Officer Brown should consider the suspect in the fourth robbery as a suspect in

(A) Robbery No. 1, but not Robbery No. 2 or Robbery No. 3
(B) Robbery No. 1 and Robbery No. 2, but not Robbery No. 3
(C) Robbery No. 2 and Robbery No. 3, but not Robbery No. 1
(D) Robbery No. 1, Robbery No. 2, and Robbery No. 3.

98. Officer Stanley obtained the following information regarding a call for help:

Time of Occurrence:	6:40 A.M.
Place of Occurrence:	452 Hull Street, Apt. 4A
Crime:	Rape
Victim:	Jane Allen
Suspect:	Male, white

Officer Stanley is completing a report on the incident. Which one of the following expresses the above information *most clearly* and *accurately*?

(A) Raped at 452 Hull Street, at 6:40 A.M., was Jane Allen in Apt. 4A by a white male.

(B) At 6:40 A.M., Jane Allen was raped by a white male living at 452 Hull Street, Apt. 4A.

(C) A white male at 452 Hull Street, Apt. 4A raped Jane Allen at 6:40 A.M.

(D) At 6:40 A.M., Jane Allen was raped at 452 Hull Street, Apt. 4A, by a white male.

Answer question 99 solely on the basis of the following information.

Complaint—is a report of an unlawful or improper act, or any condition that requires investigation by the Police to determine if an unlawful act has occurred.

Complaints should be recorded in a particular precinct when:

1. There is an arrest for an unlawful act in that precinct; or
2. A resident of that precinct is reported missing; or
3. A dead human body is found on the piers or in the waters bordering that precinct; or
4. Property is lost and the loss is first discovered in that precinct.

99. Police Officer Menke of the 126th Precinct is assigned to prepare the Precinct's Complaint Reports. Which one of the following situations should be recorded as a Complaint by Officer Menke?

(A) While having lunch in the 44th Precinct, Ray Shaw, a businessman who lives in the 126th Precinct, discovers that his briefcase has been stolen.

(B) David Spooner, who lives in the 126th Precinct, is arrested for possession of cocaine in the 56th Precinct.

(C) A dead human body is found floating in the West River approximately fifteen feet from the riverbank bordering the 126th Precinct.

(D) Richard Warman, of the 126th Precinct, reports that his 23-year-old daughter, who lives in the 130th Precinct, has been missing for 48 hours.

Answer question 100 solely on the basis of the following information.

Police Officers Smith and Jones are on patrol when, at approximately 10:00 A.M., James Banks runs up to the patrol car and informs the Officers that he has just been robbed. Mr. Banks is told to get into the patrol car and the Officers proceed to drive around the immediate area in search of the suspect. Mr. Banks gives the following description of the suspect:

Male, black, about 18 years old, 6'1", 190 lbs., wearing blue dungarees, red button-down shirt, red and white sneakers, blue cap, long sideburns, and has a gold front tooth.

Officer Smith is aware that this is the fourth robbery in this area during the past month. The reported descriptions of the suspects involved in the previous three robberies are as follows:

Robbery No.1—Male, black, 21 years old, 6'0", 180 lbs., wearing blue pants, red shirt, red sneakers, blue ski cap, wearing a slight beard.

Robbery No.2—Male, black, 19 years old, 6'0", 185 lbs., wearing blue jeans, red shirt, white sneakers, blue baseball cap, wearing long sideburns.

Robbery No.3—Male, black, 18 years old, 5'7", 150 lbs., wearing blue dungarees, red sweat shirt, red and white sneakers, blue hat, wearing long sideburns.

100. Based on the descriptions that were given of the suspects for the first three robberies, Officer Smith should consider the suspect in the Banks robbery as a suspect in

(A) Robbery No. 2, but not Robbery No. 1 or Robbery No. 3
(B) Robbery No. 1 and Robbery No. 2, but not Robbery No. 3
(C) Robbery No. 2 and Robbery No. 3, but not Robbery No. 1
(D) Robbery No. 1, Robbery No. 2, and Robbery No. 3.

101. Police Officer Roland responded to 233 Main Street to investigate a past burglary. Officer Roland arrived at the scene and interviewed Mrs. Joan Bates. Mrs. Bates stated that her apartment was broken into and the following items were missing:

- 1 Ring valued at $415.00
- Cash $220.00
- Coin Collection valued at $410.00
- 3 Cameras, each valued at $175.00

Officer Roland is preparing a report on the burglary. Which one of the following is the total value of the missing property and cash?

(A) $1,220.00   (C) $1,570.00
(B) $1,395.00   (D) $1,615.00

Answer questions 102 through 104 solely on the basis of the following passage.

Police Officers Ryder and Brown respond to a call concerning a past burglary in a private house located at 1296 Brentwood Road. When the Officers arrive, they are met by William Parker, who owns the house. Mr. Parker tells the Officers that he had been out of town for the entire weekend and, upon his return twenty minutes ago, discovered that the lock on his back door was broken. He also discovered that several items were missing from around his house. At this point, Officer Ryder asks Mr. Parker to show her where the burglars entered. Meanwhile Officer Brown makes a search of the immediate area. Officer Ryder's investigation reveals that the burglars cut a wire located by the front basement window in order to disable the alarm system. The burglars then forced open the lock with a metal bar of some kind. Officer Brown's search of the area uncovers no evidence. Office Ryder then asks Mr. Parker to describe the items which are missing. Mr. Parker says that his 19" color television and clock radio are gone, along with several items that were borrowed from various friends. Among the missing items are a compact disc player owned by David Mills, a videotape recorder owned by Samantha Burns, and a portable tape player with headphones owned by Roger Denning. Officer Ryder lists the missing items and the owners' names in her report and tells Mr. Parker to call the station house in the morning to obtain a report number which he can use if he files an insurance claim.

102. The thieves broke the lock of which entrance?

(A) Side
(B) Front

(C) Basement
(D) Back.

103. Which of the missing items were owned by William Parker?

(A) Color television and clock radio
(B) Compact disc player and tape player
(C) Videotape recorder and compact disc player
(D) Portable tape player and headphones.

104. What crime is this passage primarily concerned with?

(A) Arson
(B) Assault

(C) Burglary
(D) Fraud.

Answer question 105 solely on the basis of the following information.

When a person commits an offense for which a summons may be served, a Police Officer should:

1. Inform the violator of each offense committed.
2. Request that the violator show proof of identity and residence.
3. Take the violator to the station house for investigation if doubt exists concerning his identity.
4. Enter only one offense on a summons.
5. Use a separate summons for any additional offense.

105. Police Officer Hayes stops a motorist for driving through a red light and asks him for his driver's license, registration, and insurance card. The motorist apologizes to Officer Hayes and explains that he left his house in a hurry and forgot his wallet, which contains all of his identification. Officer Hayes asks the driver to state his name and address and advises him that, in addition to receiving a summons for going through the red light, he will receive three summonses for driving without his license, registration, and insurance card. The actions taken by Officer Hayes in this situation were

(A) proper, primarily because the driver may have been lying when he said that he forgot his wallet.
(B) improper, primarily because he did not take the driver to the station house.
(C) proper, primarily because there was no need to investigate further since the driver willingly gave his name and address.
(D) improper, primarily because he should have followed the driver home to check his identification.

106. Police Officer Greg responds to the apartment of a complainant who just reported a child missing. He obtains the following information.

Complainant:	Francis Fallon
Missing Child:	Johnny Red
Age of Child:	5 years old
Description of child:	Male, white, wearing a red T-shirt and blue jeans
Time and place last seen:	Thomas Park, 4:20 P.M.

Officer Greg is about to radio this information to the dispatcher. Which one of the following expresses the above information *most clearly* and *accurately*?

(A) Francis Fallon reported that Johnny Red, a 5-year-old white male, was last seen at 4:20 P.M. in Thomas Park. He was wearing a red T-shirt and blue jeans.

(B) Wearing a red T-shirt and blue jeans, Francis Fallon reported that Johnny Red was last seen at 4:20 P.M. in Thomas Park. He is a white 5-year-old male.

(C) In Thomas Park, Francis Fallon reported that 5-year-old, Johnny Red, a white male, was last seen wearing a red T-shirt and blue jeans at 4:20 P.M.

(D) At 4:20 P.M., Francis Fallon reported in Thomas Park that 5-year-old Johnny Red, a white male, was last seen wearing a red T-shirt and blue jeans.

107. Police Officer Zacks responds to 57th Avenue and Broadway and obtains the following information regarding a vandalism complaint:

Time of Occurrence:	12:00 P.M.
Place of Occurrence:	In front of 5716 Broadway
Damage:	Shattered front windshield of car
Complainant:	Daniel Molley, owner of car
Suspect:	Unidentified teenager

Officer Zacks is completing a report on the incident. Which one of the following expresses the above information *most clearly* and *accurately*?

(A) At 12:00 P.M., an unidentified teenager shattered his car's front windshield in front of 5716 Broadway reported Daniel Molley.

(B) At 12:00 P.M., in front of 5716 Broadway, an unidentified teenager shattered the front windshield of Daniel Molley's car.

(C) At 12:00 P.M., Daniel Molley reported an unidentified teenager in front of 5716 Broadway. His front car windshield was shattered.

(D) A teenager, unidentified, was in front of 5716 Broadway. At 12:00 P.M. Daniel Molley's front windshield was shattered on his car.

Answer question 108 solely on the basis of the following information.

When a juvenile, less than 16 years old, is arrested and charged as a juvenile offender, the arresting Police Officer should do the following in the order given:

1. Bring the juvenile to the station house
2. Notify parents that the juvenile is in custody and of the location of the juvenile.
3. If parents are unavailable to come to the station house, then:
   a. advise juvenile of constitutional rights; and
   b. begin questioning the juvenile.
4. If parents are coming to the station house, then:
   a. advise juvenile of constitutional rights in the parents' presence;
   b. begin questioning the juvenile in the parents' presence.
5. Prepare an Arrest Report.

108. While patrolling, Police Officer Martin observes a male juvenile carrying a gun and robbing an elderly woman. Officer Martin confiscates the gun and arrests 15-year-old Tom Hill. The Officer takes Hill to the station house. The Desk Officer advises Officer Martin to take Hill to the room selected for the questioning of juveniles. Officer Martin then contacts Hill's parents. They inform her that they will be there as soon as possible. Officer Martin should next

(A) begin questioning the juvenile about the offense
(B) prepare an Arrest Report detailing the events of the crime
(C) inform the juvenile of his constitutional rights once his parents arrive and are in the room
(D) request the parents to wait in another room during questioning.

109. While on patrol, Officer Woods responds to a robbery that occurred earlier. Officer Woods obtains the following information at the scene:

Crime:	Robbery
Time of Crime:	7:30 P.M.
Place of Crime:	1177 103rd Avenue
Victim:	Erica Russell
Suspect:	Floyd Benett
Witness:	Ben Jamin

Officer Woods is completing a report on the incident. Which one of the following expresses the above information *most clearly* and *accurately*?

(A) At 1177 103rd Avenue, Ben Jamin stated that Floyd Benett was seen robbing Erica Russell at 7:30 P.M.
(B) At 7:30 P.M., Ben Jamin witnessed Floyd Benett rob Erica Russell at 1177 103rd Avenue.
(C) At 7:30 P.M., Ben Jamin stated that he saw Floyd Benett rob Erica Russell at 1177 103rd Avenue.
(D) Ben Jamin witnessed Floyd Benett at 1177 103rd Avenue. At 7:30 P.M., Erica Russell was robbed.

110. Police Officer Joplin has finished investigating a report of Grand Larceny and has obtained the following information:

Place of Occurrence:	Orchard Street Furs, 121 Orchard Street
Time of Occurrence:	4:00 P.M.
Victim:	Sam Houston, owner of store
Crime:	$3000 stolen
Suspect:	Unknown black male

Officer Joplin is preparing a report on the incident. Which one of the following expresses the above information *most clearly* and *accurately*?

(A) Sam Houston, owner of Orchard Street Furs, located at 121 Orchard Street, reported that at 4:00 P.M. an unknown black male stole $3000 from his store.

(B) Orchard Street Furs is located at 121 Orchard Street. Sam Houston reported at 4:00 P.M. an unknown black male stole $3000 from his store.

(C) At 4:00 P.M., $3000 was stolen from the owner of Orchard Street Furs. Sam Houston was robbed by a black male at 121 Orchard Street.

(D) At 4:00 P.M., an unknown black male stole $3000. Sam Houston's store, Orchard Street Furs, is located at 121 Orchard Street.

111. Officers Reed and Shaw respond to the scene of robbery and obtain the following information from a witness:

Crime:	Bank Robbery, $20,000 stolen
Bank:	Federal Conserve Bank
Time of Crime:	2:30 P.M.
Suspect:	Female, white, armed with a shotgun
Witness:	Frank Count, bank teller

Officer Reed is recording the details of the crime in her memo book. Which one of the following expresses the above information *most clearly* and *accurately*?

(A) At 2:30 P.M., Frank Count, a bank teller at Federal Conserve Bank reported a robbery. The bank was robbed of $20,000 by a shotgun and a white female.

(B) Frank Count, a bank teller, reported that the Federal Conserve Bank was robbed of $20,000 at 2:30 P.M. by a white female armed with a shotgun.

(C) A bank teller, reported Frank Count, robbed the Federal Conserve bank of $20,000. She was white and armed with a shotgun.

(D) At 2:30 P.M., the Federal Conserve Bank was robbed of $20,000. Frank Count, a bank teller, reported a white female armed with a shotgun.

Answer question 112 solely on the basis of the following information.

When a Police Officer receives property found by someone other than a Police Officer he should:

1. Issue a receipt including a description of the property to the person delivering the property.
2. Enter the facts in the Activity Log.
3. Prepare a Property Clerk's Invoice.
4. Deliver the property and invoice to the Desk Officer.
5. Resume patrol.

112. Arlene Harris found a brown leather wallet containing twenty dollars and two credit cards. She approached Police Officer Taylor, who was patrolling on the corner of Concorde and Broadway. Officer Taylor took the wallet and handed Ms. Harris a signed note which stated: "Received property from Ms. Arlene Harris." He thanked Ms. Harris for her honesty and then entered the events including Ms. Harris' address and telephone number in his Activity Log. He then went directly to the precinct where he prepared a Property Clerk's Invoice which he gave, along with the wallet, to Sgt. Mead, the Desk Officer. Officer Taylor then returned to patrol. In this situation Officer Taylor's actions were

(A) proper, primarily because he thanked Ms. Harris for her honesty
(B) improper, primarily because he should have asked Ms. Harris to take the wallet to the precinct
(C) proper, primarily because he did not leave his post to return the wallet
(D) improper, primarily because he did not give Ms. Harris a proper receipt for the wallet.

113. Police Officer Hoff responds to the scene of a hit-and-run accident and obtains the following information:

Occurrence:	Woman hit by a speeding car
Time of Occurrence:	1:30 P.M.
Location of Occurrence:	35th Avenue between 4th and 5th Streets
Description of Car:	Green Ford
Victim:	Lois Nettle
Injuries:	Broken right leg

Officer Hoff is radioing for an ambulance. Which one of the following expresses the above information *most clearly* and *accurately*?

(A) Lois Nettle broke her right leg between 4th and 5th Streets on 35th Avenue. At 1:30 P.M., a woman was hit by a speeding green Ford.
(B) A car hit Lois Nettle and broke her right let at 1:30 P.M. A green Ford was speeding on 35th Avenue between 4th and 5th Streets.
(C) Lois Nettle broke her right leg when a speeding green Ford hit her at 1:30 P.M. on 35th Avenue between 4th and 5th Streets.
(D) At 1:30 P.M., a green Ford was speeding. On 35th Avenue, between 4th and 5th Streets Lois Nettle broke her right leg when she was hit.

Answer questions 114 through 116 solely on the basis of the following passage.

Police Officers Wilson and Mills receive a radio call to investigate an auto accident involving injuries. Upon their arrival, Officer Mills approaches a Mustang convertible which had been driven into the side of an Oldsmobile sedan. There is also a small Dodge truck several feet away which had crashed into a fire hydrant. Officer Mills immediately determines that no one is injured and radios the dispatcher to cancel the ambulance. Meanwhile, Officer Wilson interviews Sam Thomas, who is the owner and driver of the Mustang. Mr. Thomas states that he was driving south on Bedford Avenue when a large Oldsmobile pulled out of a parking lot in front of him. Mr. Thomas goes on to say that he immediately hit his brakes but slid into the side of the Oldsmobile. Officer Mills interviews Thomas Parker, who is the driver of the Oldsmobile. Mr. Parker admits that he drove out of the parking lot without looking for oncoming traffic. He tells Officer Mills that he is not used to driving and borrowed the Oldsmobile from his brother, Harold Parker, who is the owner of the car. Finally, Officer Wilson interviews Rutger Schmidt, who is the driver of the Dodge truck. Mr. Schmidt indicates that, in an attempt to avoid the accident, he swerved out of the way, lost control of the truck, and ran into a fire hydrant. Mr. Schmidt tells Officer Wilson that he works for the Acme Exterminating Company, which owns the truck. Following the interviews, the two Officers write their accident report and indicate the damage to each vehicle. The Mustang had a damaged front bumper and grill, and broken headlights; the Oldsmobile had a dented driver's side quarter panel; the Dodge truck had a crumpled bumper and blown right front tire.

114. Who was the owner of the Oldsmobile sedan?

(A) Sam Thomas

(B) Thomas Parker

(C) Harold Parker

(D) Rutger Schmidt

115. What was damaged on the Dodge truck?

(A) Driver's side quarter panel.

(B) Bumper and right front tire.

(C) Tailgate and tail lights.

(D) Front bumper, grill, and headlights.

116. The driver of which vehicle was the primary cause of the accident?

(A) The Mustang convertible

(B) The Patrol Car

(C) The Dodge truck

(D) The Oldsmobile sedan.

Answer question 117 solely on the basis of the following information.

Upon observing a vehicle accident, a Police Officer should do the following in the order given:

1. Park the patrol car so that it will not block traffic.
2. Determine if there are any injuries and request an ambulance if needed.
3. Divert traffic if necessary.
4. Obtain drivers' licenses, vehicle registrations, and insurance identification cards of the drivers involved.
5. Have vehicles removed from the roadway.
6. Determine the cause of the accident.

117. Officer Jackson responds to the scene of an accident. Upon arrival, Officer Jackson parks his patrol car in a spot where it is not blocking traffic. As he approaches the intersection on foot, he sees that a taxicab and a white Toyota have been involved in a head-on collision. He also notices that a large crowd has gathered around the damaged vehicles. Traffic is backed up in all directions leading into the intersection, and a man who is bleeding from the head is lying on the roadway. The next step Officer Jackson should take is to

(A) request an ambulance
(B) direct traffic away from the accident
(C) have the vehicles removed from the roadway
(D) determine the cause of the accident.

118. Police Officer Boyle was driving his patrol car in the snow when he was involved in a car accident. The following information was obtained at the scene of the accident:

Place of Occurrence: Intersection of Canal and Church Streets
Time of Occurrence: 10:15 A.M.
Vehicle Number: 5729
Damage to Vehicle: Hood, right fender, and windshield
Injuries Sustained by Officer: Two broken arms.

Police Officer Nevins is completing a report on the accident. Which one of the following expresses the above information *most clearly* and *accurately*?

(A) Police Officer Boyle had two broken arms at 10:15 A.M. Vehicle 5729 was in a car accident at the intersection of Canal and Church Streets. It has a damaged hood, right fender, and windshield.
(B) At 10:15 A.M., vehicle 5729 and Police Officer Boyle were in a car accident. At the intersection of Canal and Church Streets they suffered two broken arms, a damaged hood, right fender, and windshield.
(C) Vehicle 5729 had a damaged hood, right fender, and windshield at 10:15 A.M. At the intersection of Canal and Church Streets Police Officer Boyle had two broken arms in a car accident.
(D) At 10:15 A.M., Police Officer Boyle was in a car accident at the intersection of Canal and Church Streets. Officer Boyle suffered two broken arms, and vehicle 5729 sustained damage to the hood, right fender, and windshield.

Answer question 119 solely on the basis of the following information.

Juvenile—a child who is at least seven years of age but less than sixteen years of age.

A juvenile report should be prepared for the following:

1. All violations and offenses except felonies, unlawful assembly, and photographable offenses.
2. Petty violations.
3. A juvenile in need of supervision.
4. An intoxicated juvenile.
5. A stranded juvenile.
6. A runaway juvenile (New York City resident).

119. Police Officer Fillmore apprehends Walter Gardiner, who is fifteen years old. Walter was participating in a political demonstration in front of his 5th Avenue apartment in Manhattan. The protesters did not have a valid permit allowing them to demonstrate at that location. A witness states that she saw Walter drinking alcohol, but P.O. Fillmore sees no indication that the youth is intoxicated. The Officer believes that the youth's parents were also participants in the demonstration. Walter has no previous arrest record. Officer Fillmore decides to prepare a Juvenile Report for unlawful assembly for Walter. The action taken by Police Officer Fillmore is

(A) improper, primarily because a Juvenile Report should not be prepared for unlawful assembly
(B) proper, primarily because Walter is a New York City resident who has not reached his sixteenth birthday
(C) improper, primarily because Walter has the right to express his political beliefs
(D) proper, primarily because a Juvenile Report should be prepared for a juvenile who has been drinking.

120. Police Officer Frankle responds to the scene of an abused child. Officer Frankle obtains the following information:

Complaint:	Gladys Jones
Date of Complaint:	October 12, 1988
Time of Complaint:	2:00 P.M.
Name of Child:	Henry Worth
Child's Injuries:	Bruises to face and arms

Police Officer Frankle is notifying the Bureau of Child Welfare about this incident. Which of the following expresses the above information *most clearly* and *accurately*?

(A) On October 12, 1988, Henry Worth had bruises on his face and arms, reported Gladys Jones at 2:00 P.M.
(B) With bruises to the face and arms, Gladys Jones reported Henry Worth on October 12, 1988, at 2:00 P.M.
(C) On October 12, 1988, at 2:00 P.M., Gladys Jones reported that Henry Worth had bruises on his face and arms.
(D) Henry Worth, with bruises to his face and arms, reported Gladys Jones on October 12, 1988 at 2:00 P.M.

Answer question 121 solely on the basis of the following information.

Burglary 1st Degree—occurs when a person knowingly enters or remains unlawfully in a dwelling with intent to commit a crime therein, and when, in entering or while in the dwelling or in immediate flight from it, he or another participant in the crime:

1. Is armed with explosives or a deadly weapon; or
2. Causes physical injury to any person who is not a participant in the crime; or
3. Displays what appears to be a pistol, revolver, rifle, shotgun, machine gun, or other firearm.

Dwelling—a building which is usually occupied by a person living there at night.

121. Which one of the following situations is the best example of Burglary in the First Degree?

(A) Carrying only a flashlight, Thomas Jackson climbs through the dining room window of the Bentley estate and steals $20,000 worth of jewelry.
(B) Bill Watson breaks into a house to steal a VCR. While in the house he sees Mrs. Campbell. Watson then pulls out a gun and tells her to give him her VCR or he will kill her.
(C) Joe Smith and Mark Star, each carrying revolvers, unlawfully break into an office building to commit a robbery. While inside the building they hear a noise and try to run out. On their way out, Star pushes Smith to the ground, causing him physical injury.
(D) Tommy Taylor breaks into a department store at 2:00 A.M. to steal a television set. When a security guard confronts him, Taylor pulls out a gun and pushes the guard to the ground, causing him physical injury.

Answer question 122 solely on the basis of the following information.

To ensure fair and proper proceedings when investigations are conducted, a Police Officer must do the following in the order given:

1. Inform the suspect that he must appear in a lineup for identification in connection with the crime.
2. Arrest the suspect if he does not agree to voluntarily appear in the lineup.
3. Notify the detective supervisor who will personally supervise the lineup.
4. Give the suspect Miranda Warnings if he is to be questioned before or after the lineup.

122. Police Officers Shore and Thompson are looking for a male who was involved in a robbery and stabbing. A witness to the crime gives the Officers a description that matches the description of a person named Rodney Pitts. The Officers find Mr. Pitts at his home and tell him that he must appear in a lineup because he fits the description of a man who committed a robbery and stabbing. Mr. Pitts angrily denies his involvement with the crimes, but agrees to take part in the lineup. The next step the Officers should take is to

(A) tell Mr. Pitts that he must appear in a lineup
(B) contact the detective supervisor
(C) place the suspect under arrest
(D) advise Mr. Pitts of Miranda Warnings.

123. Police Officer Pepper responds to a shooting and obtains the following information:

Victim:	John Rice
Suspect:	Rudy Johnson
Witness:	Mary Rice, wife of victim
Location:	Rudy's Bar, 1492 York Avenue
Weapon:	.38 caliber revolver
Injury:	Wound to left leg

Officer Pepper is preparing a report on the incident. Which one of the following expresses the above information *most clearly* and *accurately*?

(A) Rudy Johnson, witnessed by his wife Mary Rice shot John Rice with a .38 caliber revolver in Rudy's Bar, 1492 York Avenue. Mr. Rice had a wound to his left leg.
(B) With a wound to the left leg, Mary Rice witnessed Rudy Johnson shoot John Rice in Rudy's Bar at 1492 York Avenue. Mr. Johnson had a .38 caliber revolver.
(C) Mary Rice witnessed Rudy Johnson shoot her husband, John Rice, with a .38 caliber revolver in Rudy's Bar at 1492 York Avenue. Mr. Rice was wounded in the left leg.
(D) Rudy Johnson was in Rudy's Bar at 1492 York Avenue. Mary Rice witnessed her husband shot by a .38 caliber revolver in the left leg.

124. Police Officers Simon and Peters receive a call to respond to a possible child abuse case. The following information was obtained by the Officers:

Occurrence:	Child found alone in apartment
Time of Occurrence:	11:00 P.M.
Place of Occurrence:	463 Lott Street, Apt. 3A
Child Found By:	Deborah Fields, neighbor
Child:	Angela Bolds, three years old
Parent of Child:	Mary Bolds, mother

Officers Simon and Peters are completing a report for the Bureau of Child Welfare. Which one of the following expresses the above information *most clearly* and *accurately*?

(A) Angela Bolds, three years old, was found in Apt. 3A of 463 Lott Street, by herself without her mother, Mary Bolds, by a neighbor who is named Deborah Fields at 11:00 P.M.

(B) At 463 Lott Street, Apt. 3A, Deborah Fields, a neighbor, found Angela Bolds, who is three years old, by herself in her apartment. Her mother, Mary Bolds, was not home at 11:00 P.M.

(C) Deborah Fields, a neighbor, found Angela Bolds, three years old, by herself in Apt. 3A at 11:10 P.M. The child's mother, Mary Bolds, who resides at 463 Lott Street, was not home.

(D) At 11:00 P.M., Deborah Fields, a neighbor, found three-year-old Angela Bolds alone in Apt. 3A of 463 Lott Street. Mrs. Fields stated that the child's mother, Mary Bolds, was not at home.

125. Police Officer Johnson responds to the scene of an assault and obtains the following information:

Time of Occurrence:	8:30 P.M.
Place of Occurrence:	120-18 119th Avenue, Apt. 2A
Suspects:	John Andrews, victim's ex-husband and unknown white male
Victim:	Susan Andrews
Injury:	Broken right arm

Officer Johnson is preparing a complaint report on the incident. Which one of the following expresses the above information *most clearly* and *accurately*?

(A) Susan Andrews was assaulted at 120-18 119th Avenue, Apt. 2A. At 8:30 P.M. her ex-husband, John Andrews, and an unknown white male broke her arm.

(B) At 8:30 P.M., Susan Andrews was assaulted at 120-18 119th Avenue, Apt, 2A by her ex-husband, John Andrews, and an unknown white male. Her right arm was broken.

(C) John Andrews, an unknown white male, and Susan Andrews's ex-husband, assaulted and broke her right arm at 8:30 P.M., at 120-18 119th Avenue, Apt. 2A.

(D) John Andrews, ex-husband of Susan Andrews, broke her right arm with an unknown white male at 120-18 119th Avenue, at 8:30 P.M. in Apt. 2A.

Answer questions 126 through 128 solely on the basis of the following passage.

Police Officer Lombardo was dispatched to the scene of an apparently dead human body. His supervisor and another Officer were at the scene, as were two paramedics. The paramedics, Pete Lizzo and Erick Clark, had just pronounced the body dead at 6:55 p.m. There were no relatives present and a neighbor, Eddie Torres, told Officer Lombardo that the dead person lived alone and had no family. Mr. Torres agreed to be a witness to the search of the premises. Officer Lombardo knew that the police were required to voucher or hold all valuables and important papers for safekeeping if a close relative did not live with the dead person. The apartment was filled with a large number of possessions including two gold rings, a gold watch, $200 in cash, and kitchen and living room furniture. They also found an old black and white television set, old clothing, and numerous kitchen utensils. In a tin box, the Officer found a birth certificate, social security card, and the dead person's diary. After the search was completed, the jewelry, cash, birth certificate, and social security card were vouchered. Eddie Torres signed Officer Lombardo's memo book.

126. Of the following, which items were vouchered by Officer Lombardo?

(A) Two gold rings, a gold watch, a social security card, birth certificate, and $200 in cash

(B) A gold watch, two gold rings, $200 cash, a diary, and a social security card

(C) A birth certificate, social security card, diary, jewelry, and $200 cash

(D) A social security card, two gold watches, a gold ring, a birth certificate, and $200 cash.

127. The search was witnessed by

(A) a neighbor
(B) a relative
(C) a police officer
(D) a paramedic.

128. Officer Lombardo vouchered the dead person's property because

(A) the paramedics were present
(B) a supervisor was not available
(C) there was only one witness
(D) there was no relative living with the dead person.

Answer question 129 solely on the basis of the following information.

When Police Officers arrive at the scene of a fire, they should do the following in the order given:

1. Send an alarm or make sure one has been sent.
2. Direct a responsible person to remain at the alarm box in order to direct fire vehicles.
3. Park the patrol car in a location that will not interfere with fire-fighting operations.
4. Warn and assist occupants in evacuation of building.
5. Upon arrival of fire vehicles, establish police lines beyond the fire apparatus and hydrants in use.

129. While on patrol, Police Officers Gannett and James see flames and smoke coming from the top floor of an apartment building and notice that the Fire Department is not on the scene. Officer Gannett double-parks his vehicle in front of the building. Officer James immediately walks to the alarm box on the corner, pulls the alarm, and awaits the arrival of the Fire Department. The next step Officer Gannett should take is to

(A) ask the building landlord to find an alarm box and direct Fire Department vehicles
(B) enter the building in order to warn and evacuate occupants
(C) establish police lines so that fire vehicles will be able to get to the building
(D) park his patrol car in a spot where it will not block fire vehicles.

130. While on patrol, Officers Banks and Thompson see a man lying on the ground bleeding. Officer Banks records the following details about the incident:

Time of Incident:	3:15 P.M.
Place of Incident:	Sidewalk in front of 517 Rock Avenue
Incident:	Tripped and fell
Name of Injured:	John Blake
Injury:	Head wound
Action Taken:	Transported to Merry Hospital

Officer Banks is completing a report on the incident. Which one of the following expresses the above information *most clearly* and *accurately*?

(A) At 3:15 P.M., Mr. John Blake was transported to Merry Hospital. He tripped and fell injuring his head on the sidewalk in front of 517 Rock Avenue.
(B) Mr. John Blake tripped and fell on the sidewalk at 3:15 P.M. in front of 517 Rock Avenue. He was transported to Merry Hospital while he sustained a head wound.
(C) Mr. John Blake injured his head when he tripped and fell on the sidewalk in front of 517 Rock Avenue at 3:15 P.M. He was transported to Merry Hospital.
(D) A head was wounded on the sidewalk in front of 517 Rock Avenue at 3:15 P.M. Mr. John Blake tripped and fell and was transported to Merry Hospital.

Answer question 131 solely on the basis on the following information.

When assigned to investigate a complaint, a Police Officer should

1. Interview witnesses and obtain facts.
2. Conduct a thorough investigation of circumstances concerning the complaint.
3. Prepare a Complaint Report.
4. Determine if the Complaint Report should be closed or referred for further investigation.
5. Enter Complaint Report on the Complaint Report Index and obtain a Complaint Report Number at the station house.

131. While on patrol, Police Officer John is instructed by his supervisor to investigate a complaint by Mr. Stanley Burns, who was assaulted by his brother-in-law, Henry Traub. After interviewing Mr. Burns, Officer John learns that Mr. Traub has been living with Mr. Burns for the past two years. Officer John accompanies Mr. Burns to his apartment but Mr. Traub is not there. Officer John fills out the Complaint Report and takes the report back to the station house where it is entered on the Complaint Report Index and assigned a Complaint Report Number. Officer John's actions were

(A) improper, primarily because he should have stayed at Mr. Burns' apartment and waited for Mr. Traub to return in order to arrest him
(B) proper, primarily because after obtaining all the facts, he took the report back to the station house and was assigned a Complaint Report Number
(C) improper, primarily because he should have decided whether to close the report or refer it for further investigation
(D) proper, primarily because he was instructed by his supervisor to take the report from Mr. Burns even though it involved his brother-in-law.

132. Police Officers are sometimes required to respond to family disputes and, when appropriate, refer a person to Family Court for counseling or other appropriate services. In which one of the following situations would it be most appropriate for an Officer to refer the person involved to Family Court?

(A) A husband who is threatening to harm his wife because she spends too much money.
(B) Two sisters arguing over the use of the telephone.
(C) Three roommates arguing about their recent rent increase.
(D) A mother yelling at her 16-year-old son for failing his history test.

Answer questions 133 through 140 on the basis of the following sketches. The first face on top is a sketch of an alleged criminal based on witnesses' descriptions at the crime scene. One of the four sketches below that face is the way the suspect looked after changing appearance. Assume that NO surgery has been done on the suspect.

133.

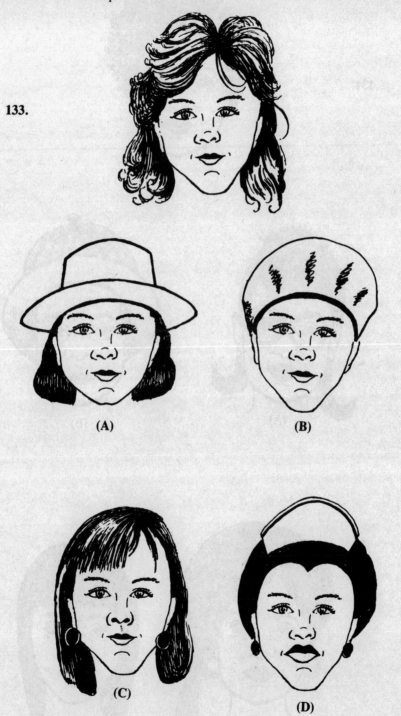

(A)   (B)

(C)   (D)

134.

(A)

(B)

(C)

(D)

135.

(A)

(B)

(C)

(D)

136.

(A) (B)

(C) (D)

137.

138.

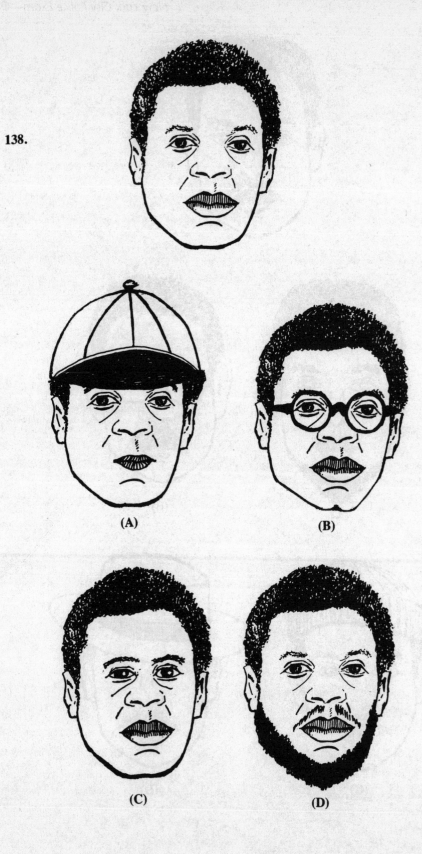

139.

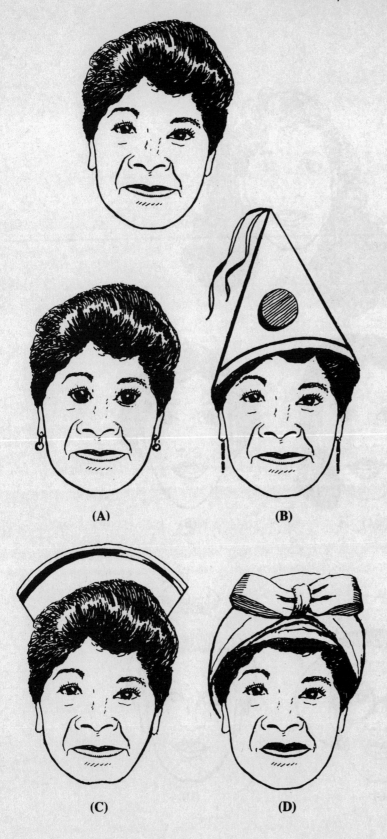

(A)

(B)

(C)

(D)

140.

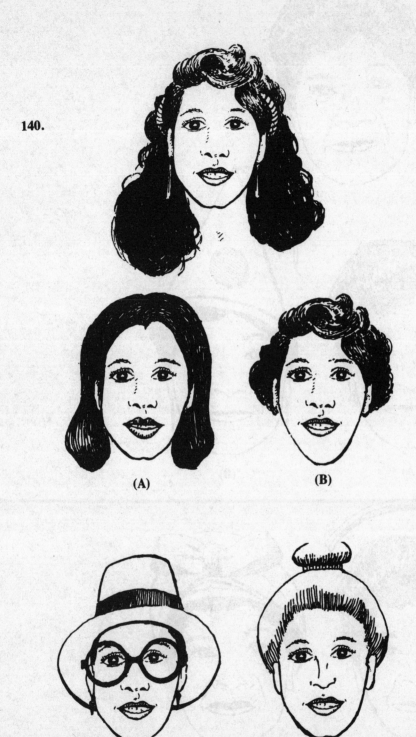

(A)

(B)

(C)

(D)

Please check your Answer Sheet to make sure that you have written in and blackened your Social Security number correctly. If you have not yet written in and blackened your Social Security number, please do so immediately. If you have incorrectly written in or blackened your Social Security number, please correct the mistake immediately. Failure to correctly blacken your Social Security number may result in your Answer Sheet not being rated.

PROTEST PROCEDURE

Any candidate wishing to file a protest to one or more key answers on this examination must submit an original and four copies of the protest, together with supporting evidence, to PROTEST—Police Officer, Department of Personnel, 220 Church Street, NY, NY 10013. Protests will be accepted for a period of thirty (30) days beginning October 31, 1988. Protests must be *received* by the last day of the protest period (November 30, 1988).

Protests must be submitted in the following form. For each proposed key answer you protest, you must start a new page and each page must be headed by the following: Examination title, examination number, question number, test date, your Social Security Number. The protest must include a statement explaining why the answer you selected is as good as or better than the proposed key answer, and must include any additional supporting evidence you wish to submit. You may not modify or add to your protest once it is submitted. However, you may submit separate protests to additional questions within the thirty (30) day protest period.

After you have prepared the four copies, print your name and address on the original pages only and sign the last page of the original protest. Do not include your name or address on any other copies. You must print *only* your Social Security Number on each page of the four copies. *PROTESTS SENT WITHOUT THE FOUR COPIES WILL NOT BE CONSIDERED!*

In order to be informed of the availability of the Validation Board Report for this test, please include a postage-paid, self-addressed, business-size envelope with your protests.

RECORD YOUR ANSWERS IN THIS TEST BOOKLET
BEFORE THE LAST SIGNAL

ANSWER SHEET COLLECTION—When you finish the test, remain seated and signal the monitor to collect your answer sheet. Leave the building quickly and quietly.

DO NOT telephone this Department to request information on the progress of the rating of this test. Such information will *NOT* be given. You will be notified individually by mail of your rating after all papers have been rated. Notify this Department promptly in writing of any change of your address. You should indicate your Social Security Number and the title and number of the examination in any correspondence to the Department of Personnel with respect to this examination.

TAKE THIS QUESTION BOOKLET WITH YOU

PROPOSED ANSWER KEY FOR WRITTEN TEST
HELD ON OCTOBER 29, 1988

1. B	29. D	57. D	85. D	113. C
2. A	30. D	58. C	86. C	114. C
3. D	31. B	59. A	87. B	115. B
4. C	32. C	60. A	88. D	116. D
5. B	33. A	61. B	89. B	117. A
6. D	34. D	62. A	90. D	118. D
7. A	35. D	63. C	91. A	119. A
8. D	36. B	64. C	92. A	120. C
9. C	37. C	65. D	93. C	121. B
10. A	38. C	66. B	94. C	122. B
11. D	39. D	67. A	95. B	123. C
12. A	40. A	68. C	96. A	124. D
13. C	41. C	69. D	97. B	125. B
14. B	42. A	70. C	98. D	126. A
15. C	43. D	71. A	99. C	127. A
16. B	44. C	72. B	100. B	128. D
17. D	45. B	73. D	101. C	129. D
18. B	46. D	74. A	102. D	130. C
19. A	47. B	75. B	103. A	131. C
20. C	48. C	76. A	104. C	132. A
21. D	49. D	77. D	105. B	133. B
22. C	50. A	78. D	106. A	134. C
23. C	51. C	79. C	107. B	135. D
24. D	52. C	80. B	108. C	136. A
25. B	53. B	81. A	109. B	137. A
26. C	54. B	82. D	110. A	138. D
27. A	55. D	83. A	111. B	139. B
28. B	56. B	84. B	112. D	140. C

ANSWER EXPLANATIONS

1. **(B)** You may not have considered the ambulance to be parked; you may not have remembered that the ambulance was on Elm Street. However, you must choose from among four choices. Of the choices offered, only an ambulance appears anywhere in the picture.

2. **(A)** The only bus is a Northside Bus.

3. **(D)** The man with a gun, dark glasses, and a necklace in his hand is wearing a white shirt with black dots.

4. **(C)** The cab that is undergoing a tire change has been pulled up in a towaway zone.

5. **(B)** The car that is angled across Elm Street near the man lying in the roadway bears the license plate 8K46. This is the only license plate visible in the picture.

6. **(D)** There is a man standing at the open second-floor window of M & P Music World.

7. **(A)** You probably noticed that the robbery at knifepoint was occurring at the corner and that the streets were Brady and 7th. You do have to focus on tiny details like East and West, or in this case simply E.

8. **(D)** There is a violinist standing mid-block, just in front of the Blair Savings Bank.

9. **(C)** The young man with the knife is wearing a black baseball cap, a short-sleeved white shirt, and plaid trousers.

10. **(A)** The person in the lower right-hand corner who is holding a gun is a bearded white male wearing light-colored pants and a plaid shirt with sleeves rolled up.

11. **(D)** The purse-snatcher running towards the subway has the number 94 on his shirt. From these last three questions, you should recognize that you must direct your attention especially to pictures of people who appear to be involved in some sort of wrongdoing. Focus in on both appearance and location.

12. **(A)** The family dispute was in Apartment 1928. The call came from Mrs. Debra Lacoste in Apartment 1930, obviously a neighbor.

13. **(C)** The officers were parked in front of 945 Howard Street, but the disturbance was at 779 Seward Street in Apartment 1928.

14. **(B)** The Order of Protection stated that Mr. Ross was not to see his children, yet he had come to his wife's apartment (also against the order) to visit the children. This was the direct cause for the arrest. Ross yelled at his wife, not at his children. Paragraphs that are full of details like this one tend to ask very specific questions, which are answered by careful reading and attention to the details. Since this is not a memory series, you may look back to check the facts. Careful initial reading with underlining of facts should save you time.

15. **(C)** Again, careful reading is the key. The word that governs the correct answer is "intentionally."

16. **(B)** Pay special attention to questions that offer you a set procedure to follow in numbered steps. Officer Jones has given reasonable aid with the blanket and has radioed for an ambulance. The call was made only 15 minutes ago; it is not yet time to call again. The correct procedure is to post a responsible person (John Rutherford, the business partner, is a good choice) outside to direct the medics.

17. **(D)** This is a relatively easy judgment question. Obviously, the activity that must arouse greatest suspicion in an area plagued by burglaries is a door-to-door check, presumably to learn which premises are unattended.

18. **(B)** All four choices include all the necessary information; therefore, your task is to choose the best organized statement. Remember that other officers must rely on the information to pursue the suspect. They must know: time, place, full description and clothing of suspect, and direction of flight. If information is given in haphazard order, as in (C) "approximately 6 feet tall five minutes ago," valuable time will be lost while the message is interpreted.

19. **(A)** Some "clearly and accurately" questions are more obvious than others. Here the statement in choice (A) is so far superior in organization to any of the others that you have no doubt. This type of question gives you a chance to prove the logic and orderliness of your thinking.

20. **(C)** You should be catching on to this type of question. All information that logically belongs together must be presented together. Thus, we must know who belongs to which car and who sustained which injury. There might be an even better way to express the information, but you must choose the best way offered.

21. **(D)** The pistol license expired on September 9, 1988, and the date of this incident is September 10, 1988. Directive #4 states that the person must be taken to the station house if the license has expired.

22. **(C)** Approach this question by counting the elements that are common to the greatest number of accounts. Choices (A) and (C) both begin with P-518 whereas the other two witnesses have given quite different versions, so chances are that either (A) or (C) is correct. As a fourth digit, "8" appears twice while "5" is only reported once, so consider (C) to be the most likely answer. Go on to the final digit. "6" is reported three times, and (C) is one of the times it is reported. While you have no guarantee of accuracy, (C) is the best choice based upon common elements.

23. **(C)** Officer Anderson has reported to the location of the complainant and has obtained a description of the missing person. Before she can begin the search, she must find out where the missing person was last seen.

24. **(D)** In choice (C) nothing is taken. In the other three choices, no property is valued at more than one thousand dollars nor are firearms taken. In choice (D) the value of the property is only $20, but the property is taken directly from the person of the victim, so the action is classified as Grand Larceny in the Fourth Degree.

25. **(B)** The organization: who is involved, description of the person, what happened, when, and where.

26. **(C)** Choices (A) and (D) are ridiculous. The stolen auto was not arrested nor was Michael Wadsworth arrested for driving at 51st Street and 8th Avenue. (B) is not incorrect, but (C) reads much more smoothly and sensibly.

27. **(A)** Take this step by step. The robberies take place on Lott Avenue between E. 98th Street and Hughes Place. Only choice (A) offers you

this location, so you need search no farther for the correct answer. If more than one choice had named the same blocks, you would have had to make your choice on the basis of days of the week and possibly time of day as well.

28. **(B)** The rapes seem to occur on Mondays and Wednesdays, so Officer Wells should not be working a weekend patrol. Since the rapes take place in the morning, choice (B), weekdays from 7:30 A.M. to 3:30 P.M., would seem the most effective period for rape control.

29. **(D)** Prisoners have been known to hang themselves with shoelaces. The other three choices offer no conceivable danger.

30. **(D)** The officer has found and removed a weapon, but this find was only incidental to the process of handcuffing. Regulations state that the officer must actually search the prisoner and the nearby area for weapons and evidence before advising the prisoner of his legal rights.

31. **(B)** This choice identifies the victim, tells where he lives, when and where the crime took place, what happened, and the nature and value of the stolen property.

32. **(C)** Ms. Starr lives in Apartment 1402, on the 14th floor. Mr. Babbit lives in Apartment 1407, obviously the same floor. Recognize this as the beginning of a series of detail questions. Refer to the passage as needed.

33. **(A)** Officer Grice is qualified in the recovery of fingerprints.

34. **(D)** The first burglary occurred on December 5. The last burglary occurred on December 6. Peter Remo was arrested ten days after the last burglary, December 16.

35. **(D)** Ms. Starr's lock had been stuffed with toothpicks. It was Ms. Chung's lock that was stuffed with chewing gum.

36. **(B)** Officer Molina has ascertained the facts, has assured that Ms. Martin does not need medical attention, and has learned that Mr. Martin has left the apartment. She is up to step 4 and must now begin searching the area for Mr. Martin.

37. **(C)** Regulation 1 states that the person should be handcuffed with hands behind back. The

activity was improper because it was against regulations. The narrative illustrates the reason for this regulation by telling of the blow to the side of Officer Lewis's head. You do not need to know the reasons for regulations; you must simply follow them.

38. **(C)** This is a "greatest number of common elements" question. The descriptions of witnesses (C) and (D) are almost identical. You should certainly consider that the vehicle was a brown Ford truck with the license number 1845. Since three witnesses saw the letter on the plate as "G" and only one as "C," go with "G."

39. **(D)** Officer Frey has properly followed procedure to this point. Reading the description along with the regulations, you know that Officer Frey has completed step 3, has removed the wallet and papers, and must now go to step 4, entering in the Memo Book a list of the property removed.

40. **(A)** The date is August 31. Why is the woman wearing a winter overcoat? Could she be planning to hide objects under that coat? Watch her.

41. **(C)** Try the routes to see which one works. Dusty Road is not a through street from Hampton Drive, so eliminate (A). Maple Road is one-way eastbound, so neither (B) nor (D) can be correct. Choice (C) works.

42. **(B)** To choose the answer, do exactly what Officer Gladden did. Locate the intersection of Beach Drive and Anderson Street. With pencil or finger follow the route, turning the map as needed to be sure you are keeping right and left straight. You should end up headed East on Main Street.

43. **(D)** Only this choice satisfies the requirement of both the goods' being stolen and knowing possession.

44. **(C)** Where date and time are indicated in a report, the most coherent summary usually begins with this information. Focus first on the choice that begins with date and time, but do not take it for granted. Be sure to read it through to be certain that it includes all other pertinent information in logical arrangement.

45. **(B)** The report must make it clear just who was abused, who is accused of the abusing,

who has made the report, and where the abused and abusers may be found. You can be certain only from choice (B).

46. **(D)** The arithmetic is simple. Don't forget the value of the leather bag itself.

2 watches at $500 each	=	$1000
4 necklaces at $315 each	=	1260
cash of $519	=	519
1 ring at $400	=	400
leather bag at $200	=	+ 200
total	=	$3379

47. **(B)** The rapist might easily wear different clothing on different days so you must concentrate on the physical description. The rapist in #2 seems to be younger and thinner than the others and has short hair. The other descriptions are quite similar.

48. **(C)** It is the middle of the night, and the police have removed a child from his home and placed him in temporary housing. The next step, according to printed procedure, is to try to locate a parent.

49. **(D)** The officer has enough information—make and color of offending car and its license plate number—to make an arrest at a later time. The driver of the Ford is a reckless driver who has left the scene of an accident, but no victim was abandoned bleeding in the street and no heinous crime was committed. Considering the danger to self and public caused by Officer Jordan's 80-M.P.H. weaving through traffic, we must conclude that Officer Jordan used bad judgment in continuing the pursuit.

50. **(A)** This question does not ask for your judgment but only for which of four choices expresses the information most clearly and accurately. Choice (A) is best.

51. **(C)** Clearly the suspect is male, white, and in his 20s. Three witnesses agree that he was wearing a black hat and red sneakers. Choice (C) contains the greatest number of common elements.

52. **(C)** In this question, you must make a judgment as to which is the greatest medical emergency. A heart attack requires the most immediate medical attention.

53. **(B)** This is a well-written report. It states the nature of the problem: a missing person;

describes the missing person; and tells when and where that person was last seen.

54. **(B)** Miss Holmes called the police on January 14. She told them that the man had threatened her two days earlier, January 12.

55. **(D)** Officer Jones found the revolver while searching the suspect's right front waistband.

56. **(B)** Miss Holmes said that the threat had occurred in front of her home at 113 Lowell Street.

57. **(D)** The gun appeared to be legally registered. Fitz was arrested because Miss Holmes identified him as the person who had threatened her earlier.

58. **(C)** All other versions are hopelessly garbled.

59. **(A)** This is the best statement of what happened to whom, when, and where. It makes clear the identity of the witness.

60. **(A)** In this case, the officers may reasonably omit step 3 and follow the instruction at 4b. An address book is not a lethal weapon. There is no basis for the officers to believe that their lives are in danger, so they have no right to search the man's clothing. They did, however, stop and frisk him, so they must prepare a Stop and Frisk Report.

61. **(B)** Clearly, the event described in choice (B) represents the use of force in stealing June's bag.

62. **(A)** The suspect in murder #2 is too young. The suspect in murder #3, while a tall man, is estimated at a full 5" shorter than the suspect in the most recent murder. The suspect in murder #1 fits the current description very closely.

63. **(C)** Police officers are trained and equipped to deal with robbery, vandalism, and recovered property. While the police might well deal with crowd control at the site of a spill of poisonous liquid, the main problem is the concern of other departments.

64. **(A)** The steps must be followed in order. Upon arrival at Central Booking, Leon must be put into a cell that does not contain adult prisoners.

65. **(D)** Sometimes you may have to read over a description a number of times to pick up

a single word on which the answer depends. Step 3 states that the officer must present shield *and* identification card. The description says only that Officer Dana presented her shield to Officer Baskin before signing the receipt.

66. **(B)** The information could be stated even more clearly, but choice (B) is the best of the four offered.

67. **(A)** The sentence is a bit awkward, but it is accurate and does get its message across clearly.

68. **(C)** Narrow your choices as quickly as possible. The larcenies occur on Amboy Place between Pitt Avenue and East Avenue. Of course, this means that they occur equally on Amboy Place between East Avenue and Pitt Avenue. Narrow to (B) and (C). Larcenies occur on Sundays and Mondays, so choose (C). You would need to consider the time of day only if two answer choices led you to both the correct blocks and days of the week.

69. **(D)** The robberies occur on Fridays and Saturdays, so eliminate (A) and (B) as choices that do not span those days. The robberies occur from 1 to 3 P.M., so Officer Jones would not be very effective in reducing robberies in the choice (C) night shift.

70. **(C)** Look over the choices and decide which represents an emergency life-and-death situation that might be disastrous if not handled correctly. You would want the benefit of your supervisor's experience.

71. **(A)** The firing of a rifle into the stands is so obvious a case of total disregard for human life and creating grave risk of death to others that the other choices would have to be very convincing. (C) is pure accident; (B) is a threat to one's own life, not the life of another; (D) is recklessness with risk of injury rather than death.

72. **(B)** Officer Vasquez has been busy and has properly investigated the automobile. Up to this point, she has not fulfilled any of the duties required upon recovery of a stolen vehicle. Therefore, she must now enter the details in her Memo Book.

73. **(D)** Officer O'Rourke met the victim on a southbound #8 train.

74. **(A)** The officer met the victim at 5:25 A.M. She reported that she had been assaulted about a half hour before, at about 4:55 A.M.

75. **(B)** The arrested suspect was wearing a white shirt and the same color pants as the day before, black.

76. **(A)** On April 7, Officer O'Rourke entered the subway station intending to take a #7 train to Queens. However, when he recognized the suspect and observed him attempting to snatch a purse, he pursued the man and instead boarded a train to Manhattan.

77. **(D)** This is a clear and accurate statement.

78. **(D)** This report is clear, accurate, and complete.

79. **(C)** The police officers have conducted their interview, during which they learned of the presence of the knife that was dropped. The knife constitutes evidence. They must now search for the knife.

80. **(B)** Apartment 1A is at 416 Blum Street. Narrow to (B) or (D). The 1A sales are midday sales, so 9:00 A.M. to 5:00 P.M. is the best time to patrol.

81. **(A)** The officers did all the right things. The driver's license had been revoked, not merely suspended, so arrest was mandated.

82. **(D)** A police officer must always hesitate to use his gun in a crowd because of the danger to innocent bystanders. In this case, however, the man with the axe is already presenting a clear and present danger to the people who surround him. A well-aimed shot to the man with the axe may preserve the safety of a far greater number. The officer must take this calculated risk.

83. **(A)** This is a difficult incident to describe in only a few words. Choice (A) does it most clearly.

84. **(B)** This is the only statement that makes sense.

85. **(D)** Choice (A) would get them there, but it is the long way around; Surf Avenue is one-way west, eliminate (B); Prospect Street is one-way north, eliminate (C). (D) is quick and legal.

86. **(C)** Eliminate (A) because Surf is one-way westbound; eliminate (B) because it is an unnecessarily long route; eliminate (D) because Prospect is one-way northbound. (C) is direct and permissible.

87. **(B)** Choice (D) entails too long a route; (A) and (C) are prohibited by one-way streets. (B) works well. Follow the routes yourself to answer map questions.

88. **(D)** This is a simple arithmetic problem. Be careful not to count the handbag twice.

Cash of $150	=	$150
3 bracelets at $95 each	=	285
2 rings at $70 each	=	140
1 handbag at $159	=	+ 159
total	=	$734

89. **(B)** The suspect in Rape 1 has the wrong color hair and what is described as a highly visible scar. Since this scar was not reported in any of the other rapes, the man is probably only a suspect in Rape 1. The rapist in Rape 2 is too old. The descriptions of the rapists in Rape 3 and Rape 4 contain one major discrepancy, namely the location of the earring. Victims do make mistakes. The correspondence of the descriptions in all other details, including the left arm tattoo, makes the identity likely. Even if you were to disagree about the possibility of a victim's mistaking which ear, you would have to choose (B). You are not offered a choice that discounts all three previous rapists.

90. **(D)** This is the only clear and accurate statement.

91. **(A)** According to the printed procedure, Highway Police Officers conduct the alcohol test at the precinct station house. The next step in this case is to send for these officers.

92. **(A)** Reconstruct the number as best you can based on the principle of frequently occurring elements. The digits 8-2-3-2 all appear in three of the four eyewitness accounts in these respective positions. Of the final digits, only "4" appears more than once. Your choice must be far from certain, but in balance (A) is the best bet.

93. **(C)** Officer Ryan has interviewed both complainant and violator. The violator, Mr. Nelson, is very cooperative and agrees at once to correct the violation. There is no need for

a summons. Skip step 5 and enter a report in the Memo Book.

94. **(C)** The woman has gone through a stop sign, a serious moving violation. The fact that she missed the stop sign because she was putting on lipstick does not constitute extenuating circumstances. On the contrary, she was truly negligent.

95. **(B)** Walker did not steal the property. He fully intended to return the car to Mr. Smith after the weekend. Barnes consciously stole the valuable car, drove it without authorization, and resold it. His actions constituted both Grand Larceny Second Degree and Unauthorized Use of the Vehicle.

96. **(A)** Choice (B) is hopelessly garbled. Choice (C) leaves doubt as to who was carrying a TV and a VCR. Choice (D) is accurate but is awkwardly stated; (A) is better.

97. **(B)** The suspect in Robbery 3 is too old. Descriptions of the robbers in No. 1 and No. 2 coincide quite closely with Officer Harris's suspect in terms of age, height, weight, and moustache.

98. **(D)** The statement clearly states when, who, what, where, and by whom.

99. **(C)** The dead body found in the waters off the precinct must be reported as a Complaint in the precinct. In (A) the loss is discovered outside the precinct; in (B) the unlawful act is committed outside the precinct; in (D) the missing person resides outside the precinct.

100. **(B)** Although he fits in most respects, the suspect in Robbery 3 is too small. Victims' estimates of height and weight may vary, but not to so great a degree. The other two suspects closely resemble the current suspect.

101. **(C)** This problem presents no pitfalls.

1 ring at	=	$415
cash at	=	220
coin collection at	=	410
3 cameras at $175 each	=	+ 525
total	=	$1570

102. **(D)** The thieves broke the lock of the back door. They cut a wire at the basement window.

103. **(A)** The 19″ color television and clock radio belonged to Parker himself. The other items were borrowed from his friends.

104. **(C)** You, as an applicant, are not expected to know the classification of crimes, but this answer is given in the first sentence. Officers Ryder and Brown responded to a call concerning a burglary.

105. **(B)** Since the driver was unable to produce proof of identity and residence, doubt existed concerning his identity. The regulations state that if there is doubt concerning the identity of the violator, the violator must be taken to the station house.

106. **(A)** Only this statement correctly sorts out who made the report, who is missing, description of missing person, and time and place of last sighting.

107. **(B)** This is a clear, simple statement.

108. **(C)** Since Hill's parents are on their way, Officer Martin must be patient and wait for them to arrive. Only after the parents are in the room, should Officer Martin advise Tom Hill of his rights and begin questioning him about the offense.

109. **(B)** This statement is clear and accurate. Choice (C) confuses time of the crime with time of the report.

110. **(A)** Clear and accurate.

111. **(B)** If choice (B) were not offered, (D) would be acceptable. (B) is clearer. (A) mistakenly states that the bank was robbed by a shotgun; (C) states that a bank teller robbed the bank.

112. **(D)** The receipt should include a description of the property.

113. **(C)** You might think it more accurate to state that Lois Nettle's right leg was broken when the car hit her, as in choice (B). However, (C) gets the total message across much more clearly. For purposes of the ambulance crew, it is sufficient to know that the leg is broken.

114. **(C)** Thomas Parker was the driver of the Oldsmobile, but his brother, Harold Parker, was its owner. This begins a series of ques-

tions of fact, which may be answered by careful reading of the passage.

115. **(B)** The Dodge truck had a crumpled bumper and blown right front tire.

116. **(D)** The driver of the Oldsmobile sedan caused the accident by pulling out of a parking lot without looking for oncoming traffic.

117. **(A)** By now you should be aware that personal injuries always must receive the first attention. This is confirmed by the printed regulations as the first priority after the officer gets out of the car.

118. **(D)** Only this last statement tells what happened and to whom and to what.

119. **(A)** The regulation clearly states that unlawful assembly is a violation or offense for which a juvenile report should *not* be prepared.

120. **(C)** Date, time, who made the report, what was reported. Clearly and accurately stated.

121. **(B)** Only choice (B) fulfills all the requirements for Burglary in the First Degree: Watson is armed, he breaks into a dwelling, and in addition he threatens the owner with his gun. In (A) there is no weapon and no injury; in (C) the building is not a dwelling and the injured is party to the crime; in (D) though the suspect is armed and the guard is injured, the building is not a dwelling.

122. **(B)** Mr. Pitts has, however reluctantly, agreed to appear in the lineup. Since he has agreed to appear, he should not be arrested. The detective supervisor should be notified to expect him.

123. **(C)** This is the only statement that is clear, complete, and accurate.

124. **(D)** All the statements give all the information, but (D) is the clearest statement.

125. **(B)** This statement is by far the clearest and most accurate.

126. **(A)** Read carefully. The facts are there.

127. **(A)** Eddie Torres, a neighbor, served as witness to the search and signed the Memo Book.

128. **(D)** Regulations require that the police voucher the property of any deceased who has no relative living with him or her.

129. **(D)** Officer Gannett double-parked in front of the building so Officer James could jump out and send the alarm. The police car now represents an obstacle to the firefighters. Gannett must move the police car before entering the building to assist in evacuation of tenants.

130. **(C)** Only one statement is clear and accurate.

131. **(C)** Officer John neglected to make a decision as to whether the report should be closed or referred for further investigation.

132. **(A)** A threat of bodily harm might best be dealt with by professional counseling arranged through Family Court. The other disputes are routine household occurrences that pose no threat to anyone's safety.

133. **(B)** Focus on distinctive features. (A) has the wrong chin; (C) has a scar or cleft between nose and lips; (D) has the wrong lips.

134. **(C)** Choice (A) has the wrong nose; (B) has the wrong lips; (D) has the wrong chin.

135. **(D)** Choice (A) has the wrong nose; (B) has the wrong eyes (glasses may make the eyes appear larger, but B's are more deeply set); (C) has the wrong lips.

136. **(A)** Choice (B) has the wrong ears; (C) has the wrong mouth; (D) has the wrong nose.

137. **(A)** Choice (B) has the wrong ears; (C) has a more narrow lower face; (D) has the wrong nose.

138. **(D)** Choice (A) has the wrong lips; (B) has a cleft chin; (C) has the wrong eyes. A dramatic change of hairstyle on head or face often makes an effective change of appearance. If you are having difficulty choosing the disguised face, give special attention to the hair.

139. **(B)** Choice (A) has the wrong eyes; (C) has the wrong chin; (D) has the wrong lips.

140. **(C)** Choice (A) has the wrong lips; (B) has the wrong chin; (D) has the wrong nose.

ANSWER SHEET

New York City Exam—October 24, 1987

1. Ⓐ Ⓑ Ⓒ Ⓓ   2. Ⓐ Ⓑ Ⓒ Ⓓ   3. Ⓐ Ⓑ Ⓒ Ⓓ   4. Ⓐ Ⓑ Ⓒ Ⓓ   5. Ⓐ Ⓑ Ⓒ Ⓓ

6. Ⓐ Ⓑ Ⓒ Ⓓ   7. Ⓐ Ⓑ Ⓒ Ⓓ   8. Ⓐ Ⓑ Ⓒ Ⓓ   9. Ⓐ Ⓑ Ⓒ Ⓓ   10. Ⓐ Ⓑ Ⓒ Ⓓ

11. Ⓐ Ⓑ Ⓒ Ⓓ   12. Ⓐ Ⓑ Ⓒ Ⓓ   13. Ⓐ Ⓑ Ⓒ Ⓓ   14. Ⓐ Ⓑ Ⓒ Ⓓ   15. Ⓐ Ⓑ Ⓒ Ⓓ

16. Ⓐ Ⓑ Ⓒ Ⓓ   17. Ⓐ Ⓑ Ⓒ Ⓓ   18. Ⓐ Ⓑ Ⓒ Ⓓ   19. Ⓐ Ⓑ Ⓒ Ⓓ   20. Ⓐ Ⓑ Ⓒ Ⓓ

21. Ⓐ Ⓑ Ⓒ Ⓓ   22. Ⓐ Ⓑ Ⓒ Ⓓ   23. Ⓐ Ⓑ Ⓒ Ⓓ   24. Ⓐ Ⓑ Ⓒ Ⓓ   25. Ⓐ Ⓑ Ⓒ Ⓓ

26. Ⓐ Ⓑ Ⓒ Ⓓ   27. Ⓐ Ⓑ Ⓒ Ⓓ   28. Ⓐ Ⓑ Ⓒ Ⓓ   29. Ⓐ Ⓑ Ⓒ Ⓓ   30. Ⓐ Ⓑ Ⓒ Ⓓ

31. Ⓐ Ⓑ Ⓒ Ⓓ   32. Ⓐ Ⓑ Ⓒ Ⓓ   33. Ⓐ Ⓑ Ⓒ Ⓓ   34. Ⓐ Ⓑ Ⓒ Ⓓ   35. Ⓐ Ⓑ Ⓒ Ⓓ

36. Ⓐ Ⓑ Ⓒ Ⓓ   37. Ⓐ Ⓑ Ⓒ Ⓓ   38. Ⓐ Ⓑ Ⓒ Ⓓ   39. Ⓐ Ⓑ Ⓒ Ⓓ   40. Ⓐ Ⓑ Ⓒ Ⓓ

41. Ⓐ Ⓑ Ⓒ Ⓓ   42. Ⓐ Ⓑ Ⓒ Ⓓ   43. Ⓐ Ⓑ Ⓒ Ⓓ   44. Ⓐ Ⓑ Ⓒ Ⓓ   45. Ⓐ Ⓑ Ⓒ Ⓓ

46. Ⓐ Ⓑ Ⓒ Ⓓ   47. Ⓐ Ⓑ Ⓒ Ⓓ   48. Ⓐ Ⓑ Ⓒ Ⓓ   49. Ⓐ Ⓑ Ⓒ Ⓓ   50. Ⓐ Ⓑ Ⓒ Ⓓ

51. Ⓐ Ⓑ Ⓒ Ⓓ   52. Ⓐ Ⓑ Ⓒ Ⓓ   53. Ⓐ Ⓑ Ⓒ Ⓓ   54. Ⓐ Ⓑ Ⓒ Ⓓ   55. Ⓐ Ⓑ Ⓒ Ⓓ

56. Ⓐ Ⓑ Ⓒ Ⓓ   57. Ⓐ Ⓑ Ⓒ Ⓓ   58. Ⓐ Ⓑ Ⓒ Ⓓ   59. Ⓐ Ⓑ Ⓒ Ⓓ   60. Ⓐ Ⓑ Ⓒ Ⓓ

61. Ⓐ Ⓑ Ⓒ Ⓓ   62. Ⓐ Ⓑ Ⓒ Ⓓ   63. Ⓐ Ⓑ Ⓒ Ⓓ   64. Ⓐ Ⓑ Ⓒ Ⓓ   65. Ⓐ Ⓑ Ⓒ Ⓓ

66. Ⓐ Ⓑ Ⓒ Ⓓ   67. Ⓐ Ⓑ Ⓒ Ⓓ   68. Ⓐ Ⓑ Ⓒ Ⓓ   69. Ⓐ Ⓑ Ⓒ Ⓓ   70. Ⓐ Ⓑ Ⓒ Ⓓ

71. Ⓐ Ⓑ Ⓒ Ⓓ   72. Ⓐ Ⓑ Ⓒ Ⓓ   73. Ⓐ Ⓑ Ⓒ Ⓓ   74. Ⓐ Ⓑ Ⓒ Ⓓ   75. Ⓐ Ⓑ Ⓒ Ⓓ

76. Ⓐ Ⓑ Ⓒ Ⓓ   77. Ⓐ Ⓑ Ⓒ Ⓓ   78. Ⓐ Ⓑ Ⓒ Ⓓ   79. Ⓐ Ⓑ Ⓒ Ⓓ   80. Ⓐ Ⓑ Ⓒ Ⓓ

81. Ⓐ Ⓑ Ⓒ Ⓓ   82. Ⓐ Ⓑ Ⓒ Ⓓ   83. Ⓐ Ⓑ Ⓒ Ⓓ   84. Ⓐ Ⓑ Ⓒ Ⓓ   85. Ⓐ Ⓑ Ⓒ Ⓓ

86. Ⓐ Ⓑ Ⓒ Ⓓ   87. Ⓐ Ⓑ Ⓒ Ⓓ   88. Ⓐ Ⓑ Ⓒ Ⓓ   89. Ⓐ Ⓑ Ⓒ Ⓓ   90. Ⓐ Ⓑ Ⓒ Ⓓ

91. Ⓐ Ⓑ Ⓒ Ⓓ   92. Ⓐ Ⓑ Ⓒ Ⓓ   93. Ⓐ Ⓑ Ⓒ Ⓓ   94. Ⓐ Ⓑ Ⓒ Ⓓ   95. Ⓐ Ⓑ Ⓒ Ⓓ

96. Ⓐ Ⓑ Ⓒ Ⓓ   97. Ⓐ Ⓑ Ⓒ Ⓓ   98. Ⓐ Ⓑ Ⓒ Ⓓ   99. Ⓐ Ⓑ Ⓒ Ⓓ   100. Ⓐ Ⓑ Ⓒ Ⓓ

101. Ⓐ Ⓑ Ⓒ Ⓓ   102. Ⓐ Ⓑ Ⓒ Ⓓ   103. Ⓐ Ⓑ Ⓒ Ⓓ   104. Ⓐ Ⓑ Ⓒ Ⓓ   105. Ⓐ Ⓑ Ⓒ Ⓓ

106. Ⓐ Ⓑ Ⓒ Ⓓ   107. Ⓐ Ⓑ Ⓒ Ⓓ   108. Ⓐ Ⓑ Ⓒ Ⓓ   109. Ⓐ Ⓑ Ⓒ Ⓓ   110. Ⓐ Ⓑ Ⓒ Ⓓ

111. Ⓐ Ⓑ Ⓒ Ⓓ   112. Ⓐ Ⓑ Ⓒ Ⓓ   113. Ⓐ Ⓑ Ⓒ Ⓓ   114. Ⓐ Ⓑ Ⓒ Ⓓ   115. Ⓐ Ⓑ Ⓒ Ⓓ

116. Ⓐ Ⓑ Ⓒ Ⓓ   117. Ⓐ Ⓑ Ⓒ Ⓓ   118. Ⓐ Ⓑ Ⓒ Ⓓ   119. Ⓐ Ⓑ Ⓒ Ⓓ   120. Ⓐ Ⓑ Ⓒ Ⓓ

121. Ⓐ Ⓑ Ⓒ Ⓓ   122. Ⓐ Ⓑ Ⓒ Ⓓ   123. Ⓐ Ⓑ Ⓒ Ⓓ   124. Ⓐ Ⓑ Ⓒ Ⓓ   125. Ⓐ Ⓑ Ⓒ Ⓓ

126. Ⓐ Ⓑ Ⓒ Ⓓ   127. Ⓐ Ⓑ Ⓒ Ⓓ   128. Ⓐ Ⓑ Ⓒ Ⓓ   129. Ⓐ Ⓑ Ⓒ Ⓓ   130. Ⓐ Ⓑ Ⓒ Ⓓ

131. Ⓐ Ⓑ Ⓒ Ⓓ   132. Ⓐ Ⓑ Ⓒ Ⓓ   133. Ⓐ Ⓑ Ⓒ Ⓓ   134. Ⓐ Ⓑ Ⓒ Ⓓ   135. Ⓐ Ⓑ Ⓒ Ⓓ

136. Ⓐ Ⓑ Ⓒ Ⓓ   137. Ⓐ Ⓑ Ⓒ Ⓓ   138. Ⓐ Ⓑ Ⓒ Ⓓ   139. Ⓐ Ⓑ Ⓒ Ⓓ   140. Ⓐ Ⓑ Ⓒ Ⓓ

141. Ⓐ Ⓑ Ⓒ Ⓓ   142. Ⓐ Ⓑ Ⓒ Ⓓ   143. Ⓐ Ⓑ Ⓒ Ⓓ   144. Ⓐ Ⓑ Ⓒ Ⓓ   145. Ⓐ Ⓑ Ⓒ Ⓓ

146. Ⓐ Ⓑ Ⓒ Ⓓ   147. Ⓐ Ⓑ Ⓒ Ⓓ   148. Ⓐ Ⓑ Ⓒ Ⓓ   149. Ⓐ Ⓑ Ⓒ Ⓓ   150. Ⓐ Ⓑ Ⓒ Ⓓ

TEAR HERE

PRACTICE EXAMINATION 2

DEPARTMENT OF PERSONNEL

Social Security No. _____

Room No. _____

Seat No. _____

School _____

POLICE OFFICER SERIES
EXAMINATION NO. 7009

First Memory Booklet
October 24, 1987

DO NOT OPEN THIS BOOKLET UNTIL THE SECOND SIGNAL IS GIVEN!

Write your Social Security Number, Room Number, Seat Number, and School in the appropriate spaces at the top of this page.

You *must* follow the instructions found on the TEST INSTRUCTION SHEET.

ANYONE DISOBEYING ANY OF THE INSTRUCTIONS FOUND ON THE TEST INSTRUCTION SHEET MAY BE DISQUALIFIED— RECEIVE A ZERO ON THE ENTIRE TEST.

This booklet contains one scene. Try to remember as many details in the scene as you can. You should pay equal attention both to objects and to people shown in the scene

DO *NOT* WRITE OR MAKE *ANY* NOTES WHILE STUDYING THE SCENE.

DO NOT OPEN THIS BOOKLET UNTIL THE SECOND SIGNAL IS GIVEN!

[NOTE: You will have five (5) minutes to study the scene shown.]

The New York City Department of Personnel makes no commitment, and no inference is to be drawn, regarding the content, style, or format of any future examination for the position of Police Officer.

DEPARTMENT OF PERSONNEL

Social Security No. _____

Room No. _____

Seat No. _____

School _____

POLICE OFFICER SERIES
EXAMINATION No. 7009

Second Memory Booklet
October 24, 1987

DO NOT OPEN THIS BOOKLET UNTIL THE FOURTH SIGNAL IS GIVEN!

Write your Social Security Number, Room Number, Seat Number, and School in the appropriate spaces at the top of this page.

You *must* follow the instructions found on the TEST INSTRUCTION SHEET.

ANYONE DISOBEYING ANY OF THE INSTRUCTIONS FOUND ON THE TEST INSTRUCTION SHEET MAY BE DISQUALIFIED— RECEIVE A ZERO ON THE ENTIRE TEST.

This booklet contains Questions 1 through 6, which are based on Scene 1 as shown in the First Memory Booklet. Answer Questions 1 through 6 after the fourth signal. At the *FIFTH SIGNAL*, you should turn to Scene 2. Try to remember as many details in the scene as you can. You should pay equal attention both to objects and to people shown in the scene.

DO NOT OPEN THIS BOOKLET UNTIL THE FOURTH SIGNAL IS GIVEN!

[NOTE: You will have five (5) minutes to study the scene shown.]

The New York City Department of Personnel makes no commitment, and no inference is to be drawn, regarding the content, style, or format of any future examination for the position of Police Officer.

Answer questions 1 through 6 solely on the basis of sketch number 1.

1. Which one of the following is printed on the side of the black vehicle with the open hood?

   (A) Richard Printing   (C) Bob's Painters
   (B) Archie's Business School   (D) Nature's Food.

2. When is parking prohibited on East Avenue?

   (A) Monday–Friday, 7:00 A.M. to 11:00 P.M.
   (B) Friday–Saturday, 7:00 P.M. to 11:00 A.M.
   (C) Monday–Saturday, 7:00 A.M. to 11:00 A.M.
   (D) Friday–Saturday, 7:00 P.M. to 11:00 P.M.

3. Which one of the following is printed on the side of the white vehicle on Bay Street?

   (A) Bob's Painters   (C) Guido's
   (B) Uptown Express   (D) Fast Movers.

4. The man standing on the sidewalk with the woman is wearing

   (A) black pants and is holding a white jacket
   (B) a white jacket and black pants
   (C) white pants and is holding a black jacket
   (D) a black jacket and white pants.

5. Which one of the following is shown as a one-way street?

   (A) East Avenue   (C) Jewel Street
   (B) Bay Street   (D) West Avenue.

6. How many men are standing next to the station wagon with the hood up?

   (A) one   (C) three
   (B) two   (D) four.

DEPARTMENT OF PERSONNEL

The City of New York

Social Security No. ____________
Room No. ____________
Seat No. ____________
School ____________

POLICE OFFICER SERIES
EXAMINATION NO. 7009

Question Booklet
October 24, 1987

Written Test: Weight 100
Time Allowed: 5 Hours

DO NOT OPEN THIS BOOKLET UNTIL THE SEVENTH SIGNAL IS GIVEN!

Record your answers on the official Answer Sheet before the last signal. If you wish, you may also record your answers in the Question Booklet before the last signal is given. This will be your only official record of answers.

This Question Booklet contains procedures and definitions which are to be used to answer certain questions. These procedures and definitions are not necessarily those of the New York City Police Department. However, you are to answer these questions solely on the basis of the material given.

After the seventh signal is given, open this Question Booklet and begin to work. You will have 5 hours to complete this test.

You may make notes in this booklet and use the scrap paper on your desk. If you need additional scrap paper, ask the monitor.

Remember, only your official Answer Sheet will be rated, so be sure to mark *all* your answers on the official Answer Sheet before the eighth signal. *No* additional time will be given for marking your answers after the test has ended.

DO NOT OPEN THIS BOOKLET UNTIL THE SEVENTH SIGNAL IS GIVEN!

The New York City Department of Personnel makes no commitment, and no inference is to be drawn, regarding the content, style, or format of any future examination for the position of Police Officer.

Answer questions 7 through 12 solely on the basis of sketch number 2.

7. What words are written on the shirt of the man carrying a knife?

   (A) Beach Bum
   (B) Grateful Dead
   (C) He-Man
   (D) Big Blue.

8. Which one of the following best describes the victim of the crime?

   (A) white female, striped pants, and blonde hair
   (B) white female, dark hair, and black and white blazer
   (C) Asian female, black pants, wearing glasses
   (D) black female, striped pants, and white blazer.

9. A man is shown taking something from a woman's purse. The man is using his

   (A) right hand, and the purse is on the woman's right shoulder
   (B) left hand, and the purse is on the woman's right shoulder
   (C) right hand, and the purse is on the woman's left shoulder
   (D) left hand, and the purse is on the woman's left shoulder.

10. The youth who is holding a knife is wearing

   (A) jeans and a jacket
   (B) shorts and a short-sleeve shirt
   (C) jeans and a short-sleeve shirt
   (D) shorts and a T-shirt.

11. Which store has a "closed" sign in its window?

   (A) Ave. R. Discount
   (B) Gourmet Supermarket
   (C) Book Store
   (D) Rubber Stamps.

12. The Electronics store is located

   (A) on Ave. R
   (B) at the corner of Ave. R and E. 3rd St.
   (C) on E. 3rd St.
   (D) at the corner of Ave. R and W. 3rd St.

Please check your Answer Sheet to make sure that you have written in and blackened your Social Security number correctly. If you have not yet written in and blackened your Social Security number, please do so immediately. If you have incorrectly written in or blackened your Social Security number, please correct the mistake immediately. Failure to correctly blacken your Social Security number may result in your Answer Sheet NOT being rated.

Answer questions 13 and 14 solely on the basis of the following information.

Police Officer Thomas is aware that within his assigned sector all rapes occur on Clark Street, all robberies occur on Gaston Street, and all assaults occur on Pine Grove Avenue. Most robberies occur on Wednesdays and Fridays, most rapes occur on Tuesdays and Thursdays, and most assaults occur on Mondays and Tuesdays. Most rapes occur between 7:00 A.M. and 11:30 A.M., most assaults occur between 2:30 P.M. and 5:00 P.M., and most robberies occur between 3:30 P.M. and 9:30 P.M.

13. Officer Thomas would most likely be able to reduce the number of robberies if he patrolled

    (A) Pine Grove Avenue on Wednesdays from 8:00 A.M. to 4:00 P.M.
    (B) Gaston Street on Wednesdays from midnight to 8:00 A.M.
    (C) Gaston Street on Fridays from 4:00 P.M. to midnight
    (D) Clark Street on Mondays from 2:00 P.M. to 10:00 P.M.

14. To reduce the number of rapes, Officer Thomas is assigned to work a steady tour. For this purpose it would be most appropriate for Officer Thomas to work

    (A) Saturday through Wednesday, 8:00 A.M. to 4:00 P.M.
    (B) Thursday through Monday, 2:00 P.M. to 10:00 P.M.
    (C) Monday through Friday, 5:00 P.M. to 1:00 A.M.
    (D) Sunday through Thursday, 6:00 A.M. to 2:00 P.M.

15. Police Officer Salley has been selected to serve on a special task force designed to identify possible locations of drug sales in the precinct. He is assigned a post at the intersection of Rochester Avenue and Bergen Street between the hours of 9:00 A.M. and 5:00 P.M., Mondays through Fridays.

    Which one of the following observations made by Officer Salley most likely indicates possible drug activity?

    (A) A continuous flow of people frequent Benny's Grocery Store and leave without packages.
    (B) A hot dog vendor arrives at the Bergen Street construction site each day at 11:30 A.M. and leaves at 2:00 P.M.
    (C) Many of the students from Rochester Avenue Elementary School go into Harry's Candy Store after school.
    (D) Many students from Bergen Street High School gather in the video arcade on Rochester Avenue during lunch periods and after school.

16. Police Officer Gattuso responded to a report of a robbery and obtained the following information regarding the incident:

Place of Occurrence:	Princess Grocery, 6 Sutton Place
Time of Occurrence:	6:00 P.M.
Crime:	Robbery of $200
Victim:	Sara Davidson, owner of Princess Grocery
Description of Suspect:	White, female, red hair, blue jeans, and white T-shirt
Weapon:	Knife

Officer Gattuso is preparing a report on the incident. Which one of the following expresses the above information *most clearly* and *accurately*?

(A) Sara Davidson reported at 6:00 P.M. her store Princess Grocery was robbed at knifepoint at 6 Sutton Place. A white woman with red hair took $200 from her wearing blue jeans and a white T-shirt.

(B) At 6:00 P.M. a red-haired woman took $200 from 6 Sutton Place at Princess Grocery owned by Sara Davidson, who was robbed by the white woman. She was wearing blue jeans and a white T-shirt and used a knife.

(C) In a robbery that occurred at knifepoint, a red-haired white woman robbed the owner of Princess Grocery. Sara Davidson, the owner of the 6 Sutton Place store which was robbed of $200, said she was wearing blue jeans and a white T-shirt at 6:00 P.M.

(D) At 6:00 P.M., Sara Davidson, owner of Princess Grocery, located at 6 Sutton Place, was robbed of $200 at knifepoint. The suspect is a white female with red hair wearing blue jeans and a white T-shirt.

Answer question 17 solely on the basis of the following information.

Murder 1st Degree—occurs when a person intentionally causes the death of another person.

17. Which one of the following situations is the best example of Murder in the First Degree?

(A) Sam is riding the train with Brenda who suddenly passes out, stops breathing, and dies even though Sam attempts to revive her.

(B) Jennifer shoots and kills her husband after a friend tells her that her husband is seeing another woman.

(C) A taxi driver goes through a red light because he is in a hurry and runs over Albert, breaking his arm and leg.

(D) Joe is standing on a very crowded subway platform when he accidentally pushes an elderly woman who falls onto the tracks and is killed by an oncoming train.

18. Police Officer Martinez responds to a report of an assault and obtains the following information regarding the incident:

Place of Occurrence:	Corner of Frank and Lincoln Avenues
Time of Occurrence:	9:40 A.M.
Crime:	Assault
Victim:	Mr. John Adams of 31-20th Street
Suspect:	Male, white, 5′11″, 170 lbs., dressed in gray
Injury:	Victim suffered a split lip
Action Taken:	Victim transported to St. Mary's Hospital

Officer Martinez is completing a report on the incident. Which one of the following expresses the above information *most clearly* and *accurately*?

(A) At 9:40 A.M., John Adams was assaulted on the corner of Frank and Lincoln Avenues by a white male, 5′11″, 170 lbs., dressed in gray, suffering a split lip. Mr. Adams lives at 31-20th Street and was transported to St. Mary's Hospital.
(B) At 9:40 A.M., John Adams was assaulted on the corner of Frank and Lincoln Avenues by a white male, 5′11″, 170 lbs., dressed in gray, and lives at 31-20th Street. Mr. Adams suffered a split lip and was transported to St. Mary's Hospital.
(C) John Adams, who lives at 31-20th street, was assaulted at 9:40 A.M. on the corner of Frank and Lincoln Avenues by a white male, 5′11″, 170 lbs., dressed in gray. Mr. Adams suffered a split lip and was transported to St. Mary's Hospital.
(D) Living at 31-20th Street, Mr. Adams suffered a split lip and was transported to St. Mary's Hospital. At 9:40 A.M., Mr. Adams was assaulted by a white male, 5′11″, 170 lbs., dressed in gray.

Answer question 19 solely on the basis of the following information.

Police Officer Hooks has been instructed by his Precinct Commander to identify the locations in his patrol area where particular patterns of complaints have been reported. In reviewing recent complaint reports, Officer Hooks finds that most noise complaints occur on Beeker Street between Bay Boulevard and 79th Avenue. Larceny complaints are reported along Sutton Place between Church Street and Jerome Avenue. The majority of complaints concerning double-parked cars occur on Main Street between Flushing Street and Ocean Boulevard. Most of the larcenies occur between 7:00 A.M. and 10:00 A.M., the noise complaints between 11:00 P.M. and 2:00 A.M., and the complaints regarding double-parked cars between 1:00 P.M. and 4:00 P.M.

19. Officer Hooks is working a 1:00 P.M. to 9:00 P.M. shift. From which area should he receive the most complaints?

(A) Sutton Place between Jerome Avenue and Church Street.
(B) Beeker Street between Bay Boulevard and 79th Avenue.
(C) Main Street between Flushing Street and Ocean Boulevard.
(D) Main Street between Jerome Avenue and Church Street.

Answer questions 20 through 23 solely on the basis of the following passage.

Police Officer Richards, performing an 8:00 A.M. to 4:00 P.M. tour of duty, is designated as the station house cell block attendant. During Officer Richards' patrol, he hears moaning sounds coming from cell block number six, which is occupied by Sam Galvez. Mr. Galvez is complaining of abdominal pain and requests to go to the hospital. Officer Richards follows the procedure for a prisoner requiring medical attention by requesting that an ambulance respond to the precinct and also notifying the Desk Officer, Lt. Schwinn, who is talking with Captain Small. When the Emergency Medical Service attendants arrive, Officer Richards escorts them toward the cell block. John Ross, a medical attendant, determines after a brief examination of Mr. Galvez that his pain is probably due to his appendix.

John Ross and Jack Ryan, the other medical attendant, recommend that the prisoner be removed to the hospital. Lieutenant Schwinn assigns Police Officer Ellen Gray to rear handcuff Mr. Galvez and escort him to the hospital in the ambulance. At the hospital, Mr. Galvez is seen by Dr. Keegan, the attending physician, who requests that Officer Gray remove the handcuffs so he may conduct a complete physical examination. Officer Gray complies with Dr. Keegan's request. After Dr. Keegan examines the patient, he recommends that Mr. Galvez be admitted for an appendectomy. Police Officer Gray notifies the Hospitalized Prisoner Unit at the Court Division, completes the entries on the Medical Treatment of Prisoners form, and remains with Mr. Galvez until the arrival of a uniformed Police Officer who relieves her.

20. Who assigned Officer Gray to accompany the prisoner?

(A) Police Officer Richards   (C) Police Officer Ryan
(B) Captain Small   (D) Lieutenant Schwinn.

21. The Medical Treatment of Prisoner form was completed by the

(A) escorting officer   (C) desk officer
(B) cell block attendant   (D) medical attendant.

22. Prior to examining Mr. Galvez, Dr. Keegan requested that Officer Gray

(A) handcuff Mr. Galvez
(B) leave the examination room
(C) remove the handcuffs from Mr. Galvez
(D) submit a copy of the Medical Treatment form.

23. Officer Gray obtained the medical diagnosis from Dr. Keegan and then notified the

(A) Hospitalized Prisoner Unit at the Court Division
(B) Emergency Medical Service attendant, John Ross
(C) Desk Officer, Lieutenant Schwinn
(D) Cell Block Attendant, Police Officer Richards.

24. The Commanding Officer of each precinct often assigns Police Officers to special conditions patrols which are designed to handle problems unique to that precinct. Officers Martin and Spector are assigned to a special narcotics vehicle. Which one of the following should they give the most attention to as a possible drug dealing location?

    (A) A schoolyard where a group of fifteen youths are playing basketball and listening to the radio at 4:30 P.M.
    (B) A street corner where a group of people are standing next to an out-of-order telephone at 3:30 A.M.
    (C) Outside a YMCA center where a group of kids are getting on bicycles at 10:30 P.M.
    (D) Near an outdoor pool where twenty teenagers are waiting for an approaching bus at 4:00 P.M.

    Answer question 25 solely on the basis of the following information.

    While reviewing crime statistics for his patrol area, Police Officer Jones, of the 25th Precinct, notices that most of the homicides occur between 1:00 A.M. and 3:00 A.M., chain snatches between 10:00 A.M. and 2:00 P.M., and assaults between 5:00 A.M. and 6:00 A.M. Most of the homicides seem to occur on Thursdays, most of the chain snatches on Fridays, and most of the assaults on Fridays and Saturdays.

25. Police Officer Jones is instructed to work a steady tour that would allow him to concentrate on homicides and assaults within his patrol area. In order to do this it would be most appropriate for Officer Jones to work

    (A) 1:00 A.M. to 9:00 A.M., Monday through Friday
    (B) 5:00 A.M. to 1:00 P.M., Tuesday through Saturday
    (C) Midnight to 8:00 A.M., Wednesday through Sunday
    (D) 10:00 A.M. to 6:00 P.M., Monday through Friday.

    Answer question 26 solely on the basis of the following information.

    Assault 3rd Degree—occurs when a person intentionally causes physical injury to another person.

26. Which one of the following situations is the best example of Assault in the Third Degree?

    (A) Jennifer and Joe were talking on a street corner when Sam approached Jennifer, snatched her pocketbook, and fled.
    (B) Arthur and Jennifer were standing on a street corner arguing over Jennifer's daughter when Arthur punched Jennifer in the face, causing her mouth to bleed.
    (C) Sam and Arthur were arguing on a street corner when Sam's head was struck and bruised by a brick falling from a nearby building.
    (D) In order to avoid paying a debt, Sam ran away from Joe, who was chasing after him on foot. Joe was then hit by a passing car.

27. The following information was obtained by Police Officer Adams at the scene of an auto accident:

Date of Occurrence:	August 7, 1987
Place of Occurrence:	541 W. Broadway
Time of Occurrence:	12:45 P.M.
Drivers:	Mrs. Liz Smith and Mr. John Sharp
Action Taken:	Summons served to Mrs. Liz Smith

Officer Adams is completing a report on the accident. Which one of the following expresses the above information *most clearly* and *accurately*?

(A) At 541 W. Broadway Mr. John Sharp and Mrs. Liz Smith had an auto accident at 12:45 P.M. Mrs. Smith received a summons on August 7, 1987.

(B) Mrs. Liz Smith received a summons at 12:45 P.M. on August 7, 1987 for an auto accident with Mr. John Sharp at 541 W. Broadway.

(C) Mr. John Sharp and Mrs. Liz Smith were in an auto accident. At 541 W. Broadway on August 7, 1987 at 12:45 P.M. Mrs. Smith received a summons.

(D) On August 7, 1987 at 12:45 P.M. at 541 W. Broadway, Mrs. Liz Smith and Mr. John Sharp were involved in an auto accident. Mrs. Smith received a summons.

28. Police Officer Gold and his partner were directed by the radio dispatcher to investigate a report of a past burglary. They obtained the following information at the scene:

Date of Occurrence:	April 2, 1987
Time of Occurrence:	Between 7:30 A.M. and 6:15 P.M.
Place of Occurrence:	124 Haring Street, residence of victim
Victim:	Mr. Gerald Palmer
Suspect:	Unknown
Crime:	Burglary
Items stolen:	Assorted jewelry, $150 cash, T.V., VCR

Officer Gold must complete a report on the incident. Which one of the following expresses the above information *most clearly* and *accurately*?

(A) Mr. Gerald Palmer stated that on April 2, 1987, between 7:30 A.M. and 6:15 P.M., while he was at work, someone broke into his house at 124 Haring Street and removed assorted jewelry, a VCR, $150 cash, and a T.V.

(B) Mr. Gerald Palmer stated while he was at work that somebody broke into his house on April 2, 1987 and between 7:30 A.M. and 6:15 P.M. took his VCR, T.V., assorted jewelry, and $150 cash. His address is 124 Haring Street.

(C) Between 7:30 A.M. and 6:15 P.M. on April 2, 1987 Mr. Gerald Palmer reported an unknown person at 124 Haring Street took his T.V., VCR, $150 cash, and assorted jewelry from his house. Mr. Palmer said he was at work at the time.

(D) An unknown person broke into the house at 124 Haring Street and stole a T.V., VCR, assorted jewelry, and $150 cash from Mr. Gerald Palmer. The suspect broke in on April 2, 1987 while he was at work, reported Mr. Palmer between 7:30 A.M. and 6:15 P.M.

Answer question 29 solely on the basis of the following information.

When a Police Officer observes a person in custody or possession of a rifle or shotgun in public, the Officer should do the following in the order given:

1. Determine if person possesses a valid permit or certificate of registration.
2. Inform person not possessing permit or certificate of registration that:
   a. he may accompany the Officer to the precinct and surrender the firearm; or
   b. he may surrender the firearm at the scene, after which a receipt will be given.
3. Serve a summons returnable to appropriate criminal court.
4. Make a prompt arrest if violator refuses to surrender weapon.
5. Prepare a Property Clerk's Invoice and voucher weapons as evidence.

29. Police Officers Stromm and Rivers receive a call from the radio dispatcher that a male black, wearing sunglasses, is creating a disturbance in front of Joe's Grocery Store, located at 592 Pit Avenue. When they arrive, the Officers observe a male fitting the description showing the rifle to a small crowd that has gathered. The man, identified as Jerry Perkins, informs the Officers that he does not have a permit for the rifle and has no intention of accompanying them to the precinct to surrender his gun. The next thing that the Officers should do is

(A) promptly place Perkins under arrest at the scene
(B) inform Perkins that a receipt will be given him if he surrenders the weapon on the spot
(C) issue Perkins a summons returnable to the appropriate criminal court
(D) inform Perkins that he must have a valid permit or certificate of registration.

Answer question 30 solely on the basis of the following information.

Police Officers must sometimes rely on eyewitness accounts of incidents, even though eyewitnesses may make mistakes with regard to some details.

30. While on patrol, Police Officers Black and Beck receive a call from the radio dispatcher regarding a bank robbery in progress. When they arrive on the scene, they see that one of the bank employees has been wounded. While Officer Beck attends to the wounded employee, Officer Black interviews four witnesses who saw a man carrying a gun get into a blue late-model Cadillac and flee from the scene. The following are license plate numbers that were observed by the witnesses. Which one of these plates should Officer Black consider most likely to be the correct one?

(A) N.J. Plate ACE-1780
(B) N.Y. Plate ADE-1780
(C) N.Y. Plate BDE-1780
(D) N.J. Plate ADE-1680.

31. While on patrol, Police Officers Morris and Devine receive a call to respond to a reported burglary. The following information relating to the crime was obtained by the Officers:

Time of Occurrence:	2:00 A.M.
Place of Occurrence:	2100 First Avenue
Witness:	David Santiago
Victim:	John Rivera
Suspect:	Joe Ryan
Crime:	Burglary, video tape recorder stolen

The Officers are completing a report on the incident. Which one of the following expresses the above information *most clearly* and *accurately*?

(A) David Santiago, the witness reported at 2:00 A.M. he saw Joe Ryan leave 2100 First Avenue, home of John Rivera, with a video tape recorder.

(B) At 2:00 A.M., David Santiago reported that he had seen Joe Ryan go into 2100 First Avenue and steal a video tape recorder. John Rivera lives at 2100 First Avenue.

(C) David Santiago stated that Joe Ryan burglarized John Rivera's house at 2100 First Avenue. He saw Joe Ryan leaving his house at 2:00 A.M. with a video tape recorder.

(D) David Santiago reported that at 2:00 A.M. he saw Joe Ryan leave John Rivera's house, located at 2100 First Avenue, with Mr. Rivera's video tape recorder.

Answer question 32 solely on the basis of the following information.

When a Police Officer responds to an incident involving the victim of an animal bite, the Officer should do the following in the order given:

1. Determine the owner of the animal.
2. Obtain a description of the animal and attempt to locate it for an examination if the owner is unknown.
3. If the animal is located and the owner is unknown, comply with the Care and Disposition of Animal procedure.
4. Prepare a Department of Health form 480BAA and deliver it to the Desk Officer with a written report.
5. Notify the Department of Health by telephone if the person has been bitten by an animal other than a dog or cat.

32. Police Officer Rosario responds to 1225 South Boulevard where someone has been bitten by a dog. He is met by John Miller who informs Officer Rosario that he was bitten by a large German Shepard. Mr. Miller also states that he believes the dog belongs to someone in the neighborhood but does not know who owns it. Officer Rosario searches the area for the dog but is unable to find it. What should Officer Rosario do next?

(A) Locate the owner of the animal.
(B) Notify the Department of Health by telephone.
(C) Prepare a Department of Health form 480BAA.
(D) Comply with the Care and Disposition of Animal procedure.

33. The following details were obtained by Police Officer Howard at the scene of a hit and run accident:

Place of Occurrence:	Intersection of Brown Street and Front Street.
Time of Occurrence:	11:15 A.M.
Victim:	John Lawrence
Vehicle:	Red Chevrolet, License Plate 727PQA
Crime:	Leaving the scene of an accident

Officer Howard is completing a report on the incident. Which one of the following expresses the above information *most clearly* and *accurately*?

(A) A red Chevrolet license plate 727PQA hit John Lawrence. It left the scene of the accident at 11:15 A.M. at the intersection of Brown and Front Streets.

(B) At 11:15 A.M., John Lawrence was walking at the intersection of Brown Street and Front Street when he was struck by a red Chevrolet, license plate 727PQA, which left the scene.

(C) It was reported at 11:15 A.M. that John Lawrence was struck at the intersection of Brown Street and Front Street. The red Chevrolet, license plate 727PQA, left the scene.

(D) At the intersection of Brown Street and Front Street, John Lawrence was the victim of a car at 11:15 A.M. which struck him and left the scene. It was a red Chevrolet license plate 727PQA.

34. Police Officer Donnelly has transported an elderly male to Mt. Hope Hospital after finding him lying on the street. At the hospital, Nurse Baker provided Officer Donnelly with the following information:

Name:	Robert Jones
Address:	1485 E. 97th St.
Date of Birth:	May 13, 1917
Age:	70 years old
Type of Ailment:	Heart condition

Officer Donnelly is completing an Aided Report. Which one of the following expresses the above information *most clearly* and *accurately*?

(A) Mr. Robert Jones, who is 70 years old, born on May 13, 1917, collapsed on the street. Mr. Jones, who resides at 1485 E. 97th Street, suffers from a heart condition.

(B) Mr. Robert Jones had a heart condition and collapsed today on the street, and resides at 1485 E. 97th Street. He was 70 years old and born on May 13, 1917.

(C) Mr. Robert Jones, who resides at 1485 E. 97th Street, was born on May 13, 1917, and is 70 years old, was found lying on the street from a heart condition.

(D) Mr. Robert Jones, born on May 13, 1917, suffers from a heart condition at age 70 and was found lying on the street residing at 1485 E. 97th Street.

35. Police Officers on patrol are often called to a scene where a response from the Fire Department might be necessary. In which one of the following situations would a request to the Fire Department to respond be most critical?

(A) A film crew has started a small fire in order to shoot a scene on an October evening.
(B) Two man-hole covers blow off on a September afternoon.
(C) Homeless persons are gathered around a trash can fire on a February morning.
(D) A fire hydrant has been opened by people in the neighborhood on a July afternoon.

Answer question 36 solely on the basis of the following information.

Upon coming into possession of found property, a Police Officer should do the following in the order given:

1. Issue a receipt to person delivering property if other than a Police Officer.
   a. If property is turned in at station house, Station House Clerk will prepare a Property Clerk's Invoice and give finder a copy as a receipt.
   b. If property is delivered to a Police Officer on patrol, prepare a receipt including a description of the property and signature of receiving Officer.
2. Enter facts in memo book.
3. Prepare worksheet of Property Clerk's Invoice.
4. Deliver property and worksheet to Station House Officer.
5. Verify accuracy of Property Clerk's Invoice by signing name in the appropriate box.

36. Police Officer Bestwell, while on patrol, finds a black leather purse near a subway entrance. The bag contains a wallet with personal papers and other miscellaneous items. After logging the items that were contained in the bag into his memo book, Officer Bestwell asks Mrs. Robinson, a witness, to sign the book to verify that he found the property and that he was going to deliver it to the station house. Officer Bestwell's next step should be to

(A) give Mrs. Robinson a receipt describing the property
(B) have the Station House Clerk prepare a Property Clerk's Invoice and give a copy to Mrs. Robinson
(C) prepare a worksheet of the Property Clerk's Invoice
(D) deliver property and Property Clerk's Invoice to the Station House Officer.

37. Police Officer Rogers was dispatched to investigate a report of drugs being sold. The Officer obtained the following information:

Place of Occurrence:	In front of 109-30 Hollis Avenue
Time of Occurrence:	Between 3:00 P.M. and 6:00 P.M.
Reporter:	Mrs. Williams, who resides at 109-30 Hollis Avenue
Crime:	Drug sales
Suspects:	Male students from PS 182

Officer Rogers is preparing a report on the investigation. Which one of the following expresses the above information *most clearly* and *accurately*?

(A) Mrs. Williams reports between the hours of 3:00 P.M. and 6:00 P.M. drugs are sold. She lives at 109-30 Hollis Avenue where a group of boys from PS 182 sell drugs outside of her home.

(B) Male students selling drugs from PS 182 are creating a problem for Mrs. Williams. She reports this takes place in front of her home. She resides at 109-30 Hollis Avenue. The sales take place from 3:00 P.M. to 6:00 P.M.

(C) Drugs are being sold in front of 109-30 Hollis Avenue. Mrs. Williams reported a group of boys from PS 182 are responsible in front of her home at 109-30 Hollis Avenue. The drugs sell from 3:00 P.M. to 6:00 P.M.

(D) Mrs. Williams reports that a group of boys from PS 182 are selling drugs in front of her home at 109-30 Hollis Avenue. She further reports that the drug sales occur between 3:00 P.M. to 6:00 P.M.

Answer question 38 solely on the basis of the following information.

Rape 1st Degree—occurs when a male engages in sexual intercourse with a female:

1. by forcible compulsion; or
2. who is incapable of consent by reason of being physically helpless; or
3. who is less than eleven years old.

38. Liz and Marie while returning home from school walked by a wooded area near their home. The girls, both 10 years old, were spotted by their neighbor, Mr. Walls, who invited them to his house for ice cream. The girls followed Mr. Walls home where Joe, Mr. Walls' friend, joined them. After finishing their ice cream, the girls decided to go home but were unable to leave because Joe had locked the door. The girls were pushed into a room by Joe and Mr. Walls. The men then tore the girls' clothes off and tied them to a bed. Mr. Walls engaged in sexual intercourse with the girls while Joe watched. Who should be charged with Rape 1st Degree?

(A) Mr. Walls should be charged with Rape 1st Degree but Joe should not.

(B) Joe should be charged with Rape 1st Degree but Mr. Walls should not.

(C) Joe and Mr. Walls should both be charged with Rape 1st Degree.

(D) Neither Joe nor Mr. Walls should be charged with Rape 1st Degree.

Answer questions 39 through 40 solely on the basis of the following map. The flow of traffic is indicated by the arrows. If there is only one arrow shown, then traffic flows only in the direction indicated by the arrow. If there are two arrows shown, then traffic flows in both directions. You must follow the flow of traffic.

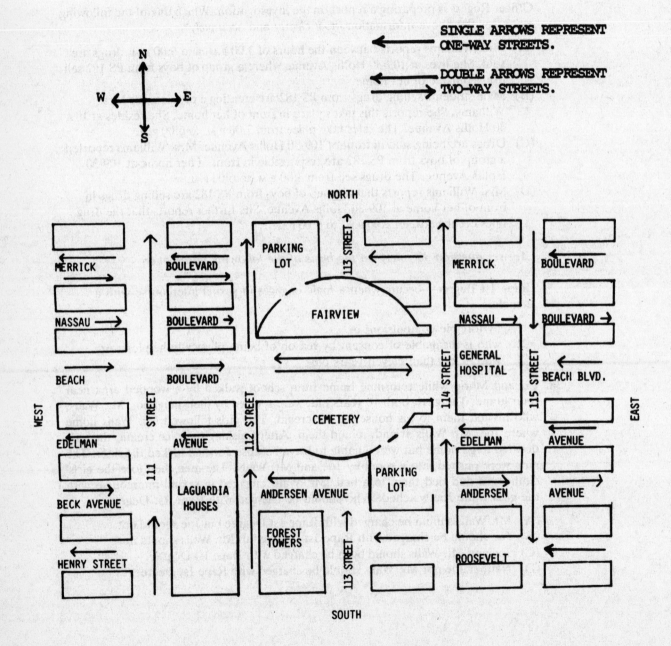

39. Police Officers Glenn and Albertson are on 111th Street at Henry Street when they are dispatched to a past robbery at Beach Boulevard and 115th Street. Which one of the following is the shortest route for the Officers to follow in their patrol car, making sure to obey all traffic regulations?

(A) Travel north on 111th Street, then east on Edelman Avenue, then north on 112th Street, then east on Beach Boulevard, then north on 114th Street, then east on Nassau Boulevard, then one block south on 116th Street.

(B) Travel north on 111th Street, then east on Beach Boulevard, then north on 114th Street, then east on Nassau Boulevard, then one block south on 115th Street.

(C) Travel north on 111th Street, then east on Merrick Boulevard, then two blocks south on 115th Street.

(D) Travel north on 111th Street, then east on Nassau Boulevard, then south on 112th Street, then east on Beach Boulevard, then north on 114th Street, then east on Nassau Boulevard, then one block south on 115th Street.

40. Later in their tour, Officers Glenn and Albertson are driving on 114th Street. If they make a left turn to enter the parking lot at Andersen Avenue, and then make a U-turn, in what direction would they now be headed?

(A) North   (C) East
(B) South   (D) West

41. On Monday, October 12, Police Officers Reynolds and Cornan responded to a past burglary at the Electronic Center. The manager of the store stated that the following merchandise was taken:

- 2 Portable tape players, each valued at $99.00
- 3 Compact Disc players, each valued at $290.00
- 5 Telephone sets, each valued at $50.00
- 1 VCR valued at $470.00
- 1 TV set valued at $600.00
- 1 Stereo rack system valued at $975.00
- 1 Walkman stereo valued at $70.00

In addition to the above items, the manager told the Officers that his calculator, worth $50, was also taken from behind the counter.

Officer Reynolds is preparing a Complaint Report on the burglary. Which one of the following is the total value of the property stolen?

(A) $2,554.00   (C) $3,433.00
(B) $2,604.00   (D) $3,483.00.

Answer Question 42 through 46 solely on the basis of the following passage.

At 10:30 P.M., while parked in front of a clothing store at 1925 First Avenue, Police Officers Cole and Reese received a radio call to investigate a possible burglary at 1423 Second Avenue. The Officers were to meet the complainant in front of the location given by the dispatcher.

Upon arriving at the scene, the Officers were met by Mr. Rivers, the owner of the Melody Grocery Store located at 1425 Second Avenue. He explained that he had called the police because he noticed the bicycle shop next door had been left open. Mr. Rivers further stated that the shop owner, Mr. Rose, usually closes at 9:00 P.M. Mr. Reyes, who lives at 1923 First Avenue and works with Mr. Rivers, noticed that the store gate had been partially closed and upon checking saw that the lights were off and the door was not locked.

At 10:40 P.M., Police Officer Reese radioed for a Supervisor before entering the premises. Sgt. Parker arrived ten minutes later and supervised a search to find out if the owner was sick, injured, or incapacitated somewhere in the store. The results proved negative. Apparently nothing had been taken or disturbed and there were no visible signs of a forced entry. The Sergeant instructed Officer Reese to guard the premises while his partner contacted Police Officer Craig, the Precinct Telephone Switchboard Operator, who would check the precinct merchant index file and then notify Mr. Rose of the situation.

42. The Sergeant supervised a search to determine if

(A) the store was being burglarized
(B) the owner was sick or injured
(C) the store had been ransacked
(D) the owner was working late.

43. The Police dispatcher received a call regarding a possible burglary at

(A) 1423 Second Avenue
(B) 1923 First Avenue
(C) 1425 Second Avenue
(D) 1925 First Avenue.

44. What type of business was left unsecured?

(A) Florist Shop
(B) Bicycle Shop
(C) Grocery Store
(D) Clothes Store.

45. At what time did the Sergeant arrive?

(A) 10:30 P.M.   (C) 10:45 P.M.
(B) 10:40 P.M.   (D) 10:50 P.M.

46. Which Police Officer would attempt to contact the store owner?

(A) Reese   (C) Craig
(B) Parker   (D) Cole.

47. While on patrol, Police Officer Willis responds to a report of unusual odors at an apartment complex. The following information was obtained by the Officer:

Place of Occurrence:	173 Concord Avenue, Apartment 17
Time of Occurrence:	1:10 A.M.
Caller:	Mrs. Denise Mathis
Odors:	Gas and ammonia
Source of Odors:	Janitor's supply room
Action Taken:	Fire Department called

Officer Willis is completing a report on the incident. Which one of the following expresses the above information *most clearly* and *accurately*?

(A) At 173 Concord Avenue, Apartment 17, the smell of gas and ammonia prompted Mrs. Denise Mathis to call 911. The Fire Department responded to the scene of the janitor's supply room. It was 1:10 A.M.

(B) Mrs. Denise Mathis smelled gas and ammonia from her home at 173 Concord Avenue, Apartment 17. She called 911. The source was found in the janitor's supply room after being noticed at 1:10 A.M. and the Fire Department was called.

(C) At 1:10 A.M., Mrs. Denise Mathis of 173 Concord Avenue, Apartment 17, smelled gas and ammonia, and called 911. The odors were found to be coming from the janitor's supply room. The Fire Department was called to the scene.

(D) Unusual odors of gas and ammonia were noticed by Mrs. Denise Mathis at 173 Concord Avenue, Apartment 17 at 1:10 A.M. The janitor's supply room was responsible. She called 911. The Fire Department was called.

Answer question 48 solely on the basis of the following information.

Police Officers must sometimes rely on eyewitness accounts of incidents, even though eyewitnesses may make mistakes with regard to some details.

48. While crossing the street, ten-year-old Nerissa King is struck by a car at the corner of James Street and Paul Avenue. Police Officer Lou responds to the scene and questions four witnesses who saw the vehicle that struck Nerissa. The following are descriptions of the vehicle given by the witnesses. Which one of these descriptions should Officer Lou consider most likely to be correct?

(A) Red Ford Mustang, NY Plate 2198 CAT
(B) Red Ford Mustang, NY Plate 2998 KAT
(C) Burgundy Ford Pinto, NY Plate 2198 CAT
(D) Red Ford Mustang, NY Plate 2198 COT

49. Police Officer Kelly responds to a call from the radio dispatcher regarding a small boy who has fallen down while running in a school yard. Officer Kelly has obtained the following information:

Time of Incident:	8:00 A.M.
Place of Incident:	PS 27 school yard at 1313 Thorn Lane
Victim:	Henry Ruiz
Injury:	Broken right index finger

Officer Kelly is writing a report on the incident. Which one of the following expresses the above information *most cleary* and *accurately*?

(A) While running in the PS 27 school yard, Henry Ruiz broke his right index finger. At 8:00 A.M. an accident occurred at 1313 Thorn Lane.

(B) At 8:00 A.M., a little boy broke his finger in the school yard at 1313 Thorn Lane. Henry Ruiz was running and it was his right index finger he broke at PS 27.

(C) Henry Ruiz fell down while running at 8:00 A.M. at 1313 Thorn Lane. The small boy broke his right index finger in the school yard of PS 27.

(D) At 8:00 A.M. in the school yard of PS 27, 1313 Thorn Lane, Henry Ruiz fell down while running and broke his right index finger.

50. Police Officer Covatti was on patrol when he received the following information relating to a person in need of assistance:

Place of Occurrence:	Canal Street and Ludlow Place
Date of Occurrence:	May 25
Person Aided:	Unidentified woman, unconscious and bleeding from the head
Reporter:	Laura Gallo
Disposition:	Victim transported by ambulance to Beth Israel Hospital

Officer Covatti is about to enter the details regarding this incident in his memo book. Which one of the following expresses the above information *most clearly* and *accurately*?

(A) An unconscious woman was transported to Beth Israel Hospital by ambulance. Laura Gallo reported that she was bleeding from the head at the corner of Canal Street and Ludlow Place on May 25th. She was unidentified.

(B) On May 25th, Laura Gallo reported that there was an unconscious woman bleeding from the head on the corner of Canal Street and Ludlow Place. An ambulance responded and transported the woman, who was unidentified, to Beth Israel Hospital.

(C) Laura Gallo reported that there was an unconscious unidentified woman bleeding from the head on the corner of Canal Street and Ludlow Place. On May 25th, an ambulance transported the woman to Beth Israel Hospital.

(D) An ambulance transported an unconscious woman, bleeding from the head, to Beth Israel Hospital. On May 25th, Laura Gallo reported that an unidentified woman was on the corner of Canal Street and Ludlow Place.

Answer question 51 solely on the basis of the following information.

When transporting emotionally disturbed people, a Police Officer should:

1. Have person removed to the hospital in an ambulance.
   a. Restraining equipment including handcuffs may be used if patient is violent or resists.
   b. When possible, a female patient being transported should be accompanied by another female or by an adult member of her immediate family.
2. Ride in body of ambulance with patient.
   a. Two police officers are needed if more than one patient is being transported.
   b. If an ambulance is not available and the situation warrants, transport the patient to the hospital by patrol car, if able to do so with reasonable restraint.

51. On Monday, while working an 8:00 P.M. to 4:00 A.M. shift, Police Officer Crown is assigned to patrol the Broadway-Lafayette subway station. At 2:15 A.M. he observes a middle-aged man wearing only red shorts pacing up and down the platform yelling, "Aliens are coming. Aliens are coming." Officer Crown approaches the man, later identified as Robert Grover, and asks, "What's the matter?" Mr. Grover begins swinging his arms at the Officer and shouts, "Don't touch me. When the next train comes, I'm jumping in front of it." Officer Crown immediately handcuffs him and calls for an ambulance. When it arrives, Officer Crown places Mr. Grover into the back of the ambulance. Just as the ambulance is about to leave for the hospital, Police Officer Cook arrives with two emotionally disturbed females, both in handcuffs. The women are placed into the ambulance along with Mr. Grover. Officer Cook stays behind to console Mrs. Susan Helms, the mother of one of the two females. Officer Crown accompanies Mr. Grover and the females to the hospital, telling Officer Cook, "I'll see you later at the hospital." In this situation, the actions taken by the Officer were

(A) proper, primarily because Officer Cook attempted to console Mrs. Helms, the mother of one of the women
(B) improper, primarily because Officer Crown handcuffed Mr. Grover without good cause
(C) proper, primarily because Officer Cook accompanied the females to the hospital in an ambulance
(D) improper, primarily because Officer Crown accompanied more than one patient to the hospital

Answer questions 52 and 53 solely on the basis of the following information.

Police Officer Malone is instructed by his supervisor to analyze the crime statistics in his patrol sector in order to reduce the number of burglaries, auto thefts, and robberies. Through his analysis, Officer Malone finds that a large percentage of the burglaries take place on East 99th Street, the majority of auto thefts along East 100th Street, and most of the robberies on Park Avenue. The burglaries occur after most people go to bed, the auto thefts during the afternoon rush hours, and the robberies during the evening hours. For the most part, burglaries take place on Thursdays and Fridays, auto thefts on Mondays and Wednesdays, and robberies on Fridays and Saturdays.

52. Officer Malone would be most effective in reducing the number or burglaries and robberies if he patrolled from

(A) 9:00 P.M. to 5:00 A.M., Wednesday through Sunday, on E. 99th Street and Park Avenue
(B) 8:00 A.M. to 4:00 P.M., Monday through Friday, on E. 99th and E. 100th Streets
(C) noon to 8:00 P.M., Wednesday through Sunday, on E. 99th Street and Park Avenue
(D) 1:00 A.M. to 9:00 A.M., Friday through Tuesday, on Park Avenue and E. 100th Street.

53. In order to most effectively reduce the number of auto thefts in his sector, Officer Malone's Supervisor asked him to work a steady tour that would allow him to concentrate on that crime. For this purpose it would be most appropriate for Officer Malone to work

(A) Tuesday through Saturday, 3:00 A.M. to 11:00 A.M.
(B) Saturday through Wednesday, 8:00 A.M. to 4:00 P.M.
(C) Monday through Friday, 4:00 P.M. to midnight
(D) Monday through Friday, midnight to 8:00 A.M.

54. It is sometimes necessary for a Police Officer to call for back-up assistance in certain situations. In which one of the following situations would it be most appropriate for Police Officers to call for back-up?

(A) A group of people playing a radio loudly in the park.
(B) Two children fighting in front of a school.
(C) A shop owner who wants a drunk removed from his doorway.
(D) Two men shaking sticks at each other while arguing in front of a bar.

Answer question 55 solely on the basis of the following information.

Police Officers coming into possession of a recovered weapon are required to voucher it by taking the following steps in the order given:

1. Unload ammunition from the chamber or magazine.
2. Scratch an identifying mark on the side of each cartridge case removed from the weapon.
3. Place the ammunition in an envelope.
4. Write "Ammunition Removed from Firearm" and the weapon's serial number (if available) across the face of the envelope.
5. Place additional ammunition, other than that removed from firearm, in a separate envelope.
6. Deliver the firearm and ammunition to the Desk Officer of the precinct of occurrence.

55. Police Officer Black is acting as vouchering officer for recovered weapons at the Midtown South Precinct. He is given a loaded .357 magnum revolver and 20 additional rounds of ammunition to be vouchered. Officer Black removes the bullets from the revolver's chamber and, with a nail, engraves "P.O.B." on the side of each cartridge case. He then places the bullets into a large brown envelope and writes "Ammunition Removed from Firearm" and the revolver's serial number across the envelope's face. The next step Officer Black should take is to

(A) scratch an identifying mark on each of the additional 20 rounds of ammunition
(B) put the additional 20 rounds of ammunition in another envelope
(C) give the revolver and bullets to the Desk Officer of the precinct where the revolver was recovered
(D) scratch an identifying mark on the barrel of the revolver.

Answer question 56 solely on the basis of the following information.

Police Officers Davis and Lewis are assigned to cover Sector A. They have been working this area for six months now and have noticed that a lot of the rapes take place on Saturdays, most of the drug sales take place on Fridays and Saturdays, and the majority of the robberies occur on Mondays and Fridays. The primary hours when the rapes occur are between 3:00 P.M. and 10:00 P.M., the drug sales take place between 9:00 A.M. and 6:00 P.M., and the robberies happen between 1:00 P.M. and midnight.

56. The Officers are instructed to work a steady tour that would allow them to concentrate on robberies and rapes within their patrol area. For this purpose it would be most appropriate for the Officers to work

(A) 3:00 P.M. to 11:00 P.M., Thursday through Monday
(B) 10:00 A.M. to 6:00 P.M., Tuesday through Saturday
(C) 8:00 A.M. to 4:00 P.M., Monday through Friday
(D) 4:00 P.M. to midnight, Wednesday through Sunday.

Answer questions 57 through 59 solely on the basis of the following passage.

Police Officers Wilson and Jost are assigned to a patrol car and receive a call from the dispatcher to respond to a shooting at 236 Bever Street between Hoyt and Clinton Avenues. The two Officers arrive at the scene at 5:20 P.M. and see a man, later identified as David Smith of 242 Bever Street, lying on the sidewalk and bleeding from the chest. An ambulance arrives at 5:35 P.M. and the attendant, Peter Johnson, pronounces Mr. Smith dead from a gunshot wound on the left side of the chest. Officer Jost begins to walk along Bever Street looking for witnesses. Suddenly, William Jones comes out of his store, located at 239 Bever Street, and tells Officer Jost that he heard a gunshot at 5:15 P.M. and saw two white males going through the victim's pockets. Meanwhile, Walter Garvey, of 247 Bever Street, approaches Officer Wilson and tells him that he saw the victim fall to the ground and then observed two white males search the victim before they ran west on Bever Street toward Clinton Avenue. Mr. Garvey describes one suspect as having blond hair and wearing a blue jacket and black jeans, and the other suspect as having brown hair and wearing a white jacket and blue jeans.

After interviewing Mr. Jones, Officer Jost is approached by Doris Finkle, owner of the Sweet Shop located at 238 Bever Street. She tells him that the victim was walking along Bever Street when two white males came from behind and pushed Mr. Smith against the wall. She also says that a man with blond hair started talking to the victim when suddenly a man wearing a white jacket fired a gun and Mr. Smith fell to the ground. Mrs. Finkle tells the Officer that the two suspects searched the victim and then ran away.

57. Who pronounced David Smith dead?

(A) William Jones
(B) Doris Finkle
(C) Peter Johnson
(D) Walter Garvey.

58. Which of the following persons was the first to report hearing a gunshot?

(A) Police Officer Jost
(B) Walter Garvey
(C) Peter Johnson
(D) William Jones.

59. Who was the first witness to give a description of the suspects' clothing?

(A) Mrs. Finkle
(B) Mr. Garvey
(C) Mr. Jones
(D) Mr. Johnson.

60. Police Officers Carrano and Lee have responded to the scene of a burglary and obtained the following information:

Place of Occurrence:	289 Orchard Street
Time of Occurrence:	1:35 A.M.
Witness:	Ms. Perez
Suspect:	A Female Hispanic, 5'10", 140 lbs., wearing a black jacket and blue jeans
Crime:	Burglary of a clothing store, three coats taken

Officers Lee and Carrano are filing the initial report on the incident. Which one of the following expresses the above information *most clearly* and *accurately*?

(A) At 1:35 A.M., Ms. Perez reported a woman stole three coats while wearing a black jacket and blue jeans in the store at 289 Orchard Street. The Hispanic is 5'10" and 140 lbs.

(B) A female Hispanic witnessed by Ms. Perez was wearing blue jeans and a black jacket. A store at 289 Orchard Street was robbed of three coats by a suspect weighing 140 lbs. at 5'10" at 1:35 A.M.

(C) Ms. Perez witnessed a burglary when she saw a woman steal three coats. She was wearing blue jeans and a black jacket. At 1:35 A.M., she burglarized a store at 289 Orchard Street. The Hispanic suspect was 5'10" and 140 lbs.

(D) At 1:35 A.M., Ms. Perez reportedly saw a female Hispanic steal three coats from a store at 289 Orchard Street. The suspect was described as being 5'10", 140 lbs., wearing blue jeans and a black jacket.

61. Police Officer Sanchez has just finished investigating a report of a rape and has obtained the following information:

Time of Occurrence:	9:10 A.M.
Place of Occurrence:	Tony's Bodega, 109 Victory Boulevard
Victim:	Joyce Rivera, employee
Crime:	Rape
Suspect:	Male, white, carrying a gun

Officer Sanchez is completing a report on the incident. Which one of the following expresses the above information *most clearly* and *accurately*?

(A) Joyce Rivera is an employee at Tony's Bodega located at 109 Victory Boulevard. She reported that at 9:10 A.M. a white male went into the Bodega and raped her at gun point.

(B) While working in Tony's Bodega, located at 109 Victory Boulevard, Joyce Rivera reported at 9:10 A.M., she was raped at gun point by a male white.

(C) The time was 9:10 A.M., when a white male went into Tony's Bodega and pointed a gun at an employee. He then raped Joyce Rivera. The Bodega is located at 109 Victory Boulevard.

(D) At 9:10 A.M., Joyce Rivera reported that she was in Tony's Bodega, located at 109 Victory Boulevard. A white male went in and raped her while she was working at gun point.

Answer question 62 solely on the basis of the following information.

When evidence is required for presentation in court a Police Officer must do the following:

1. Request evidence from Officer assigned to Property Clerk facility where it is stored.
2. Give the Officer the Property Clerk's Invoice Number.
3. Present shield and identification card.
4. If the evidence is held by the court, obtain a receipt and notify the Property Clerk's Office.
5. If the evidence is not held, return all evidence to the Property Clerk's Office.

62. Police Officer Johnson of the 105th Precinct was notified to appear in Queens Supreme Court to testify in a case involving an arrest he made the previous month. Officer Johnson needed the evidence, which consisted of two 9mm pistols and one hunting knife, before he could testify. Officer Johnson went to the 112th Precinct, where the Property Clerk's Office is located, gave the invoice number for the evidence and presented his shield and I.D. card. Officer Johnson obtained the evidence and proceeded to the court house. After four hours of testimony by various witnesses, the trial was adjourned for the day and the weapons were taken into custody by the court officer. After obtaining a receipt, Officer Johnson returned to the 105th where he completed his tour. In this situation the actions taken by Officer Johnson were

(A) proper, primarily because he obtained a receipt for the evidence before going to court
(B) improper, primarily because he did not notify the Property Clerk's Office
(C) proper, primarily because he presented his shield and I.D. card to obtain the evidence from the court officer
(D) improper, primarily because he did not return the evidence before ending his tour.

63. Captain Rutherford assigns Police Officer Haskel to a post in the Washington Avenue subway station. Officer Haskel is informed that there has been an increase in chain snatchings at the location, and he is instructed to observe anyone who looks suspicious. Which one of the following situations should Officer Haskel monitor more closely?

(A) A teenage boy who is standing on the platform and constantly checking the time on his watch.
(B) A man wearing a white robe selling incense and jewelry on the platform.
(C) A woman who has been standing against a post for the past hour watching passengers as they exit trains.
(D) Two teenagers walking down the stairs and onto an awaiting train.

64. Police Officer Mercardo has been assigned to inspect patrol car #785 for its equipment and general condition. The following information has been obtained by the Officer:

1. Total mileage of car: 76,561
2. Exterior of car: poor
   a. Broken right headlight
   b. Dents on right fender and right door
   c. Front tires flat
3. Interior of car: poor
   a. Seats ripped
   b. Dashboard lights broken
   c. Glove compartment door missing

Officer Mercardo is completing a report on his inspection of the car. Which one of the following expresses the above information *most clearly* and *accurately*?

(A) Patrol car #785 has a total mileage of 76,561 miles and is in poor condition in that the exterior of the car has a broken right headlight. It also has flats on both front tires and dents are on right fender and door. The interior of the car shows ripped seats and no glove compartment door with the dashboard lights broken.

(B) Patrol car #785, which is in poor condition, has a total mileage of 76,561 miles. The exterior of the car has a broken right headlight and dents on the right fender and right door. Both front tires are flat. The interior of the car reveals that the seats are ripped, the dashboard lights don't work, and the door to the glove compartment is missing.

(C) Patrol car #785 has on the exterior a broken right headlight, dents to the fender and door which can be found on the right side, and two flat tires in the front. For the interior, the seats are ripped, the dashboard lights are broken, and the glove compartment needs to be fixed. The general condition of the car is poor, which has a total mileage of 76,561.

(D) Patrol car #785 has in the interior ripped seats and a missing glove compartment door. Also the dashboard lights don't come on. The condition of the car is poor, it has a total mileage of 76,561 miles on it. The exterior of the car has two front tires that are flat, a broken right headlight and dents to the right fender. The door is also dented.

Answer question 65 solely on the basis of the following information.

Police Officers may become involved in cases regarding children who are lost. When a lost child is brought to a Police Officer, the Officer should do the following in the order given:

1. Notify Desk Officer and radio dispatcher.
2. Conduct a brief investigation in vicinity of place where child was found.
3. Bring child to the Precinct station house if parents or relatives are not found.
4. Prepare an Aided Report.
5. Telephone Missing Persons Squad and give a description.
6. Complete captions on Aided Report and process in normal manner.

65. Police Officer Davis, while assigned to patrol on White Street, was approached by Mr. Franklin, the custodian at 274 Lafayette Street, and a small child. Mr. Franklin explained that he found the child walking alone on the fifth floor of his building. Officer Davis radioed the dispatcher, telephoned his Desk Officer, and then escorted the child to the station house. When Officer Davis arrived at the precinct, the Desk Officer reminded him that, prior to bringing the child in, Officer Davis should have

(A) prepared an Aided Report
(B) called the radio dispatcher
(C) notified the Missing Persons Squad
(D) made inquiries in the building about the child.

66. Police Officer Cohen is on patrol and receives a call to respond to a disturbance at a local grocery store. The following information is given to the Officer at the scene:

Place of Occurrence:	Joe's Mini-Mart
Complainant:	Tom Callas
Crime:	Loitering and using abusive language
Suspect:	Male, Hispanic
Action Taken:	The suspect was removed from premises

Officer Cohen is completing a report on the incident. Which one of the following expresses the above information *most clearly* and *accurately*?

(A) Tom Callas called the Police because a male Hispanic was loitering and using abusive language in Joe's Mini-Mart. The male Hispanic was removed from the premises by Police.
(B) A male Hispanic was removed from Joe's mini-Mart. Tom Callas called the Police. He was loitering and using abusive language when he was removed from the premises.
(C) At Joe's Mini-Mart, a male Hispanic was loitering and using abusive language. Tom Callas called the Police. They removed him from the premises.
(D) The Police removed a male Hispanic from Joe's Mini-Mart. Tom Callas called them because he was loitering and using abusive language.

Answer questions 67 and 68 solely on the basis of the following information.

Upon notification or observation of a vehicle accident, a Police Officer should do the following in the order given:

1. Park radio motor patrol car behind vehicles involved so that traffic will not be blocked.
2. Determine if there are any injuries and request an ambulance if needed.
3. Divert traffic if necessary.
4. Obtain the drivers license, vehicle registration, and insurance identification card of driver(s) so that required information can be recorded.
5. Determine the cause of the accident by inquiry and observation.
6. Prepare one copy of Police Accident Report.

67. While on Highway Patrol, Police Officer Quinn witnesses a serious three vehicle accident and immediately stops to assist. While exiting his patrol car, he notices that one of the drivers involved in the accident is bleeding heavily from the mouth and that a serious traffic condition is developing on both sides of the intersection. The next step Officer Quinn should take is to

(A) reduce congestion by diverting the traffic
(B) request drivers licenses, vehicle registrations, and insurance cards from the drivers
(C) obtain medical assistance for the injured
(D) radio for a tow truck to remove accident vehicles.

68. Police Officers Velazquez and Degas are on vehicle patrol and passing through an intersection when a pedestrian flags them down to report a traffic accident. Officer Velazquez stops behind the vehicles involved in the accident, gets out of the car, and asks the two drivers if anyone is injured. They both say that they are all right. Officer Velazquez then asks them for their licenses, registrations, and insurance cards. Officer Degas notices that traffic is beginning to back up at the intersection, so she starts to direct traffic around the accident. The next step that Officers Velazquez and Degas should take is to

(A) request that an ambulance respond to the scene
(B) divert traffic if necessary
(C) prepare one copy of a Police Accident Report
(D) determine the cause of the accident.

69. During his last tour of duty, Police Officer Meehan observed a robbery in progress and arrested the suspect. The following details are related to the robbery:

Place of Occurrence:	Corner of Ludlow and Rivington Streets
Date of Occurrence:	June 10
Weapon:	.357 Magnum
Crime:	Robbery

Officer Meehan is completing a request for departmental recognition for this arrest. Which one of the following expresses the above information *most clearly* and *accurately*?

(A) On June 10th, I apprehended a perpetrator without assistance on the corner of Ludlow and Rivington Streets. I observed a robbery in progress and recovered a .357 Magnum.

(B) On June 10th, I observed a robbery in progress on the corner of Ludlow and Rivington Streets. I apprehended the perpetrator without assistance and recovered a .357 Magnum.

(C) I observed a robbery in progress and without assistance I apprehended the perpetrator with a .357 Magnum. This took place on the corner of Ludlow and Rivington Streets. The incident occurred on June 10.

(D) On June 10th, I recovered a .357 Magnum when I observed a robbery in progress. I apprehended the perpetrator on Ludlow and Rivington Streets without assistance.

Answer question 70 solely on the basis of the following information.

After a suspicious person has been stopped, questioned, and frisked, the Police Officer should do the following in the order given:

1. Request the person's name and address.
2. Prepare a Stop and Frisk report.
3. Enter the details in the Activity Log.
4. Inform the supervisor of the facts.
5. Submit a Stop and Frisk report to the Desk Officer.
6. Get the Precinct Log number.

70. Police Officer O'Boyle is dispatched to investigate a suspicious male with a knife in Van Cortland Park. When the Officer arrives on the scene, he notices a male fitting the description he has been given. Officer O'Boyle stops, questions, and frisks the male but finds nothing on him. What should the Officer do next?

(A) Inform his supervisor of the facts.
(B) Prepare a Stop and Frisk report.
(C) Request the person's name and address.
(D) Enter the details in the Activity Log.

Answer question 71 solely on the basis of the following information.

During the winter, when the temperature drops below 32° and the Department of Health declares a Cold Weather Emergency, Police Officers are required to:

1. Require all homeless people to go to a shelter.
2. Give transportation to homeless people looking for shelter.
3. If a homeless person refuses to go to a shelter and has no home, use force if necessary to get the person to a hospital for psychiatric evaluation.

71. It is 3:00 A.M. on a Tuesday and the temperature has dropped from 34° to 28°. A Cold Weather Emergency has just been declared. During his patrol, Police Officer Georgia notices a middle-aged woman lying near a metal grate on the sidewalk near the corner of Main Street and Craig Avenue. The woman is surrounded by shopping bags and appears to be disoriented. The Officer asks her where she lives and she says "many places." He asks if she has any friends or relatives and she says that she does not know anyone. The Officer asks her if she would like to go to a shelter and she refuses. When asked for identification, she hands the Officer a wallet containing a few meaningless scraps of paper. The Officer then calls for a supervisor and an ambulance to transport her to a hospital for psychiatric evaluation. In this situation, the actions taken by Officer Georgia were

(A) improper, primarily because the woman had not committed a crime or bothered anyone
(B) proper, primarily because she was obviously in need of psychiatric evaluation
(C) improper, primarily because the woman was more in need of shelter than of a psychiatric evaluation
(D) proper, primarily because the woman had refused shelter despite the Cold Weather Emergency.

Answer question 72 solely on the basis of the following information.

Criminal Sale of a Controlled Substance 5th Degree—occurs when a person knowingly and unlawfully sells a controlled substance, such as cocaine, marihuana, heroin.

Sell means to sell, give or dispose of to another, or to offer or agree to do the same.

72. Which one of the following situations is the best example of Criminal Sale of a Controlled Substance in the Fifth Degree?

(A) James and Cathy dispose of six vials of cocaine by burying them in their back yard.
(B) Harry and Jack sit in a stairwell and pass a lit pipe filled with marihuana between them.
(C) Thomas opens his dresser drawer and exchanges a bag full of cocaine for a bag of marihuana.
(D) John laces his neighbor's dog food with heroin.

Answer question 73 solely on the basis of the following information.

After arresting a suspect, Police Officers are required to take fingerprints in order to establish positive identification. When taking fingerprints, Police Officers must do the following in the order given:

1. Police Officers should be extremely careful when fingerprinting to have no weapons on their person.
2. Inform person to relax hands and fingers and let the Officer do the rolling.
3. Prepare fingerprint charts as follows:
   a. Two copies of Criminal Fingerprint Record
   b. One copy of FBI Fingerprint Chart
   c. One copy of N.Y. State Fingerprint Chart
4. In the case of a juvenile, prepare one copy of N.Y. State Juvenile Fingerprint Chart.
5. Whenever arrested persons are fingerprinted, palm prints and photographs may also be taken.

73. Police Officer Lane has arrested a juvenile and is about to process his arrest. Before taking the fingerprints, Officer Lane hands his revolver to Lt. Cronin, who secures it in the weapons locker. The youth is told to relax his hands and fingers and to let Officer Lane do the rolling. The Officer begins to prepare two Criminal Fingerprint Records, and FBI Fingerprint Chart and a N.Y. State Fingerprint Chart. After completing this, the next step Officer Lane should take is to

(A) take palm prints and photographs of the juvenile
(B) prepare an additional Criminal Fingerprint Record
(C) deliver the fingerprint reports to the appropriate agency
(D) prepare a N.Y. State Juvenile Fingerprint Chart.

74. Police Officer Roach responded to the home of Audrey Seager regarding a past burglary. Ms. Seager reported that, while she was at work, someone broke into her home and stole the property listed below. She further stated that a piece of her luggage worth approximately $150.00 was also taken and was probably used by the robber to carry the following property out of her apartment:

- 2 35mm Cameras, each valued at $289.00
- 2 Video Cassette Recorders, each valued at $329.00
- Miscellaneous jewelry valued at $455.00
- Cash $350.00
- Stock certificates valued at $1,500.00

Officer Roach is completing a Complaint Report. Which one of the following is the total value of the property and cash stolen from Ms. Seager?

(A) $2,923.00   (C) $3,691.00
(B) $3,073.00   (D) $3,991.00.

Answer question 75 solely on the basis of the following information.

Serious Physical Injury—injury that creates a substantial risk of death, or serious and prolonged disfigurement, prolonged impairment of health, or loss or impairment of function of any bodily organ.

Assault 2nd Degree—occurs when, with intent to cause physical injury to another, a person causes such injury to such person or to a third person by means of a deadly weapon or dangerous instrument.

Manslaughter 1st Degree—occurs when, with intent to cause serious physical injury to another, a person causes death to that person or to a third person.

Murder 2nd Degree—occurs when, with intent to cause the death of another, a person causes the death of such person or a third person.

75. Police Officers Harris and Linden were dispatched to Clare's Bar. Upon their arrival they observed two dead bodies lying on the floor. After interviewing witnesses at the bar, they learned that an elderly man known as "Whiskey Bill" had given the victims home-made liquor. Whiskey Bill was placed under arrest. During the interrogation, Bill admitted that he knew that the liquor would be fatal if someone drank it, but he wanted to get even with Joe, who was one of the victims. It would be most appropriate for the Officers to charge Bill with

   (A) Murder 2nd Degree
   (B) Serious Physical Injury
   (C) Assault 2nd Degree
   (D) Manslaughter 1st Degree.

Answer question 76 solely on the basis of the following information.

Police Officer Miller is assigned to the 72nd Precinct and observes that most of the rapes in his sector are committed on Bay Street between President Street and Alabama Street. All the assaults are committed on Nelson Street between Carroll Street and Lewis Street, and all the homicides are committed on Third Avenue between Tinton Street and Union Street. Most of the rapes happen on Thursdays and Fridays between 10:00 P.M. and 2:00 A.M.; the assaults on Saturdays between 10:00 A.M. and 1:00 P.M.; and most of the homicides on Saturdays and Sundays between 1:00 A.M. and 4:00 A.M.

76. Officer Miller would most likely be able to reduce the number of homicides by patrolling

   (A) Bay Street on Thursdays and Fridays between 10:00 P.M. and 2:00 A.M.
   (B) Alabama Street on Saturdays between 10:00 A.M. and 1:00 P.M.
   (C) Carroll Street on Wednesdays between 11:00 A.M. and 3:00 P.M.
   (D) Third Avenue on Saturdays and Sundays between 1:00 A.M. and 4:00 A.M.

Answer questions 77 through 79 solely on the basis of the following map. The flow of traffic is indicated by the arrows. If there is only one arrow shown, then traffic flows only in the direction indicated by the arrow. If there are two arrows shown, then traffic flows in both directions. You must follow the flow of traffic.

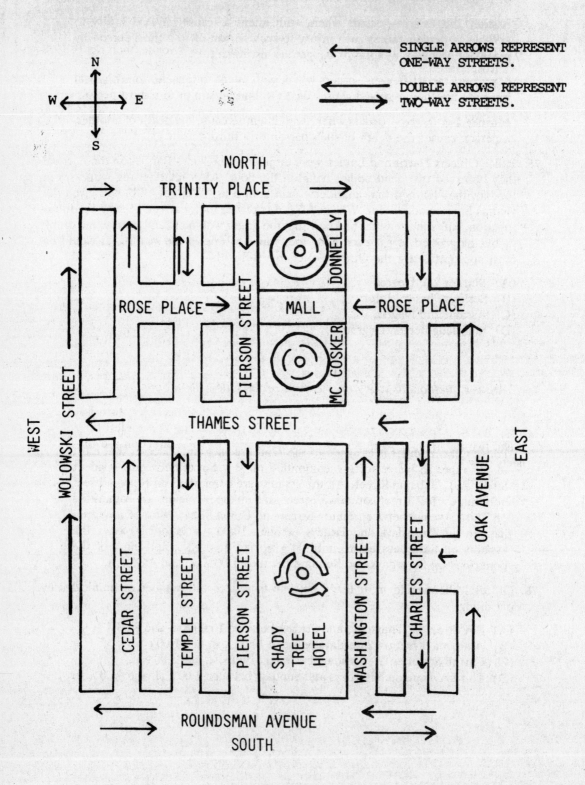

77. Police Officers Simms and O'Brien are located at Roundsman Avenue and Washington Street. The radio dispatcher has assigned them to investigate a motor vehicle accident at the corner of Pierson Street and Rose Place. Which one of the following is the shortest route for them to take in their patrol car, making sure to obey all traffic regulations?

    (A) Travel west on Roundsman Avenue, then north on Temple Street, then east on Thames Street, then north on Pierson Street to Rose Place.
    (B) Travel east on Roundsman Avenue, then north on Oak Avenue, then west on Rose Place to Pierson Street.
    (C) Travel west on Roundsman Avenue, then north on Temple Street, then east on Rose Place to Pierson Street.
    (D) Travel east on Roundsman Avenue, then north on Oak Avenue, then west on Thames Street, then north on Temple Street, then east on Rose place to Pierson Street.

78. Police Officers Sears and Castro are located at Cedar Street and Roundsman Avenue. They are called to respond to the scene of a burglary at Rose Place and Charles Street. Which one of the following is the shortest route for them to take in their patrol car, making sure to obey all traffic regulations?

    (A) Travel east on Roundsman Avenue, then north on Oak Avenue, then west on Rose Place to Charles Street.
    (B) Travel east on Roundsman Avenue, then north on Washington Street, then east on Rose Place to Charles Street.
    (C) Travel west on Roundsman Avenue, then north on Wolowski Street, then east on Trinity Place, then south on Charles Street to Rose Place.
    (D) Travel east on Roundsman Avenue, then north on Charles Street to Rose Place.

79. Police Officer Glasser is in an unmarked car at the intersection of Rose Place and Temple Street when he begins to follow two robbery suspects. The suspects go south for two blocks, then turn left for two blocks, then make another left turn for one more block. The suspects realize they are being followed and make a left turn and travel two more blocks and then make a right turn. In what direction are the suspects now headed?

    (A) North
    (B) South
    (C) East
    (D) West

80. Police Officer Ross has been assigned to investigate a recent increase in the number of token booth hold-ups committed by pairs of youths in the Chambers Street Station. He has been instructed to pay special attention to any activity that appears to be suspicious. Which one of following situations should Officer Ross monitor more closely?

(A) A male youth talking to the token clerk while the clerk is counting money.
(B) A youth looking at a subway map near the booth while holding a black canvas bag.
(C) One youth standing by the token booth while his friend waits on the stairs.
(D) Two female youths engaged in fistfight near the turnstile.

Answer question 81 solely on the basis of the following information.

When a prisoner in custody is admitted to a hospital, the arresting Police Officer should do the following in the order given:

1. Notify Desk Officer in the precinct of arrest.
2. Search male prisoner at hospital in presence of witnesses if prisoner was removed from scene of arrest directly to hospital.
3. Have hospital personnel search female prisoners.
4. Search prisoner's personal clothing, after removal by hospital personnel, for weapons, evidence, or contraband.
5. Give hospital authorities receipt for property received.
6. Enter in Activity Log list of property removed and any information necessary to process arrest.
7. Report to precinct of arrest to continue arrest processing when relieved by guarding Officer.

81. While Police Officer Smith was arresting Michelle Hart for the robbery of a jewelry store, Ms. Hart suffered an asthma attack and had to be hospitalized immediately. Officer Smith requested that an ambulance respond to the scene and informed Lt. Brandon, the Desk Officer in the precinct, of details regarding the arrest. He then rode to the hospital in the ambulance with his prisoner. After informing hospital personnel of the circumstances concerning the arrest, the next thing Officer Smith should do is

(A) report to the precinct of arrest and continue arrest processing
(B) search the prisoner in presence of hospital personnel
(C) enter in his Activity Log the time of arrest and identity of prisoner
(D) direct hospital personnel to search the prisoner.

Answer question 82 solely on the basis of the following information.

When a person is arrested for possession of a firearm, the arresting Officer should:

1. Seize the weapon.
2. Base the charge on the violation of Penal Law or Administrative Code.
3. Prepare the Request for Laboratory Examination form.
4. Bring weapon and Request form to the Ballistics Unit.
5. After examination by Ballistics Unit, deliver weapon to Property Clerk with Property Clerk's Invoice.

82. Police Officer Livingston has received a call from the dispatcher regarding shots fired. Upon arriving at the scene, Officer Livingston finds a loaded 9mm automatic pistol in the possession of John Blake. Officer Livingston secures the firearm and arrests John Blake, charging him with Criminal Use of a Firearm in the 1st Degree, a violation of the Penal Law. Once at the station house, Officer Livingston is instructed to prepare a form requesting a Laboratory Examination of the firearm. After this has been completed, Officer Livingston leaves the form with his supervisor and takes the firearm to the Ballistics Unit, where it is examined. It is learned that the gun was used in a number of crimes, including the shooting of a Police Officer. Officer Livingston delivers the gun to the Property Clerk's Office with a Property Clerk's Invoice. Officer Livingston's actions were

    (A) improper, primarily because the laboratory request was not brought to the Ballistics Unit
    (B) proper, primarily because the gun was brought to the Ballistics Unit where it was learned that the gun was used in other crimes
    (C) improper, primarily because the Property Clerk's Invoice should have been given to his supervisor after it was completed
    (D) proper, primarily because Mr. Blake was charged with Criminal Use of a Firearm in the First Degree, a violation of the Penal Law.

83. Police Officers are sometimes required to request emergency transportation for seriously injured people. For which one of the following people would it be most appropriate for a Police Officer to request emergency transportation?

    (A) A pregnant woman who complains of feeling faint.
    (B) An elderly man who has been drinking complains about his vision.
    (C) A young boy who is roller-skating falls down and is knocked unconscious.
    (D) A teenage girl slips while ice-skating and limps off the ice.

Answer questions 84 through 87 solely on the basis of the following passage.

On May 10, at 5:30 P.M., Police Officers Swift and Monroe were on routine patrol when they were dispatched to 1180 Albany Avenue, Apartment 3C on an assault in progress. They arrived at the apartment at 5:40 P.M. and were met by Mr. Raymond Ambrose. Mr. Ambrose said he called the police because he heard yelling and screaming coming from Apartment 3A, but it had since stopped. Mr. Ambrose told the Officers that the tenant in 3A, Helen Gray, lived alone ever since her divorce.

Officer Monroe knocked on the door of Apartment 3A and noticed that the door was partially opened. The Officers cautiously entered the apartment, which appeared to have been ransacked. Officer Swift checked the fire escape while his partner searched the bedroom where he found Mrs. Gray, unconscious, lying on the floor and bleeding heavily from the head. A blood-covered baseball bat was found next to her. The Officer called for an ambulance to respond while Officer Swift tried to gather information from neighbors.

Mary Grable, age 68, of Apartment 3B; Ben Grim, age 16, of Apartment 1A; and Angela Arnold, age 27, of 1162 Albany Avenue were standing in the hallway. Ms. Arnold stated that she and Mrs. Gray are close friends and she became concerned when she saw Stuart Gray in the neighborhood around 5:10 P.M. Ms. Arnold told Officer Swift, "Since they've been divorced, Stuart visits Helen to get money to support a 'crack' habit, and it always leads to an argument." Grable said she had heard a commotion, but didn't know who was involved. Grim told Officer Swift that he saw Stuart Gray running from the building at about 5:35 P.M. with blood on his hands and shirt.

Paramedics arrived at 5:50 P.M. and transported Mrs. Gray to the hospital where she died at 6:30 P.M. without regaining consciousness. Stuart Gray was arrested at 7:15 the next morning at the home of his mother, Valerie Gray, and was charged with the homicide.

84. From the information given, it is most likely that the crime was committed between

(A) 5:10 A.M.–5:35 A.M.
(B) 5:10 P.M.–5:35 P.M.
(C) 5:30 P.M.–5:35 P.M.
(D) 5:30 P.M.–5:50 P.M.

85. Who was the first person to find Mrs. Gray?

(A) Officer Monroe
(B) Mr. Ambrose
(C) Officer Swift
(D) Ms. Arnold.

86. Whose information tied Stuart to the crime?

(A) Ms. Arnold and Ben Grim
(B) Mr. Ambrose and Ms. Arnold
(C) Ben Grim and Valerie Gray
(D) Ms. Arnold and Ms. Grable.

87. Stuart Gray was arrested on

(A) May 10 at 6:30 P.M.
(B) May 11 at 7:15 P.M.
(C) May 10 at 7:15 A.M.
(D) May 11 at 7:15 A.M.

88. The following details were obtained by Police Officer Dwight at the scene of a family dispute:

Place of Occurrence:	77 Baruch Drive
Victim:	Andrea Valdez, wife of Walker
Violator:	Edward Walker
Witness:	George Valdez, victim's brother
Crime:	Violation of Order of Protection
Action Taken:	Violator arrested

Police Officer Dwight is preparing a report on the incident. Which one of the following expresses the above information *most clearly* and *accurately*?

(A) George Valdez saw Edward Walker violate his sister's Order of Protection at 77 Baruch Drive. Andrea Valdez's husband was arrested for this violation.
(B) Andrea Valdez's Order of Protection was violated at 77 Baruch Drive. George Valdez saw his brother-in-law violate his sister's Order. Edward Walker was arrested.
(C) Edward Walker was arrested for violating an Order of Protection held by his wife, Andrea Valdez. Andrea's brother, George Valdez, witnessed the violation at 77 Baruch Drive.
(D) An arrest was made at 77 Baruch Drive when an Order of Protection held by Andrea Valdez was violated by her husband. George Valdez, her brother, witnessed Edward Walker.

Answer question 89 solely on the basis of the following information.

Endangering the Welfare of a Child—occurs when a person knowingly acts in a manner likely to be injurious to the physical, mental, or moral welfare of a male child less than 16 years old or a female child less than 17 years old.

89. Which one of the following situations is the best example of Endangering the Welfare of a Child?

(A) John spanks his seven-year-old son because he has been misbehaving in school.
(B) Linda slaps her sixteen-year-old brother for punishing her child.
(C) Beverly leaves her four-year-old son unattended to go to a party in the next building.
(D) Gary sends his twelve-year-old daughter to her room with no dinner for bringing home a bad report card.

90. Police Officer Clay responds to the scene of a found child where he obtains the following information:

Child's Name:	Craig Gildae
Age:	4 years
Location Found:	Wandering around in front of 501 E. 204th Street
Description:	Male, white, blond hair, blue eyes, wearing red overalls, white T-shirt, and blue high-top sneakers.

Officer Clay is about to transmit this information to the radio dispatcher. Which one of the following expresses the above information *most clearly* and *accurately*?

(A) In front of 501 E. 204th Street a male white, Craig Gildae, was found wandering around with blond hair, blue eyes, wearing a white T-shirt, red overalls, and blue high-top sneakers. The child is four years old.

(B) Four-year-old Craig Gildae was found wandering around in front of 501 E. 204th Street. He is a male, white, blond hair, blue eyes, wearing red overalls, a white T-shirt, and blue high-top sneakers.

(C) A blond hair, blue-eyed male was found wandering around wearing red overalls, white T-shirt, and blue high-top sneakers. Four-year-old Craig Gildae was found in front of 501 E. 204th Street.

(D) Found wandering around in front of 501 E. 204th Street male, white, with blond hair, blue eyes, wearing red overalls, white T-shirt, and blue high-top sneakers identified as four-year-old Craig Gildae.

91. The following details were obtained by Police Officer Jackson at the scene of a robbery:

Place of Occurrence:	Chambers Street, northbound A platform
Victim:	Mr. John Wells
Suspect:	Joseph Miller
Crime:	Robbery, armed with knife, wallet taken
Action Taken:	Suspect arrested

Officer Jackson is completing a report on the incident. Which one of the following expresses the above information *most clearly* and *accurately*?

(A) At Chambers Street northbound A platform Joseph Miller used a knife to remove the wallet of John Wells while waiting for the train. Police arrested him.

(B) Mr. John Wells, while waiting for the northbound A train at Chambers Street, had his wallet forcibly removed at knifepoint by Joseph Miller. Joseph Miller was later arrested.

(C) Joseph Miller was arrested for robbery. At Chambers Street John Wells stated that his wallet was taken. The incident occurred at knifepoint while waiting on northbound A platform.

(D) At the northbound Chambers Street platform, John Wells was waiting for the A train. Joseph Miller produced a knife and removed his wallet. He was arrested.

Answer question 92 solely on the basis of the following information.

When a Police Officer stops a vehicle and discovers that the operator is driving with a suspended or revoked drivers license, the Officer should do the following in the order given:

1. Confiscate the driver's license.
2. Prepare a Seized Drivers License Report.
3. Give operator of vehicle a receipt for license.
   a. If operator has two or more unrelated suspensions, or his license has been revoked for any reason, remove the motorist to the precinct of arrest and process a Desk Appearance Ticket.
   b. If operator has one or more suspensions regarding the same violation, a Universal Summons should be issued.
4. Do not mark or mutilate license in any manner.
5. Have the violator's vehicle parked in a legal parking area until the registered owner can arrange to have the vehicle removed from the scene by a licensed operator.

92. Police Officers Harris and Lowe are on patrol in their radio car when they stop a vehicle driven by Dennis Clarke. Clarke, whose license had been suspended once before for speeding, was driving over the speed limit. Officer Harris confiscates Clarke's license, prepares the required report, and issues him a receipt for his license. The next thing Officer Harris should do is

(A) have Clarke park his vehicle in a legal parking area until he can arrange to have a licensed operator remove it
(B) issue Clarke a Universal Summons and have him drive his vehicle to his home
(C) remove Clarke to the precinct and process him for a Desk Appearance Ticket
(D) issue Clarke a Universal Summons and have his car parked in a legal parking area.

93. Police Officer Hayes is informed by Sergeant Holt that drugs are being sold from autos on Officer Hayes' post. He is directed to observe stopped vehicles if he believes the occupants' actions are suspicious. Which one of the following should Officer Hayes consider most suspicious?

(A) Two men sit in a parked auto in front of a school yard during recess and after school.
(B) An auto drops off a man and then quickly speeds away.
(C) A car service driver reads a newspaper and is parked in the same spot for 45 minutes.
(D) Four teenagers sit in a parked convertible by a busy recreation area while listening to a radio.

Answer question 94 solely on the basis of the following information.

Upon uncovering illegal drugs during an investigation, Police Officers should do the following in the order given:

1. Bring the drugs to the station house of the precinct where the discovery was made.
2. Notify the Station House Officer.
3. Prepare a Property Clerk's Invoice.
4. Request a laboratory analysis of the drugs.
5. Mark the drugs for future identification.
6. Request specially secured envelopes from the Station House Officer.
7. Deliver the drugs to the laboratory.

94. In the course of a drug investigation in the 2nd Precinct, Police Officer Wells has come into possession of 100 vials of refined cocaine. He brought his find to the Station House Officer in the 2nd Precinct, filled out a Property Clerk's Invoice, and called for a laboratory analysis of the narcotics, He then labelled each individual vial so that the vials could be identified by other Officers if necessary. The next step Officer Wells should take is to

(A) deliver the drugs to the laboratory
(B) consecutively number all the vials of cocaine with the Officer's initials
(C) ask the Station House Officer for specially secured envelopes
(D) prepare a request for a laboratory examination of the drugs.

Answer question 95 solely on the basis of the following information.

Theft of Services—occurs when a person intentionally fails to pay or avoids the payment of lawful charges for any public transportation service.

95. Which one of the following is the best example of Theft of Services?

(A) A shabbily dressed elderly man crawls under a turnstile in a subway station to retrieve a quarter he accidentally dropped. When a train pulls into the station, he retrieves the quarter and quickly gets on.
(B) In the middle of dinner at a restaurant, Tom and Janet complain about the quality of service. They refuse to pay their bill and immediately leave the restaurant and hail a taxi.
(C) Harry is driving home and pulls up to a toll booth to pay a quarter toll. Harry misses the coin box with the quarter and drives away.
(D) John hails a cab to take him to his office. When he arrives he realizes that he has no cash with him and asks the cab driver to wait while he gets some from his office safe.

96. Police Officer Bellows responds to a report of drugs being sold in the lobby of an apartment building. He obtains the following information at the scene:

Time of Occurrence:	11:30 P.M.
Place of Occurrence:	1010 Bath Avenue
Witnesses:	Mary Markham, John Silver
Suspect:	Harry Stoner
Crime:	Drug Sales
Action Taken:	Suspect was gone when Police arrived

Officer Bellows is completing a report of the incident. Which one of the following expresses the above information *most clearly* and *accurately*?

(A) Mary Markham and John Silver witnessed drugs being sold and the suspect flee at 1010 Bath Avenue. Harry Stoner was conducting his business at 11:30 P.M. before Police arrival in the lobby.

(B) In the lobby, Mary Markham reported at 11:30 P.M. she saw Harry Stoner, along with John Silver, selling drugs. He ran from the lobby at 1010 Bath Avenue before Police arrived.

(C) John Silver and Mary Markham reported that they observed Harry Stoner selling drugs in the lobby of 1010 Bath Avenue at 11:30 P.M. The witnesses stated that Stoner fled before Police arrived.

(D) Before Police arrived, witnesses stated that Harry Stoner was selling drugs. At 1010 Bath Avenue, in the lobby, John Silver and Mary Markham said they observed his actions at 11:30 P.M.

97. While on patrol, Police Officer Fox receives a call to respond to a robbery. Upon arriving at the scene, he obtains the following information:

Time of Occurrence:	6:00 P.M.
Place of Occurrence:	Sal's Liquor Store at 30 Fordham Road
Victim:	Sal Jones
Suspect:	White male wearing a beige parka
Description of Crime:	Victim was robbed in his store at gunpoint

Officer Fox is completing a report on the incident. Which one of the following expresses the above information *most clearly* and *accurately*?

(A) I was informed at 6:00 P.M. by Sal Jones that an unidentified white male robbed him at gunpoint at 30 Fordham Road while wearing a beige parka at Sal's Liquor Store.

(B) At 6:00 P.M., Sal Jones was robbed at gunpoint in his store. An unidentified white male wearing a beige parka came into Sal's Liquor Store at 30 Fordham Road, he told me.

(C) I was informed at 6:00 P.M. while wearing a beige parka an unidentified white male robbed Sal Jones at gunpoint at Sal's Liquor Store at 30 Fordham Road.

(D) Sal Jones informed me that at 6:00 P.M. he was robbed at gunpoint in his store, Sal's Liquor Store, located at 30 Fordham Road, by an unidentified white male wearing a beige parka.

Answer question 98 solely on the basis of the following information.

Police Officer Daily has been informed by Sergeant Newman that there have been three purse snatches on his post during the past two weeks. The description of each of the suspects is as follows:

Incident No. 1—Male, black, 24 years old, 5'9", 185 lbs., scar on left side of face, blue dungarees, white sneakers, long brown hair, earring in right ear.

Incident No. 2—Male, black, about 25 years old, 170 lbs., 5'9", long black hair, black dungarees, white sneakers, white tank top, scar on right side of face.

Incident No. 3—Male, black, 27 to 30 years old, 5'8", 190 lbs., long curly hair, blue T-shirt, earring in left ear, black sneakers, black dungarees, tattoo on right arm.

On April 20, Police Officer Daily arrested a suspect during an attempted purse snatch. The description of the suspect is as follows:

Incident No. 4—Male, black, 5'9", 180 lbs., 23 years old, white tank top, white sneakers, long, straight brown hair, black dungarees, gold earring in right ear, scar on left side of face.

98. Based on the above descriptions of the suspects in the first three incidents, Officer Daily should consider the suspect in the fourth purse snatching as a suspect in

(A) Incident No. 1, but not Incident No. 2 or Incident No. 3
(B) Incident No. 3, but not Incident No. 1 or Incident No. 2
(C) Incident No. 1 and Incident No. 2, but not Incident No. 3
(D) Incident No. 2 and Incident No. 3, but not Incident No. 1.

Answer question 99 solely on the basis of the following information.

Robbery—occurs when a person steals property by using or threatening the immediate use of physical force upon another person.

99. Which one of the following is the best example of Robbery?

(A) Bill casually bumps into Raymond, removes Raymond's wallet from his back pocket, and runs away.
(B) Carol and John are approached by Marty, who takes their money after saying he would slash Carol's face with a knife.
(C) Karen approaches Grace, who is sleeping on the train, slices her purse strap with a razor, grabs the purse and walks away.
(D) Fred threatens to find Peter's daughter and hurt her if Peter does not hand over his gold watch.

100. The following details were obtained by Police Officer Connors at the scene of a bank robbery:

Time of Occurrence:	10:21 A.M.
Place of Occurrence:	Westbury Savings and Loan
Crime:	Bank Robbery
Suspect:	Male, dressed in black, wearing a black woolen face mask
Witness:	Mary Henderson of 217 Westbury Avenue
Amount Stolen:	$6141 U.S. currency

Officer Connors is completing a report on the incident. Which one of the following expresses the above information *most clearly* and *accurately*?

(A) At 10:21 A.M. the Westbury Savings and Loan was witnessed being robbed by Mary Henderson of 217 Westbury Avenue. The suspect fled dressed in black with a black woolen face mask. He left the bank with $6141 in U.S. currency.

(B) Dressed in black wearing a black woolen face mask, Mary Henderson of 217 Westbury Avenue saw a suspect flee with $6141 in U.S. currency after robbing the Westbury Savings and Loan. The robber was seen at 10:21 A.M.

(C) At 10:21 A.M., Mary Henderson, of 217 Westbury Avenue, witness to the robbery of the Westbury Savings and Loan, reports that a male, dressed in black, wearing a black face mask, did rob said bank and fled with $6141 in U.S. currency.

(D) Mary Henderson, of 217 Westbury Avenue, witnessed the robbery of the Westbury Savings and Loan at 10:21 A.M. The suspect, a male, was dressed in black and was wearing a black woolen face mask. He fled with $6141 in U.S. currency.

Answer question 101 solely on the basis of the following information.

Police Officers sometimes have to make notifications to the Bureau of Child Welfare when they determine that a child may have been abused, maltreated, or neglected.

101. In which one of the following cases would it be most appropriate for a Police Officer to notify the Bureau of Child Welfare?

(A) A woman is pulling a screaming child across the street while the traffic light is about to turn red against them.

(B) A man is spanking his son with his bare hand because his son refused to get out of the swimming pool when he was told to.

(C) A mother is cooking with hot oil while her children are running around in the kitchen. One bangs into the stove and burns his hand slightly.

(D) A father is playing softball in the park while his infant takes a nap alone in their apartment.

102. At the scene of a dispute, Police Officer Johnson made an arrest after obtaining the following information:

Place of Occurrence:	940 Baxter Avenue
Time of Occurrence:	3:40 P.M.
Victim:	John Mitchell
Suspect:	Robert Holden, arrested at scene
Crime:	Menacing
Weapon:	Knife
Time of arrest:	4:00 P.M.

Officer Johnson is completing a report of the incident. Which one of the following expresses the above information *most clearly* and *accurately*?

(A) John Mitchell was menaced by a knife at 940 Baxter Avenue. Robert Holden, owner of the weapon, was arrested at 4:00 P.M., twenty minutes later, at the scene.

(B) John Mitchell reports at 3:40 P.M. he was menaced at 940 Baxter Avenue by Robert Holden. He threatened him with his knife and was arrested at 4:00 P.M. at the scene.

(C) John Mitchell stated that at 3:40 P.M. at 940 Baxter Avenue he was menaced by Robert Holden, who was carrying a knife. Mr. Holden was arrested at the scene at 4:00 P.M.

(D) With a knife Robert Holden menaced John Mitchell at 3:40 P.M. The knife belonged to him and he was arrested at the scene of 940 Baxter Avenue at 4:00 P.M.

103. Officer Nieves obtained the following information after he was called to the scene of a large gathering:

Time of Occurrence:	2:45 A.M.
Place of Occurrence:	Mulberry Park
Complaint:	Loud music
Complainant:	Mrs. Simpkins, 42 Mulberry Street, Apartment 25
Action Taken:	Police Officer dispersed the crowd

Officer Nieves is completing a report on the incident. Which one of the following expresses the above information *most clearly* and *accurately*?

(A) Mrs. Simpkins, who lives at 42 Mulberry Street, Apartment 25, called the Police to make a complaint. A large crowd of people were playing loud music in Mulberry Park at 2:45 A.M. Officer Nieves responded and dispersed the crowd.

(B) Officer Nieves responded to Mulberry Park because Mrs. Simpkins, the complainant, lives at 42 Mulberry Street, Apartment 25. Due to a large crowd of people who were playing loud music at 2:45 A.M., he immediately dispersed the crowd.

(C) Due to a large crowd of people who were playing loud music in Mulberry Park at 2:45 A.M., Officer Nieves responded and dispersed the crowd. Mrs. Simpkins called the Police and complained. She lives at 42 Mulberry Street, Apartment 25.

(D) Responding to a complaint by Mrs. Simpkins, who resides at 42 Mulberry Street, Apartment 25, Officer Nieves dispersed a large crowd in Mulberry Park. They were playing loud music. It was 2:45 A.M.

104. While patrolling the subway, Police Officer Clark responds to the scene of a past robbery where he obtains the following information:

Place of Occurrence:	Northbound E train
Time of Occurrence:	6:30 P.M.
Victim:	Robert Brey
Crime:	Wallet and jewelry taken
Suspects:	2 male whites armed with knives

Officer Clark is completing a report on the incident. Which one of the following expresses the above information *most clearly* and *accurately*?

(A) At 6:30 P.M., Robert Brey reported he was robbed of his wallet and jewelry. On the northbound E train, two white males approached Mr. Brey. They threatened him before taking his property with knives.
(B) While riding the E train northbound, two white men approached Robert Brey at 6:30 P.M. They threatened him with knives and took his wallet and jewelry.
(C) Robert Brey was riding the E train at 6:30 P.M. when he was threatened by knives by two whites. The men took his wallet and jewelry as he was traveling northbound.
(D) Robert Brey reports at 6:30 P.M. he lost his wallet to two white men as well as his jewelry. They were carrying knives and threatened him aboard the northbound E train.

Answer question 105 solely on the basis of the following information.

Whenever a Police Officer responds to the scene of a family offense, the Officer should do the following in the order given:

1. Determine all the facts.
2. Obtain medical assistance if requested or need is apparent.
3. Determine if:
   a. a crime has been committed; or
   b. an Order of Protection has been obtained by complainant.
4. Arrest offender if a crime has been committed.

105. Police Officers Harley and Morris are dispatched to the scene of a family dispute at 734 E. 108th Street, Apartment 2E. As the Officers enter the apartment, they see a man and a woman struggling on the floor while cursing at each other. The Officers immediately separate the two, who are identified as Herbert and Mary Jones. Officer Harley attempts to question the two individuals to determine what happened, while Officer Morris keeps them separated. Both parties blame each other for starting the fight. Although neither spouse seems to be physically hurt, Mrs. Jones insists she be examined by a doctor. What should the Officers do next?

(A) Call for medical assistance.
(B) Arrest Mr. Jones for committing the offense.
(C) Find out if Mrs. Jones has obtained an Order of Protection.
(D) Determine whether a family offense has been committed by either spouse.

Answer questions 106 through 109 solely on the basis of the following passage.

While returning to the 15th Precinct from court, Police Officer Moody encountered an armed robbery in progress outside of 238 Madison Street. When the perpetrator saw the Officer, he fled into the building and attempted to enter the second floor apartment of Maria Vasquez. Ms. Vasquez had previously opened the door when she heard the noise downstairs. When Ms. Vasquez saw the perpetrator approaching her with a gun in his hand, she immediately closed and locked the door. Since the perpetrator was not able to gain entrance to the apartment, he jumped out of the hallway window and hid in the courtyard. When Officer Moody arrived at the bottom of the second floor stairway he heard Ms. Vasquez crying hysterically from inside the apartment. He banged on the door and called to her to see if she was all right. Ms. Vasquez did not speak English and, thinking it was the perpetrator, she refused to open the door. As a result, Officer Moody assumed that the woman was being held hostage by the perpetrator. Officer Moody immediately stepped away from the door, advised the radio dispatcher of the circumstances, and requested back-up assistance.

Every sector car in the precinct responded to assist Officer Moody and each, with the exception of sectors Adam and Charlie, took up a strategic location outside of the building. Officers O'Connor and Torres, of sector Adam, went up to the second floor to guard the apartment door with Officer Moody. Officer Perez, of sector Charlie, went up to the roof. Officer Donadio, also of sector Charlie, started to enter the courtyard when he observed the perpetrator hiding in the bushes. Officer Donadio quickly took cover behind the cement wall entrance of the courtyard and ordered the perpetrator at gun point to surrender. The perpetrator surrendered his weapon and allowed himself to be easily apprehended. Officer Donadio then advised the other Officers by radio that the perpetrator was in custody and that Ms. Vasquez was not being held hostage.

106. Which Officer went up to the roof?

(A) Officer O'Connor   (C) Officer Donadio
(B) Officer Perez   (D) Officer Moody.

107. Officer Moody chased the perpetrator because

(A) he was trying to get into the apartment of Maria Vasquez
(B) he was holding Maria Vasquez hostage
(C) he was attempting to commit an armed robbery
(D) he jumped out the second floor hallway window.

108. Which Officer was *not* on the second floor?

(A) Officer Moody   (C) Officer O'Connor
(B) Officer Torres   (D) Officer Donadio.

109. While Officer Moody was standing at the bottom of the stairs, the suspect was

(A) in Ms. Vasquez's apartment
(B) in the courtyard
(C) on the roof
(D) on the second floor fire escape.

Answer question 110 solely on the basis of the following information.

Police Officers must sometimes rely on eyewitness accounts of incidents, even though eyewitnesses may make mistakes with regard to some details.

110. While coming from the bank, Sal Shure was mugged and killed at the corner of W. 238th Street and Oxford Avenue. Police Officer Farris responds to the scene and questions four witnesses who saw the person that killed Shure. The following are descriptions of the suspect given by the witnesses. Which one of these descriptions should Officer Farris consider most likely to be correct?

(A) Male, white, 5'9", 185 lbs., brown hair, black eyes.
(B) Male, Hispanic, 5'11", 175 lbs., brown hair, brown eyes.
(C) Male, white, 5'10", 190 lbs., black hair, hazel eyes.
(D) Male, white, 5'11", 190 lbs., brown hair, brown eyes

111. Police Officer Johnson has just finished investigating a report of a burglary and has obtained the following information:

Place of Occurrence:	Victim's residence
Time of Occurrence:	Between 8:13 P.M. and 4:15 A.M.
Victim:	Paul Mason of 1264 Twentieth Street, Apartment 3D
Crime:	Burglary
Damage:	Filed front door lock

Officer Johnson is preparing a report of the incident. Which one of the following expresses the above information *most clearly* and *accurately*?

(A) Paul Mason's residence was burglarized at 1264 Twentieth Street, Apartment 3D, between 8:13 P.M. and 4:15 A.M. by filing the front door lock.
(B) Paul Mason was burglarized by filing the front door lock and he lives at 1264 Twentieth Street, Apartment 3D, between 8:13 P.M. and 4:15 A.M.
(C) Between 8:13 P.M. and 4:15 A.M. the residence of Paul Mason, located at 1264 Twentieth Street, Apartment 3D, was burglarized after the front door lock was filed.
(D) Between 8:13 P.M. and 4:15 A.M., at 1264 Twentieth Street, Apartment 3D, after the front door lock was filed, the residence of Paul Mason was burglarized.

Answer question 112 solely on the basis of the following information.

Grand Larceny 4th Degree—occurs when a person steals property and when:

1. The value of the property is greater than one thousand dollars; or
2. The property consists of secret scientific material; or
3. The property consists of a credit card; or
4. The property, regardless of its nature and value, is taken from the body or clothing of another person; or
5. The property, regardless of its nature and value, is obtained through fear.

112. Which one of the following is the best example of Grand Larceny in the Fourth Degree?

(A) Jim finds a briefcase on the downtown 'E' train. Inside the briefcase he notices an envelope which contains $900.00. He removes the money from the envelope and exits the train, leaving the briefcase behind.

(B) Jane finds on the street a wallet, which contains several papers and an American Express card, which she sends back to the company.

(C) Bruce, a gang member, goes into an all-night produce market and orders the owner, Mr. Wong, to pay him $50.00 for protection or his store will be destroyed. Mr. Wong refuses and dials 911 as Bruce flees from the store.

(D) Without Elaine's knowledge, Grace removes a costume jewelry bracelet valued at about $15.00 from Elaine's wrist.

113. Police Officer Lowell has just finished investigating a burglary and has received the following information:

Place of Occurrence:	117-12 Sutphin Boulevard
Time of Occurrence:	Between 9:00 A.M. and 5:00 P.M.
Victim:	Mandee Cotton
Suspects:	Unknown

Officer Lowell is completing a report on this incident. Which one of the following expresses the above information *most clearly* and *accurately*?

(A) Mandee Cotton reported that her home was burglarized between 9:00 A.M. and 5:00 P.M. Ms. Cotton resides at 117-12 Sutphin Boulevard. Suspects are unknown.

(B) A burglary was committed at 117-12 Sutphin Boulevard reported Mandee Cotton between 9:00 A.M. and 5:00 P.M. Ms. Cotton said unknown suspects burglarized her home.

(C) Unknown suspects burglarized a home at 117-12 Sutphin Boulevard between 9:00 A.M. and 5:00 P.M. Mandee Cotton, homeowner, reported.

(D) Between the hours of 9:00 A.M. and 5:00 P.M. it was reported that 117-12 Sutphin Boulevard was burglarized. Mandee Cotton reported that unknown suspects are responsible.

Answer question 114 solely on the basis of the following information.

When a prisoner in custody requires medical or psychiatric treatment, a Police Officer should do the following in the order given:

1. Request an ambulance and remove prisoner to hospital directly from place of arrest, if necessary.
   a. Accompany prisoner to hospital.
   b. Notify Desk Officer.
2. Handcuff prisoner, hands in rear, before transporting.
3. Remain with prisoner at all times in hospital.
4. Request room change if security is inadequate.
5. Do not remove handcuffs, unless requested by attending physician.
6. Remain immediately outside room and attempt to maintain visual contact, even if requested to leave examination room after informing physician of circumstances of arrest.

114. Police Officer Schultz calls for an ambulance to remove a prisoner from the precinct to Grant Hospital's Emergency Room due to chest pains which the prisoner is experiencing. The Desk Officer, Lt. Collins, orders Officer Schultz to ride in the ambulance with the prisoner and reminds him to rearcuff the prisoner before removing him from the holding cell. Officer Schultz does so and escorts the prisoner into the ambulance. When they arrive at the hospital, Officer Schultz questions Dr. Carson about the security status of the Emergency Room. Dr. Carson informs Officer Schultz that they haven't had any problems since the hospital opened ten years ago. Officer Schultz's next step should be to

(A) remove the prisoner's handcuffs to allow Dr. Carson to examine him
(B) describe the details of the prisoner's arrest to Dr. Carson
(C) keep an eye on the prisoner if requested to leave the examining room by Dr. Carson
(D) ask Dr. Carson to examine the prisoner in a more secure location in the hospital.

Answer question 115 solely on the basis of the following information.

Under certain circumstances, Police Officers are authorized to search a person suspected of having committed a crime.

115. Which of the following people would a Police Officer most likely search?

(A) A person who is suspected by a store owner of selling watches on the street without a license.
(B) A motorist who is stopped by a Traffic Enforcement Agent for going through a red light.
(C) A poorly dressed man who is obviously intoxicated staggering down the street.
(D) A man who is recognized by a woman as being recently involved in an armed robbery.

Answer question 116 solely on the basis of the following information.

Larceny—occurs when a person, without the use of threat of force, wrongfully takes, obtains, or withholds property from the owner.

Robbery—occurs when a person uses, or threatens the immediate use of, force on the victim or an another person in the course of stealing property.

Burglary—occurs when a person knowingly and unlawfully enters or remains in a building with intent to commit a crime therein.

116. Kevin Watts follows Jane Robinson, his ex-girlfriend, to her home one night after work and decides that he wants to make her pay for breaking off their engagement. While Jane is in the kitchen preparing her dinner, Kevin climbs up the fire escape and enters her bedroom through the window. He then threatens to beat Jane "to a pulp" if she tries to stop him from taking her cash, jewelry, and television set. Kevin takes her property and leaves. In this situation, Watts should be charged with

(A) Burglary and Larceny
(B) Burglary and Robbery
(C) Robbery and Larceny
(D) Robbery, Burglary, and Larceny.

117. Police Officer Dale has just finished investigating a report of attempted theft and has obtained the following information:

Place of Occurrence:	In front of 103 W. 105th Street
Time of Occurrence:	11:30 A.M.
Victim:	Mary Davis
Crime:	Attempted theft
Suspect:	Male, black, scar on right side of face
Action Taken:	Drove victim around area to locate suspect

Officer Dale is preparing a report on the incident. Which one of the following expresses the above information *most clearly* and *accurately*?

(A) Mary Davis was standing in front of 103 W. 105th Street when Officer Dale arrived after an attempt to steal her pocketbook failed at 11:30 A.M. Officer Dale canvassed the area looking for a black male with a scar on the right side of his face with Ms. Davis in the patrol car.
(B) Mary Davis stated that, at 11:30 A.M., she was standing in front of 103 W. 105th Street when a black male with a scar on the right side of his face attempted to steal her pocketbook. Officer Dale canvassed the area with Ms. Davis in the patrol car.
(C) Officer Dale canvassed the area by putting Mary Davis in a patrol car looking for a black male with a scar on the right side of his face. At 11:30 A.M. in front of 103 W. 105th Street she said he attempted to steal her pocketbook.
(D) At 11:30 A.M., in front of 103 W. 105th Street, Officer Dale canvassed the area with Mary Davis in a patrol car who said that a black male with a scar on the right side of his face attempted to steal her pocketbook.

118. While on patrol, Police Officer Santoro received a call to respond to the scene of a shooting. The following details were obtained at the scene:

Time of Occurrence:	4:00 A.M.
Place of Occurrence:	232 Senator Street
Victim:	Mike Nisman
Suspect:	Howard Conran
Crime:	Shooting
Witness:	Sheila Norris

Officer Santoro is completing a report on the incident. Which one of the following expresses the above information *most clearly* and *accurately*?

(A) Sheila Norris stated at 4:00 A.M. she witnessed a shooting of her neighbor in front of her building. Howard Conran shot Mike Nisman and ran from 232 Senator Street.

(B) Mike Nisman was the victim of a shooting incident seen by his neighbor. At 4:00 A.M. Sheila Norris saw Howard Conran shoot him and run in front of their building. Norris and Nisman reside at 232 Senator Street.

(C) Sheila Norris states that at 4:00 A.M. she witnessed Howard Conran shoot Mike Nisman, her neighbor, in front of their building at 232 Senator Street. She further states she saw the suspect running from the scene.

(D) Mike Nisman was shot by Howard Conran at 4:00 A.M. His neighbor, Sheila Norris, witnessed him run from the scene in front of their building at 232 Senator Street.

Answer question 119 solely on the basis of the following information.

When a Police Officer arrives at a scene where there is a dead human body, the Officer should do the following in the order given:

1. Request an ambulance and a patrol supervisor.
2. Exclude unauthorized persons from the scene.
3. Obtain the names of witnesses and keep them at the scene if the death is suspicious.
4. Screen the area from public view, if possible.
5. Cover the body with waterproof covering if publicly exposed.

119. Police Officer Wong is dispatched to 365 E. 52nd Street. Upon arriving, he sees a man who is apparently dead and lying face down in an alley behind the building. Officer Wong immediately calls for an ambulance and his patrol supervisor. While waiting, the Officer notices that a large crowd is beginning to gather around the uncovered body. The next step Officer Wong should take is to

(A) cover the body with a waterproof covering
(B) keep unauthorized people away from the scene
(C) screen the area from public view
(D) obtain the names of witnesses.

120. Police Officer Taylor responds to the scene of a serious traffic accident in which a car struck a telephone pole, and obtains the following information:

Place of Occurrence: Intersection of Rock Street and Amboy Place
Time of Occurrence: 3:27 A.M.
Name of Injured: Carlos Black
Driver of Car: Carlos Black
Action Taken: Injured taken to Beth-El Hospital

Officer Taylor is preparing a report on the accident. Which one of the following expresses the above information *most clearly* and *accurately*?

(A) At approximately 3:27 A.M. Carlos Black drove his car into a telephone pole located at the intersection of Rock Street and Amboy Place. Mr. Black, who was the only person injured, was taken to Beth-El Hospital.

(B) Carlos Black, injured at the intersection of Rock Street and Amboy Place, hit a telephone pole. He was taken to Beth-El Hospital after the car accident that occurred at 3:27 A.M.

(C) At the intersection of Rock Street and Amboy Place, Carlos Black injured himself and was taken to Beth-El Hospital. His car hit a telephone pole at 3:27 A.M.

(D) At the intersection of Rock Street and Amboy Place at 3:27 A.M., Carlos Black was taken to Beth-El Hospital after injuring himself by driving into a telephone pole.

121. While on patrol in the Jefferson Housing Projects, Police Officer Johnson responds to the scene of a Grand Larceny. The following information was obtained by officer Johnson:

Time of Occurrence: 6:00 P.M.
Place of Occurrence: Rear of Building 12A
Victim: Maria Lopez
Crime: Purse snatched
Suspect: Unknown

Officer Johnson is preparing a report on the incident. Which one of the following expresses the above information *most clearly* and *accurately*?

(A) At the rear of Building 12A, at 6:00 P.M., by an unknown suspect, Maria Lopez reported her purse snatched in the Jefferson Housing Projects.

(B) Maria Lopez reported that at 6:00 P.M. her purse was snatched by an unknown suspect at the rear of the Building 12A in the Jefferson Housing Projects.

(C) At the rear of Building 12A, Maria Lopez reported at 6:00 P.M. that her purse had been snatched by an unknown suspect in the Jefferson Housing Projects.

(D) In the Jefferson Housing Projects, Maria Lopez reported at the rear of Building 12A that her purse had been snatched by an unknown suspect at 6:00 P.M.

Answer question 122 solely on the basis of the following information.

Criminal Possession of Stolen Property 2nd Degree—occurs when a person knowingly possesses stolen property with intent to benefit himself or a person other than the owner, or to prevent its recovery by the owner, and when:

1. The value of the property exceeds two hundred fifty dollars; or
2. The property consists of a credit card; or
3. The person is a pawnbroker or is in the business of buying, selling, or otherwise dealing in property; or
4. The property consists of one or more firearms, rifles, or shotguns.

122. Which one of the following is the best example of Criminal Possession of Stolen Property in the Second Degree?

   (A) Mary knowingly buys a stolen camera valued at $225.00 for her mother's birthday.
   (B) John finds a wallet containing $100.00 and various credit cards. John keeps the money and turns the credit cards in at his local precinct.
   (C) Mr. Varrone, a pawnbroker, refuses to buy Mr. Cutter's stolen VCR valued at $230.00.
   (D) Mr. Aquista, the owner of a toy store, knowingly buys a crate of stolen water pistols valued at $260.00.

123. Police Officer Dale has just finished investigating a report of menacing and obtained the following information:

Time of Occurrence:	10:30 P.M.
Place of Occurrence:	(Hallway) 77 Hill Street
Victim:	Grace Jackson
Suspect:	Susan, white female, 30 years of age
Crime:	Menacing with a knife

   Officer Dale is preparing a report on the incident. Which one of the following expresses the above information *most clearly* and *accurately*?

   (A) At 10:30 P.M., Grace Jackson was stopped in the hallway of 77 Hill Street by a 30-year-old white female known to Grace as Susan. Susan put a knife to Grace's throat and demanded that Grace stay out of the building or Susan would hurt her.
   (B) Grace Jackson was stopped in the hallway at knife point and threatened to stay away from the building located at 77 Hill Street. The female who is 30 years of age known as Susan by Jackson stopped her at 10:30 P.M.
   (C) At 10:30 P.M. in the hallway of 77 Hill Street Grace Jackson reported a white female 30 years of age put a knife to her throat. She knew her as Susan and demanded she stay away from the building or she would get hurt.
   (D) A white female 30 years of age known to Grace Jackson as Susan stopped her in the hallway of 77 Hill Street. She put a knife to her throat and at 10:30 P.M. demanded she stay away from the building or she would get hurt.

Answer questions 124 through 126 solely on the basis of the following passage.

Police Officer Berman has been assigned to a steady post from Hartman Boulevard to Bement Street on Forest Avenue for the past two years. Officer Berman's duties involve walking along Forest Avenue and in and out of stores talking with the people on his post to ensure that everything is all right. While on duty at 11:30 on Saturday morning, Officer Berman walks into Pete Arturo's Boutique, which is normally filled with female customers because of the type of merchandise sold there. Today the Officer sees only three young men in the store. Officer Berman looks around and notices that Pete is not in sight. Officer Berman notices a thin man whom he has never seen behind the register. Officer Berman decides to ask for Mrs. Arturo, knowing that Pete is not married, because he suspects that something is wrong. The thin man replies with a smile, "She will be in a little later." Officer Berman then walks out of the boutique and calls for back-up assistance on a possible robbery in progress. At 11:40, Police Officers Fernandez and Heck arrive at the side of Arturo's Boutique. Five minutes later Police Officer Jones arrives in his scooter. The Officers are now waiting for a Supervisor to arrive so they can proceed with the plan of action which they have already discussed. Two minutes after Officer Jones arrives, Sgt. Demond pulls up with his driver, Police Officer Ricco, and gathers all of the information. Sgt. Demond then calls the boutique by phone, identifies himself, and advises the man who answers to give himself up so that nobody will get hurt. Sgt. Demond also tells the man on the phone that he has the store surrounded and will give them five minutes to surrender. The three men walk out of the boutique with Mr. Arturo, who is unharmed. Officer Berman recovers three loaded .38 caliber revolvers from the suspects.

124. How many police personnel responded to Officer Berman's call for assistance?

    (A) Four   (C) Six
    (B) Five   (D) Seven.

125. At what time did Sgt. Demond arrive at the boutique?

    (A) 11:40 A.M.   (C) 11:45 A.M.
    (B) 11:42 A.M.   (D) 11:47 A.M.

126. Which of the following Officers arrived in the scooter?

    (A) Berman   (C) Jones
    (B) Fernandez   (D) Heck.

Answer questions 127 through 129 solely on the basis of the following information.

Police Officer Keenan has been ordered to improved the traffic flow on his post by issuing summonses on West 231st Street from Maple Lane to Kingsway Avenue. Officer Keenan has noticed that, between 8:00 A.M. and 10:00 A.M. at W. 231st and Maple Lane, cars park in the bus stop on the north side of the street. This has forced the buses to stop in the middle of the street, blocking traffic for several minutes at a time. In addition, from 10:00 A.M. to 3:00 P.M., cars double park on both sides of W. 231st Street from Maple Lane to Kingsway Avenue, which slows the traffic throughout the day. Officer Keenan has also noticed that from 4:00 P.M. to 6:00 P.M. cars park in the bus stop on the south side of W. 231st Street and Kingsway Avenue, again forcing the buses to stop in the middle of the street.

127. Officer Keenan would be most effective at improving the traffic condition between 8:00 A.M. and 9:00 A.M. by issuing summonses

(A) between Kingsway Avenue and Maple Lane
(B) on the north side of W. 231st Street and Maple Lane
(C) on the south side of W. 231st Street and Maple Lane
(D) between Kingsway Avenue and W. 231st Street.

128. In order to keep traffic flowing between noon and 1:00 P.M., Officer Keenan should issue summonses on

(A) the north side of Kingsway Avenue
(B) both sides of Maple Lane
(C) both sides of W. 231st Street
(D) the south side of Kingsway Avenue.

129. To keep traffic flowing between 5:00 P.M., and 6:00 P.M., Officer Keenan should issue summonses on the

(A) south side of W. 231st Street and Kingsway Avenue
(B) south side of W. 231 Street and Maple Lane
(C) north side of W. 231st Street and Kingsway Avenue
(D) north side of W. 231st Street and Maple Lane.

130. Police Officer Bennett responds to the scene of a car accident and obtains the following information from the witness:

Time of Occurrence: 3:00 A.M.
Victim: Joe Morris, removed to Methodist Hospital
Crime: Struck pedestrian and left the scene of accident
Description of Auto: Blue 1984 Thunderbird, license plate BOT-3745

Officer Bennett is preparing an Accident Report. Which one of the following expresses the above information *most clearly* and *accurately*?

(A) Joe Morris, a pedestrian, was hit at 3:00 A.M. and removed to Methodist Hospital. Also a blue Thunderbird, 1984 model left the scene, license plate BOT-3745.

(B) A pedestrian was taken to Methodist Hospital after being struck at 3:00 A.M. A blue automobile was seen leaving the scene with license plate BOT-3745. Joe Morris was knocked down by a 1984 Thunderbird.

(C) At 3:00 A.M. Joe Morris, a pedestrian, was struck by a blue 1984 Thunderbird. The automobile, license plate BOT-3745, left the scene. Mr. Morris was taken to Methodist Hospital.

(D) Joe Morris, a pedestrian at 3:00 A.M. was struck by a Thunderbird. A 1984 model, license plate BOT-3745, blue in color left the scene and the victim was taken to Methodist Hospital.

Answer question 131 solely on the basis of the following information.

Burglary—occurs when a person knowingly enters or remains unlawfully in a building with the intent to commit a crime therein.

131. Which one of the following situations is the best example of Burglary?

(A) John Moss, an employee at the Forever Toys Warehouse, enters the locked warehouse at 10:30 P.M. through an open window in order to get his wallet, which he had forgotton in his desk when he left work at 5:30 P.M.

(B) Mary Hargrove, not wanting to walk around the block to get to the train station, decides to take a short-cut by slipping through a hole in the fence and walking across a field. There are signs posted that state the field is a restricted area and unauthorized persons would be prosecuted. Although Hargrove is not authorized to be on the property, she continues anyway.

(C) Wayne Moore, after being locked out of his home by his wife, goes to a neighbor's house in the hope that he would be able to spend the night. Although the neighbors are not home, Moore notices that a window leading to the basement is unlocked. He climbs through the window and falls asleep on a basement sofa.

(D) Harold Weeks decides to steal from an antique store valuable items, which he will later sell. Weeks enters the premises by picking the lock on the back door and is confronted by the owner before he is able to take anything.

Answer questions 132 through 134 solely on the basis of the following passage.

Police Officer Smith was reassigned to the Parkhill Housing Complex, which consists of nine 8-story buildings. He was told that nine rapes had occurred in the last eight days in the complex and all had taken place between 9:00 A.M. and 6:00 P.M. On May 2, Officer Smith was working the 10:00 A.M. to 6:00 P.M. shift. At the beginning of Officer Smith's shift his supervisor, Sergeant Larry, gave him the suspected rapist's description, which had been obtained on April 27 from Nancy Lewis, one of the rape victims. The suspect was described as a male, black, 6'2", aproximately 210 lbs., having a light complexion and the word "Budda" tattooed on his left forearm.

While on patrol several blocks from the Parkhill Complex at noon of the same day, Officer Smith was called by the dispatcher and told to respond to a complaint at 110 Park Avenue, Apartment 3C, located in the complex. Upon his arrival at the apartment, he was met by Mary Wilson, who told him that her 16-year-old daughter Tammy had just been raped in the building elevator. Tammy stated that when she entered her building, a black male, approximately 26 years old, about 6'1", wearing a suit, had been waiting for the elevator. She also told Officer Smith that when she entered the elevator with this man, he forced her to the floor, raped her and pushed her out of the elevator on the 7th floor.

On May 3, at 8:00 A.M., an individual fitting the description given by Ms. Lewis was apprehended in front of 55 Hill Street, another building in the Parkhill Complex. The suspect's name was John Jones. At 12:30 P.M. of the same day, Ms. Wilson and Ms. Lewis went to the Precinct Station House and identified John Jones as the person who raped them.

132. Who was the first person to give Officer Smith a description of the rapist?

(A) Sergeant Larry
(B) Tammy Wilson
(C) Mary Wilson
(D) Nancy Lewis.

133. Where was Tammy Wilson raped?

(A) In the elevator at 55 Hill Street
(B) On the 5th floor at 110 Park Avenue
(C) In the elevator at 110 Park Avenue
(D) On the 7th floor at 55 Hill Street.

134. John Jones was apprehended

(A) the same day as the rape of Nancy Lewis
(B) the day after the rape of Nancy Lewis
(C) the same day as the rape of Tammy Wilson
(D) the day after the rape of Tammy Wilson.

135. At 11:30 A.M., Police Officers Newman and Johnson receive a radio call to respond to a reported robbery. The Officers obtained the following information:

Time of Occurrence:	11:20 A.M.
Place of Occurrence:	Twenty-four hour newsstand at 2024 86th Street
Victim:	Sam Norris, owner
Amount Stolen:	$450.00
Suspects:	Two male whites

Officer Newman is completing a complaint report on the incident. Which one of the following expresses the above information *most clearly* and *accurately*?

(A) At 11:20 A.M. it was reported by the newsstand owner that two male whites robbed $450.00 from Sam Norris. The twenty-four hour newsstand is located at 2024 86th Street.

(B) At 11:20 A.M., Sam Norris, the newsstand owner, reported that the twenty-four hour newsstand located at 2024 86th Street was robbed by two male whites who took $450.00.

(C) Sam Norris, the owner of the twenty-four hour newsstand located at 2024 86th Street, reported that at 11:20 A.M. two white males robbed his newsstand of $450.00.

(D) Sam Norris reported at 11:20 A.M. that $450.00 had been taken from the owner of the twenty-four hour newsstand located at 2024 86th Street by two male whites.

Answer question 136 solely on the basis of the following information.

Police Officers are often required to handle cases where the occupant of a residence has died. Upon arrival at the scene of a dead human body, Police Officers should do the following in the order given:

1. Request an ambulance and patrol supervisor to respond.
2. Determine if the death is suspicious or of natural causes.
3. Determine facts and notify the Desk Officer as soon as possible.
4. Notify station house and get aided and complaint report numbers.
5. Notify medical examiner and get log number
6. Notify precinct Detective Unit.
7. If apparent homicide or suicide notify Crime Scene Unit.

136. Police Officer Casin and his supervisor, Sgt. Velez, are in Apartment 1-H at 3333 Hudson Parkway. The occupant of the apartment, Tom Acheson, age 65; is lying face up on the kitchen floor, dead. The ambulance attendant is present and informs the Sergeant that the occupant died of natural causes and has probably been dead for about four days. Officer Berberich arrives on the scene and Sgt. Velez gives Officer Berberich the above information instructing him to make the proper notifications. Which one cf the following should Officer Berberich notify first?

(A) The Desk Officer
(B) The precinct Detective Unit
(C) The occupant's immediate family
(D) The medical examiner.

137. While on patrol, Police Officer Adams is dispatched to investigate a reported burglary. When he arrives, Officer Adams is informed by Ms. Bond, an artist, that when she returned home from an appointment, she found that her front door had been forced open and the following pieces of her artwork were missing:

   - 3 Sculptures, each valued at $2000.00
   - 2 Oil paintings, each valued at $500.00
   - 1 Ceramic vase valued at $375.00
   - 1 Portrait valued at $2500.00
   - 2 Small watercolors, each valued at $75.00

   In addition to the artwork, Ms. Bond told Officer Adams that a brooch and bracelet, each valued at $250.00, and $50.00 in cash were also missing. Officer Adams is preparing a Complaint Report on the burglary. Which one of the following is the total value of the property and cash stolen?

   (A) $5,450.00
   (B) $5,750.00
   (C) $10,325.00
   (D) $10,575.00.

   Answer question 138 solely on the basis of the following information.

   Police Officers are often required to respond to the scene of a serious crime, such as robbery, rape, or burglary. When a Police Officer responds to a crime scene, he should do the following in the order given:

   1. Interview the complainant and witnesses, obtain the facts, and gather evidence.
   2. Conduct a thorough field investigation.
   3. Prepare a Complaint Report.
   4. Determine if the complaint should be closed or referred for further investigation.

138. Police Officers Pastorino and Longo are driving down Longwood Avenue near Snyder Street while on patrol. They notice that a woman, later identified as Grace Thomas, is lying on the sidewalk in front of 1237 Snyder Street. Officer Pastorino approaches her, notices that she has sustained a minor stab wound on her left arm, and radios for an ambulance. Officer Longo then asks the victim to explain what happened. She tells him that she has just been robbed and assaulted and gives a description of the suspect. Meanwhile, Officer Pastorino searches the area thoroughly and finds a knife but no witnesses. The next step that the Officers should take is to

   (A) prepare a Complaint Report
   (B) determine if the complaint should be closed or referred for further investigation
   (C) conduct a thorough field investigation
   (D) interview the complainant and witnesses.

Answer question 139 solely on the basis of the following information.

Dwelling—a building that is usually occupied by a person lodging there at night.

Burglary 1st Degree—occurs when a person knowingly enters or remains unlawfully in a dwelling at night with the intent to commit a crime therein, and when, while entering or while in the dwelling, or in immediate flight therefrom, he or another participant in the crime:

1. Is armed with explosives or a deadly weapon; or
2. Causes physical injury to any person who is not a participant in the crime; or
3. Uses or threatens the immediate use of a dangerous instrument; or
4. Displays what appears to be a pistol, revolver, rifle, shotgun, machine gun, or other firearm.

139. Which one of the following situations is the best example of Burglary in the First Degree?

(A) Sam enters Joanne's apartment by breaking the lock on her door in order to get warm during the cold weather.
(B) Ernest remains in Doreen's Department Store after store hours and removes five diamond rings from the showcase. On his way out, he injures a security guard who tries to apprehend him.
(C) Roger enters the courtyard of a large apartment building and breaks a bedroom window with the butt of his pistol in order to gain entry. The tenant awakens moments later and sees Roger leaving through the window with her VCR.
(D) At 2:00 A.M. on a Sunday, Kevin enters Tom's 24-Hour Deli, removes two cases of beer without paying for them, and runs to an awaiting vehicle.

140. While on patrol, Police Officers Carter and Popps receive a call to respond to an assault in progress. Upon arrival they receive the following information:

Place of Occurrence:	27 Park Avenue
Victim:	John Dee
Suspect:	Michael Jones
Crime:	Stabbing during a fight
Action Taken:	Suspect arrested

The Officers are completing a report on the incident. Which one of the following expresses the above information *most clearly* and *accurately*?

(A) In front of 27 Park Avenue, Michael Jones was arrested for stabbing John Dee during a fight.
(B) Michael Jones was arrested for stabbing John Dee during a fight in front of 27 Park Avenue.
(C) During a fight, Michael Jones was arrested for stabbing John Dee in front of 27 Park Avenue.
(D) John Dee was stabbed by Michael Jones, who was arrested for fighting in front of 27 Park Avenue.

Answer question 141 solely on the basis of the following information.

When a child under ten years of age is reported to be missing, a Police Officer should:

1. Respond to the scene and interview the complainant in order to obtain details, including an accurate description of the child and the location where last seen.
2. Notify Desk Officer of details.
3. Start an immediate search for the child.
4. Request Patrol Supervisor to respond.

141. Police Officers Cippillone and Carey are dispatched to 2501 Richmond Road to investigate a report of a missing child. When the Officers arrive at the location, they are told by Mr. and Mrs. William that their eight-year-old daughter Jill was due back from her friend's house three hours ago and she has still not returned. The Williams describe Jill as 4'3" tall, having brown hair, green eyes and weighing 60 lbs. She was wearing a yellow dress and a white sweater when she left home. The Officers ask the Williams for the name and address of Jill's friends, particularly the last one she had visited. After obtaining this information, the Officers notify their Desk Officer and begin a thorough search for Jill. After a half hour, Officer Carey finds Jill inside a nearby candy store and returns her to her parents' home. Officer Cippillone informs the Desk Officer of the situation and both Officers go back out on patrol. In this situation the actions taken by the Officers were

(A) proper, primarily because they conducted a thorough search and located Jill
(B) improper, primarily because they should have broadcasted Jill's description to other Officers over the radio
(C) proper, primarily because they were able to locate the child without the help of their supervisor
(D) improper, primarily because the Patrol Supervisor should have been requested.

Answer questions *142* through *150* on the basis of the following sketches. The first face on top is a sketch of an alleged criminal based on witnesses' descriptions at the crime scene. One of the four sketches below that face is the way the suspect looked after changing appearance. *Assume that NO surgery has been done on the suspect.* Select the face that is most likely that of the suspect.

142.

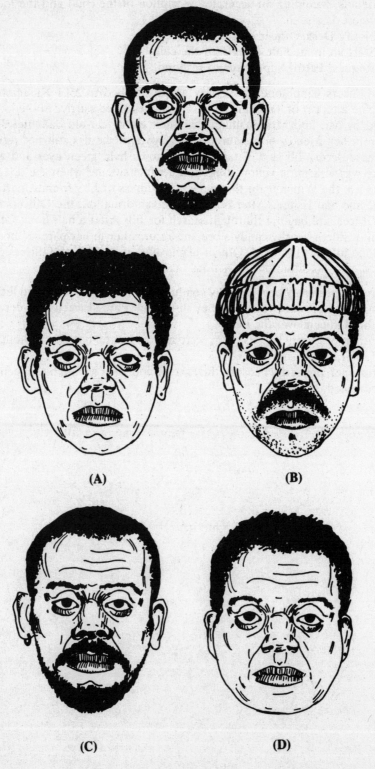

(A)

(B)

(C)

(D)

143.

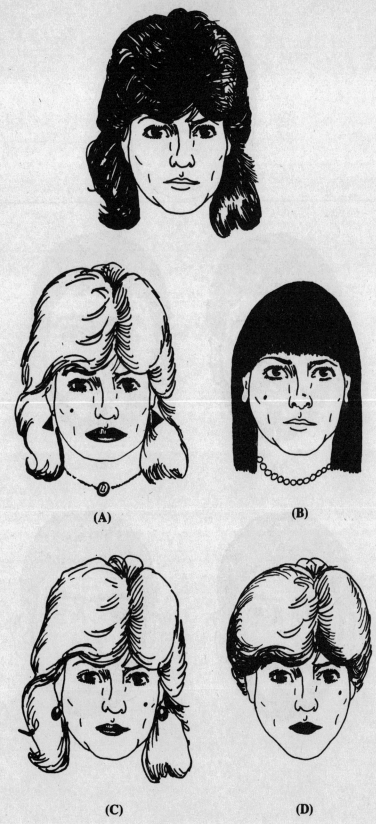

(A)　　　　　　　(B)

(C)　　　　　　　(D)

144.

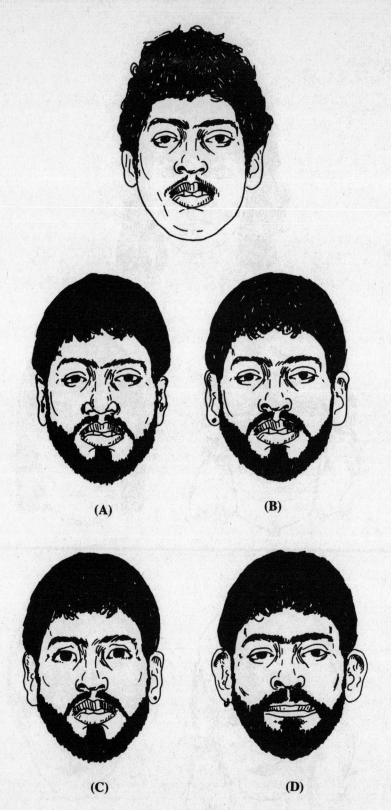

(A)   (B)

(C)   (D)

145.

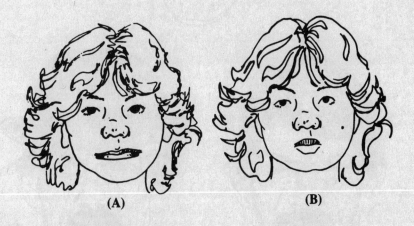

(A)　　　　　　　　　　(B)

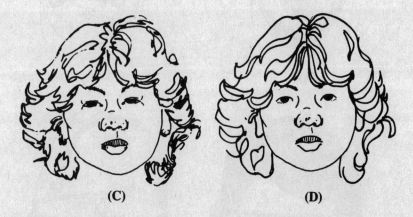

(C)　　　　　　　　　　(D)

146.

(A)

(B)

(C)

(D)

147.

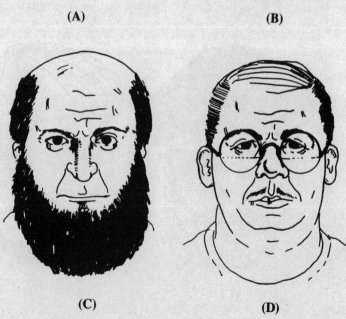

(A)

(B)

(C)

(D)

148.

(A) (B)

(C) (D)

149.

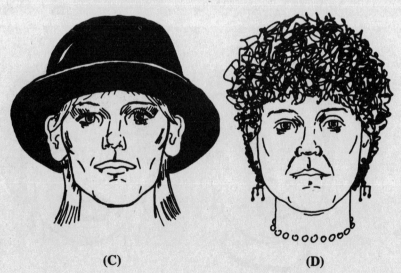

(A)   (B)

(C)   (D)

150.

(A)   (B)

(C)   (D)

Please check your Answer Sheet to make sure that you have written in and blackened your Social Security number correctly. If you have not yet written in and blackened your Social Security number, please do so immediately. If you have incorrectly written in or blackened your Social Security number, please correct the mistake immediately. Failure to correctly blacken your Social Security number may result in your Answer Sheet *not* being rated.

PROTEST PROCEDURE

Any candidate wishing to file a protest to one or more key answers on this examination must submit an original and four copies of the protest, together with supporting evidence, to PROTEST-Police Officer, Department of Personnel, 220 Church Street, NY, NY 10013. Protests will be accepted for a period of thirty (30) days beginning October 26, 1987. Protests must be *received* by the last day of the protest period (November 25, 1987).

Protests must be submitted in the following form. For each proposed key answer you protest, you must start a new page and each page must be headed by the following: Examination title, examination number, question number, test date, your Social Security Number. The protest must include a statement explaining why the answer you selected is as good as or better than the proposed key answer, and must include any additional supporting evidence you wish to submit. You may not modify or add to your protest once it is submitted. However, you may submit separate protests to additional questions within the thirty (30) day protest period.

After you have prepared the four copies, print your name and address on the original pages only and sign the last page of the original protest. Do not include your name or address on any other copies. You must print *only* your Social Security Number on each page of the four copies. PROTESTS SENT WITHOUT THE FOUR COPIES WILL NOT BE CONSIDERED!

In order to be informed of the availability of the Validation Board Report for this test, please include a postage-paid, self-addressed business-size envelope with your protests.

RECORD YOUR ANSWERS IN THIS TEST BOOKLET BEFORE THE LAST SIGNAL.

ANSWER SHEET COLLECTION—When you finish the test, remain seated and signal the monitor to collect your answer sheet. Leave the building quickly and quietly.

DO NOT telephone this Department to request information on the progress of the rating of this test. Such information will *NOT* be given. You will be notified individually by mail of your rating after all papers have been rated. Notify this Department promptly in writing of any change of your address. You should indicate your Social Security Number and the title and number of the examination in any correspondence to the Department of Personnel with respect to this examination.

TAKE THIS QUESTION BOOKLET WITH YOU

FINAL ANSWER KEY FOR WRITTEN TEST
HELD ON OCTOBER 24, 1987

1. C	31. D	61. A	91. B	121. B
2. C	32. C	62. B	92. D	122. D
3. D	33. B	63. C	93. A	123. A
4. A	34. A	64. B	94. C	124. B
5. B	35. B	65. D	95. A	125. D
6. B	36. C	66. A	96. C	126. C
7. A	37. D	67. C	97. D	127. B
8. B	38. A	68. D	98. A	128. C
9. D	39. B	69. B	99. B	129. A
10. C	40. C	70. C	100. D	130. C
11. D	41. D	71. D	101. D	131. D
12. A	42. B	72. B	102. C	132. A
13. C	43. A	73. D	103. A	133. C
14. D	44. B	74. C	104. B	134. D
15. A	45. D	75. A	105. A	135. C
16. D	46. C	76. D	106. B	136. A
17. B	47. C	77. C	107. C	137. D
18. C	48. A	78. A	108. D	138. A
19. C	49. D	79. A	109. B	139. C
20. D	50. B	80. C	110. D	140. B
21. A	51. D	81. D	111. C	141. D
22. C	52. A	82. A	112. D	142. A
23. A	53. C	83. C	113. A	143. C
24. B	54. D	84. B and/or C	114. B	144. B
25. C	55. B	85. A	115. D	145. D
26. B	56. A	86. A	116. B	146. A
27. D	57. C	87. D	117. B	147. B
28. A	58. D	88. C	118. C	148. D
29. B	59. B	89. C	119. B	149. B
30. B	60. D	90. B	120. A	150. C

ANSWER EXPLANATIONS

1. **(C)** The black car in the lower left portion of the picture with its hood open is the station wagon of Bob's Painters. The other choices are all business establishments in the picture.

2. **(C)** The only "No Parking" sign in the picture, and it is indeed on East Avenue, reads NO PARKING MON.—SAT. 7 A.M.—11 A.M.

3. **(D)** A white panel truck belonging to Fast Movers is parked on Bay Street.

4. **(A)** The man standing on the sidewalk talking to the woman in the dotted dress is wearing dark pants and a long-sleeved white shirt. He is holding a white jacket.

5. **(B)** The ONE WAY sign is on the signpost pointing in the direction of Bay Street. This is a certain answer. The sign that prohibits left turns into West Avenue does not necessarily indicate that West Avenue is a one-way street. The left turn may be prohibited only in the interest of traffic flow.

6. **(B)** There are two men attempting to determine the problem with the Bob's Painters station wagon. A woman is sitting in the car waiting.

7. **(A)** When studying pictures for memory questions, be sure to pay special attention to the people who may be involved in any sort of criminal activities. The shirt of the man with a knife says "Beach Bum."

8. **(B)** The crime in the question has nothing to do with the knife. The crime is the pickpocketing in progress. The victim is a white woman (note the legs) with dark hair and a black and white jacket.

9. **(D)** The woman's bag is hanging on her left shoulder. The pickpocket is reaching across his body with his left arm and is lifting the wallet with his left hand.

10. **(C)** The young man with the knife is wearing jeans and a short-sleeved shirt.

11. **(D)** 1802 Avenue R, a Rubber Stamps store, has a "closed" sign in its window. This question is a reminder that a police officer must be aware of all circumstances on the post. A store that is closed or out of business should not show much activity. Movement or lights should be cause for investigation.

12. **(A)** The Electronics store is located mid-block on Avenue R at number 1806. The store could not be at a corner because there is no space between it and either number 1804 or number 1808.

13. **(C)** All robberies occur on Gaston Street, so immediately narrow your choices to (B) and (C). The robberies generally occur in late afternoon and early evening so a 4:00 P.M. to midnight patrol would be most effective in reducing robberies.

14. **(D)** Since most rapes occur on Tuesdays and Thursdays, rape patrol must be conducted on those days. Eliminate choices (A) and (B). Since rapes occur between 7:00 A.M. and 11:30 A.M., Officer Thomas should be on the post from 6:00 A.M. to 2:00 P.M.

15. **(A)** The legitimate reason for people to go to a grocery store is to buy groceries. One or two people might come out empty-handed because they did not find what they wanted, but a steady stream of empty-handed patrons is cause for suspicion. The other choices describe very normal activities.

16. **(D)** Who was robbed and by whom? Who was wearing what? When and where did it happen? Choice (D) tells it best.

17. **(B)** Jennifer has a motive and intentionally kills her husband. In (D) the death is accidentally caused; in (A) the death is from natural causes; in (C) there is no death.

18. **(C)** Only this statement clearly expresses where the victim lives, where the assault occurred, the clothing of the suspect, and the nature of the injury. Organization is the key to this type of question.

19. **(C)** The 1:00 P.M. to 9:00 P.M. shift entirely encompasses the 1:00 P.M. to 4:00 P.M. period during which the major complaint concerns double-parked cars. The majority of double-parked car complaints come from the area of Main Street between Flushing Street and Ocean Boulevard.

20. **(D)** A fairly long reading passage, which is filled with names and details, is usually followed by a series of questions about those details. Read this type of passage with pencil in hand, and mark details that you think may

be important. The questions are meant only to test the accuracy of your reading, not your memory for the details, so you may keep referring to the passage while finding the answers. In the second sentence of the second paragraph, Lieutenant Schwinn assigns Officer Ellen Gray to handcuff and escort the prisoner.

21. **(A)** In the last sentence, Officer Gray, the escorting officer, completes the Medical Treatment of Prisoners form.

22. **(C)** The doctor requested that the handcuffs be removed so that he could conduct a complete physical examination.

23. **(A)** This information is given in the last sentence.

24. **(B)** This is a police judgment question. The drug dealing is most likely where people are congregated for no visible purpose. The youngsters playing basketball after school are busy; the children leaving the YMCA by bicycle at 10:30 P.M. may be running a risk of accident, but they do not give rise to suspicion for drug dealing. The bus stop is a normal place for people to congregate. But, what are those people doing at 3:30 A.M. next to the phone booth?

25. **(C)** This is not a difficult question, but you do have to pay close attention. The crimes, on which Officer Jones is to concentrate, appear to occur during the early morning hours (between 1:00 A.M. and 6 A.M.), so narrow to choices (A) and (C). Thursday, Friday, and Saturday appear to be the heaviest crime days in the area, so Wednesday through Sunday are the better days for Jones to work.

26. **(B)** Arthur committed Assault Third Degree when he intentionally punched Jennifer in the face and caused her mouth to bleed.

27. **(D)** Most often if the list of facts includes data and time of occurrence, the best organization of the information begins with date and time. You may save time by looking first at answer choices beginning with date and time if offered. In this question, the date, time, and place organization is the clearest.

28. **(A)** The best organization in this instance begins with a brief introductory statement and then continues with date, time, and description of the incident.

29. **(B)** Perkins has said that he has no intention of accompanying the officers to the precinct, but not that he will not surrender the rifle. He should be arrested only if he refuses to surrender the weapon. First, he must be informed that he may surrender the rifle on the spot and receive a receipt.

30. **(B)** Since two witnesses agree that the plate began with ADE, consider that they are probably correct. Three witnesses agree that the numbers were 1780, so they are likely to be right. The disagreement as to state is somewhat surprising, but you must base your conclusion on the elements recalled in common by the greatest number of witnesses and choose plate ADE-1780.

31. **(D)** This is a well-organized sentence that gives all the necessary information clearly and accurately.

32. **(C)** In questions based upon stated regulations and fact situations, you must limit your answer to the information on the test paper, even if you have other information or knowledge. In this question, do not allow yourself to be distracted by your concern for the dog-bite victim. According to these regulations, since Officer Rosario is unable to find the dog, he must next prepare the Department of Health Form 480BAA.

33. **(B)** This is a well-organized statement that gives all the facts.

34. **(A)** All the statements are accurate and give the information unambiguously. Choose the one that gives the information in the most reasonable order and that reads most smoothly.

35. **(B)** Man-hole covers do not simply blow off. There must be something unusual going on under the streets. The Fire Department is best equipped to investigate the causes of explosions. The contained fires in (A) and (C) should be watched but do not represent a present emergency. The Fire Department should be made aware of the open hydrant, but they need not be called to the scene.

36. **(C)** Officer Bestwell has entered a description of the items into his memo book and must now prepare a worksheet of the Property Clerk's Invoice. Mrs. Robinson does not need a receipt since she is not the person who found or turned in the property.

37. **(D)** All of the choices get the message across, but choice (D) is clearest and simplest to understand.

38. **(A)** Mr. Walls had sexual intercourse with girls under the age of eleven by forcible compulsion. He is guilty of Rape First Degree. Joe may be guilty of a number of illegal acts, but he did not have intercourse with the girls so is not guilty of Rape First Degree.

39. **(B)** Choice (D) would be possible, but it is a much longer route. (A) is incorrect because Edelman Avenue is one way westbound; (C) is incorrect because Merrick Boulevard does not go through to 115th Street.

40. **(C)** Follow the route. The officers are driving north, they turn left, which is west. A U-turn will head them in the opposite direction, which is east.

41. **(D)** This is an arithmetic problem. When adding up the list, do not forget to include the calculator.

2 tape players at $99 each	=	$198
3 compact disc players at $290 each	=	870
5 telephone sets at $50 each	=	250
1 VCR at $470	=	470
1 TV set at $600	=	600
1 stereo rack system at $975	=	975
1 Walkman stereo at $70	=	70
1 calculator at $50	=	+ 50
total		$3,483

42. **(B)** This is a reading-for-details series of questions. The Sergeant supervised a search to determine if the owner was sick, injured, or otherwise incapacitated.

43. **(A)** The first sentence tells of a possible burglary at 1423 Second Avenue.

44. **(B)** 1423 Second Avenue was a bicycle shop.

45. **(D)** At 10:40 P.M. Officer Reese radioed for a Supervisor who arrived ten minutes later, at 10:50 P.M.

46. **(C)** Police Officer Craig, the Precinct Telephone Switchboard Operator, would attempt to contact the store owner.

47. **(C)** This statement gives all the information in the most logical order.

48. **(A)** Three witnesses agree that the car was a red Ford Mustang; three witnesses agree that the plate number was 2198; two witnesses agree that the plate ended with CAT. Choice (A) includes the greatest number of common elements.

49. **(D)** The details are uncomplicated. The report should be equally straightforward.

50. **(B)** There are few details. Choice (B) expresses them well, leaving no doubt as to what happened and to whom.

51. **(D)** The regulation states: "Two police officers are needed if more than one patient is being transported." Here there are three patients.

52. **(A)** This question is not as time-consuming as it first appears. Burglaries and robberies seem to occur at night. Only choice (A) suggests a nighttime patrol, so you needn't concern yourself with days of the week or location of patrol.

53. **(C)** The auto thefts occur on Mondays and Wednesdays during evening rush hours, roughly 3:30 P.M. to 7:00 P.M., so a Monday through Friday, 4:00 P.M. to midnight tour should be most effective.

54. **(D)** In stepping in to stop a flight between armed persons, a police officer runs some risk of personal injury. Back-up assistance should help break up the fight more efficiently and with less danger.

55. **(B)** Read the steps and the narrative description carefully. The next step, in order, is to place the additional ammunition into another envelope.

56. **(A)** Robberies and rapes occur in the afternoon and night, so eliminate (B) and (C). The days of the week that are most important to cover are Monday, Friday, and Saturday. Choice (D) would leave Monday uncovered, so (A) is the answer.

57. **(C)** The ambulance attendant, Peter Johnson, pronounced Smith dead.

58. **(D)** William Jones came out of his store and reported hearing a gunshot at 5:15 P.M.

59. **(B)** Walter Garvey described the hair color and clothing of the two suspects.

60. **(D)** Only this statement makes clear descriptions of witness, suspect, and action.

61. **(A)** This is the only clear and accurate statement.

62. **(B)** Regulation item 4 requires that the police officer notify the Property Clerk's Office if evidence is held by the court.

63. **(C)** The teenage boy who keeps looking at his watch could be putting on a guise of waiting for a train in order to avoid special attention; but the woman, who has stood for a full hour without showing any impatience that the person she is awaiting has not arrived, must arouse greater suspicion and should be monitored more closely.

64. **(B)** There is no question that this is a well-organized report, which presents all the information clearly and accurately.

65. **(D)** Item 2 says that the officer should conduct a brief investigation in the vicinity of the place where the child was found. This means that the officer should have inquired within the building to learn if anyone was missing a child or if anyone had any information about this particular youngster.

66. **(A)** This is the simplest statement and clearly includes all the facts.

67. **(C)** The officer's first act at the scene of the accident must be to request medical assistance for the injured.

68. **(D)** No one was injured, so an ambulance is unnecessary; Officer Degas is already diverting the traffic. Now the officers must attempt to determine the cause of the accident so that they will have complete information to enter on the Police Accident Report.

69. **(B)** This is a short statement that includes all of the facts clearly and accurately.

70. **(C)** The activity described has all occurred before the list of procedures even begins. Therefore, the officer is now at the top of the list. The first official act must be to request the person's name and address.

71. **(D)** Officer Georgia has followed regulations. The homeless woman refused shelter during the Cold Weather Emergency, so Officer Georgia was required to have her hospitalized.

72. **(B)** Since, by the definition, "sell" means "give to another," and since Harry and Jack have been giving the marihuana pipe to each other, Harry and Jack have been involved in Criminal Sale of a Controlled Substance Fifth Degree. No one else sold or gave to another.

73. **(D)** The suspect is a juvenile so, following the printed procedure, the next step is to prepare a N.Y. State Juvenile Fingerprint Chart.

74. **(C)** Multiply and add as indicated. Do not forget about the suitcase.

2 35mm Cameras at $289 each	=	$578
2 Video Cassette Recorders at $329 each	=	658
Miscellaneous jewelry	=	455
Cash	=	350
Stock Certificates totalling	=	1500
Luggage	=	+ 150
total	=	$3,691

75. **(A)** Whiskey Bill knew that the liquor would be fatal and deliberately gave some to Joe to drink. Bill's action constitutes Murder Second Degree.

76. **(D)** The homicides are all on Third Avenue, and only one choice suggests that Officer Miller should patrol Third Avenue. Spend no extra time on a question that can be answered so easily.

77. **(C)** Choice (D) is also possible but is by no means the shortest route. (A) is impossible because Thames Street is one way westbound; (B) is impossible because Rose Place is not a through street.

78. **(A)** Choice (C) is not really a bad one, but it is somewhat longer than (A). (B) cannot be taken because Rose Place at Washington Street is one way westbound; (D) cannot be taken because Charles Street is one way southbound.

79. **(A)** Put yourself in the driver's seat and follow the route, turning the map as needed to

be certain of right and left from the driver's point of view. Starting at Rose Place and Temple Street, go south two blocks to Roundsman Avenue. Turn left and go east for two blocks to Washington Street. Turn left and travel one block north to Thames Street. Turn left and go two more blocks west to Temple Street. The final right turn will leave you headed north.

80. **(C)** The youth looking at a subway map while holding a black canvas bag might very well raise suspicion; however, this question speaks of pairs of youths who have been conducting the hold-ups. Since you are looking for two youths, and in (C) one boy appears to be acting as a lookout, choice (C) represents the pair that should be monitored closely.

81. **(D)** The prisoner was removed from the scene of the arrest directly to the hospital and so must be searched at the hospital. Since the prisoner, Michelle Hart, is female, Officer Smith must direct hospital personnel to conduct the search.

82. **(A)** Directive 4 requires that both weapon and Request for Laboratory Examination form be brought to the Ballistics Unit.

83. **(C)** A fall that renders a person unconscious is a serious injury. It requires emergency transportation for medical assistance.

84. **(B)** or **(C)** Eliminate choice (A) at once; the crime was committed in the afternoon, not in the morning. Stuart Gray was seen running from the building at 5:35 P.M., so the crime had to have been committed before that time. Stuart Gray was seen nearby at about 5:10 P.M., so the crime could not have been committed before that time. The question asks for the "most likely" time. The best answer is choice (B). The time span 5:10 to 5:35 allows for Gray to have entered the apartment, argued, hit Mrs. Gray over the head, rummaged through drawers to find money for his crack habit, and run off. (C) is acceptable as an answer because it is also possible that Gray went through drawers as Valerie Gray argued with him and that he hit her over the head as his last act before exiting the apartment. Since the

crime had to have been committed no later than 5:35 and the time span 5:30 to 5:35 is offered, there is no reason to accept choice (D) as an answer, even though it might technically be correct.

85. **(A)** Officer Swift checked the fire escape while his partner, Officer Monroe, searched the bedroom where he found Mrs. Gray.

86. **(A)** Ben Grim saw Stuart Gray run from the building with blood on his hands. Ms. Arnold's statement, of having seen Gray in the neighborhood before the crime, ties him only very circumstantially. However, Ben Grim must be part of the answer, and Valerie Gray having never regained consciousness cannot be part of the answer, so (A) is the only choice.

87. **(D)** The homicide took place on May 10. Gray was arrested at 7:15 the next morning, that is, on May 11 at 7:15 A.M.

88. **(C)** This is a clear and accurate statement of the facts.

89. **(C)** A parent is permitted to reasonably discipline a child. A mother's leaving a four-year-old at home alone for purposes of her partying can offer no benefit to the child. Quite to the contrary, a child is not equipped to deal with emergencies and might even cause them. This is a good example of Endangering the Welfare of a Child.

90. **(B)** This information is presented in logical, useful order.

91. **(B)** This statement keeps the parties straight and tells what happened.

92. **(D)** Clarke has one previous suspension for the same violation so should be issued a Universal Summons. No person may operate a motor vehicle with a suspended license, so Clarke must park his car in a legal area and arrange for a licensed operator to fetch it.

93. **(A)** The most suspicious car is that in which two men sit near the schoolyard during recess and after school. It is difficult to think of a legitimate reason for their being there, and they must be closely observed. The car

service driver could be selling drugs and using his legitimate role as a cover, and the teenagers could be selling drugs from their car, but the question asks which is *most suspicious*.

94. **(C)** Officer Wells has proceeded through step 5 and has marked the separate vials of drugs. He must now move to step 6 and request specially secured envelopes from the Station House Officer.

95. **(A)** The man crawled under the turnstile and then rode the subway train. Had he not intended to avoid payment, he could have dropped a token into the turnstile, gone through and then retrieved the quarter. The diners in (B) refused to pay for food, not for transportation services. In (C), Harry paid even though his payment may not have registered.

96. **(C)** All other choices are very unclear.

97. **(D)** Only this choice makes clear when and where the crime was committed and leaves no doubt as to who was wearing a beige parka.

98. **(A)** All suspects are within the same age, height, and weight range. The suspects in incidents 1 and 4 have three features in common that are not reported in suspects 2 and 3. These are long brown hair, not common in blacks and therefore highly significant, a scar on the left side of the face, and an earring in the right ear.

99. **(B)** Choices (A) and (C) involve stealing without physical force. In choice (D) there is threat of physical force, but not threat of *immediate* force and nothing is stolen. In (B), on the other hand, the threat is real and immediate and the money is stolen.

100. **(D)** All of the other choices present the information inaccurately and with much room for doubt as to real meaning.

101. **(D)** Instances (A) and (B) represent normal disciplinary action by parents. (C) is a household accident. It is the duty of parents to care for their defenseless and helpless infants. Leaving a baby at home alone, to go out to play softball out of sight and earshot may well constitute neglect.

102. **(C)** When two people of the same sex are involved in an interaction, you must take special care to use their names more often to avoid confusion of "he," "him," and "his." Choice (C) keeps both people and time sequence straight.

103. **(A)** This is the best organized and simplest statement.

104. **(B)** All four statements present the information accurately, but choice (B) is clearest.

105. **(A)** The officers do not perceive a need for medical attention, but Mrs. Jones has requested it. According to step 2, the officers must obtain medical assistance if it is requested.

106. **(B)** Officer Perez of sector Charlie went up to the roof.

107. **(C)** Go back to the first sentence. Officer Moody encountered an armed robbery in progress and chased the perpetrator.

108. **(D)** Officer Donadio was in the courtyard.

109. **(B)** Read carefully. By the time Officer Moody arrived at the bottom of the second floor stairway, the suspect had jumped out the hall window and was in the courtyard.

110. **(D)** Three witnesses agree that the suspect is a white, non-Hispanic male, so immediately eliminate (B). The array of estimates of height leads to infer that the man is on the taller side, so narrow to (C) and (D). Three witnesses recall that the man had brown hair and dark eyes; so (D), as the description with the greatest number of common elements, is the best choice.

111. **(C)** This statement is clear, logical and accurate.

112. **(D)** This constitutes Grand Larceny Fourth Degree because the bracelet, even though inexpensive, was removed from the victim's body. (A) is not the answer because the value of the stolen property is less than one thousand dollars and the property was not taken from the person of another nor obtained through fear. In (B) the credit card is not stolen. In (C) a threat is made but nothing is stolen.

113. **(A)** The information is sketchy and simple. There is no need to complicate it with a confusing report.

114. **(B)** The doctor has not requested that Officer Schultz remove the handcuffs, so he should not do so at this time. Officer Schultz must now inform Dr. Carson of the details of the prisoner's arrest.

115. **(D)** A man who is recognized as being recently involved in an armed robbery is most certainly a person suspected of having committed a crime. The Police Officer is authorized to search him.

116. **(B)** Larceny and robbery cannot occur at the same time, since one entails the use or threat of force, while the other occurs only without force. Kevin Watts threatened to beat Jane up, then stole her property. He committed robbery. Watts also unlawfully entered the apartment by way of the fire escape for purposes of robbery, thereby committing burglary as well.

117. **(B)** This is by far the most clear and accurate statement.

118. **(C)** This statement includes all of the facts and expresses them clearly.

119. **(B)** According to the prescribed order of actions to be taken, Officer Wong must now keep unauthorized people away from the scene. In answering questions, remember to be bound by the printed instructions that accompany the question.

120. **(A)** This is a well-organized, useful statement.

121. **(B)** All the other statements are garbled.

122. **(D)** The stolen water pistols that Mr. Aquista buys are only toys, not firearms, but their value is in excess of $250 so his purchase with knowledge of their stolen status constitutes Criminal Possession of Stolen Property Second Degree. (A) does not qualify because the value of the camera is under $250.

123. **(A)** This statement gets all the facts straight and expresses them clearly.

124. **(B)** The officers who responded to Officer Berman's call for back-up assistance are: Officers Fernandez and Heck; Officer Jones (on a scooter); and Sergeant Desmond with his driver, Officer Ricco.

125. **(D)** Officers Fernandez and Heck arrived at 11:40. Officer Jones arrived five minutes later, at 11:45. Sergeant Demond arrived two minutes after Jones, at 11:47.

126. **(C)** We know that Officer Berman was walking. There is no information as to how Officers Fernandez and Heck arrived. The passage tells us that Jones arrived by scooter.

127. **(B)** Between 8:00 A.M. and 10:00 A.M., the traffic problem is caused by cars parked in the bus stop on the north side of West 231st Street and Maple Lane.

128. **(C)** Midday traffic congestion is created by the cars that double-park on both sides of West 231st Street.

129. **(A)** During the evening rush hour, cars park in the bus stop on the south side of West 231st Street and Kingsway Avenue.

130. **(C)** This statement is clear, accurate, and well organized.

131. **(D)** Although Weeks did not actually steal anything, he broke into the store with intent to steal, and his action therefore constitutes burglary. No other choice involves criminal intent.

132. **(A)** Sergeant Larry gave Officer Jones the description of the rapist as reported by Nancy Lewis.

133. **(C)** Tammy Wilson was raped in the elevator at 110 Park Avenue, then was pushed out of the elevator at the 7th floor.

134. **(D)** Tammy Wilson was raped on the same day that Officer Smith was given the description of the rapist, May 2. John Jones was apprehended on May 3, the day after the rape of Tammy Wilson.

135. **(C)** Only this choice accurately states that the robbery occurred at 11:20 A.M. All other choices give 11:20 A.M. as the time of the report of the robbery.

136. **(A)** Whether the death is suspicious or of apparently natural causes, the first person to be notified is the Desk Officer.

137. **(D)** Read carefully so as to be sure to include all items in your total. Don't miss the brooch and the bracelet *each* valued at $250.

3 sculptures at $2000 each	=	$6,000
2 oil paintings at $500 each	=	1,000
1 ceramic vase at $375	=	375
1 portrait at $2500	=	2,500
2 small watercolors at $75 each	=	150
1 brooch at $250	=	250
1 bracelet at $250	=	250
cash of $50	=	+ 50
total		$10,575

138. **(A)** The officers have interviewed the complainant and have thoroughly searched the area for evidence. Since there are no witnesses, their next act must be to prepare a Complaint Report.

139. **(C)** There is no question that entry of a bedroom at night, pistol in hand, and stealing a VCR constitutes Burglary First Degree. Choice (B) fits all the requirements for Burglary First Degree except that a department store is not a dwelling.

140. **(B)** All the statements do make clear who was stabbed, who was arrested, and where it happened. Choice (B) makes the statement most clearly.

141. **(D)** The officers did not follow through on all required procedures. They should have requested a Patrol Supervisor.

142. **(A)** Choice (B) has a different chin; (C) has different nostrils and a pierced right ear rather than left; (D) has a totally different shape head and face.

143. **(C)** Choice (A) has a different shape chin; (B) has different ears; (D) has a different chin. The beauty marks and heavy glossed lips are cosmetic changes only and cannot be used as a basis of comparison.

144. **(B)** Choice (A) has a different nose and ears; (C) has different eyes; (D) has different ears and lips. The hole from a pierced ear is difficult to remove so is significant if the comparison face has one. It is easy to pierce an ear, so the addition of a hole in an ear of one of the choices is meaningless.

145. **(D)** Choice (A) has a different mouth; (B) has different face shape and different eyes; (C) has different eyes.

146. **(A)** The beard effectively disguises the distinctive chin, but choice (A) must be your man because (B) and (D) have wrong chins and (C) has different eyes and ears.

147. **(B)** Choice (A) has a different chin (look carefully through the stubble on the comparison face); choice (C) has an entirely different nose; (D) has different ears.

148. **(D)** Choice (A) has different eyes and nose; (B) has a different chin; (C) has a different nose. The dark glasses and beard leave few features with which to judge (D), but nose, mouth and ears match exactly and all other choices have been eliminated.

149. **(B)** Choice (C) is clearly not the answer because she has very different ears and lips; (D) has a different nose. The decision between (A) and (B) is more difficult, but (B) is the answer because (A) has eyes that are quite a bit farther apart. As you practice at home, you can check this with a ruler. If faced with this type of need for measurement at the exam, mark distances off at the edge of a piece of paper, perhaps your answer sheet.

150. **(C)** Both (A) and (B) have noses that rule them out. Choice (D) has eyes that are set more deeply than those of the comparison face. This is not an easy determination. The eyes on (C) look larger, but you must remember that makeup can create illusions. If you find yourself having difficulty choosing a face, do give consideration to the effectiveness of various disguises. The sophisticated hairdo of (C) makes for a greater contrast from the original than the hairdo on (D), which, while shorter, still frames the face.

ANSWER SHEET FOR PRACTICE EXAMINATION 3

1. Ⓐ Ⓑ Ⓒ Ⓓ   2. Ⓐ Ⓑ Ⓒ Ⓓ   3. Ⓐ Ⓑ Ⓒ Ⓓ   4. Ⓐ Ⓑ Ⓒ Ⓓ   5. Ⓐ Ⓑ Ⓒ Ⓓ

6. Ⓐ Ⓑ Ⓒ Ⓓ   7. Ⓐ Ⓑ Ⓒ Ⓓ   8. Ⓐ Ⓑ Ⓒ Ⓓ   9. Ⓐ Ⓑ Ⓒ Ⓓ   10. Ⓐ Ⓑ Ⓒ Ⓓ

11. Ⓐ Ⓑ Ⓒ Ⓓ   12. Ⓐ Ⓑ Ⓒ Ⓓ   13. Ⓐ Ⓑ Ⓒ Ⓓ   14. Ⓐ Ⓑ Ⓒ Ⓓ   15. Ⓐ Ⓑ Ⓒ Ⓓ

16. Ⓐ Ⓑ Ⓒ Ⓓ   17. Ⓐ Ⓑ Ⓒ Ⓓ   18. Ⓐ Ⓑ Ⓒ Ⓓ   19. Ⓐ Ⓑ Ⓒ Ⓓ   20. Ⓐ Ⓑ Ⓒ Ⓓ

21. Ⓐ Ⓑ Ⓒ Ⓓ   22. Ⓐ Ⓑ Ⓒ Ⓓ   23. Ⓐ Ⓑ Ⓒ Ⓓ   24. Ⓐ Ⓑ Ⓒ Ⓓ   25. Ⓐ Ⓑ Ⓒ Ⓓ

26. Ⓐ Ⓑ Ⓒ Ⓓ   27. Ⓐ Ⓑ Ⓒ Ⓓ   28. Ⓐ Ⓑ Ⓒ Ⓓ   29. Ⓐ Ⓑ Ⓒ Ⓓ   30. Ⓐ Ⓑ Ⓒ Ⓓ

31. Ⓐ Ⓑ Ⓒ Ⓓ   32. Ⓐ Ⓑ Ⓒ Ⓓ   33. Ⓐ Ⓑ Ⓒ Ⓓ   34. Ⓐ Ⓑ Ⓒ Ⓓ   35. Ⓐ Ⓑ Ⓒ Ⓓ

36. Ⓐ Ⓑ Ⓒ Ⓓ   37. Ⓐ Ⓑ Ⓒ Ⓓ   38. Ⓐ Ⓑ Ⓒ Ⓓ   39. Ⓐ Ⓑ Ⓒ Ⓓ   40. Ⓐ Ⓑ Ⓒ Ⓓ

41. Ⓐ Ⓑ Ⓒ Ⓓ   42. Ⓐ Ⓑ Ⓒ Ⓓ   43. Ⓐ Ⓑ Ⓒ Ⓓ   44. Ⓐ Ⓑ Ⓒ Ⓓ   45. Ⓐ Ⓑ Ⓒ Ⓓ

46. Ⓐ Ⓑ Ⓒ Ⓓ   47. Ⓐ Ⓑ Ⓒ Ⓓ   48. Ⓐ Ⓑ Ⓒ Ⓓ   49. Ⓐ Ⓑ Ⓒ Ⓓ   50. Ⓐ Ⓑ Ⓒ Ⓓ

51. Ⓐ Ⓑ Ⓒ Ⓓ   52. Ⓐ Ⓑ Ⓒ Ⓓ   53. Ⓐ Ⓑ Ⓒ Ⓓ   54. Ⓐ Ⓑ Ⓒ Ⓓ   55. Ⓐ Ⓑ Ⓒ Ⓓ

56. Ⓐ Ⓑ Ⓒ Ⓓ   57. Ⓐ Ⓑ Ⓒ Ⓓ   58. Ⓐ Ⓑ Ⓒ Ⓓ   59. Ⓐ Ⓑ Ⓒ Ⓓ   60. Ⓐ Ⓑ Ⓒ Ⓓ

61. Ⓐ Ⓑ Ⓒ Ⓓ   62. Ⓐ Ⓑ Ⓒ Ⓓ   63. Ⓐ Ⓑ Ⓒ Ⓓ   64. Ⓐ Ⓑ Ⓒ Ⓓ   65. Ⓐ Ⓑ Ⓒ Ⓓ

66. Ⓐ Ⓑ Ⓒ Ⓓ   67. Ⓐ Ⓑ Ⓒ Ⓓ   68. Ⓐ Ⓑ Ⓒ Ⓓ   69. Ⓐ Ⓑ Ⓒ Ⓓ   70. Ⓐ Ⓑ Ⓒ Ⓓ

71. Ⓐ Ⓑ Ⓒ Ⓓ   72. Ⓐ Ⓑ Ⓒ Ⓓ   73. Ⓐ Ⓑ Ⓒ Ⓓ   74. Ⓐ Ⓑ Ⓒ Ⓓ   75. Ⓐ Ⓑ Ⓒ Ⓓ

76. Ⓐ Ⓑ Ⓒ Ⓓ   77. Ⓐ Ⓑ Ⓒ Ⓓ   78. Ⓐ Ⓑ Ⓒ Ⓓ   79. Ⓐ Ⓑ Ⓒ Ⓓ   80. Ⓐ Ⓑ Ⓒ Ⓓ

81. Ⓐ Ⓑ Ⓒ Ⓓ   82. Ⓐ Ⓑ Ⓒ Ⓓ   83. Ⓐ Ⓑ Ⓒ Ⓓ   84. Ⓐ Ⓑ Ⓒ Ⓓ   85. Ⓐ Ⓑ Ⓒ Ⓓ

86. Ⓐ Ⓑ Ⓒ Ⓓ   87. Ⓐ Ⓑ Ⓒ Ⓓ   88. Ⓐ Ⓑ Ⓒ Ⓓ   89. Ⓐ Ⓑ Ⓒ Ⓓ   90. Ⓐ Ⓑ Ⓒ Ⓓ

91. Ⓐ Ⓑ Ⓒ Ⓓ   92. Ⓐ Ⓑ Ⓒ Ⓓ   93. Ⓐ Ⓑ Ⓒ Ⓓ   94. Ⓐ Ⓑ Ⓒ Ⓓ   95. Ⓐ Ⓑ Ⓒ Ⓓ

96. Ⓐ Ⓑ Ⓒ Ⓓ   97. Ⓐ Ⓑ Ⓒ Ⓓ   98. Ⓐ Ⓑ Ⓒ Ⓓ   99. Ⓐ Ⓑ Ⓒ Ⓓ   100. Ⓐ Ⓑ Ⓒ Ⓓ

101. Ⓐ Ⓑ Ⓒ Ⓓ   102. Ⓐ Ⓑ Ⓒ Ⓓ   103. Ⓐ Ⓑ Ⓒ Ⓓ   104. Ⓐ Ⓑ Ⓒ Ⓓ   105. Ⓐ Ⓑ Ⓒ Ⓓ

106. Ⓐ Ⓑ Ⓒ Ⓓ   107. Ⓐ Ⓑ Ⓒ Ⓓ   108. Ⓐ Ⓑ Ⓒ Ⓓ   109. Ⓐ Ⓑ Ⓒ Ⓓ   110. Ⓐ Ⓑ Ⓒ Ⓓ

111. Ⓐ Ⓑ Ⓒ Ⓓ   112. Ⓐ Ⓑ Ⓒ Ⓓ   113. Ⓐ Ⓑ Ⓒ Ⓓ   114. Ⓐ Ⓑ Ⓒ Ⓓ   115. Ⓐ Ⓑ Ⓒ Ⓓ

116. Ⓐ Ⓑ Ⓒ Ⓓ   117. Ⓐ Ⓑ Ⓒ Ⓓ   118. Ⓐ Ⓑ Ⓒ Ⓓ   119. Ⓐ Ⓑ Ⓒ Ⓓ   120. Ⓐ Ⓑ Ⓒ Ⓓ

121. Ⓐ Ⓑ Ⓒ Ⓓ   122. Ⓐ Ⓑ Ⓒ Ⓓ   123. Ⓐ Ⓑ Ⓒ Ⓓ   124. Ⓐ Ⓑ Ⓒ Ⓓ   125. Ⓐ Ⓑ Ⓒ Ⓓ

126. Ⓐ Ⓑ Ⓒ Ⓓ   127. Ⓐ Ⓑ Ⓒ Ⓓ   128. Ⓐ Ⓑ Ⓒ Ⓓ   129. Ⓐ Ⓑ Ⓒ Ⓓ   130. Ⓐ Ⓑ Ⓒ Ⓓ

131. Ⓐ Ⓑ Ⓒ Ⓓ   132. Ⓐ Ⓑ Ⓒ Ⓓ   133. Ⓐ Ⓑ Ⓒ Ⓓ   134. Ⓐ Ⓑ Ⓒ Ⓓ   135. Ⓐ Ⓑ Ⓒ Ⓓ

136. Ⓐ Ⓑ Ⓒ Ⓓ   137. Ⓐ Ⓑ Ⓒ Ⓓ   138. Ⓐ Ⓑ Ⓒ Ⓓ   139. Ⓐ Ⓑ Ⓒ Ⓓ   140. Ⓐ Ⓑ Ⓒ Ⓓ

141. Ⓐ Ⓑ Ⓒ Ⓓ   142. Ⓐ Ⓑ Ⓒ Ⓓ   143. Ⓐ Ⓑ Ⓒ Ⓓ   144. Ⓐ Ⓑ Ⓒ Ⓓ   145. Ⓐ Ⓑ Ⓒ Ⓓ

146. Ⓐ Ⓑ Ⓒ Ⓓ   147. Ⓐ Ⓑ Ⓒ Ⓓ   148. Ⓐ Ⓑ Ⓒ Ⓓ   149. Ⓐ Ⓑ Ⓒ Ⓓ   150. Ⓐ Ⓑ Ⓒ Ⓓ

TEAR HERE

PRACTICE EXAMINATION 3

MEMORY BOOKLET

Directions: You will be given 10 minutes to study the six "Wanted Posters" below and to try to remember as many details as you can. You may not take any notes during this time.

WANTED FOR ASSAULT

Name: John Markham
Age: 27
Height: 5' 11"
Weight: 215 lbs.
Race: Black
Hair color: black
Eye color: brown
Complexion: dark
Identifying marks: eagle tattoo
   on back of right hand; very
   hard of hearing
Suspect is a former boxer.
   He favors brass knuckles as
   his weapon.

WANTED FOR RAPE

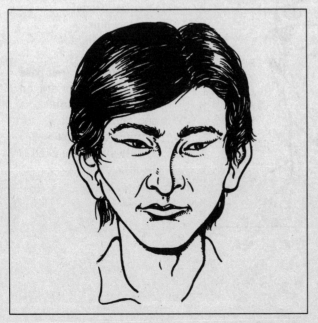

Name: Arthur Lee
Age: 19
Height: 5' 7"
Weight: 180 lbs.
Race: Asian
Hair color: black
Eye color: brown
Complexion: medium
Identifying marks: none
Suspect carries a pearl
   handled knife with an
   eight-inch curved blade.
   He tends to attack victims
   in subway passageways.

WANTED FOR ARMED ROBBERY

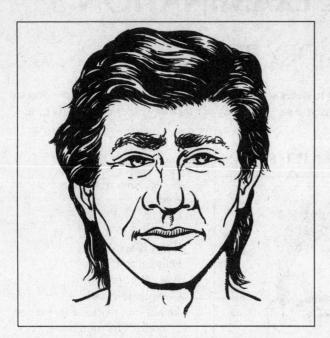

Name: Antonio Gomez
Age: 31
Height: 5' 6"
Weight: 160 lbs.
Race: Hispanic
Hair color: brown
Eye color: brown
Complexion: medium
Identifying marks: missing last finger of right hand; tattoo on back says "Mother"; tattoo on left biceps says "Linda"; tattoo on right biceps says "Carmen"
Suspect was seen leaving the scene in a stolen yellow 1987 Corvette. He carries a gun and must be considered dangerous.

WANTED FOR CAR THEFT

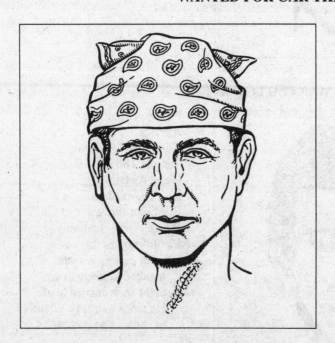

Name: Robert Miller
Age: 24
Height: 6' 3"
Weight: 230 lbs.
Race: White
Hair color: brown
Eye color: blue
Complexion: light
Identifying marks: tracheotomy scar at base of neck; tattoo of dragon on right upper arm
Suspect chain smokes unfiltered cigarettes. He always wears a red head scarf.

WANTED FOR MURDER

Name: Janet Walker
Age: 39
Height: 5' 10"
Weight: 148 lbs.
Race: Black
Hair color: black
Eye color: black
Complexion: dark
Identifying marks: large hairy
    mole on upper left thigh;
    stutters badly
Suspect has frequently been
    arrested for prostitution.
    She often wears multiple
    ear and nose rings.

WANTED FOR ARSON

Name: Margaret Pickford
Age: 42
Height: 5' 2"
Weight: 103 lbs.
Race: White
Hair color: red
Eye color: green
Complexion: light
Identifying marks: known
    heroin addict with track
    marks on forearms; walks
    with decided limp because
    left leg is shorter than right
Suspect has a child in foster
    care in Astoria. She
    usually carries two large
    shopping bags.

TEST QUESTION BOOKLET

3 hours—90 questions

Directions: Now that the Memory Booklets have been collected, you have three hours in which to answer the test questions. The first ten questions are based on the information given on the "Wanted Posters." Answer these questions first. Then proceed directly to the remaining 80 questions. Choose the best answer to each question and mark its letter on your answer sheet.

1. Which of the following suspects may have committed a crime in order to support a drug habit?

(A)

(C)

(B)

(D)

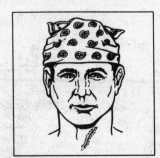

2. Which one of the following is missing a finger? The suspect wanted for

(A) rape　　　　　　　　　　　(C) murder
(B) assault　　　　　　　　　　(D) armed robbery

3. Which of the suspects is most likely to be found in the subway?

(A) John Markham　　　　　　　(C) Arthur Lee
(B) Margaret Pickford　　　　　(D) Robert Miller

4. Which of these suspects has a dragon tattoo?

(A)

(C)

(B)

(D)

5. Which is an identifying mark of this suspect?

(A) deafness
(B) a large mole
(C) a tattoo that reads "Mother"
(D) needle tracks

6. Which one of the following is considered to be the most dangerous?

(A)

(C)

(B)

(D)

7. Which of these suspects is known to be a parent?

(A) The suspect who stutters   (C) The smoker
(B) The former boxer   (D) The suspect who limps

8. Which of these suspects escaped the scene of the crime in a stolen car?

(A)

(C)

(B)

(D)

9. Which of these suspects would have the hardest time running from the police?

(A) The heroin addict   (C) The suspect who wears lots of jewelry

(B) The suspect who is nearly deaf   (D) The suspect with brass knuckles in his pocket

10. Which of these suspects is wanted for rape?

(A)

(C)

(B)

(D)

11. Police Officer Barros has received a report of a chain snatching and has obtained the following information:

Date of Occurrence:	August 12, 1993
Place of Occurrence:	In front of 4312 Third Avenue
Time of Occurrence:	5:10 P.M.
Incident:	Chain snatching
Victim:	Marina Marzycki, age 35, of 887 West Houston Street
Witness:	Bonita Bonds, age 56, of 4309 Third Avenue
Suspect:	White male, about 18 years of age, 5' 9", 165 lbs., dark brown hair, clean-shaven

Officer Barros is preparing a report on the incident. Which one of the following expresses the above information *most clearly* and *accurately*?

(A) Marina Marzycki of 887 West Houston Street had her chain snatched in front of 4309 Third Avenue by a white male. Bonita Bonds saw it at 5:10 P.M.
(B) A 5' 9", 165 lbs. white male of 4312 Third Avenue snatched the chain of Marina Marzycki, age 35, at 5:10 P.M.
(C) On August 12 at 5:10 P.M., Bonita Bonds of 4309 Third Avenue witnessed a chain snatching in front of 4312 Third Avenue. It was committed by an 18-year-old clean-shaven white male with brown hair.
(D) Bonita Bonds says that Marina Marzycki's chain was snatched at 887 West Houston Street by a medium-sized teenager.

12. Officer Hollis has just issued a summons to a driver and has obtained the following information:

Time of Occurrence: 4:08 A.M.
Place of Occurrence: Baylor Boulevard between 16th Street and Highland Road
Offense: Illegal U-turn
Driver: Robert Richards, Jr., age 29
Address of Driver: 92 Carolina Street

Officer Hollis is making an entry in his memo book regarding the incident. Which one of the following expresses the above information *most clearly* and *accurately*?

(A) Robert Richards, Jr., age 29, made a U-turn at 92 Carolina Street. I arrested him.
(B) At 4:08 A.M. I stopped Robert Richards of 92 Carolina Street for making an illegal U-turn on Baylor Boulevard.
(C) 29-year-old Robert Richards, Jr. made an illegal U-turn on Baylor Boulevard at 92 Carolina Street. It was early this morning.
(D) When Robert Richards, Jr., age 29, made an illegal U-turn on Baylor Boulevard between 16th Street and Highland Road, I gave him a summons at 92 Carolina Street at 4:08.

13. Police officers are sometimes required to respond to the scene of a traffic accident involving two vehicles. In situations in which one of the drivers involved in the accident has left the scene before the arrival of a police officer, the responding officer must use the following procedures in the order given:
1. Question the driver of the remaining vehicle as to the license plate number of the vehicle which fled.
   a. If the complete license plate number is known, call Vehicle Inquiry Section to determine name and address of owner.
   b. Write down name and address of owner of vehicle which fled.
   c. Give name and address of owner of vehicle which fled to driver remaining at scene of accident.
2. Obtain from driver remaining at scene all details of the accident including description of vehicle which fled.
3. Call Stolen Vehicle Desk.
4. Prepare Complaint Form in duplicate.

Police Officer Yoshida has arrived at the scene of a traffic accident involving two cars. One of the drivers fled the scene immediately after the impact, but the driver of the remaining vehicle, Louis Santangelo, did notice that the last three digits of the license plate were 7-9-7, and he gives this information to Officer Yoshida. Which one of the following actions should Officer Yoshida take next?

(A) Call Vehicle Inquiry Section to determine name and address of owner.
(B) Call Stolen Vehicle Desk.
(C) Write down name and address of Louis Santangelo.
(D) Ask Santangelo for a description of the other car and for details of the accident.

14. Police officers must occasionally transport prisoners in the radio patrol car to the station house for booking. In such situations, police officers must follow these procedures, in the order given:

1. Obtain permission from the patrol supervisor or station house supervisor to transport the prisoner in a radio patrol car.
2. Search and handcuff prisoner before placing prisoner in car.
3. Notify the radio dispatcher at the start of the trip.
4. Search prisoner area of car for weapons, drugs, or other property when trip is over.
5. Record all details of trip in activity log.
6. Inform police telephone switchboard operator of details of trip.

Police Officers Mutt and Jeff are transporting a prisoner in their radio patrol car for booking. Upon arrival at the station house they should

(A) search the prisoner area of the car for weapons, drugs, or other personal property
(B) notify the radio dispatcher that they have arrived
(C) record all details of the trip in the activity log
(D) inform the police telephone switchboard operator of the details of the trip

15. Officer O'Callaghan has noticed that in her sector most of the burglaries occur on Walnut Street, most of the robberies occur on Maple Street, and most of the auto thefts occur on Oak Street. Most of the robberies take place between 4:00 P.M. and 10:00 P.M. Most of the auto thefts occur between 9:00 P.M. and 3:00 A.M. Most of the burglaries occur between 11:00 P.M. and 6:00 A.M. Robberies occur most frequently on Wednesdays and Fridays. Most of the burglaries occur on Tuesdays and Saturdays. Most of the auto thefts occur on Wednesdays and Thursdays.

Officer O'Callaghan would be most likely to reduce the number of robberies by patrolling

(A) Walnut Street on Wednesdays and Fridays between 4:00 P.M. and 10:00 P.M.
(B) Maple Street on Wednesdays and Fridays between 4:00 P.M. and midnight
(C) Maple Street on Wednesdays and Thursdays between 4:00 P.M. and 10:00 P.M.
(D) Walnut Street on Tuesdays and Fridays between 9:00 P.M. and 3:00 A.M.

16. BURGLARY is committed when a person enters or remains in a building in which he or she has no right to be, intending to commit a crime. According to the definition given, which one of the following is the best example of a burglary?

(A) Jason, a teenager, props open a stairwell door for later getaway, then hides in a men's room at the department store's closing time. Just as Jason is about to steal an expensive camera, he is startled by the approach of a night watchman and runs from the store empty-handed.
(B) Mrs. Green enters a large discount store to buy a new battery for her smoke alarm. After waiting ten minutes in the check-out line, she pops the battery into her purse and leaves the store without paying.
(C) George trusts to luck and passes a gas station without filling up. Within a few miles, he runs out of gas. As George is walking back to the gas station, a thunder storm blows up and he runs into a nearby barn to take shelter among the cows.
(D) While the office manager is away from her desk, a coworker from another floor pulls open a desk drawer and takes the office manager's wallet from her pocketbook.

17. Transit Police Officer Padula has responded to a complaint of drug sales in a subway entrance stairwell. Officer Padula obtains the following information at the scene:

Time of Occurrence:	6:15 A.M.
Place of Occurrence:	Stairwell of northbound entrance, 50th Street Station, Broadway line
Witnesses:	Mary Jones, age 58, homeless Tom Harriman, age 25, 1189 Ninth Ave.
Suspect:	Hispanic male about age 20 wearing torn blue jeans and long-sleeved plaid shirt; known as "Tony"
Crime:	Drug sales
Action taken:	Suspect ran onto northbound #1 train.

Officer Padula must file a report of this incident. Which one of the following expresses the above information *most clearly* and *accurately*?

(A) Tony was selling drugs in the Broadway subway station but he got away on the #1. Mary Jones and Tom Harriman saw him.
(B) At 6:15 this morning a homeless man named Tony sold drugs to Mary Jones who lives on Ninth Avenue and Tom Harriman in a plaid shirt. This happened in the 50th Street subway station. He got away.
(C) At 6:15 A.M. Tom Harriman sold drugs to a homeless man called Tony in the northbound 50th Street subway station. Mary Jones said that he escaped to 1189 Ninth Avenue.
(D) Tom Harriman of 1189 Ninth Avenue and Mary Jones, homeless, report that a man called Tony wearing torn blue jeans and a plaid shirt was selling drugs in the northbound 50th Street Broadway stairwell at 6:15 A.M. The suspect escaped on a northbound #1 train.

Answer questions 18-23 on the basis of the following paragraph:

On Friday, February 2, at 8:30 A.M., Assistant Bridge Operator, Henry Jones, started to clean the walk of the Avenue X Bridge. It was snowing heavily, and the surface of the road was slippery. At 8:32 A.M., Jones saw a westbound station wagon skid and strike a westbound sedan about 50 feet from the barrier. Both cars were badly damaged. The station wagon overturned and came to rest eight feet from the barrier. The driver of the station wagon, Harriet White, was thrown clear and landed in the middle of the road. The other car was smashed against the barrier. The driver of the sedan, Tom Green, was pinned behind the steering wheel and suffered cuts about the face. Jones called the Bridge Operator, Frank Smith, who telephoned for an ambulance. First aid was given to both drivers. They were taken to the Avenue W Hospital by an ambulance driven by James Doe which had arrived upon the scene at 9:07 A.M. Police Officer John Brown, Badge No. 71162, had arrived before the ambulance and recorded all the details of the accident including the statements of Henry Jones and of Jack Black, another eyewitness.

18. The station wagon was driven by

(A) Jane Brown   (C) Harriet White
(B) Jane White   (D) Harriet Brown

19. The barrier was

(A) struck by the sedan   (C) struck by both cars
(B) struck by the station wagon   (D) not struck by either car

20. Tom Green was the

(A) driver of the ambulance
(B) driver of the sedan
(C) other eyewitness
(D) police officer

21. The woman driver

(A) was pinned behind the wheel
(B) suffered face cuts
(C) was thrown clear
(D) was trapped in the car

22. The name of the Bridge Operator was

(A) Frank Smith
(B) John Smith
(C) Henry Jones
(D) Frank Jones

23. When the accident occurred,

(A) the station wagon was 20 feet from the barrier
(B) the cars were 50 feet from the barrier
(C) the sedan was 60 feet from the barrier
(D) the sedan was 8 feet from the barrier

24. Foreign diplomats cannot be arrested or personally served with a summons. When a police officer arrives at the scene of an incident involving a diplomat, the officer must:

1. Take necessary action to protect life and property.
2. Obtain the name and title of the diplomat and his government.
   a. Ask to see the diplomat's identification.
   b. If the diplomat cannot produce identification, telephone the Operations Unit for verification.
3. If a vehicle bearing DPL license plates is unoccupied, illegally parked, and creating a safety hazard, place a summons on the windshield.

As Police Officer Schuman is patrolling her assigned area, she is approached by an agitated citizen carrying a black bag. The gentleman identifies himself as Dr. Forster. Dr. Forster has been called by the hospital to attend to a patient, but a double-parked car with DPL license plates is blocking his car. Officer Schuman notices that there is a person sitting in the back seat of the car with DPL plates. The passenger identifies himself as a diplomat and produces identification. He does not move the car. Officer Schuman suggests to Dr. Forster that he had better take a cab to the hospital. Schuman writes a parking summons and places it on the windshield of the vehicle. Police Officer Schuman's action in giving the car a parking summons is

(A) appropriate; because the car created a safety hazard in blocking a doctor's car
(B) inappropriate; Schuman should have checked first with the Operations Unit
(C) appropriate; a summons cannot be handed to a diplomat but may be placed on a diplomat's car
(D) inappropriate; the car was not unoccupied

25. Housing Police Officers, whether patrolling on foot or in a vehicle, are often the first to notice fires in apartment buildings. A Housing Police Officer who spots a fire must:

1. Send an alarm or make sure one has been sent.
2. Direct a responsible person to remain at the alarm box to direct fire engines if fire is not in view.
3. Park patrol car so as to divert traffic to prevent interference with firefighting operations.
4. Warn and assist occupants in evacuation of building.
5. Take appropriate action to protect lives and property.

Housing Police Officer Patel is patrolling the interior streets of a large city housing project in his patrol car when he sees smoke pouring from a third story window of a building that faces into another courtyard. Officer Patel uses his police radio to call in the fire alarm and to give the precise location of the fire. What should Officer Patel do next?

(A) Ask a woman who is walking her dog to wait at the corner to direct firefighters to the fire.
(B) Park the patrol car so that it blocks all access to the courtyard on which the fire building faces.
(C) Enter the building to alert residents.
(D) Grab a hall fire extinguisher and enter the burning apartment.

26. Police Officer Martinez is investigating a report of a stolen vehicle. He has collected the following information:

Date of Occurrence:	March 3 or March 4
Time of Occurrence:	between 9 P.M. and 7:30 A.M.
Occurrence:	stolen car
Location:	in front of 3626 Kings Highway
Description of car:	mauve 1992 Honda Civic, 4-door, NY plate 673 NYG
Owner:	Gloria Garland of 1618 East 24th Street

Officer Martinez must file a stolen car report. Which of the following expresses the information *most clearly* and *accurately*?

(A) Someone stole Gloria Garland's mauve 1992 Honda Civic in front of 1618 East 24th Street at night.
(B) Honda Civic number 673 NYG, was stolen on the night of March 3 at 3626 Kings Highway says Gloria Garland.
(C) A mauve 4-door 1992 Honda Civic, NY 673 NYG, was stolen by Gloria Garland of 3626 Kings Highway around midnight of March 3 at 1618 East 24th Street.
(D) Gloria Garland of 1618 East 24th Street reports that her mauve 1992 Honda Civic, NY 673 NYG, was stolen during the night of March 3-4. It had been parked near 3626 Kings Highway.

27. While on foot patrol on July 6, Police Officer Cartozian is stopped by a pedestrian and is told that a little boy in the neighborhood has been bitten by a dog. Officer Cartozian investigates and gathers the following information:

Date of Occurrence:	July 5
Occurrence:	dog bite, lower right leg
Victim:	Nicholas Christophe, age 8
Address of Victim:	612 Tenth Avenue, Apt. 3L
Witness:	Mary Murta of 721 Ninth Avenue
Location of Occurrence:	in front of 718 Ninth Avenue
Description of dog:	mixed-breed, black and white, spaniel-sized
Location of dog:	unknown

With the current rabies epidemic, Officer Cartozian takes this report very seriously and transmits the information right away to the precinct and to the canine control unit. Which of the following expresses the information *most clearly* and *accurately*?

(A) Nicholas Cristophe was bitten on the leg by a little black and white dog yesterday. He is eight years old and lives at 721 Ninth Avenue, Mary Murta said.
(B) Eight-year-old Nicholas Cristophe of 612 Tenth Ave. was bitten by a small to mid-size black and white mutt on July 5. Mary Murta of 721 Ninth Avenue observed this from her window.
(C) Mary Murta of 721 Ninth Avenue reports a black and white dog bite of Nicholas Christophe on his right leg yesterday.
(D) A black and white dog of 718 Ninth Avenue bit Nicholas Christophe on his leg at 612 Tenth Avenue. He is eight, says Mary Murta, a witness.

28. **CRIMINAL MISCHIEF** is committed when

1. A person intentionally damages property belonging to another and the amount of the damage is $250 or more; or
2. A person intentionally damages property in any amount by means of an explosive.

According to the definition given, which one of the following is the best example of criminal mischief?

(A) On the last night of the school year, Jim and Ben put a lighted cherry bomb into the Marlin's $90 mailbox, blowing away the mailbox.
(B) A noisy party at the Brown's house is disturbing Mary's concentration on the book she is reading. Mary angrily goes into the street and scratches one guest's car with a letter opener. Repair of the paint job costs $180.
(C) Peter is admiring Paul's new B-B gun. The gun fires and the stray B-B shatters the O'Brien's $400 living room picture window.
(D) Katie's foot slips off the brake pedal and her mother's car, which she is driving without her mother's permission, smashes into a utility pole. Damage to the car is $2500 and to the pole $300.

29. Chief Jones is concerned with the recent increase in crime. He has noticed that assaults tend to occur between 11 A.M. and 2:00 P.M.; most robberies occur between 8:00 P.M. and 1:00 A.M.; and peak hours for murders are from 3:00 A.M. to 6:00 A.M. Assaults are most common on Tuesdays and Thursdays; robberies on Sundays and Mondays; and murders on Thursdays and Saturdays. A high percentage of assaults occur on Avenue B; robbery is a major problem on Second Avenue; murders are frequently committed on Thurston Avenue. Officer Smith has been assigned to try to reduce the number of robberies. Smith should be certain to patrol

(A) Second Avenue from 9:00 P.M. to midnight Tuesday through Friday
(B) Thurston Avenue from 11:00 P.M. to 4:00 A.M. Friday through Sunday
(C) Second Avenue from 7:30 P.M. through 12:00 P.M. Saturday through Tuesday
(D) Avenue B from 10:00 A.M. through 4:00 P.M. Wednesday, Sunday, and Monday

30. Housing Police Officer Tomassi has taken into custody a man caught running from the scene of an apartment burglary with a pillow case slung over his shoulder. At the station house the booking sergeant takes inventory of the contents of the pillowcase. The contents consist of:

2 silver candlesticks, each valued at	$ 110.00
1 diamond bracelet valued at	$1200.00
3 18-kt. gold chains, each valued at	$ 250.00
Cash in the sum of	$ 719.00

What is the total value of the contents of the pillowcase?

(A) $2279   (C) $2889
(B) $2639   (D) $2989

Answer questions 31-33 on the basis of the following map. The flow of traffic is indicated by the arrows. You must follow the flow of traffic.

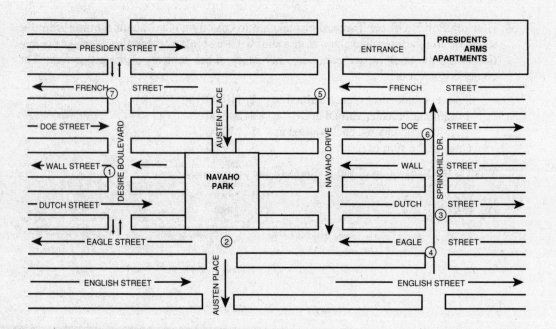

31. If you are located at point (1) and travel north three blocks, then turn east and travel one block, then turn south and travel five blocks, then turn west and travel one block, you will be closest to point

(A) 2

(C) 5

(B) 3

(D) 7

32. You are located at Desire Boulevard and Wall Street and receive a call to respond to the corner of Dutch Street and Springhill Drive. Which of the following is the most direct route for you to take in your patrol car, making sure to obey all traffic regulations?

(A) Travel two blocks south on Desire Boulevard to Eagle Street, then three blocks east to Springhill Drive, then north one block to Dutch Street.

(B) Travel three blocks north on Desire Boulevard to President Street, then one block east to Navaho Drive, then two blocks south to Austin Place, then one block east to Springhill Drive, then two blocks to Dutch Street.

(C) Travel two blocks north on Desire Boulevard to French Street, then three blocks east to Springhill Drive, then three blocks south to Dutch Street.

(D) Travel one block north on Desire Boulevard to Doe Street, then east two blocks to Navaho Drive, then south two blocks to Dutch Street, then east one block to Springhill Drive.

33. The call to Dutch Street and Springhill Drive turns out to be a false alarm, but your patrol car radio suddenly alerts you to a disturbance in the entryway of the President's Arms Apartments. You must get to the site of the disturbance in the quickest legal way. You should go:

(A) North three blocks on Springhill Drive to French Street, then turn left onto French Street and go one block to Navaho Drive, then turn right and go one block on Navaho Drive to the entrance.

(B) North three blocks on Springhill Drive to French Street, then turn left onto French Street and follow it to Desire Boulevard, then go right onto Desire Boulevard one block to President Street, then go east on President Street to the apartment house entrance.

(C) South one block on Springhill Drive to Eagle Street, then go west on Eagle Street to Desire Boulevard, then turn right onto Desire Boulevard and follow it five blocks to President Street, then go east on President Street into the entrance.

(D) North one block on Springhill Drive to Wall Street, then west on Wall Street one block to Navaho Drive, then south on Navaho Drive two blocks to Eagle Street, then follow Eagle Street west to Desire Boulevard, then turn right onto Desire Boulevard and go to President Street, then turn right onto President Street and go to the entrance.

34. CRIMINALLY NEGLIGENT HOMICIDE is committed when an individual behaves in such a way that his or her behavior creates a substantial risk for others, unintentionally causing the death of a person. According to the definition given, which of the following is the best example of criminally negligent homicide?

(A) In a burst of impatience, Roger pulls out from behind a school bus in order to pass it. As he comes alongside the bus, Roger realizes that the traffic signal ahead is red. Roger puts on a spurt of speed to pull into the space ahead of the bus, not noticing the motorcycle that has stopped for the light. Roger's car strikes the motorcycle, throwing the driver, Rosa, from her seat and killing her instantly.

(B) As a member of a ring of drug dealers, Jim has taken on the task of eliminating the leader of a rival drug distributor. Jim plants a bomb under the hood of the car regularly driven by the drug distributor, John Doe. Doe enters the car, turns on the ignition, and is killed by the explosion. Pieces of the car fly about the street and sidewalk seriously injuring a number of passers by.

(C) George Herman comes home from work early one afternoon and finds his wife, Helen, in bed with Tom Jones. Furious, Herman takes his unlicensed revolver from the glove compartment of his car and shoots both Helen and Tom Jones. Both die within hours of the shooting.

(D) Peter Piper enters the First National Bank, gun in hand, and orders the tellers and patrons to lie on the floor face down. He then proceeds to take cash and jewelry from the patrons one at a time. Piper warns everyone not to move. Molly Malone raises her head to get a good look at the robber. Piper shoots her dead.

35. Police Officer Wassersug is approached by a young boy who tells her that he has spotted what appears to him to be a dead body in the weeds near the bicycle path along the river. Officer Wassersug investigates for herself and further speaks to the boy. She assembles the following information:

Occurrence:	Discovery of body of fully clothed Asian female in early 20s
Date of Discovery:	Sunday, April 30
Time of Discovery:	11:25 A.M.
Location:	Bicycle path, Hudson riverbank near 112th Street
Witness:	Amahl Hussein, age 11
Identity of Victim:	unknown

Officer Wassersug is preparing a report of this incident for the detective squad. Which of the following conveys all the information *most clearly* and *accurately*?

(A) A woman was found by Amahl Hussein on the Hudson bicycle path. He is 11 years old, and he doesn't know her.

(B) There is a body near the bicycle path along the Hudson River at 112th Street. She is an Asian woman, and Amahl Hussein, an 11-year-old, found her.

(C) The body of an unknown Asian woman was found at 11:30 A.M. Sunday, April 30, by 11-year-old Amahl Hussein along the Hudson bicycle path near 112th Street.

(D) On Sunday, April 30, Amahl Hussein found a dead body of a woman near the bicycle path. He said he didn't know her or why she died, but she had her clothes on.

36. Police Officer Castelhano has arrived at the scene of a hit and run accident. He has looked over the situation and has questioned a witness. He has made these notes:

Occurrence:	Hit and run accident
Location:	Intersection of Jerome Avenue and Willow Street
Victim:	Elderly black man
Witness:	Moira Wong of 630 Jerome Avenue, Apt. 5G
Vehicle:	Late-model red two-door sports car with out-of-state license plate

Officer Castelhano has already radioed for an ambulance and is writing up this event in his memo book. Which of the following expresses the information *most clearly* and *accurately*?

(A) A very old black man was hit by Moira Wong in a red sports car at 630 Jerome Avenue, Apt. 5G.
(B) Moira Wong was hit by an elderly black man at the intersection of Jerome Avenue and Willow Street. The red sports car was from out of state.
(C) Moira Wong of 630 Jerome Avenue, Apt. 5G, saw an elderly black man being hit by a red sports car at Jerome and Willow.
(D) A red sports car from out of state hit an old black man in front of Moira Wong at 630 Jerome Avenue.

37. A police officer who has determined that a child with whom he or she is in contact has run away from home should do the following in this order:

1. Bring the child to the Precinct.
2. Prepare Juvenile Report (PD-902).
3. Interview child to determine whereabouts of parent or guardian.
    a. Attempt to contact parent or guardian.
    b. If parent or guardian appears, release child to custody of parent or guardian.
    c. If parent or guardian cannot be reached or refuses to appear, contact Runaway Unit.

Transit Police Officer Schmidt has determined that the nine-year-old boy he has observed hanging about in the subway station all morning has run away from home. He takes the child to the Precinct, asks him his name, address, and telephone number, and goes to the telephone to call his parents. Officer Schmidt has acted

(A) properly; he had to call the parents so as to release child to their custody
(B) improperly; he should have first inquired where the parents could be found at that time
(C) properly; children should not be permitted to hang around in subway stations
(D) improperly; he should have first prepared a Juvenile Report

38. A desk officer who receives a report that a suicide is being attempted must do the following in this order:

1. Ask the precise location where the attempt is occurring.
2. Ask for the sex and race of the attempter, approximate age and name if known.
3. Ask for the name of the person reporting the attempt.
4. Request the address from which the report is coming.
5. Ask if the caller knows the victim. If so,
   a. ask about motive
   b. request names of others who might be of influence in dissuading victim

Police Officer Swenson at the Precinct desk receives a telephoned report from a caller that a woman is about to jump off a bridge. Officer Swenson first asks, "Which bridge?" What should Swenson do next?

(A) Ask, "From what number are you calling?"
(B) Ask, "Can you tell me the race and age of the jumper?"
(C) Ask, "Is the person threatening suicide a man or a woman?"
(D) Notify the rescue squad at once.

39. DISORDERLY CONDUCT is committed when with intent to cause public inconvenience, annoyance, or alarm, or recklessly creating a risk thereof, a person engages in fighting or in violent, tumultuous, or threatening behavior. According to the definition given, which one of the following is the best example of disorderly conduct?

(A) Tom, Dick, and Harry spend much of the evening on Harry's back porch with three six-packs of beer. Then they go into the cemetery and push over a number of headstones.
(B) Lorraine tells her father that there is something wrong with the brakes on her bicycle. Her father puts off looking at the bicycle. Lorraine loses control, flies over the handlebars, and is seriously injured.
(C) For Barry's bachelor party, his friends rent a room at a neighborhood restaurant. The party is very boisterous and rowdy.
(D) Ronald suspects that he did not get the job that he had applied for because David told the boss untruths about Ronald. Ronald goes to David's house and rings the doorbell. When David opens the door, Ronald punches him in the nose.

40. Police Officer Hua has noticed that most of the robberies in her sector occur on Greene Street, most of the auto thefts occur on Linda Lane, and most of the assaults occur on Battle Hill. The robberies occur most frequently between 6:00 P.M. and 10:00 P.M., the auto thefts most frequently occur between 9:00 P.M. and 2:00 A.M., and the assaults tend to occur between 6:00 A.M. and 9:00 A.M. and between 3:00 P.M. and 7:00 P.M. The departmental schedule is about to be altered, and Officer Hua's supervisor is asking for recommendations as to which shifts should be assigned more officers in order to reduce the general crime rate. Officer Hua should recommend that more officers should be assigned to patrol from

(A) Midnight to 8:00 A.M.
(B) 8:00 A.M. to 4:00 P.M.
(C) Noon to 8:00 P.M.
(D) 4:00 P.M. to midnight

41. A small art gallery on Police Officer Bannai's regular patrol has been burglarized. The owner of the gallery, Karel White, has prepared this inventory of missing objects:

2 small bronze sculptures, each valued at	$4500
5 oil paintings, each valued at	$ 930
3 porcelain urns, each valued at	$2220
7 framed prints, each valued at	$ 90
contents of cash register	$ 436

By what formula should Officer Bannai calculate the value of the missing property?

(A) 2 + 4500 + 5 + 930 + 3 + 2220 + 7 + 90 + 436
(B) 2 (4500) + 5 (930) + 3 (2220) + 7 (90) + 436
(C) (2 + 5 + 3 + 7)(4500 + 930 + 2220 + 90 + 436)
(D) (2 + 5 + 3 + 7)(4500 + 930 + 2220 + 90) + 436

42. Police officers are required to respond to areas where persons have become ill or been injured and to render necessary aid, take corrective action, and prepare prescribed forms. Upon arrival at a scene at which aid is required, a police officer should:

1. Render reasonable aid to sick or injured person.
2. Request an ambulance or doctor, if necessary.
3. Wait in view to direct the ambulance or assign some responsible person to do so.
4. If ambulance does not arrive in 20 minutes, make another call.
5. Accompany unconscious or unidentified aided person to hospital in body of ambulance.

Off-duty Police Officer McGonnigle is in the vicinity of a construction site where a heavy steel beam has fallen from the roof and struck a woman passing by on the sidewalk. Officer McGonnigle runs to the scene and finds that the woman is unconscious and is bleeding profusely from a wound to the groin. The first thing Officer McGonnigle should do is

(A) identify himself as a police officer
(B) send for an ambulance
(C) attempt to stop the bleeding by applying pressure
(D) reassure the woman that he will go to the hospital with her

43. Police Officers Makowski and Sevast report in their patrol car to the scene of a just-completed armed robbery of a small shop. In the course of questioning the shop-owner, they gather the following information:

Occurrence:	Knifepoint robbery; $300 cash
Time of Occurrence:	4:23 P.M.
Location:	Barbara's Boutique, 1717 Third Avenue
Victim:	Barbara Betancourt, owner
Witness:	Althea Goulbourne of 836 Madison Road, customer
Suspect:	white female, slight build, red hair, wearing white jeans and a blue tank top

While Officer Sevast attempts to calm and comfort the victim, Officer Makowski must write up this incident. Which of the following expresses the information *most clearly* and *accurately*?

(A) Barbara Betancourt reported at 4:23 P.M. her store Barbara's Boutique was robbed at knifepoint at 1717 Third Avenue. A white woman with red hair took $300 from her wearing white jeans and a blue tank top. Althea Goulbourne watched.

(B) At 4:23 P.M. a red-haired woman took $300 from 836 Madison Road at Barbara's Boutique owned by Barbara Betancourt, who was robbed by a white woman. She was wearing white jeans and a blue tank top and used a knife.

(C) In a robbery that occurred at knifepoint, a red-haired white woman robbed the owner of Barbara's Boutique. Barbara Betancourt, the owner of the 1717 Third Avenue store, was robbed of $300. Althea Goulbourne said that she was wearing white jeans and a blue tank top at 4:23 P.M.

(D) At 4:23 P.M. Barbara Betancourt, owner of Barbara's Boutique, located at 1717 Third Avenue, was robbed of $300 at knifepoint. The suspect is a white female with red hair, wearing white jeans and a blue tank top. Althea Goulbourne of 836 Madison Road witnessed the holdup.

44. Transit Police Officer Trujillo is walking through a subway train which is stalled between stations and comes upon a very pregnant woman writhing on the floor. Passengers in the car are screaming that the woman is about to give birth. There is no way for Officer Trujillo to make the train move, so he delivers the baby. He then jots in his memo book the following information:

Occurrence:	Assisted childbirth, apparently healthy black male infant
Location:	#5 subway car, northbound, between 96th and 103rd Streets
Time:	9:13 P.M.
Mother:	Joan Jordan, 21, 852 St. Nicholas Ave.
Witnesses:	Donato Venezia, conductor, badge 84632
	Laura Wint, 456 East 125th Street
	Carola Cortinez, 9876 Montgomery Ave.

Officer Trujillo must write up this exciting event. Which of the following expresses the information *most clearly* and *accurately*?

(A) Joan Jordan, 21, of 852 St. Nicholas Avenue gave birth to a baby boy in a stalled northbound #5 subway car between 96th and 103rd Streets at 9:13 P.M. Assisting and witnessing were Conductor Donato Venezia, badge 84632, and passengers Laura Wint and Carola Cortinez.

(B) A black baby boy was born on the #5 going north above 93rd Street in a stalled train to Joan Jordan who is 21 and lives at 852 St. Nicholas Avenue. Conductor Donato Venezia says the baby seems healthy. Witnesses were Laura Wint, badge 84632, and Carola Cortinez from Montgomery Street.

(C) Joan Jordan of 852 St. Nicholas Avenue who is 21 says that she had a black baby boy on the subway when it was stuck. Laura Wint of 456 West 125th Street and Carola Cortinez of 9876 Montgomery Street were there.

(D) Laura Wint of 456 East 125th Street and Carola Cortinez of 9876 Montgomery Street were there when the baby was born. It is a healthy black boy said Donato Venezia and Joan Jordan, his mother.

45. Police officers assigned to transport prisoners to court should follow these procedures, in the order given:

1. Obtain an official Prisoner List Form of the prisoners who are due in court.
2. Make certain that the prisoners placed in chains are the same as those listed on the Prisoner List Form and take a head count.
3. Ride in transporting vehicle and keep constant watch of prisoners.
4. Make certain that prisoners are taken to holding area at destination.
5. Contact Station House Supervisor for next assignment.

Police Officers Yahtze and Wilen have been assigned by the Station House Supervisor to take a group of prisoners to court. While Officer Wilen takes a head count, Officer Yahtze checks to be certain that these are the prisoners named on the Prisoner List Form. This action by Officer Yahtze is

(A) proper; Officer Yahtze is watching the prisoners at all times
(B) improper; Officer Yahtze should have put the prisoners in chains
(C) proper; checking against the Prisoner List Form and taking a head count should be done at the same time
(D) improper; Officer Yahtze should have made certain that the prisoners were taken to the holding area

Answer questions 46-48 on the basis of the following map.

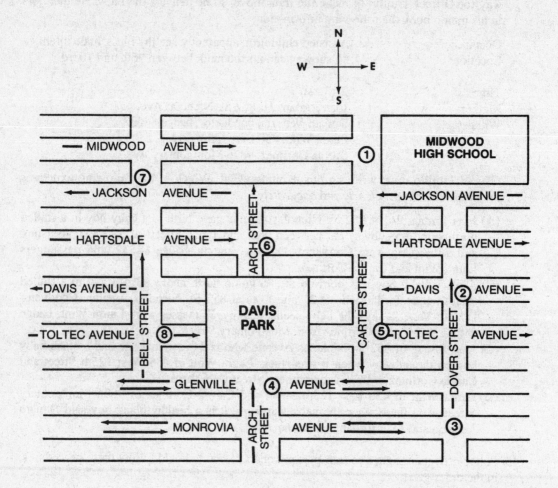

46. You are located at Carter Street and Davis Avenue. You receive a call to respond to a traffic accident at the intersection of Midwood Avenue and Carter Street. Which one of the following is the most direct route for you to take in your patrol car, making sure to obey all traffic regulations?

(A) Travel south on Carter Street for one block, then one block east on Toltec Avenue, then three blocks north on Dover Street, then one block west on Jackson Avenue, then one block north on Carter Street.

(B) Travel two blocks south on Carter Street, then west for two blocks on Glenvilie Avenue, then north for five blocks on Bell Street, then one block east on Midwood Avenue.

(C) Travel one block east on Davis Avenue, then two blocks north on Dover Street, then three blocks west on Jackson Avenue, then north for one block on Bell Street, then one block east on Midwood Avenue.

(D) Travel two blocks south on Carter Street, then east for one block on Glenville Avenue, then north for four blocks on Dover Street, then west for three blocks on Jackson Avenue, then north for one block on Bell Street, then east for one block on Midwood Avenue.

47. If you are located at point (4) and travel west for one block, turn north and travel three blocks, then turn east and travel one block, then turn north and travel one block, and then turn west for one block, you will be closest to point

(A) 7   (C) 1
(B) 6   (D) 8

48. You are located at Davis Avenue and Bell Street. You receive a call of a burglary in progress at Glenville Avenue and Dover Street. Which of the following is the most direct route for you to take in your patrol car, making sure to obey all traffic regulations?

(A) Travel south for two blocks on Bell Street, then east for three blocks on Glenville Avenue.
(B) Travel north three blocks on Bell Street, then east for one block on Midwood Avenue, then south for five blocks on Carter Street, then one block east on Glenville Avenue.
(C) Travel north one block on Bell Street, the east for two blocks on Hartsdale Avenue, then south for three blocks on Carter Street, then one block east on Glenville Avenue.
(D) Travel north one block on Bell Street, then east for three blocks on Hartsdale Avenue, then south for three blocks on Dover Street.

49. When confronted with a report of a missing person, a police officer should request the following information, in this order:

1. Sex of missing person
2. Age of missing person
3. Name of missing person
4. Name and relationship of person making the report.
5. Place and time missing person was last seen.
6. Physical description of person and clothing.

As she rounds a corner on foot patrol, Police Officer Susannah Moses is accosted by a tearful, hysterical woman. The woman blurts out, "My baby she missing." The first question Officer Moses should ask is

(A) "Where did you lose the baby?"   (C) "How old is the baby?"
(B) "Is the baby a boy or a girl?"   (D) "Are you the baby's mother?"

50. Police Officer Jaime Veldez, riding alone in his patrol car in the early morning of November 12, spots an active fire. Officer Veldez quickly notes the following information:

Location of fire:	112 Lorelei Lane, just north of Industrial Highway
Time of report:	3:12 A.M.
Type of structure:	plastics warehouse
Origin of fire:	unknown
Extent of involvement:	active and total; heavy, foul-smelling smoke

Officer Veldez must radio an alarm right away. Which of the following conveys all the information *most clearly* and *accurately*?

(A) A plastics warehouse caught fire all by itself at 3:12 A.M. today at 112 Lorelei Lane. It is north of Industrial Highway and smoking.

(B) There is a big fire at the plastics warehouse at Industrial Highway, North and 112 Lorelei Lane right now. It is November 12 and it is 3:12 A.M. so no one is at work, but it smells awful.

(C) A fire at 112 Lorelei Lane, a plastics warehouse, is burning out of control for unknown reasons north of Industrial Highway. Someone should put it out.

(D) It is 3:12 A.M. and I am approaching a major fire at the plastics warehouse at 112 Lorelei Lane just north of Industrial Highway. The smoke is heavy and may well be toxic.

51. ROUTINE SICK AT HOME — The New York City police department classifies as routine sick at home a call for service in which a sick person is aided at his or her residence and:

a. Is conscious and properly identified;
b. No other police service or notification is required;
c. No dependent adults or uncared for children are in the household; and
d. No other investigation is needed.

According to the definition above, which of the following should be entered in a police officer's log as a routine sick at home call?

(A) Myrtle Cubbage, age 97, became dizzy in her apartment and fell to the living room floor. Her full-time live-in aide, Millie Mohan, was unable to lift her, so called emergency services. Police Officer Ataturk responded to the call, helped Ms. Mohan in lifting Ms. Cubbage to her bed, and found Ms. Cubbage's vital signs to be normal. Ms. Mohan thanked Officer Ataturk for his assistance and assured him that she had the situation well under control.

(B) Police Officer Barbini responded to the call of Hattie Cool who had cut herself very badly while splitting a three-day-old bagel. Officer Barbini noted that the baby appeared to be safely sleeping in his crib and called for an ambulance to transport Ms. Cool to the emergency room to have her hand sutured.

(C) Officer Kaliopolis was called to an apartment house airshaft where she found an unidentified man lying unconscious on the ground. Officer Kaliopolis summoned an ambulance and accompanied the victim to the hospital.

(D) Jimmy Jordan, age 9 and home alone, felt very nauseated and began vomiting. Police Officer Llewellyn, responding to Jimmy's call, found him feeling much better but frightened at having been sick all by himself.

52. Carol White, a woman with a record of convictions for prostitution, has been pointed out to police by a man who admits to having been her client and now accuses her of rifling his pockets while he slept. Upon booking, Ms. White's valuables are removed from her possession and are inventoried. Among the items taken from Carol White are:

1 woman's watch valued at	$ 80
2 woman's rings, each valued at	$120
1 pair earrings valued at	$ 40
1 woman's purse containing	$356
1 man's watch valued at	$625
2 gold chains, each valued at	$110
1 man's alligator wallet valued at	$250
containing: 6 bills @	$ 50
10 bills @	$ 20
5 bills @	$ 5
7 bills @	$ 1

What was the total value of the inventoried items taken from Carol White?

(A) $2113.

(B) $2338.

(C) $2343.

(D) $2443.

53. Transit Police Officer Maloney is concerned with serious crimes committed in subway stations. He has noticed that most robberies occur in the Atlantic Avenue station, most assaults occur in the Clark Street station, and most rapes occur in the Chambers Street station. Most rapes occur between 9:00 P.M. and midnight; most robberies occur between 6:00 P.M. and 8:00 P.M.; and most assaults occur between 7:00 P.M. and 11:00 P.M. Officer Maloney works a 4:00 P.M. to midnight tour and divides his time among these three stations. In order to reduce the number of assaults, Officer Maloney should patrol

(A) Chambers Street station between 8:00 P.M. and 11 P.M.

(B) Clark Street station between 8:30 P.M. and 11:00 P.M.

(C) Atlantic Avenue station between 4:00 P.M. and 8:00 P.M.

(D) Clark Street Station between 4:00 P.M. and 8:00 P.M.

54. Police Officer Assad has stopped and given a summons to a motorist who neglected to come to a full stop at a flashing red light and has collected the following information:

Occurrence:	Ignoring flashing red light
Place of Occurrence:	Intersection of Weaver Street and Murray Avenue
Time of Occurrence:	8:17 A.M.
Driver:	Dorothy Harris, age 54
Address of Driver:	137 Rockledge Road
License number:	NYSS53824179940 — expired

Officer Assad is making an entry of this incident in his memo book. Which of the following expresses the above information *most clearly* and *accurately*?

(A) 54-year old Dorothy Harris drove through the flashing red light at Weaver Street and Murray Avenue. Her license expired.

(B) At 8:17 A.M., Dorothy Harris of 137 Rockledge Road, age 54, drove through the red flasher at Weaver and Murray. Her driver's license, NYSS53824179940 had expired, and I gave her a summons.

(C) Dorothy Harris of 137 Weaver Street ignored a red flashing light at an intersection at 8:17 A.M. She is 54 years old, and her license has expired so I handed her a summons.

(D) At the intersection of Murray Avenue and Rockledge Road, at 8:17 A.M., Dorothy Harris, a 54-year old woman with an expired driver's license, ignored the red flasher. The license number was NYSS53824179940.

55. Police Officer Phansonboom on foot patrol has surprised a suspect in the process of breaking into a car. He has taken the suspect into custody and has obtained the following information:

Suspect:	Nick Harrison, age 17
Address of Suspect:	8768 East 99th Street
Crime:	Attempted auto theft
Location of Crime:	in front of Kimberly Hotel
Date of Occurrence:	March 19
Time of Occurrence:	6:12 A.M.

Officer Phansonboom must write up his arrest for the booking officer. Which of the following expresses this information *most clearly* and *accurately*?

(A) Nick Harrison, age 17, who lives at the Kimberly Hotel, 8768 East 99th Street, tried to steal a car on March 19 at 6:12 A.M.
(B) 17-year old Nick Harrison tried to steal a car in front of the Kimberly Hotel, 8768 East 99th Street, at 6:12 A.M. on March 19th.
(C) On March 19th at 6:12 A.M., Nick Harrison, 17, of 8768 East 99th Street attempted to steal a car from the front of the Kimberly Hotel.
(D) The 17 year old suspect, Nick Harrison of 8678 East 99th Street, attempted to steal a car parked in front of the Kimberly Hotel at 6:12 on the morning of March 19.

56. A police officer who stops a person under suspicion for driving under the influence of alcohol should follow this procedure:

1. Ask the driver to step out of the vehicle.
2. Pat down the driver for weapons.
3. Ask to see license and registration.
4. Ask driver to walk a straight line.
5. Smell breath.
6. Bring driver to police station for chemical testing.

Police Officer Gambino has been following a driver who has been weaving back and forth across the center line of the highway. Officer Gambino pulls the driver to the shoulder and asks to see her driver's license and registration. Officer Gambino has acted:

(A) correctly, because the driver was weaving as if intoxicated
(B) incorrectly, because the driver might have been armed
(C) correctly, because there was alcohol on the driver's breath
(D) incorrectly, because Officer Gambino should first have asked the driver to get out of the car

57. Police officers responding to the scene of suspected domestic violence should:

1. Announce themselves clearly and request admittance.
2. Step away from the doorway to await authorization to enter.
3. If not admitted, force door.
4. Disengage family members and interview separately.
5. If charges are placed, take accused into custody.

Police Officers Ng and Singh report to the an apartment upon the urgent call of a neighbor reporting shouted threats. Officer Ng calls out, "Police, open up." The officers step aside as the door opens. The apartment residents, Gina Girton and Arthur Ogilvy, sheepishly tell the officers that they have been rehearsing their parts in a play and apologize that they have gotten so loud as to disturb the neighbors. The next thing Officers Ng and Singh should do is

(A) leave the apartment
(B) interview Girton and Ogilvy in separate rooms
(C) serve Girton and Ogilvy with a summons for making so much noise
(D) ask if either Girton or Ogilvy wishes to accuse the other

58. Upon returning home from a weekend visit to their grandchildren Dr. and Mrs. O'Leario discover that their home has been ransacked. Police Officer Mbwana arrives to investigate and asks the O'Learios for a list of missing objects. The list includes:

1 color television set valued at	$ 950
2 small black and white TVs, each valued at	$ 150
1 VCR valued at	$ 475
1 home entertainment center, including CD player, tape deck, and 2 speakers, valued at	$2300
Sterling silver service for 12 valued at	$3000

In addition, the intruders destroyed two triple-insulated glass sliding door panels valued at $600 each. By what formula should Officer Mbwana calculate the O'Learios' loss?

(A) $950 + $150 x 2 + $475 + $2300 + ($3000 × 12) + $600
(B) 2($950 + $150) + $475 + 2($2300) + $3000 + 2($600)
(C) $950 + 2($150) + $475 + $2300 + $3000
(D) $950 + 2($150) + $475 + $2300 + $3000 + 2($600)

59. FELONY MURDER is committed when a person, acting alone or with others, commits or attempts to commit the crimes of robbery, burglary, kidnapping, arson, or rape and in the course and furtherance of such crime, or immediate flight therefrom, he, or another participant, if there be any, causes the death of a person other than one of the participants. According to the definition above, which of the following is the best example of the crime of felony murder?

(A) John, Tom, and Frank enter the Tiny Tots Toy Factory through a skylight in hopes of hijacking a loaded truck sitting in one of the bays. While the three are wending their way down through the dark factory, Tom steps into an open elevator shaft, falls three stories, and is killed.

(B) Hank and Harry kidnap a wealthy furniture manufacturer, bury him in a deep pit, and demand ransom from the executive's family. As negotiations drag on, the buried executive suffocates and dies.

(C) Dan and Don accept a contract from Jerry to torch an abandoned building which Jerry owns so that he can collect insurance money. Unknown to Dan, Don, or Jerry, homeless Millicent has been living in the building. Millicent runs from the building in flames and is fortunately rescued by Tillie who is passing by. Tillie rolls Millicent in the dirt, extinguishing the fire, and summons an ambulance which takes Millicent to a hospital for treatment of third degree burns.

(D) Charley patronizes Polly the prostitute. Polly displeases Charley, and Charley slashes her face badly with a razor.

60. Police Officer Cheung has been sent to investigate a report of a missing person. In the course of her interview of the person who made the report, Officer Cheung gathers the following information:

Occurrence:	Disappearance of senile adult
Name of Missing Person:	Annie Hall
Date of report:	Wednesday, August 11
Date of disappearance:	Tuesday, August 10
Description of Missing Person:	White female, age 70, 5' 1", 98 lbs., gray hair, green eyes, wearing colorful flowered housedress and sandals
Location last seen:	Lotus Lake Park
Reported by:	Jane Thompson, daughter, of 66 Ferris Boulevard

Officer Cheung must prepare a bulletin for other members of the department. Which of the following expresses the information *most clearly* and *accurately*?

(A) Annie Hall is missing. Her daughter, Jane Thompson lost her in the park wearing a colorful flowered housedress and sandals. She is 70 and senile and 5' 1".

(B) Jane Thompson, age 66, reports her mother Annie Hall to be missing since Tuesday, August 10 in Lotus Lake Park. Annie Hall is 5' 1", 98 lbs, with gray hair and green eyes. She is wearing a flowered housedress and is senile and 70.

(C) Jane Thompson of 66 Ferris Boulevard reports that her mother, Annie Hall, age 70 and senile, has been missing since Tuesday, August 10. Annie Hall, 5' 1", 98 lbs. with gray hair and green eyes, was last seen in Lotus Lake Park wearing a colorful housedress and sandals.

(D) Annie Hall is missing. Annie is the mother of Jane Thompson who lost her on Ferris Boulevard on August 11. Annie is short and thin with gray hair and green eyes and a colorful dress. She is senile and might be in Lotus Lake Park.

61. Housing Police Officer Hernandez has been sent to the scene of a mugging. Officer Hernandez collects the following information:

Occurrence: Mugging
Location: Elevator, Building 15, Mellow Hills Houses
Time: 4:10 P.M.
Victim: Belinda Bass, 51, Apt. 153-G
Witness: Esme Golden, 28, Building 13
Suspect: Teenage Hispanic male, 5' 6", slight build, black jeans, denim jacket

Officer Hernandez must write up this incident. Which of the following expresses the information *most clearly* and *accurately*?

(A) Esme Golden, 28, who lives in building 13 of Mellow Hills Houses saw a slim teenage Hispanic male in black jeans and a denim jacket mug Belinda Bass of Apt. 153-G in the elevator of Building 15 at 4:10 P.M.
(B) Belinda Bass, 51, of building 13 in Mellow Hills Houses was mugged by a teenage Hispanic male in the elevator at 4:10. Esme Golden who lives in Apt. 153-G saw the boy mug her in black jeans and a blue denim jacket.
(C) A teenage Hispanic male about 5' 6" in black jeans and a denim jacket mugged Belinda Bass in the elevator of Mellow Hills Houses. She is 28. Esme Golden who lives there too saw it.
(D) A mugging happened at 4:10 P.M. in an elevator in Apt. 153-G of Mellow Hills Houses. Belinda Bass got mugged. Esme Golden saw it. The mugger was a Hispanic teenager in black jeans. He was short and slight.

62. When arresting a person who must be transported to the station house in a one-man patrol car, a police officer should:

1. Handcuff the suspect with hands behind the suspect's back.
2. Search the suspect for weapons, drugs, or evidence.
3. Seat the suspect in the right passenger location in the rear seat of the patrol car.
4. Escort the suspect to station house and inform desk officer of the charges.
5. Place suspect in cell and remove handcuffs.

Police Officer Davidson is arresting a suspect whom she has observed jumping up and stomping on the hoods of parked cars. Officer Davidson handcuffs the suspect with his hands behind his back. Then she searches him and removes three glassine envelopes of heroin from his pants pockets. The next thing Officer Davidson should do is

(A) radio the station house to inform the desk officer of the charges
(B) place the suspect in the right front seat of the patrol car so that she can observe him while driving to the station house
(C) place the suspect in the back seat of the patrol car and shackle his feet so that he cannot escape
(D) place the suspect in the right rear seat and drive to the station house

63. If a police officer has good cause to suspect that a person has committed or is about to commit a crime, the officer may stop the person and do the following:

   1. Ask for identification.
   2. Request an explanation of the person's behavior.
   3. Pat down the person for weapons.
   4. If pat down suggests hidden weapons conduct full search of clothing; confiscate weapon.
   5. Arrest person.

   On a hot summer afternoon, Police Officer Sharif observes a woman coming out of Dicey's Department Store in a bulging woolen overcoat. Officer Sharif stops the woman and asks for identification. Then Officer Sharif asks why the woman is dressed so warmly. The woman says that the store is air-conditioned. Officer Sharif pats down the woman, but she is so well padded that he can feel no weapons. Officer Sharif then searches the woman. Sharif's action is

   (A) proper; the woman is obviously a shoplifter and shoplifters must be searched
   (B) improper; Sharif did not feel any weapons so should not have searched the woman
   (C) proper; a weapon could have easily been concealed under or among the layers and bundles under the woman's coat
   (D) improper; there was no reason for Officer Sharif to suspect that the woman had committed or was about to commit a crime

64. **MURDER** is committed when a person, following a period of lengthy planning, intentionally causes the death of another person. According to the above definition, which of the following is the best example of murder?

   (A) Tyrone, a jealous husband, suspects that his wife is having an affair with Errol. Tyrone buys a cheap gun from a man in the street and sits in his parked car just around the corner from Errol's home. Errol comes out of his home and walks to the bus stop to wait for a bus to take him to work. As Errol waits, Tyrone shoots him dead.
   (B) Mary tells John that her father has been molesting her for many years and she would like to see him dead. John and Mary together purchase explosives, and John wires Mary's father's car so that it will explode when he turns the ignition key. Mary's mother borrows her husband's car and is instantly killed when it explodes.
   (C) Cliff and Connie are drug addicts in need of money to buy drugs. They enter the bank, guns in hand, announcing, "This is a stickup." They observe a teller reaching for an alarm button, and Cliff shoots the teller. The teller dies on the way to the hospital.
   (D) Mike does not like to see derelicts lying in doorways. As he passes a drunken man sound asleep, he responds to a sudden urge and lights a match to the man's threadbare trousers. The man lives three weeks, then succumbs to his burns.

65. Police Officer McQueen has become aware of a pattern of drug sales in his sector. The drug "store" seems to be set up in Apt. 4-D at 711 Eighth Avenue from 10:00 A.M. to 2:00 P.M., on the sixth floor landing at 945 West 12th Street from 4:00 P.M. to 8:00 P.M., and in the alleyway behind 87 Blarney Way from 7:30 P.M. to close to midnight. Drug sales are heaviest on Eighth Avenue on Mondays, Tuesdays, and Wednesdays; on Blarney Way on Fridays, Saturdays, and Sundays; and on West 12th Street on Wednesdays, Thursdays, and Fridays. Officer McQueen can have the greatest effect on drug sales by patrolling

(A) Eighth Avenue and West 12th Street on Wednesday from 1:00 P.M. to 6:00 P.M.
(B) West 12th Street and Blarney Way from 5:00 P.M. to 10:00 P.M. on Friday
(C) Thursday from 3:00 A.M. to 10:00 A.M. on Eighth Avenue and Blarney Way
(D) Blarney Way and West 12th Street on Saturday from 3:00 P.M. to 9:00 P.M.

66. Police Officer Regis has been summoned by the superintendent of an apartment building who reports a foul odor coming from Apt. 2-B. When no one responds to Officer Regis's request to open the door, Regis breaks in and discovers a body on the couch. Officer Regis assembles the following information:

Occurrence:	Discovery of dead body
Victim:	Horace Manning, age 83
Location:	19 May Avenue, Apt. 2-B
Time of discovery:	1:15 P.M.
Witness:	Florence Kreplach, superintendent
Cause of death:	unknown

Officer Regis must prepare a report for the Medical Examiner's Department. Which of the following expresses the information *most clearly* and *accurately?*

(A) Florence Kreplach, the superintendent, found the dead body of Horace Manning, age 83, in 2-B at 1:15. It smells.
(B) Horace Manning, 83, of 19 May Avenue, Apt. 2-B, died at 1:15 P.M. today. Florence Kreplach, the superintendent, smelled him. She does not know why he died.
(C) At 1:15 P.M. the body of 83-year old Horace Manning was discovered in his apartment, 2-B at 19 May Avenue. The superintendent, Florence Kreplach, had smelled a bad odor.
(D) From unknown causes, Horace Manning who was 83 died in his apartment at 19 May Avenue at 1:15, Florence Kreplach, the superintendent said. She noticed the odor in Apt. 2-B.

67. Police Officer Nygaard is making an inventory of the belongings of a deceased who lived alone and died in her apartment. The items include:

1 gold wedding band valued at	$ 110.00
1 silver necklace valued at	$ 70.00
2 bracelets with semiprecious stones, each valued at	$ 50.00
1 marcasite brooch valued at	$ 150.00
contents of purse, total value	$ 37.89

What is the sum total value of the items inventoried?

(A) $417.89
(B) $428.89
(C) $467.89
(D) $468.89

68. Routine procedure upon arresting a suspect is to take fingerprints for purposes of positive identification. Fingerprinting is done in the following manner:

1. Ask person to relax hands and fingers and let the officer do the rolling.
2. Prepare the fingerprint charts as follows:
   a. Two copies of Criminal Fingerprint Record
   b. One copy of FBI Fingerprint Chart
   c. One copy of State Fingerprint Chart
   d. If juvenile, one copy of State Juvenile Fingerprint Chart
3. Prepare two copies of palm prints.
4. Take photographs, full face and profile.

Police Officer Taormina responds to a call from Mitchell Rubin, owner of Motown Cleaners. Rubin complains of a woman who keeps darting behind the counter and tearing up plastic garment bags. The woman, who appears to be about 23 years of age, refuses to give her name or address. Officer Taormina takes her to the station house, asks her to relax her hands and fingers, and begins to roll fingerprints. Taormina prepares two sets for the woman's criminal record, one set for the FBI, and one set for the State Fingerprint Chart. Next Officer Taormina should

(A) prepare a set of fingerprints for the State Juvenile Chart
(B) check the records to see if this woman is known to the police
(C) take front face and profile photographs of the woman in duplicate
(D) take palmprints

69. The bank manager has summoned Police Officer Goola with an excited account of a break-in at the bank. Here is what he told to Officer Goola:

Occurrence:	Break-in, bank and vault
Date of Occurrence:	During the night January 5-6
Time of Occurrence:	Between 5:30 P.M. and 8:00 A.M.
Place of Occurrence:	First Fidelity Bank, Green Mall branch
Reporter:	Walter Briggs, bank manager
Crime discovered by:	Marsha Szymborska, vault officer
Missing objects:	Contents of safe deposit boxes 138 to 266 and one large canvas money sack, serial #9088098

Officer Goola must write up this event for the department's investigators and for a preliminary report to be sent to the Treasury Department. Which of the following expresses the information *most clearly* and *accurately*?

(A) During the night of January 5-6, thieves broke into the vault of the Green Mall branch of First Fidelity Bank and took contents of over 100 safe deposit boxes in money sack #9088098. The crime was discovered by the vault officer, Marsha Szymborska, after 8:00 A.M., January 6, and was reported by the bank manager, Walter Briggs.
(B) Marsha Szymborska discovered that the bank had been robbed when she came to work at 5:30 on January 6. She said that safe deposit boxes 138-266 had been emptied into a money sack. The bank manager, Walter Briggs, told me that the bank is in the Green Mall and the money sack was #9088098.
(C) Walter Briggs, the manager of First Fidelity Bank, told me that Marsha Szymborska broke into the vault of safe deposit boxes 138-266 and took a money sack #9088098. This happened between closing on January 5 and opening on January 6 at the Green Mall.
(D) A money sack #9088098 is missing from First Fidelity Bank in Green Mall full of safe deposit boxes 138-266 said Marsha Szymborska and Walter Briggs between 5:30 P.M. and 8:00 A.M. on January 5th or 6th.

70. A police officer making an arrest must do the following in the order given:

1. Inform the prisoner of the reason for the arrest, unless the prisoner is caught in the act of committing the crime.
2. Handcuff the prisoner's hands behind his or her back.
3. Search the prisoner and the area around the prisoner for weapons and evidence.
4. Recite "Miranda Warnings" to prisoner.
5. Be sure that prisoner understands legal rights before questioning.

Police Officer Polisario patrolling the city park comes upon Harold Painter shooting squirrels with a single barrel shotgun. Officer Polisario handcuffs Painter's hands behind his back, searches Painter for ammunition, and walks around the area picking up dead squirrels. He then carefully explains Painter's legal rights to him. Officer Polisario is acting

(A) properly; dead squirrels should not be permitted to lie around
(B) improperly; Painter should have been told why he was being arrested
(C) properly; he handcuffed the prisoner's hands behind his back before searching him or the area
(D) improperly; there was no reason to search because the gun was in plain sight

71. MENACE is committed when a person, by physical threat, intentionally places, or attempts to place, another person in a state of fear of imminent and serious physical injury. According to the above definition, which of the following is the best example of menace?

(A) In his eagerness to get on the bus, Steve pushes Barney aside and kicks him as he rushes up the steps.
(B) Sol has had a fierce argument with his girlfriend who is Clara's mother. In an attempt to get even with his girlfriend, he sends a letter to Clara in which he threatens to kidnap her.
(C) In the crowded entry to the baseball stadium, Kyle reaches for the flap of Beverly's pocketbook and attempts to open it. Beverly slaps his hand away.
(D) Lonnie calls Charlene every day at 7:00 P.M. and again at 9:30 P.M. As soon as Charlene answers the phone, Lonnie hangs up.

72. Police Officer Barton arrives at the scene of a street fight. He jots down the following information:

Occurrence:	street fight
Location:	in front of Hennesey's Bar
Time:	11:34 P.M.
Participants:	Tom Jones, 20, of 35 Ocean Drive
	John Smith, 41, bartender, of 683 Tompkins Drive
	Bill Brown, 26, of 76 Pye Place
Witnesses:	Gerald Jerome, 38, of 11 Oregon St.
	Elizabeth Adz, 34, of 99 E. 9th St.

After breaking up the fight, Officer Barton must write up the incident for his daily activity report. Which of the following expresses the information *most clearly* and *accurately?*

(A) John Smith, the bartender at Hennesey's Bar, threw out Tom Jones who was only 20, and then there was a big fight. Gerald Jerome who lives at 11 Oregon Street joined the fight. I broke it up at 11:34 P.M. while Elizabeth Adz watched.
(B) There was a fight in front of Hennesey's Bar at 11:34 P.M. The fighters were 20-year old Tom Jones of 35 Ocean Drive, the bartender John Smith of 683 Tompkins Drive, and Bill Brown, age 34. The fight was witnessed by Elizabeth Adz and Gerald Jerome who watched it.
(C) Tom Jones, 20, of 35 Ocean Drive got into a fight with John Smith, 41, the bartender, and Bill Brown, 26, of 76 Pye Place in front of Hennesey's Bar around 11:30 P.M. The fight was seen by Elizabeth Adz of 99 E. 9th Street and Gerald Jerome, 38, of 11 Oregon Street.
(D) At a fight in Hennesey's Bar, 683 Tompkins Avenue, the bartender, John Smith, fought with Tom Jones, 20, and Bill Brown, 26, who lives at 76 Pye Place. The witnesses who came to the fight were Elizabeth Adz, 34, of 99 E. 9th St. and Gerald Jerome.

73. Police Officer Zorah has been called to the home of a woman who has an Order of Protection against her estranged husband but is being harassed by him. At the woman's home, Officer Zorah collects the following information:

Occurrence:	Violation of Order of Protection
Location:	78 Highland Way, upstairs apt.
Time:	5:56 A.M.
Complainant:	Rita Rogers, 25
Accused:	Benjamin Rogers, 27, 986 Central Avenue, apt. 14
Activity:	Breaking and entering, threat of rape

Officer Zorah must write up this incident. Which of the following expresses the information *most clearly* and *accurately?*

(A) Rita Rogers, 25, under Order of Protection, says that at 5:56 A.M. her husband, Benjamin Rogers, 27, almost raped her upstairs at 986 Central Avenue.
(B) At 5:56 A.M. Benjamin Rogers, 27, of 986 Central Avenue, broke into the upstairs apartment at 78 Highland Way and threatened to rape his wife Rita Rogers, 25, though under court order to stay away from her.
(C) Rita Rogers complained that her husband Benjamin Rogers, in violation of court order, broke into her apartment at 5:56 A.M. in apartment 14 upstairs and tried to rape her at 78 Highland Way.
(D) Rita Rogers, 25, of 78 Highland Way was under court Order of Protection from her husband Benjamin Rogers who raped her upstairs at 5:56 A.M. when he broke in. He lives at 986 Central Avenue and is 27.

74. HARASSMENT is committed when a person intends to harass, annoy, or alarm another person and does so by striking, shoving, kicking, or otherwise subjecting the other person to physical contact. According to the above definition, which of the following is the best example of harassment?

(A) Peter's dog has overturned Darlene's garbage can once too often, and Darlene is tired of cleaning up the mess. Darlene sprinkles rat poison on chicken bones in the garbage can.

(B) As he is trying to get off a very crowded subway car, Bruce tugs a folded newspaper from Philip's arm, thinking it is his own.

(C) In hopes of extorting money, Michael writes letters to Jackson, threatening to expose an extramarital affair in which Jackson has been involved unless Jackson pays him handsomely.

(D) Six-foot-two inch Lawrence grabs five-foot-seven-inch Eric by the shoulders and shakes him hard while saying, "Stay away from my little brother. If I catch you smoking reefer with him, I'll shake you to death."

75. A Police Officer who responds to the scene of a serious crime should proceed as follows:

1. Look quickly over the scene and assess the nature and severity of the crime.
2. Interview the complainant and witnesses.
3. Gather evidence.
4. Prepare a Complaint Report.
5. Determine if complaint can be closed or where it should be referred for further investigation.

Police Officer Yves Montand on foot patrol discovers an unconscious middle-aged well-dressed man lying in the gutter. Officer Montand rolls the man over and notes that the man is lying in a small pool of blood and has a gunshot wound to the shoulder but that he is not bleeding profusely. Officer Montand radios for an ambulance. The next thing Montand should do is

(A) interview the man
(B) look for a bullet
(C) decide where to refer the case for further investigation
(D) interview the witnesses

76. If a suspect being taken into custody has sustained wounds in the course of committing the crime or being taken into custody, the arresting officer should do the following:

1. Handcuff the prisoner with hands behind his or her back.
2. Request an ambulance and ride in the ambulance with the prisoner.
3. Check with hospital personnel as to security of area of hospital in which prisoner is being held and examined.
4. Inform physician about circumstances of arrest.
5. Remain with prisoner at all times.
6. Remove handcuffs only upon request by attending physician.

Police Officer Acholonu has successfully resolved a hostage situation by shooting the alleged hostage taker in the leg. While other officers are caring for the needs of the hostages, Acholonu handcuffs the prisoner with her hands behind her back and sends for an ambulance. Acholonu rides to the hospital with the prisoner, then asks about security in the emergency room in which the prisoner is to be examined and assisted. Satisfied that security is tight, Acholonu goes into the physician's office to explain the charges and the source of the injury to the doctor. Acholonu's actions are

(A) appropriate; he rode in the ambulance with the prisoner
(B) inappropriate; he should have removed the handcuffs so that the physician could better examine the prisoner
(C) appropriate; he had to explain the circumstances of the case to the physician
(D) inappropriate; he should not have left the prisoner alone in the examining room

77. LARCENY is committed when a person intentionally deprives another of property or wrongfully takes, obtains, or withholds property from the owner of that property without the use of force, violence, or threat of injury. According to this definition, the best example of larceny is:

(A) Carmen has just taken a swim in the public pool and is in the locker room getting dressed. She notices that the door to the adjacent locker is ajar, reaches in, and takes a $20 bill from the wallet in the locker.
(B) Penelope's mother has asked her to run a number of errands. Penelope is willing to help out, but is impatient and eager to complete the errands quickly because it is almost time for a favorite television program. She sees a bicycle lying on a front lawn on her way to the store. Penelope takes the bicycle and rapidly completes the errands. On her way back, she carefully replaces the bicycle where she had found it.
(C) Bentley holds out a toy gun and says to the delivery truck driver, "Your money or your life." The truck driver looks carefully, then says, "Go ahead and shoot." Bentley runs away.
(D) As Eugene is attempting to pry open her pocketbook, Tara reaches down to push his hand away. Eugene cuts the strap of the pocketbook, slashing Tara's arm slightly, and runs off with the pocketbook.

78. CRIMINAL TRESPASS is committed when a person enters or remains in a building he has no right to be in and, while there, possesses, or has knowledge of another person accompanying him possessing a weapon. According to the above definition, which of the following is the best example of criminal trespass?

(A) Dean and Kent discover that a side door of a warehouse has inadvertently been left unlocked. They slip in after dark in hope of finding something they would like to steal. They manage to elude the armed night watchman.

(B) Somehow Bridgitte is in a room overlooked by museum guards at closing time and gets locked into the museum. She sets off a fire alarm to alert authorities to her plight.

(C) Scott and Ian have hidden behind a pile of cartons and have remained in the sporting goods store after its closing for the night. As they prepare to help themselves to expensive equipment, Ian says, "I hear a noise." Scott replies, "Don't worry, I have a gun."

(D) Diane, a homeless person, beds down for the night on a subway platform. At the other end of the same platform, sleeps Douglas with a knife in his pocket.

79. Police Officer Paik receives information about a cock fight in progress. Officer Paik investigates, then sends for reinforcements. Paik begins making notes while waiting for backup officers to make the arrest. At the booking, he completes these notes:

Occurrence:	cock fight and gambling
Location:	basement, 58 West 158th St.
Time:	11:30 P.M.
Principal participants:	Bill Rice, 39, 62 W. 158th St.
	Joe Frost, 43, 12 E. 143rd St.
Gamblers:	Phil Pott, 27, 980 Broadway
	Don Rose, 28, 134 E. 143rd St.
Informant:	anonymous Hispanic woman, about 22 yrs.

Officer Paik must write up this incident for his daily activity log. Which of the following expresses the information *most clearly* and *accurately?*

(A) Bill Rice, 39, of 62 W. 158th St. and Joe Frost, 43, of 12 E. 143rd St. were fighting and Phil Pott, 27, of 980 Broadway and Don Rose, 28, of 134 E. 143rd St. were gambling said an unknown 22-yr. old woman.

(B) Bill Rice who lives at 62 W. 158th St. and Joe Frost who lives at 12 E. 143rd St. were having a cock fight in the basement of Bill Rice's building at 11:30 P.M. A 22-yr. old woman and Phil Pott and Don Rose placed bets.

(C) 39-yr. old Bill Rose of 62 W. 158th St. fought the cock of 43-yr. old Joe Frost at 58 W. 158th St. in the basement at 11:30 P.M. The anonymous witness, who is about 22, said that there were gamblers from 980 Broadway and E. 143rd St. too.

(D) At 11:30 P.M. a Hispanic woman told me of a cock fight in the basement of 58 W. 158th St. I found Bill Rice, 39, of 62 W. 158th St. and Joe Frost, 43, of 12 E. 143rd St. fighting their birds. Phil Pott of 980 Broadway and Don Rose of 134 E. 143rd St. were betting on the fight.

80. Police Officer Jorgenson is dispatched to investigate an allegation of child abuse in progress. Officer Jorgenson collects the following information:

Complaint: Child abuse
Location: 1530 East 18th St., Apt.7A
Complaint by: Martje vanDam, 79, Apt.7E
Alleged victim: Jonathan Grant, age 9
Alleged abusers: Mary Grant, mother, and Jack Frost, her boyfriend
Finding: Allegation unfounded

Officer Jorgenson is preparing a report of this incident. Which of the following expresses the information *most clearly* and *accurately?*

(A) Martje vanDam said that Mary Grant and Jack Frost were beating Jonathan Grant. They weren't.
(B) Mary Grant and Jack Frost, Apt.7A, 1530 East 18th Street, were accused by Martje vanDam, age 79, of Apt.7E, of abusing Mary Grant's 9-year old son Jonathan Grant. I found no signs of child abuse.
(C) Mary Grant and Jack Frost, who is her boyfriend, said that they did not abuse Jonathan Grant at Apt.7E. Martje vanDam of 1530 East 18th Street said they did. She is 79.
(D) Jonathan Grant, 9, of Apt.7A, 1530 East 18th St., was not abused by his mother or her boyfriend even though Martje vanDam of Apt.7E said he was.

81. Jared Kevy parked his BMW in a municipal parking garage overnight. The next morning, he discovered that the car had been broken into. He told police officers that missing items consisted of:

1 radio valued at	$900
1 tape player valued at	$655
9 tapes, each valued at	$ 12
15 bridge tokens, each valued at	$ 6
1 winter coat valued at	$237

By what formula should police calculate the value of the missing items?

(A) $900 + $655 + (9 + 15)($12 + $6) + $237
(B) $900 + $655 + (9)($12) + (15)($6) + $237
(C) $900 + $655 + $9 + $12 + $15 + $6 + $237
(D) $900 + $655 + (9)(15) + ($12)($6) + $237

82. If a police officer discovers a vehicle which appears to have been abandoned, the officer should do the following:

1. Make a memo book entry describing the vehicle and the location at which the vehicle was found.
2. Notify the desk officer and request a registration check.
3. Check registration and vehicle identification number against stolen automobile files.
4. Arrange for removal of vehicle.
5. Notify owner.

Police Officer Fulco covering a regular beat in a patrol car, has noticed a badly battered red Camaro that has not been moved from a spot too close to a crosswalk for a full week. Officer Fulco makes a memo book entry, notifies the desk officer, and requests a registration check. Next, Officer Fulco should

(A) arrange for removal of the vehicle
(B) notify the owner
(C) check the stolen automobile files
(D) write a complete report

83. Police officers happening upon a crime in progress must take special care to safeguard their own lives and the lives of citizens who happen to be in the vicinity of the crime. The order in which to proceed is as follows:

1. Clear the immediate vicinity of casual bystanders quickly and as unobtrusively as possible.
2. Stand to the sides of the outer doorway and announce their presence as police officers.
3. Draw weapons and enter premises.
4. Clear premises of bystanders.
5. Attempt to overpower perpetrators.
6. Do not shoot unless necessary to save innocent lives.

Police Officers Rose and Redhead happen to walk by a liquor store in time to see an armed holdup in progress. Officer Rose orders all bystanders in the street to move away at once. Officer Redhead stands to one side of the doorway and announces, "Police officers; drop your weapons." The startled robber drops his gun to the floor. Officer Redhead then draws his gun and enters the liquor store. Officer Redhead is acting

(A) properly; he is entering the scene of a crime in progress
(B) improperly; the robber has dropped his gun so the police officer should not draw his
(C) properly; he was right to clear customers from the store before shooting
(D) improperly; he should have attempted to overpower the robber before drawing his gun

84. Transit Police Officer Urinyi riding a subway car realizes that a small girl sitting on a seat is unaccompanied and that her face is tear-streaked. Officer Urinyi approaches the child and gathers the following information:

Location:	Northbound A train, between 42nd Street and 59th Street
Date:	Tuesday, June 5
Time:	10:40 A.M.
Occurrence:	Lost child
Name of Child:	Linda LoCicero
Description:	white female approximately 4 yrs. old, blond hair, gray eyes, about 3 ft. tall, wearing red shorts, white blouse, and sandals; address unknown

Officer Urinyi must call in this report to the supervisor for broadcast to precincts and the Missing Persons Bureau. Which of the following expresses the information *most clearly* and *accurately*?

(A) Linda LoCicero was left on the A train at 10:40 A.M. on Tuesday, June 5. She is about 4 and blond and is lost between 42nd Street and 59th Street. She doesn't know where she lives.
(B) A 4-year-old blond girl named Linda LoCicero is riding the A train all alone from 42nd Street to 59th Street and is going north. She wears white shorts, a red t-shirt, and red sneakers.
(C) At 10:40 this morning, Tuesday, June 5, I found a small blond girl alone on the northbound A train between 42nd Street and 59th Street. Her name is Linda LoCicero. She has on red shorts, a white blouse, and sandals and is unable to give her address.
(D) This morning Linda LoCicero, about 4, was riding alone on the A train from 42nd Street to 59th Street on Tuesday at 10:40 A.M. She is about 3 feet tall and is blond. She lives in the northbound direction in red shorts and a white blouse.

85. ARSON is committed when an individual intentionally starts a fire that causes damage to a building or that ignites an explosion. According to this definition, which of the following is the best example of arson?

(A) Lou and Pete have had too much to drink and are looking for trouble. They pass a man they identify as being gay, wrestle him to the ground, pour lighter fluid on him, and set him afire.

(B) Jenny is taking a short cut through a used car lot and is smoking a cigarette. She absently tosses away her cigarette which lands in a puddle of gasoline that has leaked under a car. The gasoline bursts into flame, the flames lick the car, and the car explodes.

(C) As Sheldon is driving along a heavily wooded section of highway, his old car shudders and smoke pours from under the hood. Sheldon jumps out and into the street just as the car explodes. Fire from the car ignites dry leaves and soon grows into a major forest fire.

(D) Bob has been working for farmer White for six months without a raise and is very angry. He starts a fire in the chicken yard, and soon the chicken coop goes up in flames. Many chickens perish.

Answer questions 86 through 90 on the basis of the following sketches. The first face on top is a sketch of an alleged criminal based on witnesses' descriptions at the crime scene. One of the four sketches below that face is the way the suspect might look after changing his or her appearance. Assume that NO surgery has been done on the suspect's face.

86.

(A)   (C)

(B)   (D)

87.

(A)

(C)

(B)

(D)

88.

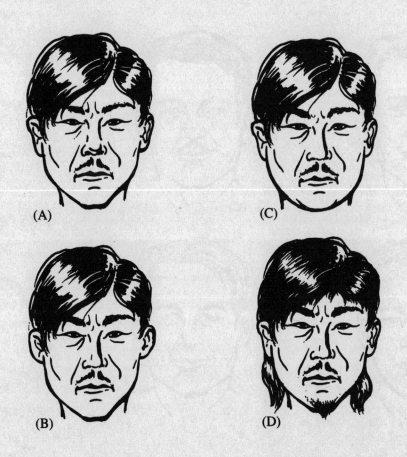

(A)

(C)

(B)

(D)

89.

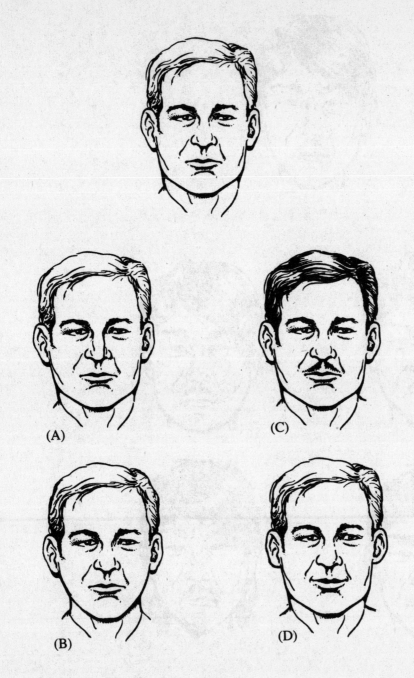

90.

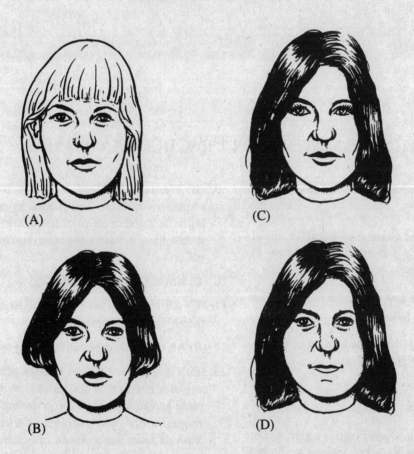

(A)

(C)

(B)

(D)

ANSWER KEY FOR PRACTICE EXAMINATION 3

1. B	11. C	21. C	31. A	41. B	51. A	61. A	71. B	81. B
2. D	12. B	22. A	32. D	42. C	52. C	62. D	72. C	82. C
3. C	13. D	23. B	33. B	43. D	53. B	63. C	73. B	83. A
4. A	14. A	24. D	34. A	44. A	54. B	64. A	74. D	84. C
5. B	15. B	25. C	35. C	45. C	55. C	65. B	75. B	85. D
6. B	16. A	26. D	36. C	46. B	56. D	66. C	76. D	86. B
7. D	17. D	27. B	37. D	47. A	57. A	67. C	77. A	87. B
8. C	18. C	28. A	38. B	48. C	58. D	68. D	78. C	88. D
9. A	19. A	29. C	39. A	49. B	59. B	69. A	79. D	89. C
10. C	20. B	30. C	40. D	50. D	60. C	70. C	80. B	90. B

EXPLANATORY ANSWERS FOR PRACTICE EXAMINATION 3

1. **(B)** Margaret Pickford is a known heroin addict.

2. **(D)** Antonio Gomez is wanted for armed robbery. He is missing the last finger of his right hand.

3. **(C)** Arthur Lee often attacks his victims in subway passageways.

4. **(A)** Robert Miller has a tattoo of a dragon on his right upper arm.

5. **(B)** Janet Walker has a large hairy mole on her upper left thigh.

6. **(B)** Antonio Gomez carries a gun. Arthur Lee carries a wicked looking knife, but Lee is not offered among the choices.

7. **(D)** Margaret Pickford, who walks with a limp because her left leg is shorter than her right, has a child in foster care so obviously is a parent.

8. **(C)** Antonio Gomez escaped from the scene of a recent armed robbery in a stolen yellow 1987 Corvette.

9. **(A)** Margaret Pickford, who is a drug addict, has a severe limp caused by one leg's being shorter than the other so would have a hard time running from police.

10. **(C)** Arthur Lee is wanted for rape.

11. **(C)** All other choices confuse addresses thereby giving misinformation.

12. **(B)** All other choices confuse locations.

13. **(D)** The complete license number of the vehicle that fled is not known, so the name and address of its owner cannot be immediately determined. Officer Yoshida must get as much information as possible from the remaining driver.

14. **(A)** The trip is over upon arrival at the station house. This is the time to search the prisoner area of the car.

15. **(B)** Robberies occur most frequently on Maple Street on Wednesdays and Fridays between 4:00 P.M. and 10:00 P.M. Patrolling from 4:00 P.M. to midnight certainly covers the time span.

16. **(A)** Burglary occurs when there is intent to commit a crime in a building in which the burglar has no right to be at that time. The crime itself need not actually occur. In (B) and (D) the perpetrators are legitimately in the buildings and had not entered for purposes of committing crimes. In (C) there is neither crime nor intent to commit a crime.

17. **(D)** None of the other choices covers the facts.

18-23. If you made any mistakes, read again.

24. **(D)** The car was not unoccupied.

25. **(C)** Officer Patel used his radio, so firefighters already know the location of the fire. Surely he should not block the entrance; firefighters must be able to reach the fire. Residents must be alerted and evacuated to safety. Firefighters are best equipped to put out the fire.

26. **(D)** Choices (A) and (C) get it all wrong. (B) is incomplete.

27. **(B)** Only this choice gives all the needed information correctly.

28. **(A)** The damage, though not expensive, was caused by an explosion. In (B) the cost of the damage without an explosion does not place it into the criminal mischief category. In (C) and (D) there is no intent.

29. **(C)** The robberies are on Second Avenue on Sundays and Mondays between 8:00 P.M. and 1:00 A.M. Patrolling from 7:30 through 12:00 P.M. in the appropriate place on the appropriate days should help to reduce robberies.

30. **(C)** silver candlesticks

$2 \times \$110 =$	$\$ 220.00$
diamond bracelet	1200.00
18-kt. gold chains	
$3 \times \$250 =$	$\$ 750.00$
cash	$+ 719.00$
	$\$2889.00$

31. **(A)**

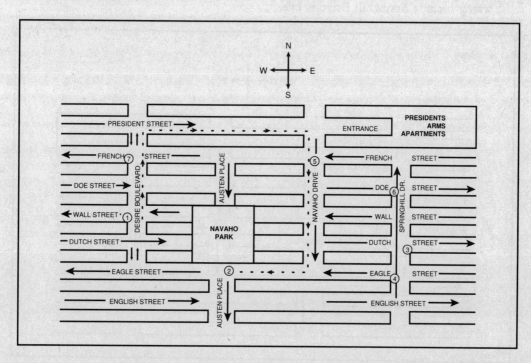

32. **(D)** Choice (A) is wrong because Eagle Street is one-way westbound; **(B)** is wrong because going south on Navaho Drive will never get you to Austin Place, which is parallel to Navaho; (C) is wrong because French Street is one-way westbound.

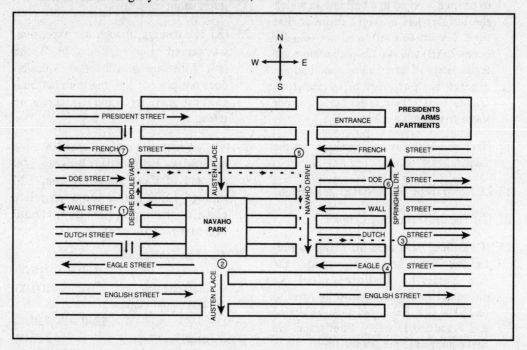

33. **(B)** Choice (A) is wrong because Navaho Drive is one-way southbound; (C) is wrong because Springhill Drive is one-way northbound; (D) is legal but it most certainly is not the shortest route.

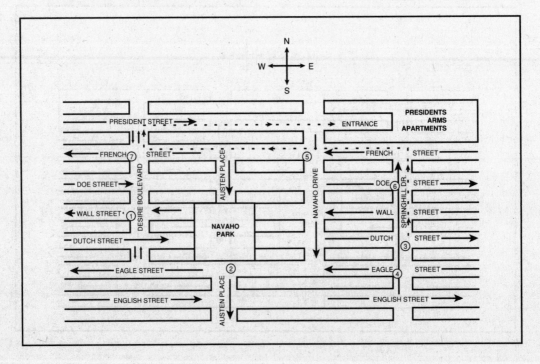

34. **(A)** Roger's reckless driving caused an innocent death. In all other choices, the deaths were caused intentionally, though some were not premeditated.

35. **(C)** All other choices give incomplete information.

36. **(C)** Choices (A) and (B)confuse the victim and the perpetrator; in (D) the location is wrong.

37. **(D)** Officer Schmidt skipped the step in which he should have prepared the Juvenile Report.

38. **(B)** The caller told the officer that the threatening suicide is a woman, and Officer Swenson has already determined the location of the attempt. The next facts to be gathered are race and age of person involved.

39. **(A)** The only reason to go into a cemetery and to push over headstones is to annoy and to cause public inconvenience. In (B) and (C) there is no intent. In (D) the intent is to do real harm, not merely to alarm. The offense is greater than disorderly conduct.

40. **(D)** Most crimes occur in this time span.

41. **(B)** In words, this formula reads: two times $4500 for the bronze sculptures plus five times $930 for the oil paintings plus three times $2220 for the porcelain urns plus seven times $90 for the framed prints plus $436.

42. **(C)** First aid comes first.

43. **(D)** Choice (A) gives no details on the witness; (B) has the address of the robbery wrong; in (C) it is unclear who was wearing white jeans and a blue tank top.

44. **(A)** This choice omits addresses of the witnesses, but all other information is clear and complete. All other choices are garbled and incomplete or erroneous.

45. **(C)** This is step 2.

46. **(B)** Choice (A) is wrong because Carter Street is one-way southbound; (C) is wrong because Davis Avenue is one-way westbound; (D) is legal but unnecessarily long and roundabout.

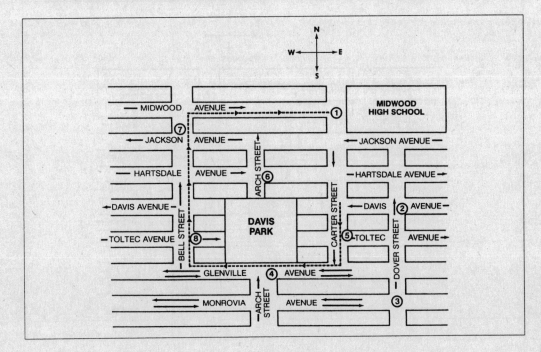

47. (A)

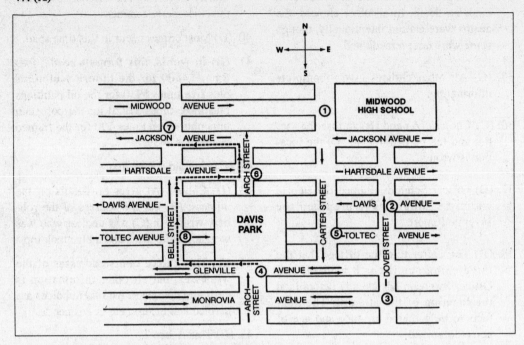

48. (C) Choice (A) is wrong because Bell Street is one-way northbound; (B) is legal but longer than necessary; (D) is wrong because Dover Street is one-way northbound.

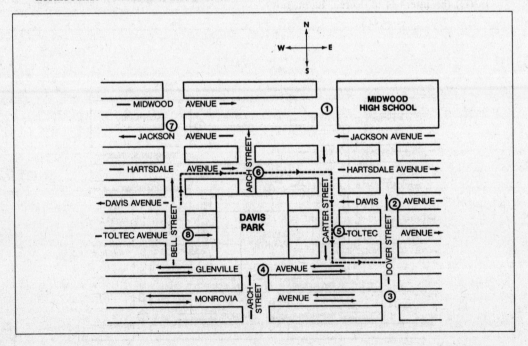

49. **(B)** The statement blurted by the hysterical woman is made in broken English; there is no verb. Foreign-born persons often have difficulty mastering English pronouns. To be certain that the woman is not confused, Officer Moses should ask whether the baby is a boy or a girl as directed in the official procedures.

50. **(D)** All the choices place the fire correctly and give the most vital information, but (D) is clearest and most easily followed.

51. **(A)** In choice (B) action was required and there was an infant in the household; in (C) further action was taken; in (D) there was a child needing care.

52. **(C)**

woman's watch		$ 80
woman's rings	2 × $120 =	240
earrings		40
woman's purse		356
man's watch		625
gold chains	2 × $110 =	220
man's alligator wallet		250
$50 bills	6 × $ 50 =	300
$20 bills	10 × $ 20 =	200
$ 5 bills	5 × $ 5 =	25
$ 1 bills	7 × $ 1 = +	7
		$2,343

53. **(B)** The greatest number of assaults occur in the Clark Street station during the late evening and early night hours.

54. **(B)** Choices (A) and (C) give incomplete information. In (D), the location of the incident is incorrect.

55. **(C)** Choices (A) and (B) confuse locations of crime and residence; (D) reverses digits in the suspect's address.

56. **(D)** These rules are for the officer's protection. The suspect should be removed from the vehicle and checked for weapons before license and registration are requested.

57. **(A)** The officers correctly followed procedures for gaining entrance to the apartment. Having learned that there is no problem and that the occupants are ready to cooperate with their neighbors in toning down the volume, they should leave.

58. **(D)** In words, this formula reads: $950 for the color TV plus two times $150 for the black-and-white TVs plus $475 for the VCR plus $2300 for the home entertainment center plus $3000 for the silver service plus two times $600 for the door panels.

59. **(B)** In (A) one of the participants dies; in (C) and (D) nobody dies.

60. **(C)** Choice (A) is incomplete and a bit confusing as to who was wearing the housedress; in (B) the daughter is reported to be only four years younger than the mother; (D) confuses both date and location.

61. **(A)** None of the other choices identifies the location at which the mugging occurred.

62. **(D)** The procedure does not specify foot shackles, so the officer should seat the suspect in the right passenger location and drive to the station house.

63. **(C)** Officer Sharif has good reason to suspect that the woman is concealing something, quite possibly a weapon, under her inappropriate clothing.

64. **(A)** In all other choices there was no lengthy planning for the death of the person who was killed.

65. **(B)** Friday is a heavy drug sale day on both West 12th Street and Blarney Way and the time span 5:00 P.M. to 10:00 P.M. fits into the sales hours of 4:00 P.M. to midnight.

66. **(C)** Choice (A) gives incomplete information. (B) and (D) incorrectly fix a time of death.

67. **(C)**

gold wedding band		$110.00
silver necklace		70.00
bracelets	2 x $50.00 =	100.00
marcasite brooch		150.00
contents of purse		37.89
		$467.89

68. **(D)** The suspect is not a juvenile, so the next step is to take palmprints.

69. **(A)** Choice (B) does not identify the bank; (C) and (D) are garbled and incorrect.

70. **(C)** The search at this point was for spent cartridges and dead squirrels. Painter did not need to be told what he was doing wrong. Firing guns in city parks is illegal.

71. **(B)** In choice (A) there is no intent; in (C) the fear is of pickpocketing not of physical harm; in (D) there is no threat.

72. **(C)** Choice (A) gives incomplete information; (B) has Bill Brown's age wrong and doesn't fully identify the witnesses; (D) assumes that the bartender lives in the bar.

73. **(B)** Choice (A) has the location of the incident wrong; (C) is a bit confused and does not adequately identify Benjamin Rogers; (D) erroneously accuses Rogers of rape rather than of attempted rape.

74. **(D)** Choice (C) presents an intimidating situation, but since there is no physical contact, it does not fit the definition of harassment.

75. **(B)** The man is unconscious so cannot be interviewed, and there is no mention of witnesses. (One can assume that witnesses might have drawn the officer's attention to the man in the gutter rather than leaving it to the officer to stumble upon him.) Officer Montand should now look for evidence such as a bullet.

76. **(D)** Careful reading of the procedure indicates that the doctor should be briefed in the examining room so that the officer may remain with the prisoner.

77. **(A)** In (B) the property is not withheld; in (C) nothing is taken; (D) does involve violence so does not fulfill the requirements of the definition of larceny.

78. **(C)** In (A) the armed watchman is not accompanying the trespassers, so their offense is not criminal trespass; in (B) there is no weapon and in (D) there is no knowledge.

79. **(D)** Choice (A) misses the point that there was a cock fight; choice (B) places the cock fight in the wrong building and makes the informant a participant; (C) confuses names and is very garbled.

80. **(B)** Choice (A) is very incomplete; (C) and (D) are stated very childishly.

81. **(B)** In words, this formula reads: $900 for the radio plus $655 for the tape player plus nine times $12 for the tapes plus fifteen times $6 for the bridge tokens plus $237 for the coat.

82. **(C)** The next step is to determine if the car has been stolen.

83. **(A)** Both officers have followed the proper steps.

84. **(C)** All other choices are garbled and less complete than this one.

85. **(D)** In (A) there is no building; in (B) there is no intent; in (C) there is neither intent nor a building.

86. **(B)** The suspect in choice (A) has larger eyes; the suspect in choice (C) has different ears; the suspect in choice (D) has a fuller face.

87. **(B)** The suspect in choice (A) has a smaller nose; the suspect in choice (C) has a fuller face and fuller lips; the suspect in choice (D) has lighter eyes and thinner lips.

88. **(D)** The suspect in choice (A) has a different nose; the suspect in choice (B) has different ears; the suspect in choice (C) has an entirely different head and face shape.

89. **(C)** The suspect in choice (A) has a much finer nose; the suspect in choice (B) has a narrower jaw structure; the suspect in choice (D) has different ears.

90. **(B)** The suspect in choice (A) has a smaller nose; the suspect in choice (C) has lighter eyes and a wider mouth; the suspect in choice (D) has a fuller face and thinner lips.

ANSWER SHEET FOR PRACTICE EXAMINATION 4

1. Ⓐ Ⓑ Ⓒ Ⓓ   2. Ⓐ Ⓑ Ⓒ Ⓓ   3. Ⓐ Ⓑ Ⓒ Ⓓ   4. Ⓐ Ⓑ Ⓒ Ⓓ   5. Ⓐ Ⓑ Ⓒ Ⓓ

6. Ⓐ Ⓑ Ⓒ Ⓓ   7. Ⓐ Ⓑ Ⓒ Ⓓ   8. Ⓐ Ⓑ Ⓒ Ⓓ   9. Ⓐ Ⓑ Ⓒ Ⓓ   10. Ⓐ Ⓑ Ⓒ Ⓓ

11. Ⓐ Ⓑ Ⓒ Ⓓ   12. Ⓐ Ⓑ Ⓒ Ⓓ   13. Ⓐ Ⓑ Ⓒ Ⓓ   14. Ⓐ Ⓑ Ⓒ Ⓓ   15. Ⓐ Ⓑ Ⓒ Ⓓ

16. Ⓐ Ⓑ Ⓒ Ⓓ   17. Ⓐ Ⓑ Ⓒ Ⓓ   18. Ⓐ Ⓑ Ⓒ Ⓓ   19. Ⓐ Ⓑ Ⓒ Ⓓ   20. Ⓐ Ⓑ Ⓒ Ⓓ

21. Ⓐ Ⓑ Ⓒ Ⓓ   22. Ⓐ Ⓑ Ⓒ Ⓓ   23. Ⓐ Ⓑ Ⓒ Ⓓ   24. Ⓐ Ⓑ Ⓒ Ⓓ   25. Ⓐ Ⓑ Ⓒ Ⓓ

26. Ⓐ Ⓑ Ⓒ Ⓓ   27. Ⓐ Ⓑ Ⓒ Ⓓ   28. Ⓐ Ⓑ Ⓒ Ⓓ   29. Ⓐ Ⓑ Ⓒ Ⓓ   30. Ⓐ Ⓑ Ⓒ Ⓓ

31. Ⓐ Ⓑ Ⓒ Ⓓ   32. Ⓐ Ⓑ Ⓒ Ⓓ   33. Ⓐ Ⓑ Ⓒ Ⓓ   34. Ⓐ Ⓑ Ⓒ Ⓓ   35. Ⓐ Ⓑ Ⓒ Ⓓ

36. Ⓐ Ⓑ Ⓒ Ⓓ   37. Ⓐ Ⓑ Ⓒ Ⓓ   38. Ⓐ Ⓑ Ⓒ Ⓓ   39. Ⓐ Ⓑ Ⓒ Ⓓ   40. Ⓐ Ⓑ Ⓒ Ⓓ

41. Ⓐ Ⓑ Ⓒ Ⓓ   42. Ⓐ Ⓑ Ⓒ Ⓓ   43. Ⓐ Ⓑ Ⓒ Ⓓ   44. Ⓐ Ⓑ Ⓒ Ⓓ   45. Ⓐ Ⓑ Ⓒ Ⓓ

46. Ⓐ Ⓑ Ⓒ Ⓓ   47. Ⓐ Ⓑ Ⓒ Ⓓ   48. Ⓐ Ⓑ Ⓒ Ⓓ   49. Ⓐ Ⓑ Ⓒ Ⓓ   50. Ⓐ Ⓑ Ⓒ Ⓓ

51. Ⓐ Ⓑ Ⓒ Ⓓ   52. Ⓐ Ⓑ Ⓒ Ⓓ   53. Ⓐ Ⓑ Ⓒ Ⓓ   54. Ⓐ Ⓑ Ⓒ Ⓓ   55. Ⓐ Ⓑ Ⓒ Ⓓ

56. Ⓐ Ⓑ Ⓒ Ⓓ   57. Ⓐ Ⓑ Ⓒ Ⓓ   58. Ⓐ Ⓑ Ⓒ Ⓓ   59. Ⓐ Ⓑ Ⓒ Ⓓ   60. Ⓐ Ⓑ Ⓒ Ⓓ

61. Ⓐ Ⓑ Ⓒ Ⓓ   62. Ⓐ Ⓑ Ⓒ Ⓓ   63. Ⓐ Ⓑ Ⓒ Ⓓ   64. Ⓐ Ⓑ Ⓒ Ⓓ   65. Ⓐ Ⓑ Ⓒ Ⓓ

66. Ⓐ Ⓑ Ⓒ Ⓓ   67. Ⓐ Ⓑ Ⓒ Ⓓ   68. Ⓐ Ⓑ Ⓒ Ⓓ   69. Ⓐ Ⓑ Ⓒ Ⓓ   70. Ⓐ Ⓑ Ⓒ Ⓓ

71. Ⓐ Ⓑ Ⓒ Ⓓ   72. Ⓐ Ⓑ Ⓒ Ⓓ   73. Ⓐ Ⓑ Ⓒ Ⓓ   74. Ⓐ Ⓑ Ⓒ Ⓓ   75. Ⓐ Ⓑ Ⓒ Ⓓ

76. Ⓐ Ⓑ Ⓒ Ⓓ   77. Ⓐ Ⓑ Ⓒ Ⓓ   78. Ⓐ Ⓑ Ⓒ Ⓓ   79. Ⓐ Ⓑ Ⓒ Ⓓ   80. Ⓐ Ⓑ Ⓒ Ⓓ

81. Ⓐ Ⓑ Ⓒ Ⓓ   82. Ⓐ Ⓑ Ⓒ Ⓓ   83. Ⓐ Ⓑ Ⓒ Ⓓ   84. Ⓐ Ⓑ Ⓒ Ⓓ   85. Ⓐ Ⓑ Ⓒ Ⓓ

86. Ⓐ Ⓑ Ⓒ Ⓓ   87. Ⓐ Ⓑ Ⓒ Ⓓ   88. Ⓐ Ⓑ Ⓒ Ⓓ   89. Ⓐ Ⓑ Ⓒ Ⓓ   90. Ⓐ Ⓑ Ⓒ Ⓓ

91. Ⓐ Ⓑ Ⓒ Ⓓ   92. Ⓐ Ⓑ Ⓒ Ⓓ   93. Ⓐ Ⓑ Ⓒ Ⓓ   94. Ⓐ Ⓑ Ⓒ Ⓓ   95. Ⓐ Ⓑ Ⓒ Ⓓ

96. Ⓐ Ⓑ Ⓒ Ⓓ   97. Ⓐ Ⓑ Ⓒ Ⓓ   98. Ⓐ Ⓑ Ⓒ Ⓓ   99. Ⓐ Ⓑ Ⓒ Ⓓ   100. Ⓐ Ⓑ Ⓒ Ⓓ

101. Ⓐ Ⓑ Ⓒ Ⓓ   102. Ⓐ Ⓑ Ⓒ Ⓓ   103. Ⓐ Ⓑ Ⓒ Ⓓ   104. Ⓐ Ⓑ Ⓒ Ⓓ   105. Ⓐ Ⓑ Ⓒ Ⓓ

106. Ⓐ Ⓑ Ⓒ Ⓓ   107. Ⓐ Ⓑ Ⓒ Ⓓ   108. Ⓐ Ⓑ Ⓒ Ⓓ   109. Ⓐ Ⓑ Ⓒ Ⓓ   110. Ⓐ Ⓑ Ⓒ Ⓓ

111. Ⓐ Ⓑ Ⓒ Ⓓ   112. Ⓐ Ⓑ Ⓒ Ⓓ   113. Ⓐ Ⓑ Ⓒ Ⓓ   114. Ⓐ Ⓑ Ⓒ Ⓓ   115. Ⓐ Ⓑ Ⓒ Ⓓ

116. Ⓐ Ⓑ Ⓒ Ⓓ   117. Ⓐ Ⓑ Ⓒ Ⓓ   118. Ⓐ Ⓑ Ⓒ Ⓓ   119. Ⓐ Ⓑ Ⓒ Ⓓ   120. Ⓐ Ⓑ Ⓒ Ⓓ

121. Ⓐ Ⓑ Ⓒ Ⓓ   122. Ⓐ Ⓑ Ⓒ Ⓓ   123. Ⓐ Ⓑ Ⓒ Ⓓ   124. Ⓐ Ⓑ Ⓒ Ⓓ   125. Ⓐ Ⓑ Ⓒ Ⓓ

126. Ⓐ Ⓑ Ⓒ Ⓓ   127. Ⓐ Ⓑ Ⓒ Ⓓ   128. Ⓐ Ⓑ Ⓒ Ⓓ   129. Ⓐ Ⓑ Ⓒ Ⓓ   130. Ⓐ Ⓑ Ⓒ Ⓓ

131. Ⓐ Ⓑ Ⓒ Ⓓ   132. Ⓐ Ⓑ Ⓒ Ⓓ   133. Ⓐ Ⓑ Ⓒ Ⓓ   134. Ⓐ Ⓑ Ⓒ Ⓓ   135. Ⓐ Ⓑ Ⓒ Ⓓ

136. Ⓐ Ⓑ Ⓒ Ⓓ   137. Ⓐ Ⓑ Ⓒ Ⓓ   138. Ⓐ Ⓑ Ⓒ Ⓓ   139. Ⓐ Ⓑ Ⓒ Ⓓ   140. Ⓐ Ⓑ Ⓒ Ⓓ

141. Ⓐ Ⓑ Ⓒ Ⓓ   142. Ⓐ Ⓑ Ⓒ Ⓓ   143. Ⓐ Ⓑ Ⓒ Ⓓ   144. Ⓐ Ⓑ Ⓒ Ⓓ   145. Ⓐ Ⓑ Ⓒ Ⓓ

146. Ⓐ Ⓑ Ⓒ Ⓓ   147. Ⓐ Ⓑ Ⓒ Ⓓ   148. Ⓐ Ⓑ Ⓒ Ⓓ   149. Ⓐ Ⓑ Ⓒ Ⓓ   150. Ⓐ Ⓑ Ⓒ Ⓓ

TEAR HERE

PRACTICE EXAMINATION 4

MEMORY BOOKLET

Directions: You will be given 10 minutes to study the scene below and to try to notice and remember as many details as you can. You may not take any notes during this time.

TEST QUESTION BOOKLET

Time: 2 hours, 45 minutes—85 questions

Directions: Now that the Memory Booklets have been collected, you have 2 hours and 45 minutes in which to answer the test questions. The first 14 questions are based on the scene that you just studied. Answer these questions first. Then proceed directly to the remaining 71 questions. Choose the best answer to each question and mark its letter on your answer sheet.

Answer questions 1–14 on the basis of the scene in the memory booklet.

1. A person arriving at this reception area by elevator and wishing to go to room 2-J would have to walk past the

(A) information desk
(B) exit
(C) wall clock
(D) director's office

2. The person in the personnel manager's doorway is a

(A) white woman wearing a business suit
(B) man with a gun
(C) well-dressed man wearing glasses
(D) well-dressed man not wearing glasses

3. The time at which this hostage situation is occurring is

(A) 10:25
(B) 11:20
(C) 4:40
(D) 5:45

4. The person who is bald is

(A) blind
(B) requesting information
(C) sitting beside an umbrella
(D) holding a newspaper

5. The total number of people in this scene is

(A) 6
(B) 8
(C) 9
(D) 11

6. The weapon carried by the kneeling man is

(A) no weapon
(B) a handgun
(C) a machete
(D) a submachine gun

7. The receptionist is

   (A) talking on the telephone
   (B) consulting the appointment book
   (C) left handed
   (D) wearing her hair in corn rows

8. The number of floors serviced by this elevator is

   (A) 4
   (B) 5
   (C) 6
   (D) 7

9. On the table in front of the person with both feet on the floor is

   (A) *Health* magazine
   (B) a pile of newspapers
   (C) *Elle* magazine
   (D) an ashtray

10. The youngest person in this scene

    (A) is wearing a ponytail
    (B) is not wearing glasses
    (C) came with a dog
    (D) is sitting with feet crossed at the ankles

11. The person holding the automatic rifle

    (A) has it pointed at the receptionist
    (B) is wearing work clothes
    (C) is being watched by a dog
    (D) is equipped with lots of ammunition

12. The person with right leg crossed over left is

    (A) a black woman
    (B) seated in front of *New York* magazine
    (C) a terrorist
    (D) wearing high-heeled sandals

13. At the end of the bench next to the black man is

    (A) a potted plant
    (B) an umbrella stand
    (C) an umbrella
    (D) a floor lamp

14. On the floor between the elevator and the stairs is

    (A) a water cooler
    (B) a waste container
    (C) a coat rack
    (D) nothing at all

15. Police Officer Ruiz on patrol in a residential area arrives at the scene of a fire and, after speaking with a bystander on the street, makes the following notes:

Place of occurrence:	1520 Clarendon Road, Brooklyn
Time of occurrence:	6:32 A.M.
Type of building:	two-family frame dwelling
Event:	fire; suspected arson
Suspect:	male, white, approx. 6-foot, wearing jeans
Witness:	Mary Smith of 1523 Clarendon Road, Brooklyn

Officer Ruiz must now write up a report of the incident. Which of the following expresses the information *most clearly, accurately, and completely?*

(A) At 6:32 A.M. Mary Smith of 1523 Clarendon Road, Brooklyn, saw a white male wearing approximately 6-foot blue jeans running from the building across the street.

(B) A white male wearing blue jeans ran from the house at 1520 Clarendon Road at 6:32 A.M. Mary Smith saw him.

(C) At 6:32 A.M. a 6-foot white male wearing blue jeans ran from a burning two-family frame structure at 1520 Clarendon Road, Brooklyn. He was observed by a neighbor, Mary Smith.

(D) A two-family frame house is on fire at 1520 Clarendon Road in Brooklyn. A white male in blue jeans probably did it. Mary Smith saw him run.

16. As a student at the police academy, you are handed the following scenario: Police Officer Wu, assigned to the transit division, reports to a token booth and obtains this information from a sobbing woman.

Time of occurrence:	1:22 A.M.
Place of occurrence:	uptown-bound platform, 59th Street Station, 7th Avenue line
Victim:	Juana Martinez
Crime:	purse snatching
Description of suspect:	unknown, fled down steps to lower platform

Officer Wu must now call in an alert to the police dispatcher. Which of the following expresses the information *most clearly, accurately, and completely?*

(A) Juana Martinez had her purse snatched on the subway platform at 59th Street Station. She didn't see him.

(B) A purse was just snatched by a man who ran down the steps from the 7th Avenue token booth at 59th Street Station. Her name is Juana Martinez.

(C) It is 1:22 A.M. The person who snatched Juana Martinez' purse is downstairs at 59th Street Station.

(D) I am at 59th Street Station, uptown-bound 7th Avenue token booth. A Juana Martinez reports that her purse was just snatched by a man who fled down the steps to a lower platform.

17. Police officers assigned to patrol in a radio car are instructed to adhere to the following rules concerning the use of the police radios in patrol cars:

    1. The use of the radio is to be restricted to performance of duty only.
    2. All conversations should be to the point and as short as possible.
    3. Names of people are not to be used.
    4. All conversations should begin by identifying the vehicle by number.
    5. A message received is to be acknowledged by "ten-four."

    Police Officers Abel and Flynn apprehend two men in the act of robbing a jewelry store. They place the men in Patrol Car 14 and radio in a report of the activity. Which one of the following messages would be in conformance with the procedure specified?

    (A) "Officers Abel and Flynn, car one-four, proceeding to station house with two prisoners."
    (B) "Car one-four, proceeding to station house with two prisoners."
    (C) "Car one-four, Officers Abel and Flynn, proceeding to station house with two prisoners."
    (D) "Car one-four, proceeding to station house with prisoners Bossey and Warren."

18. Quite often a police officer is required to give assistance to an injured person. Upon responding to a call to assist an injured person, a police officer should be guided by the following procedure:

    1. Administer first aid.
    2. Call for medical assistance.
    3. Call again if the ambulance does not respond within 20 minutes.
    4. Accompany the injured person to the hospital if he or she is unconscious or unidentified.
    5. Witness the search of an unconscious or unidentified person.
    6. Attempt to identify the person who is unconscious or unidentified by a search of his or her property.

    Officer Alcorn, while on patrol, observes a man lying in the front yard of a four-family house. Upon questioning, the man reveals that he fell while repairing the roof of his house. He says he is in a great deal of pain and is unable to move. Officer Alcorn summons an ambulance and gives the man first aid. He then requests that the man give him his name, but the man refuses. The ambulance arrives in 15 minutes, and Officer Alcorn resumes patrol. Officer Alcorn failed to fulfill his obligations in this incident because he

    (A) did not make a second call for the ambulance when the man was in great pain
    (B) failed to accompany the man to the hospital
    (C) did not attempt to locate a physician while waiting for the ambulance
    (D) failed to relieve the injured man's pain through the administration of proper first aid

Questions 19 and 20 are based on the following situation:

On a hot summer afternoon, three prisoners are missing from the state penitentiary located on the wooded outskirts of a small upstate city. Their means of escape has not yet been established, so search parties are dispatched near and far.

19. Police car 43 leaves the city traveling west on highway 9. After three miles, the car makes a right turn onto route 21. Two miles up route 21, a dirt road forks off in a diagonal right. Car 43 turns onto the dirt road and continues until it reaches a farmhouse on the right hand side of the road. The car turns into the driveway and both officers get out. When the driver gets out, in which direction is she facing?

(A) Northeast
(B) Southwest
(C) East
(D) South

20. Correction Officers English and Miller leave the prison by the south gate, turn right, and run into the woods. They run half way around a large boulder that lies directly in their path, and continue looking to the right and to the left. They stop and peer into a dense clump of bushes on their left. In what direction are they looking?

(A) East
(B) North
(C) South
(D) West

21. Taxes are deducted each pay period from the amount of salaries or wages, including payments for overtime, paid to law enforcement personnel in excess of the withholding exemptions allowed under the Internal Revenue Act. The amount of tax to be withheld from each payment of wages to any employee will be determined from the current official table of pay and withholding exemptions to be found on page 32 of the employee manual. The paragraph best supports the statement that salaries of law enforcement personnel

(A) do not include overtime
(B) are determined by provisions of the Internal Revenue Act
(C) are paid from tax revenues
(D) are subject to tax deductions

22. A police officer on foot patrol is stopped by a man who shouts that a neighbor's child has just been raped. The officer goes to the scene of the alleged crime and is told by the hysterical mother that her eight-year-old daughter was raped in the apartment while she was in the basement with the laundry. The child is crying and bleeding on the bed. The mother screams that she believes the man is on the roof. The police officer should *first*

(A) call for medical assistance
(B) attempt to calm the hysterical mother
(C) go to the roof to search for the accused man
(D) question the child as to what actually took place

23. At 11 A.M. on Saturday, June 11, Police Officer Szulk on bicycle patrol in Highland Park is approached by a boy walking a dog. The boy tells officer Szulk of a body to which his dog has just led him. Officer Szulk accompanies the boy to the dog's find and notes the following:

Location:	underbrush about 80 yards south of Civil War Monument, Highland Park
Occurrence:	discovery of body of fully clothed Hispanic female in early 20s
Reporter:	Bill Sawyer, age 12
Identity of victim:	unknown

Officer Szulk is about to call his precinct to report this incident and to request assistance. Which of the following conveys all the information *most clearly, accurately, and completely?*

(A) A woman was found by Bill Sawyer in the park near the Civil War Monument. He doesn't know her.
(B) The body of an unknown Hispanic woman was found at 11 A.M. by 12-year-old Bill Sawyer's dog in the Highland Park underbrush south of the Civil War Monument.
(C) There is a body in the underbrush in Highland Park. She is a Hispanic woman and Bill Sawyer, a 12-year-old with a dog, found her.
(D) On Saturday, June 11, Bill Sawyer found a body of a dead woman all dressed up in the park with his dog.

24. Police Officer Rios is investigating a furniture store break-in which evidently had occurred during the previous night. She compiles the following information:

Location:	Berger's Furniture Store, 1509 Orchard Street
Incident:	burglary
Date of event:	night of Tuesday, May 3 to Wednesday, May 4
Time of event:	between 9:40 P.M. and 8:15 A.M.
Reporter:	Mo Berger, owner, of 108 West 12th Street
Damage:	broken window; empty cash register

Officer Rios must write up a report of this incident for follow-up. Which of the following expresses the information *most clearly, accurately, and completely?*

(A) Mo Berger had a burglary between closing on May 3 and opening May 4. He got a broken window and they emptied the cash register.
(B) Berger's Furniture Store at 1509 West Orchard Street had a burglary at night on May 3rd. They broke a window and took the money.
(C) Mo Berger of 108 West 12th Street reports that his Berger's Furniture Store on 1509 Orchard Street was broken into between 9:40 P.M. May 3 and 8:15 A.M. May 4. Contents of the cash register are missing.
(D) Mo Berger's Furniture Store was burgled through a broken window on 1509 Orchard Street during the night May 3–4. The burglars took everything out of the cash register. Mr. Berger lives at 108 West 12th Street and keeps the store open from 8:15 A.M. to 9:40 P.M.

Answer questions 25 and 26 solely on the basis of the following procedure:

Police officers responding to complaints of loud or violent disagreements between members of a family are directed to follow the procedure below:

1. When knocking on the door of the premises in which the dispute is taking place, do not stand directly in front of it.
2. Separate the parties taking part in the dispute by taking them into different rooms.
3. Attempt to calm the people involved while interviewing them.
4. Stay out of the dispute; do not take sides.
5. If an insult is directed at you, ignore it.
6. Advise the parties in the argument where they may go for counseling.
7. Do not say anything that will direct the people's anger at you.
8. Make no arrests unless one of the participants is hurt.

25. Officers Claymore and Peron, arriving at the scene of a family dispute, separate a screaming couple into different rooms. The wife shouts that her husband is having an affair with his secretary and that she is going to file for divorce. The wife picks up the ringing telephone, listens briefly, and then slams it down. She shouts to her husband, "Your secretary just called, but she didn't leave a message." At his point, it would be proper for one of the police officers to advise that the

    (A) husband end this affair at once
    (B) wife go ahead with her divorce plans
    (C) wife trust her husband
    (D) couple seek the help of local marriage counselors

26. Two officers respond to a complaint of gunshots and loud arguing taking place in an apartment. They approach the apartment and hear a television set playing. They stand in front of the door, knock on it, and are told to enter. A man and a woman are sitting on a couch watching a murder mystery on television. The couple states that they have been watching the program for almost two hours. The officers evaluate the situation and decide that a mistake has been made. They apologize and leave. One of the actions taken by the officers does not conform to the procedure for dealing with this type of situation. This occurred when they

    (A) determined that a mistake had been made and then apologized and left the premises
    (B) interviewed both people in the same room
    (C) investigated the complaint even though they could hear no argument
    (D) stood in front of the door while knocking on it

27. The term *homicide* means

    (A) manslaughter
    (B) murder
    (C) killing of one person by another person
    (D) death caused by a felony

Answer questions 28 and 29 on the basis of the following definitions:

Assault is committed when a person intentionally causes physical injury to another person or when a person acting recklessly causes physical injury to another person.

Harassment is committed when an individual, with intent to annoy or frighten another individual, does strike, shove, kick, or subject that individual to physical contact or attempts or threatens to do the same, or uses abusive or obscene language, or makes an obscene gesture in a public place, or follows a person in a public place, or repeatedly engages in conduct which serves no legitimate purpose but which results in alarming or seriously annoying another person.

Reckless Endangerment is committed when a person, failing to exercise caution, engages in conduct which creates a substantial risk of serious injury to another person.

28. As a result of a dispute over a parking space, Anne Blount and Bea Wallace engage in an argument during which Blount pushes Wallace in an attempt to scare her. Wallace is not hurt, but she makes an obscene gesture in the direction of Blount. Referring to the definitions given, which one of the following best describes the incident?

    (A) Blount committed assault, and Wallace committed harassment.
    (B) Blount and Wallace both committed harassment.
    (C) Neither Blount nor Wallace committed harassment.
    (D) Wallace committed assault, and Blount committed harassment,

29. William Hammer, fully intending to scare James Bates, drives his car at high speed in the direction of Bates who quickly jumps out of the path of the vehicle. In turning in the direction of Bates, Hammer narrowly misses Fred Collins, a bystander. Neither Bates nor Collins is injured. According to the definitions, Hammer

    (A) did not commit an assault against Bates or Collins
    (B) did not commit a crime
    (C) committed an assault against Bates and Collins
    (D) committed an assault against Collins only

30. Police Officer Polara answers a motorist's request for directions by telling the motorist to: "Proceed south, as you are now headed, for two blocks; turn right at the traffic light and, at the next intersection, turn right again. Immediately after you see a gas station on your right, make a left turn and go one block. You will see the store you are seeking on your left." In what direction will the car be traveling when the motorist reaches his destination?

    (A) North
    (B) South
    (C) East
    (D) West

31. A police officer attempting to extract information from a witness should not ask questions that can be answered by a "yes" or "no." A police officer is interviewing a witness to a car accident that resulted in serious injury to two people. The officer has reason to believe that the car involved went through an intersection against the light. Of the following, the proper question for the officer to ask the witness would be:

    (A) Did you see the car go through a red light?
    (B) Can you recall if the light turned red before the car went through the intersection?
    (C) What color was the light at the time the car went through the intersection?
    (D) Was the light red when the car went through the intersection?

32. Police Officer Dobbo is alerted by radio to go to an apartment in which there is a child in distress. The information is:

Location:	97 West 98th Street, Apt. 2-B
Time of call:	1:32 P.M.
Name of caller:	Martha Ho
Child:	Barney Ho, 21 months
Event:	head caught between spokes of chair back

Now that she has dealt with this emergency, Officer Dobbo must make a record for her activity log. Which of the following expresses the information *most clearly, accurately, and completely?*

(A) At 1:32 P.M. Martha Ho of 97 West 98th Street, Apt. 2-B, requested assistance for Barney Ho, aged 21 months, who was caught in a chair. I removed a spoke from the chair back and released the child.

(B) Barney Ho, 21 months, got his head stuck in a chair. His mother called at 1:32 P.M., and I went and got his head out. This was in Apt. 2-B.

(C) Martha Ho, mother of Barney Ho, a 21-month old little boy, of 98 West 97th Street called at 1:32 P.M. because Barney had his head stuck in a chair. I got him out of the chair by removing a spoke from the back.

(D) When Barney Ho got his head stuck at 1:32 P.M., his mother called from 97 West 98th Street and asked for someone to come and help him in Apt. 2-B. The chair should be thrown out.

33. Police Officer Neilly is approached by a woman along his post. The woman tells him that she would like to file a complaint against the husband of her employer. This is the information that Office Neilly takes down:

Date:	March 30
Complainant:	Janina Klinski, age 34
Address of complainant:	5630 Grand Concourse, Apt. 3-W
Accused:	Joseph Johns, mid-50s
Address of accused:	120 Palisades Heights, Apt. 19-A
Complaint:	sexual abuse

Officer Neilly informs the woman of the proper legal procedures for filing this complaint. Then he records his conversation with Ms. Klinski in his log book. Which of the following expresses the information *most clearly, accurately, and completely?*

(A) Janina Klinski who lives at 5630 Grand Concourse, Apt. 3-W, says that she was sexually abused on March 30 by an older man, Joseph Johns.

(B) On March 30, Janina Klinski, 34, of 5630 Grand Concourse, Apt. 3-W, complained that she had been sexually abused by Joseph Johns of 120 Palisades Heights, Apt. 19-A, the husband of her employer.

(C) Joseph Johns, who is in his 50s, sexually abused Janina Klinski on March 30, she said. Janina Klinski works for Joseph Johns' wife at 5630 Grand Concourse, Apt. 3-W.

(D) Janina Klinski said that Joseph Johns sexually abused her at 120 Palisades Heights, Apt. 19-A, where she worked for Mrs. Johns on March 30. Janina Klinski is 34 years old, and Joseph Johns is in his mid-50s.

34. Beverly Bowers, who has been convicted of aggravated assault and who has exhausted all appeals, surrenders herself at the Women's Correctional Facility to serve her sentence. Ms. Bowers hands over her purse, and the contents of her wallet are inventoried thus:

5 $20 bills

7 $10 bills

13 $5 bills

2 $1 bills

9 quarters

21 dimes

17 nickels

8 pennies

How much money was in Ms. Bowers' purse?

(A) $237.88
(B) $242.28
(C) $243.06
(D) $244.68

Answer questions 35 and 36 on the basis of the following procedure:

1. When a prisoner requests medical attention or is in apparent need of it, the police officer should arrange for the prisoner to be promptly examined by a doctor.
2. In the event that a prisoner is in need of medical treatment, the police officer should notify a supervisor immediately so that an ambulance can be summoned. Prisoners who are drug addicts and who are in need of treatment for their addiction should be taken to a hospital by a radio car.
3. Under no circumstances should a police officer prescribe any medication for a prisoner.
4. A police officer should not attempt to diagnose a prisoner's illness or injury and should not attempt to treat the prisoner except in a situation where first aid is required. First aid should be administered promptly.
5. A doctor is the only one authorized to administer medicine to a prisoner. When a doctor is not available, the police officer in charge of the prisoner should then give him or her the medicine and watch him or her take it.

35. Alan Fox, a prisoner well known to police because of his long record, is in custody when he claims that he has a severe headache as a result of being badly beaten. There are no apparent signs of a physical injury, but the prisoner is demanding medical attention. The police officer in charge of Alan Fox should

(A) consider the prisoner's long record before deciding to call a doctor
(B) give the prisoner two aspirins
(C) ignore the prisoner's request for medical attention since there are no apparent physical injuries
(D) see that Alan Fox is promptly examined by a doctor

36. It is a hot summer day, and Officer Stone has in his custody a prisoner who is a drug addict. The prisoner opens his shirt to reveal a large unhealed wound which is obviously infected. Officer Stone suggests to the prisoner that he call a doctor in to examine him, but the prisoner refuses, saying the wound is of no consequence. In this instance, Officer Stone should

   (A) request that his supervisor call an ambulance
   (B) closely examine the wound in order to evaluate its severity
   (C) adhere to the prisoner's wishes and do nothing about the matter
   (D) take the prisoner at once to a hospital in a radio car

37. Detectives assigned to investigate violent crimes with no obvious motive and no apparent witnesses must direct their whole effort toward success in their work. If they wish to succeed in such investigations, their work will be by no means easy, smooth, or peaceful; on the contrary, they will have to devote themselves completely and continuously to a task that requires all their ability.

   The paragraph best supports the statement that an investigator's success depends most upon

   (A) ambition to advance rapidly in rank
   (B) persistence in the face of difficulty
   (C) training and experience
   (D) superior ability

38. A police officer should not ask leading questions, that is, questions which suggest the answer that the officer desires. A police officer is called to the scene of an accident that involved a red and a green car. It would be proper for the officer to ask a witness to the accident,

   (A) "You observed the red car hit the green car, didn't you?"
   (B) "Did you see the green car hit the red car?"
   (C) "The red car caused the accident, didn't it?"
   (D) "Just what caused the accident between the red car and the green car?"

39. As part of an exercise at the police academy, a recruit is given the following information to organize into a short report:

Location:	northwest corner of Smith Street and Tenth Avenue
Date:	August 2
Time:	3:35 P.M.
Event:	fire hydrant fully opened without sprinkler cap
Suspect:	unidentified white male, approximately 20 years old, 5 ft. 10 in., 160 lb., wearing blue jeans and torn white sneakers.
Witnesses:	neighborhood children

Which of the following expresses this information *most clearly, accurately, and completely?*

(A) On August 2 at 3:35 P.M., the fire hydrant at the northwest corner of Smith Street and Tenth Avenue was fully opened with water gushing from it without a water-saving sprinkler cap. Neighborhood children reported that an unfamiliar white teenager wearing blue jeans and torn white sneakers had probably opened the hydrant.

(B) The fire hydrant at the corner of Smith and Tenth was opened by a 20-year old, average height and weight man in blue jeans and torn sneakers this hot and sticky afternoon around 3:30 the children said.

(C) Some neighborhood children said that the fire hydrant had been opened by a white man they didn't know who was about standard size with blue jeans and torn sneakers. The date is August 2; the time 3:35 P.M.

(D) The northwest fire hydrant at Smith Street and Tenth Avenue was opened on August 2 at 3:35 P.M. The children playing in the water do not know who did it.

40. In another police academy exercise, a recruit is handed the following information collected by a police officer arriving at the scene of a robbery immediately after it had occurred:

Time:	5:28 P.M.
Place:	Aneke's Bridal Fashions, 280 Second Avenue
Reporter:	Aneke Blau, owner
Event:	knife-point robbery; $200 taken
Suspect:	white woman, red hair, blue jeans, white T-shirt

The police officer is calling in a report so that cars in the vicinity can search for the suspect. Which of the following expresses this information *most clearly, accurately, and completely?*

(A) Aneke Blau reported at 5:28 P.M. her store Aneke's Bridal Fashions was robbed at knifepoint at 280 Second Avenue. A white woman with red hair took $200 from her wearing blue jeans and white T-shirt.

(B) At 5:28 P.M. a red-haired woman took $200 from 280 Second Avenue at Aneke's Bridal Fashions owned by Aneke Blau who was robbed by a white woman. She was wearing blue jeans and a white T-shirt and used a knife.

(C) In a robbery that occurred at knifepoint, a red-haired white woman robbed the owner of Aneke's Bridal Fashions. Aneke Blau, the owner of the 280 Second Avenue store was robbed of $200. She said she was wearing blue jeans and white T-shirt at 5:28 P.M.

(D) Just before 5:28 P.M., Aneke Blau, owner of Aneke's Bridal Fashions located at 280 Second Avenue was robbed of $200 at knifepoint. The suspect is a white female with red hair, wearing blue jeans and white T-shirt.

41. In taking a report of a missing person, a police officer must request the following information in the following order:

1. Sex of missing person
2. Age of missing person
3. Name of missing person
4. Name and relationship of person making the report
5. Place and time missing person was last seen
6. Physical description of person and clothing
7. Other special identifying features

Police Officer Manning is practically bowled over by a hysterical, tearful woman who is wailing, "My baby she missing." Officer Manning's first question should be:

(A) Where did you lose the baby?
(B) How old is the baby?
(C) Is the baby a boy or a girl?
(D) Are you the baby's mother?

42. Police Officer Klein leaves the police garage by the western gate, makes a left turn and begins to cover her assigned area. After four blocks, Officer Klein turns west. When Officer Klein has driven five more blocks, she is passed by a speeding car going in the opposite direction. She makes a quick U-turn and follows the speeding car. After eight blocks, the speeding car turns left, loses control, and crashes into a telephone pole. The location of the crash is

(A) in front of the police garage
(B) due south of the police garage
(C) southeast of the police garage
(D) northeast of the police garage

Answer questions 43 and 44 on the basis of the following definitions:

Burglary is committed when an individual, without authorization, enters or remains in a building with the intent of committing a crime.

Criminal mischief is committed when a person intentionally damages the property of another person, having no right to do so nor any reasonable ground to believe that he has the right to do so.

Larceny is committed when a person intentionally deprives another of property or wrongfully takes, obtains, or withholds property from the owner of that property without the use of force, violence, or threat of injury. Larceny is committed, for example, when property is obtained under false pretenses, finding and not returning lost property, or the intentional issuance of a bad check.

Robbery is committed when a person, against another person's will, takes property from that person.

43. Jane Wills finds a diamond ring on the sidewalk of a busy street. She keeps it. According to the definitions, Wills committed

(A) the crime of larceny
(B) the crime of burglary
(C) the crime of robbery
(D) none of the listed crimes

44. Elwood Tompkins is waiting at a bus station to hand over a package of expensive jewelry to a representative of the XYZ Transfer Company. Phil Shore learns of the shipment and decides to steal the package. He goes to the bus station, presents himself to Tompkins, and says he is from XYZ. Tompkins gives Shore the package believing he is from XYZ. Shore is not armed. The definitions indicate that Shore committed the crime of

(A) robbery
(B) burglary
(C) criminal mischief
(D) larceny

Answer questions 45 through 47 on the basis of the following procedure:

A police officer responding to a situation that involves a person or persons who seem to be dead should take the following steps:

1. The officer should assume that the person is alive unless the officer is absolutely sure that he or she is dead.
2. If the officer is absolutely sure that the person is dead, and if the body is in public view, the body should be covered with a waterproof covering.
3. The officer should summon a sergeant to the scene.
4. The officer should immediately call the homicide detectives if the death is suspicious.
5. The body should be searched for identification if the death took place in a public area. In the event that the death took place in the home of a person who lived alone, both the body and the home are to be searched. All searches must be witnessed by a sergeant.
6. Property of a dead person may be released only to a relative who lived with the deceased.
7. Do not notify relatives or family of a death over the telephone. However, if you receive a call from a relative concerning the person's condition, you may inform the relative of the death.

45. A police officer is summoned to the scene of an accident. The victim, a young woman, is lying on the street, apparently dead. She is surrounded by bystanders. In this situation, the officer should first

(A) cover the body with a waterproof covering
(B) notify the homicide detectives
(C) search the body to determine its identity
(D) check to see if the woman is alive

46. A police officer is sent to the apartment of an elderly man who obviously has been dead for a few days. The officer closes the door to the apartment and is now alone with the body. His first act should be to

(A) summon a sergeant
(B) search the apartment
(C) search the body
(D) cover the body

47. A police officer, while searching the home of a dead man who had lived alone, is approached by the man's sister who requests permission to remove a few family albums from the apartment. The officer, in this instance, should

(A) give her the albums since she is the dead man's sister
(B) not give her the albums since she did not live with the dead man
(C) give her the albums since they contain only family pictures
(D) not give her the albums until she proves that she is the deceased's sister

48. Police Officer Ling reports to her precinct from a corner police call box six blocks north of the precinct house along her assigned patrol route. She turns left at that corner, walks one block, and turns left again. After walking three more blocks, Officer Ling turns right, walks two full blocks, and checks in from another corner call box. The call box from which Officer Ling is now calling is located

(A) 4 blocks north and 2 blocks east of the precinct house
(B) 3 blocks north and 3 blocks east of the precinct house
(C) 3 blocks north and 3 blocks west of the precinct house
(D) 2 blocks north and 4 blocks west of the precinct house

49. As Officer Ling stands at the call box, she witnesses a car sideswiping a parked car almost directly in front of her and continuing on its way at a high speed. This is the information that Officer Ling rapidly takes note of:

Location:	in front of 158 Broome Street, just south of Potter Avenue
Incident:	sideswipe of parked car by speeding car; hit and run
Damage:	removed right side mirror and badly smashed right front fender
Description of speeding car:	red two-door Honda Accord, approximately 1994; no occupants besides male driver; New Jersey license plate beginning 7T4, traveling west
Description of damaged car:	black four-door Saturn SL-1, 1993, license plate Connecticut XYZ-123

Officer Ling is on foot and cannot pursue the speeding car, but she can transmit the information directly to the sergeant with whom she is checking in. Which of the following expresses the needed information *most clearly, accurately and completely?*

(A) A speeding red car and driver from New Jersey and going west just hit a black four-door 1993 Saturn, Connecticut license plate XYZ-123 on Broome Street.
(B) A red two-door Honda Accord, New Jersey license plate beginning 7T4, with only male driver, last seen traveling west on Broome Street near Potter at high speed after hitting black Saturn on right side.
(C) A black 1993 four-door Saturn SL-1 parked in front of 158 Broome Street just south of Potter Avenue was just hit and damaged by a red two-door Honda Accord from New Jersey that was speeding and didn't stop. It is speeding west.
(D) A speeding car, a red two-door Honda Accord from Connecticut, license plate beginning 7T4, just sideswiped a black Saturn in front of 158 Broome Street. Its only occupant is the male driver, and the car is speeding west.

50. Police Officer Jonas assigned to the housing division is patrolling a large city housing project in his car when he notices an elderly gentleman wandering aimlessly in circles. The man tells Officer Jonas that thinks that his name is Bob and that he once lived here but was kidnapped by aliens in a flying saucer and just escaped. Officer Jonas puts the man in his car and radios the following information to his sergeant:

Incident:	lost, disoriented adult
Location:	Orchard Houses, southeast sector, in front of Building 3
Description:	white male, about 80, 5 ft. 7 in., weight 150, thin gray hair, blue eyes, wearing gray pants, white shirt, and green windbreaker, "Bob"

Which of the following expresses the information *most clearly, accurately, and completely?*

(A) An old man who might be Bob says that he was left in front of Building 3 by aliens who kidnapped him. He is about 5 ft. 7 in, weighs about 150 lbs. and has thin gray hair and blue eyes. He is wearing gray pants, white shirt, and a windbreaker.

(B) Bob is an old man who was kidnapped by aliens and returned to Orchard Houses where he lives in Building 3. He is confused wearing gray pants, a white shirt, and a green windbreaker. He has gray hair and blue eyes and is average size.

(C) A confused white man, about 80, was found in front of Building 3, southeast sector, Orchard Houses. The man is about 5 ft. 7 in, weighs about 150 lbs. and has thin gray hair and blue eyes. He is wearing gray pants, white shirt, and a windbreaker and is uncertain of his name and his residence.

(D) A man with thin gray hair and blue eyes wearing gray pants, a white shirt, and a green windbreaker says he is Bob who was left by aliens in front of Orchard Houses where he used to live before they kidnapped him. He is 5 ft. 7 in. and weighs 150 lbs.

Answer questions 51 and 52 on the basis of the following Employee Leave Regulations:

As a full-time permanent city employee under the Career and Salary Plan, Officer Peter Smith earns an "annual leave allowance." This consists of a certain number of days off a year with pay and may be used for vacation, for personal business, or for observing religious holidays. During his first 8 years of city service, he will earn an "annual leave allowance" of 20 days off a year (an average of 1–2/3 days off a month). After he has finished 8 full years of working for the city, he will begin earning an additional 5 days off a year. His "annual leave allowance" will then be 25 days a year and will remain at this amount for 7 full years. He will begin earning an additional 2 days off a year after he has completed a total of 15 years of city employment.

A "sick leave allowance" of 1 day a month is also given to Officer Smith, but it can be used only in case of actual illness. When Smith returns to work after using "sick leave allowance," he *must* have a doctor's note if the absence is for a total of more than 3 days, but he may also be required to show a doctor's note for absences of 1, 2, or 3 days.

51. According to the preceding passage, Mr. Smith's "annual leave allowance" consists of a certain number of days off a year that he

(A) does not get paid for
(B) gets paid for at time and a half
(C) may use for personal business
(D) may not use for observing religious holidays

52. According to the preceding passage, when he uses "sick leave allowance," Mr. Smith may be required to show a doctor's note

(A) even if his absence is for only 1 day
(B) only if his absence is for more than 2 days
(C) only if his absence is for more than 3 days
(D) only if his absence is for 3 days or more

Answer questions 53 and 54 on the basis of the drawing below. This drawing shows some vital interior parts of a police revolver and the order in which they fit together.

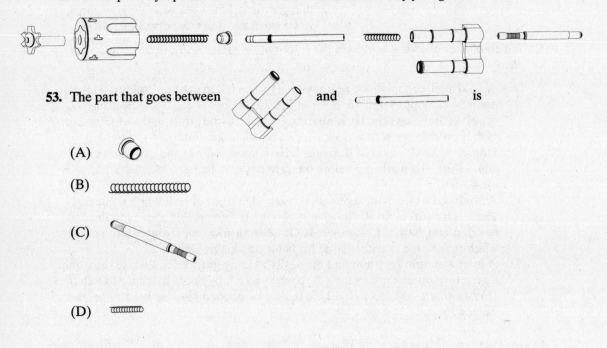

53. The part that goes between 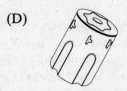 and is

(A)

(B)

(C)

(D)

54. The part that does NOT belong to this portion of the revolver is

(A)

(B)

(C)

(D)

55. Police officers are often assigned to the scene of a fire to control traffic and, at times, to close off a street to all traffic except emergency vehicles. Two officers assigned to this duty arrive in a radio car which they park across one end of a street, blocking traffic. After locking their radio car, they then proceed to the other end of the street on foot to block off traffic at that end. The action taken by these police officers should be considered

(A) improper, because they should have remained in their car in order to be able to move quickly if they were needed
(B) proper, since a person who may have started the fire would be effectively trapped
(C) improper, because their car was left unattended and therefore could not be moved to permit emergency vehicles to enter
(D) proper, because the street is now closed to all but emergency vehicles

56. While on routine patrol, Police Officer Kalb is approached by a furious citizen who complains about nighttime activity in the church parking lot next door to his home. These are the facts collected by Officer Kalb:

Date:	July 21
Time:	10:30 A.M.
Complainant:	Peter Lynch of 168 Carman Road
Complaint:	nighttime noise, rowdiness, drinking, drag racing, and sex in parking lot of St. Mary's Church at 170 Carman Road

Officer Kalb is writing up a report of this complaint. Which of the following expresses the information *most clearly, accurately, and completely?*

(A) Peter Lynch of St. Mary's on 170 Carman Road says the parking lot should be locked at 10:30 A.M. People drink there at night, and he doesn't like it.
(B) Peter Lynch of 168 Carman Road complains of nighttime noise and rowdiness in the parking lot of St. Mary's at 170 Carman. He demands police action, perhaps padlocking of the lot at night.
(C) There is drinking and sex in the St. Mary's parking lot at night at 170 Carman Road. Peter Lynch says the police should do something on July 21st.
(D) Padlocking the parking lot of St. Mary's might be the solution to nightly distur-

bances at 170 Carman Road according to Peter Lynch of 168 Carman Road at 10:30 A.M. on July 21st.

57. It is mid-January, and many members of the precinct house staff are out with the flu. Officer Seguaro is covering the dispatcher's desk on an emergency basis. Officer Seguaro receives a call reporting alleged child abuse and consults the following rules for the procedure to be followed in prescribed order:

1. Ask for the name, address, and telephone number of the caller.
2. Ask for the name and address of the person being abused.
3. Ask the nature of the abuse.
4. Ask for the name of the abuser.
5. Dispatch police to the scene of the alleged abuse.
6. If the reporter is at a location not proximate to the scene of the abuse and abused, dispatch police to interview caller.
7. Ask caller his or her relationship to abused and abuser.
8. Assure caller that all information will be kept confidential.

Officer Seguaro asks the caller his name, address, and telephone number, then asks for the name and address of the person being abused. She learns that the caller lives in the apartment directly across the hall from the little girl who is being beaten by a shouting male, unidentified since the beating is taking place behind closed doors. Officer Seguaro immediately dispatches a patrol car to the scene. The next thing for Officer Seguaro to do is

(A) dispatch another patrol car to interview the caller
(B) ask the caller his relationship to the abused
(C) ask the names of likely suspects
(D) assure the caller that all information will be kept confidential

58. As part of a police academy exercise, you are handed the following set of facts:

Date of event:	February 26 or February 27
Time of event:	between 10 P.M. and 8 A.M.
Event:	stolen car
Location:	in front of 10–15 Moss Place between Harlan Blvd. and Montrose Pike
Description:	red 4-door 1989 Mazda 626, NY plate PYD 123
Owner:	Donald Tramp

Which of the following expresses this information *most clearly, accurately and completely?*

(A) Donald Tramp's car was stolen in front of Harlan Boulevard and Moss Place at 10–15 on February 26 or 27. It is a red 4-door Mazda
(B) A red 4-door 1989 Mazda 26 was stolen by Donald Tramp on February 26 or 27 between 10 P.M. and 8 A.M. Its plate is PYD 123.
(C) From the front of 10–15 Moss Place between Harlan Blvd. and Montrose Pike overnight between February 26 and 27 was stolen the red Mazda of Donald Tramp.
(D) Donald Tramp reports that his red 4-door 1989 Mazda 626, bearing NY plates PYD 123 was stolen from the front of 10–15 Moss Place between Harlan Boulevard and Montrose Pike during the night of February 26–27.

59. Part of the training at the police academy involves preparing reports that are useful to various divisions within the police department. Crimes and criminals are often pursued and investigated from more than one angle, yet all investigators begin with the same report. Officer Monroe has taken these details from a woman who has just been raped:

Location:	583 Cooper Terrace, elevator
Time:	2:25 P.M.
Occurrence:	rape and robbery
Weapon:	knife
Perpetrator:	white male, approx. 25 yrs., slight build, medium height, wearing blue jeans and red T-shirt
Items stolen:	pocketbook, pearl ring, cameo brooch
Victim:	Bella Luciano, age 67, of 583 Cooper Terrace

Officer Monroe must prepare a report to be used in apprehending the criminal, recovering the property, and securing the premises. Which of the following expresses the information *most clearly, accurately, and completely?*

(A) A 25-year-old white male raped 67-year-old Bella Luciano with a knife in the elevator. He robbed her too.
(B) At 2:15 P.M. a man raped Bella Luciano in the elevator of 583 Cooper Terrace and robbed her of her pocketbook, pearl ring, and cameo brooch.
(C) A white male, approximately 25 years of age, slightly built and of medium height, wearing blue jeans and a red T-shirt robbed and raped at knifepoint Bella Luciano, age 67, in the elevator of 583 Cooper Terrace at 2:15 P.M. Items stolen were: pocketbook, pearl ring, and cameo brooch.
(D) A pocketbook, pearl ring, and cameo brooch were stolen at knifepoint from Bella Luciano when a man raped her in the elevator. He was 67 years old, medium sized, and wearing blue jeans and a red T-shirt.

60. A fire truck with lights flashing and siren wailing pulled out of the firehouse and headed north towards the site of a fire. After one block, the fire truck turned right. At the next corner it turned right again, proceeding for two blocks before turning left. At successive corners, the fire truck then turned right and right again. At the next intersection, an impatient motorist crossed the path of the fire truck, and the fire truck hit the car on its right side. In which direction was the car traveling?

(A) North
(B) South
(C) East
(D) West

61. Police Officer D'Onofrio is the first to arrive at the scene of a one-car accident in which a motorist has wrapped his car around a tree. Gasoline is pouring from the ruptured tank and smoke is escaping from the popped hood. The motorist is bleeding profusely from a bad gash on his neck, is slumped unconscious in a contorted position, and has a visibly broken arm. The *first* thing Officer D'Onofrio should do is

(A) apply pressure on the wound to stop the bleeding
(B) pull the man from the car
(C) splint and bandage the broken arm
(D) apply mouth-to-mouth artificial respiration to restore the man to consciousness

62. A police officer who becomes aware of an unsafe condition with regard to sidewalks or streets along his or her patrol must promptly notify the city department that is responsible for repairing the unsafe condition. The procedure for making this notification is as follows:

1. Note the nature of the unsafe condition in the memo book.
2. Enter the exact location of the unsafe condition in the memo book.
3. Phone or radio the desk officer at the precinct house with information about the unsafe condition and its location.
4. If the unsafe condition is a malfunctioning traffic signal, notify the Traffic Department. Police Officer Mardikian sits four full minutes in his patrol car at the intersection of Broadway and West 128th Street waiting for a red light that refuses to turn green. He pulls up at the curb and writes in his memo book that a traffic signal located at Broadway and West 128th Street is out of order and will not change. From his car he radios to his precinct house and tells the desk officer of this unsafe condition. The next action Officer Mardikian must take is to

(A) notify the Traffic Department
(B) jump out and direct traffic
(C) note in his memo book the time that he notified the precinct house
(D) continue to cover his assigned patrol route

Answer questions 63 and 64 on the basis of the following procedure:

Preservation of life is a police officer's highest responsibility. Safeguarding members of the public is the officer's first duty, but then self-preservation takes precedence over guaranteeing all civil rights to all people. The Stop and Frisk procedure was instituted to protect police officers along with protecting the public and protecting property. The procedure is:

1. Follow the person and observe to determine if there is cause to suspect that the person has committed, is committing, or is about to commit a crime.
2. If there is cause for suspicion, stop the person, request identification and an explanation for his or her behavior.
3. Frisk if the explanation or nature of suspicious behavior lead the officer to believe that he or she may be physically injured or killed.
4. Search if the frisk leads to suspicion that the individual is concealing a weapon.
5. Confiscate the weapon unless the individual produces a permit.
6. Arrest the person for illegal possession of a weapon.

63. Just after 11 P.M., Police Officer Poplis patrolling a commercial district that has recently been the target of night time break-ins finds herself following a man who is walking slowly, peering into darkened windows, and trying doorknobs. Officer Poplis should now

(A) stop and frisk the man so that he does not injure or kill her
(B) continue following the man to see if he will break into a store
(C) stop the man and ask him to identify himself and to explain his conduct
(D) ignore the man and cover the remainder of her post to discourage break-ins

64. At 3:30 A.M., Police Officer Moro turns a corner and comes upon two men in their twenties who are alternately shouting at each other and caressing one another. Some of the words that pass between them are threats of bodily harm. Officer Moro approaches the two men, asks for identification and for an explanation of what is going on. The young men assure Officer Moro that this is simply a lovers' quarrel and that their threats are merely words. Officer Moro should now

(A) ask the men why they are quarreling
(B) frisk the men to be certain they will not harm each other or him
(C) search for concealed weapons
(D) leave the men alone and move on

Answer question 65 on the basis of the following definitions:

Felony murder is committed when a person, acting alone or with others, commits or attempts to commit the crimes of robbery, burglary, kidnapping, arson, or rape, and in the course and furtherance of such crime, or immediate flight therefrom, he, or another participant, if there be any, causes the death of a person other than one of the participants. **Murder** is committed when a person, following a period of lengthy planning, intentionally causes the death of another person.

65. The difference between murder and felony murder is that

(A) in murder someone is killed; in felony murder the crime may be attempted
(B) in the case of felony murder some other crime must be committed along with the murder
(C) murder is planned; felony murder may be incidental to another crime
(D) felony murder is part of a calculated crime; murder may be impulsive upon extreme provocation or emotional stress

Answer questions 66 and 67 on the basis of the following paragraph:

Proper firearms training is one phase of law enforcement that cannot be ignored. No part of the training of a law officer is more important or more valuable. The officer's life, and often the lives of his or her fellow officers, depend directly upon skill with the weapon he or she is carrying. Proficiency with the revolver is not attained exclusively by the volume of ammunition used and the number of hours spent on the firing line. Supervised practice and the use of training aids and techniques help make the shooter. It is essential to have a good firing range where new officers are trained and older personnel practice in scheduled firearms sessions. The fundamental points to be stressed are grip, stance, breathing, sight alignment, and trigger squeeze. Coordination of thought, vision, and motion must be achieved before the officer gains confidence in shooting ability. Attaining this ability will make the student a better officer and enhance his or her value to the force.

66. The paragraph best supports the statement that

(A) skill with weapons is a phase of law enforcement training that is too often ignored
(B) the most useful and essential single factor in the training of a law officer is proper firearms training
(C) the value of an officer to the force is enhanced by the officer's self-confidence and coordination
(D) the lives of law enforcement officers always depend directly upon the skill with weapons displayed by fellow officers

67. The word *stance* as used in this paragraph means

(A) attitude
(B) opinion
(C) angle of head
(D) placement of feet

68. An off-duty police officer visiting a friend in another city stops to fill his tank with gasoline and discovers a holdup in progress at the gas station. When he identifies himself as a law officer, the robber takes off at high speed and the officer gives chase. They proceed west on the highway for three miles. Then they make a right turn off the highway onto a secondary road for another mile and a half, and then a left turn onto a dirt road. Driving at high speed on the dirt road, the holdup man's car develops a flat tire. The man jumps out of the driver's seat and runs directly into the woods. The police officer follows on foot, but loses sight of his suspect. The officer then turns around to walk back to his car. In what direction is he walking?

(A) North
(B) South
(C) East
(D) West

69. As a student at the police academy you are handed the following scenario: Police Officer Hakim on routine nighttime patrol in a commercial area discovers that the front door of the dark liquor store is not locked. She carefully opens the door a crack and hears sounds inside. Prudently she steps away from the door and radios for backup. Three fellow officers promptly arrive to reinforce her. They open the door and surprise the burglars into surrender without firing a shot. Here are the details:

Location: Sam's Spirits, 250 Main Street
Date: Tuesday, May 9
Time: 1:20 A.M.
Event: break-in; attempted theft
Officers involved: Peter Nwazota, Amy Zadrozny, and Frank O'Kun
Suspects: Seth Dowling and Tim Farr

Officer Hakim must file a report about this incident. Which of the following expresses the information *most clearly, accurately, and completely?*

(A) Seth Dowling and Tim Farr broke into the liquor store at 1:20 on Tuesday, May 9. Peter Nwazota, Amy Zadrozny, Frank O'Kun, and I captured them.
(B) At 1:20 A.M. on Tuesday, May 9 a break-in was discovered at Sam's Spirits, 250 Main Street. With backup assistance of Peter Nwazota, Amy Zadrozny, and Frank O'Kun, the suspects Seth Dowling and Tim Farr were peacefully arrested.
(C) Peter Nwazota, Amy Zadrozny, and Frank O'Kun helped me take Seth Dowling and Tim Farr into custody when they broke in to Sam's Spirits on Tuesday night at 1:20 A.M.
(D) Theft of the liquor store at 250 Main Street was averted on May 9 at 1:20 A.M. when the suspects were surprised and didn't shoot at Peter Nwazota, Amy Zadrozny, Tim Farr, and me.

70. When summoned to a location at which there is a street fight in which the participants are armed with knives and a large crowd is watching, a police officer must follow this procedure in precise order:

1. Call for reinforcements.
2. Await arrival of reinforcements.
3. Firmly demand that the participants stop fighting at once.
4. Ask spectators to step back.
5. Restrain spectators.
6. With assistance of other officers, grab fighters from behind and forcibly separate them.
7. Confiscate weapons.

Police Officer Fisher has reported to the scene of a street fight. He has sent for reinforcements who have just arrived. He has demanded that the participants stop fighting, but they are still wielding their knives at one another. Officer Fisher should now

(A) draw his gun and fire into the air
(B) grab spectators from behind and restrain them
(C) ask the spectators politely to step out of the way
(D) confiscate the weapons

71. At the scene of an apparent homicide, the following procedure must be rigidly followed:

1. Pull on gloves.
2. Check for signs of life in all victims.
3. If any victim is alive, summon ambulance without delay.
4. Make a quick sketch of the scene so as to show relative locations and positions of bodies, weapons, possible points of entry and exit, and both large and small objects.
5. Seal off premises and permit access only to police and medical personnel.
6. Remain at premises until a superior officer arrives.

Police Officer Blitz arrives at an apartment in which a small massacre has taken place. Two men and a woman are lying face down in the living room with bullet holes in the backs of their heads. A teenage girl is lying face up on a bed with her neck slashed.

A baby is lying in its crib with a stomach wound. Officer Blitz pulls on her gloves, takes out a pocket mirror, and holds the mirror to each person's mouth. The mirror fogs slightly when she holds it to the baby's mouth, so Officer Blitz immediately calls for an ambulance. She then opens her memo book to an empty page and makes a rough sketch of this scene of carnage. The doorbell rings and Officer Blitz learns that the person at the door lives in this apartment. Officer Blitz should now

(A) check this occupant of the apartment for injuries and possible need for medical care
(B) refuse admittance to this person
(C) leave because the owner of the apartment has returned
(D) cover the bodies

72. Police Officer vanNorden, who has just completed a special course in suicide prevention mediation, is summoned over his radio to the North River Bridge where a young man has climbed to the top of a suspension tower and is threatening to jump. Officer vanNorden discovers that the man speaks hesitant English so requests a backup interpreter. With the assistance of Gloria Ariza, vanNorden succeeds in talking the man down, though not in learning his name, and makes these notes in his book:

Location:	central suspension tower on west side of North River Bridge
Time:	5:10 P.M.
Event:	threatened suicide
Description:	23-year-old Hispanic male, slight build, about 5 ft. 8 in., primary language Spanish, wearing denim cutoffs, gray tank top, and canvas sneakers. Name not revealed. Individual just learned that he is HIV positive.
Assisting personnel:	Gloria Ariza, certified interpreter, civilian police employee

Officer vanNorden must prepare a report to enter into his activity record and to transmit to psychiatrists who will examine and treat the threatened suicide at the city hospital. Which of the following expresses the information *most clearly, accurately, and completely?*

(A) An HIV positive 23-year-old Hispanic male speaking Spanish tried to jump off the North River Bridge at 5:10 P.M. Gloria Ariza talked him out of it wearing denim cutoffs, gray tank top, and canvas sneakers.

(B) A 23-year-old Spanish-speaking male wearing denim cutoffs, gray tank top, and canvas sneakers is 5 ft. 8 in. and has a slight build. He is HIV positive and doesn't know his name. He wanted to jump off the North River Bridge but Gloria Ariza and I told him not to so he didn't.

(C) At 5:10 P.M. Police Officer Gloria Ariza and I convinced an unidentified 23-year-old Hispanic male, about 5 ft. 8 in., slightly built, HIV positive, and wearing denim cutoffs, gray tank top, and canvas sneakers, not to jump from a suspension tower of the North River Bridge.

(D) At 5:10 P.M. an unidentified 23-year-old Hispanic male, about 5 ft. 8 in., slightly built, wearing denim cutoffs, gray tank top, and canvas sneakers, threatened to jump from the central suspension tower on the west side of the North River Bridge. Spanish interpreter Gloria Ariza and I dissuaded him despite the fact that he is HIV positive.

Answer questions 73 and 74 on the basis of the map below. The flow of traffic is indicated by the arrows. If there is only one arrow shown, then traffic flows only in the direction indicated by the arrow. If there are two arrows shown, then traffic flows in both directions. You must follow the flow of traffic.

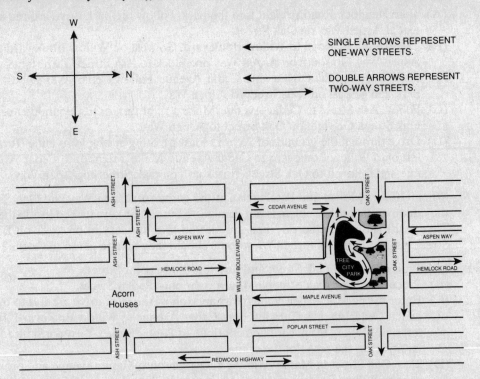

SINGLE ARROWS REPRESENT
ONE-WAY STREETS.

DOUBLE ARROWS REPRESENT
TWO-WAY STREETS.

73. Police Officers Patel and Mohan are in their patrol car on Ash Street at the corner of Hemlock Road when they receive word of a car being vandalized on Aspen Way at the corner of Oak Street. Which is the fastest legal route for the officers to take to apprehend the vandals?

(A) Take Hemlock Road straight into the park. Follow the park drive around and exit at Aspen Way on Oak Street.

(B) Take Hemlock Road to Willow Boulevard. Go west on Willow Boulevard to Aspen Way. Go south on Aspen Way one block to Ash Street. Turn right onto Ash Street and right again onto Cedar Avenue. Follow Cedar Avenue past the park and go east on Oak Street to Aspen Way.

(C) Follow Ash Street to Cedar Avenue. Make a right turn onto Cedar Avenue to Oak Street. Go right on Oak Street to Aspen Way.

(D) Drive through the grounds of Acorn Houses, exiting at Maple Avenue. Turn left onto Willow Boulevard to Cedar Avenue. Make a right onto Cedar Avenue and follow it to Oak Street. Turn south on Oak Street to Aspen Way.

74. When Officers Mohan and Patel arrive at the corner of Aspen Way and Oak Street, they discover that the problem is not vandalism but rather keys locked inside the car. They assist is opening the car, then are alerted to a burglary in progress on Poplar Street just south of Oak Street. What route should they take to get to the scene?

(A) Proceed east on Oak Street and turn left onto Poplar Street.

(B) Proceed east on Oak Street and turn right onto Poplar Street.

(C) Enter the park at Aspen Valley Way and follow the park drive around to the exit at Cedar Avenue. Turn left onto Cedar Avenue to Willow Boulevard. Turn left onto Willow Boulevard and continue to Poplar Street. Turn north into Poplar Street to the scene of the crime.

(D) Take Oak Street to Maple Avenue. Turn right onto Maple Avenue and proceed to Willow Boulevard. Make a left onto Willow Boulevard for one block, then another left onto Poplar Street.

75. An assumption commonly made in regard to the reliability of testimony is that when a number of persons report the same matter, those details upon which there is an agreement may generally be considered substantiated. Experiments have shown, however, that there is a tendency for the same errors to appear in the testimony of different individuals, and that, apart from any collusion, agreement of testimony is no proof of dependability. This paragraph suggests that

(A) if the testimony of a group of people is in substantial agreement, it cannot be ruled out that those witnesses have not all made the same mistake

(B) if details of the testimony are true, all witnesses will agree to it

(C) if most witnesses do not independently attest to the same facts, the facts cannot be true

(D) unless there is collusion, it is impossible for a number of persons to give the same report

76. Police officers must be trained in the safe and efficient operation of motor vehicles. Principles and techniques are thoroughly explained in the classroom before students are allowed to participate in the actual performance of practical exercises. Under close supervision and guidance, the students train until they recognize their personal limitations as well as limitations of the vehicle. The training curriculum should include courses in: highway response; defensive driving; skid control; transportation of prisoners; pursuit driving; evasive maneuver driving techniques; and accident investigation. The paragraph best supports the statement that

(A) it is important for police officers to understand the principles of motor vehicle operation

(B) the training curriculum is specific to the special requirements of police driving

(C) police officers have personal limitations so must be closely supervised

(D) vehicle maintenance is an important part of police driver training

77. Police Officer Thorkelson has just assisted the victim of a hit-and-run accident. He has seen the victim safely removed by ambulance and has made these notes in his memo book:

Location:	intersection of Grand Street and Myrtle Avenue
Occurrence:	hit and run accident
Victim:	very old Asian man, unconscious
Witness:	Joan Johnson of 332 Grand Street, Apt. 3B
Vehicle:	blue sports car with Texas license plates
Response by:	EMS ambulance #453; driver: Bo Barron; EMT: Hansi Kohl

Officer Thorkelson must now file a report about this incident. Which of the following expresses the information *most clearly, accurately and completely?*

(A) A very old Asian man was hit by Joan Johnson in a blue sports car at 332 Grand Street, Apt. 3B. EMS ambulance #453 took him away with Bo Barron and Hansi Kohl in attendance.

(B) Joan Johnson was hit by a very old Asian man at the intersection of Grand Street and Myrtle Avenue. The blue sports car was from Texas, and the ambulance was #453 driven by Bo Barron and EMT Hansi Kohl.

(C) Joan Johnson of 332 Grand Street, Apt. 3B reported that a very old Asian man was hit by a blue sports car at Grand and Myrtle. EMS ambulance #453 with Bo Barron driving and Hansi Kohl, EMT, responded and took the unconscious victim to the hospital.

(D) A blue sports car from Texas killed an old Asian man in front of Joan Johnson of 332 Grand Street, Apt. 3B. Bo Barron and EMT Hansi Kohl picked him up in EMS ambulance #453.

78. Police Officer Lovely, speeding in response to an emergency alert on his car radio, misjudges a tight right turn and hits a fire hydrant. Officer Lovely is not injured and the fire hydrant is not damaged, but the police car sustains a broken headlight and dented fender. Here are the facts:

Date:	Monday, June 3
Time:	10:46 A.M.
Location:	southeast corner of High Street and Low Avenue
Event:	collision with fire hydrant making right turn from northbound High Street en route to stabbing at Low Avenue and Middle Road
Damage:	broken headlight and dented right fender of police car #99, 1995 Chevrolet Corsica

Officer Lovely must file a report of this incident. Which of the following expresses the information *most clearly, accurately, and completely?*

(A) At 10:46 A.M. on Monday, June 3, on my way to the stabbing at Low Avenue and Middle Road, I hit the fire hydrant at the corner of High Street and Low Avenue. No one was hurt, but the right headlight was broken and the right fender of police car #99, a 1995 Chevrolet Corsica, was dented.

(B) A 1995 Chevrolet #99 police car broke a headlight and dented its right fender hitting a fire hydrant at Low Avenue and Middle Road going to a stabbing on June 3 at 10:46 A.M.

(C) On my way to a stabbing at 10:46, I broke a headlight and dented the right front fender of car #99 by hitting a fire hydrant. The hydrant is at High Street and Low Avenue. The car is a 1995 Chevrolet Corsica. I am fine.

(D) A fire hydrant at High Street and Low Avenue hit the broken headlight and dented right front fender of Chevrolet Corsica car #99 on the way to a stabbing on Monday, June 3. There were no injuries and no damage.

79. Police Officer Mroz leaves the diner at which he just drank a cup of coffee and proceeds to drive south on highway 6. He turns left onto Tobacco Road, then right onto Bonnie Lane, and right again onto Bank Street. As he is proceeding straight ahead on Bank Street, the railroad gate drops in front of him and he hears a train whistle approaching on his right. In what direction is the train traveling?

(A) North
(B) South
(C) East
(D) West

80. A police officer who observes a merchant selling liquor to a person who appears to the officer to be underage should take the following steps in this order:

1. Ask the purchaser for identification.
2. If the purchaser is a minor, as defined by the liquor laws, ask to see what identification was shown to the salesclerk.
3. Ask the salesperson what identification the purchaser presented.
4. If the salesperson did not request adequate proof, serve a summons on the person and on the establishment.
5. If the minor presented fraudulent proof, take the minor into custody.

Police Officer Murphy on foot patrol passes a liquor store and observes a youth leaving with a brown paper bag in his hand. Officer Murphy suspects that the youth is underage, stops him, and asks to see his identification. The young man produces a driver's license which indicates that he is 21 years of age and a picture ID from his place of employment.

Officer Murphy should now

(A) ask the salesperson what identification the young man presented
(B) release the young man and serve a summons on the salesclerk
(C) release the young man and continue patrolling her post
(D) take the young man into custody

81. When stopping a driver whom the officer suspects of being under the influence of alcohol or drugs, a police officer should follow this procedure:

1. Ask for driver's license and automobile registration.
2. Shine flashlight into driver's eyes and observe reaction of pupils.
3. Ask driver to step out of car.
4. Pat down driver for weapons.
5. Mark straight line on pavement or shoulder and ask driver to walk on it.
6. Ask driver to touch nose.

Police Officer Perry has stopped a car that has been wandering from side to side across the road. Officer Perry has followed proper procedure and has just asked the driver to step outside of the car. Next Officer Perry should

(A) check the driver's license and registration that the driver handed him
(B) sniff the driver's breath
(C) shine his flashlight into the driver's eyes while asking him to touch his nose
(D) pat the driver down for weapons

82. A police car exits the police station parking lot from its north exit and proceeds straight ahead until it comes to a traffic circle. The car travels counterclockwise two-thirds of the way around the circle and exits on the spoke street at that point on the circle. After four blocks, the car makes a right turn. In what direction is the car headed?

(A) North
(B) Northwest
(C) West
(D) Southwest

83. A police officer should never put his or her own life in jeopardy except to save the life of a member of the public that he or she is sworn to protect. An officer encountering a situation that is illegal and potentially volatile, but not immediately dangerous to the participants, should proceed in this manner:

   1. Call for backup.
   2. Observe quietly and inconspicuously until backups arrive in adequate numbers.
   3. Draw weapons in a show of strength,
   4. Request that the activity cease at once.
   5. Shoot only if seriously threatened.
   6. Take participants into custody.
   7. Disperse bystanders.

   Police Officer Smith on foot patrol in a congested immigrant neighborhood hears unusual sounds coming from an alley along his post. He peers carefully into the alley and slowly works his way towards its end. At the end of the alley is a cellar door, and at the base of the steps is a makeshift arena in which a cockfight is taking place. Bettors and handlers are excitedly waving pistols and beer cans. Spectators are also participating in the excitement. Officer Smith backs a short distance into the alley and radios for heavy reinforcements. Officer Smith should now

   (A) watch the activity from the alley
   (B) enter the cellar and merge with the crowd to watch
   (C) quietly shoo away the bystanders
   (D) leave the alley to wait for reinforcements

84. Police Officer Dayan is patrolling the area near an elementary school and observes a man sitting in a white car stopping and speaking to children as they pass. Some children stop and face the window so that Officer Dayan cannot tell exactly what is going on. Officer Dayan approaches the car, and the man suddenly speeds off in a westbound direction on Ocean Avenue. She then interviews some children and takes these notes:

Location:	side entrance of PS 36
Time:	8:22 A.M.
Suspect:	white man, mid-30s in white Buick Skylark, approx. 1993, New York plates including letters TY
Incident:	attempted drug sales
Witnesses:	Mary Jelko, age 10, of 127 Woodruff Place
	Robert Tank, age 9, of 876 Caledonian Court

   Officer Dayan radios a description of the man and car to the dispatcher. She then prepares a report of the incident. Which of the following expresses the information *most clearly, accurately, and completely?*

   (A) Mary Jelko, a 10-year-old who lives on Woodruff Place and Robert Tank, who is only 9 and lives on Caledonian Court, said that a man in a white car was trying to sell them reefers outside PS 36 before school at the side entrance.
   (B) A white man in a white Buick, New York plates with TY on them, tried to sell drugs to Mary Jelko, age 10, of 876 Caledonian Court and Robert Tank, age 9, of 127 Woodruff Place at 8:22 this morning at PS 36. He went west.
   (C) At 8:22 this morning at the side entrance of PS 36, a white man in a white Buick Skylark with New York plates including the letters TY attempted to sell drugs to 10-year-old Mary Jelko of 127 Woodruff Place and 9-year-old Robert Tank of 876 Caledonian Court. The suspect was last seen driving west on Ocean Avenue.
   (D) A white man with New York license plates sells drugs to children at PS 36 on Ocean Avenue in the morning before school. Mary Jelko, 10, who lives at 127 Woodruff Court and Robert Tank, 9, who lives at 876 Caledonian Place told me about it. The man drove away very fast going west.

85. Police Officer Davis patrolling the park by motorcycle on a bitterly cold day hears cries from the direction of the partially frozen lake. He runs to the sound and sees that a large dog has fallen through the ice in a shallow area near the edge of the lake. A teenage girl is calling to the dog and shouting that someone should save it. Officer Davis radios for immediate assistance from a car with blankets, then wades in and rescues the dog. In the warm police car that arrives promptly, Officer Davis dries the dog and takes these notes:

Location:	south shore of Muddy Lake, Clover Park
Date:	February 4
Time:	4:10 P.M.
Incident:	rescued dog that fell through ice in shallow water
Dog's owner:	Peggy Wilson, 15, of 1979 Sunrise Drive, Apt. 12B
Assisted by:	Officer Kalish in police car #66

When Officer Davis is warm and dry, he writes up a report of this incident. Which of the following expresses the information *most clearly, accurately, and completely?*

(A) Peggy Wilson's dog fell through the ice into Muddy Lake in Clover Park at 4:10 P.M. I rescued it and police car #66 with Officer Kalish helped me.

(B) At 4:10 P.M. on February 4, a dog owned by Peggy Wilson who is 15 years old and lives at 1979 Sunset Drive, Apt. 12 B was rescued from the icy water in the lake by Officer Kalish of police car #66.

(C) Peggy Wilson who is 15 years old was in Muddy Lake in Clover Park with her dog at 4:10 P.M. through the ice. Officer Kalish in police car #66 answered my radio call and we rescued her at 1979 Sunrise Drive, Apt. 12B on February 4.

(D) On February 4 at 4:10 P.M. at the shallow end of Muddy Lake in Clover Park, I rescued the dog of 15-year-old Peggy Wilson of Apt. 12B, 1979 Sunrise Drive. Officer Kalish of car #66 assisted with warming and transportation.

ANSWER KEY FOR PRACTICE EXAMINATION 4

1. B	12. D	23. B	34. B	45. D	56. B	67. D	78. A
2. D	13. D	24. C	35. D	46. A	57. B	68. A	79. B
3. A	14. B	25. D	36. A	47. B	58. D	69. B	80. C
4. D	15. C	26. D	37. B	48. C	59. C	70. C	81. D
5. C	16. D	27. C	38. D	49. B	60. A	71. B	82. B
6. B	17. B	28. B	39. A	50. C	61. B	72. D	83. A
7. C	18. B	29. A	40. D	51. C	62. A	73. C	84. C
8. C	19. A	30. D	41. C	52. A	63. C	74. D	85. D
9. A	20. C	31. C	42. C	53. D	64. D	75. A	
10. B	21. D	32. A	43. A	54. B	65. C	76. B	
11. C	22. A	33. B	44. D	55. C	66. B	77. C	

EXPLANATORY ANSWERS FOR PRACTICE EXAMINATION 4

1. **(B)** A sign on the wall indicates that rooms 2I-S are to the right. The stairs are to the right of the elevator.

2. **(D)** The man peeking from the personnel manager's office is not wearing glasses.

3. **(A)** The time indicated on the clock is 10:25. If there is a clock, expect a time question.

4. **(D)** The bald black man has a newspaper on his lap.

5. **(C)** There are nine people in the scene. Always count people in a memory picture.

6. **(B)** The kneeling terrorist has a handgun.

7. **(C)** The receptionist has close-cropped hair and is looking straight ahead. She is holding a pencil in her left hand, so it is reasonable to assume that she is left-handed.

8. **(C)** The indicator above the elevator goes from L to 5. This makes six in all.

9. **(A)** The woman terrorist has both boots on the floor. *Health* magazine is on the table in front of her.

10. **(B)** The young boy is sitting on one leg and is not wearing glasses. The seeing-eye dog undoubtedly came with the blind woman.

11. **(C)** The seated woman terrorist is wearing an army camouflage jumpsuit and has her gun pointed at the opposite bench. The dog is watching her. It is the man terrorist who is obviously carrying extra ammunition.

12. **(D)** The Hispanic woman sitting in front of the pile of newspapers is wearing high-heeled sandals and has her right leg crossed over her left.

13. **(D)** The floor lamp is next to the black man. The potted plant is next to the receptionist's desk; the umbrella is leaning on the opposite bench; there is no umbrella stand.

14. **(B)** There is a waste container between elevator and stairs. Neither water cooler nor coat rack are shown in this scene.

15. **(C)** Choices (A) and (B) neglect to mention the fire. (D) leaves out the time and expresses an opinion. A report should be factual; not conjectural.

16. **(D)** Only this statement gives all relevant information in logical order. Choice (A) does not give adequate location information; the other choices are garbled.

17. **(B)** Rule 3 prohibits use of names over the radio.

18. **(B)** Rule 4 of the procedure indicates that Officer Alcorn should have accompanied the man to the hospital since the man refused to identify himself.

19. **(A)**

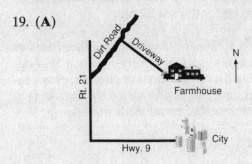

20. **(C)**

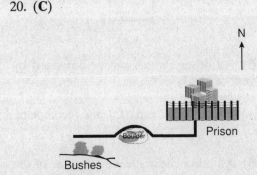

21. **(D)** The paragraph tells us that the payroll department complies with IRS regulations in withholding taxes from salaries and wages. The IRS determines the tax, not the salaries.

22. **(A)** The most important thing is to get medical help for the child.

23. **(B)** Officer Szulk wants assistance. He must be specific about his location.

24. **(C)** Choice (D) includes all the information, but (C) is clearer.

25. **(D)** Rule 4 explains why the other choices are wrong. Choice (D) conforms with rule 6.

26. **(D)** The officers violated rule 1. The officers had no way of knowing that there was no gun and no argument. If there were, a knock at the door might easily provoke a shot at the door.

27. **(C)** The dictionary definition of *homicide* is "the killing of one person by another."

28. **(B)** Both committed harassment: Blount because she pushed Wallace in an attempt to scare her and Wallace because she made an obscene gesture at Blount.

29. **(A)** Hammer did not injure either Bates or Collins so he is not guilty of assault. Without a full list of definitions of all crimes, you cannot state that he committed no crime. In fact, Hammer was intentionally reckless.

30. **(D)**

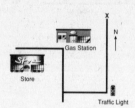

31. **(C)** All other choices can be answered by "yes" or "no."

32. **(A)** Choices (B) and (D) are incomplete. (C) has the address wrong.

33. **(B)** All other choices leave out some of the information.

34. **(B)**
$20 × 5 = $100.00
$10 × 7 = 70.00
$ 5 × 13 = 65.00
$ 1 × 2 = 2.00
$ .25 × 9 = 2.25
$ .10 × 21 = 2.10
$ .05 × 17 = .85
$ .01 × 8 = .08
_____
$242.28

35. **(D)** Rule 1. An officer should never assume the responsibility of deciding whether or not a prisoner requires the services of a doctor.

36. **(A)** Rule 2 governs. It is apparent that the prisoner requires medical attention even though there is no emergency. Medical attention is required for the prisoner's wound, not for his drug addition, therefore an ambulance should be called.

37. **(B)** In saying that investigators must devote themselves completely though the work may not be easy, smooth, or peaceful, the paragraph is saying that they must be persistent in the face of difficulty.

38. **(D)** All other choices are leading questions.

39. **(A)** This is the only choice that gives time, date, location, and description of a suspect.

40. **(D)** Who was robbed and by whom? Who was wearing what? When and where did it happen? Choice **(D)** tells it best.

41. **(C)** The rule states that the first question must relate to the sex of the missing person. The fact that the woman referred to the baby as "she" is no guarantee that the baby is a girl. Confusion of pronouns is very common among people for whom English is not the primary language, especially in time of stress.

42. **(C)**

43. **(A)** According to the definition of *larceny*, one may be considered guilty of this crime if found property is not returned to its owner. Since the question makes no reference to a search for the rightful owner, one must assume intent to keep the ring.

44. **(D)** *Larceny* also involves obtaining property under false pretenses, the situation here.

45. **(D)** In compliance with Rule 1, the first thing the officer must do is ascertain that the woman is indeed dead.

46. **(A)** The officer is certain that the man is dead, and the body is in the apartment not in public view. Rule 3 requires that the officer now summon a sergeant to the scene.

47. **(B)** The sister did not live with the dead man so, according to Rule 6, the albums may not be released to her.

48. **(C)**

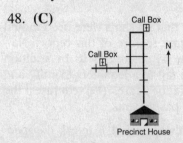

49. **(B)** At this moment police cars in the area would need as much information as possible about the offending car. Details about the car that was hit, aside from color, are not relevant to pursuit. Choices (A) and (C) give incomplete descriptions; choice (D) has the state of registration wrong.

50. **(C)** Since the man is clearly confused, the information he has given about his residence or former residence, how he arrived at this location, and possibly even his name should not be reported as fact. Physical description of the man is very important for purposes of establishing his identity and of finding a responsible person to claim him.

51. **(C)** The second sentence lists the permissible uses of annual leave allowance.

52. **(A)** According to the last sentence of the paragraph, he *may* be required to show a doctor's note for absences of 1, 2, or 3 days.

53. **(D)**

54. **(B)**

55. **(C)** The officers were assigned to close off the street to all traffic except emergency vehicles. They have used poor judgment. Their unattended parked police car cannot be easily moved to permit arriving emergency vehicles to enter the street.

56. **(B)** Choices (A) and (C) are both garbled and incomplete. (D) is accurate, but (B) is far clearer.

57. **(B)** Officer Seguaro has followed the procedure properly through step 5. Since the caller is just across the hall from the location of the child abuse, there is no reason to send a second car. The caller has already said that he does not know the identity of the abuser, so there is no point to asking his relationship to the abuser. But, the caller might be related to the child being beaten. Officer Seguaro must ask.

58. **(D)** This is an all-inclusive description. (B) is wrong; (A) is garbled; (C) neglects to describe the car.

59. **(C)** This report is correct and very complete. (A) gives neither description nor address; (B) neglects to describe the perpetrator; and (D) describe the man wrong and omits the location.

60. **(A)**

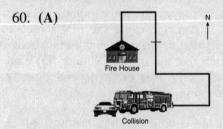

61. **(B)** The car is hot and is leaking gasoline. An explosion is a very real and imminent danger. Officer D'Onofrio must get the victim and himself away from the car as quickly as possible, even at the risk of causing the victim some harm by moving him. Officer D'Onofrio's second act should be to apply pressure to stop the bleeding. Artificial respiration restores breathing, not consciousness. The arm can wait.

62. **(A)** According to the rules as stated, Officer Mardikian is now responsible for notifying the Traffic Department to repair the signal light. You might expect that the desk officer could notify the Traffic Department and that the officer would be better utilized directing traffic, but you must answer exam questions on the basis of the rules as printed. Actual procedures may, of course, be different.

63. **(C)** Officer Poplis has already followed the man. His walking slowly and peering into windows might just be a way of killing time, but his trying doorknobs is clear reason to suspect that he intends to commit a crime. Asking for identification and explanation for the behavior is the proper next step.

64. **(D)** Officer Moro should be satisfied that a crime has not been committed, is not being committed, and will not be committed. The reason for the quarrel is none of his business. It is time for Police Officer Moro to move on.

65. **(C)** The definitions make it quite clear that murder is planned and intentional while felony murder refers to accidental death that occurs during commission or *attempted commission*—which is why (B) is wrong—of another crime.

66. **(B)** If no part of the training of a law officer is more important or more valuable (sentence 2), then clearly the most useful and essential single factor in the training of a law officer is proper firearms training. Choice (A) is incorrect because the first sentence says only that firearms training *cannot* be ignored not that it *is* ignored. Choice (D) is an overstatement; lives often depend directly upon weapons skills, but not always.

67. **(D)** In describing standing posture, *stance* refers specifically to placement of feet.

68. **(A)**

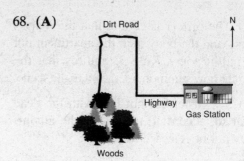

69. **(B)** The fact that no shots were fired should be an important feature of this report. Neither (A) nor (C) mentions it. In addition these choices fail to adequately identify and locate the liquor store. (D) confuses the names of the participants.

70. **(C)** The next step, step 4, is to ask the spectators to get out of the way.

71. **(B)** Rule 5 is very clear. Access is permitted only to police and medical personnel.

72. **(D)** Choices (A) and (B) are incomplete and poorly stated. Was Gloria Ariza wearing denim cutoffs? (C) includes the information quite clearly, but incorrectly identifies the civilian interpreter as a police officer.

73. **(C)** Choice (A) is incorrect because one cannot exit the park at Aspen Way; (B) is legal but is surely not the quickest, most direct route; (D) is incorrect because Ash Street is westbound, so the officers cannot enter the grounds of Acorn Houses from Ash and Hemlock. (D) is further impossible because Oak Street runs east, not south.

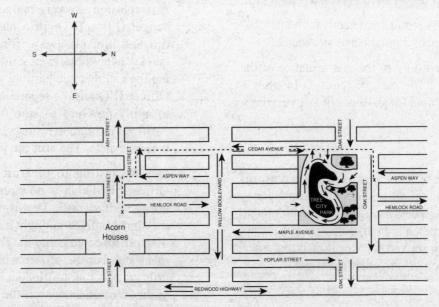

74. **(D)** Choice (A) is incorrect because a left turn onto Poplar will take them away from the scene of the burglary; (B) is incorrect because Poplar is one-way northbound and a right off Oak would send them south; (C) is an unnecessarily long and circuitous route.

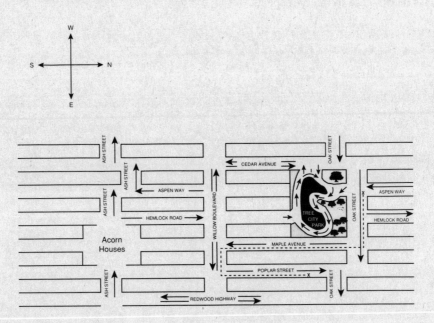

75. **(A)** Just as *agreement of testimony is no proof of dependability,* so agreement of testimony is no proof of undependability; they can all make the same mistake either way.

76. **(B)** The paragraph lists some of the specialized courses in the police driving curriculum.

77. **(C)** Even though this report omits the useful information that the car had Texas plates, it is by far the most clear and accurate of the choices. (A) is garbled with respect to suspect and location; (B) misidentifies participants; (D) overstates—the victim is unconscious, not dead.

78. **(A)** Choice (B) mislocates the fire hydrant; (C) is written childishly and leaves out the date; (D) blames the fire hydrant for the accident and implies that the damage had already been done before the accident.

79. **(B)**

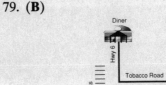

80. **(C)** The facts as presented indicate that Officer Murphy's suspicion was unfounded. The young man is of legal age, and there is no reason to question the salesperson.

81. **(D)** Now that the driver is outside of the car, step 4 is to pat him down for weapons.

82. **(B)**

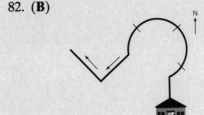

83. **(A)** Officer Smith has gotten only to step 2. He should stay right where he is and observe until his backups arrive.

84. **(C)** Choice (A) inadequately describes man and car; (B) confuses the addresses of the children; (D) is incomplete in many respects.

85. **(D)** Choice (A) inadequately describes Peggy Wilson; (B) credits Officer Kalish with the rescue; (C) places Peggy Wilson in the lake with her dog.

Answer Sheet for Practice Examination 5

1. Ⓐ Ⓑ Ⓒ Ⓓ
2. Ⓐ Ⓑ Ⓒ Ⓓ
3. Ⓐ Ⓑ Ⓒ Ⓓ
4. Ⓐ Ⓑ Ⓒ Ⓓ
5. Ⓐ Ⓑ Ⓒ Ⓓ
6. Ⓐ Ⓑ Ⓒ Ⓓ
7. Ⓐ Ⓑ Ⓒ Ⓓ
8. Ⓐ Ⓑ Ⓒ Ⓓ
9. Ⓐ Ⓑ Ⓒ Ⓓ
10. Ⓐ Ⓑ Ⓒ Ⓓ
11. Ⓐ Ⓑ Ⓒ Ⓓ
12. Ⓐ Ⓑ Ⓒ Ⓓ
13. Ⓐ Ⓑ Ⓒ Ⓓ
14. Ⓐ Ⓑ Ⓒ Ⓓ
15. Ⓐ Ⓑ Ⓒ Ⓓ
16. Ⓐ Ⓑ Ⓒ Ⓓ
17. Ⓐ Ⓑ Ⓒ Ⓓ
18. Ⓐ Ⓑ Ⓒ Ⓓ
19. Ⓐ Ⓑ Ⓒ Ⓓ
20. Ⓐ Ⓑ Ⓒ Ⓓ

21. Ⓐ Ⓑ Ⓒ Ⓓ
22. Ⓐ Ⓑ Ⓒ Ⓓ
23. Ⓐ Ⓑ Ⓒ Ⓓ
24. Ⓐ Ⓑ Ⓒ Ⓓ
25. Ⓐ Ⓑ Ⓒ Ⓓ
26. Ⓐ Ⓑ Ⓒ Ⓓ
27. Ⓐ Ⓑ Ⓒ Ⓓ
28. Ⓐ Ⓑ Ⓒ Ⓓ
29. Ⓐ Ⓑ Ⓒ Ⓓ
30. Ⓐ Ⓑ Ⓒ Ⓓ
31. Ⓐ Ⓑ Ⓒ Ⓓ
32. Ⓐ Ⓑ Ⓒ Ⓓ
33. Ⓐ Ⓑ Ⓒ Ⓓ
34. Ⓐ Ⓑ Ⓒ Ⓓ
35. Ⓐ Ⓑ Ⓒ Ⓓ
36. Ⓐ Ⓑ Ⓒ Ⓓ
37. Ⓐ Ⓑ Ⓒ Ⓓ
38. Ⓐ Ⓑ Ⓒ Ⓓ
39. Ⓐ Ⓑ Ⓒ Ⓓ
40. Ⓐ Ⓑ Ⓒ Ⓓ

41. Ⓐ Ⓑ Ⓒ Ⓓ
42. Ⓐ Ⓑ Ⓒ Ⓓ
43. Ⓐ Ⓑ Ⓒ Ⓓ
44. Ⓐ Ⓑ Ⓒ Ⓓ
45. Ⓐ Ⓑ Ⓒ Ⓓ
46. Ⓐ Ⓑ Ⓒ Ⓓ
47. Ⓐ Ⓑ Ⓒ Ⓓ
48. Ⓐ Ⓑ Ⓒ Ⓓ
49. Ⓐ Ⓑ Ⓒ Ⓓ
50. Ⓐ Ⓑ Ⓒ Ⓓ
51. Ⓐ Ⓑ Ⓒ Ⓓ
52. Ⓐ Ⓑ Ⓒ Ⓓ
53. Ⓐ Ⓑ Ⓒ Ⓓ
54. Ⓐ Ⓑ Ⓒ Ⓓ
55. Ⓐ Ⓑ Ⓒ Ⓓ
56. Ⓐ Ⓑ Ⓒ Ⓓ
57. Ⓐ Ⓑ Ⓒ Ⓓ
58. Ⓐ Ⓑ Ⓒ Ⓓ
59. Ⓐ Ⓑ Ⓒ Ⓓ
60. Ⓐ Ⓑ Ⓒ Ⓓ

61. Ⓐ Ⓑ Ⓒ Ⓓ
62. Ⓐ Ⓑ Ⓒ Ⓓ
63. Ⓐ Ⓑ Ⓒ Ⓓ
64. Ⓐ Ⓑ Ⓒ Ⓓ
65. Ⓐ Ⓑ Ⓒ Ⓓ
66. Ⓐ Ⓑ Ⓒ Ⓓ
67. Ⓐ Ⓑ Ⓒ Ⓓ
68. Ⓐ Ⓑ Ⓒ Ⓓ
69. Ⓐ Ⓑ Ⓒ Ⓓ
70. Ⓐ Ⓑ Ⓒ Ⓓ
71. Ⓐ Ⓑ Ⓒ Ⓓ
72. Ⓐ Ⓑ Ⓒ Ⓓ
73. Ⓐ Ⓑ Ⓒ Ⓓ
74. Ⓐ Ⓑ Ⓒ Ⓓ
75. Ⓐ Ⓑ Ⓒ Ⓓ
76. Ⓐ Ⓑ Ⓒ Ⓓ
77. Ⓐ Ⓑ Ⓒ Ⓓ
78. Ⓐ Ⓑ Ⓒ Ⓓ
79. Ⓐ Ⓑ Ⓒ Ⓓ
80. Ⓐ Ⓑ Ⓒ Ⓓ

81. Ⓐ Ⓑ Ⓒ Ⓓ
82. Ⓐ Ⓑ Ⓒ Ⓓ
83. Ⓐ Ⓑ Ⓒ Ⓓ
84. Ⓐ Ⓑ Ⓒ Ⓓ

TEAR HERE

PRACTICE EXAMINATION 5

The time allowed for the entire examination is 3   hours.

Directions: Each question has four suggested answers, lettered (A), (B), (C), and (D). Decide which one is the best answer, and on the sample answer sheet, locate the question number and darken the area corresponding to your answer choice with a soft pencil.

Questions 1 through 15 are to be answered on the basis of the description of the police action which follows. You will have ten minutes to read and study the description. Then you will have to answer the 15 questions about the incident without referring back to the description of the incident.

Police Officers Smith and Jones were working a midnight to 8 A.M. tour of duty. It was a Saturday morning in the month of July and the weather was clear. At about 4:30 A.M., Officers Smith and Jones received a radio call reporting a burglary in progress at 777 Seventeenth Street, the address of an appliance store.

Upon their arrival at the scene, the officers could not find evidence of a break-in. However, as the officers continued their investigation, they heard noises coming from the rear of the building. As the officers raced to the rear of the building, they saw four people alighting from the roof, by way of a ladder, and climbing over a fence that leads to the rear of a warehouse. As the officers climbed over the fence, they observed two of the people running into an alleyway on the west side of the warehouse and the other two people running into a parking lot on the east side of the warehouse.

Officer Smith, using a walkie-talkie, called for assistance and proceeded to give chase after the two persons who entered the alley. The description of the two individuals was as follows: One was a male white, wearing light pants, a blue shirt, and white sneakers, with long blond hair, and carrying what appeared to be a portable T.V. set. The other was also a male white, wearing dungarees, a white T-shirt, and cowboy boots, with short dark hair, and carrying what appeared to be a portable cassette-stereo-radio.

417

Officer Jones continued to give chase to the two individuals who had entered the parking lot. The description of these two individuals was as follows: One was a male Hispanic, wearing dark pants, a yellow shirt, and dark shoes, with long dark hair, and carrying what appeared to be a video recorder. The other was a male black, wearing dungarees, a white T-shirt, and white sneakers, with a bald head, and carrying what appeared to be a baseball bat and portable T.V. set.

As Officer Smith emerged from the alley onto the sidewalk, he again observed the two individuals he had been chasing. They were entering a dark blue Chevrolet with New York license plates, beginning with the letters AKG. The vehicle drove west on Seventh Street. The male with the long blond hair appeared to be driving.

As Officer Jones reached the parking lot, he observed the two individuals he was pursuing speed off in a white station wagon, heading west on Seventh Street. The license plates could not be discerned. Officer Jones found a broken portable T.V. set in the parking lot.

Officer Smith broadcast this additional information, and both officers then quickly returned to their radio car to conduct a search of the area.

Do not refer back to the description while answering questions 1 through 15.

1. Officers Smith and Jones responded to a "burglary in progress" call at approximately

   (A) midnight
   (B) 8:00 A.M.
   (C) 4:30 P.M.
   (D) 4:30 A.M.

2. This suspects in the burglary gained entrance to the store by

   (A) breaking a front window
   (B) breaking a rear window
   (C) breaking in from an adjoining warehouse
   (D) using a ladder to get to the roof.

3. The suspects, when fleeing from the burglary,

   (A) all ran into an alleyway
   (B) all ran into a parking lot
   (C) all ran into a warehouse
   (D) went in different directions.

4. The male white with the long blond hair was carrying what appeared to be a

   (A) portable T.V. set
   (B) portable cassette-stereo-radio
   (C) video recorder
   (D) portable cassette player.

5. The male Hispanic was carrying what appeared to be a

   (A) video recorder
   (B) portable cassette-stereo-radio
   (C) portable T.V. set
   (D) portable cassette player.

6. The male white with the short hair was carrying what appeared to be a

   (A) portable T.V. set
   (B) portable cassette-stereo-radio
   (C) video recorder
   (D) portable cassette player

7. The suspect wearing cowboy boots was the

   (A) male white with long blond hair
   (B) male black
   (C) male Hispanic
   (D) male white with short hair.

8. The suspect wearing light pants and blue shirt was the

   (A) male black
   (B) male white with long blond hair
   (C) male Hispanic
   (D) male white with short hair.

9. The suspect wearing dark pants and a yellow shirt was the

   (A) male white with long blond hair
   (B) male black
   (C) male white with short hair
   (D) male Hispanic.

10. When the suspects were fleeing, the two male whites entered a

    (A) blue station wagon with unknown license plates
    (B) white station wagon with New York license plates beginning with the letters AKG
    (C) blue Chevrolet with New York license plates beginning with the letters AKG
    (D) white Chevrolet with unknown license plates.

11. From reading the description of the incident, one could assume

    (A) that Seventh Street is one way westbound
    (B) that Seventh Steet is a two-way street
    (C) that Seventh Street is one way eastbound
    (D) none of the above.

12. Upon entering the parking lot, Officer Jones found a broken portable T.V. set that has apparently been dropped by the

    (A) male white with blond hair
    (B) male white with dark hair
    (C) male black
    (D) male Hispanic.

13. The male black was

    (A) bald, and wearing dark pants, a yellow shirt, and dark shoes
    (B) bald, wearing dungarees, a white T-shirt, and white sneakers
    (C) wearing dungarees, a white T-shirt, and cowboy boots, and had dark hair
    (D) bald, and wearing light pants and a blue shirt.

14. The suspect who was carrying the baseball bat was also carrying what appeared to be a

    (A) portable T.V. set
    (B) video recorder
    (C) portable cassette-stereo-radio
    (D) portable cassette player.

15. A description of the suspects was broadcast to other police units so that they could assist in searching the area. This was done by
    (A) both Officers Jones and Smith as they both had walkie-talkies
    (B) Officer Jones as he had a walkie-talkie
    (C) Officer Smith as he had a walki-talkie
    (D) both officers upon returning to their radio car.

16. In the investigation of a homicide case, it is desirable to have photographs taken of the body in its original condition and position. Of the following, the best reason for this practice is that the photographs
    (A) show the motive for the hoimicide and thus indicate likely suspects
    (B) indicate if the corpse has been moved in any way
    (C) form a permanent record of the body and the scene of the crime
    (D) reveal the specific method used in committing the homicide.

17. A police officer hears two shots fired and proceeds in the direction of the shots. He comes upon an intoxicated man who is angrily screaming at a woman. The officer notices that the handle of a pistol is protruding from the man's pocket and orders him to surrender the pistol. The man apparently ignores the order and continues screaming at the woman. For the officer now to fire a warning shot over the man's head would be
    (A) bad; it is quite possible that the man is so intoxicated that he did not clearly hear or understand the officer's order
    (B) bad; the officer should realize that an intoxicated person is not entirely responsible for his actions
    (C) good, the warning shot will impress the man with the seriousness of the situation
    (D) good; since the man had already fired twice, the officer should take no further chances.

18. The practice of writing down confessions while a suspect is being questioned is
    (A) bad, chiefly because the time taken to put a confession into written form may prove to be a waste of time since it may later be declared to be inadmissible as evidence in court
    (B) bad, chiefly because this may cause the suspect to withhold information when he or she knows that the confession is being recorded
    (C) good, chiefly because the suspect cannot claim at a later date that the information was obtained by force
    (D) good, chiefly because the suspect is thereby given more time to gather his or her thoughts and give the information wanted by the police.

19. It is important for a police officer to be thoroughly familiar with the street locations, house numbers, and alleys on his or her post. In the event that the police officer is searching for a prowler reported to be on his or her post, this familiarity will be of greatest value in that it will enable the police officer to
    (A) capture the prowler more quickly by going directly to the usual haunts of those previously arrested for the same violation
    (B) anticipate possible avenues of flight which the prowler might take from the location where he was reported seen.
    (C) conduct a systematic search of the surrounding area
    (D) know which buildings are unoccupied and search for the prowler there first.

20. An escaped prisoner has been wounded and is lying flat on his stomach with his head turned to one side. The one of the following directions from which a police officer should approach the prisoner in order to make it most difficult for the prisoner to fire quickly and accurately at the police officer is from the side
    (A) directly behind the prisoner's head
    (B) facing the top of the prisoner's head
    (C) facing the prisoner's face
    (D) facing the prisoner's heels.

21. A gas main explosion has caused some property damage. Examination by an emergency repair crew clearly indicates that no further explosions will occur. Nevertheless, rumors are circulating that more explosions and greater damage are going to occur. This situation has resulted in a high degree of fear among local residents. The best of the following actions for a police officer on duty at the scene to take *first* would be to

(A) ignore the rumors since they are false and no real danger exists

(B) inform the people of the true circumstances of the emergency

(C) question several people at the scene in an attempt to determine the source of the rumors

(D) order everyone to leave the area quickly and in an orderly fashion.

22. A police officer finds a young child wandering about a residential neighborhood. After unsuccessfully questioning the child as to the location of his home, the officer phones police headquarters and is informed that no child meeting the description given by the officer has been reported as lost. The officer decides to make inquiries about the child in the immediate area before taking any other action. This action is advisable chiefly because

(A) the child's parents probably know of his whereabouts since no report of the missing child has been received at headquarters

(B) the child has probably been away from home only a short time since no report of the missing child has been received at headquarters

(C) the child is less likely to become emotionally disturbed if he remains in his own neighborhood

(D) young children, when lost, never wander more than a short distance from home.

23. While a police officer in plain clothes is following and watching a suspect in a homicide case, the officer becomes convinced that the suspect realizes he is being watched. The suspect's identity is known to the police, but he is also known to have changed his place of residence frequently during the past few months. The officer does not have sufficient evidence to arrest the suspect at this time. Of the following, the best action for the officer to take is to

(A) approach the suspect, inform him that he is being followed, and demand an explanation of his suspicious past conduct

(B) continue to follow the suspect until an opportunity is presented for the officer to telephone for a replacement

(C) continue to follow the suspect since he will probably commit an illegal act eventually

(D) discontinue following the suspect and attempt to gain evidence by other means.

24. While issuing a summons to the manager of a movie theater for allowing a child under 16 to remain in the theater without a parent or guardian at an R-rated movie, a police officer requests identification from the manager. The manager hands his wallet to the officer and says that his operator's license is in the wallet. The officer should not accept the wallet mainly

(A) because the sorting of papers and cards contained in the wallet would be too time consuming for the officer

(B) to discourage the manager from any possible bribery offer

(C) to lessen the possibility that the manager will later claim that money or papers were taken from the wallet

(D) to minimize the temptation for the officer to look at papers or cards of a personal nature.

25. Probationary Police Officers A and B are given a special assignment by the sergeant. Officer B does not fully understand some of the instructions given by the sergeant concerning the carrying out of the assignment. Of the following, it would be best for Officer B to

    (A) proceed with those parts of the assignment he understands and ask for an explanation from the sergeant when he can go no further
    (B) observe Officer A's work carefully in order to determine how the assignment is to be carried out
    (C) ask the sergeant to explain that portion of the instructions which he does not fully understand before starting the assignment
    (D) suggest to Officer A that he supervise the operation since he probably understands the sergeant's instructions better.

26. A police officer responds at night to a telephone complaint that a prowler has been observed at a particular location. The officer arrives at the location and notices someone who appears to fit the description of the prowler previously given by the complainant. In approaching this individual, it would be best for the police officer to

    (A) consider this individual to be a potentially dangerous criminal
    (B) avoid taking any precautionary measures since there is no way of knowing whether any offense has been committed
    (C) consider that this individual is probably harmless and is only a "Peeping Tom"
    (D) fire a warning shot over the man's head.

27. A police officer has been asked by a merchant on his post to recommend the best make of burglar alarm for his store. The chief reason why the police officer should not make any specific recommendation is that

    (A) he does not have enough technical knowledge of the operation of burglar alarms
    (B) the merchant may interpret the officer's recommendation as an official police department endorsement
    (C) such a recommendation would imply that the police are incapable of protecting the merchant's property
    (D) he is not likely to know the prices of the various makes and models available.

28. Two police officers in a radio patrol car stop a car which they recognize as having been reported stolen. The police officers immediately separate the two occupants of the car and proceed to question them apart from each other. Of the following, the most important reason for questioning them separately is to

    (A) give each suspect an opportunity to admit guilt out of the presence of the other suspect
    (B) prevent the suspects from agreeing on an explanation of their presence in the car
    (C) prevent the errors which may arise when attempting to record in a notebook two separate statements being made at the same time
    (D) determine which of the two suspects actually planned the theft of the car.

29. While on patrol, you are informed by the manager of a supermarket that an object which appears to be a homemade bomb has been discovered in his market. Your first reaction should be to

    (A) go to the market amd make sure that everyone leaves it immediately
    (B) go to the market, examine the bomb, and then decide what action should be taken
    (C) question the manager in detail in an effort to determine whether this really is a bomb
    (D) telephone the bomb squad for instructions as to how the bomb should be rendered harmless.

30. A police officer on post would be most likely to make a regular hourly signal-box call to the precinct, rather than an immediate call, when he or she

    (A) discovers that a traffic signal light is not functioning properly
    (B) discovers what appears to be an abandoned car on the post
    (C) notices a street name sign which has been damaged
    (D) overhears a conversation relating to a possible disturbance between two groups of teenagers.

31. The most reasonable advice that a police officer can give to a merchant who asks what he should do if he receives a telephone call from a person he doesn't recognize regarding an alleged emergency at his store after ordinary business hours is that the merchant should go to the store and, if police officers are not at the scene, he should

(A) continue past the store and call the police for assistance
(B) continue past the store, and return and enter it if there doesn't appear to be an emergency
(C) enter the store and ascertain whether the alleged emergency exists
(D) enter the store only if there is no one apparently loitering in the vicinity.

32. A police officer is asked by a citizen for directions to a candy store which the officer knows is under observation for suspected bookmaking activity. In such a situation, the police officer should

(A) give the proper directions to the citizen
(B) give the proper directions to the citizen but explain that the store is under observation
(C) pretend not to know the location of the store
(D) tell the citizen that he may be arrested if the store is raided.

33. Whenever a crime has been committed, the criminal has disturbed the surroundings in one way or another by his or her presence. The *least* valid deduction for the police to make from this statement is that

(A) clues are thus present at all crime scenes
(B) even the slightest search at crime scenes will turn up conclusive evidence
(C) the greater the number of criminals involved in a crime, the greater the number of clues likely to be available
(D) the completely clueless crime is rarely encountered in police work

34. It is suggested that a suspect should not be permitted to walk in or about the scene of a crime where fingerprints may be present until a thorough search has been made for such evidence. This suggested procedure is

(A) good; the suspect would, if permitted to walk about the scene, smear all fingerprints that might be found by police investigators
(B) bad; the return of a suspect to the scene of a crime provides an opportunity to obtain additional fingerprints from the suspect
(C) good; if the suspect handled any objects at the scene, the value of any original fingerprints, as evidence, might be seriously impaired
(D) bad; the return of a suspect to the scene of a crime provides an opportunity to identify objects that had been handled during the commission of the crime.

35. A police officer is the first one to arrive at the scene of a murder. The suspect offers to make a statement concerning the crime. The police officer refuses to accept the statement. The officer's action was

(A) good; interrogation of suspects should be performed by experienced detectives
(B) poor; the suspect may later change his mind and refuse to make any statement
(C) good; the officer will be too busy maintaining order at the scene to be able to accept the statement
(D) poor; a statement made by the suspect would quickly solve the crime.

Answer questions 36 through 45 on the basis of the following legal definitions.

Burglary is committed when a person enters a building to commit a crime therein.

Larceny is committed when a person wrongfully takes, obtains, or withholds the property of another.

Robbery is the forcible stealing of property. If a person, while committing a larceny, uses or threatens the *immediate* use of force, the crime changes from larceny to robbery.

Sexual Abuse is committed when a person subjects another person to sexual contact without the second person's consent or when a person has sexual contact with another person less than 17 years of age. (A person less than 17 years of age cannot legally consent to any sexual conduct.) "Sexual contact" may be defined as touching the sexual or other intimate parts of a person to achieve sexual gratification.

Sexual Misconduct is committed when a male has sexual intercourse with a consenting female who is at least 13 years of age but less than 17 years of age.

Harassment is committed when a person intends to harass, annoy, or alarm another person and does so by striking, shoving, kicking, or otherwise subjecting the other person to physical contact.

Assault is committed when a person unlawfully causes a physical injury to another person.

36. James Kelly enters the home of Mary Smith with the intention of taking Mary's portable T.V. set. While Kelly is in the apartment, Mary wakes up and attempts to retrieve her T.V. set from Kelly. Kelly punches Mary in the face and flees with the T.V. set. Kelly can be charged with

(A) burglary and larceny
(B) burglary only
(C) robbery and larceny
(D) burglary and robbery.

37. John Brown enters a department store with the intention of doing some shopping. Brown has a .38 caliber revolver in his coat pocket and also has a criminal conviction for armed robbery. As he passes the jewelry counter, he notices an expensive watch lying on the showcase. He checks to see if anyone is watching him, and, when he feels that he is not being observed, he slips the watch into his pocket and leaves the store. Brown could be charged with

(A) larceny
(B) burglary and larceny
(C) burglary and robbery
(D) robbery.

38. Tom Murphy enters a crowded subway car. He positions himself behind a woman and starts to touch her buttocks with his hand. The woman becomes very annoyed and starts to move away. As she does so, Murphy reaches into her pocketbook and removes $10. He then exits the train at the next station. Murphy could be charged with

(A) robbery, larceny, and sexual misconduct
(B) burglary, robbery, and sexual abuse
(C) burglary, larceny, and sexual misconduct
(D) larceny and sexual abuse.

39. Ed Saunders entered the apartment of Jane Robers with the intent to sexually abuse her. However, Robers was not at home and Saunders left the apartment. Saunders could be charged with

(A) sexual abuse
(B) sexual misconduct
(C) burglary
(D) none of the above as a crime did not take place because Robers was not at home.

40. Frank Taylor entered the apartment of his 16-year-old girlfriend, Doris, to have sexual intercourse with her. Doris consented to this sexual conduct and they engaged in intercourse. Taylor could be charged with

(A) burglary
(B) sexual misconduct
(C) both burglary and sexual misconduct
(D) no crime as Doris consented to the activity.

41. Brian Jones asks his 17-year-old girlfriend, Mary, if she would like to go to a motel and have sexual intercourse. She agrees and they go to the motel. Jones could be charged with

(A) burglary
(B) sexual misconduct
(C) both burglary and sexual misconduct
(D) no crime as she consented to the activity.

42. Bill is at a party at Joan's house. An argument ensues among several of the guests. Bill overhears Helen make a derogatory comment about him. He walks up to Helen and demands she "apologize or else." Helen refuses to apologize; Bill slaps her in the face and then rushes from the apartment. Bill could be charged with

(A) assault
(B) burglary and assault
(C) harassment
(D) burglary and harassment.

43. Joe is on his way to work. He is in a very bad mood. As he enters the warehouse where he works, he slips and falls to the floor. This only escalates his foul mood. As he is getting up, he sees a fellow worker who had made some unkind remarks to him two days before. Joe picks up a piece of board that is lying on the floor, walks up to the other worker, and hits him across the arm. This causes the other worker to suffer a broken arm. Joe could be charged with

(A) assault
(B) burglary and assault
(C) harassment
(D) none of the above as Joe was emotionally upset.

44. Jim enters a school through a rear window at 2:00 A.M. He wants to take a movie projector that he knows is kept in a specific room. He enters the room, takes the projector, and starts to leave when he is confronted by a security guard. The guard attempts to grab Jim; however, Jim slips away. As the guard again attempts to apprehend him, Jim swings the projector, striking the guard in the face. The guard falls to the floor unconscious and suffers a broken nose. Jim could be charged with

(A) burglary, larceny, and robbery
(B) robbery, larceny, and assault
(C) burglary, larceny, and assault
(D) burglary, robbery, and assault.

45. Sue invites Tom to her apartment for dinner. After dinner, Tom decides that he would like to have a sexual encounter with Sue. She attempts to discourage his advances. Tom then proceeds to hold her down on the couch and to fondle her breasts and touch her private parts. When Sue starts to scream, Tom rushes from the apartment. Tom could be charged with

(A) burglary and sexual abuse
(B) burglary and sexual misconduct
(C) sexual abuse
(D) no crime as Sue invited him to her apartment.

46. It is important that the police give proper attention to the investigation of apparently minor, as well as major, complaints made by citizens. Of the following, the one which is the most valid reason for doing so is that

(A) minor complaints may be of great importance in the mind of the complainant
(B) minor complaints are more readily disposed of
(C) minor complaints may be an indication of a serious police problem
(D) police efficiency is determined by the attitude shown towards citizens complaints.

47. Hearsay evidence may be defined as testimony by one person that another person told him or her about a criminal act which that other person had witnessed. Hearsay evidence is usually not admissible in a criminal trial mainly because

(A) hearsay evidence is consistently biased and deliberately distorted
(B) hearsay evidence is usually not relevant to the issues of the case
(C) such evidence is usually distorted by both the original witness and the person to whom the observations were stated
(D) the actual witness to the criminal act is not being examined under oath.

48. "Arrests should not be given too much weight in the appraisal of a police officer's performance since a large number of arrests does not necessarily indicate that a good police job is being done." This statement is

(A) true, factors other than the number of arrests made must also be considered in judging police effectiveness

(B) false; the basic job of the police is to suppress crime and the surest measure of this is the number of arrests made

(C) true; arrest figures are not indicative in any way of a police officer's efficiency

(D) false; although some police officers are in a better position to make arrests than others, the law of averages should operate to even this out.

49. "Arson is a particularly troublesome crime for the police." Of the following statements, the one which is the *most* important reason why this is so is that

(A) arsonists usually seek the protection of darkness for their crimes

(B) arson occurs so infrequently that the police lack a definite approach for combatting it

(C) important evidence is frequently destroyed by the fire itself.

(D) witnesses find it difficult to distinguish arsonists from other criminals.

50. "Undoubtedly, the police have an important contribution to make to the welfare of youth." Of the following, the principal reason for this is that

(A) effectiveness is a result of experience and the police have had the longest experience in youth work

(B) no other agency can make use of the criminal aspects of the law as effectively as the police

(C) the police are in a strategic position to observe children actually or potentially deliquent and the conditions contributing thereto

(D) welfare agencies lack an understanding of the problems of youth.

51. An apparently senile man informs a police officer that he is returning from a visit to his daughter and that he is unable to find his way back home because he has forgotten his address. Of the following courses of action, the *first* one that should be taken by the officer is to

(A) question the man in an effort to establish his identity

(B) request the police missing persons section to describe to you any person recently reported as missing

(C) suggest that the man return to his daughter for travel directions to his home

(D) telephone a description of the man to the precinct station house.

52. Of the following facts about a criminal, the one which would be of most value in apprehending and identifying the criminal would be that he

(A) drives a black 1980 Chevrolet sedan with chrome license-plate holders

(B) invariably uses a .38 caliber Colt blue steel revolver with walnut stock and regulation front sight

(C) talks with a French accent and has a severe stutter

(D) usually wears three-button single-breasted "Ivy League" suits with white oxford cloth button-down-collar shirts

53. A pawnshop dealer has submitted to the police an accurate and complete description of a wristwatch which he recently purchased from a customer. The one of the following factors that would be most important in determining whether this wristwatch was stolen is the

(A) degree of investigative perservance demonstrated by the police

(B) exactness of police records describing stolen property

(C) honesty and neighborhood reputation of the pawnbroker

(D) time interval between the purchase of the wristwatch by the pawnbroker and the report made to the police.

54. A police officer at the scene of a serious vehicular accident requests two witnesses to the accident not to speak to each other until each one has given a statement to the officer concerning the accident. The most likely reason for this request by the police officer is that if the witnesses were allowed to speak to each other at this time they might

(A) become involved in a violent quarrel over what actually occurred

(B) change their opinion so that identical statements to the police would result

(C) discuss the possibility of a bribe offer to either of them by one of the operators involved in the accident

(D) have their original views of the accident somewhat altered by hearing each other's view of the accident.

55. "Tests have shown that sound waves set up by a siren have a greater intensity ahead than at either side or at the rear of a police car." On the basis of this quotation, it would be most reasonable for the operator of a police car, when responding to the scene of an emergency and using the siren, to expect that a motorist approaching an intersection from

(A) a side street may not stop his vehicle as soon as a more distant motorist directly ahead of the police car

(B) directly ahead may not stop his vehicle as soon as a more distant motorist approaching from the rear of the police car

(C) directly ahead may not stop his vehicle as soon as a more distant motorist approaching from the side of the police car

(D) the rear of the police car may stop his vehicle before the less distant motorist approaching from a side street.

56. A police officer is guarding the entrance of an apartment in which a homicide occurred. While awaiting the arrival of the detectives assigned to the case, the officer is approached by a newspaper reporter who asks to be admitted. The police officer refuses to admit the reporter. The officer's action was

(A) wrong; the police should cooperate with the press

(B) right; the reporter might unintentionally destroy evidence if admitted

(C) wrong; experienced newspaper reporters can be trusted to act intelligently in situations such as this.

(D) right; this reporter should not be given an advantage over other reporters.

57. A phone call is received at police headquarters indicating that a burglary is now taking place in a large loft building. Several radio motor patrol teams are dispatched to the scene. In order to prevent the escape of the burglars, the two police officers arriving first at the building, knowing that there is at least one entrance on each of the four sides of the building, should first

(A) station themselves at diagonally opposite corners outside of the building

(B) enter the building and proceed to search for the criminals

(C) station themselves at the most likely exit from the building

(D) enter the building and remain on the ground floor attempting to keep all stairways under observation.

58. Soon after being appointed a police officer, you decide that some of the rules and regulations of the police department are unwise. It would be best for you to

(A) carry out these rules and regulations regardless of your opinion

(B) make any changes that you decide are necessary

(C) not do your job until some changes are made

(D) disregard these rules and regulations and use your own good judgment.

59. In most cases, a written report about a serious accident is better than an oral report, mainly because a written report

(A) includes more of the facts

(B) can be referred to later

(C) takes less time to prepare

(D) is more accurate.

60. Officers assigned to regular posts for an extended period of time should try to establish friendly relations with the people in the area. For officers to follow this procedure is generally

(A) advisable, mainly because the officers will be more likely to get the cooperation of the residents when needed

(B) inadvisable, mainly because it will take the officer's attention away from their regular duties

(C) advisable, mainly because it will help officers to impress their superior officers

(D) inadvisable, mainly because the people may be encouraged to take advantage of this friendliness to commit minor violations.

Assume that a police officer at a certain location is equipped with a two-way radio to keep him in constant touch with his security headquarters. Radio messages and replies are given in code form, as follows:

Radio Code for Situation	J P M F B
Radio Code for Action to be Taken	o r a z q
Radio Response for Action Taken	1 2 3 4 5

Assume that each of the above capital letters is the radio code for a particular type of situation, that the small letter below each capital letter is the radio code for the action a police officer is directed to take, and that the number directly below each small letter is the radio response the police officer should make to indicate what action was actually taken.

In each of the following questions, 61 through 66, the code letter for the action directed (Column 2) and the code number for the action taken (Column 3) should correspond to the capital letters in Column 1.

- If only Column 2 is different from Column 1, mark your answer (A).
- If only Column 3 is different from Column 1, mark your answer (B).
- If both Column 2 and Column 3 are different from Column 1, mark your answer (C).
- If both Columns 2 and 3 are the same as Column 1, mark your answer (D).

SAMPLE QUESTION

Column 1	Column 2	Column 3
JPFMB	orzaq	12453

The code letters in Column 2 are correct, but the numbers "53" in Column 3 should be "35." Therefore, the correct answer is (B).

	Column 1	Column 2	Column 3
61.	PBFJM	rqzoa	25413
62.	MPFBJ	zrqoa	32541
63.	JBFPM	oqzra	15432
64.	BJPMF	qaroz	51234
65.	PJFMB	rozaq	21435
66.	FJBMP	zoqra	41532

Answer questions 67 through 76 solely on the basis of the following narrative and Assistance Report. The report contains 20 numbered boxes. First read the narrative and the information given concerning the form, and then study the form thoroughly before answering the questions.

It was 9:30 A.M., Sunday, June 14, 1989. Officers Whelan and Murphy of the 2nd Precinct, riding in patrol car 1294, received a radio call of an injury at the N.W. corner of Seventh Avenue and 83rd Street. The location of the injury was within the confines of the 3rd Precinct; however, the 3rd Precinct did not have any cars available to respond.

Upon arriving at the scene, Officers Whelan and Murphy found a male white, approximately 28 years of age, lying on the sidewalk. The man was bleeding moderately from a cut on the forehead. When questioned by the officers, the man identified himself as John Mandello, and he stated that someone ran up behind him and pushed him to the ground, causing him to strike his head on the sidewalk. The person who pushed him to the ground also took a wallet containing $100 from his rear left pocket. Officer Whelan informed Mr. Mandello that an ambulance was on the way. Mr. Mandello stated that he would take care of the injury himself and did not want any medical assistance.

Officer Whelan cancelled the ambulance and proceeded to take the information to be included in the report. As he was doing so, Officer Whelan noticed that the corner street light was not working.

Just as Officer Whelan was finishing getting the information, he and Officer Murphy heard what sounded like brakes screeching and cars colliding. The two officers ran around the corner and saw a car on the southeast corner sidewalk of 82nd Street and Seventh Avenue. They also observed a van, lying on its side, in the intersection of 82nd Street and Seventh Avenue. Officer Murphy ran back to his patrol and car and put in a call for an additional 2nd Precinct patrol car to handle traffic conditions. The accident had occurred within the confines of the 2nd Precinct.

Officer Whelan checked the car that was on the sidewalk. The car, after colliding with the van, apparently mounted the sidewalk and went through the front window of a men's clothing store, setting off the burglar alarm. The driver was lying on the front seat with moderate bleeding from a cut on his head and had what appeared to be a broken arm. The driver of the car was identified as Joe Serrano, a male white, 29 years of age, residing at 384 Lincoln Place, Apt. 4E, Brooklyn, NY.

Officer Murphy went to the van and, with the help of several passersby, pulled the driver out. The driver was unconscious. A search of the unconscious van driver's wallet identified him as Juan Rodriguez, a male Hispanic, 24 years of age, residing at 98 Fourth Avenue, Apt. 1, Newark, NJ.

An ambulance from Washington Hospital arrived at the scene. The ambulance attendant, John Francis, administered first aid to both drivers who were then removed to Washington Hospital.

Further investigation produced two witnesses to the accident. The first witness was Mary Randolph of 876 First Avenue, Apt. 2S, NYC; the second was Helen Sweeney of 684 Broadway, Apt. A, NYC. The witnesses stated to Police Officer Whelan that the traffic light at the intersection of 82nd Street and Seventh Avenue was not working.

Mr. Thomas Serrano of 384 Lincoln Place, Apt. 4E, phone 287-8777 was notified that his brother, Joe, was admitted to Washington Hospital. The admission number for Joe Serrano was 18764.

No friends or relatives of Juan Rodriguez could be notified that he was admitted to Washington Hospital. His admission number was 18763.

ASSISTANCE REPORT

1. Date	2. Last name First name M.I.	3. Age	4. Sex	5. Color

6. Time	7. Residence (including county, apt. # & Zip Code)

8. Location of occurrence (including county, apt. # & Zip code)

9. Illness or injury	10. Precinct and report number

11. Check:	12. Taken to:
☐ sick ☐ mentally ill ☐ injured ☐ dead	Name of ☐ hospital ( ) ☐ morgue ( )

13. Admission number	14. Name of Doctor or ambulance attendant

15. Person notified	Relationship

16. Witnesses

17. Remarks

18. Additional required reports (Check appropriate boxes, if any)
   ☐ Crime report   ☐ Morgue report
   ☐ Vehicle accident report   ☐ Street injury report

19. Other agency notifications

20. Reporting Officer

   Rank   Name   Number   Precinct

A police officer is required to prepare an Assistance Report whenever an occurrence which requires that a person receive medical aid or assistance comes to the officer's attention. However, if a person is sick at his or her own residence, an Assistance Report is not required. The officer then need only make a log book entry.

Box #1 will indicate the date that the report is being prepared. If the occurrence happened on a date that is different from the date of the report, the date of occurrence will be listed under Remarks, box #17. The reason for the delay in reporting the incident will also be noted under Remarks, box #17.

Box #8 will give the specific location of the occurrence, i.e., 374 First Street, Apt. 1D; Front of 374 First Street on sidewalk; N.W. corner of 86th Street and First Avenue.

Box #9 will indicate, to the best of your knowledge, the illness or injury sustained, i.e., cut on forehead, dizziness, etc. The official doctor's or hospital's diagnosis, if available, will be listed under Remarks, box #17.

Box #10 will list the precinct of the site of the incident and the precinct report number.

Check the appropriate circumstance in box #11.

Check the appropriate disposition in box #12. If a person is treated at his or her home and is not removed to another location, no report is required. If a person is removed to a hospital or morgue, check the appropriate box and list the name of the hospital or morgue. If a person refuses medical assistance, write "refused assistance" in box #12. If a person is treated at another location other than his or her home and is not removed to a hospital or morgue, state such facts under Remarks, box #17.

The hospital admission number is listed in box #13 only if a relative or a friend cannot be notified that the person is being admitted to the hospital.

Box #14 will indicate the name of the doctor or ambulance attendant who treated the individual.

Box #15 will list the name and address of the friend or relative who was notified of the person's admission to the hospital. The relationship of the person notified to the person admitted will also be listed, i.e., friend, wife, brother, etc.

Box #16 will indicate the names and addresses of any witnesses.

Box #17 will contain a short description of the incident.

Box #18, check the appropriate box for any additional forms that may be needed. Check *crime report* if medical assistance was made necessary as the result of a criminal act. Check *vehicle accident report* if the incident involved a motor vehicle accident. Check *morgue report* if the individual involved dies. Check *street injury report* if the person was injured as a result of a defect in a street or sidewalk.

Box #19 will list the names of any other city agencies that may have to be notified, i.e., damaged or broken traffic or street lights—Traffic Department; potholes in the street or broken sidewalks—Department of Highways; broken or damaged fire hydrants or water mains—Department of Water Supply, etc.

Box #20 will contain the rank, name, and command of the police officer making the report.

All other boxes not specifically mentioned are self-explanatory.

Questions 67 through 70 are to be answered solely on the basis of the information relating to the case of John Mandello.

67. An assistance report

(A) would not be required because Mr. Mandello refused medical assistance

(B) would not be required; only a police officer's log entry would be necessary

(C) would be required, and the precinct that would be listed in box #10 would be the 2nd Precinct

(D) would be required, and the precinct number that would be listed in box #20 would be the 2nd Precinct.

68. In box #9, the officer would

(A) enter the official hospital diagnosis when it became available

(B) enter the description of the illness or injury in his own words

(C) make a reference to see box #17, Remarks, for the official diagnosis

(D) enter "refused medical assistance."

69. In box #18, the officer would check the box(es) for

(A) street injury report, because Mr. Mandello was injured when his head struck the sidewalk

(B) street injury report, because the injury was incurred when Mr. Mandello's head struck the sidewalk, and crime report, because he was apparently the victim of a robbery

(C) crime report only

(D) No additional report would be required because Mr. Mandello refused medical assistance.

70. In box #19, the officer would

(A) enter Traffic Department

(B) enter Department of Highways

(C) enter both Traffic Department and Department of Highways

(D) make no entry as no additional agency would have to be notified.

Answer questions 71 through 76 based on the information given regarding Joe Serrano and Juan Rodriguez.

71. Box #13 would be

(A) filled in only in the case of Mr. Serrano

(B) filled in only in the case of Mr. Rodriguez

(C) filled in the cases of both Mr. Serrano and Mr. Rodriguez

(D) left blank in both cases.

72. The official hospital diagnoses of Mr. Serrano's injuries were a laceration of the forehead and a fracture of the right arm. This information would

(A) be listed in box #17, Remarks

(B) be listed in box #9, Illness or injury

(C) be listed in box #14 next to the doctor's name

(D) not be listed in the report.

73. In regard to the proper preparation of the Assistance Report, select the correct answer from the choices given below.

(A) In box #10, the number of the precinct that would be entered would be the 2nd Precinct.

(B) In box #20, the number of the precinct that would be entered would be the 3rd Precinct.

(C) In box #10, the number of the precinct that would be entered would be the 3rd Precinct.

(D) The admission number for Mr. Serrano, 18763, would be entered in box #13.

74. In box #18, the additional report(s) that would be required is (are)

(A) a crime report

(B) a street injury report

(C) a vehicle accident report

(D) a vehicle accident report and a crime report.

75. Based on the information given by the witnesses, box #19 would contain the name(s) of which other agency or agencies?

    (A) Traffic Department
    (B) Traffic Department and Highway Department
    (C) Highway Department
    (D) Building Department.

76. In preparing the Assistance Report,

    (A) the caption "Sick" would be checked in box #11
    (B) the relationship of the person notified in the case of Mr. Serrano would be "father" and would be entered in box #15
    (C) the location of the occurrence would be the intersection of 83rd Street and Seventh Avenue and would be entered in box #8
    (D) the name John Francis would be entered in box #14.

Answer questions 77 through 80 on the basis of the information given in the following passage.

The public often believes that the main job of a uniformed officer is to enforce laws simply by arresting people. In reality, however, many of the situations that an officer deals with do not call for the use of the power of arrest. In the first place, an officer spends much of his or her time *preventing* crimes from happening, by spotting potential violations or suspicious behavior and taking action to prevent illegal acts. In the second place, many of the situations in which officers are called on for assistance involve elements like personal arguments, husband-wife quarrels, noisy juveniles, or emotionally disturbed persons. The majority of these problems do not result in arrests and convictions, and often they do not even involve illegal behavior. In the third place, even in situations where there seems to be good reason to make an arrest, an officer may have to exercise very good judgement. There are times when making an arrest too soon could touch off a riot, or could result in the detention of a minor offender while major offenders escaped, or could cut short the gathering of necessary on-the-scene evidence.

77. The passage implies that most citizens

    (A) will start to riot if they see an arrest being made
    (B) appreciate the work that law enforcement officers do
    (C) do not realize that making arrests is only a small part of law enforcement
    (D) never call for assistance unless they are involved in a personal argument or a husband-wife quarrel.

78. According to the passage, one way in which law enforcement officers can prevent crimes from happening is by

    (A) arresting suspicious characters
    (B) letting minor offenders go free
    (C) taking action on potential violations
    (D) refusing to get involved in husband-wife fights.

79. According to the passage, which of the following statements is *not* true of situations involving emotionally disturbed persons?

    (A) It is a waste of time to call on law enforcement officers for assistance in such situations.
    (B) Such situations may not involve illegal behavior.
    (C) Such situations often do not result in arrests.
    (D) Citizens often turn to law enforcement officers for help in such situations.

80. The last sentence in the passage mentions "detention of minor offenders." Of the following, which best explains the meaning of the word "detention" as used here?

    (A) Sentencing someone
    (B) Indicting someone
    (C) Calling someone before a grand jury
    (D) Arresting someone.

Answer questions 81 through 84 on the basis of the information given in the following passage.

Automobile tire tracks found at the scene of a crime constitute an important link in the chain of physical evidence. In many cases, these are the only clues available. In some areas, unpaved ground adjoins the highway or paved streets. A suspect will often park his or her car off the paved portion of the street when committing a crime, sometimes leaving excellent tire tracks. Comparison of the tire track impressions with the tires is possible only when the vehicle has been found. However, the initial problem facing the police is the task of determining what kind of car probably made the impressions found at the scene of the crime. If the make, model, and year of the car which made the impressions can be determined, it is obvious that the task of elimination is greatly lessened.

81. The one of the following that is the most appropriate title for this passage is

(A) The Use of Automobiles in the Commission of Crimes

(B) The Use of Tire Tracks in Police Work

(C) The Capture of Criminals by Scientific Police Work

(D) The Positive Identification of Criminals Through Their Cars.

82. When searching for clear signs left by the car used in the commission of a crime, the most likely place for the police to look would be on the

(A) highway adjoining unpaved streets

(B) highway adjacent to paved streets

(C) paved streets adjacent to a highway

(D) unpaved ground adjacent to a highway.

83. Automobile tire tracks found at the scene of a crime are of value as evidence in that they are

(A) generally sufficient to trap and convict a suspect

(B) the most important link in the chain of physical evidence

(C) often the only evidence at hand

(D) circumstantial rather than direct.

84. The primary reason that the police try to determine the make, model, and year of the car involved in the commission of a crime is to

(A) compare the tire tracks left at the scene of the crime with the type of tires used on cars of that make

(B) determine if the mud on the tires of the suspected car matches the mud in the unpaved road near the scene of the crime

(C) reduce, to a large extent, the amount of work involved in determining the particular car used in the commission of a crime

(D) alert the police forces to question the occupants of all automobiles of this type.

ANSWER KEY FOR PRACTICE EXAMINATION 5

1. D	21. B	41. D	61. D	81. B
2. D	22. B	42. C	62. C	82. D
3. D	23. B	43. A	63. B	83. C
4. A	24. C	44. D	64. A	84. C
5. A	25. C	45. C	65. D	
6. B	26. A	46. C	66. A	
7. D	27. B	47. D	67. D	
8. B	28. B	48. A	68. B	
9. D	29. A	49. C	69. C	
10. C	30. C	50. C	70. A	
11. D	31. A	51. A	71. B	
12. C	32. A	52. C	72. A	
13. B	33. B	53. B	73. A	
14. A	34. C	54. D	74. C	
15. C	35. B	55. A	75. A	
16. C	36. D	56. B	76. D	
17. A	37. A	57. A	77. C	
18. B	38. D	58. A	78. C	
19. B	39. C	59. B	79. A	
20. A	40. C	60. A	80. D	

EXPLANATORY ANSWERS FOR PRACTICE EXAMINATION 5

1. **(D)** Refer to the third sentence of the description.

2. **(D)** The officers observed the suspects alighting from the roof by way of a ladder.

3. **(D)** The two male whites ran into an alleyway and the male black and male Hispanic ran into a parking lot.

4. **(A)** This information is included in the description of the male white with long blond hair.

5. **(A)** This information is included in the description of the male Hispanic.

6. **(B)** This information is included in the description of the male white with short hair.

7. **(D)** This information is included in the description of the male white with short hair.

8. **(B)** This information is included in the description of the male white with long blond hair.

9. **(D)** This information is included in the description of the male Hispanic.

10. **(C)** This is the description of the vehicle in which the two male whites fled.

11. **(D)** The description states only that the escape vehicles fled west on Seventh Street. There is no information as to what type of street Seventh Street is.

12. **(C)** Both the male black and male Hispanic entered the parking lot. However, it was the male black who was carrying what appeared to be a portable T.V. set.

13. **(B)** This information is included in the description of the male black.

14. **(A)** This information is included in the description of the male black.

15. **(C)** The description refers only to Officer Smith using a walkie-talkie and broadcasting information.

16. **(C)** Photographs form a permanent record of how the crime scene appeared when the police arrived. These pictures can be used at a criminal trial to show how the crime scene looked.

17. **(A)** There is no immediate danger to the officer or to the woman since the gun is in the man's pocket. Therefore, it is not necessary or proper for the officer to fire a shot. The officer should repeat his order before taking any further action.

18. **(B)** If the suspect observes that notes are being taken, he or she may freeze up or not talk as freely because he knows that what he or she is saying will become part of the permanent record.

19. **(B)** Being familiar with the post allows a police officer to anticipate the easiest avenues of escape from specific locations.

20. **(A)** The prisoner would either have to roll over or turn his head completely around to see the officer in order to shoot accurately. The time required for this type of movement would allow the officer to take cover or to fire the first shot.

21. **(B)** Ignoring the rumors or not supplying the true circumstances of the emergency as soon as they are available only increases the fear people may have and may result in a possible panic situation.

22. **(B)** If a child has been missing for an extended period of time, police headquarters usually would have received information concerning the child.

23. **(B)** If the plainclothes officer were to stop following the suspect now, he would be difficult to locate again since he is known to have changed residences frequently.

24. **(C)** The police officer should always request that only the needed identification papers be produced. If the police officer accepts the wallet and goes through it for identification papers, there is a possibility that a complaint could be made that money and other personal items were missing when the wallet was returned.

25. **(C)** If a police officer doesn't fully understand the instructions given by a supervisor, the officer should immediately ask for clarification from the person giving the instructions so that he or she can carry out the assignment properly.

26. **(A)** A police officer should always be alert and on guard until the nature of the situation in which he or she is involved is made completely clear.

27. **(B)** Police officers and police departments should never recommend a specific product or business. Endorsements tend to indicate favoritism and police officers should always be impartial.

28. **(B)** Suspects and witnesses should always be questioned separately so that the description that one person gives does not influence the description given by any other persons at the scene.

29. **(A)** If there is the slightest chance that the object could be a bomb, all persons should be removed from the location for safety reasons.

30. **(C)** All of the other choices require immediate police action; a damaged street name sign does not.

31. **(A)** The call could be a set-up for robbing both the owner and his store. If there were a real emergency, the police would most likely be on the scene.

32. **(A)** The citizen may have a legitimate reason for going to the store. Information regarding a criminal investigation should not be divulged to the public.

33. **(B)** In most cases it takes a thorough search of the crime scene to uncover the clues left by the criminal. Most clues in and of themselves are not conclusive. However, when used collectively, they form the foundation for proving the guilt or innocence of the suspect.

34. **(C)** In a criminal prosecution, it would have to be shown that the fingerprints were found prior to the suspect's walking around or entering the scene.

35. **(B)** A statement should be taken as soon as the suspect offers to make one. The suspect may feel an immediate need to tell someone what happened. A delay in taking the statement may cause the suspect to remain silent about the matter.

36. **(D)** The situation fits both the definition of burglary (to enter a building to commit a crime) and of robbery (stealing by force—in this case, the punch in the face).

37. **(A)** John Brown can be charged with larceny only as there was no intent to commit a crime when he entered the store, and there was no force used.

38. **(D)** The charges are sexual abuse (touching of the buttocks) and larceny (taking $10 from the pocketbook). No force was used to remove the money, thus eliminating the charge of robbery.

39. **(C)** To charge a person with burglary, it only must be shown that the building was entered with the intention of committing a crime therein. (In this case, the crime was sexual abuse.) Despite the fact that Saunders was not successful in committing the crime he intended, the intention was there.

40. **(C)** Taylor's intention for entering the apartment was to have sexual intercourse with his 16-year-old girlfriend, a crime because she is less than 17 years of age. He could be charged with burglary (intent to commit a crime) and sexual misconduct (sexual intercourse with a female less than 17 years of age).

41. **(D)** Mary is 17 years old and gave her consent.

42. **(C)** There was neither any intention to commit a crime when Bill entered the building nor was there any injury incurred. For the charge to be assault, there must be some kind of injury.

43. **(A)** Joe had no intent to commit a crime before he entered the warehouse. He caused an injury to a fellow worker, a broken arm, by his actions; therefore, the charge of assault could be preferred. Emotional disturbance is not a valid excuse for such actions.

44. **(D)** The charges are burglary (entering the school with the intention of taking a movie projector), robbery (using force on the security guard to take the projector), and assault (causing an injury, the broken nose, to the security guard).

45. **(C)** Because Tom used force to touch Sue's private parts, he could be charged with sexual abuse. Since there was no intention to commit the crime prior to his entering her apartment, the possibility of a burglary charge is eliminated.

46. **(C)** Minor complaints, when properly investigated, can show a pattern of conduct that could lead to a major problem for the police.

47. **(D)** With the exception of a few narrowly defined situations, the courts demand that actual witnesses be examined under oath.

48. **(A)** A police officer does a multitude of things other than arrest people. The officer responds to sick, injured, and emotionally disturbed people calling for help. He or she handles vehicle accidents, family disputes, lost children, traffic problems, and so on. The officer's effectiveness should be based on how the officer handles the entire spectrum of his or her duties rather than on the number of arrests he or she makes in a given period of time. (C) is not the best answer because of the exclusionary word *any*. Arrest figures are some indication of a police officer's efficiency.

49. **(C)** Fire destroys valuable clues that are usually found at a crime scene. Investigation is made considerably more difficult as a result.

50. **(C)** When the police observe potential delinquent-producing conditions, they can take immediate action to correct them.

51. **(A)** By questioning the man first, the officer may be able to ascertain who he is and where he lives, and thereby return him to his home without any further delay.

52. **(C)** The suspect's accent and stuttering are more or less permanent conditions. The other habits mentioned could be readily changed as needed.

53. **(B)** Police descriptions must be accurate in order to match the article to the complainant. For example, just listing the watch as a yellow metal man's wristwatch would fit thousands of complaints of lost or stolen watches.

54. **(D)** Witnesses and suspects should always be separated when being questioned or giving statements so that the statement one makes does not influence what the others might say.

55. **(A)** This information is stated clearly in the quotation itself.

56. **(B)** Until a crime scene is properly searched and investigated, no one other than those assigned directly to the case should be allowed to enter the area because of the possibility that valuable evidence will be destroyed.

57. **(A)** By stationing themselves in this manner, the two officers would be able to observe all four sides of the building.

58. **(A)** In order to function effectively, police departments have specific rules and regulations that must be followed. Individual police officers must follow the rules; they cannot change or disregard these rules because they think they are unwise or unnecessary. All changes will be made by the chiefs of the respective departments.

59. **(B)** With the passage of time, accurate mental recall of an incident decreases. Written reports should always be prepared for future reference, especially if the case may go to court.

60. **(A)** Once the people in the neighborhood get to know the police officer who is regularly assigned, they are more likely to cooperate. People don't generally cooperate with strangers, even if the stranger is a police officer.

61. **(D)** All the letters in Column 2 and all the numbers in Column 3 are in sequence with the capital letters in Column 1.

62. **(C)** When compared to Column 1, the letters (Column 2) z, q, o, and a and the numbers (Column 3) 5 and 4 are out of sequence.

63. **(B)** When compared to Column 1, all the letters in Column 2 are in their proper sequence, however, the numbers 2 and 3 in Column 3 are out of sequence.

Assistance Report on John Mandello Completed with Information Supplied

ASSISTANCE REPORT				
1. Date 6/14/89	**2. Last name First name M.I.** Mandello, John	**3. Age** Approx. 28	**4. Sex** M	**5. Color** W
6. Time 9:30 A.M.	**7. Residence (including county, apt. # & Zip Code)**			

8. Location of occurrence (including county, apt. # & Zip code)

N.W. Corner, Seventh Avenue and 83rd Street, New York

9. Illness or injury Cut on forehead	**10. Precinct and report number** 3

11. Check: ☐ sick ☐ mentally ill ☒ injured ☐ dead	**12. Taken to:** Refused assitance ☐ hospital ☐ morgue	**Name of** ( ) ( )

13. Admission number	**14. Name of Doctor or ambulance attendant**

15. Person notified	**Relationship**

16. Witnesses

17. Remarks

Victim was pushed from behind; fell to sidewalk and struck forehead; wallet containing $100.00 was removed from pocket.

18. Additional required reports (Check appropriate boxes, if any)
☒ Crime report   ☐ Morgue report
☐ Vehicle accident report   ☐ Street injury report

19. Other agency notifications

Traffic Department

20. Reporting Officer

Rank	Name Whelan	Number	Precinct 2

Assistance Report on Juan Rodriquez Completed with Information Supplied

ASSISTANCE REPORT					
1. Date 6/14/89	**2. Last name First name M.I.** Rodriguez, Juan	**3. Age** 24	**4. Sex** M	**5. Color** Hispanic	

6. Time
Shortly after 9:30 A.M.

7. Residence (including county, apt. # & Zip Code)
98 Fourth Ave., Apt. 1, Newark, N.J.

8. Location of occurrence (including county, apt. # & Zip code)
82 Street and Seventh Ave, New York, N.Y.

9. Illness or injury
Unconscious

10. Precinct and report number
2nd

11. Check:
☐ sick ☐ mentally ill
☒ injured ☐ dead

12. Taken to:
☒ hospital (Washington)
☐ morgue ( ) Name of

13. Admission number
18763

14. Name of Doctor or ambulance attendant
John Francis, ambulance attendant

15. Person notified

Relationship

16. Witnesses
Mary Randolph, 876 First Ave., Apt. 2S, N.Y.C.
Helen Sweeney, 684 Broadway, Apt. A, N.Y.C.

17. Remarks
Collision of car and van at intersection of inoperative signal. Car mounted sidewalk and entered window of men's clothing store, setting off burglar alarm. Both drivers injured. No other injuries.

18. Additional required reports (Check appropriate boxes, if any)
☐ Crime report   ☐ Morgue report
☒ Vehicle accident report   ☐ Street injury report

19. Other agency notifications
Traffic

20. Reporting Officer

Rank   Name   Number   Precinct 2

Assistance Report on Joe Serrano Completed with Information Supplied

ASSISTANCE REPORT

1. Date	2. Last name First name M.I.	3. Age	4. Sex	5. Color
6/14/89	Serrano, Joe	29	M	W

6. Time
Shortly after 9:30 A.M.

7. Residence (including county, apt. # & Zip Code)
384 Lincoln Place, Apt. 4E, Brooklyn, N.Y. (Kings)

8. Location of occurrence (including county, apt. # & Zip code)
82nd St. and Seventh Ave., N.Y.C.

9. Illness or injury
bleeding from cut on head; possible broken arm

10. Precinct and report number
2nd

11. Check:
☐ sick   ☐ mentally ill
☒ injured   ☐ dead

12. Taken to:
☒ hospital (Washington)
☐ morgue ( )
Name of

13. Admission number

14. Name of Doctor or ambulance attendant
John Francis, ambulance attendant

15. Person notified
Thomas Serrano   384 Linclon Place, Apt. 4E
Brooklyn, N.Y.   287-8777

Relationship
brother

16. Witnesses
Mary Randolph, 876 First Ave, Apt. 25, N.Y.C.
Helen Sweeney, 684 Broadway, Apt. A, N.Y.C.

17. Remarks
Collision of car and van at intersection of inoperative signal. Car mounted sidewalk and entered window of men's clothing store setting off burglar alarm. Hospital diagonsis of forehead laceration and right arm fracture. Other driver injured.

18. Additional required reports (Check appropriate boxes, if any)
☐ Crime report   ☐ Morgue report
☒ Vehicle accident report   ☐ Street injury report

19. Other agency notifications
Traffic

20. Reporting Officer

Rank   Name   Number   Precinct 2

64. **(A)** When compared to Column 1, all the numbers in Column 3 are in their proper sequence; however, the letters a and o in Column 2 are out of sequence.

65. **(D)** When compared to Column 1, all the letters in Column 2 and all the numbers in Column 3 are in proper sequence.

66. **(A)** When compared to Column 1, all the numbers in Column 3 are in proper sequence, however, the letters r and a in Column 2 are out of sequence.

67. **(D)** The person is treated at a location other than his home. If he were treated at home, a report would not be required. The reporting officer is from the 2nd Precinct. The incident occurred in the 3rd Precinct.

68. **(B)** The directions for box #9 state that the officer will enter the nature of the illness or injury to the best of his or her knowledge.

69. **(C)** Mr. Mandello was the victim of a robbery; therefore, a crime report is required. A street injury report is not required because he was not injured as a result of a defect in the sidewalk.

70. **(A)** As he was taking the information for the Assistance Report, Officer Whelan noticed that the corner streetlight was not working.

71. **(B)** An admission number is required only when a relative or friend can't be notified that a person was admitted to a hospital. This is true only in the case of Mr. Rodriguez.

72. **(A)** The directions for preparing the report state that the official diagnosis will be listed in box #17, Remarks.

73. **(A)** The incident involving Mr. Serrano and Mr. Rodriguez occurred in the 2nd Precinct. Mr. Serrano's admission number is not recorded because his brother was notified that he was taken to the hospital. In addition, the number listed for Mr. Serrano in choice (D) is incorrect.

74. **(C)** Only a vehicle accident report is required. There was no crime involved and the accident was not caused by a defect in the roadway, thus eliminating a street injury report.

75. **(A)** The witnesses state that the traffic light was not working, therefore the Traffic Department should be notified.

76. **(D)** John Francis was the ambulance attendant who responded. The victims were not sick; they were injured. Mr. Serrano's brother, not his father, was notified as to his injury in an accident which occurred on Seventh Avenue and 82nd Street.

77. **(C)** Refer to the first sentence of the passage.

78. **(C)** Refer to the third sentence of the passage.

79. **(A)** It is stated in the fourth sentence that many of the situations in which police assistance is required involve emotionally disturbed persons.

80. **(D)** A police officer arrests; the courts sentence, indict, or call people before a grand jury. Detention is holding in custody.

81. **(B)** The passage talks exclusively about tire tracks. No mention is made of autos being used in the commission of crimes, of scientific police work, or of positive identification through cars.

82. **(D)** Refer to sentences 3 and 4 of the passage.

83. **(C)** Refer to the second sentence of the passage.

84. **(C)** Refer to the last sentence of the passage.

THE POLICE ACADEMY

The First Step in Your Law Enforcement Career

BY STEVE ALBRECHT

ABOUT THE AUTHOR

Steve Albrecht is nationally known for his written work on police officer safety and tactics. He has been with the San Diego Police Department since 1984, first as a regular officer and now as a reserve. He is a member of the American Society of Law Enforcement Trainers and contributes articles to police publications across the country. He is the author of *STREETWORK: The Way To Police Officer Safety & Survival* (Paladin) and is co-author, with John Morrison, of *CONTACT & COVER: Two-Officer Suspect Control* (Charles C. Thomas).

THE POLICE ACADEMY

Police work is one of the few professions—besides baseball umpiring—where you have to start out perfect and get better each day. It's also a profession that puts a tremendous emphasis upon training. You'll start the first day of your law enforcement career in a training mode and continue with it every day after that. As long as you wear the badge of a police officer, you will spend a large part of your time learning on the job.

This job requires you to carry an extraordinarily broad range of knowledge. During an average patrol shift, you'll be called upon to solve a variety of problems, mediate disputes, investigate criminal cases, and respond to any number of different service requests ranging from the life-threatening to the mundane.

New police officers like to think of themselves as true "crime fighters." Equipped with a badge, gun, and uniform, many new cops envision themselves chasing "bad guys," making dozens of felony arrests, and solving major crimes on a constant basis. Unfortunately, this is not really how the job goes. Studies of law enforcement tell us you'll probably spend only 20 percent of your patrol time actually in an enforcement position. The rest of the time you'll answer citizen complaints, questions, and requests, write reports, participate in administrative or training tasks, or just randomly patrol your area waiting for calls.

The 20-percent figure that relates to enforcement—issuing citations, making arrests, and protecting life and property—is certainly an important part of your job as a police officer, but it's really only one of your many functions.

Our society is a diverse and ever-changing place, filled with people who have different cultural backgrounds, ethical values, and moral standards. The residents of a city interact with the police in a variety of matters, not just during enforcement situations. Since enforcement is such a small part of your job, you have to bring other "people" skills to bear. The citizens of this country look to the police for protection and service, and by its nature, police work is a reactive, service "business."

If you have been hired as a police officer, you have already met a number of high standards. You've passed a series of rigorous mental, physical, medical, and psychological tests. And you have convinced key city and police department personnel that you have the high morals, positive ethical values, and stable personality traits needed to do the job in a humane and intelligent manner.

But surviving the hiring process is only the start of your exposure to the world of police service. The next phase of your development as an officer—your introduction to law enforcement—begins in the Police Academy.

It's here that you will spend the next four to six months of your life, learning what it means to be a police officer. In the sections that follow, you'll get a complete overview of a typical police academy facility, including the information you'll need to have before you begin your training. Some information may not exactly match what you already know or what you've been told about the police academy in your area, but most of it pertains to the overall police training experience.

Different agencies require different things from their police officer trainees. Some police departments—like the LAPD—stress extensive physical training sessions and spend a significant amount of time teaching recruits to speak Spanish. This emphasis on second-language skills reflects the cultural necessities of the area.

Other agencies—like the San Diego Police Department—have established a "phase training" program where police officer trainees rotate back and forth between academy classes and actual participation in street patrol with senior Field Training Officers. This hands-on experience helps to prepare new officers for the stress of police work by introducing them to it in carefully controlled stages.

Some police academies require the recruits to live at the facility—much like the military. Federal and state law enforcement agencies usually require their trainees to live on-site, while city and county academies allow their cadets to commute from home.

Other police training centers operate in conjunction with state universities or with local community college facilities. But no matter how or where the academy for your agency functions, the values you learn are the same.

On the west coast or east, from a small midwestern training center or from a large southern regional facility that covers an entire state, you'll come away from your academy experience with the following traits and abilities:

- **Discipline.** You will know how to take orders and give them, especially during moments of extreme stress.
- **Teamwork.** You will recognize the need to work together as a unit, either with a partner or even with several dozen other officers.
- **Camaraderie.** You will establish personal friendships that last for your entire career and beyond.
- **Esprit-de-corps.** You will forge an intense commitment to your "brothers and sisters in arms" that permeates your working relationships and even your entire way of life.
- **Courtesy, tact, and control.** You will use these traits to handle any situation, politely, safely, humanely, and above all, professionally.
- **Tactical survival skills.** You will receive the best officer safety material available and learn the latest patrol theories designed to save your life.
- **Professionalism.** You will become a total law enforcement professional, taught to protect and serve with skill and a strong sense of commitment that the career you have chosen is both right and necessary in our society today.

Pre-Academy Preparations

Your entrance into the police academy really begins long before you get there. An old police maxim fits here: Forewarned is forearmed. The more you can prepare yourself—both mentally and physically—for the rigors of academy training, the better you'll do. This may sound simplistic and obvious, but the reasoning is clear. A little preparation before you start can save you from an enormous amount of hardship later.

Police academy training instructors can all remember police officer candidates who had all the "on paper" qualifications to make it to the academy. Typically, these people seemed to have it all. They scored well on written tests, showed impressive skills during the many interviews, and even had the strength and health to pass the physical and medical tests. But once they arrived at the academy—with its built-in stressors and physical requirements—they folded under the pressure.

In some instances, people who reach the academy stage find themselves quite disillusioned by the pressure, the workload, and the physical side of police work. This disillusionment often leads to their dismissal because of low test scores and poor physical performance. More frequently, they quit on their own.

To get through a typical police academy, you need more than just high test scores and physical strength; you need mental toughness as well. The biggest, "baddest," or smartest people don't always make it because the police academy calls for so many other characteristics from its students. Humility, internal courage, and enthusiasm count for just as much as physical virtues.

Another common mistake comes when new enrollees underestimate the amount of classroom study required. Most academy programs are designed around a college curriculum, offering from 12 to 18 units to officer-graduates. To learn and retain this much material, academy students have to spend much of their off-time studying their notes and reading their textbooks. With today's academy programs, it's just not possible to "wing it" and get by without extensive study. The classroom work is demanding and calls for mental discipline. Scanning your criminal law book and reading a few cryptic notes will not suffice. If you don't devote a substantial portion of your off-hours to studying this large amount of material, you won't make it to graduation day.

The skills you bring to the academic portion of the academy are largely in place when you get there. You may want to review some books on how to study efficiently, take good notes, and manage your time effectively. You will learn and succeed in the police academy by maximizing your in-class time, working at home at a specific pace, and following a planned study schedule.

But except for reviewing some helpful techniques, there is very little you can do to improve upon the common sense you already carry. Reading legal textbooks and police training manuals may give you an idea of what to expect, but for the most part, your instructors will teach you everything you'll need to know to function in the field.

Since you can't really prepare for the academic rigors, you can focus your attention on one key area you can improve: your level of physical fitness.

Most academy physical fitness programs stress the same three elements: upper body strength, cardiovascular endurance, and joint and muscle flexibility. The key to your success in these demanding areas starts with your pre-academy fitness level. It's just not possible to "work" yourself into shape once you get there. You've probably seen or heard stories about professional athletes who come to training camp for their sport grossly overweight or out of shape. They quickly fall behind their teammates and spend most of their time in a catch-up position.

Being out of shape is just as demanding mentally as it is physically. Since your body is under tremendous stress during hard exercise, your mind cannot "relax" either. If you couple this exercise-induced stress with the additional pressures from the academy training officers and competition from your classmates, you can find yourself far behind in a short period of time.

If you train correctly and work hard before your academy classes begin, you'll find the exercise programs much easier than if you don't. You don't want to start off with the handicap of being out of shape. Come to the academy in the best shape of your life, and try to improve upon that once the physical training sessions begin.

In some academy programs, you'll be given a list of equipment to purchase before you arrive. In some cases, your department will give you various items; in others, you'll have to buy them. Usually, you're required to buy your uniforms, dress jacket, cold and rainy weather clothes, footwear, and leather gear.

Most departments will give you a duty weapon, a baton, a helmet, a whistle, Mace, and other similar department-issue items. These items belong to the agency, even though you will use them for your entire career. Should you decide to leave the department, you'll need to return any equipment issued to you.

A few police agencies issue a badge and a photo identification card to trainees just before the academy formally begins. If your agency does this, you'll get instructions on how and when to wear your badge, including some careful admonishments about off-duty considerations and the potential for misuse and abuse of your new authority.

Most agencies see the badge and police officer ID card as something to be earned through hard work and dedication and issue it only after you complete the academy, usually at the graduation ceremony.

In most programs, you'll be given the textbooks, paperwork, report forms, and other written materials needed to complete the academic portions of the academy.

If your agency requires you to buy uniforms and leather gear, do yourself a favor and buy the best you can afford. Shopping at cut-rate uniform or police equipment shops can lead to problems later. With uniforms, your appearance is critical to your professionalism, inside the academy and later, out in the field. Don't skimp here. Buy quality uniforms and have them tailored to fit your body.

Nowhere is this sense of quality more important than with your leather gear and police equipment. The quality and durability of your holster, handcuff case, and baton ring could affect your safety. Respected, namebrand equipment may save you from injuries or death; poor-quality "knockoffs" could threaten your survival if they fail. Buy the best leather gear and equipment you can afford and then take care of it as if your life depended on it, because it just might.

With an understanding of the nature of police work, the goals of police academy training, and the mental and physical preparations you'll need, you're ready to look at academy life—one of the most exciting and demanding parts of your law enforcement career.

Dealing with the "Boot Camp" Environment

It's no secret that the police academy is much like military basic training. As in the military, you'll be required to respond to orders quickly, march in a structured fashion to and from various locations, salute when necessary, answer your training officers with a stout "Yes Sir!" or "Yes Ma'am!" when called upon, and generally assume a role of the classic "cadet," "recruit," or "trainee." It seems as if the academy training officers are always yelling and mostly at you. There are good reasons for this: discipline, obedience, and unity are the orders of the day.

On the first day of the academy, the training officers in charge of your class will carefully point out the rules and regulations of the facility. They'll also teach you how to walk, how to talk, how to act, and how to move on command. Any attempt at horseplay, showing off, or other childish moves that jeopardize the safety and success of your classmates will be met with swift and decisive punishment.

As one veteran instructor puts it, "Unless you want to spend all of your time doing pushups or writing 500-word essays on the importance of discipline, you had better 'toe the mark' and do what we tell you."

There are many reasons most police training academies follow this military model. Some are based upon safety concerns (especially when dealing with firearms, defensive tactics, pursuit-driving and other potentially dangerous training programs), others relate to the need to unite, train, and control a large group of people in a minimum amount of time, and still others are linked to the histories and traditions of that particular agency.

Police work is similar to the military in more than just its use of titles—Officer, Sergeant, Lieutenant, Captain, Commander, Chief, etc. Both organizations deal with life-and-death situations in many hostile environments. Each requires its people to respond to specific orders during periods of great personal danger and stress. With these similarities in mind, it's not surprising the police department trains just like the military. In many foreign countries, the police and the military work in conjunction with each other, even to the point of near interchangeability.

Some new recruits are quite comfortable with this enormous emphasis on the paramilitary. Other trainees find it terrifying and have a hard time concentrating on the tasks at hand. The people who seem to react the best are those who have had actual prior military experience. They still remember how to march and how to speak to superiors, so they have a significant edge over their classmates. The academy training officers usually recognize or identify these people and assign them "squad leader" roles to help the others. Learning from your peers is easier than learning from a large man in a khaki uniform who seems to take great delight in yelling at you.

Most officers who have gone through the academy experience will say that after a short period, it becomes easier to respond in this military fashion. What seems foreign and difficult at first will get easier, especially if you concentrate and work hard to conform. Still, you'll do much better if you can develop a thick skin before you begin the academy program. The trick is to follow the orders, complete the tasks you're given, and show effort and enthusiasm at all times. Don't take any verbal abuse from your training officers or instructors as a personal attack.

Rest assured that these people have your best interests in mind. They want you to make it to graduation day, and they will never hit you, curse you, or allow you to do anything unsafe or dangerous. Keep in mind that they aren't picking on you. They're merely exercising their lungs and reinforcing the level of discipline that must pervade the academy setting. It's all for your own good, although it's often difficult to keep this in mind as you complete your fiftieth pushup on a hot summer day.

One key tenet of police work is the strong sense of camaraderie and unity. Large academy classes are often broken into two separate squads and each competes against the other for the top class honors. Some academy classes, like those of the LAPD, use full-size military flags with their class colors, emblem, and slogan printed on them. Many academy classes have a "fight" slogan which they yell out at the beginning and end of each day, before each break, and during rigorous physical training sessions. These class mottos serve to reinforce the concepts of teamwork, unity of command, tradition, pride, and aggressiveness—all good qualities for today's police officers.

The concept of the "Thin Blue Line" —that the police are the first and only defense against the criminals and other bad people in our society—continually permeates the academy training process. The training officers want you to think and act as individuals, but never at the expense of the group. They will teach you how to help each other survive not only the academy process but life on the streets as well.

This concept runs throughout the academy experience, probably because most times law enforcement is a lonely profession. Few people would go out of their way to help a police officer in dire need, either because they dislike the police or, more likely, because they don't want to "get involved."

As a solo patrol officer making a traffic stop at 2:00 a.m., you can feel that help is a world away. But when the chips are down, your brothers and sisters in arms will drop whatever they're doing and race to your side—no questions asked.

How many other professions offer this kind of support? Where else can you find someone willing to risk his or her life for you when necessary? Above all else, law enforcement is a team effort, and the academy teaches this to you each day.

The rewards and punishments doled out by your training officers have a "one size fits all" flavor. You'll usually be rewarded as a group, and punished as one too. Class unity is a constant goal, so if one trainee violates the rules, his or her associates may share the blame. This isn't to say that individual punishments don't exist, but rather that the instructors use their knowledge of group dynamics to teach discipline and order by involving everyone.

The best way to deal with the discipline and paramilitary structure of academy training is to accept it as a part of your law enforcement training process. Don't take anything too personally—it won't last forever. Monitor your stress level the best you can, and realize that your training officers want you to succeed.

Classroom Conduct

The time you spend in the academy classroom environment represents about 60 percent of your total training time. You'll spend another 20 percent of time involved with physical training and defensive tactics activities, and you'll spend the last 20 percent outside the classroom, with driving and firearms training, role plays, and trips to off-site agencies. Since you'll spend the majority of your training time in class, it helps to know what to expect, what to ask, and how to respond to questions, orders, and requests.

Your day will usually begin outside the classroom—in uniform and in orderly rows, ready for a careful inspection. Under the direction of your training officers, you and your classmates will practice marching short distances. Then you'll line up for a uniform and equipment inspection, listen to some announcements about the activities of the day, and then "fall out" for the classroom lectures.

Most police academy courses are taught by experienced, highly qualified veteran officers. The positions of academy training officer and academy course instructor are highly coveted jobs, so the competition among officers is fierce. This competition almost guarantees that you will get some of the finest teachers available. These people know their subjects and can spice the classroom lectures with some carefully chosen "war stories" that illustrate the need to do things correctly in the field.

The course material itself is specifically written and created to stress the most important parts of each subject. There is very little "fat" in a standard police academy curriculum. The organizers know they have only a limited amount of time to teach you and your classmates a wide variety of necessary information. As such, nearly everything your instructors discuss relates to material you must know to pass an exam.

The instructors who teach the various academy subjects are responsible for explaining certain core material mandated by the state. Each state has its own learning requirements for its police officers, and the instructors are expected to teach to these criteria. This isn't to say that you won't hear an abundance of stories, bad jokes, or inside police gossip, just that you can expect the bulk of the classroom material to relate to specific, testable material you'll need to remember later in the academy and later in your career.

Academy classroom etiquette is similar to that of most college-type classrooms, with a few important exceptions. In a college class, the room level is fairly informal, and the discussions usually bounce back and forth between students and the teacher. In the academy, discipline in the classroom is much more important. To ask a question, you'll usually need to raise your hand, wait to be called on, and stand and address the instructor formally, "Sir, Trainee Jones. I wanted to ask about . . . . "

While this kind of formality is popular with your training officers, it's usually less important to the instructors, who will tell you how to address them once their class begins. This formal style serves a few purposes. It shows respect to the instructors; it helps build a foundation of discipline in the classroom; and it allows each student to speak without interruption.

Most academy subjects are taught in blocks of instruction, ranging from two-hour overviews to 80-hour, in- depth looks. Lectures for these blocks, however, usually last for 50 minutes at a time to allow for frequent breaks. At many academies the break procedure is the same: get dismissed by the instructor, "fall in" to ranks outside the classroom, wait to be marched to the break area by a training officer or chosen student, and then get dismissed for a break. Returning to the classroom is usually less structured, as long as you come back on time for the next lecture session.

Lectures

It's hard to overstress the importance of good study habits. Academy courses are dense and force you to cover a lot of material in a short period. Your success in the classroom lies in your ability to take good notes, ask appropriate questions when you need further clarification, study efficiently, and score well on the exams.

In most academy classes, you must score at least a 70 to pass the exams. If you fail an exam, you'll usually be given one opportunity to "remediate" or retake that exam. If you fail the exam the second time you could fail out of the academy program—"wash out," to put it bluntly. While this sounds harsh, it does illustrate the need for good study habits and hard work.

Effective studying starts with good notetaking. One of the easiest ways to take notes efficiently is to use a technique called "mind-mapping." To use this method, start with a clean sheet of paper and write the title or the subject of the lecture right in the center of the page. From there, draw lines that radiate from the center, attaching a word, phrase, or key piece of information to each line. Each time you hear a new piece of information, start a new line or add it to an existing line. Some people call these "spider diagrams" because they look like webs. They are also called "mind-maps" because the ideas look like cities and the lines look like roads.

Anytime you take notes in an academy lecture, be sure to listen carefully to the instructor. He or she will usually tell you what material you'll "see again," meaning that it relates to test questions. Make extra notes about these items and study them in particular later.

Since most academy courses are taught in core modules, that's how you'll take the exams as well—in sections. Instead of one huge 500-question test that covers all your knowledge, you'll usually take a series of 10- to- 50-question multiple-choice tests on each subject. Most academies use multiple-choice exams because they're easier to create and grade, and aren't completely subjective in the grading, as are essay tests.

In most cases, the test will follow the conclusion of the last block of instruction for that subject. That means you'll have a test about every two weeks. You'll know from your master schedule when each subject concludes and when the exam blocks will arrive. This gives you ample time to plan your study sessions accordingly.

In the interest of speed and accuracy, many academies use electronic scoring machines to grade exams. Since many of the tests are reused with future classes, you'll mark your answers on a special tally sheet rather than on the test itself. This method has many benefits, besides making life easier for your training officers who have to grade each test. Because the machine can score several hundred exams in a short period, you can get the results back immediately. This can do wonders for your morale, because you won't have to worry about your scores overnight or, worse, over a weekend. You get immediate feedback; 70 percent and above is a passing grade, and anything below that means you have to retake the test.

Some academy programs allow you to retake a failed exam the next day. Others will let you take it at the end of the same day, allowing you ample study time to prepare again. It's important that you pass the first time. A failed exam can put you behind your fellow classmates and add to your mental burdens. The academy program is stressful enough without having to retake exams. Further, you run the risk of expulsion if you don't pass the make-up exams.

After you've received your test papers back, your training officers will go over each test question and each answer with the entire class. Here, you can learn from your mistakes and reinforce the material you've learned. Remember again that the academy program continues to build upon your knowledge. The more you can retain and recall, the better you'll do on future exams.

This question-and-answer exam review serves an even more important purpose: it gives you the right to have certain test questions thrown out if a majority of your fellow classmates got the wrong answer as well. Say, for example, you took an extensive exam on first aid procedures. If your instructor gave you one answer and the test asks for something completely different, you can ask to have that question deleted. This protects your grade and tells the training officers and instructors what parts of the lectures they might need to improve.

If you're a bit apprehensive about the amount of study involved in the academy, consider getting some help from your fellow classmates. One of the best ways to study is in groups. Informal study sessions are usually held at a student's home or some other convenient meeting place. Besides the obvious benefits of review and reinforcement, these study sessions also offer a good way to get to know your fellow officers.

However you study—alone or in groups—make sure you stay on track and current with the material. As with most college-type classes, academy courses usually require some cumulative knowledge, meaning that things you learned in the first week will apply to courses that come later.

Since you now know the academy classroom format, you'll want to know more about the specific subjects of study. What follows is an annotated list of topics covered during a typical academy program. While a few of these topics may not pertain to your individual agency, the list helps you know what to expect. Don't think that you'll have to know anything about these subjects before you get to the academy. Your instructors will make sure you know each one thoroughly before you leave.

Academy Subjects

Here's an overview of the criminal law classes, patrol theory, first aid, and evidence courses required to graduate. The subjects may differ in scope and content, since different academies stress different subjects. For the most part, this list represents the core of a typical police academy program.

ALCOHOLIC BEVERAGE CONTROL LAWS. This subject deals with the rules and regulations surrounding alcoholic beverage sales and distribution, including types of liquor store, bar, and restaurant licenses; underage minors violations; and the enforcement of similar vice laws. Patrol officers and detectives spend a good deal of their time dealing with alcohol-related problems in bars, taverns, and liquor stores. This class gives information crucial to the law enforcement aspects of these problems.

CHEMICAL WEAPONS TRAINING. Although most of the chemical weapons training calls for outdoor activities (and exposures), there is a significant amount of class time involved too. You'll learn the dynamics of chemical weapon assaults; chemical weapon types and ingredients; effective usage as a defensive weapon; first aid; and proper suspect handling techniques after exposure.

CITATIONS. The training involves how and when to write citations for traffic, misdemeanor, drug, and alcohol violations. This section uses sample citation forms to illustrate the written formats. Since "cite" writing makes up a large part of the police patrol function, the lectures include specific officer safety techniques. You'll be given several "street scenarios" and will be asked to write a variety of sample citations for each.

COMMUNITY RELATIONS. Since our cities are represented by a growing and diverse number of ethnic groups, this section explains the customs of many races and how to build better cultural relations; meet community needs; follow noncultural, unbiased standards for law enforcement; conduct community meetings; form citizen awareness groups; make citizen contacts; suggest referrals and recommend social service agencies; and create crime and drug prevention programs for neighborhoods, businesses, and schools.

CONSTITUTIONAL LAW. Here you'll learn more about the Constitution, the Bill of Rights, and the amendments that relate specifically to the judicial system and to police work. This information is especially useful when coupled with patrol practices involving search and seizure, laws of arrest, interrogation, report writing, and court testimony.

CORRECTIONS. This module follows the booking procedures for arrested suspects, including bail; in-custody care; probation and parole; city and county jail procedures; the roles and functions of the Sheriff's Department; and an overview of the state prison system.

THE COURT SYSTEM. This overview covers the entire judicial process, including trials, hearings, and arraignments; pleas and plea bargains; complaints; indictments; appeals; felony and misdemeanor cases; district and city attorneys; subpoenas; traffic court; family court; and juvenile court. You'll learn more about the arrest "cycle," from the initial arraignment and the preliminary hearing to the jury selection, the court case, the verdict, and the sentencing hearing.

COURTROOM TESTIMONY. Focusing on courtroom etiquette and preparedness, this section explains court procedures, testimony techniques, and the use of reports as a prosecution and defense tool. You'll probably see a mock trial, with careful explanations of your role in the court proceedings.

CRIMINAL LAWS. This section is one of the most comprehensive parts of academy training. It covers all phases of the law as it pertains to police work, such as the laws of arrest; search and seizure rules; stop and frisk requirements; detentions; the definitions of "reasonable suspicion" and "probable cause"; "Miranda" warnings; laws relating to property crimes, personal crimes, the Penal Code, Health & Safety codes, juvenile crimes, Welfare & Institution codes, and the Vehicle Code; citizens' arrests; and powers of arrest and release. This section is often taught by ranking district attorneys, city attorneys, or, in some cases, former police officers who have themselves become prosecuting attorneys.

DEADLY FORCE ISSUES. Another of the important core elements in any academy training program, this section will utilize highly focused and detailed discussions, role playing, and video training simulations. The issues themselves include use of firearms; warning shots; "fleeing felon" decisions; the use of shotguns; the use-of-force continuum; deadly force decision-making techniques; stress control; and the potential for civil or criminal liability actions against officers who misuse deadly force.

DEATH CASES. This topic includes death case procedures, crime scene and evidence protection, report writing, and an overview of the Coroner's Office.

DEFENSIVE TACTICS. Another important core element in your academy training, the defensive tactics module emphasizes the defensive rather than offensive side of effective suspect control. It includes classroom lectures; gymnasium training; armed and unarmed handcuffing procedures; armed and unarmed self-defense; baton training; the carotid neck restraint; search procedures; the use of chemical weapons; high-risk arrest tactics; crowd and riot control; and the potential for civil liability of officers who misuse defensive tactics, arrest and control procedures, or police weaponry.

DISTURBANCE CALLS. Since many officers are killed or injured while handling disturbance calls, this section explains the dynamics of disturbance calls; one- and two-officer safety issues; conflict management; cultural issues; family fights; child custody cases; emotionally disturbed persons; domestic violence; social services and referrals; report procedures; and arrest criteria.

DRIVER'S LICENSES. Taught by State Motor Vehicle investigators, this class explains the issuance and use of driver's licenses, ID cards, vehicle license plates, and VIN numbers. You'll see examples of fraudulent documents to help you recognize them in the field.

DUI ARRESTS. Because drunk driving arrests are growing in response to public awareness, this section shows how to identify, stop, arrest, and book the suspected driver. It includes discussions and examples of the Field Coordination Test; officer safety factors; accident scenes involving the drinking driver; public safety issues; awareness campaigns; arrest, impound, and booking procedures; reports; State Motor Vehicle requirements; and potential civil liability problems.

EVIDENCE. Patrol officers are often called on to collect and recover evidence from crime scenes. This course explains collection techniques; impounding procedures; chain of custody; how to take photos and make crime scene diagrams; fruits of the crime; instrumentalities of the crime; and practical exercises to help recover trace amounts of evidence, such as fingerprints, hairs, fibers, and soil.

FIREARMS TRAINING. This is another significant core module, involving classroom lectures; gun safety rules; range practice; two-hand, one hand, barricade, prone, and stress shooting; reloading; cleaning the weapon; shotgun training; and weapons identification.

FIRST AID TRAINING. While this course probably won't make you a paramedic, it does provide enough information to allow you to stabilize most injury cases, from minor problems to life-threatening wounds. The subjects include first aid application and theory; CPR certification; field problems and role play; and first aid testing and certification.

INTERVIEWS AND INTERROGATIONS. Since most crimes come to police attention "after the fact," a police investigation is only as good as the officer asking the questions. This course teaches techniques for interviewing victims and witnesses; techniques for interrogating suspects; and the dynamics of human communication, including "active listening," body language, and lie detection.

OFFICER SAFETY AND SURVIVAL. Police work is a dangerous profession and is getting more so each day. This class is probably one of the most demanding and powerful sections of the academy. This no-nonsense module looks at mental and physical awareness; patrol theory; radio call response; low- and high-risk arrest tactics; assaults involving knives, guns, and other weapons; disarmings; gun retention; role plays; the use of force; uses of gun, baton, and defensive tactics; stress control; and the "survival" mindset.

PATROL THEORY. This section teaches trainees how to patrol the streets, either on a foot beat or from the seat of a police car. It explains the proper response to radio calls, self-initiated activity, citations, field interviews, and referrals. It covers crimes in progress; building searches; using the police radio; car stops; pedestrian stops; observation techniques; officer safety; officer survival; and modern patrol practices.

PENAL CODE. Coupled with detailed explanations in the law section, the discussion of the Penal Code shows officers how to use this law book and explains the crime elements, violations, and enforcement sections.

PHYSICAL TRAINING LECTURES. More than a few police officers in this country die of heart attacks. Some of these attacks are brought on by poor dietary habits, lack of exercise, and far too much stress. Other officers are forced into early retirement because of chronic back and knee ailments. The PT classroom module discusses health issues that relate to police officers, including diet and exercise plans, injury prevention, and stress control.

POLICE HISTORY AND ETHICAL PRINCIPLES. A course module will offer an overview of the history and principles of law enforcement in the U.S.; ethics and conduct; on- and off-duty habits; individual department policies and procedures; the police chain of command; and the administration of justice in the community.

REPORT WRITING. You'll spend most of your career writing reports of some type. This important module explains the nature and scope of police reports; terminology, procedures, and forms; narratives; interviews and interrogations; crime cases; arrest reports; impounds; narcotics arrests; drunk driver arrest reports; auto theft reports and recoveries; crime descriptions; courtroom procedures; and civil liability precautions.

TRAFFIC ACCIDENT INVESTIGATION. This section explains the proper procedures to be used to respond to vehicle accidents, including safe response; flare patterns; injuries; evidence; vehicle impounds; collision reports; victim, driver, and witness statements; traffic direction; scene protection; measurements; and collision investigation techniques.

VEHICLE CODE. This course offers detailed explanations of state traffic laws. The discussion of the Vehicle Code shows officers how to use this law book in the field, including the administrative and enforcement sections, and specific traffic violations to remember.

VEHICLE OPERATIONS. A typical police patrol officer will spend more time behind the wheel of a police car than at nearly any other on-duty activity. This important section includes classroom study; emergency vehicle traffic laws; emergency vehicle operations; pursuit driving techniques; pursuit policies; accident prevention; and civil liability issues.

Physical Training

While the classroom portion of your academy training takes up the bulk of your time, you will spend a significant part of your days and weeks doing some kind of physical training (PT). How well you do during these PT sessions will depend upon two things: your level of fitness before the academy begins and your ability to work hard and ignore the pain and discomfort that come with difficult physical exercise. The good news is that you can control each of these factors. The bad news is that if you don't, you may fail the academy program.

Like classroom work, police academy physical training can be extremely difficult. If you aren't prepared for it in advance, you'll fall behind your classmates, add to your existing stress level, risk the wrath of your training officers, and possibly even get dismissed from the academy.

Police work is a physically and mentally demanding occupation. It takes place in all kinds of weather, in some of the worst neighborhoods imaginable, and under the most difficult stressors a human being can face. Police work can be painful, involving severe bodily injury and even death to the officer. It requires upper and lower body strength, flexibility, cardiovascular stamina, and lastly, plain old-fashioned guts. If you lack some of these physical requirements, fear not, because academy PT sessions will teach you to overcome physical pain and carry on.

The best way to succeed in PT is to be in shape before it begins. Some hard work on your part before the academy starts will save you much grief later. It's just not possible to get in shape when you get there. You don't have the luxury of time (or a stress-free training environment) to help you ease your way into it.

If you have any preconceived notions about police officers being the largest people around, get rid of them. The old days of the burly, door-filling cops on the beat are over. Today's officers are leaner, more health conscious, and more fit than ever before. More officers are exercising, eating correctly, quitting smoking, and actually working to reduce their on- and off-duty stresses.

Your personal PT program should begin at least four months before the actual academy starts. This will give you plenty of time to get physically and mentally ready for the classroom courses and PT sessions. Consider these four steps as a part of your pre-academy training plan.

QUIT SMOKING

If you don't smoke, don't start. As stressful as police work can be, a cigarette won't help any. Taking up the habit to kill time or calm your nerves is just a bad idea. Health studies tell us that heavy smokers face more sick days, higher health-care bills, and more respiratory problems than nonsmokers.

If you do smoke, it's time to quit. The police academy theory of PT is based on one idea: constant movement. If you aren't running somewhere at double-time speed, you'll be marching or walking quickly. If you're a medium-to-heavy smoker, you will pay the price during these training and marching sessions. Quit now and give your lungs a break. You'll need the oxygen later on those long training runs, and you'll certainly see a definite improvement in your fitness level.

Many progressive police academies actively discourage smoking. They know how harmful it is to the health and safety of their new officers, so they create barriers that make it hard for you to continue smoking, such as no "smoke breaks," restricted smoking areas, and added peer pressure from training officers and fellow classmates to give up the habit.

LOSE WEIGHT

If you can lose any extra weight before the academy, you'll find it very easy to keep it off once the PT sessions start. In fact, you may even find you have to eat more food, more frequently, just to maintain your current weight. If you go through your academy program during hot summer or cold winter months, you'll probably need to increase your intake of calories and fluids to keep up. The PT sessions can take a lot out of you.

Proper weight control also makes it easier for you to run long distances. Since it's no longer necessary to be built like a pro football player to work as a police officer, you should focus your pre-academy training efforts toward slimming down to a leaner body weight. Many new recruits who spent hours in the health spa "pumping iron" have found the extra muscle bulk actually hindered their performance. Carrying extra weight, even if it's mostly muscle, can slow you down.

The trick is to be strong and muscular, without any unnecessary muscle mass or fat to carry around. Unless you're an experienced athlete with years of work behind you, don't try to bring any extra muscle weight to the academy. If you're too heavy, you're probably too slow as well. Lean and mean is the idea here. You can certainly lift weights before and during the academy, but keep the weights light and the number of repetitions high to "tone up" rather than "bulk up."

Start a sensible diet program when you begin your pre-academy conditioning program. Lose the extra weight slowly and safely by drinking plenty of water, taking vitamins, and eating a balanced and reduced-calorie diet as you train. Just remember you'll have to carry any extra pounds with you on those long academy training runs.

Walk / Run / Sprint

If you're more than a weekend athlete, you're probably already used to running or jogging at least three or four times per week. If so, continue your present training pace and add some long runs, some sprints and speed work, and plenty of pre- and post-run stretching to your workouts. If you don't run regularly, do yourself a favor and start your training by walking first. Many overeager police cadets have set themselves back with serious injuries by overtraining. Go to the bookstore and get a good book on walking. Follow the advice concerning the choice of shoes, walking courses, and training times. Start slowly, work hard during every session, and focus on strengthening your leg and back muscles as you walk. Some carefully planned walking workouts will prepare your body safely and efficiently for the runs to follow.

Once you've worked up to a brisk walking pace, you can start your pre-academy running program. The secret here again is not to overdo it and risk an injury that could set you back for months. Run at a "talking pace"—a speed where you can hold a conversation without gasping—for the first few weeks. Make sure you have a good pair of running shoes—not tennis or basketball sneakers—that support your ankles and protect your legs from the inevitable pounding from hard running surfaces.

While some experts say you can run on a near-daily basis, as long as you alternate one "hard" day with one "easy" day, other sports trainers aren't so sure. A good rule of thumb is to run every other day and rest your legs, lungs, and heart on your off days. Many people like to run on Mondays, Wednesdays, and Fridays, with a longer distance run on Sunday. Then they rest Monday and start up again Tuesday with the every-other-day pace. Pick a schedule that works for you and stick with it. If you want to increase your mileage, go up about 10 percent every other week. For example, if you can run 10 total miles per week with little difficulty, go up to 11, and so on.

Too much running can cause you a host of problems, from blisters to shin splints, and even stress fractures and broken bones. Be sensible, run "softly" on well-cushioned surfaces, and concentrate on quality training sessions rather than quantity. Run in a way that causes you to roll along heel to toe, rather than on the balls of your feet. Run straight upright, so that your body doesn't bounce. If the horizon in front of you shakes about, you're probably moving your upper body too much.

To give you some variety during your running workouts, you may want to try some "wind sprints." Go to a local high school football field and pace off 40 yards. Try running a few warmup sprints at half-speed and then "kick it into gear." Run six to ten full-speed sprints to get your heart rate up and increase your leg-muscle flexibility. Sprint workouts offer a good change of pace and can prepare you for a variety of academy running assignments. Remember to stretch before and after every running workout, especially if you plan to do any sprinting.

Use Your Body Weight

If you were to get a dime for every push-up you'll do in the police academy, you could retire at an early age. The standard gym-class pushup is a mainstay of most academy PT sessions. You'll do them as punishment in a group; you'll do them as punishment for an individual mistake; and you'll do them by the carload in your formal PT sessions.

As you're doing these pushups with your classmates, you'll all collectively wonder when your training officers will get tired and ask you to stop. Unfortunately, they have several secret weapons at their disposal. First, if they get tired, they simply stand up and continue counting. So while they've stopped at 37, you have to go on until 50. Secondly, if they get tired at 50, they just ask another instructor to take over until you reach 100. Lastly, if you don't yell loudly during the count portion, these fine instructors will pretend they lost track, and you'll have to start again from pushup number one!

Seriously, since the pushup exercise is so much a part of academy PT, you'll want to do many hundreds of them as part of your pre-academy training program. As with most body-weight resistance exercises, pushups get easier the more you do them.

As with running, if you haven't done this type of exercise in some time, you'll need to start slowly. Give yourself small goals and try to meet them each day. Start with 10 pushups per session, go to 25, and then go to 50. Increase the number of times you practice pushups from once or twice per day on up to 10 times per day. Use good form, breathe correctly (inhale going down, exhale coming up), and stick with them. The more you do now, the easier they are to do later, especially when a large, uniformed man is yelling in your ear.

Like pushups, situps are another standard-issue academy exercise. And while pushups build your arms, shoulders, and chest, situps strengthen your abdominal muscles and, to a lesser extent, your lower back and hip joint area. Many police officers have had to retire early with long-term medical disabilities because of weak backs. Many of these problems stem from the constant wear and tear on your stomach muscles. Police gun belts, bullet-proof vests, heavy shoes, and other equipment can add up to 30 pounds to an officer's body weight. This can cause stomach muscles to sag and become more prone to injuries like hernias, ruptures, and lateral low-back ailments.

Do your back and stomach a favor. Start a situp program with your pushup regimen. Choose a target number and meet it every day. Use good form; don't pull on the back of your neck with your hands; and protect your seat with a towel or pad.

Lastly, many training academies ask their officers to do pullups as a part of PT. The typical pullup movement requires an above-average amount of upper-body strength and it offers a good way to show improvements in overall fitness levels. As with your pre-academy conditioning exercises, start slowly and build yourself up to multiple pullup sets. If you can't do one pullup, make that your goal and work hard to achieve it. Use your determination and concentrate on good form. Try to do one, five, or ten more of everything than you did in the previous day.

The paramilitary model that covers the classroom discipline in the academy also reaches the PT sessions. Those trainees with prior military experience will be fairly comfortable with the group exercise process. If you don't have a military background, you'll have to make a few adjustments.

Most academy PT classes run for one hour to one hour and fifteen minutes. Some sessions will take place early in the morning, before classes begin; others will start just before lunch, and still others will cover the last hour of the work day. Nearly every session will include a running program followed by a vigorous session of mat work, which includes the usual pushups, situps, leg lifts, abdominal crunches, pullups, and even bar dips.

You'll begin with a set of warm-ups and calisthenics, which you'll do as a group, counting loudly enough to impress your training officers. From there, you'll form two single-file lines and begin the run of the day.

Running in formation like this takes a careful step. Too close and you'll stomp on the person in front of you; too far away and you'll risk falling behind. Since most training runs are held on the roads around the academy facility, you'll need to pay strict attention to the terrain and the potential hazards in the street, such as curbs, fire hydrants, and mail boxes.

A few academy classes like to run in the traditional Army style, with everyone staying together and running at a comfortable pace so the slowest runner can keep up. Most PT instructors, however, prefer to start the class together and then let the faster runners set the pace. This tends to spread the group out in a long line, but it allows everyone to work at a rate that is personally best. To keep the "gazelles" under control, a training officer will often set a fast pace and keep everyone else behind. Another training officer will anchor the end of the line to encourage the stragglers with a few well-chosen words and to push them along.

If you're out of shape, this spread-out method can be unbearable. Just when you catch up to the leaders of the pack—who jog in place until you arrive—they start up again, giving you no break whatsoever. This should tell you how important pre-academy fitness is to your mental and physical health. Unless you want your eardrums to ring with the howls of your training officers, get in shape and be ready to run at a brisk pace when necessary.

The only thing that makes this kind of running enjoyable—besides knowing that it can't last forever—is the cadence calling. Just like the military, many academies use marching songs and rhymes to encourage the recruits and take their minds off their labored breathing. These songs, limericks, and marching poems are always inspirational, usually motivational, and occasionally humorous. They also encourage group unity, promote discipline, and help to pass the time a bit.

After a stimulating run, it's off to the gym room or exercise area for some more calisthenics. You will usually line up in rows and begin a whole series of pushups and situps. These exercises aren't particularly difficult, but coupled with the running program, they can really tire you out.

As with all PT exercises, the more you can do before the academy begins, the easier it will be for you to complete each exercise session. During all sessions, try to stay up with the training officers and match them exercise for exercise. You'll improve your conditioning, and this makes for a better impression among your peers and trainers.

If your PT program takes place before class begins, you'll probably have just enough time to shower and dress for the start of the day. If the session ends at lunch or at the close of the day, take some extra time to eat properly and drink plenty of fluids, especially water. If you eat sensibly, minimizing the junk food, sodas, and fast-food items, you'll help your physical performance and feel better as well.

Besides the obvious cardiovascular and upper-body strength benefits, most academy

PT sessions are designed to build the muscles of the abdomen, lower back, and back and knee joints. Since so many officers suffer career-threatening health problems in these vital areas, injury prevention is a critical part of your overall fitness plan while you attend the academy. Tell your instructors anytime you feel any unusual pains or anything other than normal muscle soreness.

Work hard to keep your knee joints strong and flexible. Concentrate on your stomach muscles to prevent back and stomach injuries. Run carefully and efficiently to avoid any foot or leg problems. Think of your academy PT sessions as the gateway to a career of lifelong fitness and injury prevention.

Arrest and Control Classes

Many academies have a "mat room" especially designed for police defensive training. This area is covered with thick wrestling-style mats, and there are usually heavy boxing-type "body punching" bags in various locations around the room. The mats help protect you during defensive tactics training, and the bags are for baton strikes and punching practice.

You'll spend most of your time in the mat room doing PT work—pushups, situps, etc. Except for the classroom courses, you'll go through most of your arrest and control classes and defensive tactics work here, too.

Notice the key word "defensive." By its nature, police work is filled with opportunities for officers to prevent physical confrontations. We use defensive rather than offensive movements for a variety of reasons, besides just to protect ourselves. The defensive mode promotes better officer safety tactics; it's more effective as a suspect control technique; and it prevents undue civil liability suits against officers and their departments.

The days of the baton-swinging, head-beating officer are long over. With the potential for unlawful injuries to suspects and the tremendous risk of civil liability for excessive force, police academies have turned their attention towards defensive tactics that protect officers and suspects alike.

Some trainers like to teach judo "safe-falling" techniques, tumbling movements, ground and foot fighting movements, boxing and wrestling techniques, and other "street" fighting maneuvers.

For these defensive tactics drills, you'll partner up with a fellow classmate. Most of these activities call for one officer to be "the cop" and one to be "the crook." You'll switch back and forth as you practice the hands-on techniques over the one- to two-hour class sessions.

Whether you're learning to use the police baton, a handcuffing technique, or an empty-hand control technique, the key to your success in defensive tactics training lies in correct practice and repetition. You must exercise the proper control to protect yourself and your partner from injuries. Some officers have been badly injured during these sessions because of an overzealous partner or because they failed to practice safely and carefully. On the other hand, the only way you'll learn to perform these techniques correctly (and safely) is to practice them over and over again.

The human body, in terms of police training, thrives on repetition. Constant, unrelenting practice involving several hundred or even several thousand repetitions will build a sense of "muscle memory" into your brain and muscles. With sufficient practice, each of these moves can become almost instinctive, requiring no thought, just action.

Your defensive tactics training instructors know this, so you'll spend most of your time learning new techniques and drilling with them over and over again. The more you can practice in the gym, the better you will follow the techniques in the field, where it really counts.

Many hands-on techniques for police work are based on the martial art aikido, which focuses on wrist, elbow, and shoulder-joint pressures and throwing techniques. You won't need any previous martial arts experience to learn these movements, but you may want to review some aikido or other martial arts books at the bookstore or library. Sometimes it helps to see these grappling techniques as they are broken down in step-by-step photographs.

Police baton training in the academy depends upon the equipment used by your local agency. Some police departments use the straight baton and others use an expandable straight baton. Some agencies train officers to use the PR-24 side-handle baton and others prefer the Orcutt Police Nunchakus. Whatever equipment you use, keep these rules in mind: train safely—these are potentially deadly weapons—and train consistently, using many drills and repetitions to hone your skills.

Dress Codes

Most academies require their trainees to maintain three different types of uniform: the dress uniform, the arrest and control uniform, and the PT uniform. Each serves its own purpose. Since the word "uniform" is defined as "official clothing; one that does not vary," you can imagine that police academy clothing is all the same. You will dress exactly the same as your classmates, even down to the color of your socks. You'll also have the same haircut, the same color dress shoes, and, hopefully, the same enthusiastic attitude. Only your training officers and instructors will dress differently from you, and they do not particularly encourage your individuality.

The dress uniform is usually the uniform of the agency that hired you. Some academies have trainees wear the actual uniform of the police agency, while others use a training uniform of blue or khaki brown. In the latter example, you would begin wearing the traditional uniform of your agency at your graduation. In any case, the dress uniform is usually worn during the classroom sessions.

The arrest and control uniform also varies. Most cadets wear "nametag" T-shirts with their last names printed on the front and back for ease in identification (and yelling at). Some academies have trainees wear T-shirts, standard blue jeans, and running shoes for defensive tactics classes, while other classes use T-shirts, sweatpants, and running shoes. In either case, the purpose of the uniform is comfort, durability, freedom of movement, easy identification, and safety. Few academies want their people to wrestle and fight in dress uniforms, since it's expensive to fix torn clothes.

The PT uniform consists of the "nametag" T-shirt, running shorts, white socks, and running shoes. This uniform is used strictly for PT sessions because it's cool and comfortable and allows free movement.

For nearly every defensive tactics session, you'll use the arrest and control uniform. You'll also wear your gunbelt, baton, and unloaded handgun. Since safety is a constant issue, every arrest and control session starts with a handgun inspection to make certain no live ammunition is anywhere near your gun. Then after a quick warm-up session involving some stretching and pushups, you'll begin the course of instruction for the day.

Role Plays

A weary patrol officer once said that all of police work is just "street theater." This refers to a cop's ability to portray certain characters while out in the field. In some cases, you'll have to be the concerned and empathetic helper when talking to an emotionally disturbed or suicidal person. In others, you'll have to play the "heavy," the strict authoritarian figure, especially in the face of certain violence. And in others, you may have to act as if you aren't the slightest bit afraid, even though, inside, you may be shaking like a leaf. Police patrol work requires much of its officers, and playing different roles is just part of the job. You learn to play these parts in the police academy.

As the academy training begins to wind down, your training officers and instructors will begin to give you more autonomy, more leeway in your decision-making activities. You'll still have the discipline that is a part of academy life, but you'll be placed in certain situations and be asked to respond like a professional law enforcement officer. These situations are called "role plays," and they resemble small theater skits in that they call for you to act out a part and respond to other people doing the same.

In a typical role-play scenario, you and your partner will be asked to answer a radio call regarding some in-progress or after-the-fact crime. You'll go to the scene, meet the participants, and take the appropriate police action. During this role-play scenario, your training officers and instructors will supervise your actions and grade your performance. Here, under the controlled conditions of the academy, you can make mistakes and learn from them. You don't always have that luxury in the field, where your mistakes could cost your life.

These role plays could involve something simple, like a burglary report, or something life-threatening, like a liquor store robbery or a high-risk vehicle stop. In each example, you'll be expected to respond just as you would if it were a live, real-life field problem. Now is the time to put your skills and training to use. Your success in these role plays in the academy can mean continued success on the streets later.

Weapons Training

Besides the role-playing work, you will spend a significant portion of your academy time at the police range, practicing with your duty firearm. Coupled with your classroom training on deadly force issues, the firearms module is critical to your development as a professional police officer.

Anytime you are not at a police range or in some other training capacity, you are responsible for every bullet that leaves your gun. These days, it just doesn't matter that an officer says he or she "meant to do the right thing." Civil liability and deadly force go hand in hand. You must know when to draw your weapon and how to operate it safely. The instructors at the police range will teach you how to do both.

As with the movements you make in the defensive tactics and arrest and control classes, safety and repetition are the keys to your success on the firing line. You must always realize that you are holding a loaded handgun, capable of delivering deadly force in a split-second. Discipline and attention to the details of safety are the rules of the police range. Rest assured that your instructors will make sure you pay attention and follow their explicit directions.

Some police agencies favor the standard .38-caliber police handgun while others are going with the 9mm semi-automatic pistol. There are arguments pro and con for each, but whatever gun you're given, treat it as if it were a member of your family. Barring damage or malfunction, you will carry that gun for the rest of your police career. You may have to call upon it to save your life or the life of someone else.

Your instructors will show you how to shoot your weapon from a variety of hand and body positions. You'll learn how to clean it, disassemble and reassemble it, and carry and draw it in a stressful situation. You'll probably shoot over one thousand rounds before your academy training ends—sometimes at night, sometimes in bright sunlight. You'll shoot lefthanded and right, from your knees, from your stomach, and from behind barricades of all shapes and sizes. You'll shoot at close range and over long distances, under timed conditions, with a partner, and on your own.

Since most law enforcement agencies use the standard police shotgun, you'll learn just as much about that weapon as you will about your handgun. By the end of your training, you'll know how to break the shotgun down into pieces and rebuild it. You'll shoot it in a variety of positions, settings, and lighting conditions, using different ammunition loads. Other agencies use police rifles, involving similar training and repetition as with the police shotgun.

As in the role plays, at the range you'll be under the watchful eyes of your training officers and firearms instructors. And like the role-play exercises, the police range is the place to make mistakes and learn from them. Any mistake involving a firearm that you make in the street could end in a tragedy.

Emergency Vehicle Driving

Other outdoor academy work will take place on the driving course. Since you'll spend the majority of your random patrol time behind the wheel of a car, you'll need some extensive training in emergency vehicle driving. Some large-city law enforcement agencies average over one police equipment accident per day. Not only is it expensive to repair these cars, but an accident often results in injuries to officers and civilians and the distinct possibility of a court case against the officer and the department.

Because your instructors assume you already have some average or better-than-average behind-the-wheel skills, the driving portion of your academy training usually focuses on emergency techniques to help you during high-risk pursuit-type operations. This includes "speed" braking, driving in reverse, "slalom" turn driving, high-speed turning, and skid control. Because you spend so much time behind the wheel—and a moving car can be just as much of a deadly weapon as a gun—it's essential that you appreciate your degree of responsibility every time you operate a police vehicle in a normal or emergency situation.

Field Trips

Some academies send their trainees out to various criminal justice facilities for some familiarization training. Most recruits enjoy these short "field trips" because a trip offers a change of pace and gets the recruits away from the day-to-day grind of the academy. Usually, the instructor for that particular subject will lead a tour or arrange to have a representative take the recruits around the facility.

Because officers will interact with other public service agencies, it helps to know where these places are located and how they operate. Your academy may schedule tours and short trips to the facilities listed below.

CITY AND COUNTY JAIL TOUR. Since many city law enforcement agencies contract their custodial inmate services with the county sheriff, deputies rather than police officers will work in these facilities. A jail tour helps new officers understand the booking and detention procedures as well as the duties and responsibilities of the sheriff's department for inmate housing, transportation, and care inside the jail. Some academy classes will tour both the men's and the women's detention facilities on separate days.

JUVENILE HOLDING CENTERS. Because juvenile inmates are held in locations separate from those for adults, officers will tour the youth facilities. The laws and restrictions surrounding the housing of juvenile inmates are quite strict, so trainees will have to learn how arrest and booking procedures differ from those of adult suspects.

FAMILY AND CHILD PROTECTIVE SERVICES. Many cities have social service facilities to care for abandoned, abused, or injured children. These places also care for foster children, wards of the court, and other children involved in noncriminal matters that come to the attention of the police.

COURTHOUSE TOUR. This tour covers the city or county courthouses and explains to new officers how and where the trials take place. Coupled with the classroom lectures that cover courtroom procedures, this trip takes recruits through the criminal justice cycle that begins after an arrest is made.

CORONER'S OFFICE TOUR. Usually an exciting and fascinating trip, the Coroner's Office tour supplements the classroom lectures for death cases and crime scene investigations. In some cities, police recruits will watch an actual autopsy. Members of the Coroner's Office will explain when an autopsy is necessary in a death case and how the evidence is collected, analyzed, and processed. Many trainees find this tour quite informative—once they get over the initial shock of being around so many dead bodies.

These field trips give recruit officers a different perspective about the criminal justice process and the social service organizations in their area. The trips also expose recruits to other available sources of help and information once they get into the field. These trips, combined with the classroom lectures, exercises, and tests, help put some reality into the academy training.

Graduation and Beyond

The only event more important than starting the academy is finishing it. And the only day more exciting than the first one is graduation day. Here you'll see the payoff, the culmination of your hard work, the sweat, the exams, and the extra effort.

Graduation Day is an exciting time for all new officers. The drudgery of the academy is finally over. No more marching, saluting, or those heavy doses of discipline. You can now dispense with the constant stream of "yes sirs" and "yes ma'ams" that have been a part of your vocabulary for the past months. It's time to celebrate your efforts with a graduation ceremony steeped in the tradition and history of your agency. You'll get your badge—a centuries-old symbol of the public trust. You'll also get to meet your police chief and the command staff. It's a proud moment for your relatives and loved ones, and it's an even prouder moment for you. Celebrate your accomplishments and salute your fellow classmates.

The Field Officer Training Phase

There's an old saying in law enforcement that goes, "The academy teaches you to be a police officer and the streets teach you to be a cop." The distinction is an important one.

The material you learned in the academy is a valuable and necessary part of your development as a police officer, but the only way you can earn the title of "street cop" is to hit the streets and prevent crime. Rest assured that you won't be asked to do this by yourself. For the first few months of your patrol career, you'll be under the wing of an experienced Field Training Officer (FTO).

Some new officers say the Field Training phase is even more stressful and difficult than the academy. This may be because the academy is a relatively safe environment. Nobody can assault or injure you there, and except for all the yelling and screaming done by the training officers, it's a fairly calm place. The streets, on the other hand, are rarely calm and hardly offer much safety, especially in some of the more vehemently anti-police neighborhoods.

For all its stresses, the academy is still a structured, orderly place well-suited for learning. Street patrol, with its hours of boredom interspaced with minutes of high excitement, offers a much more difficult learning environment. It's indeed possible to magnify the consequences of your mistakes, especially when it comes to your safety, the safety of your partner, and that of the people you're supposed to protect. The ever-present news media hardly help the situation; your mistakes can now be captured for eternity on videotape. You're now in the "fishbowl," under constant public scrutiny, with many eyes upon you.

To minimize the mistake process and make sure you learn to be a good, safe street cop, most police agencies have developed an entire program based on the training needs of new officers. Your initial meeting with your partner, the Field Training Officer, will include your introduction to the "bible" of street policing, the Critical Task book. Other agencies may refer to it differently, perhaps as the Patrol Guide, but however it's called, the book is basically a checklist of your duties and responsibilities as a patrol officer.

Just as it's titled, the Critical Task book is a book filled with various critical and essential police tasks that you must identify and complete with the approval of your FTO. Your FTO will explain each of the tasks, ranging from checking the equipment in your police car before the beginning of a shift, to proper radio procedures, to handling domestic disturbance calls, to high-risk arrests, to issuing parking citations, to working with the computer records back at the station, to writing complete and effective reports. If you do something as a police officer, you'll find it in this Critical Task book.

You may even be asked to complete "homework" assignments, ranging from map book location problems to sample arrest and crime case reports. You'll complete these assignments on your own and turn them in on time.

Besides teaching you how to do this demanding job safely and effectively, your FTO will document your daily activities on paper. The FTO's report includes an evaluation of your work habits, strengths, weaknesses, mistakes, and good points. Depending upon the length of time you spend with your FTO, he or she will write biweekly evaluation reports to show that you are "on schedule" and progressing in a timely manner.

These biweekly reports are reviewed by the training division personnel who also monitor your progress and by a number of other supervisors up the line. Rest assured that your agency wants you to make it through this street patrol training phase and to become a full-fledged member of the department. Officers who can work alone or without constant supervision offer the best service to their department. The Field Training Phase teaches you how to work alone and with a partner.

The length of the Field Training Phase varies from agency to agency. Some departments put new academy graduates through a four-month program, rotating their partners, shift hours, and duty areas each month. Others will cycle new officers back and forth each month between the academy classroom and the field until they graduate. Other departments will send a new officer to his or her permanent duty assignment immediately upon graduation, with no area or shift rotation at all. Still other agencies will assign new graduates to one station for their entire one-year (or 18-month) probationary period. After they clear probation, they can request a transfer to another station.

During this critical probationary period, the officer must work hard and meet all of the required job performance objectives. Probationary officers have very few civil service rights and can be quickly terminated for crucial mistakes, judgment errors, or hazardous off-duty incidents. Where the veteran officer may have some protection from discharge by the civil service board, the probationary officer does not. The probationary period forces new officers to demonstrate their skills and knowledge to the police agency that hired them.

Getting through the field training phase is quite similar to succeeding in the academy: listen, do as you're told, ask questions when necessary, and practice doing the right things over and over again. Your FTO will suggest ways to do the job more effectively. Take what you learn from each training officer you encounter in the field. Just like the academy training officers and course instructors, the Field Training Officers in your department are chosen for their police skills and their ability and desire to train new officers to function in the field. They're usually the finest officers in the department.

Listen to their suggestions, take their criticisms in stride, and learn from your mistakes. Don't rationalize your behavior with statements like, "What I really meant to do was . . . ." or "I meant to do that but didn't because . . . ." Your FTO partners will try to give you the benefit of their experience. Watch how they work, observe their safety habits, and make these part of your own operating plan. Learn from them and continually tell yourself you can do this job safely and successfully.

Recruiting studies show that for every one person a police agency hires and puts through an academy, it turns away nearly 90 applicants, for one reason or another. Police work truly is a profession for an elite and qualified few. Consider yourself part of a proud and honorable calling.

Many people in this country admire law enforcement and have the utmost respect and admiration for police officers. Plenty of people will tell you, "You know, I always thought I could be a cop." The difference between them and you is that you put forth the effort and did what was asked. You have become a law enforcement officer.

APPENDIX
PHYSICAL FITNESS COURSE

In the law enforcement universe, much of the hiring decision is based upon the candidate's physical status. Considering the demands made upon the law enforcement officer's body, the emphasis on physical fitness is entirely reasonable. From your own standpoint as a serious candidate, it makes sense to devote at least as much attention to preparing your body for the physical test as to preparing your mind for the written exam.

Obviously, if you are considering yourself as a law enforcement officer candidate, you consider yourself a healthy, physically fit person. Even so, it would be wise to consult with your own doctor before proceeding. Tell your doctor about the type of work you have in mind, describe the physical demands, and ask for an assessment of your potential to withstand these rigors. If your doctor foresees any potential problems, either in passing the exams or in facing the demands of the job, discuss corrective measures and remedial programs right now. Follow the medical advice you receive concerning diet and general lifestyle. If the jurisdiction to which you are applying provides you with a description of the physical performance test you must take, describe it to your doctor. You may be able to pick up special tips to prepare yourself to do well on your exam. Your doctor may have a physical conditioning program to recommend. If not, design your own program. You may find the following suggestions prepared by the President's Council on Physical Fitness convenient to follow just as printed or helpful as you tailor-make a fitness program to your own needs and time requirements.

Defining Fitness

Physical fitness is to the human body what fine tuning is to an engine. It enables us to perform up to our potential. Fitness can be described as a condition that helps us look, feel and do our best. More specifically, it is:

"The ability to perform daily tasks vigorously and alertly, with energy left over for enjoying leisure-time activities and meeting emergency demands. It is the ability to endure, to bear up, to withstand stress, and to carry on in circumstances where an unfit person could not continue and is a major basis for good health and well-being."

Physical fitness involves the performance of the heart, the lungs, and the muscles of the body. And, since what we do with our bodies also affects what we can do with our minds, fitness influences to some degree qualities such as mental alertness and emotional stability.

As you undertake your fitness program, it's important to remember that fitness is an individual quality that varies from person to person. It is influenced by age, sex, heredity, personal habits, exercise and eating practices. You can't do anything about the first three factors. However, it is within your power to change and improve the others where needed.

KNOWING THE BASICS

Physical fitness is most easily understood by examining its components, or "parts." There is widespread agreement that these four components are basic:

CARDIORESPIRATORY ENDURANCE—the ability to deliver oxygen and nutrients to tissues, and to remove wastes, over sustained periods of time. Long runs and swims are among the methods employed in measuring this component.

MUSCULAR STRENGTH—the ability of a muscle to exert force for a brief period of time. Upper-body strength, for example, can be measured by various weight-lifting exercises.

MUSCULAR ENDURANCE—the ability of a muscle, or a group of muscles, to sustain repeated contractions or to continue applying force against a fixed object. Pushups are often used to test endurance of arm and shoulder muscles.

FLEXIBILITY—the ability to move joints and use muscles through their full range of motion. The sit-and-reach test is a good measure of flexibility of the lower back and backs of the upper legs.

BODY COMPOSITION is often considered a component of fitness. It refers to the makeup of the body in terms of lean mass (muscle, bone, vital tissue, and organs) and fat mass. An optimal ratio of fat to lean mass is an indication of fitness, and the right types of exercises will help you decrease body fat and increase or maintain muscle mass.

A Workout Schedule

How often, how long, and how hard you exercise, and what kinds of exercises you do should be determined by what you are trying to accomplish. Your goals, your present fitness level, age, health, skills, interest, and convenience are among the factors you should consider. For example, an athlete training for high-level competition would follow a different program than a person whose goals are good health and the ability to meet work and recreational needs.

Your exercise program should include something from each of the four basic fitness components described previously. Each workout should begin with a warmup and end with a cooldown. As a general rule, space your workouts throughout the week and avoid consecutive days of hard exercise.

Here are the amounts of activity necessary for the average, healthy person to maintain a minimum level of overall fitness. Included are some of the popular exercises for each category.

WARMUP—5–10 minutes of exercises such as walking, slow jogging, knee lifts, arm circles or trunk rotations. Low intensity movements that simulate movements to be used in the activity can also be included in the warmup.

MUSCULAR STRENGTH—a minimum of two 20-minute sessions per week that include exercises for all the major muscle groups. Lifting weights is the most effective way to increase strength.

MUSCULAR ENDURANCE—at least three 30-minute sessions each week that include exercises such as calisthenics, pushups, situps, pullups, and weight training for all the major muscle groups.

CARDIORESPIRATORY ENDURANCE—at least three 20-minute bouts of continuous aerobic (activity requiring oxygen) rhythmic exercise each week. Popular aerobic conditioning activities include brisk walking, jogging, swimming, cycling, rope-jumping, rowing, cross-country skiing, and some continuous action games like racquetball and handball.

FLEXIBILITY—10–12 minutes of daily stretching exercises performed slowly, without a bouncing motion. This can be included after a warmup or during a cooldown.

COOL DOWN—a minimum of 5–10 minutes of slow walking, low-level exercise, combined with stretching.

A Matter of Principle

The keys to selecting the right kinds of exercises for developing and maintaining each of the basic components of fitness are found in these principles:

SPECIFICITY—pick the right kind of activities to affect each component. Strength training results in specific strength changes. Also, train for the specific activity you're interested in. For example, optimal swimming performance is best achieved when the muscles involved in swimming are trained for the movements required. It does not necessarily follow that a good runner is a good swimmer.

OVERLOAD—work hard enough, at levels that are vigorous and long enough to overload your body above its resting level, to bring about improvement.

REGULARITY—you can't hoard physical fitness. At least three balanced workouts a week are necessary to maintain a desirable level of fitness.

PROGRESSION—increase the intensity, frequency and/or duration of activity over periods of time in order to improve.

Some activities can be used to fulfill more than one of your basic exercise requirements. For example, in addition to increasing cardiorespiratory endurance, running builds muscular endurance in the legs, and swimming develops the arm, shoulder and chest muscles. If you select the proper activities, it is possible to fit parts of your muscular endurance workout into your cardiorespiratory workout and save time.

MEASURING YOUR HEART RATE

Heart rate is widely accepted as a good method for measuring intensity during running, swimming, cycling and other aerobic activities. Exercise that doesn't raise your heart rate to a certain level and keep it there for 20 minutes won't contribute significantly to cardiovascular fitness.

The heart rate you should maintain is called your **target heart rate.** There are several ways of arriving at this figure. One of the simplest is: **maximum heart rate** (220 – age) × 70%. Thus, the target heart rate for a 40-year-old would be 126.

Some methods for figuring the target rate take individual differences into consideration. Here is one of them:

1. Subtract age from 220 to find **maximum heart rate.**

2. Subtract resting heart rate (see below) from maximum heart rate to determine **heart rate reserve.**

3. Take 70% of heart rate reserve to determine **heart rate raise.**

4. Add heart rate raise to resting heart rate to find **target rate.**

Resting heart rate should be determined by taking your pulse after sitting quietly for five minutes. When checking heart rate during a workout, take your pulse within five seconds after interrupting exercise because it starts to go down once you stop moving. Count pulse for 10 seconds and multiply by six to get the per-minute rate.

The Program

The program below assumes that you have not been putting all of your muscles to any consistent use and that you are starting from close to "couch potato" status. If you are already in pretty good shape, you might be able to start more quickly. But do not overdo. A gradual build-up makes sense.

The program starts with an orientation or "get-set" series of exercises that will allow you to bring all major muscles into use easily and painlessly.

There are then five graded levels.

As you move from one to the next, you will be building toward a practical and satisfying level of fitness.

By building gradually, progressively, you will be building soundly.

WHAT THE EXERCISES ARE FOR

There are three general types—warmup exercises, conditioning exercises and circulatory activities.

The warmup exercises stretch and limber up the muscles and speed up the action of the heart and lungs, thus preparing the body for greater exertion and reducing the possibility of unnecessary strain.

The conditioning exercises are systematically planned to tone up abdominal, back, leg, arm and other major muscles.

The circulatory activities produce contractions of large muscle groups for relatively longer periods than the conditioning exercises—to stimulate and strengthen the circulatory and respiratory systems.

The plan calls for doing 10 mild exercises during the orientation period and, thereafter, the warmup exercises and the seven conditioning exercises listed for each level. The first six exercises of the orientation program are used as warmup exercises throughout the graded levels.

When it comes to the circulatory activities, you choose one each workout. Alternately running and walking ... skipping rope ... running in place. All are effective. You can choose running and walking on a pleasant day and one of the others for use indoors when the weather is inclement. You can switch about for variety.

How You Progress

A sound physical conditioning program should take into account your individual tolerance—your ability to execute a series of activities without undue discomfort or fatigue. It should provide for developing your tolerance by increasing the work load so you gradually become able to achieve more and more with less and less fatigue and with increasingly rapid recovery.

As you move from level to level, some exercises will be modified so they call for increased effort.

Others will remain the same, but you will build more strength and stamina by increasing the number of repetitions.

You will be increasing your fitness another way, as well.

At level 1, your objective will be to gradually reduce, from workout to workout, the "breathing spells" between exercises until you can do the seven conditioning exercises without resting. You will proceed in the same fashion with the more difficult exercises and increased repetitions at succeeding levels.

You will find the program designed—the progression carefully planned—to make this feasible. You will be able to proceed at your own pace, competing with yourself rather than with anyone else—and this is of great importance for sound conditioning.

Note: Gradually speeding up, from workout to workout, the rate at which you do each exercise will provide greater stimulation for the circulatory and respiratory systems and also help to keep your workouts short. However, the seven conditioning exercises should not be a race against time. Perform each exercise correctly to insure maximum benefit.

How Long at Each Level

Your objective at each level will be to reach the point where you can do all the exercises called for, for the number of times indicated, without resting between exercises.

But, start slowly.

It cannot be emphasized enough that by moving forward gradually you will be moving forward solidly, avoiding sudden strains and excesses that could make you ache and hold you back for several days.

If you find yourself at first unable to complete any exercises—to do continuously all the repetitions called for—stop when you encounter difficulty. Rest briefly, then take up where you left off and complete the count. If you have difficulty at first, there will be less and less with succeeding workouts.

Stay at each level for at least three weeks. If you have not passed the prove-out test at the end of that time, continue at the same level until you do. The prove-out test calls for performing—in three consecutive workouts—the seven conditioning exercises without resting and satisfactorily fulfilling the requirement for one circulatory activity.

A Measure of Your Progress

You will, of course, be able to observe the increase in your strength and stamina from week to week in many ways—including the increasing facility with which you do the exercises at a given level.

In addition, there is a 2-minute step test you can use to measure and keep a running record of the improvement in your circulatory efficiency, one of the most important of all aspects of fitness.

The immediate response of the cardiovascular system to exercise differs markedly between well-conditioned individuals and others. The test measures the response in terms of pulse rate taken shortly after a series of steps up and down onto a bench or chair.

Although it does not take long, it is necessarily vigorous. Stop if you become overly fatigued while taking it. You should not try it until you have completed the orientation period.

THE STEP TEST

Use any sturdy bench or chair 15–17 inches in height.

Count 1—Place right foot on bench.
Count 2—Bring left foot alongside of right and stand erect.
Count 3—Lower right foot to floor.
Count 4—Lower left foot to floor.

REPEAT the 4-count movement 30 times a minute for two minutes.

THEN sit down on bench or chair for two minutes.

FOLLOWING the 2-minute rest, take your pulse for 30 seconds. Double the count to get the per-minute rate. (You can find the pulse by applying middle and index finger of one hand firmly to the inside of the wrist of the other hand, on the thumb side.)

Record your score for future comparisons. In succeeding tests—about once every two weeks—you probably will find your pulse rate becoming lower as your physical condition improves.

Three important points:

1. For best results, do not engage in physical activity for at least 10 minutes before taking the test. Take it at about the same time of day and always use the same bench or chair.

2. Remember that pulse rates vary among individuals. This is an individual test. What is important is not a comparison of your pulse rate with that of anybody else—but rather a record of how your own rate is reduced as your fitness increases.

3. As you progress, the rate at which your pulse is lowered should gradually level off. This is an indication that you are approaching peak fitness.

YOUR PROGRESS RECORDS

Charts are provided for the orientation program and for each of the five levels.

They list the exercises to be done and the goal for each exercise in terms of number of repetitions, distance, etc.

They also provide space in which to record your progress—(1) in completing the recommended 15 workouts at each level, (2) in accomplishing the three prove-out workouts before moving on to a succeeding level, and (3) in the results as you take the step test from time to time.

A sample chart and progress record for one of the five levels is shown below.

You do the warmup exercises and the conditioning exercises along with one circulatory activity for each workout.

Check off each workout as you complete it. The last three numbers are for the prove-out workouts, in which the seven conditioning exercises should be done without resting. Check them off as you accomplish them.

You are now ready to proceed to the next level.

As you take the step test—at about 2-week intervals—enter your pulse rate.

When you move on to the next level, transfer the last pulse rate from the preceding level. Enter it in the margin to the left of the new progress record and circle it so it will be convenient for continuing reference.

Sample	**Goal**	
Warmup Exercises	Exercises 1–6 of Orientation program	
Conditioning Exercises	Uninterrupted repetitions	
1. Bend and stretch	10	
2. Sprinter	6	
3. Sitting stretch	15	
4. Knee pushup	12	
5. Situp (fingers laced)	10	
6. Leg raiser	10 each leg	
7. Flutter kick	30	
Circulatory activity (choose one each workout)		
Jog-walk (jog 50, walk 50)	$^1/_2$ mile	
Rope (skip 30 secs.; rest 60 secs.)	3 series	
Run in place (run 100, hop 25—2 cycles)	3 minutes	
Water activities (see pages 500–501)		
Your progress record 1 2 3 4 5 6 7 8 9 10 11 12		13 14 15
Step test (pulse)		Prove-out workouts

Getting Set—Orientation Workouts

With the series of mild exercises listed in the chart which follows and described on the next two pages, you can get yourself ready—without severe aches or pains—for the progressive conditioning program.

Plan to spend a minimum of one week for preliminary conditioning. Don't hesitate to spend two weeks or three if necessary for you to limber up enough to accomplish all the exercises easily and without undue fatigue.

Note: The police officer physical performance test is identical for both men and women because all police officers must be able to perform all tasks. The demands of police work do not cater to weakness of any form. The women who can meet the physical standards take their places as full-fledged police officers sharing equally in duties, responsibilities, risks and hard work.

There are, of course, real physiological differences between men and women. Some conditioning exercises are modified in recognition of these differences. Women with the potential to pass the police officer physical performance test should find that the women's program described here, if followed faithfully, should prepare them well.

The Program for Women

Orientation Program: Women   Goal

Conditioning Exercises	Repetitions
*1. Bend and stretch	10
*2. Knee lift	10 left, 10 right
*3. Wing stretcher	20
*4. Half knee bend	10
*5. Arm circles	15 each way
*6. Body bender	10 left, 10 right
7. Prone arch	10
8. Knee pushup	6
9. Head and shoulder curl	5
10. Ankle stretch	15
Circulatory activity (choose one each workout)	
Walking	$^1/_2$ mile
Rope (skip 15 secs.; rest 60 secs.)	3 series

* *The first six exercises of the orientation program will be used as warmup exercises throughout the graded levels.*

Step Test Record—After completing the orientation program, take the 2-minute step test. Record your pulse rate here: _____. This will be the base rate with which you can make comparisons in the future.

1. Bend and Stretch

Starting position: Stand erect, feet shoulder-width apart.
Action: Count 1. Bend trunk forward and down, flexing knees. Stretch gently in attempt to touch fingers to toes or floor. Count 2. Return to starting position.
Note: Do slowly; stretch and relax at intervals rather than in rhythm.

2. Knee Lift

Starting position: Stand erect, feet together, arms at sides.
Action: Count 1. Raise left knee as high as possible, grasping leg with hands and pulling knee against body while keeping back straight. Count 2. Lower to starting position. Counts 3 and 4. Repeat with right knee.

3. Wing Stretcher

Starting position: Stand erect, elbows at shoulder height, fists clenched in front of chest.
Action: Count 1. Thrust elbows backward vigorously without arching back. Keep head erect, elbows at shoulder height. Count 2. Return to starting position.

4. Half Knee Bend

Starting position: Stand erect, hands on hips.
Action: Count 1. Bend knees halfway while extending arms forward, palms down. Count 2. Return to starting position.

5. Arm Circles
Starting position: Stand erect, arms extended sideward at shoulder height, palms up.
Action: Describe small circles backward with hands. Keep head erect. Do 15 backward circles. Reverse, turn palms down and do 15 small circles forward.

6. Body Bender
Starting position: Stand, feet shoulder-width apart, hands behind neck, fingers interlaced.
Action: Count 1. Bend trunk sideward to left as far as possible, keeping hands behind neck. Count 2. Return to starting position. Counts 3 and 4. Repeat to the right.

7. Prone Arch
Starting position: Lie face down, hands tucked under thighs.
Action: Count 1. Raise head, shoulders, and legs from floor. Count 2. Return to starting position.

8. Knee Pushup
Starting position: Lie on floor, face down, legs together, knees bent with feet raised off floor, hands on floor under shoulders, palms down.
Action: Count 1. Push upper body off floor until arms are fully extended and body is in straight line from head to knees. Count 2. Return to starting position.

9. Head and Shoulder Curl
Starting position: Lie on back, hands tucked under small of back, palms down.
Action: Count 1. Tighten abdominal muscles, lift head and pull shoulders and elbows off floor. Hold for four seconds. Count 2. Return to starting position.

10. Ankle Stretch
Starting position: Stand on a stair, large book, or block of wood, with weight on balls of feet and heels raised.
Action: Count 1. Lower heels. Count 2. Raise heels.

Circulatory Activities
WALKING—Step off at a lively pace, swing arms and breathe deeply.
ROPE—Any form of skipping or jumping is acceptable. Gradually increase the tempo as your skill and condition improve.

Women: Level One	Goal
Warmup Exercises	Exercises 1–6 of Orientation program
Conditioning Exercises	Uninterrupted repetitions
1. Toe touch	5
2. Sprinter	8
3. Sitting stretch	10
4. Knee pushup	8
5. Situp (arms extended)	5
6. Leg raiser	5 each leg
7. Flutter kick	20
Circulatory activity (choose one each workout)	
Walking (120 steps a minute)	$1/_2$ mile
Rope (skip 30 sec.; rest 60 secs.)	2 series
Run in place (run 50;	2 minutes

straddle hop 10—2 cycles)
Water activities (see pages 500–501)
Your progress record 1 2 3 4 5 6 7 8 9 10 11 12   13 14 15
Step test (pulse)   Prove-out workouts

---

1. Toe Touch

Starting Position: Stand at attention.

Action: Count 1. Bend trunk forward and down, keeping knees straight, touching fingers to ankles. Count 2. Bounce and touch fingers to top of feet. Count 3. Bounce and touch fingers to toes. Count 4. Return to starting position.

2. Sprinter

Starting position: Squat, hands on floor, fingers pointed forward, left leg fully extended to rear.

Action: Count 1. Reverse position of feet in bouncing movement, bringing left foot to hands, extending right leg backward—all in one motion. Count 2. Reverse feet again, returning to starting position.

3. Sitting Stretch

Starting position: Sit, legs spread apart, hands on knees.

Action: Count 1. Bend forward at waist, extending arms as far forward as possible. Count 2. Return to starting position.

4. Knee Pushup

Starting position: Lie on floor, face down, legs together, knees bent with feet raised off floor, hands on floor under shoulders, palms down.

Action: Count 1. Push upper body off floor until arms are fully extended and body is in straight line from head to knees. Count 2. Return to starting position.

5. Situp (Arms Extended)

Starting position: Lie on back, legs straight and together, arms extended beyond head.

Action: Count 1. Bring arms forward over head, roll up to sitting position, sliding hands along legs, grasping ankles. Count 2. Roll back to starting position.

6. Leg Raiser

Starting position: Right side of body on floor, head resting on right arm.

Action: Lift left leg about 24" off floor, then lower it. Do required number of repetitions. Repeat on other side.

7. Flutter Kick

Starting position: Lie face down, hands tucked under thighs.

Action: Arch the back, bringing chest and head up, then flutter kick continuously, moving the legs 8"–10" apart. Kick from hips and with knees slightly bent. Count each kick as one.

Circulatory Activities

WALKING—Maintain a pace of 120 steps per minute for a distance of 1/2 mile. Swing arms and breathe deeply.

ROPE—Skip or jump rope continuously using any form for 30 seconds and then rest 60 seconds. Repeat 2 times.

RUN IN PLACE—Raise each foot at least 4" off the floor and jog in place. Count 1 each time left foot touches floor. Complete number of running steps called for in chart, then do specified number of straddle hops. Complete 2 cycles of alternate running and hopping for time specified on chart.

STRADDLE HOP—*Starting position:* At attention.

Action: Count 1. Swing arms sideward and upward, touching hands above head (arms straight) while simultaneously moving feet sideward and apart in a single jumping motion. Count 2. Spring back to starting position. Two counts in one hop.

Women: Level Two	Goal
Warmup Exercises	Exercises 1–6 of Orientation program
Conditioning Exercises	Uninterrupted repetitions
1. Toe touch	15
2. Sprinter	12
3. Sitting stretch	15
4. Knee pushup	12
5. Situp (fingers laced)	10
6. Leg raiser	10 each leg
7. Flutter kick	30
Circulatory activity (choose one each workout)	
Jog-walk (jog 50, walk 50)	$\frac{1}{2}$ mile
Rope (skip 30 sec.; rest 60 secs.)	3 series
Run in place (run 80; hop 15—2 cycles)	3 minutes
Water activities (see pages 500–501)	
Your progress record 1 2 3 4 5 6 7 8 9 10 11 12	13 14 15
Step test (pulse)	Prove-out workouts

1. Toe Touch

Starting position: Stand at attention.

Action: Count 1. Bend trunk forward and down, keeping knees straight, touching fingers to ankles. Count 2. Bounce and touch fingers to top of feet. Count 3. Bounce and touch fingers to toes. Count 4. Return to starting position.

2. Sprinter

Starting position: Squat, hands on floor, fingers pointed forward, left leg fully extended to rear.

Action: Count 1. Reverse position of feet in bouncing movement, bringing left foot to hands, extending right leg backward—all in one motion. Count 2. Reverse feet again, returning to starting position.

3. Sitting Stretch

Starting position: Sit, legs spread apart, hands on knees.

Action: Count 1. Bend forward at waist, extending arms as far forward as possible. Count 2. Return to starting position.

4. Knee Pushup

Starting position: Lie on floor, face down, legs together, knees bent with feet raised off floor, hands on floor under shoulders, palms down.

Action: Count 1. Push upper body off floor until arms are fully extended and body is in straight line from head to knees. Count 2. Return to starting position.

5. Situp (Fingers Laced)

Starting position: Lie on back, legs straight and feet spread approximately 1' apart. Fingers laced behind neck.

Action: Count 1. Curl up to sitting position and turn trunk to left. Touch right elbow to left knee. Count 2. Return to starting position. Count 3. Curl up to sitting position and turn trunk to right. Touch left elbow to right knee. Count 4. Return to starting position. Score one situp each time you return to starting position. Knees may be bent as necessary.

6. Leg Raiser

Starting position: Right side of body on floor, head resting on right arm.
Action: Lift left leg about 24" off floor, then lower it. Do required number of repetitions. Repeat on other side.

7. Flutter Kick

Starting position: Lie face down, hands tucked under thighs.
Action: Arch the back, bringing chest and head up, then flutter kick continuously, moving the legs 8"–10" apart. Kick from hips with knees slightly bent. Count each kick as one.

Circulatory Activities

JOG-WALK—Jog and walk alternately for number of paces indicated on chart for distance specified.

ROPE—Skip or jump rope continuously using any form for 30 seconds and then rest 60 seconds. Repeat 3 times.

RUN IN PLACE—Raise each foot at least 4" off floor and jog in place. Count 1 each time left foot touches floor. Complete number of running steps called for in chart, then do specified number of straddle hops. Complete 2 cycles of alternate running and hopping for time specified on chart.

STRADDLE HOP—*Starting position:* At attention.

Action: Count 1. Swing arms sideward and upward, touching hands above head (arms straight) while simultaneously moving feet sideward and apart in a single jumping motion. Count 2. Spring back to starting position. Two counts in one hop.

Women: Level Three	**Goal**
Warmup	Exercises 1–6 of Orientation program
Conditioning Exercises	Uninterrupted repetitions
1. Toe touch	20
2. Sprinter	16
3. Sitting stretch (fingers laced)	15
4. Knee pushup	20
5. Situp (arms extended, knees up)	15
6. Leg raiser	16 each leg
7. Flutter kick	40
Circulatory activity (choose one each workout)	
Jog-walk (jog 50, walk 50)	$^3/_4$ mile
Rope (skip 45 secs.; rest 30 secs.)	3 series
Run in place (run 110, hop 20—2 cycles)	4 minutes
Water activities (see pages 500–501)	
Your progress record 1 2 3 4 5 6 7 8 9 10 11 12	13 14 15
Step test (pulse)	Prove-out workouts

1. Toe Touch

Starting position: Stand at attention.
Action: 1. Bend trunk forward and down, keeping knees straight, touching fingers to ankles. Count 2. Bounce and touch fingers to top of feet. Count 3. Bounce and touch fingers to toes. Count 4. Return to starting position.

2. Sprinter

Starting position: Squat, hands on floor, fingers pointed forward, left leg fully extended to rear.

Action: Count 1. Reverse position of feet in bouncing movement, bringing left foot to hands, extending right leg backward all in one motion. Count 2. Reverse feet again, returning to starting position.

3. Sitting Stretch (Fingers Laced)

Starting position: Sit, legs spread apart, fingers laced behind neck.
Action: Count 1. Bend forward at waist, reaching elbows as close to floor as possible. Count 2. Return to starting position.

4. Knee Pushup

Starting position: Lie on floor, face down, legs together, knees bent with feet raised off floor, hands on floor under shoulders, palms down.
Action: Count 1. Push upper body off floor until arms are fully flexed and body in straight line from head to knees. Count 2. Return to starting position.

5. Situp (Arms Extended, Knees Up)

Starting position: Lie on back, legs straight, arms extended overhead.
Action: Count 1. Sit up, reaching forward with arms encircling knees while pulling them tightly to chest. Count 2. Return to starting position. Do this exercise rhythmically, without breaks in the movement.

6. Leg Raiser

Starting position: Right side of body on floor, head resting on right arm.
Action: Lift left leg about 24" off floor, then lower it. Do required number of repetitions. Repeat on other side.

7. Flutter Kick

Starting position: Lie face down, hands tucked under thighs.
Action: Arch the back, bringing chest and head up. Then flutter kick continuously, moving the legs 8"–10" apart. Kick from hips with knees slightly bent. Count each kick as one.

Circulatory Activities

JOG-WALK—Jog and walk alternately for number of paces indicated on chart for distance specified.
ROPE—Skip or jump rope continuously using any form for 45 seconds and then rest 30 seconds. Repeat 3 times.
RUN IN PLACE—Raise each foot at least 4" off floor and jog in place. Count 1 each time left foot touches floor. Complete number of running steps called for in chart, then do specified number of straddle hops. Complete 2 cycles of alternate running and hopping for time specified on chart.
STRADDLE HOP—*Starting position:* At attention.
Action: Count 1. Swing arms sideward and upward, touching hands above head (arms straight) while simultaneously moving feet sideward and apart in a single jumping motion. Count 2. Spring back to starting position. Two counts in one hop.

Women: Level Four	Goal
Warmup Exercises	Exercises 1–6 of Orientation program
Conditioning Exercises	Uninterrupted repetitions
1. Toe touch (twist and bend)	15 each side
2. Sprinter	20
3. Sitting stretch (alternate)	20
4. Pushup	8
5. Situp (arms crossed, knees bent)	20
6. Leg raiser (whip)	10 each leg

7. Prone arch (arms extended)	15

Circulatory activity (choose one each workout)

Jog-walk (jog 100, walk 50)	1 mile
Rope (skip 60 secs.; rest 30 secs.)	3 series
Run in place (run 145, hop 25—2 cycles)	5 minutes

Water Activities (see pages 500–501)

Your progress record 1 2 3 4 5 6 7 8 9 10 11 12	13 14 15
Step test (pulse)	Prove-out workouts

1. Toe Touch (Twist and Bend)

Starting position: Stand, feet shoulder-width apart, arms extended over head, thumbs interlocked.

Action: Count 1. Twist trunk to right and touch floor inside right foot with fingers of both hands. Count 2. Touch floor outside toes of right foot. Count 3. Touch floor outside heel of right foot. Count 4. Return to starting position, sweeping trunk and arms upward in a wide arc. On the next four counts, repeat action to left side.

2. Sprinter

Starting position: Squat, hands on floor, fingers pointed forward, left leg fully extended to rear.

Action: Count 1. Reverse position of feet in bouncing movement, bringing left foot to hands, extending right leg backward—all in one motion. Count 2. Reverse feet again, returning to starting position.

3. Sitting Stretch (Alternate)

Starting position: Sit, legs spread apart, fingers laced behind neck, elbows back.

Action: Count 1. Bend forward to left, touching forehead to left knee. Count 2. Return to starting position. Counts 3 and 4. Repeat to right. Score one repetition each time you return to starting position. Knees may be bent if necessary.

4. Pushup

Starting position: Lie on floor, face down, legs together, hands on floor under shoulders with fingers pointing straight ahead.

Action: Count 1. Push body off floor by extending arms so that weight rests on hands and toes. Count 2. Lower the body until chest touches floor.

Note: Body should be kept straight, buttocks should not be raised, abdomen should not sag.

5. Situp (Arms Crossed, Knees Bent)

Starting position: Lie on back, arms crossed on chest, hands grasping opposite shoulders, knees bent to right angle, feet flat on floor.

Action: Count 1. Curl up to sitting position. Count 2. Return to starting position.

6. Leg Raiser (Whip)

Starting position: Right side of body on floor, right arm supporting head.

Action: Whip left leg up and down rapidly lifting as high as possible off the floor. Count each whip as one. Reverse position and whip right leg up and down.

7. Prone Arch (Arms Extended)

Starting position: Lie face down, legs straight and together, arms extended to sides at shoulder level.

Action: Count 1. Arch the back, bringing arms, chest and head up, and raising legs as high as possible. Count 2. Return to starting position.

Circulatory Activities

JOG-WALK—Jog and walk alternately for number of paces indicated on chart for distance specified.

ROPE—Skip or jump rope continuously using any form for 60 seconds and then rest 30 seconds. Repeat 3 times.

RUN IN PLACE—Raise each foot at least 4" off floor and jog in place. Count 1 each time left foot touches floor. Complete number of running steps called for in chart, then do specified number of straddle hops. Complete 2 cycles of alternate running and hopping for time specified on chart.

STRADDLE HOP—*Starting position:* At attention.

Action: Count 1. Swing arms sideward and upward, touching hands above head (arms straight) while simultaneously moving feet sideward and apart in a single jumping motion. Count 2. Spring back to starting position. Two counts in one hop.

Women: Level Five	Goal
Warmup Exercises	Exercises 1–6 of Orientation program
Conditioning Exercises	Uninterrupted repetitions
1. Toe touch (twist and bend)	25 each side
2. Sprinter	24
3. Sitting stretch (alternate)	26
4. Pushup	15
5. Situp (fingers laced, knees bent)	25
6. Leg raiser (on extended arm)	10 each side
7. Prone arch (fingers laced)	25
Circulatory activity (choose one each workout)	
Jog-run	1 mile
Rope (skip 2 mins.; rest 45 secs.)	2 series
Run in place (run 180, hop 30—2 cycles)	6 minutes
Water Activities (see pages 500–501)	
Your progress record 1 2 3 4 5 6 7 8 9 10 11 12	13 14 15
Step test (pulse)	Prove-out workouts

1. Toe Touch (Twist and Bend)

Starting position: Stand, feet shoulder-width apart, arms extended over head, thumbs interlocked.

Action: Count 1. Twist trunk to right and touch floor inside right foot with fingers of both hands. Count 2. Touch floor outside toes of right foot. Count 3. Touch floor outside heel of right foot. Count 4. Return to starting position, sweeping trunk and arms upward in a wide arc. On the next four counts, repeat action to left side.

2. Sprinter

Starting position: Squat, hands on floor, fingers pointed forward, left leg fully extended to rear.

Action: Count 1. Reverse position of feet in bouncing movement, bringing left foot to hands, extending right leg backward—all in one motion. Count 2. Reverse feet again, returning to starting position.

3. Sitting Stretch (Alternate)

Starting position: Sit, legs spread apart, fingers behind neck, elbows back.

Action: Count 1. Bend forward to left, touching forehead to left knee. Count 2. Return to starting position. Counts 3 and 4. Repeat to right. Score one repetition each time you return to starting position. Knees may be bent if necessary.

4. Pushup

Starting position: Lie on floor, face down, legs together, hands on floor under shoulders with fingers pointing straight ahead.

Action: Count 1. Push body off floor by extending arms so that weight rests on hands and toes. Count 2. Lower the body until chest touches floor.

Note: Body should be kept straight, buttocks should not be raised, abdomen should not sag.

5. Situp (Fingers Laced, Knees Bent)

Starting position: Lie on back, fingers laced behind neck, knees bent, feet flat on floor.

Action: Count 1. Sit up, turn trunk to right, touch left elbow to right knee. Count 2. Return to starting position. Count 3. Sit up, turn trunk to left, touch right elbow to left knee. Count 4. Return to starting position. Score one each time you return to starting position.

6. Leg Raiser (On Extended Arm)

Starting position: Body rigidly supported by extended right arm and foot. Left arm is held behind head.

Action: Count 1. Raise left leg high. Count 2. Return to starting position slowly. Repeat on other side. Do required number of repetitions.

7. Prone Arch (Fingers Laced)

Starting position: Lie face down, fingers laced behind neck.

Action: Count 1. Arch the back, legs and chest off floor. Count 2. Extend arms fully forward. Count 3. Return hands to behind neck. Count 4. Flatten body to floor.

Circulatory Activities

JOG-RUN—Jog and run alternately for distance specified on chart.

ROPE—Skip or jump rope continuously using any form for 2 minutes and then rest 45 seconds. Repeat 2 times.

RUN IN PLACE—Raise each foot at least 4" off floor and jog in place. Count 1 each time left foot touches floor. Complete number of running steps called for in chart, then do specified number of straddle hops. Complete 2 cycles of alternate running and hopping in time specified on the chart.

STRADDLE HOP—*Starting position:* At attention.

Action: Count 1. Swing arms sideward and upward, touching hands above head (arms straight) while simultaneously moving feet sideward and apart in a single jumping motion. Count 2. Spring back to starting position. Two counts in one hop.

The Program For Men

ABOUT THE PROGRAM

The program assumes you have not—recently and consistently—been exposed to vigorous, all-around physical activity ... which could be true even if you play golf once or twice a week or engage in some other sport; no one sport provides for balanced development of all parts of the body.

The plan starts with an orientation—"get-set"—series of mild exercises to limber up all major muscle groups and help assure a painless transition.

There are then five graded levels.

As you move up from one level to the next, you will be building toward a practical and satisfactory level of fitness.

By building gradually—progressively—you will be building soundly.

WHAT THE EXERCISES ARE FOR

There are three general types—warmup exercises, conditioning exercises and circulatory activities.

The warmup exercises stretch and limber up the muscles and speed up the action of the heart and lungs, thus preparing the body for greater exertion and reducing the possibility of unnecessary strain.

The conditioning exercises are systematically planned to tone up abdominal, back, leg, arm and other major muscles.

The circulatory activities produce contractions of large muscle groups for relatively longer periods than the conditioning exercises—to stimulate and strengthen the circulatory and respiratory systems.

The plan calls for doing 10 mild exercises during the orientation period and, thereafter, the warmup exercises and the seven conditioning exercises listed for each level. The first six exercises of the orientation program are used as warmup exercises throughout the graded levels.

When it comes to the circulatory activities, you select one each workout. Alternately running and walking … skipping rope … running in place. All are effective. You can switch about for variety.

HOW YOU PROGRESS

Right now, you have limited tolerance for exercise; you can do just so much without discomfort and fatigue.

A sound conditioning program should gradually stretch your tolerance. It should give unused or little-used muscles moderate tasks at first, then make the tasks increasingly more demanding so you become able to achieve more and more with less and less fatigue and with increasingly rapid recovery.

As you move from level to level, some exercises will be modified so they call for more effort. Others will remain the same but you will build strength and stamina by increasing the number of repetitions.

At level 1, your objective will be to gradually reduce, from workout to workout, the "breathing spells" between exercises until you can do the seven conditioning exercises without resting.

You will proceed in the same fashion with the more difficult exercises and increased repetitions at succeeding levels.

You will find the program designed—the progression carefully planned—to make this feasible. You will be able to proceed at your own pace, competing with yourself rather than with anyone else—and this is of great importance for sound conditioning.

Note: Gradually speeding up, from workout to workout, the rate at which you do each exercise will provide greater stimulation for the circulatory and respiratory systems and also help to keep your workouts short. However, the seven conditioning exercises should not be a race against time. Perform each exercise completely to insure maximum benefit.

WHEN AND HOW OFTEN TO WORK OUT

To be most beneficial, exercise should become part of your regular daily routine—as much as bathing, shaving, dressing.

Five workouts a week are called for throughout the program.

You can choose any time that is convenient. Preferably, it should be the same time every day—but it does not matter whether it's first thing in the morning, before dinner in the evening, just before retiring, or any other time.

The hour just before the evening meal is a popular time for exercise. The later afternoon workout provides a welcome change of pace at the end of the work day and helps dissolve the day's worries and tensions.

Another popular time to work out is early morning, before the work day begins. Advocates of the early start say it makes them more alert and energetic on the job.

Among the factors you should consider in developing your workout schedule are personal preference, job and family responsibilities, availability of exercise facilities, and weather. It's important to schedule your workouts for a time when there is little chance that you will have to cancel or interrupt them because of other demands on your time.

You should not exercise strenuously during extremely hot, humid weather or within two hours after eating. Heat and/or digestion both make heavy demands on the circulatory system, and in combination with exercise can be an overtaxing double load.

YOUR PROGRESS RECORDS

Charts are provided for the orientation program and for each of the five levels.

They list the exercises to be done and the goal for each exercise in terms of number of repetitions, distance, etc.

They also provide space in which to record your progress—(1) in completing the recommended 15 workouts at each level, (2) in accomplishing the three prove-out workouts before moving on to a succeeding level, and (3) in the results as you take the step test from time to time.

A sample chart and progress record for one of the five levels is shown below.

You do the warmup exercises and the conditioning exercises along with one circulatory activity for each workout.

Check off each workout as you complete it. The last three numbers are for the prove-out workouts, in which the seven conditioning exercises should be done without resting. Check them off as you accomplish them.

You are now ready to proceed to the next level.

As you take the step test—at about 2-week intervals—enter your pulse rate.

When you move on to the next level, transfer the last pulse rate from the preceding level. Enter it in the margin to the left of the new progress record and circle it so it will be convenient for continuing reference.

Sample	**Goal**

Sample (cont.)	Goal
Warmup Exercises	Exercises 1–6 of Orientation program
Conditioning Exercises	Uninterrupted repetitions
1. Toe touch	20
2. Sprinter	16
3. Sitting stretch	18
4. Pushup	10
5. Situp (fingers laced)	15
6. Leg raiser	16 each leg
7. Flutter kick	40
Circulatory activity (choose one each workout)	
Jog-walk (jog 100, walk 100)	1 mile
Rope (skip 60 secs.; rest 60 secs.)	3 series
Run in place (run 95, hop 15—2 cycles)	3 minutes
Water activities (see pages 500–501)	
Your progress record 1 2 3 4 5 6 7 8 9 10 11 12	13 14 15
Step test (pulse)	Prove-out workouts

GETTING SET—ORIENTATION WORKOUTS

With the series of preliminary exercises listed in the chart which follows and described on the next two pages, you can get yourself ready—without severe aches or pains—for the progressive conditioning program.

Even if these preliminary exercises should seem easy—and they are deliberately meant to be mild—plan to spend a minimum of one week with them. Do not hesitate to spend two weeks or even three if necessary for you to limber up enough so you can accomplish all the exercises easily and without undue fatigue.

Orientation Program: Men	Goal
Conditioning Exercises	*Repetitions*
*1. Bend and stretch	10
*2. Knee lift	10 left, 10 right
*3. Wing stretcher	20
*4. Half knee bend	10
*5. Arm circles	15 each way
*6. Body bender	10 left, 10 right
7. Prone arch	10
8. Knee pushup	6
9. Head and shoulder curl	5
10. Ankle stretch	15
Circulatory activity (choose one each workout)	
Walking	$1/_2$ mile
Rope (skip 15 secs.; rest 60 secs.)	3 series

* The first six exercises of the orientation program will be used as warmup exercises throughout the graded levels.

Step Test Record—After completing the orientation program, take the 2-minute step test.

Record your pulse rate here: _____. This will be the base rate with which you can make comparisons in the future.

1. Bend and Stretch

Starting position: Stand erect, feet shoulder-width apart.
Action: Count 1. Bend trunk forward and down, flexing knees. Stretch gently in attempt to touch fingers to toes or floor. Count 2. Return to starting position.
Note: Do slowly, stretch and relax at intervals rather than in rhythm.

2. Knee Lift

Starting position: Stand erect, feet together, arms at sides.
Action: Count 1. Raise left knee as high as possible, grasping leg with hands and pulling knee against body while keeping back straight. Count 2. Lower to starting position. Counts 3 and 4. Repeat with right knee.

3. Wing Stretcher

Starting position: Stand erect, elbows at shoulder height, fists clenched in front of chest.
Action: Count 1. Thrust elbows backward vigorously without arching back. Keep head erect, elbows at shoulder height. Count 2. Return to starting position.

4. Half Knee Bend

Starting position: Stand erect, hands on hips.
Action: Count 1. Bend knees halfway while extending arms forward, palms down. Count 2. Return to starting position.

5. Arm Circles

Starting position: Stand erect, arms extended sideward at shoulder height, palms up.
Action: Describe small circles backward with hands. Keep head erect. Do 15 backward circles. Reverse, turn palms down and do 15 small circles forward.

6. Body Bender

Starting position: Stand, feet shoulder-width apart, hands behind neck, fingers interlaced.
Action: Count 1. Bend trunk sideward to left as far as possible, keeping hands behind neck. Count 2. Return to starting position. Counts 3 and 4. Repeat to the right.

7. Prone Arch

Starting position: Lie face down, hands tucked under thighs.
Action: Count 1. Raise head, shoulders, and legs from floor. Count 2. Return to starting position.

8. Knee Pushup

Starting position: Lie on floor, face down, legs together, knees bent with feet raised off floor, hands on floor under shoulders, palms down.
Action: Count 1. Push upper body off floor until arms are fully extended and body is in straight line from head to knees. Count 2. Return to starting position.

9. Head and Shoulder Curl

Starting position: Lie on back, hands tucked under small of back, palms down.
Action: Count 1. Tighten abdominal muscles, lift head and pull shoulders and elbows up off floor. Hold for four seconds. Count 2. Return to starting position.

10. Ankle Stretch

Starting position: Stand on a stair, large book or block of wood, with weight on balls of feet and heels raised.

Action: Count 1. Lower heels. Count 2. Raise heels.

Circulatory Activities

WALKING—Step off at a lively pace, swing arms and breathe deeply.

ROPE—Any form of skipping or jumping is acceptable. Gradually increase the tempo as your skill and condition improve.

Men: Level One	Goal
Warmup Exercises	Exercises 1–6 of Orientation program
Conditioning Exercises	Uninterrupted repetitions
1. Toe touch	10
2. Sprinter	12
3. Sitting stretch	12
4. Pushup	4
5. Situp (arms extended)	5
6. Leg raiser	12 each leg
7. Flutter kick	30
Circulatory activity (choose one each workout)	
Walking (120 steps a minute)	1 mile
Rope (skip 30 secs.; rest 30 secs.)	2 series
Run in place (run 60, hop 10—2 cycles)	2 minutes
Water activities (see pages 500–501)	
Your progress record 1 2 3 4 5 6 7 8 9 10 11 12	13 14 15
Step test (pulse)	Prove-out workouts

1. Toe Touch

Starting position: Stand at attention.

Action: Count 1. Bend trunk forward and down keeping knees straight, touching fingers to ankles. Count 2. Bounce and touch fingers to top of feet. Count 3. Bounce and touch fingers to toes. Count 4. Return to starting position.

2. Sprinter

Starting position: Squat, hands on floor, fingers pointed forward, left leg fully extended to rear.

Action: Count 1. Reverse position of feet in bouncing movement, bringing left foot to hands and extending right leg backward—all in one motion. Count 2. Reverse feet again, returning to starting position.

3. Sitting Stretch

Starting position: Sit, legs spread apart, hands on knees.

Action: Count 1. Bend forward at waist, extending arms as far forward as possible. Count 2. Return to starting position.

4. Pushup

Starting position: Lie on floor, face down, legs together, hands on floor under shoulders with fingers pointing straight ahead.

Action: Count 1. Push body off floor by extending arms, so that weight rests on hands and toes. Count 2. Lower the body until chest touches floor.

Note: Body should be kept straight, buttocks should not be raised, abdomen should not sag.

5. Situp (Arms Extended)

Starting position: Lie on back, legs straight and together, arms extended beyond head.
Action: Count 1. Bring arms forward over head, roll up to sitting position, sliding hands along legs, grasping ankles. Count 2. Roll back to starting position.

6. Leg Raiser

Starting position: Right side of body on floor, head resting on right arm.
Action: Lift left leg about 24" off floor, then lower it. Do required number of repetitions. Repeat on other side.

7. Flutter Kick

Starting position: Lie face down, hands tucked under thighs.
Action: Arch the back, bringing chest and head up, then flutter kick continuously, moving the legs 8"–10" apart. Kick from hips with knees slightly bent. Count each kick as one.

Circulatory Activities

WALKING—Maintain a pace of 120 steps per minute for a distance of 1 mile. Swing arms and breathe deeply.

ROPE—Skip or jump rope continuously using any form for 30 seconds and then rest 30 seconds. Repeat 2 times.

RUN IN PLACE—Raise each foot at least 4" off floor and jog in place. Count 1 each time left foot touches floor. Complete the number of running steps called for in chart, then do specified number of straddle hops. Complete 2 cycles of alternate running and hopping for time specified on chart.

STRADDLE HOP—*Starting position:* At attention.

Action: Count 1. Swing arms sideward and upward, touching hands above head (arms straight) while simultaneously moving feet sideward and apart in a single jumping motion. Count 2. Spring back to starting position. Two counts in one hop.

Men: Level Two	Goal
Warmup Exercises	Exercises 1–6 of Orientation program
Conditioning Exercises	Uninterrupted repetitions
1. Toe touch	20
2. Sprinter	16
3. Sitting stretch	18
4. Pushup	10
5. Situp (fingers laced)	20
6. Leg raiser	16 each leg
7. Flutter kick	40
Circulatory activity (choose one each workout)	
Jog-walk (jog 100; walk 100)	1 mile
Rope (skip 1 min.; rest 1 min.)	3 series
Run in place (run 95, hop 15—2 cycles)	3 minutes
Water activities (see pages 500–501)	
Your progress record 1 2 3 4 5 6 7 8 9 10 11 12	13 14 15
Step test (pulse)	Prove-out workouts .

1. Toe Touch

Starting position: Stand at attention.
Action: Count 1. Bend trunk forward and down keeping knees straight, touching fingers to ankles. Count 2. Bounce and touch fingers to top of feet. Count 3. Bounce and touch

fingers to toes. Count 4. Return to starting position.

2. Sprinter

Starting position: Squat, hands on floor, fingers pointed forward, left leg fully extended to rear.

Action: Count 1. Reverse position of feet in bouncing movement, bringing left foot to hands, extending right leg backward—all in one motion. Count 2. Reverse feet again, returning to starting position.

3. Sitting Stretch

Starting position: Sit, legs apart, hands on knees.

Action: Count 1. Bend forward at waist, extending arms as far forward as possible. Count 2. Return to starting position.

4. Pushup

Starting position: Lie on floor, face down, legs together, hands on floor under shoulders with fingers pointing straight ahead.

Action: Count 1. Push body off floor by extending arms, so that weight rests on hands and toes. Count 2. Lower the body until chest touches floor.

Note: Body should be kept straight, buttocks should not be raised, abdomen should not sag.

5. Situp (Fingers Laced)

Starting position: Lie on back, legs straight and feet spread approximately 1' apart. Fingers laced behind neck.

Action: Count 1. Curl up to sitting position and turn trunk to left. Touch the right elbow to left knee. Count 2. Return to starting position. Count 3. Curl up to sitting position and turn trunk to right. Touch left elbow to right knee. Count 4. Return to starting position. Score one situp each time you return to starting position. Knees may be bent as necessary.

6. Leg Raiser

Starting position: Right side of body on floor, head resting on right arm.

Action: Lift left leg about 24" off floor, then lower it. Do required number of repetitions. Repeat on other side.

7. Flutter Kick

Starting position: Lie face down, hands tucked under thighs.

Action: Arch the back, bringing chest and head up, then flutter kick continuously, moving the legs 8"–10" apart. Kick from hips with knees slightly bent. Count each kick as one.

Circulatory Activities

JOG-WALK—Jog and walk alternately for number of paces indicated on chart for distance specified.

ROPE—Skip or jump rope continuously using any form for 60 seconds and then rest 60 seconds. Repeat 5 times.

RUN IN PLACE—Raise each foot at least 4" off floor and jog in place. Count 1 each time left foot touches floor. Complete number of running steps called for in chart, then do specified number of straddle hops. Complete 2 cycles of alternate running and hopping for time specified on chart.

STRADDLE HOP—*Starting position:* At attention.

Action: Count 1. Swing arms sideward and upward, touching hands above head (arms straight) while simultaneously moving feet sideward and apart in a single jumping motion. Count 2. Spring back to starting position. Two counts in one hop.

Men: Level Three	**Goal**
Warmup Exercises	Exercises 1–6 of Orientation program
Conditioning Exercises	Uninterrupted repetitions
1. Toe touch	30
2. Sprinter	20
3. Sitting stretch (fingers laced)	18
4. Pushup	20
5. Situp (arms extended, knees up)	30
6. Leg raiser	20 each leg
7. Flutter kick	50
Circulatory activity (choose one each workout)	
Jog-walk (jog 200; walk 100)	$1^1/_2$ miles
Rope (skip 1 min.; rest 1 min.)	5 series
Run in place (run 135, hop 20—2 cycles)	4 minutes
Water activity (see pages 500–501)	
Your progress record 1 2 3 4 5 6 7 8 9 10 11 12	13 14 15
Step test (pulse)	Prove-out workouts

1. Toe Touch

Starting position: Stand at attention.

Action: Count 1. Bend trunk forward and down keeping knees straight, touching fingers to ankles. Count 2. Bounce and touch fingers to top of feet. Count 3. Bounce and touch fingers to toes. Count 4. Return to starting position.

2. Sprinter

Starting position: Squat, hands on floor, fingers pointed forward, left leg fully extended to rear.

Action: Count 1. Reverse position of feet in bouncing movement, bringing left foot to hands, extending right leg backward—all in one motion. Count 2. Reverse feet again, returning to starting position.

3. Sitting Stretch (Fingers Laced)

Starting position: Sit, legs spread apart, fingers laced behind neck, elbows back.

Action: Count 1. Bend forward at waist, reaching elbows as close to floor as possible. Count 2. Return to starting position.

4. Pushup

Starting position: Lie on floor, face down, legs together, hands on floor under shoulders with fingers pointing straight ahead.

Action: Count 1. Push body off floor by extending arms, so that weight rests on hands and toes. Count 2. Lower the body until chest touches floor.

Note: Body should be kept straight, buttocks should not be raised, abdomen should not sag.

5. Situp (Arms Extended, Knees Up)

Starting position: Lie on back, legs straight, arms extended overhead.

Action: Count 1. Sit up, reaching forward with arms encircling knees while pulling them tightly to chest. Count 2. Return to starting position. Do this exercise rhythmically, without breaks in the movement.

6. Leg Raiser
Starting position: Right side of body on floor, head resting on right arm.
Action: Lift left leg about 24" off floor then lower it. Do required number of repetitions. Repeat on other side.

7. Flutter Kick
Starting position: Lie face down, hands tucked under thighs.
Action: Arch the back, bringing chest and head up, then flutter kick continuously, moving the legs 8"-10" apart. Kick from hips with knees slightly bent. Count each kick as one.

Circulatory Activities
JOG-WALK—Jog and walk alternately for number of paces indicated on chart for distance specified.
ROPE—Skip or jump rope continuously using any form for 60 seconds and then rest 60 seconds. Repeat 5 times.
RUN IN PLACE—Raise each foot at least 4" off floor and jog in place. Count 1 each time left foot touches floor. Complete number of running steps called for in chart, then do specified number of straddle hops. Complete 2 cycles of alternate running and hopping for time specified on chart.
STRADDLE HOP—*Starting position:* At attention.
Action: Count 1. Swing arms sideward and upward, touching hands above head (arms straight) while simultaneously moving feet sideward and apart in a single jumping motion. Count 2. Spring back to starting position. Two counts in one hop.

Men: Level Four	Goal
Warmup Exercises	Exercises 1–6 of Orientation program
Conditioning Exercises	Uninterrupted repetitions
1. Toe touch (twist and bend)	20 each side
2. Sprinter	28
3. Sitting stretch (alternate)	24
4. Pushup	30
5. Situp (arms crossed, knees bent)	30
6. Leg raiser (whip)	20 each leg
7. Prone arch (arms extended)	20
Circulatory activity (choose one each workout)	
Jog	1 mile
Rope (skip 90 secs.; rest 30 secs.)	3 series
Run in place (run 180, hop 25—2 cycles)	5 minutes
Water activity (see pages 500–501)	
Your progress record 1 2 3 4 5 6 7 8 9 10 11 12	13 14 15
Step test (pulse)	Prove-out workouts

1. Toe Touch (Twist and Bend)
Starting position: Stand, feet shoulder-width apart, arms extended overhead, thumbs interlocked.
Action: Count 1. Twist trunk to right and touch floor inside right foot with fingers of both hands. Count 2. Touch floor outside toes of right foot. Count 3. Touch floor outside heel

of right foot. Count 4. Return to starting position, sweeping trunk and arms upward in a wide arc. On the next four counts, repeat action to left side.

2. Sprinter

Starting position: Squat, hands on floor, fingers pointed forward, left leg fully extended to rear.

Action: Count 1. Reverse position of feet in bouncing movement, bringing left foot to hands, extending right leg backward—all in one motion. Count 2. Reverse feet again, returning to starting position.

3. Sitting Stretch (Alternate)

Starting position: Sit, legs spread apart, fingers laced behind neck, elbows back.

Action: Count 1. Bend forward to left, touching forehead to left knee. Count 2. Return to starting position. Counts 3 and 4. Repeat to right. Score one repetition each time you return to starting position. Knees may be bent if necessary.

4. Pushup

Starting position: Lie on floor, face down, legs together, hands on floor under shoulders with fingers pointing straight ahead.

Action: Count 1. Push body off floor by extending arms, so that weight rests on hands and toes. Count 2. Lower the body until chest touches floor.

Note: Body should be kept straight, buttocks should not be raised, abdomen should not sag.

5. Situp (Arms Crossed, Knees Bent)

Starting position: Lie on back, arms crossed on chest, hands grasping opposite shoulders, knees bent to right angle, feet flat on floor.

Action: Count 1. Curl up to sitting position. Count 2. Return to starting position.

6. Leg Raiser (Whip)

Starting position: Right side of body on floor, right arm supporting head.

Action: Whip left leg up and down rapidly, lifting as high as possible off the floor. Count each whip as one. Reverse position and whip right leg up and down.

7. Prone Arch (Arms Extended)

Starting position: Lie face down, legs straight and together, arms extended to sides at shoulder level.

Action: Count 1. Arch the back, bringing arms, chest and head up, and raising legs as high as possible. Count 2. Return to starting position.

Circulatory Activities

JOG—Jog continuously for 1 mile.

ROPE—Skip or jump rope continuously using any form for 90 seconds and then rest for 30 seconds. Repeat 3 times.

RUN IN PLACE—Raise each foot at least 4" off the floor and jog in place. Count 1 each time left foot touches floor. Complete number of running steps called for in chart, then do specified number of straddle hops. Complete 2 cycles of alternate running and hopping in time specified on chart.

STRADDLE HOP—*Starting position:* At attention.

Action: Count 1. Swing arms sideward and upward, touching hands above head (arms straight) while simultaneously moving feet sideward and apart in a single jumping motion. Count 2. Spring back to starting position. Two counts in one hop.

Men: Level Five (cont.)	Goal
Men: Level Five	**Goal**
Warmup Exercises	Exercises 1–6 of Orientation program
Conditioning Exercises	Uninterrupted repetitions
1. Toe touch (twist and bend)	30 each side
2. Sprinter	36
3. Sitting stretch (alternate)	30
4. Pushup	50
5. Situp (fingers laced, knees bent)	40
6. Leg raiser (on extended arm)	20 each side
7. Prone arch (fingers laced)	30
Circulatory activity (choose one each workout)	
Jog-run	3 mile
Rope (skip 2 mins.; rest 30 secs.)	3 series
Run in place (run 216, hop 30—2 cycles)	6 minutes
Water activity (see pages 500–501)	
Your progress record 1 2 3 4 5 6 7 8 9 10 11 12	13 14 15
Step test (pulse)	Prove-out workouts

1. Toe Touch (Twist and Bend)

Starting position: Stand, feet shoulder-width apart, arms extended overhead, thumbs interlocked.

Action: Count 1. Twist trunk to right and touch floor inside right foot with fingers of both hands. Count 2. Touch floor outside toes of right foot. Count 3. Touch floor outside heel of right foot. Count 4. Return to starting position, sweeping trunk and arms upward in a wide arc. On the next four counts, repeat action to left side.

2. Sprinter

Starting position: Squat, hands on floor, fingers pointed forward, left leg fully extended to rear.

Action: Count 1. Reverse position of feet in bouncing movement, bringing left foot to hands and extending right leg backward—all in one motion. Count 2. Reverse feet again, returning to starting position.

3. Sitting Stretch (Alternate)

Starting position: Sit, legs spread apart, fingers laced behind neck, elbows back.

Action: Count 1. Bend forward to left, touching forehead to left knee. Count 2. Return to starting position. Counts 3 and 4. Repeat to right. Score one repetition each time you return to starting position. Knees may be bent if necessary.

4. Pushup

Starting position: Lie on floor, face down, legs together, hands on floor under shoulders with fingers pointing straight ahead.

Action: Count 1. Push body off floor by extending arms so that weight rests on hands and toes. Count 2. Lower body until chest touches floor.

Note: Body should be kept straight, buttocks should not be raised, abdomen should not sag.

5. Situp (Fingers Laced, Knees Bent)

Starting position: Lie on back, fingers laced behind neck, knees bent, feet flat on floor.
Action: Count 1. Sit up, turn trunk to right, touch left elbow to right knee. Count 2. Return to starting position. Count 3. Sit up, turn trunk to left, touch right elbow to left knee. Count 4. Return to starting position. Score one each time you return to starting position.

6. Leg Raiser (On Extended Arm)

Starting position: Body rigidly supported by extended right arm and foot. Left arm is held behind head.
Action: Count 1. Raise left leg high. Count 2. Return to starting position slowly. Do required number of repetitions. Repeat on other side.

7. Prone Arch (Fingers Laced)

Starting position: Lie face down, fingers laced behind neck.
Action: Count 1. Arch back, legs, and chest off floor. Count 2. Extend arms forward. Count 3. Return hands to behind neck. Count 4. Flatten body to floor.

Circulatory Activities

JOG RUN—Alternately jog and run the specified distance. Attempt to increase the proportion of time spent running in each succeeding workout.
ROPE—Skip or jump rope continuously using any form for 2 minutes and then rest 30 seconds. Repeat 3 times.
RUN IN PLACE—Raise each foot at least 4" off floor and jog in place. Count 1 each time left foot touches floor. Complete number of running steps called for in chart, then do specified number of straddle hops. Complete 2 cycles of alternate running and hopping for time specified on the chart.
STRADDLE HOP—*Starting position:* At attention.
Action: Count 1. Swing arms sideward and upward, touching hands above head (arms straight) while simultaneously moving feet sideward and apart in a single jumping motion. Count 2. Spring back to starting position. Two counts in one hop.

STAYING FIT

Once you have reached the level of conditioning you have chosen for yourself, you will wish to maintain your fitness.

To do so, continue the workouts at that level.

While it has been found possible to maintain fitness with three workouts a week, ideally, exercise should be a daily habit. If you can, by all means continue your workouts on a five-times-a-week basis.

If at any point—either after reaching your goal or in the process of doing so—your workouts are interrupted because of illness or other reason for more than a week, it will be best to begin again at a lower level. If you have had a serious illness or surgery, proceed under your physician's guidance.

BROADENING YOUR PROGRAM

The exercises and activities you have engaged in are basic—designed to take you soundly and progressively up the ladder to physical fitness without need for special equipment or facilities.

There are many other activities and forms of exercise which, if you wish, you may use to supplement the basic program.

They include a variety of sports; water exercises you can use if you have access to a pool; and isometrics—sometimes called exercises without movement—which take little time (6–8 seconds each).

Isometrics

Isometric contraction exercises take very little time, and require no special equipment. They're excellent muscle strengtheners and, as such, valuable supplements.

The idea of isometrics is to work out a muscle by pushing or pulling against an immovable object such as a wall ... or by pitting it against the opposition of another muscle.

The basis is the "overload" principle of exercise physiology—which holds that a muscle required to perform work beyond the usual intensity will grow in strength. And research has indicated that one hard, 6- to 8-second isometric contraction per workout can, over a period of six months, produce a significant strength increase in a muscle.

The exercises described in the following pages cover major large muscle groups of the body.

They can be performed almost anywhere and at almost any time.

There is no set order for doing them—nor do all have to be completed at one time. You can, if you like, do one or two in the morning, others at various times during the day whenever you have half a minute or even less to spare.

For each contraction, maintain tension no more than eight seconds. Do little breathing during a contraction; breathe deeply between contractions.

And start easily. Do not apply maximum effort in the beginning.

For the first three or four weeks, you should exert only about one-half what you think is your maximum force.

Use the first three or four seconds to build up to this degree of force—and the remaining four or five seconds to hold it.

For the next two weeks, gradually increase force to more nearly approach maximum. After about six weeks, it will be safe to exert maximum effort.

Pain indicates you're applying too much force; reduce the amount immediately. If pain continues to accompany any exercise, discontinue using that exercise for a week or two. Then try it again with about 50 percent of maximum effort and, if no pain occurs, you can go on to gradually build up toward maximum.

Neck
Starting position: Sit or stand, with interlaced fingers of hands on forehead.
Action: Forcibly exert a forward push of head while resisting equally hard with hands.
Starting position: Sit or stand, with interlaced fingers of hands behind head.
Action: Push head backward while exerting a forward pull with hands.
Starting position: Sit or stand, with palm of left hand on left side of head.
Action: Push with left hand while resisting with head and neck. Reverse using right hand on right side of head.

Upper Body
Starting position: Stand, back to wall, hands at sides, palms toward wall.
Action: Press hands backward against wall, keeping arms straight.
Starting position: Stand, facing wall, hands at sides, palms toward wall.
Action: Press hands forward against wall, keeping arms straight.
Starting position: Stand in doorway or with side against wall, arms at sides, palms to-

ward legs.
Action: Press hand(s) outward against wall or doorframe, keeping arms straight.

Arms
Starting position: Stand with feet slightly apart. Flex right elbow, close to body, palm up. Place left hand over right.
Action: Forcibly attempt to curl right arm upward, while giving equally strong resistance with the left hand. Repeat with left arm.

Arms and Chest
Starting position: Stand with feet comfortably spaced, knees slightly bent. Clasp hands, palms together, close to chest.
Action: Press hands together and hold.
Starting position: Stand with feet slightly apart, knees slightly bent. Grip fingers, arms close to chest.
Action: Pull hard and hold.

Abdominal
Starting position: Stand, knees slightly flexed, hands resting on knees.
Action: Contract abdominal muscles.

Lower Back, Buttocks and Back of Thighs
Starting position: Lie face down, arms at sides, palms up, legs placed under bed or other heavy object.
Action: With both hips flat on floor, raise one leg, keeping knee straight so that heel pushes hard against the resistance above. Repeat with opposite leg.

Legs
Starting position: Sit in chair with left ankle crossed over right, feet resting on floor, legs bent at 90 degree angle.
Action: Forcibly attempt to straighten right leg while resisting with the left. Repeat with opposite leg.

Inner and Outer Thighs
Starting position: Sit, legs extended with each ankle pressed against the outside of sturdy chair legs.
Action: Keep legs straight and pull toward one another firmly. For outer thigh muscles, place ankles inside chair legs and exert pressure outward.

Water Activities

Swimming is one of the best physical activities for people of all ages—and for many of the handicapped.

With the body submerged in water, blood circulation automatically increases to some extent; pressure of water on the body also helps promote deeper ventilation of the lungs; and with well-planned activity, both circulation and ventilation increase still more.

The water exercises described on the following page can be used either as supplements to, or replacements for, the circulatory activities of the basic program. The goals for each of the five levels are shown in the chart below.

Women

Level	1	2	3	4	5
Bobs	10	15	20	50	100
Swim	5 min	10 min	15 min	—	—
Interval swimming	—	—	—	25 yds. (Repeat 10 times.)	25 yds. (Repeat 20 times.)

Men

Level	1	2	3	4	5
Bobs	10	15	25	75	125
Swim	5 min	10 min	15 min	—	—
Interval swimming	—	—	—	25 yds. (Repeat 20 times.)	50 yds. (Repeat 20 times.)

BOBBING

Starting position: Face out of water.
Action: Count 1. Take a breath. Count 2. Submerge while exhaling until feet touch bottom. Count 3. Push up from bottom to surface while continuing to exhale. Three counts to one bob.

SWIMMING

Use any type of stroke. Swim continuously for the time specified.

INTERVAL SWIMMING

Use any type of stroke. Swim moderately fast for distance specified. You can then either swim back slowly to starting point or get out of pool and walk back. Repeat specified number of times.

Weight Training

Weight training also is an excellent method of developing muscular strength—and muscular endurance. Where equipment is available, it may be used as a supplement to the seven conditioning exercises.

Because of the great variety of weight training exercises, there will be no attempt to describe them here. Both barbells and weighted dumbbells—complete with instructions—are available at most sporting goods stores. A good rule to follow in deciding the maximum weight you should lift is to select a weight you can lift six times without strain.

Sports

Soccer, basketball, handball, squash, ice hockey and other sports that require sustained effort can be valuable aids to building circulatory endurance.

But if you have been sedentary, it's important to pace yourself carefully in such sports, and it may even be advisable to avoid them until you are well along in your physical conditioning program. That doesn't mean you should avoid all sports.

There are many excellent conditioning and circulatory activities in which the amount of exertion is easily controlled and in which you can progress at your own rate. Bicycling is one example. Others include hiking, skating, tennis, running, cross-country skiing, rowing, canoeing, water skiing and skindiving.

You can engage in these sports at any point in the program, if you start slowly. Games should be played with full speed and vigor only when your conditioning permits doing so without undue fatigue.

On days when you get a good workout in sports you can skip part or all of your exercise program. Use your own judgment.

If you have engaged in a sport that exercises the legs and stimulates the heart and lungs—such as skating—you could skip the circulatory activity for that day, but you still should do some of the conditioning and stretching exercises for the upper body. On the other hand, weight-lifting is an excellent conditioning activity, but it should be supplemented with running or one of the other circulatory exercises.

Whatever your favorite sport, you will find your enjoyment enhanced by improved fitness. Every weekend athlete should invest in frequent workouts.